D1593117

The Cantatas of J.S. Bach

The Cantatas of J.S. Bach

An Analytical Guide

by

W. Murray Young

McFarland & Company, Inc., Publishers
Jefferson, North Carolina, and London

British Library Cataloguing-in-Publication data available

Library of Congress Cataloguing-in-Publication Data

Young, W. Murray, 1920–
The cantatas of J.S. Bach.

Bibliography: p. 299.
Includes index.
1. Bach, Johann Sebastian, 1685–1750. Cantatas.
2. Cantatas—18th century—Analysis, appreciation.
I. Title.
MT115.B2Y7 1989 782.2'4 89-42762

ISBN 0-89950-394-2 (lib. bdg. : 50# alk. paper) 

Manufactured in the United States of America

McFarland & Company, Inc., Publishers
Box 611, Jefferson, North Carolina 28640

To the memory of my grandmother,
my mother and my father,
and to the patient devotion of my wife

Table of Contents

Introduction **xiii**

I. The Sacred Cantatas 1

A. Composed at Mühlhausen (1707–1708) **1**

BWV 131 Aus der Tiefe rufe ich, Herr, zu dir **1**
BWV 71 Gott ist mein König **2**
BWV 196 Der Herr denkt an uns **3**
BWV 189 Meine Seele rühmt und preist **3**
BWV 150 Nach dir, Herr, verlanget mich **4**
BWV 106 Gottes Zeit ist die allerbeste Zeit **5**

B. Composed at Weimar (1708–1717) **6**

BWV 18 Gleichwie der Regen und Schnee vom Himmel fällt **7**
BWV 21 Ich hatte viel Bekümmernis **8**
BWV 199 Mein Herze schwimmt im Blut **10**
BWV 61 Nun komm, der Heiden Heiland I **11**
BWV 182 Himmelskönig, sei willkommen **12**
BWV 31 Der Himmel lacht, die Erde jubilieret **13**
BWV 185 Barmherziges Herze der ewigen Liebe **14**
BWV 161 Komm, du süsse Todesstunde **15**
BWV 162 Ach, ich sehe, jetzt da ich zur Hochzeit gehe **16**
BWV 163 Nur jedem das Seine **17**
BWV 132 Bereitet die Wege, bereitet die Bahn **18**
BWV 152 Tritt auf die Glaubensbahn **19**
BWV 155 Mein Gott, wie lang', ach lange **20**
BWV 59 Wer mich liebet, der wird mein Wort halten I **20**
BWV 70 Wachet! betet! betet! wachet! **21**
BWV 147 Herz und Mund und Tat und Leben **23**
BWV 158 Der Friede sei mit dir **24**

C. Composed at Cöthen (1717–1723) **25**

BWV 173 Erhöhtes Fleisch und Blut **25**
BWV 47 Wer sich selbst erhöhet, der soll erniedrigt werden **27**
BWV 134 Ein Herz, das seinen Jesum lebend weiss **27**
BWV 22 Jesus nahm zu sich die Zwölfe **29**
BWV 23 Du wahrer Gott und Davids Sohn **30**

D. Composed at Leipzig (1723–1734) **31**

BWV 75 Die Elenden sollen essen **31**
BWV 76 Die Himmel erzählen die Ehre Gottes **33**
BWV 24 Ein ungefärbt Gemüthe **35**
BWV 186 Ärgre dich, O Seele, nicht **36**
BWV 164 Ihr, die ihr euch von Christo nennet **37**
BWV 119 Preise, Jerusalem, den Herrn **38**
BWV 194 Höchsterwünschtes Freudenfest **40**
BWV 63 Christen, ätzet diesen Tag **42**
BWV 40 Dazu ist erschienen der Sohn Gottes **43**
BWV 64 Sehet, welch eine Liebe hat uns der Vater erzeiget **44**
BWV 16 Herr Gott, dich loben wir **46**
BWV 153 Schau', lieber Gott, wie meine Feind' **47**
BWV 65 Sie werden aus Saba alle kommen **48**
BWV 154 Mein liebster Jesus ist verloren **49**
BWV 81 Jesus schläft, was soll ich hoffen? **50**
BWV 83 Erfreute Zeit im neuen Bunde **51**
BWV 4 Christ lag in Todesbanden **52**
BWV 12 Weinen, Klagen, Sorgen, Zagen **54**
BWV 172 Erschallet ihr Lieder **55**
BWV 184 Erwünschtes Freudenlicht **56**
BWV 165 O heiliges Geist und Wasserbad **57**
BWV 179 Siehe zu, dass deine Gottesfurcht nicht Heuchelei sei **58**
BWV 69 Lobe den Herrn, meine Seele I **59**
BWV 190 Singet dem Herrn ein neues Lied **60**
BWV 73 Herr, wie du willst, so schick's mit mir **61**
BWV 144 Nimm was dein ist, und gehe hin **62**
BWV 181 Leichtgesinnte Flattergeister **63**
BWV 67 Halt im Gedächtnis Jesum Christ **64**
BWV 104 Du Hirte Israel, höre **65**
BWV 166 Wo gehest du hin? **66**
BWV 86 Wahrlich, wahrlich, ich sage euch **67**
BWV 44 Sie werden euch in den Bann tun I **68**
BWV 20 O Ewigkeit, du Donnerwort I **69**
BWV 167 Ihr Menschen, rühmet Gottes Liebe **71**
BWV 136 Erforsche mich, Gott, und erfahre mein Herz **72**
BWV 168 Tue Rechnung! Donnerwort **73**
BWV 105 Herr, gehe nicht ins Gericht **74**
BWV 46 Schauet doch und sehet, ob irgend ein Schmerz sei **75**
BWV 77 Du sollst Gott, deinen Herren, lieben **76**
BWV 8 Liebster Gott, wann werd' ich sterben? **77**
BWV 148 Bringet dem Herrn Ehre seines Namens **78**
BWV 72 Alles nur nach Gottes Willen **79**

BWV 19 Es erhub sich ein Streit **81**
BWV 195 Dem Gerechten muss das Licht **82**
BWV 157 Ich lasse dich nicht, du segnest mich denn **83**
BWV 37 Wer da glaubet und getauft wird **84**
BWV 198 Lass, Fürstin, lass noch einen Strahl (Trauerode) **85**
BWV 93 Wer nur den lieben Gott lässt walten **87**
BWV 159 Sehet, wir gehen hinauf gen Jerusalem **88**
BWV 145 Ich lebe, mein Herze, zu deinem Ergötzen **89**
BWV 171 Gott, wie dein Name, so ist auch dein Ruhm **90**
BWV 156 Ich steh' mit einem Fuss im Grabe **91**
BWV 120 Gott, man lobet dich in der Stille zu Zion **92**
BWV 188 Ich habe maine Zuversicht **94**
BWV 80 Ein feste Burg ist unser Gott **95**
BWV 89 Was soll ich aus dir machen, Ephraim? **96**
BWV 52 Falsche Welt, dir trau' ich nicht **97**
BWV 36 Schwingt freudig euch empor **98**
BWV 82 Ich habe genug **99**
BWV 84 Ich bin vergnügt mit meinem Glücke **100**
BWV 66 Erfreut euch, ihr Herzen **101**
BWV 42 Am Abend aber desselbigen Sabbaths **103**
BWV 112 Der Herr ist mein getreuer Hirt **104**
BWV 174 Ich liebe den Höchsten von ganzen Gemüte **105**
BWV 9 Es ist das Heil uns kommen her **106**
BWV 102 Herr, deine Augen sehen nach dem Glauben **107**
BWV 35 Geist und Seele wird verwirret **108**
BWV 25 Es ist nichts Gesundes an meinem Leibe **109**
BWV 29 Wir danken dir Gott, wir danken dir **110**
BWV 51 Jauchzet Gott in allen Landen **111**
BWV 27 Wer wiess, wie nahe mir mein Ende **112**
BWV 169 Gott soll allein mein Herze haben **113**
BWV 149 Man singet mit Freuden vom Sieg **114**
BWV 56 Ich will den Kreuzstab gerne tragen **116**
BWV 49 Ich geh' und suche mit Verlangen **117**
BWV 109 Ich glaube, lieber Herr, hilf meinem Unglauben **118**
BWV 55 Ich armer Mensch, ich Sündenknecht **119**
BWV 140 Wachet auf, ruft uns die Stimme **119**
BWV 129 Gelobet sei der Herr **121**
BWV 39 Brich dem Hungrigen dein Brot **122**
BWV 177 Ich ruf' zu dir, Herr Jesu Christ **123**
BWV 88 Siehe, ich will viel Fischer aussenden **124**
BWV 170 Vergnügte Ruh', beliebte Seelenlust **126**
BWV 187 Es wartet alles auf dich **127**
BWV 137 Lobe den Herren, den mächtigen König der Ehren **128**

BWV 95 Christus, der ist mein Leben **129**
BWV 98 Was Gott tut, das ist wohlgetan I **130**
BWV 60 O Ewigkeit, du Donnerwort II **131**
BWV 192 Nun danket alle Gott **133**
BWV 58 Ach Gott, wie manches Herzeleid II **134**
BWV 99 Was Gott tut, das ist wohlgetan II **135**
BWV 191 Gloria in excelsis Deo **136**
BWV 117 Sei Lob und Ehr' dem höchsten Gut **136**
BWV 97 In allen meinen Taten **138**
BWV 54 Widerstehe doch der Sünde **140**

E. Composed at Leipzig (1735–1750) **141**

BWV 143 Lobe den Herrn, meine Seele II **141**
BWV 14 Wär' Gott nicht mit uns diese Zeit **143**
BWV 85 Ich bin ein guter Hirt **144**
BWV 103 Ihr werdet weinen und heulen **145**
BWV 108 Es ist euch gut, dass ich hingehe **146**
BWV 87 Bisher habt ihr nichts gebeten in meinem Namen **148**
BWV 43 Gott fähret auf mit Jauchzen **149**
BWV 11 Lobet Gott in seinen Reichen (Himmelfahrtsoratorium) **151**
BWV 128 Auf Christi Himmelfahrt allein **153**
BWV 183 Sie werden euch in den Bann tun II **154**
BWV 74 Wer mich liebet, der wird mein Wort halten II **155**
BWV 68 Also hat Gott die Welt geliebet **156**
BWV 175 Er rufet seinen Schafen mit Namen **158**
BWV 176 Es ist ein trotzig und verzagt Ding **159**
BWV 107 Was willst du dich betrüben **160**
BWV 94 Was frag' ich nach der Welt **162**
BWV 133 Ich freue mich in dir **163**
BWV 100 Was Gott tut, das ist wohlgetan III **164**
BWV 5 Wo soll ich fliehen hin **166**
BWV 79 Gott, der Herr, ist Sonn und Schild **167**
BWV 41 Jesu, nun sei gepreiset **168**
BWV 13 Meine Seufzer, meine Tränen **169**
BWV 249 Kommt, eilet und laufet (Osteroratorium) **171**
BWV 6 Bleib' bei uns, denn es will Abend werden **173**
BWV 28 Gottlob! nun geht das Jahr zu Ende **174**
BWV 17 Wer Dank opfert, der preiset mich **176**
BWV 197 Gott ist unsre Zuversicht **177**
BWV 30 Freue dich, erlöste Schar **179**
BWV 123 Liebster Immanuel, Herzog der Frommen **181**
BWV 32 Liebster Jesu, mein

Verlangen (Dialogus) **182**
BWV 124 Meinen Jesum lass' ich nicht **184**
BWV 3 Ach Gott, wie manches Herzeleid I **185**
BWV 111 Was mein Gott will, das g'scheh allzeit **186**
BWV 92 Ich hab' in Gottes Herz und Sinn **187**
BWV 125 Mit Fried' und Freud' ich fahr' dahin **188**
BWV 126 Erhalt' uns, Herr, bei deinem Wort **190**
BWV 127 Herr Jesu Christ, wahr' Mensch und Gott **191**
BWV 1 Wie schön leuchtet der Morgenstern **192**
BWV 146 Wir müssen durch viel Trübsal in das Reich Gottes eingehen **194**
BWV 34 O ewiges Feuer. O Ursprung der Liebe **195**
BWV 2 Ach Gott, vom Himmel sieh' darein **196**
BWV 135 Ach Herr, mich armen Sünder **197**
BWV 7 Christ, unser Herr, zum Jordan kam **198**
BWV 10 Meine Seel' erhebt den Herren **199**
BWV 45 Es ist dir gesagt, Mensch, was gut ist **200**
BWV 178 Wo Gott, der Herr, nicht bei uns hält **202**
BWV 101 Nimm von uns, Herr, du treuer Gott **203**
BWV 113 Herr Jesu Christ, du höchstes Gut **204**
BWV 193 Ihr Tore zu Zion **206**
BWV 33 Allein zu dir, Herr Jesu Christ **207**
BWV 78 Jesu, der du meine Seele **208**
BWV 138 Warum betrübst du dich, mein Herz **209**
BWV 114 Ach, lieben Christen, seid getrost **211**
BWV 96 Herr Christ, der ein'ge Gottessohn **212**
BWV 130 Herr Gott, dich loben alle wir **214**
BWV 48 Ich elender Mensch, wer wird mich erlösen **215**
BWV 180 Schmücke dich, o liebe Seele **216**
BWV 38 Aus tiefer Not schrei ich zu dir **218**
BWV 115 Mache dich, mein Geist, bereit **219**
BWV 139 Wohl dem, der sich auf seinen Gott **220**
BWV 26 Ach wie flüchtig **221**
BWV 90 Es reifet euch ein schrecklich Ende **223**
BWV 62 Nun komm, der Heiden Heiland II **224**
BWV 91 Gelobet seist du, Jesu Christ **225**
BWV 110 Unser Mund sei voll Lachens **226**
BWV 57 Selig ist der Mann (Dialogus) **228**
BWV 121 Christum wir sollen loben schon **229**
BWV 151 Süsser Trost, mein Jesus kommt **231**
BWV 122 Das neugebor'ne Kindelein **231**
BWV 116 Du Friedefürst, Herr Jesu Christ **233**
BWV 50 Nun ist das Heil und die Kraft **234**
BWV 118 O Jesu Christ, mein's Lebens Licht **234**
BWV 200 Bekennen will ich seinen Namen **235**

II. The Secular Cantatas 236

A. Composed at Weimar **236**

BWV 203 Amore traditore **236**
BWV 209 Non sa che sia dolore **237**
BWV 208 Was mir behagt (Jagdkantate) **238**

B. Composed at Cöthen **240**

BWV 173a Durchlauchtster Leopold **240**
BWV 202 Weichet nur, betrübte Schatten **242**

C. Composed at Leipzig **244**

BWV 249a Entfliehet, verschwindet, entweichet, ihr Sorgen **244**
BWV 36c Schwingt freudig euch empor **246**
BWV 205 Der zufriedengestellte Aeolus **248**
BWV 207 Vereinigte Zwietracht der wechselnden Saiten **250**
BWV 207a Auf, schmetterande Töne **253**
BWV 204 Ich bin in mir vergnügt **256**
BWV 201 Geschwinde, geschwinde, ihr wirbelnden Winde (Der Streit zwischen Phoebus und Pan) **257**
BWV 211 Schweiget stille, plauder nicht (Kaffee-Kantate) **259**
BWV 213 Lasst uns sorgen, lasst uns wachen (Die Wahl des Herkules) **261**
BWV 214 Tönet, ihr Pauken! Erschallet, Trompeten! **263**
BWV 215 Preise dein Glücke, gesegnetes Sachsen **265**
BWV 206 Schleicht, spielende Wellen **267**
BWV 30a Angenehmes Wiederau, freue dich **269**
BWV 212 Mer hahn en neue Oberkeet (Bauernkantate) **271**
BWV 210 O holder Tag, erwünschte Zeit **274**

III. The Christmas Oratorio (Weihnachts-Oratorium) 277

Part 1 **277**
Part 2 **279**
Part 3 **282**
Part 4 **284**
Part 5 **285**
Part 6 **287**

Appendix A: The Sacred Cantatas by Type 291
Appendix B: Cantatas by BWV Number 293

Bibliography **299**
Index **301**

Introduction

For English-only readers of Johann Sebastian Bach's sacred and secular cantata texts, many previous translations from the German have been either too literal or too freely poetic to be readily or accurately understood. Yet it was from his libretti that Bach was motivated to compose the marvelous musical settings admired by listeners throughout the world. It seems evident, therefore, that these texts should be made available in sequential, clearly comprehensible translations, so that non-German speaking readers may gain a better insight into the meaning of each number which inspired Bach's interpretation in sound.

Although Bach's librettists for his cantatas, oratorios and passions did not always produce outstanding poetry, they did give him the key words and phrases upon which he constructed his music. Schweitzer, in his *J. S. Bach,* Vol. II, chapters XIX to XXIII, has examined the interrelation of sound, word and image (music, poetry and painting), showing how Bach applied such relationships in his composition. According to Schweitzer's analysis, the music evokes an *Affekt* or emotion from the words of the text, together with a visual concept of ideas or motives: steps, waves, tumult, calm, storms and clouds.

This tone-painting, combined with a mystical-emotional effect on the listener, is usually not fully appreciated by a non-German speaking audience because without textual comprehension, hearing and "seeing" do not occur simultaneously. Therefore, a translation and analysis of the texts from which Bach worked is essential for any non-German speaking listener wishing to understand how Bach could mold the plastic word into an emotional or pictorial experience. This book attempts to provide that essential information.

One cannot overlook the subjective interpretation by any individual of what he hears. Hence any of the present writer's feelings on a given theme may be questioned, but it is hoped that his observations or comments might be accepted as a guide by the average non-German speaking reader and listener.

The Various Types of Cantatas Composed by Bach

It should be remembered that Bach did not call his vocal compositions cantatas but rather *Stücke* (pieces), *Concerti* or *Motetti,* whether they were written for the Lutheran services or for other events. The reason could be that he, an organist and instrument player, was constantly aware of the importance of the orchestra, so that he regarded voices as other instruments for the performance of his work.

However, we shall use the term cantata to designate these vocal works, which may be divided into three general classifications (see Appendix A):

Free cantatas—the text is based directly on the Bible or a religious poem, and treated by Bach as he wished for choir and soloists.

Solo cantatas—these are without a chorus but may have a concluding chorale; they are intended for one or more soloists.

Chorale cantatas—have the material of a hymn text at the beginning and the end and possibly within the arias and recitatives.

Some of the texts were written by Bach's librettists, whose work he read and used in the following towns:

Mühlhausen—Georg Christian Eilmar.

Weimar—Erdmann Neumeister, Salomo Franck.

Cöthen—Johann Friedrich Helbig.

Leipzig—Christian Weiss, Sr.; Picander; Luther; and Mariane von Zeigler.

Bach may have been his own librettist for some of his earlier cantatas, but in some cases his authorship is uncertain according to Johann Forkel, Bach's first biographer (1802). Bach seems to have favored the chorale cantata, especially from 1735 to 1744, but chorales are featured in most of his vocal writing from Mühlhausen to Leipzig. One must remember that Bach was an organist at Arnstadt, where he played his chorale preludes before composing his first cantatas.

The Church Cantatas

In chronological order, the cities in which Bach composed his cantatas were Mühlhausen, Weimar, Cöthen and Leipzig. A progression in Bach's skill at composing is noticeable from his early efforts at Mühlhausen to his masterpieces at Leipzig, despite the duress under which he worked in this latter city, where he wrote most of his masterpieces.

Bach's choruses, usually at the beginning of a cantata, and arias which sometimes begin or lie within the piece, take their texts usually from the Old or New testament, while the chorales, customarily at the end, are based on Lutheran hymns of the sixteenth or seventeenth centuries. Thus Bach was able to integrate the Gospel word with the words of the Lutheran service to create a total effect in each cantata.

However, Bach modified many chorale tunes to suit himself, and although the congregation of his time could recognize the melody of the hymn, the words sung might or might not be heard as expected. This is especially true where a chorale is sung as cantus firmus for an aria within the cantata. The result is that two simultaneous emotional reactions occur in the listener's mind, which by association adds to the symbolism he hears in the music.

To the modern English-only listener, these hymns are less familiar; hence much of the symbolism dependent on the chorale may be difficult to understand. Close attention to the chorale text in association with the melody should lessen this difficulty. Furthermore, the tunes of some chorales have a certain metrical similarity to familiar hymns which should induce the listener to become more attentive to the actual text being sung.

As the short form of the cantata (most of them are under 30 minutes in duration) is related to the long opera format, we find similar "actors" in the persons who sing arias, recitatives, dialogues, and choruses—sometimes solo and sometimes in a duet. However, our sacred cantata "actors" represent religious personages: Jesus, the Sinner, the Disciples, the Soul, the Holy Spirit.

Bach's use of symbolism in his music comes from his harmonic illustration of certain key words or phrases in the text he sets. These may be classified as:

1. Simple words which impart a visual image: waves, serpent, angel, valley, clouds.

2. Abstract ideas which suggest a visual aspect: *weinen,* to weep; *jauchzen,* to rejoice; *glänzen (der Glanz),* to shine (the shine); *Flamme, Feuer,* flames, fire; and other verbs and nouns.

3. Verbs suggesting motion or lack of motion: *fangen,* to catch; *führen,* to lead; *schweben,* to hover, float; *treten,* to step; *schlafen,* to sleep; *ruhen,* to rest.

4. A sung or instrumental chorale quoted against an independent voice in an aria, or voices in a chorus.

The listener must note these aspects of Bach's method of composing in order to comprehend his art.

The secular cantatas follow the same principles for the musical settings of their texts.

On the Contents of This Book

No attempt has been made here to compare or rate performances of these cantatas, whether in actual concert or on any recording company's label. All the church cantatas have now been done by Helmuth Rilling and another set is being completed soon by Nikolaus Harnoncourt, so that it should be easy to obtain a copy of any cantata which interests the reader.

The church cantatas will be discussed first, chronologically insofar as possible, under the headings of BWV (Bachwerke Verseichnis) number, date, place, format; the same procedure is followed for the secular cantatas in a subsequent section. As Bach often borrowed material from his secular works (even entire cantatas) to fashion his religious ones, a note will be made where the church cantata is treated. The Christmas Oratorio, which consists of six distinct cantatas, is covered completely and placed after the secular cantatas from which many of its numbers are borrowed.

Under the heading for each work, the writer will discuss items in the German libretto which interested him (and presumably Bach too from their resultant treatment). I believe that from this text Bach deduced his imagery in musical form, from which he produced his intensely emotional appeal on his audience.

In discussing the text of soprano or alto arias, the author has used the pronoun "she," even though women's voices were never heard singing these parts in Bach's day. (Choir boys were used instead.) The author has made this decision in the belief that the feminine pronoun is more appropriate to the meaning of the text.

Cantatas included in the Bachgesellschaft but subsequently proved *not* to be the work of Bach have not been included here. Yet it is easy to see why the Bachgesellschaft included them in its lists, for they were in Bach's possession and performed by him. Most of these are also available on record or in score today.

As other books have covered Bach's biography and his instrumental works, these will be mentioned only as they affect his cantatas.

For easy reference, an index and a selected bibliography are included.

It is hoped that this book will help both listeners and performers who wish to understand Bach's artistry in translating the word into divine harmony.

I. The Sacred Cantatas

A. Composed at Mühlhausen (1707–1708)

• **Aus der Tiefe rufe ich, Herr, zu dir (Out of the Depths I Cry, Lord, to Thee)** (1707; BWV 131).

Bach composed this at the request of Georg Christian Eilmar, who was pastor of St. Mary's Church in Mühlhausen, for a mourning service after a fire that destroyed a fourth of the town, including the parish of St. Blasius where Bach had just become organist. Bach set the complete text of Psalm 130, *De Profundis,* plus two stanzas of Ringwaldt's chorale "Herr Jesu Christ, du höchstes Gut" (Lord Jesus Christ, Thou Highest Possession) (1588) in cantus firmus superimposed over the bass and tenor arias. He did not change or add to the psalm text, but took it word for word.

1. *Sinfonia.* Begins the instrumental prelude to the work, reminding one of the seventeenth century format of Buxtehude's cantatas. A somber mood is at once established by the only instruments used in the work: strings, oboe and bassoon.

2. *Chorus.* Repetition of the phrases "Aus der Tiefe" (Out of the depths), followed by "ruf'ich, Her, zu dir" (I cry, Lord, to Thee), gives the feeling that melancholy dejection has brought the petitioners to seek God's help through direct prayer. Then the mood changes to vivace, imploring urgently the Lord's attention to this prayer: ". . . die Stimme meines Flehens" (the voice of my supplication) with special emphasis on "Flehens," beseeching as a visual portrait of somebody at prayer.

3. *Aria—bass (with chorale—sopranos).* "So du willst, Herr, Sünde zurechnen" (Since Thou, Lord, will count up sins) "Herr, wer wird bestehen?" (Lord, who will stand?) The bass continues his entreaty, knowing that his sins will count against him and all other men. Then he realizes that the Lord will forgive and thereby be feared—note the stress placed on "die Vergebung" (forgiveness) and especially "fürchte" (feared) which is given a special coloratura treatment.

4. *Chorus.* The despondent gloom here begins to change into a more confident mood at the knowledge that God will help those who wait on Him. This chorus is the central high point of the cantata (a chorus and an aria before; an aria and a chorus after it). Theme: trust in God by waiting—"Meine Seele harret" (My soul waits) for His aid, "und ich hoffe auf sein Wort" (and I hope in His Word).

5. *Aria—tenor (with chorale—altos).* Length of waiting and patience are indicated in the words "von einer Morgenwache bis zu der andern" (from one morning watch until the next); a reiteration of the preceding chorus but with the chorale producing a rather mystical symbolism.

6. *Chorus.* Begins with three shouts of "Israel" by the full chorus. Hope in the Lord's mercy (die Gnade) and redemption from sin which He will give: "Und er wird Israel *erlösen* aus allen seinen Sünden." (And He will redeem Israel out of all its sins.) This passage is expressed in a joyous fugue, which brings us up from the sadness of despair to the joy of certain forgiveness. Note the emphasis on "Erlö-

sung" (redemption) and "erlösen" (redeem) to color the harmony.

This masterpiece may well have been the first original cantata written by Bach.

• **Gott ist mein König (God Is My King)** (1708; BWV 71).

The text was written by Bach or Eilmar on Psalm 74 with additions from Deuteronomy and Samuel. This was a church-performed cantata for the election of the new Town Council (Ratswahl), and was the only cantata by Bach printed during his lifetime (except a second Ratswahlkantate published at Mühlhausen, unfortunately lost). The printing of these ceremonial pieces was a customary honor paid to the new council by whoever was the town's composer at that time.

There are a full orchestra and two choral groups, which are subdivided into "coro pleno" and a smaller "senza ripieni" choir, both of which may combine into a "tutti." It almost seems as though Bach were experimenting here with voices in concerto grosso style, each section supported by one of three groups of instruments which comprise the festival orchestra: the trumpets and drums, the woodwinds, and the strings. These instrumental sections give tone to the various movements. Again, the style is similar to that of Buxtehude in his church cantatas.

1. *Chorus.* The cantata opens with two great cries of "Gott," followed by "von Alters her" (from long ages past), which focuses our attention on the everlasting majesty of our (my) King (mein König), whose help is given and whose will is done *on earth;* "auf Erden" is repeated three times in a lower register for each repetition.

2. *Aria—tenor (with chorale as cantus firmus).* The predominant pessimistic mood pictured here is that of an old man (perhaps one of the councillors?) who, at the age of eighty, wonders why he should continue the heavy burden of his life. He would like to return to his home-town, to lie in his grave beside his father and his mother. The chorale reinforces this sad image, asking that the old man be spared sin and shame, so that his grey hair not be dishonored.

3. *Choir (quartet).* They sing of consolation to the old man—May your old age be as your youth, for, as then, God is with you in everything that you do. Note the many runs on "in allem" (in all).

4. *Arioso—bass.* Very effective declamation throughout, referring to God's creation of "Tag und Nacht" (day and night) and His guiding of the order of the universe: "Du machest, dass beide, Sonn' und Gestirn, ihren gewissen Lauf haben." (Thou makest that both sun and stars have their certain course.)

This idea is extended to "Du setzet einem jeglichen Lande seine Grenze" (you set the borders for each country). The didactic strain of this arioso and of the following aria would indicate the Divine Right of the Emperor Joseph I (mentioned in the last chorus) to control politics in his Free Imperial City, Mühlhausen.

Notice the da capo aria here for the first time in Bach's usage.

5. *Aria—alto.* "Durch mächtige Kraft" (Through mighty power) continues the preceding idea of God's protection in time of war or political unrest—"Wenn Mord und Kriegessturm ... erhebt" (When murder and the storm of war arise)—in these two images derived from the nouns "Mord" (murder), "Kriegessturm" (storm of war), "Kron und Zepter bebt" (crown and scepter tremble).

Warlike images come to life in this aria through the rumble of the timpani and the abrupt repetition of the first line at the end.

6. *Chorus (Psalm 74–19).* Bach's tone-painting of this Biblical verse is the first of the many great gems in his cantatas. The pleading voices, accompanied by syncopated woodwinds, very well imitate the cooing of doves. (Bach wrote this music thirty years before Handel used bird-call themes to depict the songs of the lark and of the nightingale in his Pastorale, *L'Allegro ed Il Penseroso.*)

Although Bach's reference is somewhat obscure, the turtledoves may represent the town councillors and the townspeople of Mühlhausen, who vocally entreat the Lord that their actions will not lead them to Satan: "Du wollest dem Feinde nicht geben die Seele deiner Turteltauben." (Thou wouldst not give to the enemy the soul of Thy turtledoves.)

This chorus is exceptionally moving by virtue of its simultaneously sounding onomatopoeia of voices and recorders.

7. *Chorus.* A joyous conclusion for the full vocal and instrumental forces is heard. The new regime will bring peace and prosperity to their town, so that their *"fortune, welfare* and *great victory"* (Glück, Heil und grosser Sieg) will make their Emperor Joseph rejoice.

It is curious that Bach brings this chorus to an abrupt end at the repetition of this phrase; without at least some instrumental completion, the choir stops suddenly and so does the music. Was the composer in such a hurry to finish this chorus that he fragmented its ending, or was this the effect he wished to produce?

• **Der Herr denkt an uns (The Lord Is Mindful of Us)** (1708; BWV 196).

The libretto consists only of the verses in Psalm 115 (12 to 15), which Bach set directly. The event was a wedding in the village of Dornheim just outside Arnstadt in the church in which Bach had previously married his cousin Maria Barbara Bach in 1707. This time it was Maria Barbara's aunt who was being married to the pastor of the Dornheim church, Johann Lorenz Stauber, who had performed the ceremony for Bach and Maria Barbara.

This cantata is lightly scored for instruments (strings and organ continuo) as befits the occasion, but has soprano, tenor and bass soloists with a chorus.

1. *Sinfonia.* This introduction is very apt for the beginning of a wedding ceremony. An atmosphere of sublime peace is created by the unison strings.

2. *Chorus.* The choir expresses the calm reassurance that "Der Herr denket an uns und segnet uns" (The Lord is mindful of us and blesses us). His blessing on the present Christian congregation is symbolized in the Biblical lines: "Er segnet das Haus Israel Er segnet das Haus Aaron." (He blesses the house of Israel He blesses the house of Aaron.)

3. *Aria—soprano.* Throughout this, the joy motif is predominate; God will bless them who fear Him, whether they are humble or mighty.

4. *Duet—tenor and bass.* Here we hear a wish that God will bless the couple more and more (je mehr und mehr), them and their children yet to be born. The imagery reveals a rainfall of many gifts, coming down from Heaven like a mysterious benediction.

5. *Chorus.* Now comes the high point of the work: "Ihr seid die Gesegneten des Herrn, der Himmel und Erde gemacht hat. Amen." (Ye are the blessed of the Lord, who has made Heaven and Earth. Amen.) Notice the high tones placed on "Himmel," and the low ones given to "Erde."

The florid singing of the "Amen," which concludes the cantata in a more satisfying way than in the last chorus of BWV 71 (see previous entry), seems to waft the listener from earth to heaven. Such a conclusion is worthy of Handel's greatest "amen" choruses.

• **Meine Seele rühmt und preist (My Soul Glorifies and Praises)** (c. 1707–10; BWV 189).

This is Bach's first solo cantata (presumed to have been composed by him in the original lists of the Bach Gesellschaft), based on a paraphrase of the *Magnificat.* It is for tenor, but the solo voice really forms part of a quintet for voice, flute, oboe, violin and continuo. It shows how much Bach considered the voice to be equal to any accompanying instruments, yet having its own individual part to play in an ensemble.

The arias are all in da capo form and here we find the first use of recitatives in Italian style. This cantata is without choruses and chorales.

1. *Aria.* We hear a very forceful begin-

ning by the tenor (who represents a poor sinner) in praise of "God's grace and rich goodness" (Gottes Huld und reiche Güte) towards him. The rest of the aria is an expansion of this theme: his whole being rejoices in God, "Der mein Heil und Helfer heisst" (Who is called my salvation and helper). There is a long run on the word "erfreut" (rejoices), and also on "preist" (praises) in the da capo repeat of the first line, which the listener should find very impressive.

2. *Recitative.* When he examines his life, the tenor's declamation changes to arioso in the third line, "Gott, Gott! was hast du doch an mir getan!" (God, God, what hast Thou then to me done!) This is a statement of wonder and appreciation for all benefits he has received.

3. *Aria.* This aria does not have the same high quality of the first; it seems to be more like an arioso evolved from recitative than a true aria. The statement that God on high looks down on the world, which in turn looks down on the sinner, who yet is not forgotten by God, seems more didactic than lyrical.

4. *Recitative.* A rather standard secco declamation, with continuo only, continues to extol God for his bounty: "Er hat mir Leib und Leben Er hat mir auch das Recht zur Seligkeit Und was mich hier und dort erfreut Aus lauter Huld gegeben." (He has to me body and life He has to me also the right to blessedness And whatever me here and there rejoices From pure grace given.)

5. *Aria.* This happy lyrical conclusion gives the listener a feeling of reassurance that God's mercy is everlasting, especially for the poor, who are devoted to Him. The idea of never-ending mercy is well brought out in the verb "währet," repeated and drawn out very artistically: "Deine Güte, dein Erbarmen Währet, Gott, zu aller Zeit" (Thy goodness, Thy pity lasts, God, at all times.)

One gets the feeling that a happy confidence is always to be had if one trusts in God, as the radiance of this aria suggests.

• **Nach dir, Herr, verlanget mich (For Thee, Lord, I Long)** (c. 1708–1710; BWV 150).

The occasion for this cantata is unknown. It is still in the old style of alternating choruses and arias, without recitatives and da capo repeats. The text is based on Psalm 25 (1, 2, 5, 15) for the first three choruses, with original additions to the libretto for the soprano aria, the trio and the final chorus. Bach's arrangement of the text and his authorship have been questioned, but the music is certainly his, I feel.

The work is written for soprano, alto, tenor, bass and chorus.

1. *Sinfonia.* The orchestra, which consists of only two violins and one bassoon for the entire cantata, plays a very smooth, lulling introduction, suggestive of the "verlangen" (longing) theme, which will pervade all the rest of the numbers in the cantata.

2. *Chorus.* "Nach dir, Herr, verlanget mich" (For Thee, Lord, I long) forms the appealing invocation addressed to the Lord; this is followed by a faster tempo in the rest of the movement to denote the urgency of the pleading: "Mein Gott, ich hoffe auf dich." (My God, I hope in Thee). "Ich hoffe" is repeated four times as if to emphasize the sincerity of the belief felt.

Then we hear a tumultuous reiteration of what the speaker longs for: "Lass mich nicht zuschanden werden, dass sich meine Feinde nicht freuen über mich." (Let me not become ashamed, so that my enemies may not rejoice over me.)

3. *Aria—soprano.* Bach's treatment of this aria is highly emotional (as is also the soprano aria in his later cantatas, especially BWV 199 at Weimar), even though this aria is not in da capo form.

"Doch bin und bleibe ich vergnügt, obgleich hier zeitlich toben," has a moving emotional contrast between the lengthened "toben" (rages) and the simple statement of "vergnügt." (Still I am and remain content, although here at times rages...) Then after listing the things that beset her, symbolically pictured in "*Kreuz, Sturm* und *andere Proben* . . . Tod, Höll. . . (Cross, storm and other trials . . . death, Hell. . .), she realizes that God's Right will prevail after all her misfortunes: "Ob Unfall schlägt den treuen Knecht / Recht ist und bleibt ewig Recht." (Whether mischance strikes the faithful servant / Right is and remains always right.)

4. *Chorus.* This begins with a plea to God to lead "me" (the supplicant) in His truthfulness and teach this to me as a believer, "for Thou art the God who helps me." The concluding section, "täglich harre ich dein" (daily I wait upon Thee), seems to contain a contrast between the confidence the speaker claims in his daily waiting with the unsteady musical background of the accompanying instruments—these could represent the sound of confusion in the world surrounding the speaker.

5. *Terzett (trio)—alto, tenor, bass.* There is a marvelous word painting of nature in sweeping melody here as Bach describes a windstorm which uproots cedar trees. This produces a metaphor, for men, who think and act according to God's will are in no danger of being upset by the winds of fate: "Achtet nicht, was widerbellt" (Heed not what is contrary [to God]). There is a lively play on "widerbellt," after which the agitation subsides into a beautifully peaceful final line: "Denn sein Wort ganz anders lehrt" (For His Word quite otherwise teaches).

6. *Chorus.* A broadly sweeping choral beginning reminds us of the breezes in the Terzett, by its repeats of "stets zu dem Herrn" (always to the Lord), to where "my" eyes look. Then comes a lively fugue on the idea that the Lord will pull the believer's foot out of the net of evil—a dramatic tonal image of an escape from a snare.

7. *Chorus.* This final movement is called Ciaccona (Chaconne), a stately dance, the music of which Bach translates to form his conclusion. The majestic sweeping flow of the lines denotes that God will lead us to joy after sustaining us during our earthly pain: "Christen auf den Dornenwegen / Führen Himmels Bleibet Gott mein treuer Schutz / kraft und Segen. / Achte ich nicht Menschentrutz." (Christians on the thorny roads / Lead Heaven's strength and blessing. / If God remains my true protector, / I heed not man's defiance.)

In the last two lines, a picture is suggested—Jesus stands beside the believer to help him victoriously fight the good fight every day: "Christus, der uns steht zur Seiten / Hilft mir täglich sieghaft streiten." (Christ, Who stands at our side / Helps me daily fight victoriously.)

It is important to notice that many of Bach's religious cantatas begin on a negative theme—despair, grief or guilt—but end on a positive note of joy, consolation or hope. This cantata is a good example, in that it shows longing changing into confidence.

• **Gottes Zeit ist die allerbeste Zeit (God's Time Is the Very Best Time) [Actus tragicus]** (Possibly 1707 or 1711; BWV 106).

The date of composition of this funeral cantata is dubious, because Bach conducted it both in Mühlhausen and in Weimar for two different mourning ceremonies. It is probable that he wrote it in 1707 upon the death of his uncle, Tobias Lämmerhirt of Erfurt, and later performed it again at the funeral of the Weimar rector Philipp Grossgebauer in 1711. Perhaps one could ascribe the earlier date, as it is written in the old style, which Bach was using in Mühlhausen (alternating choruses and arias).

Bach's deep preoccupation with death and the afterlife, which we have observed in his previous cantatas, is summed up in this perfect masterpiece, whose lyrics were compiled by either Eilmar or Bach himself. This work could be the culmination of the 17th century style of cantata writing, all previous efforts leading to this great Bach elegy. This is not to say that Bach did not later return to this old style of Buxtehude and of Tunder, but when he arrived in Weimar, he suddenly began composing in the new style, advocated in the texts of Neumeister and Franck, which he would use for his compositions at the ducal chapel in the Weimar Himmelsburg (Heavenly fortress).

The libretto of BWV 106 is suitably based on both the Old and the New testaments: Psalms 90 (12) and 31 (5), Isaiah 38 (1), Ecclesiastes 14 (17), Acts 17 (28), Revelations 22 (20), Luke 23 (43), and hymns by Luther and Reusner. The theme is on the fear of death in the Old Testament, and the joy in death in the New Testament. It is scored for soprano, alto, tenor, bass as soloists, a choir and a simple orchestra, consisting of only two recorders, two violas da gamba and continuo.

1. *Sonatina.* This melancholy prelude features the two recorders in a fitting background melody for the funeral service. Their sad tones seem to evoke a picture of a mist-shrouded autumnal landscape; in fact, this image lasts throughout the cantata.

2. *Chorus.* They quietly assert that God controls our lives as long as He wills, until He calls us through death at the time He deems best. This Christian fatalism finds poignant expression in the verbs of the text: "In ihm *leben, weben,* und *sind* wir, so lange er *will.* / In ihm *sterben* wir zu rechter Zeit, wenn er *will.*" (In Him we *live, act,* and *are,* as long as He *wills.* / In Him we *die* at the right time, when He *wills.*)

Without any pause, the soloists take up the remainder of this chorus, each taking a new thought. (Note that Bach always chooses the bass voice to represent Christ.)

TENOR: "Lord, teach us to consider that we must die in order to become wise."

BASS: "Put your house in order, for you will die. / It is the old covenant: Man, thou must die!" (At this point a chorale is intoned by the instruments.)

SOPRANO: "Yes, come, Lord Jesu, come!" (The repetition of this high-soaring arioso should touch a tender spot in any listener.)

ALTO: "Into Thy Hands I commend my spirit: Thou has redeemed me, Lord, Thou faithful God."

BASS: "Today shalt thou be with Me in Paradise." (This repeated statement by the bass seems to glow with ecstasy.)

The mounting emotion to be felt in "Paradise," which is stressed, and the alto voice singing Luther's paraphrasing of the chorale *Nunc Dimittis* simultaneously, affords the listener an insight into Bach's mysticism. One feels that he too has been transfigured by the impact of such music.

"Mit Fried und Freud ich fahr dahin / In Gottes Willen. . ." (With peace and joy I travel thither / In God's will. . .) Thus intones the chorale.

Then the base fades away at the words "sanft und stille" (soft and still), leaving the chorale to give the concluding impression that death has delivered the spirit from the body: "Der Tod ist mein Schlaf worden." (Death has become my sleep.)

3. *Chorus.* This is a song of praise to God the Father, to the Son and to the Holy Spirit, whose power makes us triumphant through Jesus Christ. The block harmonies are impressive and terminate in a brilliant double fugue, repeating the "Amen" until a final single "Amen" ends the work on a hushed note.

B. Composed at Weimar (1708–1717)

These cantatas mark the beginning of Bach's decision to compose regular yearly cycles of cantatas, designated for each Sunday and sacred feast day in the church calendar. He was required to write one a month for Duke Wilhelm Ernst, to be performed in his chapel in the Himmelsburg palace. (This edifice was destroyed by fire later in the eighteenth century, after Bach's death.)

The duke engaged Bach at first as a "Cammermusicus," i.e., an instrument player on the violin or harpsichord in the duke's small orchestra. Two years later

Bach became court organist, thus being able to write a large number of works for the organ, although his purpose in moving from Arnstadt ("to compose a well-regulated church music without further vexation") appears still to have been somewhat delayed in its fulfillment.

After he had, in his frustration, sought and been offered the post of organist in the Liebfraukirche in Halle, Duke Wilhelm Ernst decided to promote Bach to Concertmeister in 1714, with the specific duty of composing and performing a new vocal work every month. Consequently, Bach, having realized his goal, declined the Halle position and decided to remain in Weimar.

It is important that one remember Bach's continual activity as instrumentalist and organist when he first settled in Weimar, as this had a bearing on the cantatas he composed from 1714 on.

Of equal importance is the fact that Bach would be constrained to adapt his musical composition to the new-style writers of religious verse, Neumeister and Franck, whose poems contain recitatives and arias in the popular eighteenth century Italian manner (i.e. da capo arias).

• **Gleichwie der Regen und Schnee vom Himmel fällt (Just as the Rain and Snow from Heaven Falls)** (1714; BWV 18).

This cantata is unusual in two respects; its development depends largely on the use of recitatives and chorales (there is only one aria), and the instrumentation consists of four violas (no violins), two recorders, a bassoon and organ continuo accompaniment.

The text is taken from Erdmann Neumeister's "Fünffache Kirchen-Andachten" (Five-fold Church Devotions): Isaiah 55 (10, 11), four clauses of Luther's Litany for the chorale backing the tenor-bass recitative, and the final chorale of Spengler's hymn, "Durch Adams Fall ist ganz verderbt" (By Adam's Fall, It Is Quite Ruined).

It is written for soprano, tenor and bass soloists with chorus.

1. *Sinfonia.* This is a chaconne for the whole instrumental ensemble. We hear a beautiful pastorale, depicting the quiet fall of rain and snow in early spring or late winter.

2. *Recitative — bass.* Here the voice of Christ gives vocal expression to the above picture in a simile: "Just as the rain and snow falls from heaven and makes the earth fertile . . . so the Word from My mouth will bear fruit in mankind." The voice seems to descend in broken phrases like raindrops splashing down in an irregular pattern. Alternating arioso sections in this recitative give this impression: "sondern feuchtet die Erde" (but fertilizes the earth); "sondern tun, das mir gefällt" (but do that which pleases Me).

3. *Recitative — tenor, bass and chorale (litany).* The tenor entreats God to send his Word like seed into his heart.

Here, as in after each section of the recitative, the choir sings parts of Luther's militant litany, which interrupt the peaceful musical description of nature which has preceded: "Du wollest deinen Geist und Kraft zum Worte geben; / Erhör uns, lieber Herre Gott!" (Thou wilt give thy Spirit and Strength to the Word; / Hear us, good Lord God!)

The bass sings a plea to God for protection against the devil's deceit "des Teufels Trug," which tries to rob us of God's Word.

The tenor mentions that many renounce Word and faith and so fall like rotten fruit, whenever they suffer the temporary pain of persecution. Bach makes a long run on "Verfolgung" (persecution) as if in anticipation of the next chorale comment: "Und uns vor des Türken und des Papsts grausamen Mord und Lästerungen" (And us protect from the terrible murder and blasphemies of the Turk and the Pope). These dangers were more threatening to Luther in his time than to Bach in his, but Bach adhered faithfully to the chorale text of his spiritual father.

The bass lists the sins that Christians commit: gluttony, Mammon (greed for money), lust and debauchery. Then the chorale implores: "Alle Irrige und Verführte wiederbringen; / Erhör uns, lieber Herre Gott!" (Bring back all those in error and led astray; / Hear us, good Lord God!)

4. *Aria—soprano.* This is like a ray of sunshine after the sermonizing of the preceding recitative. The music has a wave-like melody, possibly called to Bach's mind by the word "Netze" (nets), which the world and Satan stretch out to catch worthless souls; she, however, will hope to avoid the nets in knowing that "Mein Seelenschatz ist Gottes Wort" (My soul's treasure is God's Word). Her rejection of Satan's proffered treasures is lyrically expressed in "Fort mit allen, fort, nur fort!" (Away with all that, away, just away!) with its effective ritornello.

5. *Chorale.* The choir expresses the hope that God will not take away His Word, which He has given to "me," as protection against sin and guilt. "Wer sich nur fest darauf verlässt, / Der wird den Tod nicht schauen" (Whoever trusts firmly in His Word will not look upon death): brings us back to the original idea that God's Word falls upon us from above like rain or snow, so that we may grow like seeds to bear fruit for Him.

• **Ich hatte viel Bekümmernis (I Had Much Worry in My Heart)** (1714; BWV 21).

Both Schweitzer and Spitta attribute this libretto to Franck. It was written for any occasion, with perhaps the largest orchestra used by Bach since BWV 71, *Gott ist mein König,* in 1708: a thirteen-part instrumental group, consisting of three trombones, a drum, an oboe, a cello, two violins, a bassoon and four additional continuo instruments. The vocal force has a soprano, a tenor and a bass as soloists with a chorus. The cantata is in two parts because of its length; it is assumed that the sermon occurred between these parts, as was the custom for the longer *Hauptstücke* (main concert pieces).

With this cantata, Bach seems to have reached his maturity in his cantata style; from this point he developed full mastery of the genre. He is able to paint in musical terms the Christian's daily life, with its attendant emotions: despair and hope, agony and relief, distress and joy. The listener's ear, inner eye, and feelings are all awakened together by his treatment of the texts he sets.

The Biblical passages for this libretto are: Part I, Psalm 94 (19) and Psalm 42 (5); Part II, Psalm 116 (7) and Revelation 5 (12, 13). Also in both parts we see the use of the parable of the lost sheep, Luke 15 (1–10).

Part I

1. *Sinfonia.* A melancholy mood pervades this opening movement in a duet between the violins and the oboe, which represents the theme of Part I—the soul in despair over being lost from God, just as a lost sheep in a desolate region would be without its shepherd. The tempo seems to suggest the halting steps of the sheep, as it searches and pauses.

2. *Chorus.* "Ich hatte viel Bekümmernis in meinem Herzen" (I had much worry in my heart) begins with a repetition of "ich" three times before its amplification (also repeated) of "viel Bekümmernis." The Hamburg critic, Mattheson, criticized Bach for treating his text in this way. Yet Bach's originality is clearly seen in such a splendid vocal opening.

The dejected mood then suddenly changes into a brilliant vivace at the word "aber" (but), at which there is a significant pause to mark the change into the joy motif as a counterbalance to the first theme: "aber deine Tröstungen erquicken meine Seele" (but Thy consolations revive my soul.) This great fresco of harmonious rapture seems to banish all the trouble previously stated.

3. *Aria—soprano.* Here we have a lugubrious return to sadness, indicated by the frequency of nouns: "Seufzer, Tränen, Kummer, Not, / Ängstliches Sehnen, Furcht und Tod" (Sighs, tears, worry, need, / Anxious longing, fear and death), which appears to be unusual for

a light soprano voice, but presages the initial chorus of the later BWV 12, *Weinen, Klagen, Sorgen, Zagen.*

4. *Recitative—tenor.* The tenor utters a plaintive cry to the Lord, to ask why he has been abandoned by Him. This recalls the picture of the lost sheep in its brokenhearted declamation: "Du warest meine Lust (Thou wert my joy) . . . Ich suche dich an allen Orten (I seek Thee in all places), / Ich ruf und schrei dir nach (I call and cry after Thee. . . .)"

5. *Aria—tenor.* The word-painting in this aria is outstanding; all the images pertain to water and the sea. First we hear a repining largo theme well suited to the tenor's words about the streams of salt tears he sheds continually: "Bäche von gesalznen Zähren, / Fluten rauschen stets einher." (Brooks of salted tears, / Flow always gushing along.)

Suddenly the tempo becomes allegro to portray a storm at sea, wherein the salt tears become an ocean, dragging down a drowning man after the break-up of his ship—" Mast und Anker wollen brechen" (Mast and anchor want to break). The doomed man sees the abyss of hell, as he sinks. A dismal scene, but what astounding imagery in this aria!

6. *Chorus.* Bach concludes Part I with this magnificent chorus in the form of a prelude and fugue. The prelude solemnly asks why "my" soul is so sad and uneasy within me; the fugue comprises the second half of the chorus with great emotional stress in its lines: "denn ich werde ihm danken, dass er meines Angesichtes Hilfe und mein Gott ist." (for I shall still thank Him, that He is the help of my countenance and my God.)

This chorus seems to mark the turning point in the cantata from sadness to happiness. The music is very moving, especially with the vocal repetitions in the canon. Any listener should be overwhelmed by the sincere sentiment expressed in this chorus.

Part II

7. *Recitative—soprano, bass.* A dialogue between the Soul and Jesus, returning to the theme of the lost sheep, but giving the Lord's reassurance of His loving protection.

8. *Duet—soprano, bass.* Again in dialogue to continue the theme of the above recitative. Bach may have copied the quick vocal exchanges from the Hamburg opera, but despite criticism that it is not suitable for church music, this dialogue proves that Bach has real dramatic ability.

9. *Chorus and Chorale.* Although this chorale based on G. Neumark's hymn, "Wer nur den lieben Gott lässt walten" (Who only lets the dear God act), is not clearly distinguished when sung by one section of the choir, it nevertheless forms an impressive background to this, the longest of Bach's choruses thus far. The constantly repeated line sung by the main choir, "Sei nun wieder zufrieden, meine Seele, denn der Herr tut dir Guts" (Be now again satisfied, my soul, for the Lord does to thee good things), paints a huge vocal canvas of the Lord's majestic power of consolation. It is overpowering in its impact on the listener, as Bach uses all the voices and instruments to produce this mighty éclat for faith in God.

10. *Aria—tenor.* This is a cheerful reflection, which continues the above chorus, but on a personal level; for him, Jesus' love banishes all care and weeping and replaces them by rejoicing now.

11. *Chorus.* Another massive prelude and fugue for the entire group; the first section of the chorus sings the prelude, which reminds the listener of Handel's final chorus, "Worthy Is the Lamb" in *Messiah.* "Das Lamm, das erwürgt ist, ist würdig zu nehmen Kraft und Weisheit und Stärke und Ehre und Preis und Lob." (Revelation 5 [12]). (The Lamb, that is slaughtered, is worthy of taking power and wisdom and strength and honor and praise and laud.)

There is a remarkable piling up of nouns to inspire Bach's imagination here, and in the inverted order for the brilliant fugue which follows: "Lob und Ehre und Preis und Gewalt sei unsrem Gott von Ewigkeit zu Ewigkeit. Amen.

Alleluja!" (Laud and honor and praise and might be to our God from everlasting to everlasting. Amen. Alleluja!)

Handel uses the same prelude and fugue construction for *Messiah*'s final chorus based on the same text, but he keeps to a fugal "Amen" only, while Bach includes a florid "Alleluja" in his conclusion.

The listener should compare both choruses.

• **Mein Herze schwimmt im Blut (My Heart Swims in Blood)** (1714; BWV 199).

The unusual title for this solo soprano cantata was taken from a Neumeister text, but the rest of the libretto was by a little-known poet, Georg Christian Lehms, whose texts were frequently set by the Darmstadt court chapel composer, J.C. Graupner. The text is based on the Gospel for the day, Luke 18 (9–14), the parable of the Pharisee and the Publican.

The theme deals with the transformation of a sinner (the Publican), conscious of his sins, through regret and repentance, to the forgiveness of God.

The instrumentation is fairly light, in keeping with the solo voice: two violins, a viola, an oboe, a bassoon and string continuo.

1. *Recitative.* The soprano begins a rather lengthy account of her guilty conscience; she is ashamed of the sins she has committed: "Mein Herze schwimmt im Blut, weil mich der Sünden Brut in Gottes heiligen Augen zum Ungeheuer macht." (My heart swims in blood, because the brood of sin in God's holy eyes makes me a monster.) Furthermore as Adam's seed, my soul is robbed of all repose and Heaven is closed to me.

2. *Aria and Recitative.* The "stumme seufzer, stille Klagen" (dumb sighs, quiet moans) of the aria part show to what extent her regret has penalized her. Then in an arioso-recitative, she states that her heart is a well of hot tears; how will she be able to appease God? The da capo of the aria then restates the beginning of it.

3. *Recitative.* This movement is taken directly from Luke 18 (13)—"And the publican, standing afar off, would not lift up so much as his eyes unto heaven, but smote upon his breast, saying, God be merciful to me." The soprano declaims: "Gott sei mir Sünder gnädig" (God be merciful to me, a sinner), because I have shown atonement for my sins. This leads directly into the following aria, which is the high point of the cantata.

4. *Aria.* Its broad-sounding solemnity and heart-felt melody again remind the listener of Handel. The emotional humility expressed in "Tief gebückt und voller Reue lieg ich, liebster Gott, vor dir" (Deeply bowed and full of regret, I lie, dear God, before Thee), with its orchestral ritornello and vocal repeats, cannot fail to move any listener. In its development into "Ich bekenne meine Schuld" (I confess my guilt) and "aber habe doch Geduld mit mir!" (but do have patience with me!), we perceive the total transformation of the sinner through this prayer of repentance. The runs on the words "Reue" (regret) and "Geduld" (patience) have an intensely poignant appeal. This is certainly one of Bach's most beautiful and moving arias.

5. *Recitative.* Exceedingly short, only one line: "Auf diese Schmerzensreu fällt mir alsdann dies Trostwort bei." (At this painful repentance, occurs to me then this word of comfort.) This introduces the following chorale.

6. *Chorale.* With only string accompaniment, this hymn taken from J. Heermann's "Wo soll ich fliehen hin" (Whither Shall I Flee) is unusual because it is sung by only one soprano voice and because we would expect it to come at the end of the cantata rather than at this point. The repentant states that she will cast all her sins into the Lord's wounds, whence will come her salvation.

7. *Recitative.* This leads into the final aria which follows. She will place herself in the Lord's wounds in order to find her true resting-place, where her faith will give her gladness.

8. *Aria.* The music to show her gladness lies in the gigue tune which she sings. Here, once more, we notice Bach's interest in dance rhythms upon which to set vocal themes. Perhaps he still remembers the French tunes he had played as a violinist in Celle years before.

The joyful, rocking lilt to the music is well suited to the words: "Wie freudig ist mein Herz, da Gott versöhnet ist..." (How glad is my heart, since God is conciliated...)

"After my repentance and pain"—thus she concludes her aria, to end the cantata, without a final chorale.

• **Nun komm, der Heiden Heiland (Now Come, Savior of the Heathen) I** (1714; BWV 61).

The textual sources of this cantata are Luther's hymn of the above title for stanza 1, Revelation 3 (20) for the recitative for bass, and P. Nicolai's hymn "Wie schön leuchtet der Morgenstern" (How Beautifully Shines the Morning-Star) for the final chorale. The whole libretto was by Neumeister; Bach set it for soprano, tenor, bass and chorus. The Gospel is Matthew 21 (1–9), Christ's entry into Jerusalem.

1. *Chorus (Overture).* Bach's preoccupation with instrumental works probably induced him to compose this slow-fast-slow French overture, treating the voices and instruments on equal terms. The Gospel chosen is out of season for Advent, but in Luther's hymn, the coming of the Savior points ahead to His final triumph in overcoming death.

The first two lines of this chorus, marked *grave* (slow), are a solemn supplication to Jesus to come to us: "Nun komm, der Heiden Heiland, / Der Jungfrauen Kind erkannt," (Now come, Savior of the Heathens, / Recognized Child of the Virgin).

The next line, marked *gai* (allegro) by Bach, gives us the second movement of the overture: "Des sich wundert alle Welt" (At which the whole world wonders).

The last line of Luther's stanza then returns to the slow *(grave)* part of the overture: "Gott solch Geburt ihm bestellt" (God has ordained such a birth for him).

A mystical atmosphere is conjured up in our minds by the musical tempo of this wonderful chorale-chorus, which seems to visualize for us a pious procession singing on its way into Jerusalem.

2. *Recitative and Arioso—tenor.* In his declamation of this recitative, the tenor describes the arrival (Birth) of the Savior and the blessings He has given us. The last two lines are sung arioso to reinforce what he has stated: "Du kommst und lässt dein Licht / Mit vollem Segen scheinen." (You come and let your light / With full blessing shine on us.)

3. *Aria—tenor.* Bach's instrumental bent appears here again in the rhythm of a slow gigue to accompany this aria. The slow first part expresses the wish that Jesus come to His church and give a blessed New Year. The last part quickens to extend the blessing requested upon pulpit and altar, from which His holy teaching comes. The entire aria seems to float like a magic cloud.

4. *Recitative—bass.* This text is taken directly from Revelation 3 (20), vividly depicting Jesus standing before our door and knocking. The bass voice again represents Jesus, who wants anyone who hears Him knocking to open the door, so that they may sup together (in communion).

The musical imagery is remarkable, illustrating by the constant plucking of the strings (pizzicato) the actual knocking at the door. This is an artistic device that Bach will use again later: it makes this particular recitative one of Bach's never-to-be-forgotten numbers.

5. *Aria—soprano.* She expresses a joyful greeting at the arrival of the Savior into her own heart upon His Advent. Although she is only dust and earth, He will not disdain her.

6. *Chorale.* This closing number is very short, as it uses only a part of one stanza of Nicolai's hymn. Thus the conclusion seems out of balance with the

preceding sections. But what Bach has set is very well done, even if brief. This chorale is like the end of a prayer, supported by the full orchestra. We can almost see people, waiting for the rising of the morning star, from the context of the words "Freudenkrone" (crown of joy) and "Deiner wart ich mit Verlangen" (I wait for you with longing).

The only strangeness to be noticed in the text is that the words "Amen, Amen!" stand at the beginning instead of at the end of the stanza.

• **Himmelskönig, sei willkommen (Heavenly King, Be Welcome)** (1715; BWV 182).

For Palm Sunday, Bach set this cantata to the libretto of the Weimar court poet, Salomo Franck. This text is based on St. Matthew's account of the Passion (Matthew 21 [1–9]), Psalm 40 (7, 8), and Paul Stockmann's hymn "Jesu Leiden, Pein und Tod" (Jesus' Suffering, Pain and Death) for the chorale, as befits the Easter season. It is unusual in that it consists of only one recitative, has three arias in succession, and ends up with the chorale as the penultimate number, to which is added a final chorus (resulting in two choruses in a row). The soloists are alto, tenor, and bass with the usual chorus.

1. *Sonata.* As in BWV 61, pizzicato strings give a serious (adagio) timbre to this instrumental overture. We find the step motive strongly emphasized by them; this time Bach pictures the steady, solemn tread of a procession as it plods onwards towards Jerusalem.

2. *Chorus.* Expresses fervently the crowd's welcome to the Lord, who has taken their hearts. They want to share in His coming victory in Zion, by His conquest of their hearts. "Himmelskönig, sei willkommen, / Lass auch uns dein Zion sein!" (Heavenly King, be welcome, Let us also be your Zion!)

3. *Recitative—bass.* Represents the voice of the Lord, saying that He has come to do His Father's will. This bass arioso, taken from Psalm 40 (7, 8), imparts a mysterious overtone of foreboding, as Jesus says that He submits to God's purpose in bringing Him here.

4. *Aria—bass.* Comments on how much God loved the world, that He would send His Son as its Savior by His sacrifice. The sound of the music seems, however, to be more suited to a recitative than to an aria, because it narrates more than being lyrical.

5. *Aria—alto.* A more animated aria than the preceding: Christians must submit to the Lord in the same way as Christ submitted to God. In their belief, they should dedicate their all to Him: "Leib und Leben und Vermögen / Sei dem König itzt geweiht." (Body and life and possessions / Be dedicated now to the King.)

6. *Aria—tenor.* The most touching of these three arias, with only continuo accompaniment, reveals this Christian's devotion to Christ. Despite the troubles the world puts on him, he will adhere to the Lord, with whom he will find his reward. Notice the scene before Pilate, which is inferred in the text, and how he applies it to himself in these lines: "Schreit die Welt nur 'Kreuzige,' / So lass mich nicht fliehen, / Herr, von deinem Kreuzpanier; / Kron und Palmen find ich hier." (Cries the world only "Crucify," / So let me not flee. / Lord, from Thy Cross-banner, / Here I find crown and palms."

Mention should be made of how the word "Palmen" in this context brings us back to the celebration of this special Sunday.

7. *Chorale fantasia.* This is a stupendous movement, packed with emotion for the listener, and by its fugal development involving us in the symbolic significance of Christ's Passion and what it means for humankind. The elaborate choral fantasia abounds with the joy-motive. This is the first time that Bach has used a fantasia in a cantata chorale, and it is a masterpiece!

8. *Chorus.* This *Schlusschor* (closing chorus) returns us to Bach's usual optimism, to be observed at the end of any of his cantatas. The procession has

changed its stately, solemn pace into a happy, dancing swing. We see the welcoming crowd casting palms before the Lord, who leads the throng. The text forms their song, which they sing in chorus: "So lasset uns gehen in Salem der Freuden, / Begleitet den König in Lieben und Leiden. / Er geht voran / Und öffnet die Bahn." (So let us go into Joyful Salem, / Accompany the King in love and grief. / He goes on ahead / And opens the way.)

• **Der Himmel lacht, die Erde jubilieret (Heaven Laughs, the Earth Rejoices)** (1715; BWV 31).

This marvelous work, written for Easter Day, 21 April 1715, and performed by Bach in the Ducal Chapel of Weimar, must have thrilled its audience. There can be no doubt that Bach considered it to be one of his most successful cantatas, since he refashioned it for reperformance in Leipzig in 1724 and in 1731. Salomo Franck wrote the libretto, taken from his collection entitled *Evangelisches Andachts-Opfer* (Evangelical Devotional Offering), 1715, except for the chorale "Wenn mein Stündlein vorhanden ist" (Whenever My Last Hour Is at Hand) by N. Hermann, 1575.

Bass, tenor and soprano are the soloists with chorus. The orchestra is huge: three trumpets, timpani, four oboes, a tenor oboe (taille), a bassoon, a large string group (violins, violas, celli) and continuo. One wonders how Bach could muster all this force, when Duke Wilhelm's band was so small!

1. *Sonata.* This resounding concerto movement arrests the listener's attention immediately. The bouncy, upward surge of the music seems to transport us with it in its happy symbolic representation of the Resurrection. Toward the end, notice three repeated series of drum beats, which Bach may have intended to represent the Trinity.

2. *Chorus.* The mood of joyous gaiety continues as Heaven laughs in the song of the chorus, and all the earth rejoices also in a glorious blaze of color. Then the reason for this joy becomes apparent: "Der Schöpfer lebt! der Höchste triumphieret / Und ist von Todesbanden los." (The Creator lives! The Highest One triumphs / And is free from death's bonds.)

The allegro now changes to adagio at the mention of Christ in the grave, but at the last line, the allegro resumes with the thought that He cannot perish: "Der sich das Grab zur Ruh erlesen, / Der Heiligste kann nicht verwesen." (He, who has chosen the grave for rest, / The Most Holy cannot vanish.)

Bass, tenor and soprano will each have now a recitative (secco = unaccompanied) and an aria.

3. *Recitative—bass.* The bass does not represent Christ, here or in his following aria. He shows many changes in his declamation: allegro, adagio, andante, often in arioso, to describe our guilt, because we imprisoned Christ, whereas we should have considered Him the Alpha and Omega in our lives. Yet He lives again after death, so we too may live: "Lebt unser Haupt, so leben auch die Glieder." (If our head lives, so also live the limbs.)

4. *Aria—bass.* There is a serenity in the solemn tone of this aria, which vividly pictures how the ladder of the Cross has raised Jesus to the highest place of honor. One wonders, however, why Bach contrasts in such dark tone-colors the three questions asked in his text with the lofty-sounding invocation: "Fürst des Lebens, starker Streiter, / Hochgelobter Gottessohn!" (Prince of life, strong Champion, / Highly-praised Son of God!)

5. *Recitative—tenor.* A much brighter tone enters here with the tenor. He exhorts us to rise in spirit like Christ from death (death meaning sin and evil for us) to begin a new course of life, which will be noticed by the Savior. The text is very pictorial, as seen in the comparison of the grape-stock bearing no dead fruit, and in the imagery of the Christian leaving sin behind him, just as Christ left the stone and cloth of His tomb.

6. *Aria—tenor.* The joy-rhythm seems to underline the tenor's words in this aria. It is like a song to spring, beginning on a low key, but rising in tone, to express the singer's longing in the last half. The pulsating tempo lends musical undertones to the aria, which suggests a march in its step motif.

The tenor insists that one must remove Adam's presence within oneself in order to become perfect, as in God's likeness one ought to be. As his tone rises, he informs us: "Du musst geistlich auferstehen / Und aus Sündergräbern gehen, / Wenn du Christi Gliedmass bist." (You must be spiritually resurrected / And go out of sinners' graves, / If you are a member of Christ.)

7. *Recitative—soprano.* Continues the idea that the limb will be drawn to the head, so that she, in her flesh, will also see God.

8. *Aria and Chorale—soprano.* Spitta thought it strange that Bach should find delight in this text, which has changed in meaning from the happiness of Easter into the longing for death. This is indeed a reversal of the usual sequence (melancholy turning to joy) of the cantata librettos set by Bach heretofore. However, despite the constraint imposed by his libretto, Bach still manages to bring an optimistic, though not exactly joyful, conclusion out of this chorale aria and the final chorale.

The soprano begins her aria in an ecstatic mood of longing for death: "Letzte Stunde, brich herein, / Mir die Augen zuzudrücken!" (Last hour, break in, / To close my eyes!) Thereupon, she will see Jesus (immediately after her death, implied). She is accompanied by the tune of the final chorale, played only by the instruments. The resulting effect is like a painting of a scene of heavenly peace, superimposed on a spring landscape under the glow of evening: "Lass mich Jesu Freudenschein / Und sein helles Licht erblicken, / Lass mich Engeln ähnlich sein!" (Let me glimpse Jesus' joyous radiance / And His bright light, / Let me be like the angels!)

9. *Chorale.* Bach's treatment of this hymn is a work of art. The high trumpet parts, which embellish the lines, emphasize the journey to Heaven after death, where we will find eternal life. The image conveyed to the listener is that of a soul floating upwards and stretching out its arms to the vision of Jesus, who waits to open Heaven's gate.

• **Barmherziges Herze der ewigen Liebe (Pitying Heart of Eternal Love)** (1715; BWV 185).

Franck's paraphrased libretto for this work was so dry that Bach must have had to use all his musical skill to set it. The Gospel was Luke 6 (36–42), a part of the Sermon on the Mount, and J. Agricola's hymn "Ich ruf zu dir, Herr Jesu Christ" (I Call to Thee, Lord Jesus Christ) for the chorale which occurs in the first and last movements. Soprano, alto, tenor and bass are the soloists with chorus.

1. *Duet—soprano and tenor with Chorale.* Verbs and nouns in the strophe give Bach the necessary inspiration to perceive an idea of pleading in the voices, with which the oboe plays the melody of the chorale, beginning at just before the second line: "Barmherziges Herze der ewigen *Liebe, / Errege, bewege* mein Herze durch dich; Damit ich *Erbarmen* und *Gütigkeit übe, /* O *Flamme der Liebe, zerschmelze* du mich." (Pitying heart of eternal *love, / Inspire, move* my heart through Thee; / So that I may practice *pity* and *goodness, /* O *flame of love, melt* Thou me.)

The trilling runs on the evocative words (italicized above) suggest the warmth of God's heart-melting love towards the speaker.

2. *Recitative—alto.* Relates in uninspired didactic fashion (as did Bach in his musical setting of this section) the Biblical paraphrase of Franck: practice mercy, judge not the Lord, forgive so that you may be forgiven, practice charity so that God will repay you with interest. "Denn wie ihr messt, wird man euch wieder messen." (For as you measure, it will be measured to you again.)

3. *Aria—alto.* Vocally pictures the sowing of seed and the harvesting of the sheaves, the metaphor being that when one does good works on earth, he will rejoice at his reward in heaven. The music is an improvement on the preceding recitative, but the sermon-like tones are still dull to the listener.

4. *Recitative—bass.* Continues the preaching of the Gospel narrative: the removal of the beam from one's eye before seeing the splinter in his neighbor's eye, and the thought of the blind leading the blind. Again not very motivating for either composer or listener.

5. *Aria—tenor.* This vivace, but not da capo, aria still reminds the listener of a sermon, inasmuch as the tenor lists dogmatically those actions which make up the art of being a Christian, which have all been mentioned before in the cantata. It sounds like a summary of one's Christian duties, beginning and ending with the line, "Das ist der Christen Kunst." (That is the art of Christians.) The tempo suggests a march step with its slight pause at the end of each line, as though pacing the meaning after each idea is presented.

6. *Chorale.* The chorale melody of the duet recurs in this four-part hymn like a bridge joining the end to the beginning of the cantata. (Bach would later use this chorale to commence another cantata, BWV 177.) "Ich ruf zu dir, Herr Jesu Christ." (I call to Thee, Lord Jesus Christ.)

• **Komm, du süsse Todesstunde (Come, Thou Sweet Hour of Death)** (1715; BWV 161).

Franck was the librettist, but his text was altered by Bach. The Gospel for the day was the raising of the widow's son at Nain, Luke 7 (11–17). The chorale was C. Knoll's hymn "Herzlich tut mich verlangen," (I Long Heartily) used again in both the first number (Alto aria) and the last chorale number, like a bridge spanning all the other numbers. The usual four-part chorus appears, with the soloists being alto and tenor. The orchestra is light, two recorders, strings and organ continuo.

1. *Aria—alto (with Chorale on instruments only).* A favorite theme with Bach is the idea of death being a release from worldly problems in exchange for a happier life thereafter. In this cantata, he fully expresses death and resurrection.

A sombre note is struck immediately by the two recorders, accompanying the alto voice. Then the melody of the chorale is added by the organ, playing in the background. The effect is funereal and celestial at the same time; the whole sounds supercharged with intense emotion: "Komm, du süsse Todesstunde, / Da mein Geist / Honig speist / Aus des Löwen Munde." (Come, thou sweet hour of death, / When my spirit / Feeds on honey / Out of the lion's mouth.)

The Biblical reference is to Samson's slaying of a young lion, in the body of which he found bees and honey (Judges 14 [8]), but here referring to the sweetness imparted by death (the lion), which will enable her to greet her Savior with a kiss, as the rest of the stanza states.

2. *Recitative—tenor.* The tenor gives his reasons for wishing for death: world's joys are a burden—his only desire is to be with Christ. The words in his declamation often show melismas e.g. "Seele Qual" (soul torment) or "blasse Tod" (pale death), and the imagery of the descriptive words in the text is remarkable: "Morgenröte" (redness of morning), "Himmelswonne" (heavenly bliss).

3. *Aria—tenor.* The elegiac tone pervading the opening of this aria turns into a ray of hope in its conclusion. The tenor sings of his longing to be soon with Christ, although he knows that death will turn him into ashes and earth before this can happen. This macabre scene is then replaced by the sparkle of his coming glory: "Wird der Seele reiner Schein / Dennoch gleich den Engeln prangen." (The pure brightness of my soul / will, nevertheless, gleam like angels.) The repeated long runs on the words "Schein" (brightness) and "prangen" (gleam) have a stirring effect on the listener.

4. *Recitative—alto.* The splendid accompanying sound of recorders, organ, and finally pizzicato strings make this one of Bach's best recitatives. The alto imagines herself lying in her rose-covered grave, until Jesus wakes her to join His sheep in the heavenly pasture. One can almost visualize the two fields in this pastoral description.

As the bells in North German churches toll for funerals, so Bach sets the last two lines pizzicato for the strings to represent the motif of grief to mark the moment of her death.

5. *Chorus.* Begins with the same melancholy tonal ambience heard in the beginning aria of the cantata; this is still produced by the recorders and the organ during the first three lines: "Wenn es meines Gottes Wille, / Wünsch ich, dass des Leibes Last / Heute noch die Erde fülle," (If it is the will of my God, / I wish that my body's burden / Today yet fill the earth.)

At this point, the motif changes to joy, which continues for the remainder of the strophe: the wish is expressed that the speaker's soul become immortal in the joy of heavn. The last two lines are his ultimate plea to the Lord: "Jesu, komm und nimm mich fort! / Dieses sei mein letztes Wort." (Jesus, come and take me away! / This be my last word.)

6. *Chorale.* The chorale's tune, as heard in the first aria, returns in full song by the choir this time, still with accompaniment of recorders, organ and strings.

The meaning of the verse with its music seems to summarize all that has been sung before in this cantata, from sad burial of the body to happy transfiguration of the soul.

• **Ach, ich sehe, jetzt da ich zur Hochzeit gehe (Ah, I See, Now as I Go to the Wedding)** (1715; BWV 162).

Bach composed this charming cantata on Franck's libretto as the Hauptstück (main music piece) preceding the sermon for that particular Sunday. The Gospel was Matthew 22 (1–14)—the parable of the marriage of the king's son. Soloists are soprano, alto, tenor, bass, and the usual chorus for the final chorale based on Johann Albinus's "Alle Menschen müssen sterben" (1652) (All Men Must Die). The instrumentation has the usual violins, viola, bassoon and continuo, but to this Bach introduces a cor da tirasi (a slide trumpet or tromba with the mechanism of a trombone), used in the first aria and in the last chorale.

1. *Aria—bass.* "Ach! ich sehe, itzt, da ich zur Hochzeit gene," (Ah, I see, now as I go to the wedding). The bass expresses his fear and anxiety at being found worthy to attend the Lord's wedding feast, and not be rejected to remain in the world's confusion. On his way to the wedding (i.e. of his soul to the Lord), he notices the welter of his thoughts, represented by the opposing nouns juxtaposed in his text, which beset himself and all humanity: "Wohl und Wehe, / Seelengift und Lebensbrot, / Himmel, Hölle, Leben, Tod, / Himmelsglanz und Höllenflammen." (Weal and woe, / Poison of the soul and bread of life, / Heaven, hell, life, death, / Heaven's glow and hell's flames.) He hopes he can endure all this turmoil he sees in the world. Although the impression made by the music is tragic, the aria has a swinging melody which is very beautiful.

2. *Recitative—tenor.* From here on, all recitatives and arias are accompanied by continuo only, which gives the voices more prominence.

The tenor expresses the sentiments of the bride (i.e. mankind), who longs to be with her husband (i.e. Jesus). The wedding meal is metaphoric for the Lord's supper (communion) and those whose faith is lacking are banned from it and cursed: "Wie selig ist, den hier der Glaube leitet, / Und wie verflucht ist doch, der dieses Mahl verachtet!" (How blessed is he, whose belief leads him here, / And how cursed is he, who despises this meal!) Bach's increasing proficiency in recitative is evident in this number.

3. *Aria—soprano.* Sings with ecstasy at the possibility of being admitted to

the Lord's feast. Her urgent supplication is shown when she repeats "Jesu" three times. This ethereal theme is well interpreted by the high soprano voice.

4. *Recitative—alto.* Wishes to be dressed properly in the white silk of innocence, as befits a bride; her old Adam's garment, with its stains of sin, will be covered and purified by Christ's blood, making it white. Thus she will not be rejected, as was the guest in St. Matthew's account.

5. *Duet—alto, tenor.* Has the form of the Italian aria; it is like a two-part song, evoking a picture of a festal dance. This is Bach's first use of this type of duet-aria, in which the voices repeat each line alternately. Lovely runs on "erfreut" (rejoiced) at the end of the first line enliven this duet from its beginning.

6. *Chorale.* Bach set the seventh stanza of Johann Rosenmüller's hymn, "Alle Menschen müssen sterben" (All Men Must Die). The import of the stanza is that the bride has attained her heavenly dress and is standing now before God's throne as the wedding is concluded.

• **Nur jedem das Seine (To Each Only His Due)** (1715; BWV 163).

Schweitzer is somewhat critical of this libretto by Franck, stating that it contains little to inspire poetic imagery (*J.S. Bach,* vol II, p. 146): "It contains neither poetic ideas nor pictorial images. This, to be sure, is less the fault of the poet than of the Gospel for the day, (Matthew XXII, 15–22), that deals with the subject of the tribute money. The religious valuation of tax-paying is not a grateful theme for a cantata text."

Yet there are poetic ideas and pictorial images in the words to stir Bach's musical genius, despite the text he had to set.

It is for all four soloists (SATB) who also probably sang the final chorale (marked *Choral in simplice stylo* by Bach). The few instruments indicated—violins, viola, cello, an oboe and continuo—would seem to confirm the simple style of the chorale, as well as the whole work.

1. *Aria—tenor.* Bach's meticulous sense of order and duty would induce him to give special emphasis to the nouns in this aria following the opening line, "Nur jedem das Seine" (To each only his due).

The joy-motif permeates all the aria with its swinging rhythm, even though the thought of paying taxes imposes on us a disagreeable duty, as reflected in the italicized nouns: "Muss *Obrigkeit* haben / *Zoll, Steuern* und *Gaben,* / Man weigre sich nicht / Der *schuldigen Pflicht!*" (Must *government* have / *Duty, taxes* and *donations,* / One should not refuse / His *debt-obligations!*)

The last line of the aria brings us to the main idea: that the heart belongs only to God, while money belongs to the earth.

2. *Recitative—bass.* States that God has given us everything we possess; how are we to return it all to Him with our thanks? The one thing pleasing to Him would be our hearts, but they are at present like counterfeit coins, sullied by Satan, and must be restruck with God's likeness to be acceptable to Him.

It is interesting to note that Franck was the custodian of the Ducal museum which included a coin collection—hence his numismatic interest as seen in the poetic imagery in this bass recitative and the following bass aria.

3. *Aria—bass.* Fervently expresses the wish, accompanied by a step-motif in the music, that his heart will be the coin he will pay unto the Lord, once the coin has been restruck by Him with his shining visage thereon. We can visualize the angelic workers busy with their hammers in the scene presented by the last three lines with their metaphor and change of tempo: "Komm, arbeite, schmelz und präge, / Dass dies Ebenbild in mir / Ganz erneuert glänzen möge!" (Come, work, melt and stamp, / That this likeness in me / May shine completely renewed!)

What lyrical word-painting here!

4. *Recitative (Duet)—soprano, alto.* The two voices sing arioso and in canon mostly. They express their fear that the

genuine coin (their hearts) will be tarnished by the world, which they hate. They pray that God will fill their heart with grace, empty it of the world's lusts, and make them real Christians.

5. *Duet with Chorale—soprano, alto.* The chorale melody in the background is C. Keimann's hymn "Meinen Jesum lass ich nicht" (I Do Not Leave My Jesus) (used also later for BWV 124 in the first stanza). The voices repeat each other in canon, each line entreating the Lord to exchange their present lives for His perfect goodness. They want to do His will, not theirs: "Nimm mich mir und gib mich dir! / Nimm mich mir und meinem Willen, / Deinen Willen zu erfüllen." (Take me from myself and give me to Thee! / Take me from myself and my will, / To fulfill Thy will.) The repetition of the first line at the end of this stanza makes this duet very beautiful and artistic in its effect.

6. *Chorale.* Based on J. Heermann's hymn "Wo soll ich fliehen hin" (Whither Shall I Flee). With the light orchestral accompaniment, we hear a short but sincere prayer that God will guide "me" through His Spirit, so that I may avoid everything that might separate me from Him.

• **Bereitet die Wege, bereitet die Bahn (Prepare the Ways, Prepare the Road)** (1715; BWV 132).

This solo cantata for four voices (SATB), one oboe, strings and continuo for organ reflects Bach's interest in Italian contemporary music while he was at Weimar. Franck's libretto furnished him with an Italian-style cantata text, alternating arias and recitatives, to which Bach added a final chorale, composed on the fifth verse of E. Cruciger's hymn "Herr Christ, der einig Gottes Sohn" (Lord Christ, the Only Son of God) (1524). The result is a chamber-styled, lightly orchestrated cantata similar to those of Alessandro Scarlatti.

The Gospel was from John 1 (19–28), recalling Isaiah's prophecy of John the Baptist—Isaiah 40 (3).

1. *Aria—soprano.* The text of this first aria is Franck's poetic paraphrasing of the Scriptures for this last Sunday in Advent: "Bereitet die Wege, bereitet die Bahn! / Bereitet die Wege / Und machet die Stege / Im Glauben und Leben / Dem Höchsten ganz eben; / Messias kommt an!" (Prepare the ways, prepare the road! / Prepare the ways / And make the paths / In (your) faith and life / Quite smooth for the Highest; / Messiah is approaching!)

The soprano's florid treatment of this aria (e.g. long runs on "Bahn"), and the dance-like rhythm of the instruments with ritornello, make the first aria the high point in the cantata. Her thrice repeated utterance of "Messias kommt an!" without accompaniment shows Bach's originality in setting such an aria.

2. *Recitative—tenor.* Begins a didactic theme, secco, containing arioso interludes, telling how we must clear the way for Christ to enter our hearts through faith. "Und räume weg die Hügel und die Höhen, / Die ihm entgegenstehen! / Wälz ab die schweren Sündensteine." (And remove the hills and heights, / Which stand in His way! / Clear away the heavy stones of sin.) This is a very picturesque description for the heavy load of sin obstructing Christ's entry into our hearts.

3. *Aria—bass.* A rather lugubrious movement in which the bass voice seems to represent a priest or Christ preaching to the sinner. The Lord asks the sinner who he is and then tells him to consult his conscience and the Commandments; they will show him to be a false, hypocritical Christian.

4. *Recitative—alto.* Confesses her lack of faith in her role as sinner, and asks God to forgive her. In her baptism she promised her faith, and she now asks Jesus to help her find it again.

5. *Aria—alto.* Excellent word-painting with exuberant arabesques in the solo violin accompaniment, which may suggest flowing water. The words evoke a picture of John the Baptist, who is busily converting people from their sins, just

as Christ will do later. "Christi Glieder, ach bedenket, / Was der Heiland euch geschenket / Durch der Taufe reines Bad! / Bei der Blut—und Wasserquelle / Werden eure Kleider helle, / Die befleckt von Missetat." (Members of Christ, o consider, / What the Savior has given you / Through baptism's pure bath! / By the blood and water fountain / Your clothes become bright, / Which are soiled by misdeeds.)

6. *Chorale.* Again marked by Bach *Choral in simplice stylo* (chorale in plain style). The music for this chorale has been lost, but for modern performance, the same four-part chorale text and melody, as used at the end of BWV 164, replaced it. This tune was even more beautifully set in BWV 22, where the instrumentation is fuller: "Ertöt uns durch dein Güte, / Erweck uns durch dein Gnad." (Mortify us by Thy goodness, / Awaken us by Thy mercy.)

• **Tritt auf die Glaubensbahn (Step on the Path of Faith)** (1714 or 1715; BWV 152).

This solo cantata for soprano and bass for the Sunday after Christmas is again, like BWV 132, a personal, chamber-style piece. It is different because it lacks a final chorale; also its orchestra is unique, for it has no violins. The instruments are a recorder, an oboe, a viola d'amore (Bach's first use of this particular instrument, which he would use only twice more in secular cantatas), a viola da gamba and continuo.

The Gospel for Franck's libretto is Luke 2 (33–40), in which it is prophesied that Christ will redeem Israel. Franck's poem interprets this in the text for the bass aria and the first bass recitative.

1. *Concerto.* A fine instrumental prelude in the style of a shortened French overture (only two movements): a short adagio, followed by a rather long allegro, depicting a step-motif of someone walking happily along the road to faith.

2. *Aria—bass.* The step-motif is continued by the voice and oboe accompaniment. The bass urges us to step onto the way of faith, which the text represents as a cornerstone supporting Zion's structure: "Tritt auf die Glaubensbahn. / Gott hat den Stein geleget, / Der Zion hält und träget." (Step on the path of faith / God has laid the stone, / Which holds and bears up Zion.) This stone symbolizes Christ, both in the musical context of Bach, and the word.

The next line seems to show someone who stumbles in hesitation on this road: "Mensch, stosse dich nicht dran!" (Man, do not hesitate on it!), before the repeat of the injunction: "Tritt auf die Glaubensbahn."

3. *Recitative—bass.* Begins with the words of Simeon, taken from Luke 2 (34): "Der Heiland ist gesetzt / In Israel zum Fall und Auferstehen!" (The Savior is set for the fall and rising again [of many] in Israel!)

Then he mentions the noble stone (Christ) which withstands the evil world. A Christian should base his faith on this cornerstone where alone he will be able to find salvation and redemption.

4. *Aria—soprano.* Refers back to the "Stein" (Stone) and "Eckstein" (Cornerstone) of the previous recitative. The tonal colors here are very soft, as if one might be describing a rich jewel while beholding it glowing steadily in its own radiance. Perhaps Bach was thinking of the star which guided the Magi, since he composed this cantata so soon after Christmas.

The singer wishes that this Stone will help her faith; her high tones seem to impart to her aria an atmosphere of ethereal bliss.

5. *Recitative—bass.* Recounts how vexed the learned people of the world are, because their reasoning does not explain why God sent His Son into the world in human form. These people are spiritually blind, led astray by a blind woman-leader (personification of reason), so that they both fall into the ditch (cf. Matthew 15 [14]).

6. *Aria (Duet)—soprano, bass.* A dialogue between the Soul and Jesus, set in dance rhythm, a *loure,* showing Bach's

continuing interest in French instrumental musical forms. The emphasis is again on faith leading the way to attain the favor of Jesus, who promises us a crown after all the sadness and shame in our lives.

The Soul asks the questions and Jesus answers them in the first half, but the dialogue changes to exclamations by both singers in the last half of the duet. This duet reminds the listener of a love song between a lover and his lady to the sound of a happy dance theme. This impression will be evident again in later sacred cantata duets where Bach composes dialogues between the Soul and Jesus.

• **Mein Gott, wie lang', ach lange (My God, How Long, Oh Long)** (1716; BWV 155).

This rather brief, four-part (SATB) solo cantata for the second Sunday after Epiphany was composed on Franck's poem. The Gospel for the day is John 2 (1–11)—Christ turns water into wine at the wedding in Cana—but Franck's libretto seems to have only slight reference to it in the alto-tenor duet. Instead, Franck develops the general idea that we should turn to God in time of tribulation. God knows the right time to deliver us from trouble.

The orchestra consists of only two violins, a viola, a bassoon and continuo. The concluding chorale is stanza 12 of Paul Speratus's hymn "Es ist das Heil uns kommen her" (Our Salvation Has Come to Us) (1524).

1. *Recitative—soprano.* Recites the soul's dejection over her daily lot of sorrow, which seems to never end. She asks God how long she must endure it: "Mein Gott, wie lang', ach lange? / Des Jammers ist zuviel," (My God, how long O long? / Of lamentation there is too much,) She concludes the last two lines in coloratura arioso: "Der Freudenwein gebricht; / Mir sinkt fast alle Zuversicht." (The wine of joy fails; / In me almost all assurance sinks.)

2. *Duet—alto, tenor.* The singers play the part of comforters to the Soul in despair. Their long runs on "gelassen" (resigned), "erfreun" (gladden) and "offen" (open), together with their singing in canon with solo bassoon obbligato, make this a gently soothing and consoling number.

3. *Recitative—bass.* In this secco recitative in the role of Jesus, who speaks to the Soul, the bass tells her that He (her dearest friend) has not forsaken her. Her sorrows will not last, as He will turn her bitter tears from wormwood into the virgin honey of joy. He is only testing her love for Him through her suffering ("Er prüfet nur durch Leiden deine Liebe"). Therefore, she should let Him govern her in everything, according to His will.

4. *Aria—soprano.* The soul expresses her change to happiness in a joy-motif which graphically illustrates her idea of throwing herself into Jesus' arms: "Wirf, mein Herze, wirf dich noch / In des Höchsten Liebesarme," (Throw, my heart, do throw yourself / Into the loving Arms of the Highest,).

The idea of placing our worries on His mercy is neatly personified in the last three lines: "Lege deiner Sorgen Joch, / Und was dich bisher beladen, / Auf die Achseln seiner Gnade!" (Lay the yoke of your sorrows, / And what has burdened you until now / On the shoulders of His mercy.)

5. *Chorale.* This final hymn seems to confirm the whole thought expressed in the preceding movements: although we may think that God is sometimes not present, He is always near us in word and in spirit.

• **Wer mich liebet, der wird mein Wort halten (Whoever Loves Me Will Keep My Word) I** (1716; BWV 59).

This solo cantata for soprano and bass, with chorus for the chorale, is Bach's first version of this work (the second, BWV 74, was composed about 1735). Some Bach scholars have questioned the 1716 date for the first performance, delaying it until 1723, when it was presented at the Leipzig University Chapel for the Whitsunday service, and stating that Bach had previously composed it while he was in Cöthen. However, Whittaker says that it was performed at the Weimar castle chapel on 31 May 1716.

Neumeister was the librettist for this richly orchestrated cantata: two trumpets, timpani, two violins, a viola and continuo. The work is peculiar because there is no final chorale and there are only four numbers.

The Gospel, John 14 (23), provides the text for the duet which opens the cantata.

1. *Duet—soprano, bass.* We must remember that Bach would use a boy to sing the soprano part, and one may wonder if his voice would be strong enough to be sufficiently audible above this magnificent crescendo of sound. Certainly the soprano can be clearly heard as she sings in canon with the bass in our more modern performances. The trumpets add splendor to their voices; Bach generally used them to indicate royalty or divinity. In this case, they support Jesus' words quoted in the text: "Wer mich liebet, der wird mein Wort halten, und mein Vater wird ihn lieben, und wir werden zu ihm kommen und Wohnung bei ihm machen." (Whoever loves Me will keep my word, and my Father will love him, and We shall come to him and dwell with him.)

A most passionate and persuasive aria.

2. *Recitative—soprano.* Departs from the Gospel here, to comment on the honor God bestows on us by sending His Holy Spirit as well as His Son. Mention is made again of His dwelling in our souls, with her vocal arioso treatment of the last two lines.

3. *Chorale.* Based on stanza 1 of Luther's hymn "Komm, heiliger Geist, Herre Gott!" (Come Holy Ghost, Lord God!) (1524). The text is interesting because it states that God has collected all the people in the world, irrespective of their language, into adoration of Him. Therefore we should praise Him, as the twice repeated "Halleluja!" at the end triumphantly sings.

4. *Aria—bass.* Accompanied by the strings and continuo in a mystical aura of sound, the bass sings that God's grandeur is far above any splendor on this earth. How blessed will we be, when we shall dwell with Him in His heavenly Kingdom after our time on earth.

There is something mysterious underlying the tones of the bass voice (here not representing Christ), which could come from Bach's pietistic thinking at this moment of his composition.

• **Wachet! betet! betet! wachet! (Watch! Pray! Pray! Watch!)** (1716; BWV 70).

In the 1723 version of this cantata, which is the version we hear today, Bach has added six numbers (four recitatives and two chorales) to the 1716 libretto of Salomo Franck. The two chorales, which conclude Parts I and II of the cantata, are taken respectively from an anonymous hymn, "Freu' dich sehr, O meine Seele" (Rejoice Greatly, O My Soul) and C. Keimann's hymn "Meinen Jesum lass ich nicht" (I Do Not Leave My Jesus).

The Gospel is Matthew 25 (31–46), pertaining to the Last Judgment, which is vividly described in Bach's music throughout the entire work.

This is a choral cantata for SATB soloists with chorus; the orchestra consists of a trumpet, an oboe, a bassoon, strings and organ continuo (in its amended form).

Part I

1. *Chorus.* Right from the beginning, we hear the tumult motif to denote the end of the world. Amid the agitation of the orchestra to depict the probable confusion resulting from the chaos of the Last Day, we hear the excited cries of the faithful: "Wachet! betet! betet! wachet! / Seit bereit / Allezeit, / Bis der Herr der Herrlichkeit / Dieser Welt ein Ende machet!" (Watch! pray! pray! watch! / Be ready / At all times, / Until the Lord of glory / Makes an end to this world!)

The urgency imparted by the nervous tone of the music and the staccato vocal exclamations make this one of Bach's greatest choruses.

2. *Recitative—bass.* Compares the state of both sinners and faithful on this final day; the former will be terrified, and the latter joyful. All the instruments are used in this fine recitative to paint in emotional tones the fear-motif and the joy-motif.

3. *Aria—alto.* Sings a rather uninspired solo with cello obbligato, bassoon, and organ continuo. Bach must have had some problem with this text, as it seems to suit recitative more than aria treatment. The singer's message is that we should wake up before destruction befalls us.

The Biblical references are realistically depicted, however, in the metaphors concerning the exodus of the believers from Egyptian bondage, and in the fiery death of the sinners of Sodom: "Wann kommt der Tag, an dem wir ziehen / Aus dem Ägypten dieser Welt? / Ach! lasst uns bald aus Sodom fliehen, / Eh' uns das Feuer überfällt." (When will the day come, when we depart / Out of the Egypt of this world? / O! let us soon from Sodom flee, / Before the fire falls over us.)

4. *Recitative—tenor.* Describes how the world tries to entrap us by stretching out its nets and snares, so that in spite of our spiritual longing to do the right thing, our selfish bodies tempt us otherwise. "Der Geist ist willig, doch das Fleisch ist schwach." (The spirit is willing, but the flesh is weak.) (Matthew 26 [41])

5. *Aria—soprano.* Beautiful imagery and music, although Bach took both the vocal and the instrumental themes from Handel's bass solo found in his first opera, *Almira,* 1705. The uplifting, confident mood of joy seems to transform the previous dismal threatening into rapturous hope. The florid treatment of the final words in the first and last lines is noteworthy: "Lasst der Spötter Zungen *schmähen*. . . / Christi Wort muss fest *bestehen.*" (Let the mockers' tongues *jeer*. . . / Christ's word must *stand firm.*)

Almost as in a religious painting, Bach creates a sound-image of Jesus in Heaven through these lines in the middle of the stanza: "Es wird und muss geschehen, / Dass wir Jesum werden sehen / Auf den Wolken, in den Höhen." (It will and must happen, / That we shall see Jesus / On the clouds, in the heights.)

6. *Recitative—tenor.* States that God will protect His servants from further harm, and place them in His heavenly Eden. This short number continues the optimistic feeling expressed by the soprano aria before it.

7. *Chorale.* Concludes Part I (sung before the sermon) with a hymn of confidence, "Freu' dich sehr, O meine Seele" (Rejoice Greatly, O My Soul), which would be well known to the congregation. With all the instruments of the orchestra accompanying the voices, the meaning of the text—God calling humankind out of its valley of tears into His Eternity—would affect the audience deeply.

Part II

8. *Aria—tenor.* Franck's original 1716 text had a third line which Bach omitted in setting his 1723 version: "Der jüngste Tag wird kommen" (The last day will come). Probably, as Spitta says, "this omission is a fresh proof of how completely his mind was directed solely to the illustration of the main sentiment." (Vol. I, footnote p. 572.)

Handel's influence appears again in the tenor's happy song of confidence in God, indicated by repetitions of "seid getrost" (be comforted) to the pious, who can now lift up their heads. The aria exudes a springtime atmosphere of plant growth, metaphorically indicated for the pious souls, who will flourish in God's garden of Eden: "Zu eurer Seelen Flor! / Ihr sollt in Eden grünen, / Gott ewiglich zu dienen." (For the blossoming of your souls! / You are to thrive in Eden, / To serve God eternally.)

9. *Recitative with Chorale—bass.* Returns to the tragic description of the Judgment Day, punctuated by outbursts

on the trumpet, which also plays the melody of Luther's Advent hymn "Nun freut euch, lieben Christen, g'mein" (Now Rejoice, Dear Christians, Together) as the whole orchestra does.

The declamation is very dramatic, changing to a more cheerful strain in the last half at the thought of the Saviour's protecting arm of mercy.

10. *Aria—bass.* Again a contrast between hopeless terror and confident happiness. He begins, in a quietly peaceful tone, to greet the Resurrection Day; then comes the crash of the trumpet, with full orchestra, to signal the world falling in ruins; finally, we hear a return to a moment of calm ecstasy, as Jesus leads him to peace.

11. *Chorale.* All voices and full orchestra perform verse 5 of C. Keimann's hymn, picturing the soul longing for Jesus, and concluding with the title line of the hymn: "Meinen Jesum lass ich nicht" (My Jesus I do not leave).

• **Herz und Mund und Tat und Leben (Heart and Mouth and Deed and Life)** (1716; BWV 147).

As was the case for BWV 70, Salomo Franck wrote the libretto for only the opening chorus and the first three arias in 1716, which Bach expanded with recitativi, a fourth aria, and two chorales about 1727 for performances in Leipzig. This later version is the one we hear today.

The Gospel deals with the visit of Mary to Elizabeth, Luke 1 (39–56), which includes the text of the *Magnificat.* But there are references to this event only in some of the numbers. The central theme is praise of Christ.

This cantata is a long one in two parts, each ending with the same chorale tune, "Jesu, Joy of Man's Desiring," but based on different hymn texts. The orchestra again includes a trumpet, two oboes, a bassoon, strings and continuo. The soloists are SATB and are included also in the chorus.

Part I

1. *Chorus.* A dazzling display of Bach's genius in fugal form; a lilting rhythm of joy pervades the whole movement, so that the words of the libretto seem to come alive: "Herz und Mund und Tat und Leben / Muss von Christo Zeugnis geben / Ohne Furcht und Heuchelei, / Dass er Gott und Heiland sei." (Heart and mouth and deed and life / Must give witness of Christ / Without fear and hypocrisy, / That He is God and Savior.)

2. *Recitative—tenor.* Refers to Mary's words in the *Magnificat,* where she praises the wonders God has done for her. Then the tenor blames those who do not acknowledge God's blessings bestowed on them.

3. *Aria—alto.* Continues the same thought concerning those ungrateful souls who do not acknowledge their Savior on this earth. They will be disowned by Him in turn when He comes in glory.

4. *Recitative—bass.* Paraphrases "He hath put down the mighty from their seat" of the *Magnificat,* but explains that this comes about through "Verstockung" (stubbornness) in the character of the powerful, who refuse to accept God. On the other hand the "Elenden" (wretched people) will be redeemed by their Savior.

5. *Aria—soprano.* With solo violin accompaniment, we can visualize the believing soul who happily treads along the path towards Jesus, because He has chosen her to join Him.

6. *Chorale.* The melody for this extended chorale, as also for the chorale at the end of Part II, comes from Johann Schop's well-known tune to J. Rist's hymn "Werde munter, mein Gemüthe" (Become Cheerful, My Spirit)—i.e. Jesu, Joy of Man's Desiring. The actual hymn text sung is verse 6 of Martin Jahn's "Jesu, meiner Seelen Wonne" (Jesu, the Bliss of My Soul) (1661).

Part II

7. *Aria—tenor.* Asks Jesus to help him, so he will recognize Him as his Savior at

all times, whether in joy or in sorrow. This aria appears to be a short prayer beginning: "Hilf, Jesu, hilf" (Help, Jesus, help) and ending, "Dass stets mein Herz von deiner Liebe brenne" (That my heart may always burn from your love).

8. *Recitative—alto.* A realistic description of the unborn John's leaping in his mother's body, when Mary announces to Elizabeth that she, too, is going to give birth. The text refers back to St. Luke's Gospel for this incident: "Bereits in seiner Mutter Leibe, / Dass er den Heiland kennt, / Ob er ihn gleich noch nicht / Mit seinem Munde nennt, / Er wird bewegt, er hüpft und springet." (Already in his mother's body, / So that he knows the Savior, Although he doesn't yet name Him / With his mouth, / He becomes lively, he leaps and springs.)

9. *Aria—bass.* With spectacular trumpet accompaniment, the bass shows forth his praise: "Ich will von Jesu Wunden singen" (I want to sing of Jesus' wounds). The references in the text to lips and mouth ("Lippen" and "Mund") recall the verses in the Morning Service of both Lutheran and Anglican ritual: "O Lord, open thou our lips, / And our mouth shall shew forth thy praise."

The libretto also appears to contain an allusion to each word in the title: Herz = das schwache Fleisch (the weak flesh), Mund (mouth), Tat = Opfer (offering), Leben = seiner Liebe Bund (the covenant with His love and our lives).

God's way of acting on us is also pictured in the climactic last line with its forceful musical illustration of "heil'ges Feuer (holy fire), i.e. the Holy Spirit, which will compel us to turn to Him: "Durch heil'ges Feuer kräftig zwingen." (He will compel strongly through holy fire.)

Together with the initial chorus and the ending chorales, this aria also shines among the best numbers in this cantata.

10. *Chorale.* Repeats the melody of the chorale at the end of Part I—verse 17 of Martin Jahn's hymn: "Jesus bleibet meine Freude, / meines Herzens Trost und Saft." (Jesus remains my joy, / The comfort and sap of my heart.) The same memorable melody, repeated in order to round off the work, was destined to remain one of Bach's masterpieces for centuries yet to come.

• **Der Friede sei mit dir (Peace Be Unto You)** (1716; BWV 158).

It is probable that Franck wrote the libretto for the aria (2) and the recitative (3), as they bear on the Purification of the Blessed Virgin Mary, for which Sunday Bach originally set this cantata. However, in about 1724 for Easter Tuesday, Bach revised the original by adding an opening recitative (1) and a concluding chorale (4). Unfortunately, these texts do not follow a logical sequence, because of this revision.

The Gospel for the later Easter version, which is the one we hear today, is Luke 24 (36) where the risen Christ appears before His Disciples and says, "Peace be unto you." This greeting or blessing, "Der Friede sei mit dir," begins the cantata with the first line of the recitative.

Bach uses only a solo violin, an oboe, and organ continuo instead of an orchestra. It is a solo cantata for soprano and bass voices. Two chorales are heard, but only the last is for chorus.

1. *Recitative—bass.* A combination of secco and arioso, with the opening line, "Der Friede sei mit dir," repeated three times in the text, and "der Friede," alone, repeated on the second occasion that the line is sung (possibly to signify Christ's thrice-repeated blessing).

The bass describes (as though he were one of the apostles) how Jesus tries to calm his fearful conscience by telling him that He has annulled his name in the guilt-book and removed the curse of the law because of his sin. He has also overcome the prince of this world, who has tried to entrap his soul. Therefore he should know that God loves him through His mediator, Christ.

2. *Aria—bass, and Chorale—soprano.* A charming but long aria (non da capo) is beautifully sung by the bass, accom-

panied by the solo violin: "Welt, ade! ich bin dein müde" (World, farewell! I am tired of you).

As he proceeds, the soprano intones stanza 1 of J.G. Albinus's hymn on J. Rosenmüller's melody, beginning with the same first line but with organ accompaniment.

The bass portrays the peace and rest that he will find in Heaven, whereas the soprano's text at the same point shows the world's turmoil: "Welt, bei dir ist Krieg und Streit, / Nichts denn lauter Eitelkeit," (World, with you is war and strife, / Nothing else than pure vanity.)

Yet, at the end of the aria, both voices find peace in Heaven:

BASS: "Da bleib' ich, da hab' ich Vergnügen zu wohnen, / Da prang' ich geziert mit himmlischen Kronen." (There I remain, there I have delight to live, / There I shine adorned with heavenly crowns.)

SOPRANO: "In dem Himmel allezeit / Friede, Freud und Seligkeit." (In heaven at all times (are) / Peace, joy and blessedness.)

Few other solo cantata arias leave such an impression of artistic beauty on the listener.

3. *Recitative and arioso—bass.* The last two lines are arioso, repeating the last two lines of the bass aria (2). The bass asks the Lord to govern his mind, so that he will think as a child of peace as long as he lives on earth, and when he dies, that he may depart in peace as Simeon did. "Friede" (peace) occurs twice in the context, as if to reinforce it as the main theme here and throughout the cantata.

4. *Chorale.* Stanza 5 of Luther's Easter chorale, "Christ lag in Todesbanden" (Christ lay in death's bonds), closes the work on the well-known Easter hymn.

C. Composed at Cöthen (1717–1723)

When Bach accepted his appointment as Kapellmeister to Prince Leopold of Anhalt-Cöthen, he did not foresee that his cantata production might diminish during the years of his service in Cöthen. Unfortunately, this seems to have been the case, because Leopold wanted him to lead his augmented court band, instead of composing religious cantatas. Thus Bach's instrumental production was paramount during his sojourn in Cöthen. The four orchestral suites, the *Brandenburg Concerti* and those concerti for violin, as well as the English and the French suites for clavier and the sonatas for harpsichord, flute and violin—all this creative activity for the use of the court or his family must have left Bach little time for vocal composition. Moreover, there was little demand for religious cantatas in Cöthen, because the town had a strong tradition of Calvinism in its public worship, which forbad ornate music in its churches.

Despite this hiatus in his cantata production, Bach had found a friend in his new employer, Prince Leopold, and felt that he could happily finish his career in his service (as compared to his imprisonment in Weimar by Duke Wilhelm Ernst, just prior to his departure for Cöthen). It was during his absence, while traveling to Carlsbad with Leopold in 1720, that Maria Barbara died and was buried before his return to Cöthen.

Nevertheless, Bach had not forgotten his commitment to vocal music, as we shall see in those few cantatas which survive from his Cöthen years, mostly composed at the rate of two per year or when the Prince requested—one for New Year's Day and one for Leopold's birthday. The music for many of these has been lost, although some of the librettos remain extant.

• **Erhöhtes Fleisch und Blut (Exalted Flesh and Blood)** (c. 1718; BWV 173).

Bach's admiration and enthusiasm for Prince Leopold were evident in the Birthday Serenata, "Durchlaucht'ster Leopold" (Most Serene Highness, Leopold), which he composed for his employer soon after he arrived in Cöthen. Bach apparently wrote the flattering libretto for this secular work (BWV 173a), but we do not know who revised the text for the religious version, which was performed in Leipzig in 1724. It was probably done by Bach himself, wishing to revive the exceptional music he had written in 1718. Bach omitted two of the eight numbers in the secular Serenata (number 6, a soprana aria, and number 7, a bass aria), but retained the exact music of all the rest for BWV 173, which is the version we are treating here.

The Gospel for this Whit-Monday is John 3 (16–21), of which verse 16 appears in part at the beginning of the duet for bass and soprano.

The orchestra includes two transverse flutes (the first time Bach has used them in a cantata), a bassoon, strings and continuo.

The solo voices are SATB, which are also included in the chorus.

1. *Recitative—tenor.* Begins and ends his narrative with the apostrophe, "Erhöhtes Fleisch und Blut" (Exalted flesh and blood), and then in a tone of awe, which seems to marvel at such a mystery, goes on to explain how God put on flesh and blood, in order to become our Salvation in His child, Jesus Christ. If Bach wrote these lines, they surely reflect his pietistic thinking in regard to the divine will.

2. *Aria—tenor.* Tries to influence the audience to spread the word of God's goodness towards them, through their praise in *song* and in *music.* (Could Bach *not* have written this?) The rhythm of felicity seems to spring from every part of this song, beginning: "Ein geheiligtes Gemüte / Sieht und schmecket Gottes Güte." (A sanctified mind / Sees and tastes God's goodness.)

3. *Aria—alto.* A very tuneful melody with a pleasant felicity-motif expressing the joy our hearts, mouths, ears and eyes must feel, when we praise God for His goodness towards us.

4. *Aria and Duet—bass, soprano.* The bass and the soprano sing separate arias first; then they sing together in duet for the third part. The flutes lend celestial tone-colors to the voices, while with the strings, they play a minuet including fairly long ritornelli.

BASS: Begins with the Biblical quotation: "So hat Gott die Welt geliebt" (God so loved the world), followed by his interjection: "Sein Erbarmen / Hilft uns Armen" (His pity / Helps us poor ones). The next line returns to the Scripture: "Dass er seinen Sohn uns gibt" (That He gave us His Son), concluding with: "Gnadengaben zu geniessen, / Die wie reiche Ströme fliessen." (To enjoy gifts of mercy, / Which flow like rich streams.)

SOPRANO: Continues this song of praise: that His mercy, in men's hearts, induces them to utter their belief in Him. This is followed up in the duet.

BASS AND SOPRANO (DUET): In canon, with runs on the verbs in the last two lines, produces a very florid effect: "Da sein offenbartes Licht / Sich zu seinen Kindern *neiget,* / Und sich ihnen kräftig *zeiget.*" (Since His revealed light / *Inclines* itself to His children, / And *shows* itself strongly to them.)

5. *Recitative (Duet)—soprano, tenor.* An unusual duet to have both soloists declaim in canon and mostly arioso. Bach's mysticism appears in his musical interpretation of the textual idea: We want to bring the offering of our hearts to Thee, so that the glow of our sighs of yearning may ascend to Heaven.

6. *Chorus.* A four-part chorus in the form of another graceful minuet. Bach's love of instrumental dance styles, which is evident in his four orchestral suites composed at Cöthen, can be detected in the two minuets he used in this cantata. It is a chorus of magnificent grandeur, representing a touching prayer that God may move our spirits, so that we may perceive His gifts to us. It concludes with a mystic vision of this prayer: "Da dein Sohn uns beten heisst, / Wird es durch die Wolken dringen, / Und Erhörung auf uns bringen." (As Thy Son bids us pray, / It will press through the clouds, / And bring Thy hearing to us.)

Up to this time, Bach had never poured such emotion into a chorus. This is a superb achievement.

• **Wer sich selbst erhöhet, der soll erniedrigt werden (Whoever Raiseth Himself, He Shall Be Humbled)** (1720; BWV 47).

Bach apparently worked on the composition of this cantata while he was with Leopold in Carlsbad, presumably with the intention of performing it in Hamburg, but whether he did, during his visit to that city after Maria Barbara's death, is unknown.

He had no librettist available in Cöthen as he had in Franck in Weimar; so Bach "imported" his libretto from a writer in Eisenach, Johann Helbig, who published his "Aufmunterung zur Andacht" (Encouragement to Devotion) there in 1720.

The Gospel, which gives the impetus to this cantata at its first line, was taken from Luke 14 (11): "For whosoever exalteth himself shall be abased; and he that humbleth himself shall be exalted." The rest of the cantata amplifies this thought: pride falls before humility. It was later performed for the first time in 1726 at Leipzig.

The performers are SATB soloists, who also sing the first chorus and the final chorale. The orchestra is light: two oboes, two violins, a viola and continuo.

1. *Chorus.* Sings Christ's words, given in the title of the cantata, accompanied by the full orchestra, which plays a long introductory ritornello before the choir begins to sing. This chorus has fugal movements, which rise and fall in the voices and in the instruments to resemble a tone-painting of the proud and the humble, depicting also how their status will be reversed. Bach pictures the paradox of the text in music that sounds like an Italian concerto movement, containing the picturesque rising and falling of the voices.

2. *Aria—soprano.* Sings of the need for humility (= Demut) for any true Christian. Again, the falling and rising tones, as she interprets the text, are prominent—e.g. the low tones used to express "Demut" (twice), and the rising tones for "Hoffahrt" (arrogance) and "Stoltz" (pride). This long da capo aria seems to derive its whole message in the juxtaposition of its two middle lines: "Demut stammt aus Jesu Reich. / Hoffahrt ist dem Teufel gleich." (Humility originates in Jesus' Kingdom. / Arrogance is similar to the Devil.)

3. *Recitative—bass.* Begins his agitated declamation in very crude language, which describes man as only mud, stench, ash and earth. How can you, a poor worm, presume to have any pride, when Christ was low and humble for your sake? You ought to be ashamed, and do penance for such presumption.

4. *Aria—bass.* The idea of lowering oneself in humility continues in the verbal imagery of Jesus bending our hearts, just as we might bend a twig to test its strength: "Jesu, beuge doch mein Herze / Unter deine starke Hand, / Dass ich nicht mein Heil verscherze," (Jesu, do Thou then bend my heart / Under Thy strong hand, / So that I may not foolishly lose my salvation.)

The aria continues as a prayer that he may not fall from Heaven through the sin of pride, as did Lucifer, and that his humility will please God.

5. *Chorale.* A fine melody complements the thought in this hymn taken from Hans Sachs' "Warum betrübst du dich, mein Herze?" (Why Are You Sad, My Heart?) (1560) set to a tune dating back to the Meistersingers, which Bach's harmony transforms into a wonderful conclusion: "Der zeitlichen Ehr will ich gern entbehrn, / Du wollst mir nur das Ewge gewähm." (I will gladly dispense with temporal honor, / If Thou wilt only grant me the eternal.)

• **Ein Herz, das seinen Jesum lebend weiss (A Heart, That Knows Its Jesus to Be Living)** (1719; BWV 134).

In its original form, this cantata, BWV 134a, was a congratulatory ode to honor the birthday of Leopold of Anhalt-Cöthen, entitled "Die Zeit, die Tag' und Jahre macht" (Time, that makes days and years).

This secular homage cantata was for

two voices: a tenor in the role of "Zeit" (time), and an alto representing "Göttliche Vorsehung" (divine providence), both of which Bach retained in his textual revision for the sacred adaptation on Easter Tuesday 1729 or 1731 in Leipzig. Both libretti are supposed to have been written by Bach, and both have only a light orchestra: two oboes, two violins, a viola and continuo (as for BWV 47).

The Gospel, Luke 24 (36–47), relating how the risen Jesus appeared to the Twelve, occurs only briefly in the last two lines of the duet. Still, Bach must have worked hard at this adaptation, since three versions of the libretto are known to exist.

1. *Recitative – tenor, alto.* The tenor begins by citing that "Ein Herz, das seinen Jesum lebend weiss, / Empfindet Jesu neue Güte." (A heart, that knows its Jesus to be living, / Feels Jesus' new goodness.) Following this, he adds, ". . . and composes only on praise of its Savior."

The alto voice adds the final arioso: "Wie freuet sich ein gläubiges Gemüte!" (How a believing mind rejoices!)

2. *Aria – tenor.* In heroic style, the tenor exhorts believers to pay homage to the Lord with songs of thanks. Noteworthy are the high-noted repeats of "Auf, Gläubige" (Up, believers), with interjections of "auf" repeated in a series of ascending tones as the aria develops. Even the text dances with the felicity-motif from beginning to end. The idea of the living Savior in the title recurs in the last half of the aria (as it will again in the final chorus): "Der lebende Heiland gibt selige Zeiten, / Auf, Seelen, ihr müsset ein Opfer bereiten, / Bezahlt dem Höchsten mit Danken die Pflicht!" (The living Savior gives blessed times, / Up, souls, you must prepare an offering, / Pay your obligation to the Highest with thanks.) The thought and its musical expression make this aria especially memorable.

3. *Recitative in Dialogue – tenor, alto.* The singers alternately discourse in dialogue about how Christ defends us from the wiles of the enemy (Satan), until even the last enemy (death) is overcome by Him.

4. *Aria (Duet) – alto, tenor.* With the orchestral accompaniment playing a minuet, this long duet (ten minutes in duration) continues the theme of praise and thanks, with the joy-motif apparent in voices and instruments. The long instrumental ritornelli remind the listener of Bach's attention to his composition of the *Brandenburg Concerti* about this time. The last part of the aria is treated in florid fashion, especially in their runs on the verbs "erwechet" (awakens), "erscheint" (appears), tröstet" (consoles), and "stärket" (strengthens). Here we also find Bach's only reference to the Gospel for the day: "Der Sieger *erwecket* die freudigen Lieder, / Der Heiland *erscheinet* und *tröstet* uns wieder / Und *stärket* die streitende Kirche durch sich." (The Victor *awakens* the joyful songs, / The Savior *appears* and *consoles* us again, / And *strengthens* the militant church through Himself.)

5. *Recitative – tenor, alto.* Not in dialogue this time; the tenor narrates the first part, and the alto the last. Both express in turn their thanks to God for His protection against evil, and for His gift of salvation.

6. *Chorus.* Seems more a duet for two separate choirs of soprano and bass voices than a chorus in the usual sense. The orchestral ritornelli, before and after the vocal sections, are very long – in fact the whole chorus is much longer than the duet (4) – and again the rhythm is a *passepied* dance form akin to a minuet. The joy-motif, symbolic of Easter, pervades the whole chorus from the beginning: "Erschallet, ihr Himmel, erfreue dich, Erde, / Lobsinge dem Höchsten, du glaubende Schar!" (Resound, ye Heaven, rejoice, earth, / Sing praise to the Highest, ye believing flock!" Note the coloratura runs on "Schar."

The last line emphasizes Christ's triumph; as the melody rises, it betokens Christ's victory, which is the consolation of all believers on this earth: "Er tröstet und stellet als Sieger sich dar." (He comforts and presents Himself as Victor.)

This is another marvelous chorus which, although derived from a secular cantata, proves that Bach can apply his religious feeling to convert praise for princes into praise for God. The sacred and the secular find common ground in Bach's mystical vision expressed in his music.

• **Jesus nahm zu sich die Zwölfe (Jesus Took to Himself the Twelve and Spoke)** (1723; BWV 22).

This was Bach's *Probestück* (test piece) for the position of Cantor in St. Thomas's Church, Leipzig. He composed it at Cöthen right after cantata BWV 23, "Du wahrer Gott und Davids Sohn" (Thou True God and David's Son) which Bach had originally intended as his test piece, but had changed his mind because he felt that BWV 23 was more suitable in its format for the connoisseur aristocracy of the Cöthen court than for the Leipzig bourgeois congregation at St. Thomas's. The latter were accustomed to the regular cantata of Bach's predecessor, Johann Kuhnau: five movements, instead of the three he had set for BWV 23 in its original outlay.

Graupner had set his trial piece on the five-movement cantata format three weeks before Bach's performance. Graupner had impressed the Leipzig Council so much with it that they had chosen him to be Cantor, without even having heard Bach. Graupner, however, had to decline the position as he could not obtain his release from Darmstadt, so Bach's chance came on 7 February 1723.

It is assumed that Bach wrote the libretto for this cantata, based on Luke 18 (31–34), for Estomihi Sunday (the last Sunday before Lent, and looking forward towards Easter).

Bach uses a simple orchestra: an oboe, strings and continuo for the soloists SATB, who also serve as the choir.

1. *Arioso—tenor, bass and Chorus.* The tenor begins with the Biblical quotation, "Jesus nahm zu sich die Zwölfe und sprach: . . ." (Jesus took to Himself the Twelve and spoke: . . .). Then the bass takes the role of Jesus, declaiming in arioso that they were going up to Jerusalem to fulfill the prophecy of the Scriptures. The chorus completes the quotation, accompanied by an allegro fugue, which indicates their inability to comprehend their master.

2. *Aria—alto.* Represents a pious believer, who now wants Jesus to draw her after Himself into Jerusalem, so that she may share in His passion and understand its significance for her. The step-motif and the grief-motif, respectively, illustrate the beginning and the ending of the aria, the former on the theme of going up to Jerusalem, and the latter by this text: "Wohl mir, wenn ich die Wichtigkeit / Von dieser Leid-und Sterbenszeit" (Well for me, if I [can understand] the importance / Of this grief and time of death.)

3. *Recitative—bass.* Again we hear the step-motif, with florid runs on the words "laufen" (to run) and "Freuden" (joys) in the first and last lines. Like the alto, he desires to be present at Golgotha, so that he may understand Christ's words, which the Disciples couldn't do.

4. *Aria—tenor.* A prayer, in a lilting dance-like joy rhythm, that Christ will help him strike from his heart everything contrary to his renunciation of the flesh. Then Jesus will draw him in peace after Himself. This is the third time the verb "ziehen" (to draw) has occurred in different movements in this cantata. The melody seems to suggest a transformation in his heart, through being drawn by Christ's peace.

5. *Chorale.* Set on the same verse of E. Cruciger's hymn ("Herr Christ, der einig Gottes Sohn"—Lord Christ, the Only Son of God) as the final chorale in BWV 132, but here in a much more elaborate setting. The dance rhythm is very marked, as it was in the above tenor aria. Bach still retains his ear for a minuet, transposed from the usual instrumental context into a vocal one, despite his striving to avoid a learned, courtly ambience. Not that

this detracts from the terrific impact this chorale has on the listener. The sound and emotional appeal of this chorale make it one of Bach's greatest.

The libretto itself continues the tenor's prayer, which preceded it, in that the Lord is asked to help us change the old man into the new one: "Ertöt uns durch dein Güte, / Erweck uns durch dein Gnad: / Den alten Menschen kränke, / Dass der neu' leben mag." (Mortify us by Thy goodness, / Awaken us by Thy mercy: / The old man chastise, / So that the new may live.)

Bach took the anonymous melody for this hymn and transformed it into a down-to-earth interpretation of the text, which couldn't fail to impress the congregation, no matter who they were!

• **Du wahrer Gott und Davids Sohn (Thou True God and David's Son)** (1723; BWV 23).

Composed in Cöthen, this cantata was to have been Bach's test piece for Leipzig, but for the reasons mentioned under BWV 22 (the substitute cantata), and the fact that Bach had borrowed a final chorale of BWV 23 in his haste to complete his *St. John Passion* for Leipzig, Bach decided to replace this cantata by a completely new test piece (BWV 22). As it happened, BWV 23 was performed in 1724 just before the *St. John Passion.*

Both cantatas deal with Christ's going to Jerusalem, Luke 18 (31, 34), but this cantata stresses the episode of the healing of the two blind men in Matthew 20 (30–34). It is likely that Bach was its librettist.

The soloists are SAT with B added in the choral sections. The orchestra has two oboes, two violins, a viola and continuo, with the addition of a cornetto and three trombones for the final chorale.

1. *Duet—soprano, alto.* Bach chose the scripture from Matthew (two blind men) rather than from Luke (only one blind man), as he wished to begin with a duet. As Jesus passes by, the two blind men cry their lament: "Du wahrer Gott und Davids Sohn / . . . erbarm dich mein! / Und lass durch deine Wunderhand, / Die so viel Böses abgewandt, / Mir gleichfalls Hilf und Trost geschehen." (Thou true God and David's Son / . . . pity me! / And let through Thy wonder-hand, / Which has turned aside so much evil, / Help and comfort happen likewise for me.)

The music evokes a living picture of the Easter procession approaching and of the entreaties of the two blind men.

2. *Recitative—tenor.* Assumes the role of one of the blind men to continue their plaintive appeal to Christ: "Ach, gehe nicht vorüber" (O, don't pass us by). The instruments play the tune of the *Agnus Dei* chorale, which will close the cantata, as the tenor declaims their sad plight—abandoned at the side of the road in their blindness. He remembers the Lord's promise to serve the sick and not the healthy.

3. *Chorus—SATB.* In rondo style, the first line is repeated seven times between sections of the text. The beauty of this chorus is indescribable. It conveys the most poignant emotion to any listener who comprehends the German text. At each interpolation of the tenor and bass, after repetitions of the first line by the soprano and alto, a magnificent prayer is built up in the voices of the two blind men, who represent all believers: "Aller Augen warten, Herr, du allmächtiger Gott, auf dich, / Und die meinen sonderlich." (All eyes wait, Lord, Thou Almighty God, on Thee, / And mine particularly.)

We seem to catch a view of the crowd, moving about these blind men and listening to their prayer, which the tenor and bass (representing the crowd) supplement with their interpolations: "Gib denselben Kraft und Licht, lass sie nicht immerdar in Finsternissen! / Künftig soll dein Wink allein der geliebte Mittelpunkt aller ihrer Werke sein, / Bis du sie einst durch den Tod wiederum gedenkst zu schliessen." (Give to these same men strength and light, leave them not always in darkness! / In the future, Thy sign, alone, will be the beloved centre of all their doings, / Until one day, Thou thinkest to close their eyes again through death.)

What a stunning chorus! Any listener will certainly be enchanted by such profound sentiment.

4. *Chorale.* Breathes an atmosphere of heavenly peace throughout. However, Bach seems to have omitted it in the performances of the *St. John Passion* after 1725, as it does not seem to be included in most recorded versions. Evidently, only the second version of 1725 contained it. The petition, expressed in the German paraphrase of the *Agnus Dei,* is repeated three times, with cornetto and three trombones doubling the choir: "Christe, du Lamm Gottes, / Der du trägst die Sünd der Welt, / Erbarm dich unser." (Christ, Thou Lamb of God, / Who bears the sin of the world, / Have mercy on us.)

The florid "Amen" at the end of this movement of beautiful serenity should remind us of prayers for Jesus' aid, offered to Him on behalf of the sick.

D. Composed at Leipzig (1723–1734)

Upon his installation as Cantor in Leipzig, Bach's cantata production increased to one per week, plus additional cantatas for feast days and other events. Only during the years 1727 to 1729 was there a slackening in his rate of cantata writing, caused by several factors: the general mourning for the death of Queen Christiane Eberhardine, which meant that no cantatas were sung for over four months; Bach's compositions for the Collegium Musicum which he had taken over; Bach's disputes with the Church Council; and the pace at which he was expected to work for the Thomasschule and the four city churches. One can assume, too, that some cantatas from this period have been lost.

During the first half of his years of glorious cantata achievement in Leipzig, Bach's librettists were still Erdmann Neumeister, Salomo Franck and himself, but he also added Christian Weiss, Sr., who was the pastor of St. Thomas from 1714 to 1734, and who offered his poems to his new Cantor.

About 1725, Bach discovered another librettist, Christian Friedrich Henrici, who wrote satires and humorous verses under the pseudonym Picander and had published a cycle of religious cantata texts in 1724.

As some musicologists question many of the authors who are presumed to have written the cantata libretti of this period, I feel that we should accept the names of those librettists listed in C.S. Terry's table, added in the appendix to his translation of Forkel's biography, which I have followed for my chronology. Also, in regard to the questionable dating of each cantata, from the middle of 1724 to the middle of 1727, I have taken Terry's suggested dates, even where (especially for 1725) he has preceded the date by c. (circa).

• **Die Elenden sollen essen (The Miserable Shall Eat)** (30 May 1723; BWV 75).

This cantata was Bach's first public presentation, sung in the St. Nicolai Church the day before his official induction as Cantor. This was also the first time that the Leipzig congregation had heard a long cantata in two parts on the day preceding such an induction, so it appears that Bach wished to impress his audience right from the start.

The librettist was Pastor Christian Weiss; the Gospel was taken from Luke 16 (19–31), while Psalm 22 (26) provides the opening chorus-verse according to the Lutheran Kirchenbuch (Prayer-book).

The vocalists are SATB, with a large orchestra: a trumpet, two oboes, one oboe d'amore, a bassoon, strings and continuo.

Part I

1. *Chorus.* Deep pathos is felt immediately in the wailing lament of voices and oboes to paint a picture of grief: "Die Elenden sollen essen, dass sie satt

werden." (The miserable shall eat, so that they become filled.) Then the voices ascend as if in prayer: "und die nach dem Herrn fragen, werden ihn preisen." (and those who ask about the Lord will praise Him.) The choral conclusion changes to the joy-motif in a brilliant fugue: "Euer Herz soll ewiglich leben." (Your heart shall eternally live.)

2. *Recitative—bass.* His declamation sounds as though it were part of a sermon on the vanity of acquiring worldly wealth, since it must all disappear. Bach's librettist must have surely been Pastor Weiss for this text: "Was hilft des Purpurs Majestät, da sie vergeht?" (What avails the majesty of purple, since it vanishes?) The color-tone of purple seems to indicate the splendor of temporal royalty, and it will reappear with a different meaning in the following aria.

3. *Aria—tenor.* His melodious affirmation of faith is accompanied by all the instruments except the trumpet, which blend with his voice: "Mein Jesus soll mein alles sein." (My Jesus shall be my everything.) Then we return to the color-tone purple, but this time denoting Christ's Blood: "Mein Purpur ist sein teures Blut," (My purple is His precious Blood,).

The final word in the aria, "Freudenwein" (wine of joy), with its vocal runs, seems to be connected with the idea of purple, signifying His Blood, to complete the pictorial impression: "Und seines Geistes Liebesglut / Mein allersüsster Freudenwein." (And the love-glow of His Spirit / Is my most sweet wine of joy.)

A very picturesque aria!

4. *Recitative—tenor.* Shows contrast in his vocal interpretation of those verbs denoting the raising and the lowering of those whom God loves and those whom He curses: "Gott *stürzet* (lowers) und *erhöhet* (raises). Even the nouns are opposed: "Zeit" (time) and "Ewigkeit" (eternity), "Himmel" (heaven) and "Hölle" (hell).

5. *Aria—soprano.* An enchanting, beautiful tune with oboe d'amore obbligato, continuing the comparison between the sufferings of the Christian and those of Lazarus. Patience in adversity leads to reward hereafter: "Ich nehme mein Leiden mit Freuden auf mich. / Wer Lazarus' Plagen / Geduldig ertragen, / Den nehmen die Engel zu sich." (I take upon myself my sufferings with joy. / Who patiently endures Lazarus's torments, / Him the angels take to themselves.)

6. *Recitative—soprano.* There appears to be a trace of predestination in this recitative: God presents us with a good conscience, from which a Christian can derive much pleasure, but He also leads him through long distress to his death. The last line, however, states that what He does is well done; this leads into the chorale which closes Part I: "So ist es doch am Ende wohlgetan." (So it is yet finally well-done.)

7. *Chorale.* Based on stanza 5 of Samuel Rodigast's hymn (1674), "Was Gott tut, das ist wohlgetan" (What God Does, That Is Done Well), from which the last stanza concludes Part II also.

The thought that spiritual consolation will replace earthly cares inspires Bach to set the theme as a felicity-motif in an undulating, bouncy tune for all voices and full orchestra, accompanied by trumpet fanfares. The sermon would now follow.

Part II

1. *Sinfonia.* This is Bach's only use of a chorale tune (the trumpet plays the above chorale melody) for orchestra alone. It evokes a feeling of deep mysticism, which must have moved the congregation when they heard it right after the sermon.

2. *Recitative—alto.* Expresses her belief in God's goodness, but doubts that she has the necessary spiritual strength to extend her belief to the life hereafter.

3. *Aria—alto.* Then she realizes that Jesus can give her this spiritual strength which will complete her life. She will ask for nothing more than to receive His spirit. The mystical quality of the music as she sings "Jesus macht mich geistlich

reich" (Jesus makes me spiritually rich) gives her aria an exceptionally emotional appeal.

4. *Recitative—bass.* A rather short statement to affirm that he, who steadfastly believes in God and practices self-denial, will find himself and God, once he has renounced earthly things.

5. *Aria—bass.* Amid a sparkling trumpet obbligato, he sings of his confidence in the love Jesus has for him. His return love stems from the warmth he feels from "Jesu süsse Flammen" (Jesus' sweet flames)—these words are decorated with fine florid runs in his vocal treatment of them.

The happy joy rhythm of this aria seems to complement the motif which the alto expressed in her aria (3).

6. *Recitative—bass.* Turns back to the Gospel, stating that being poor is preferable to being rich, if one only keeps Christ in his heart: "O Armut, der kein Reichtum gleicht! / Wenn aus dem Herzen / Die ganze Welt entweicht, / Und Jesus nur allein regiert." (O poverty, which no wealth equals! / If, out of our hearts, / The whole world disappears, / And just Jesus alone reigns.)

7. *Chorale.* As for the final number in Part I: the same voices and instruments. "Was Gott tut, das ist wohlgetan" (What God Does, That Is Done Well) is the first line of this stanza also. This verse should be noticed, because it would be the title of several cantatas Bach would later compose.

The last line is interesting, because it reinforces the main idea of the cantata: Humankind would submit to God's love, protection, and guidance in daily life, even though our lot is painful: "Drum lass ich ihn nur walten." (Therefore I let only Him govern.)

• **Die Himmel erzählen die Ehre Gottes (The Heavens Tell of God's Glory)** (1723; BWV 76).

This was the twin of BWV 75, performed the next Sunday, and having the same double format in its vocalists and instrumentation. Again the librettist was Pastor Weiss; the Gospel for this Sunday was Luke 14 (16–24), but instead, Psalm 19 (1, 3) leads off the first chorus. The main theme of brotherly love is taken from the first Epistle of John 3 (13–18), which occurs in the alto aria in Part II.

Part I

1. *Chorus.* The full orchestra plays a short prelude; then the bass solo sings the first line: "Die Himmel erzählen die Ehre Gottes und die Feste verkündiget seiner Hände Werk." (The heavens tell of God's glory and the firmament proclaims His handiwork.)

Then the chorus, with full orchestra, sings the same line, followed by the tenor, who begins the fugal section: "Es ist keine Sprache noch Rede, da man nicht ihre Stimme höre." (There is no language or speech, in which one does not hear their voice.)

The three other soloists then repeat this line, and then the choir, which builds up the fugue into a mighty climax, punctuated by the trumpet. This produces a vision of total ecstasy in the universe and among humankind.

2. *Recitative—tenor.* Explains that God reveals Himself to us in nature and in the universe. It seems that Bach has painted a small picture of creation in the wave-like rhythm that accompanies the narrative, emphasized by the verbs "regen" (to stir) and "sich bewegen" (to move). The tenor then states that we should pay attention to these "Boten ohne Zahl" (innumerable messengers), metaphorically, the things God has created, which invite us to come to His feast of love.

3. *Aria—soprano.* With solo violin accompaniment playing an allegro, the step-motif in her aria implies that all people will wend their way to God through Christ. But we must listen to His voice and then hurry to Him: "Hört, ihr Völker, Gottes Stimme, / Eilt zu seinem Gnadenthron!" (Hear, ye people, God's voice, / Hurry to His throne of mercy!)

4. *Recitative—bass.* With only continuo, the bass deplores the sad state of

the world in which most men have other gods they worship. These gods sit in God's house (i.e. replace Him), so that even Christians run away from Christ to worship the power of evil.

5. *Aria—bass.* Expresses his condemnation of idolatry in the social masses. His invective is very vehement in his repetition of the first line: "Fahr hin, abgöttische Zunft!" (Go away, atheist company!) Even if they are perverted, he will honor Christ, because the Lord is the light of reason. As is usual with Bach, in mentioning divinity, the trumpet blazes forth very forcibly at this line: "Er ist das Licht der Vernunft." (He is the Light of reason.)

6. *Recitative—alto.* Preparatory to the following chorale, she summarizes how the Lord has brought humankind out of heathen darkness, and bestowed on them His Holy Spirit. Then she concludes with a fine arioso, expressive of her most heartfelt thanks: "Drum sei dir dies Gebet demütigst zugeschicht!" (Therefore may this prayer most humbly be sent to Thee!) At this moment we can visualize a kneeling crowd with heads bowed in prayer.

7. *Chorale.* Based on stanza one of Luther's hymn; "Es woll uns Gott genädig sein" (May God Wish to Be Gracious to Us). The instrumental tutti with full chorus makes this chorale seem like a vast panorama of divine majesty in sound. The prayer is in the text of the hymn: that we recognize His work throughout the universe, and that the heathen turn to God through their acquaintance with His Son.

Part II

1. *Sinfonia.* A solemn piece of chamber music; it resembles a trio sonata for oboe d'amore (used also for the first time in BWV 75), viola da gamba, and continuo. These instruments set the mood after the sermon for the theme of brotherly love, which is the main idea of this part. Bach omits the trumpet from this calm tone-poem of spacious serenity.

2. *Recitative—bass.* Wishes that God may bless the true flock, so that they may show forth and increase His honor through faith, love and sanctity. His declamation has pauses of breaks after each line, as if to stress what he has just said. The struggle against evil by the faithful is stated in the last three lines by the highlighted word "Hass" (hatred), which leads into the next aria.

3. *Aria—tenor.* "Hass nur, hasse mich recht, / Feindlichs Geschlecht!" (Only hate, really hate me, / Hostile race!)

With the verb "hasse" (hate) repeated seventeen times, Bach conjures up a miniature confrontation scene between the champion of faith and the forces of evil. The only accompaniment is the viola da gamba and the continuo: this light instrumentation allows full clarity to the tenor's voice. The staccato tempo changes to a smoother, calmer pace at the end of the aria, before the agitated da capo, in "Christum gläubig zu umfassen, / Will ich alle Freude lassen." (To embrace Christ in my belief, / I wish to leave all other joy.)

4. *Recitative—alto.* Returns to more agreeable thoughts on how Christ shows His love for her and feeds her with the manna symbolic of brotherly love.

5. *Aria—alto.* "Liebt, ihr Christen, in der Tat!" (Truly love, ye Christians!) She sings the Epistle on brotherly love, accompanied by the same instruments as in the Sinfonia. The same reverence for love that was implied in the tone-poem is now vocalized by the alto. It is like the climax to all the drama developed in the preceding movements. The elegant sweep of these final lines from the epistle recalls the origins of sacred drama in the medieval mystery plays of the church: "Jesus stirbet für die Brüder, / Und sie sterben für sich wieder, / Weil er (sie) sich verbunden hat." (Jesus dies for the brethren, / And they again die for each other, / Because He has united (them) unto Himself.)

Bach's dramatic ability, revealed in his music, is certainly much in evidence here.

6. *Recitative—tenor.* This connects the

trumpets, timpani, two flutes, three oboes, strings, and organ included in the continuo. This is one of the most impressive cantatas that Bach ever wrote; the town council had never before been honored by such regal music.

1. *Chorus.* A very lavish movement, beginning with all the instruments playing a French overture, which, in its slow-fast-slow structure, continues throughout. The chorus does not participate in the slow sections; it sings only the middle fast section: "Preise, Jerusalem, den Herrn; lobe, Zion, deinen Gott!" (Praise, Jerusalem, the Lord; praise, Zion, thy God!) "Denn er machet fest die Riegel deiner Tore, und segnet deine Kinder drinnen" (For He makes fast the bolts of thy gates, and blesses thy children inside), "Er schaffet deinen Grenzen Frieden." (He makes peace for thy borders.)

These choral sections have pauses after each line for instrumental interludes. It is a wonderful chorus, worthy of any royal court, including Versailles. Could Bach have remembered the music he had heard in the Celle court many years before?

2. *Recitative—tenor.* Extols the city of Leipzig and the country of Saxony as being favored by God, beginning and ending with: "Gesegnet Land, glückselge Stadt!" (Blessed country, fortunate town!)

3. *Aria—tenor.* The inhabitants of Leipzig were very proud of their linden trees; hence the text mentions them as the people of the lindens. Bach even manages to introduce a solemn, syncopated rhythm into the oboe accompaniment, to indicate the swaying of the branches of these trees: "Wohl dir, du Volk der Linden, / Wohl dir, du hast es gut!" (Well for thee, thou people of the lindens, / Well for thee, thou art fortunate!) He goes on to say that they are fortunate, because they have God's blessing in abundance.

4. *Recitative—bass.* Lauds the magnificence of Leipzig, which God has chosen for His heritage. There are fanfares of trumpets and drums at the beginning. Two flutes and two oboes without strings support the declamation throughout. Then he proceeds to praise the wise government from which, under God, they receive all their benefits.

5. *Aria—alto.* Apparently this text was taken from Romans 13 (1): "Let every soul be subject unto the higher powers. For there is no power but of God: the powers that be are ordained of God." This is a direct tribute to the newly elected council.

With a sprightly flute obbligato, she reasons that we should accept authority as a gift from God. The text clearly refers to the council which holds its office by God's will; Bach's religious convictions would agree.

"Die Obrigkeit ist Gottes Gabe, / Ja selber Gottes Ebenbild. / Wer ihre Macht nicht will ermessen, / Der muss auch Gottes gar vergessen: / Wie würde sonst sein Wort erfüllt?" (The government is God's gift, / Yes, even God's Likeness. / Whoever will not measure its power, / He must also even forget God: / How would His Word be fulfilled otherwise?)

6. *Recitative—soprano.* Continues to praise the new city-fathers, who have spent many sleepless hours over this election. So the people should thank God, because He has brought this day about.

7. *Chorus.* A massive fugal movement with all performers. It abounds in the joy-motif, expressive of the people's praise, indicated in the previous recitative. In its happily rolling rhythm, gradually slowing towards the end, it is a panoramic revelation to the congregation of God's influence on the ruling fathers of their town. Therefore they will want to praise Him.

8. *Recitative—alto.* Asks that God will hear their longing prayer, which comes from their mouth, their heart and their soul. This prayer will occur in the following chorale, sung by His pious people.

9. *Chorale.* Consists of the 22nd and 23rd clauses of Luther's German *Te Deum:* "Herr Gott dich loben wir" (Lord God We Praise Thee). It is plainly set,

but very effective as a final prayer for this cantata: "Hilf deinem Volk, Herr Jesu Christ, / Und segne, was dein Erbteil ist, / Wart und pfleg ihr zu aller Zeit / Und heb sie hoch in Ewigkeit! Amen." (Help Thy people, Lord Jesus Christ, / And bless, what is Thine inheritance, / Wait and care for them at all times, / And lift them into eternity! Amen.)

• **Höchsterwünschtes Freudenfest (Highest Wished-for Feast of Joy)** (1723; BWV 194).

Even before 1723, Bach was famous as an authority on organ-building and repair. He had made several journeys to inspect organs and to give organ recitals in the towns he visited (e.g. Halle, Hamburg). He often composed music to perform on those occasions.

When the church at Störmthal, a village near Leipzig, was rebuilt in 1722 and 1723, a new organ was installed in it by Zacharias Hildebrand, a pupil of the great organ-builder, Gottfried Silbermann. The money for this work was provided by the local minor nobleman, Statz Hilmor von Fullen, who asked Bach to try the new instrument. Accordingly, Bach composed a cantata for the occasion and came with all his musical forces from Leipzig to attend the dedication of the church and its organ on 2 November 1723.

Bach certified the organ as an excellent instrument. He is said to have brought his wife, Anna Magdalena, as solo soprano (unusual for a woman to perform in a church at that time) for his cantata. Bach was probably his own librettist. The text was printed with a dedication to the patron, Statz Hilmor von Fullen, whom Bach was seemingly eager to impress with this lengthy cantata.

It is likely that Bach used a now-lost suite for his musical setting of the work, probably one of his Cöthen compositions. All movements, except the recitatives, are French dance forms; no doubt he thought that this learned, aristocratic style would please von Fullen, whose musical tastes would favor those of the Dresden court, where August the Strong heard French music.

Since the dedication service was held on a Tuesday, there is no direct Gospel reference as for a Sunday cantata.

The soloists are STB, with chorus and an orchestra, consisting of three oboes, a bassoon, strings, organ and continuo.

Part I

1. *Chorus.* With organ continuo and all other instruments, the tripartite French overture form makes a stirring opening. The chorus, as in BWV 119, does not enter until the first instrumental grave movement has finished, and then sings the allegro section. The last movement repeats the grave with instruments only.

The allegro vocal section begins and ends with "Höchsterwünschtes Freudenfest" (Highest wished-for feast of joy), thus making an impressive conclusion. The intervening lines refer to the festivities of this occasion, without any Biblical allusion: "Das der Herr zu seinem Ruhme / Im erbauten Heiligtume / Uns vergnügt begehen lässt." (That the Lord to His glory / In the built sanctuary / Lets us delightedly celebrate.)

2. *Recitative—bass.* Begins the preaching, in this and the following recitatives—interesting, because they show Bach's ability to write short sermons like any clergyman, but have little musical interest.

His prayer is that God will be pleased with His new church and with the fervent singing to be offered therein.

3. *Aria—bass.* We hear a pastorale for oboes and strings, which would surely have delighted the whole congregation as much as it charms the modern listener. The runs on the words "erfüllt" (fills) and "auserlesen" (chosen) in this graceful aria are enhanced by the feeling expressed in the first two lines, repeated at the end, and referring to this church: "Was des Höchsten Glanz erfüllt, Wird in keine Nacht verhüllt." (What the glow of the Highest fills, / Becomes veiled in no night.)

4. *Recitative—soprano.* Continues the hope that their church will be worthy of God, and that He will accept their songs of praise in lieu of the sacrifice of a bullock as in the Old Testament.

5. *Aria—soprano.* The rhythm of a gavotte, played by the instruments and sung by the soprano, makes this the outstanding solo number in both parts of the cantata. Here is to be found the only Biblical reference, taken from Isaiah 6 (6–7), of the seraphim cleansing the prophet of sin by placing a live coal in his mouth. Bach uses this imagery of divine fire throughout the aria as a sin-cleansing agent and a purifying force: "Hilf, Gott, dass es gelingt, / Und dein Feuer in uns dringt, / Dass es auch in dieser Stunde / Wie in Esaiae Munde / Seiner Wirkung Kraft erhält / Und uns heilig vor dich stellt." (Help, God, that we succeed, / And Thy Fire presses into us, / So that it also in this hour, / As in Isaiah's mouth / Contains the power of its effect / And puts us holy before Thee.)

The dance rhythm does not detract from the singer's declamation of these verses; in fact, Bach has made the poetry conform to the measured tune he wished to set.

6. *Chorale.* This chorale and the final one after Part II have two verses each. This would permit the congregation to sing these hymns with which they were familiar. For this chorale, Bach uses stanzas six and seven of Johann Heermann's hymn "Treuer Gott, ich muss dir klagen." (Faithful God, I Must Complain to Thee). Following the theme of the previous aria, the metaphor of faith being kindled by a spark of God's fire recurs here.

Part II

7. *Recitative—tenor.* Exhorts the saintly members of the congregation to hasten to praise God, who is represented in this church by the Trinity. They should choose Him, since they cannot find comfort in this vain world. This sounds like a text that Bach would write, in his simple but sincere longing for God.

8. *Aria—tenor.* With only continuo accompaniment in the rhythm of a gigue, the tenor depicts a combat scene between the might of God in Heaven and the power of Satan in the world. This conflict rhythm is shown both in the gigue melody and in the words sung: "Des Höchsten Gegenwart allein / Kann unsrer Freuden Ursprung sein. / Vergene, Welt, mit deiner Pracht, / In Gott ist, was uns glücklich macht!" (Only the presence of the Highest / Can be the source of our joys. / Vanish, world with your splendor, / In God is what makes us happy!)

9. *Recitative in Duet—soprano, bass.* The soprano voices her doubts about God's helping influence on people; the bass gives reassuring answers to each of her problems. This question-and-answer dialogue continues line by line until the two vocalists unite to sing the last four lines together: "Da er den Glauben nun belohnt / Und bei uns wohnt, / Bei uns als seinen Kindern, / So kann die Welt und Sterblichkeit die Freude nicht vermindern." (Since He now rewards belief / And dwells with us, / With us as His children, / So the world and our mortality cannot diminish our joy.) We should note that Bach has rarely, if ever before, used a duet in a recitative, and this one is well done.

10. *Aria-Duet—soprano, bass.* An unusually long duet with two oboes. It was originally a minuet in form but loses some of this feature as it develops. It states that we should rejoice that God has chosen us to provide His new home: "O wie wohl ist uns geschehn, / Dass sich Gott ein Haus ersehn!" (O how well it has happened to us, / That God has chosen a house for Himself!) This number is musically interesting, but its length tends to detract from its emotional appeal.

11. *Recitative—bass.* Tells the congregation that God dwells within each of them as well as in the church. Then he encourages them to offer Him their hearts and gifts—probably referring to the communion and the collection which

would follow in the order of the service after the cantata.

12. *Chorale.* From stanzas nine and ten of Paul Gerhardt's hymn "Wach auf, mein Herz, und singe" (Wake up, My Heart, and Sing). The guidance of God is prayed for in stanza nine; in stanza ten, the prayer is that their hearts be the Lord's house, which neatly brings the congregation back to the theme of the dedication of the church and of themselves to God.

• **Christen, ätzet diesen Tag (Christians, Engrave This Day)** (1723; BWV 63).

For his first Christmas in Leipzig, Bach composed the *Magnificat* and this cantata; the cantata alone was performed by the first choir in the Nicolaikirche on Christmas morning, while both pieces were sung at the evening service in St. Thomas's church. J.M. Heineccius wrote the libretto, and it is possible that Bach had previously performed it during his visit to the Liebfraukirche in Halle, although there is no proof of this.

This cantata is unusual because it has neither Biblical reference, nor chorale, nor arias. Two choruses, one at the beginning and one at the end, frame the intervening recitatives and duets. Thus it resembles an oratorio more than a cantata in its style.

The Gospel deals with the Nativity of Christ, St. Luke 2 (1–14), but this is not quoted directly in the libretto's text. It is a free cantata for SATB and chorus with an exceptionally large orchestra: four trumpets, timpani, three oboes, a bassoon, two violins, a viola, organ and continuo.

1. *Chorus.* The opening orchestral tutti, with its blazing trumpets and drums among the other instruments, paints a picture of a festive procession. Then the chorus comes in, like the solo group of a concerto grosso, which the choruses of this cantata resemble: "Christen, ätzet diesen Tag / In Metall und Marmorsteine!" (Christians, engrave this day / In metal and marblestone!)

After an elaborate orchestral ritornello, the choir continues: "Kommt und eilt mit mir zur Krippen / Und erweist mit frohen Lippen / Euren Dank und eure Pflicht!" (Come and hasten with me to the crib / And prove with happy lips / Your thanks and your duty!)

Another instrumental interlude occurs now before the final two lines sung in canon (a striking feature of the vocal numbers throughout this cantata): "Denn der Strahl, so da einbricht, / Zeigt sich euch zum Gnadenscheine." (For the radiance, which so breaks there, / Shows itself to you as the light of mercy.)

Much emphatic repetition is placed on "Strahl" (radiance or ray of life) to highlight it.

A full da capo of the opening tutti and chorus concludes this ecstatic scene.

2. *Recitative—alto.* Blends declamation with arioso in the lengthy text. She rejoices over this wonderful day on which the Shilo (Hebraic for Messiah) was promised by God to mankind, in order to deliver Israel from the slavery of Satan. She wonders that God would send His child to be born in a manger, when the people have already forsaken Him. The last line in arioso conveys all the mystic emotion of which Bach is capable: "O unbegreifliches, doch seliges Verfügen." (O incomprehensible, yet blessed enactment!)

Neither in this, nor the other recitatives of this cantata, do we feel that Bach is sermonizing as he did in some previous ones. This is genuine, heartfelt sentiment.

3. *Duet—soprano, bass.* With oboe obbligato and organ continuo, the voices sing in canon their gratitude to God for His bounty towards them in the gift of His Son. This is expressed in the last two lines: "Denn er hat uns dies beschert, / Was uns ewig nun vergnüget." (For He has bestowed on us this, / Which now delights us eternally.)

4. *Recitative—tenor.* In secco, he states that the troubles which have oppressed Israel have turned to pure salvation and grace. They will now again find

at Christmastide. Bach composed it on a libretto by Christian Weiss, Sr., for the third day of Christmas (a Tuesday) when he was expected to produce a cantata.

The main idea shows distaste for the world's attractions, which cannot be compared to the joys of heaven. The only Gospel reference occurs in the first chorus, taken from the first Epistle of John 3 (1), which quotes it for its text, because this date was the feast day of John the Apostle. However, the rest of the cantata has nothing more to do with this nor with the Christmas story; it is concerned simply with renunciation of the world.

There are three chorales as well as a chorus for the choir, with solo numbers for soprano, alto and bass. The instruments are a cornetto, an oboe d'amore, three trombones, two violins, a viola, organ and continuo.

1. *Chorus.* Like a motet in its fugal style. Right from the beginning, the voices repeat the sections of the fugue, with the orchestra doubling the voices in a joy-motif: "Sehet, welch eine Liebe hat uns der Vater erzeiget, dass wir Gottes Kinder heissen." (See what a love the Father has shown to us, that we are called God's children.) It is a very powerful opening number.

2. *Chorale.* Expresses the joy and thanks of all Christians to be chosen as His children. It is stanza seven of Luther's hymn, "Gelobet seist du, Jesus Christ" (Praised Be Thou, Jesus Christ).

3. *Recitative—alto.* Launches into the main theme of all the remainder of the cantata: the world with its wealth is transitory, whereas her desire is for a lasting heaven: "Geh, Welt! behalte nur das Deine, / Ich will und mag nichts von dir haben, / Der Himmel ist nun meine, / An diesem soll sich meine Seele laben." (Begone, world! just keep your possessions; / I want and wish to have nothing from you. / Heaven is now mine; / On this shall my soul be refreshed.)

She ends her recitative with what she would say as the lead-in to the following chorale.

4. *Chorale.* Stanza one of G.M. Pfefferkorn's hymn, "Was frag' ich nach der Welt" (What Do I Ask of the World), which begins and ends with this line, trust in Jesus being expressed in between as the source of her pleasure.

5. *Aria—soprano.* This is the most beautiful part of the cantata. Bach must have been greatly inspired to have written such mystical music as this, with its emotional, dream-like, haunting melody of the violins. The text comes from Psalm 37 (20), paraphrased thus: "Was die Welt / In sich hält, / Muss als wie ein Rauch vergehen." (What the world / Holds within itself / Must like smoke vanish.) This picture of poignant emptiness in a desolate landscape is audibly created by Bach's pen. Nowhere has his tone-color been so touching as in this aria. In the second part of her aria, Bach's artistry is evident in the coloratura runs on the words "fest" (firmly) and "stehen" (stand): "Aber was mir Jesus gibt, / Und was meine Seele liebt, / Bleibet fest und ewig stehen." (But what Jesus gives to me, / And what my soul loves / Remains standing firmly and eternally.)

The da capo returns us to the beauty of the first part of her aria.

6. *Recitative—bass.* Feels confident that his belief will admit him to heaven, but he laments that he must stay longer on earth, before he can share the joy of heaven with Jesus. There is a peculiar tone to his declamation, which seems to reflect Bach's own longing to escape from the troubles of this world.

7. *Aria—alto.* Reiterates the desire to demand nothing of the world, provided that she inherits heaven. She would gladly give away all she has, if she can be assured that she will not eternally perish. The obbligato oboe d'amore plays in dancing rhythm to the lovely vocal treatment of the text.

8. *Chorale.* Based on stanza five of J. Franck's hymn, "Jesu, meine Freude" (Jesus, My Joy). It was modeled on a secular tune for a love song: "Flora meine Freude; meiner Seele Weide" (Flora My Joy; the Pasture of My Soul), but the

theme here is to bid good-night to the sin, pride and vice in the world. Indeed, the words "Gute Nacht" (good-night) begin four of its verses.

• **Herr Gott, dich loben wir (Lord God, We Praise Thee)** (1724; BWV 16).

Here is Bach's first cantata for 1724; it is for New Year's Day, having both libretto and its music composed by Bach. It is interesting because it is the first extant chorale cantata (the chorale tune is in the first chorus, plus a Chorale as the final number), and because it shows Telemann's influence on Bach's composition of this piece.

The soloists are ATB with chorus; the orchestra is composed of two oboes, two violins, a corno da caccia and continuo. There is no Gospel or Epistle for this day.

1. *Chorus.* An exceedingly short chorus, based on the first four lines of Luther's *Te Deum,* with all the instruments, yet very striking despite its brevity: "Herr Gott, dich loben wir, / Herr Gott, wir danken dir! / Dich, Gott Vater in Ewigkeit, / Ehret die Welt weit und breit." (Lord God, we praise Thee. / Lord God, we thank Thee! / Thou, God Father in eternity, / The world honors far and wide.)

2. *Recitative—bass.* Describes the warm devotion shown by the people at the beginning of this new year. The secco style makes this piece rather dull, but it serves to introduce the next movement, their first new song of devotion to God for this year.

3. *Aria—bass and chorus.* This superb song of rollicking merriment expresses their exuberance over God's blessing on them. It appears that this is the first time that Bach has composed an aria-chorus combination. Telemann has done so in his cantatas, and it seems that Bach has imitated him in this number. The joy-motif is so overpowering in the first line that the listener can almost hear the singers' joyous laughter, as the bass alternates with the full choir in repeating the first line: "Lasst uns jauchzen, lasst uns freuen" (Let us exult, let us rejoice). The corno da caccia gives brilliance, as it doubles the voices.

The remainder of the aria shows less verve, but its florid effect continues in its charming repeats: "Gottes Güt' und Treu' / Bleibet alle Morgen neu! / Krönt und segnet seine Hand, / Ach so glaubt, dass unser Stand / Ewig glücklich sei!" (God's goodness and fidelity / Stays every morning new! / His Hand crowns and blesses, / O then believe, that our condition / Is forever happy!) The da capo returns to the resounding jollity of the beginning verse.

4. *Recitative—alto.* Coming right after this tumultuous chorus, this declamation, with continuo only, provides a pleasant respite from the previous excitement. It is a prayer to God to protect church and school for the increase of his kingdom, so that Satan's cunning will be disturbed. May we ask Him for peace and rest and that He will water our land in order to improve it. We should be well-off, if we trust in Jesus to achieve this.

5. *Aria—tenor.* With oboe da caccia and continuo, this aria seems to resemble those of Telemann according to Spitta, but its length, with repeats and da capo, makes it more monotonous than any Telemann aria. On the merit side, it has a plaintive sort of tone, as if the singer were entreating Jesus to believe his prayer: "Geliebter Jesu, du allein / Sollst meiner Seele Reichtum sein!" (Beloved Jesus, Thou alone / Shalt be the wealth of my soul!) These lines are repeated at the end of the number and before the da capo.

6. *Chorale.* The hymn text is stanza six of Paul Eber's "Helft mir Gottes Güte preisen" (Help Me Praise God's Goodness) for New Year's. With violins and oboes, the hymn praises God's goodness and refers to the main theme of a happy new year in its last three lines: "Gib uns ein friedlich Jahre, / Vor allem Leid bewahre / Und nähr uns mildiglich." (Give us a peaceful year; / Preserve us from all sorrow / And nourish us gently.)

• **Schau', lieber Gott, wie meine Feind' (See, Dear God, How My Enemies)** (1724; BWV 153).

Despite its three chorales, probably intended for congregational participation when they occur, and two splendid arias for tenor (6) and alto (8), this cantata seems to lack a definite aim in its libretto.

The theme for this first Sunday after New Year's refers to the flight into Egypt described in Matthew 2 (13–15), but this is only briefly mentioned in the bass recitative (7), while all the other numbers deal with the attacks on Christians by their enemies, their appeals to God for help, and their trust and confidence in Him, which are mentioned in the Epistle for this Sunday in 1st Peter 4 (12–19).

It is thought that Bach wrote this libretto. It is scored for ATB soli with choir and light instrumentation: two violins, a viola and continuo.

1. *Chorale.* Sets a despondent mood, which will last right up to the penultimate number of the cantata. The text is taken from David Denicke's hymn, the first stanza: "Schau', lieber Gott, wie meine Feind' / Damit ich stets muss kämpfen, / So listig und so mächtig seind, / Dass sie mich leichtlich dämpfen." (See, dear God, how my enemies, / With whom I always must struggle, / Are so cunning and so powerful, / That they overcome me easily.)

The three enemies—the devil, the flesh and the world—are listed in the final lines. A Christian can resist them only if he has God's grace.

2. *Recitative—alto.* Pleads that God help her in her misery; she must live here among lions and dragons which seek her ruin. The personification of these fierce animals to depict the cruel people of the world is noteworthy.

3. *Aria—bass.* Represents God, saying that he will strengthen her against such vicious adversaries. Isaiah 41 (10) is the text, literally quoted, for this aria: "Fear thou not; for I am with thee. Be not dismayed; for I am thy God; I will strengthen thee; yea, I will uphold thee with the right hand of my righteousness."

4. *Recitative—tenor.* In secco, as for the alto recitative, he listens to God's consolation, but immediately thereafter relapses into despair, saying that his enemies have bent their bows to loose their arrows at him. His life is in danger; the whole world is for him a torture-pit. His only help can come from God, as he pleads in arioso: "Hilf, Helfer, hilf! errette meine Seele!" (Help, Helper, help! rescue my soul!).

5. *Chorale.* Based on stanza five of Paul Gerhardt's "Befiehl du deine Wege" (Commend Thy Ways). This stanza tells of submission to God's will, which will come to pass, in spite of all the devils who beset a Christian.

6. *Aria—tenor.* With all the defiance he can muster, he invites the evil elements to descend on him, if only he knows that God is his protector and his Savior. In amazing florid fashion, Bach combines the tumult and the wave motifs to paint a storm scene, in which the tenor invites the waves of misfortune to break over him. The flooding waters and inundating fires present, in allegory, the evils which beset him: "Stürmt nur, stürmt, ihr Trübsalswetter, / Wallt, ihr Fluten, auf mich los! / Schlagt, ihr Unglücksflammen, / Über mich zusammen, / Stört, ihr Feinde, meine Ruh," (Just storm, storm, sadness-weather; / Undulate, floods, freely over me! / Strike, flames of misfortune, / Over me together; / Disturb, ye enemies, my rest."

The last two lines of the aria then become like the calm after the storm, as he adds in a more tranquil tone: "Spricht mir doch Gott tröstlich zu: / Ich bin dein Hort und dein Erretter." (Yet God speaks to me consolingly: / I am thy Refuge and thy Savior.)

7. *Recitative—bass.* Begins to change the gloom and doom to a picture of possible happiness. He comforts himself by realizing that his troubles are much less severe than Herod's persecution of the infant Jesus, when He was driven into Egypt with His parents. His concluding arioso affirms that those who suffer here

as Christ did will be granted entry into Heaven by Him.

8. *Aria—alto.* Here we hear a definite change to the joy of heaven, as the tempo turns from andante at the beginning to allegro at the end. She affirms her belief, in charming melody, that Jesus will convert all previous sadness to joy: "Soll ich meinen Lebenslauf / Unter Kreuz und Trübsal führen, / Hört es doch im Himmel auf." (If I am to pass the course of my life / Under cross and sadness, / That stops, after all, in heaven.)

At this point the tempo quickens to the end: "Da ist lauter Jubilieren, / Daselbsten verwechselt mein Jesus das Leiden / Mit seliger Wonne, mit ewigen Freuden." (There is loud jubilation there, / For there my Jesus exchanges the pain / For blessed rapture, for eternal joy.)

This is a very well-composed aria and a tribute to Bach's art.

9. *Chorale.* This final happy frame of mind is consolidated by this concluding chorale, based on Martin Moller's "Ach Gott, wie manches Herzeleid" (O God, How Much Sorrow). Each of the three stanzas refers to parts already sung in the cantata: imitation of Christ's suffering, combat against sin, confidence in the Lord, and the desire to join Him in Heaven.

• **Sie werden aus Saba alle kommen (They Will All Come Out of Sheba)** (1724; BWV 65).

For Epiphany of this year, Bach set this libretto by Christian Weiss, Sr., or perhaps by himself. The Gospel from Matthew 2 (1–12) tells of the visit of the Magi to the stable; the Old Testament reading from Isaiah 60 (1–6) speaks of the prophecy of Christ's birth. Parts of both texts are used in this cantata.

The soloists are ATB with chorus; the orchestra has two of each of these instruments: horns, recorders, oboes da caccia, violins, and a viola with continuo. The setting is quite lavish as befits the festival.

1. *Chorus.* Bach's imagination must have been fired when he painted this panorama of camels and dromedaries in a caravan proceeding across the desert waste. The two horns begin the march theme, which is joined by the two recorders and violins in unison to produce a tone-painting depicting the oriental majesty of this procession. The chorus enters, after this short introduction, to sing the text, which is composed partly of the Old Testament and partly of the Gospel for the day: "Sie werden aus Saba alle kommen, Gold und Weihrauch bringen und des Herren Lob verkündigen." (They will all come out of Sheba, bringing gold and incense and proclaiming the Lord's praise.)

The caravan seems to halt at the end, just before the music stops.

2. *Chorale.* Takes its text from stanza four of an anonymous hymn, 1543, "Ein Kind geborn zu Bethlehem" (A Child Born in Bethlehem), which was also used in the Catholic version in Latin, "Puer natus in Bethlehem." The recorders and oboes give the voices the sound of group singing of a Christmas carol, and the congregation of St. Thomas's would be familiar with this tune. The simplicity of this chorale contrasts with the lavish splendor of the first chorus, probably to mark the difference between the rich kings and the lowly Child: "Die Kön'ge aus Saba kamen dar, / Gold, Weihrauch, Myrrhen brachten sie dar, / Alleluja!" (The kings from Sheba came there, / Gold, incense and myrrh brought they there, / Alleluja!)

3. *Recitative—bass.* In secco style, he narrates the fulfilled prophecy of Isaiah concerning the arrival of the Wise Men and their gifts to the infant. This leads him to the present time: what does he have to offer? He decides that he has only his heart to give.

The rest of the cantata will be devoted to this sole idea of offering one's heart as one's best gift to Christ.

4. *Aria—bass.* The instrumental phrases of the oboes in triple canon suggest the bowing of the Magi before the cradle, while the long runs on "Gaben"

(gifts) suggest their worthlessness: "Gold aus Ophir ist zu schlecht, / Weg, nur weg mit eitlen Gaben, / Die ihr aus der Erde brecht!" (Gold from Ophir is too base; / Away, just away with vain gifts, / Which you break out of the earth!)

Thus he continues the theme of his recitative, which he will also end with the gift of his heart: "Jesus will das Herze haben. Schenke dies, O Christenschar, / Jesu zu dem neuen Jahr!" (Jesus wants to have the heart. / Present this, O Christian flock, / To Jesus for the New Year!)

5. *Recitative — tenor.* Also in secco, he says that he humbly presents his heart and that his gifts will be the gold of faith, the incense of prayer, the myrrh of patience. He asks that Jesus will give Himself to him, so that he will become the richest man on earth.

6. *Aria — tenor.* The uninhibited joy-motif in the rhythm of this aria and the sincerity of the tenor's voice, as he prays to Christ to receive his heart and his service to Him, make this one of the loveliest of Bach's arias. The sentiment he expresses in his devotion to Christ is magnificently aided by all the instruments to produce a very touching effect on the listener: "Nimm mich dir zu eigen hin, / Nimm mein Herze zum Geschenke. / Alles, alles, wzs ich bin, / Was ich rede, tu' und denke, / Soll, mein Heiland, nur allein / Dir zum Dienst gewidmet sein." (Take me to Thyself as Thine own, / Take my heart as the present. / Everything, everything, that I am, / That I speak, do and think, / Shall, my Savior, just only / To Thee be dedicated as service.)

7. *Chorale.* Stanza ten of Paul Gerhardt's hymn, "Ich hab' in Gottes Herz und Sinn," (I Have in God's Heart and Mind) (1647). It continues the tenor's dedication to Christ, with the hope that He will guide him into useful service, so that he may increase His honor.

• **Mein liebster Jesus ist verloren (My Dearest Jesus Is Lost)** (1724; BWV 154).

Bach was the librettist of this cantata for the first Sunday after Epiphany. The Gospel was taken from Luke 2 (41–52), concerning the twelve-year old Jesus, whom his parents lost after the Passover in Jerusalem, and then found again discoursing with the doctors in the Temple.

The text adheres to this Gospel story, but changes the worry of the parents over the lost child to concern of Christians over losing their Lord. This appears in the recitatives and the arias.

The soloists are ATB with chorus. The orchestra comprises two oboes d'amore, two violins, a viola and continuo.

1. *Aria — tenor.* Expresses the same anguish that Mary must have felt when she perceived that her Son was lost. In this grief-motif, the tenor's lament represents his despair over losing Christ. It is like a sword that pierces his soul. This simile is derived from Johann Rist's hymn, "O Ewigkeit, du Donnerwort" (O Eternity, Thou Word of Thunder) (1642). Bach will later compose two cantatas with this title, BWV 20 (1725) and BWV 60 (1732), on this hymn based on Luke 2 (35). Bach paraphrases it in the third and fourth lines of this aria: "Mein liebster Jesus is verloren, / O Wort, das mir Verzweiflung bringt, / O Schwert, das durch die Seele dringt, / O Donnerwort in meinen Ohren." (My dearest Jesus is lost. / O word, that brings me despair; / O sword, that pierces through the soul; / O thunder-word in my ears.)

2. *Recitative — tenor.* Asks where he can find Jesus; no misfortune can touch him so much as the loss of his Savior.

3. *Chorale.* Introduced by the previous tenor recitative. The choir sings of the same sense of loss as the tenor, as though they represent him, praising Jesus in terms of endearment (e.g. "Jesulein" = little Jesus). The hymn is stanza two of Martin Jahn's "Jesu, meiner Seelen Wonne" (Jesus, Bliss of My Soul) (1661).

4. *Aria — alto.* Very moving in her plea to let her find Jesus. Repeats of the first line, "Jesu, lass dich finden," (Jesus, let Thyself be found), as the aria develops, are very effective, as are the second

and third lines, which evoke the imagery of her sins being thick clouds hiding Jesus from her: "Lass doch meine Sünden / Keine dicke Wolken sein." (Don't let my sins / Be like any thick clouds.) Much color is added to the aria by the oboes d'amore and the strings.

5. *Arioso—bass.* A very fine declamation, in which the bass gives Jesus' reply to His mother, Luke 2 (49). Although the bass portrays Jesus, his voice represents the man rather than the child; in this case, He is speaking to the searching Christians: "Wisset ihr nicht, dass ich sein muss in dem, das meines Vaters ist?" (Do ye not know, that I must be busy in that, which concerns my Father?)

Probably the text also relates to what Jesus said to the doctors in the Temple.

6. *Recitative—tenor.* Rejoices that he has heard Jesus' voice and thus has found Him in His Father's house (the church). He will join Him there by taking the sacrament.

7. *Duet—alto, tenor.* An entrancing, dance-like rhythm of all the instruments accompanies the vocalists in a joy-motif proclaiming their bliss. This movement is one of the most memorable duets in any of Bach's cantatas: "Wohl mir, Jesus ist gefunden, / Nun bin ich nicht mehr betrübt. / Der, den meine Seele liebt, / Zeigt sich mir zur frohen Stunden." (Well for me, Jesus is found; / Now I am saddened no more. / He, Whom my soul loves, / Shows Himself to me at the happy hour.)

Then the tempo becomes slower for the last two lines (before returning to the allegro of the da capo): "Ich will dich, mein Jesu, nun nimmermehr lassen, / Ich will dich im Glauben beständig umfassen." (I will Thee, my Jesus, now nevermore leave, / I will embrace Thee constantly in faith.)

This transformation of tempo is rare in a Bach aria.

8. *Chorale.* Stanza six of Christian Keimann's "Meinen Jesum lass' ich nicht" (My Jesus I Do Not Leave) (1658), which is the first and last line of this stanza also. The chorus sings that, if "I" go always by the side of Jesus, He will guide me through my life.

• **Jesus schläft, was soll ich hoffen? (Jesus Sleeps, What Am I to Hope For?)** (1724; BWV 81).

Just as he showed his sense of drama in the two previous cantatas, BWV 65 and BWV 154, Bach's expertise as a dramatic composer really shines in this work. The Leipzig Town Council had stated in his contract that he was not to be theatrical in his church music, but when he had such vividly descriptive incidents as in this cantata to set, his natural bent to interpret a Biblical scene in music would bring to life not only the scenario but also the persons involved as actors.

The libretto for this fourth Sunday after Epiphany cantata was probably written by Bach, although Neumann suggests Christian Weiss, Sr., and Robertson gives Erdmann Neumeister. The text adheres closely to the Gospel for this Sunday, Matthew 8 (23–27)—Jesus calms the storm on the Sea of Galilee.

Two recorders, two oboes d'amore, two violins, a viola and continuo comprise the orchestra. The vocalists are ATB with chorus.

1. *Aria—alto.* In the role of one of the disciples, she sees a storm approaching her ship and is fearful because her Master sleeps. She is very frightened, thinking that she will drown after the vessel founders in the storm. This tempest symbolizes the ocean of sin drowning the Christian soul, which she metaphorically applies to her own present predicament.

The terror-motif in the alto's voice combines with the sombre tone-colors of the instruments to reflect this fear: "Jesus schläft, was soll ich hoffen? / Seh' ich nicht / Mit erblasstem Angesicht / Schon des Todes Abgrund offen?" (Jesus sleeps, what am I to hope for? / Do I not see / With pale face / Already open the abyss of death?)

2. *Recitative—tenor.* As another disciple, he asks the Lord why He has left them in their distress, when He usually is awake beside them. He has even guided

the Wise Men by the star on the right road to find Him; why should He sleep in this moment of danger?

3. *Aria—tenor.* Sings of his fright as the storm breaks upon him. Bach must have seen the Baltic or the North Sea at least twice during his visits to Lübeck and Hamburg. Thus he can visualize the wave and tumult motifs he produces in this aria. The dashing waves and rolling billows of sound seem very realistic in this seascape conjured up by the orchestra: "Die schäumende Wellen von Belials Bächen / Verdoppeln die Wut." (The foaming waves of Belial's streams / Redouble their fury.) It is interesting to note that Bach associates the raging storm, which now bursts upon the ship, with evil sent by the malignant devil.

There is a sudden abatement of the turmoil in the adagio of the next two lines: "Ein Christ soll zwar wie Felsen stehen, / Wenn Trübsalswinde um ihn gehn," (A Christian should surely stand like a rock, / When trouble-winds go around him,). Then the fury returns in the last two lines: "Doch suchet die stürmende Flut / Die Kräfte des Glaubens zu schwächen." (Still the storming flood seeks / To weaken the strength of belief.)

4. *Arioso—bass.* In the role of Jesus, speaks the text of Matthew 8 (26): "Ihr Kleingläubigen, warum seid ihr so furchtsam?" (O ye of little faith, why are ye so fearful?)

In this realistic intonation, we seem to see Christ, just awakened from His sleep, standing before them to address them, as an actor might appear suddenly on the stage at the right moment.

5. *Aria—bass.* The dramatic action of this aria, sung by the bass in the role of Jesus, is like the climax of a play. Jesus rebukes the storm, which has returned in full fury, not heeding His words at first, but gradually abating as the aria progresses: "Schweig, aufgetürmtes Meer! / Verstumme, Sturm und Wind! / Dir sei dein Zielgesetzet / Damit mein auserwähltes Kind / Kein Unfall je verletzet." (Be quiet, towering sea! / Be silent, storm and wind! / To thee thy limit is set, / So that My chosen child / No mishap ever harms.)

The imagery of the Savior reaching out to save His chosen child of little faith (the disciple Peter or, symbolically, a modern Christian) can be imagined by the listener at this point of the aria. The da capo brings us back to the storm scene.

This is a fine example of Bach's dramatic ability; he instills life into the text via his music, and creates a miniature drama of persons and imagined stage-sets.

6. *Recitative—alto.* Gives the comments of the first disciple, whose fear is now replaced by calm, now that Jesus has quelled the storm. Her remarks are like the comments on the action by an actor in a play: "Wohl mir, mein Jesus spricht ein Wort, / Mein Helfer ist erwacht." (Well for me, my Jesus speaks a word; / My Helper has awakened.)

As Jesus removed all the disciples' worry, so He will calm all her cares, as He quietened the waves after awaking.

7. *Chorale.* Is the second stanza of Johann Franck's "Jesu, meine Freude" (Jesus, My Joy) (1653). This verse refers to to the believer's trust in Jesus to protect him from the storms of his enemies and of Satan.

Spitta's opinion of this cantata might be mentioned in conclusion: "In this cantata Bach has shown how with the smallest means he could produce the grandest results. It is beyond question one of the most stupendous productions, not only of his art but of German music at any time. In every bar it may be said that his genius reveals its full power." (Vol. II, p. 404.)

• **Erfreute Zeit im neuen Bunde (Joyful Time in the New Covenant)** (1724; BWV 83).

Since the begining of this New Year 1724, Bach's cantatas have been composed for ATB soli only without a soprano. This holds for this work also. A possible explanation is that Bach had no suitable soprano voice available—part of his first complaint to the Town Council about the lack of talent among his singers.

Bach may have set the first three movements (aria-recitative-aria) on the allegro-adagio-allegro format of the Italian concerto, and if so, we may assume that Bach's concerto in this case has been lost.

The occasion was the Feast of the Purification on Tuesday, 2 February 1724, for which Bach or Picander wrote the libretto. The Gospel was taken from Luke 2 (19–31), used in the bass recitative and in the final chorale. It is scored for two horns, two oboes, one solo violin, two violins, a viola and continuo.

1. *Aria—alto.* The violin solo, with all the other instruments, indicates that this was the first movement of a concerto. Bach has placed the alto boy's voice very distinctly, so that his enunciation is clearly heard amid the orchestral tutti. The joy-motif expressed in the main theme of this cantata—that belief in Christ will make death appear only as a state of transition to a new life of peace and rest which He has promised: "Erfreute Zeit im neuen Bunde, / Da unser Glaube Jesum hält. / Wie freudig wird zur letzten Stunde / Die Ruhestatt, das Grab bestellt!" (Joyful time in the new covenant, / Since our belief holds Jesus. / How happy will be at the last hour / The resting-place, the grave, arranged!)

This longing for death is a favorite theme in Bach's religious thought, as it was among his contemporaries.

2. *Intonation and Recitative—bass.* The intonation of the Biblical words of Simeon (the *Nunc dimittis*) is placed at the beginning and at the end of this movement, while the receitative is inserted between. This is a most unusual arrangement for a recitative. Yet the adagio intonation, giving the arioso effect at the beginning, as well as at the end, makes it one of Bach's best recitatives: "Herr, nun lässest du deinen Diener in Friede fahren, wie du gesaget hast." (Lord, now lettest Thou Thy servant depart in peace, as Thou has said.) [Recitative follows, then the intonation resumes:] "Denn meine Augen haben deinen Heiland gesehen, welchen du bereitet hast vor allen Völkern." (For my eyes have seen Thy Salvation, which Thou hast prepared before all people.)

The intervening recitative comments on death as being the entrance to eternal life—just as Simeon was willing to die, once he had seen the Child Jesus, so we should be unafraid of death, in order that we may see Him ourselves.

3. *Aria—tenor.* This may have been the last movement of the lost violin concerto. The allegro joy-motif returns in gigue rhythm, still featuring the solo violin with the voice. The believer's impatient yearning for death is reflected in the text: "Eile, Herz, voll Freudigkeit / Vor den Gnadenstuhl zu treten!" (Hasten, heart, full of joy / To step before the chair of mercy!) This aria, however, seems to have less musical quality than the first aria.

4. *Recitative—alto.* Features words denoting dark colors—"Finsternis" (darkness), "Nacht" (night), "Schatten" (shadows), "Tode" (death)—but the singer concludes optimistically on the idea that after the grave's darkness, the Lord's light will shine forth: "Ja, wenn des Grabes Nacht / Die letzte Stunde schrecklich macht, / So wirst du doch gewiss / Sein helles Licht im Tode selbst erkennen." (Yes, when the grave's night / Makes the last hour terrible, / Then you will certainly recognize / His bright light in death itself.)

5. *Chorale.* The 4th stanza of Luther's hymn, his paraphrase of the *Nunc Dimittis,* "Mit Fried' und Freud' ich fahr' dahin" (With Peace and Joy I Travel There), was usually sung at the vesper service for this festival. Its praise of Christ as the Salvation and Light of the heathen and of believers makes this chorale a suitable conclusion.

• **Christ lag in Todesbanden (Christ Lay in the Bonds of Death)** (1724; BWV 4).

While he was in Weimer, Bach had composed parts of this cantata for Easter

Sunday. It is his only cantata which follows the format of those set by Buxtehude, Pachelbel and Kuhnau, i.e., completely set on one chorale melody without recitatives.

The libretto is a seven-stanza poem by Luther, set to music by Johann Walther in 1524, "Christ ist erstanden" (Christ Has Risen). Bach adds a sinfonia to its seven numbers, varying the treatment for each, to create his first true chorale cantata.

It should be noted that Luther ended each stanza with "Halleluja." The vocalists are SATB in four-part chorus; the instruments are a cornetto, three trombones, two violins, two violas and continuo.

1. *Sinfonia.* With strings only, Bach paints the melancholy atmosphere of the tomb, but this tone rises toward the end, symbolic of the Resurrection.

2. *Chorus—SATB.* Begins with a low grief-motif, which soon changes into joy as the stanza progresses. It is a great chorale fantasia with the melody sung by the sopranos, doubled by the cornetto; the other voices are doubled by the trombones. The gloom of the first two lines—"Christ lag in Todesbanden / Für unsre Sünd' gegeben" (Christ lay in the bonds of death / Given for our sin)—soon changes to rejoicing in the rest of the stanza: "Er ist wieder erstanden / Und hat uns bracht das Leben; / Des wir sollen fröhlich sein, Gott loben und ihm dankbar sein / Und singen Halleluja, Halleluja!" (He is again risen / And has brought us life; / Therefore we should be happy, / Praise God and be thankful to Him / And sing Halleluja, / Halleluja!)

3. *Duet—soprano, alto.* In a more serious, lower tone, they say that no mortal can compel death to come or go—that death has power over us because of our sins. Yet the "Halleluja" at the end implies that we can conquer it as Christ did.

4. *Chorale—tenor.* A very forceful and clear-cut delivery of the stanza by the tenor; Jesus has come to remove sin from us and He has also taken the sting out of death, leaving it a powerless figure. The melody tumbles down to symbolize Satan's fall, finishing with a triumphant "Halleluja."

5. *Chorale—SATB.* Sung as chorale fantasia in Pachelbel style by the full chorus. The rhythm presents a tone-picture of a battle between life and death, from which life emerges victorious. The sound evokes a vast canvas by a master-painter: "Es war ein wunderlicher Krieg, / Da Tod und Leben rungen, / Das Leben behielt den Sieg, / Es hat den Tod verschlungen." (It was an amazing war, / As death and life struggled; / Life held the victory, / It has swallowed death.)

This conflict is strange because the text depicts two animals or reptiles in combat with one swallowing the other: "Wie ein Tod den andern frass" (As one death devoured the other)—"frass" means "ate" (of animals). The symbolic meaning is that Christ's death swallowed (in victory) real death and thus made a joke of dying (as the last line states).

6. *Chorale—bass.* Movingly paints the scene of the Crucifixion with Christ hanging on the Cross: "Hier ist das rechte Osterlamm, / Davon Gott hat geboten, / Das hoch an des Kreuzes Stamm / In heisser Lieb' gebraten." (Here is the real Easter Lamb, / Whom God has ordered [and] / Who high on the tree of the Cross / Burned in hot love.)

He continues to sing that his blood marks our door, so that our belief in his sacrifice will prevent the evil executioner (Satan) from harming us further.

7. *Duet—soprano, tenor.* Sing their song of triumph at this Festival in celebration of the end of sin, and to express their joy over Christ's intercession on their behalf: "So feiern wir das hohe Fest / Mit Herzensfreud und Wonne, . . . Der Sünden Nacht ist verschwunden." (So we celebrate the High Feast / With joyous heart and bliss . . . The night of sins has disappeared.) The joy-motif pervades the entire duet, the singers decorating many words: "Wonne" (bliss), "Sonne" (sun), "Gnade Glanz" (glow of grace), "Herzen" (hearts).

A fine rhythm of solemnity is heard also in the music.

8. *Chorale—SATB.* With all instruments, the choir relates how they will change the old bread of the Passover for a new bread for the soul in the body of Christ (Communion). Otherwise, they say, their faith cannot live.

• **Weinen, Klagen, Sorgen, Zagen (Weeping, Complaining, Worries, Fears)** (1724; BWV 12).

Bach had composed this cantata in its early form at Weimar in 1714. Its finished form for the third Sunday after Easter, called *Jubilate* from the motet "Jubilate Deo" performed then, was given in Leipzig in 1724.

Salomo Franck was the librettist and, as was usual with him, included no recitatives in his text. The Gospel is from John 16 (16–23), which tells of the Savior's return among His disciples, and the trials and the troubles they will endure before He changes them to joy. This theme is applied to the present Christian congregation in all movements of this cantata.

The soloists are ATB with chorus; the orchestra has trumpet, oboe, bassoon, strings and continuo.

1. *Sinfonia.* Sets the melancholy mood of the first half of the cantata in the adagio for woodwinds and strings, which seems to reflect Bach's imitation of the Italian church sonata style.

2. *Chorus.* Divided into three sections, of which the first and third are a passacaglio for chorus and orchestra. The tearful, lamenting tones present a tone-poem of the grief suffered by Christians in their daily lives: "Weinen, Klagen, / Sorgen, Zagen, / Angst und Not / Sind der Christen Tränenbrot," (Weeping, complaining, / Worries, fears, / Anxiety and need / Are the Christians' bread of tears.)

3. *Recitative—alto.* Sings with beautiful melisma the consoling text taken from Acts 14 (22): "Wir müssen durch viel Trübsal in das Reich Gottes eingehen." (We must go through much tribulation into the Kingdom of God.) Her declamation makes this seem more arioso than recitative, especially with the supporting bassoon and strings.

4. *Aria—alto.* An emotional song with only oboe and continuo; it marks the end of the pervading despondency up to this number. She brings her intense feeling out of her text, which teaches that resignation to suffering is what Christ experienced on earth, before He could ascend into heaven: "Kreuz und Krone sind verbunden, / Kampf und Kleinod sind vereint. / Christen haben alle Stunden / Ihre Qual und ihren Feind, / Doch ihr Trost sind Christi Wunden." (Cross and crown are bound together, / Struggle and jewel are united. / Christians have in every hour / Their torment and their enemy, / Yet Christ's wounds are their comfort.)

5. *Aria—bass.* Sings in a happy step-motif, saying that he will follow after Christ and never leave Him, whether in well-being or in adversity. There is a joyous tone of confidence in his voice, denoting his happy decision.

6. *Aria—tenor (with Chorale).* With the trumpet playing the chorale, "Jesu, meine Freude" (Jesus, My Joy), he sings of the necessity of keeping faith in Jesus, despite all hardships and pain, because these will soon pass away. We seem to perceive the Savior speaking these words of comfort to the believer. The textual imagery reveals an appealing scene: a blossoming landscape after a rainstorm has passed over (just as our pain will disappear, to be replaced by blessing). "Sei getreu, alle Pein / Wird doch nur ein Kleines sein. / Nach dem Regen / Blüht der Segen, / Alles Wetter geht vorbei. / Sei getreu, sei getreu!" (Be faithful, all pain / Will then only be a little thing. / After the rain / Blooms the blessing; / All bad weather passes by. / Be faithful, be faithful!) This aria is the best movement in the cantata.

7. *Chorale.* With full orchestra, it is based on S. Rodigast's "Was Gott tut, das ist wohlgetan" (What God Does, That Is Done Well).

transferred its melody to the Quoniam section of his *Short Mass in G* also.

4. *Recitative—bass.* The publican is the topic for this second recitative, as the Pharisee was for the first. Bach tries to illustrate the story of the publican by associating the words of the text with the music he sets in very artistic and lyrical style: "Wer so von innen wie von aussen ist, / Der heisst ein wahrer Christ. / So war der Zöllner in dem Tempel, / Der schug in Demut an die Brust, / Und legte sich nicht selbst ein heilig Wesen bei;" (Whoever is thus from within as from without, / He is called a true Christian. / So was the publican in the Temple, / Who struck on his breast in humility, / And did not ascribe a holy nature to himself.)

He continues by saying that even if one commits no crimes, he should not therefore imagine himself to be angelic, since he may still have other sins. His final lines in arioso state what must be done: "Bekenne Gott in Demut deine Sünden, / So kannst du Gnad und Hilfe finden!" (Confess humbly to God your sins; / Then you can find mercy and help!)

This extortion ends the denunciation of the preceding movements.

5. *Aria—soprano.* In her imploring vocal tones, accompanied by oboe da caccia and continuo, she appears to be a penitent sinner standing before God. Hers is the best movement in the cantata; again Bach borrowed it for the *Qui tollis* movement in another of his *Short Masses* (this one in A) at a later date.

What is surprising about this text is that some of the words are rather coarse to have been written by a clergyman: "Meine Sünden kränken mich / Als ein *Eiter* in Gebeinen. / Hilf mir, Jesu, Gottes Lamm, / Ich versink' im tiefen *Schlamm!*" (My sins afflict me / Like a *pus* in the bones. / Help me, Jesus, God's Lamb, / I am sinking in the deep *slime!*)

6. *Chorale.* It is the first verse of Christoph Tietze's hymn "Ich armer Mensch, ich armer Sünder" (I Poor Man, I Poor Sinner) (1663), set to Georg Neumark's tune for "Wer nur den lieben Gott lässt walten" (Whoever Lets Dear God Govern). The verse continues to implore God's mercy on us sinners, and the choir brings out this prayer very harmoniously.

• **Lobe den Herrn, meine Seele (Praise the Lord, My Soul) I** (1724; BWV 69).

In its original form, BWV 69a, this cantata was for the Inauguration of the Town Council (Ratswahl), but Bach performed it also on the preceding Sunday, the twelfth after Trinity. Subsequently he revised it into its present form (BWV 69) for another Ratswechsel celebration in 1730.

The librettist is unknown, but it may have been Christian Weiss, Sr. The Gospel for the original version was Mark 7 (31–37), the healing of the deaf-mute, but references to this, which occur in the two recitatives of BWV 69a, were omitted in the substitutes Bach composed for them in 1730. The only Biblical quotation appears in the opening chorus (Psalm 103 [2]).

The soloists are SATB with a four-part chorus. The orchestra is lavishly regal: three trumpets, timpani, three oboes, a bassoon, two violins, a viola and continuo.

1. *Chorus.* The altos and tenors, joined by the sopranos and basses, begin by singing the first half of the verse, which is then repeated by all groups in unison, before they begin a double fugue. The first fugue is begun by the tenors in florid style and the second by the sopranos, who sing the last half of the verse. The two fugues are combined at the end. The da capo return has magnificent impact. This chorus provides the overall theme of the cantata: praise of the Lord by the congregation and by the Town Council: "Lobe den Herrn, meine Seele, und vergiss nicht, was er dir Gutes getan hat!" (Praise the Lord, my soul, and do not forget what good things He has done for you!)

This is without any doubt one of Bach's most brilliant and powerful choruses.

2. *Recitative—soprano.* She describes God's favors to us: He caused us to be born, He supports us with life as He does all His creatures. She wants to do her utmost to express her praise to Him in song.

3. *Aria—alto.* With oboe, bassoon and violin accompaniment, she proceeds to carry out the soprano's intention (in the above recitative) to praise God in this, her song of thanksgiving: "Meine Seele, / Auf! erzähle, / Was dir Gott erwiesen hat!" (My soul, / Arise! tell, / What God has shown thee!)

The rhythm reminds us of a sort of lullaby which, however, does not seem to fit the thought expressed in the last lines of the text, where the joy-motif barely glimmers through: "Rühme seine Wundertat, / Lass dem Höchsten zu gefallen / Ihm ein frohes Danklied schallen!" (Praise His wonderful doing. / Let in order to please the Highest, / To Him a happy song of thanks resound!)

4. *Recitative—tenor.* He continues their thanks to God and prays that He will give wisdom to the new government and protection to their country. He hopes that God will chastise His people, but not refuse them His help.

5. *Aria—bass.* His moving prayer, with woodwinds and strings doubling the continuo, is one of Bach's superlative arias for bass. The emotional fervor of this prayer increases in intensity toward the end with dramatic effect. His prayer seems to become that of the listener as well as of the singer. "Mein Erlöser und Erhalter, / Nimm mich stets in Hut und Wacht! / Steh' mir bei in Kreuz und Leiden, / Alsdann singt mein Mund mit Freuden: / Gott hat alles wohl gemacht." (My Redeemer and Preserver, / Take me always in Thy care and guard! / Stand by me in suffering and sorrow; / Then my mouth sings with joy: / God has done all things well.) The joy-motif at the end of the aria still reflects the element of praise, which has been the theme in every movement.

6. *Chorale.* This wonderfully climactic conclusion, with full orchestra and chorus, is based on Luther's stanza three of Psalm 67: "Let the people praise thee, O God: let all the people praise thee." It is the same verse and anonymous melody that Bach used to compose the final chorale for BWV 76, "Die Himmel erzählen," but here treated somewhat differently in one great, elaborate hymn of praise. The joy-motif is featured throughout, right to the final "Amen"!

• **Singet dem Herrn ein neues Lied (Sing to the Lord a New Song)** (1725; BWV 190).

With this cantata for New Year's Day, we begin the 1735 cycle, although Bach must have composed it in 1724. The librettist is unknown. Picander revised the text for another performance in 1730 to celebrate the Jubilee of the Augsburg Confession. The original work was incomplete, missing the first two numbers, which were reconstructed in 1948 and added to the 1725 text. It is this reconstructed form which is performed today.

As with BWV 69, this cantata is intended to praise God, and therefore it has the same rich instrumentation: three trumpets, timpani, three oboes, two violins, a viola and continuo. The soli are ATB with full four-part chorus.

1. *Chorus and Chorale.* The chorus takes its text from Psalm 149 (1) and Psalm 150 (4, 6). The chorale verses of Luther's German *Te Deum* are inserted within the chorus lines and are sung separately in unison by the choir. The chorus sings in two fugal sections, the first in their first two lines, and the second in their last line: "Singet dem Herrn ein neues Lied! Die Gemeine der Heiligen soll ihn loben! / Lobet ihn mit Pauken und Reigen, lobet ihn mit Saiten und Pfeifen! (chorale)—Herr Gott, dich loben wir! / Alles, was Odem hat, lobe den Herrn! / (chorale)—Herr Gott, wir danken dir! / Alleluja!" (Sing to the Lord a new song! The congregation of the Saints shall praise Him! / Praise Him with drums and dance, praise Him with strings and pipes! / (chorale)—Lord

God, we praise Thee! / Everything that has breath, praise the Lord! / (chorale)—Lord God, we thank thee! / Halleluja!)

With the chorale interjections, the effect is astounding.

2. Chorale and Recitative—bass, tenor, alto. Each soloist in the above order declaims a part of the recitative, while the choir sings the *Te Deum* lines at the beginning of the number and after each soloist.

The bass expresses his thanks for God's blessing in this New Year; the tenor thanks Him for having protected their country and their city from famine, pestilence and war in the past year; the alto says that we should humbly fold our hands in prayer to Him to give thanks for His daily watch over us throughout our lives.

3. *Aria—alto.* There is a dance-like rhythm to this aria that reminds the listener of Bach's courtly music which he had composed at Cöthen. We can see a picture of the Lord as her good shepherd, Who will lead her and the other sheep of Zion into green pastures (Psalm 23). The peacefully lilting music seems to give an image of the tranquil meadows of heaven.

4. *Recitative—bass.* In this long secco number, the imagery of the shepherd with His sheep is prolonged. The bass wants to be counted among Christ's flock and have His guidance in the coming year.

5. *Duet—tenor, bass.* With oboe d'amore obbligato accompaniment, the pastoral atmosphere is retained from the two previous movements. The joy-motif predominates, except for the penultimate line, where a reference to the Passion conjures up a passing cloud over this idyllic contentment: "Jesus hilft mir durch sein Blut," (Jesus helps me through His Blood,).

It should be noted that each line of the duet begins with "Jesus" to focus our attention on the source of our happiness.

6. *Recitative—tenor.* He asks the Lord to give His blessing on His anointed, on church and school, on dedicated teachers, and on the Council and the judges in the law-courts.

7. *Chorale.* The text is stanza two of J. Herman's New Year's hymn, "Jesu, nun sei gepreiset" (Jesus, Now Be Praised). An interesting feature is the obbligato trumpet, which plays a fanfare after each pair of lines. All vocal and instrumental forces produce a resounding hymn praising God's glory, thus creating a dazzling conclusion.

• **Herr, wie du willst, so schicks mit mir (Lord, As Thou Wilt, So Send It to Me)** (c. 1725; BWV 73).

The author of this libretto for the third Sunday after Epiphany is unknown. He ignores the Gospel for this Sunday, Matthew 8 (1–13)—Jesus heals the leper and the centurion's servant—and instead, concentrates the theme on obedience to God's will, which is the basis of the first number in the cantata. This is the first stanza of Caspar Bienemann's hymn, which is the title of this cantata.

The soli are STB with chorus. The orchestra has two oboes, two violins, a viola, a horn *or* organ obbligato, and continuo. The reason for the choice of horn or organ may have depended on the availability of a corno player when Bach performed this work, his second chorale cantata.

1. *Chorale and Recitative—TBS.* It is a surprise to hear the chorale verses of Bienemann's hymn blended in with the recitative, which the three soloists declaim in sequence. All the sections are sung separately; it is the first time that Bach has set such a combination.

The choir begins with a chorale fantasia on the first two lines of the hymn. The remaining verses are continued between the tenor-bass and the bass-soprano recitatives. As each soloist proclaims the sufferings he must endure throughout his imperfect life, the choir sings, to give him consolation through submission to God's will. As Christians, they must accept their fate as God has decreed it to be.

Bach has created a dramatic scene between soloists and chorus in this splendid number. The chorale stanza with Bach's fantasia treatment clearly introduces the main theme of a Christian's acceptance of his fate in accordance with God's will:

CHORUS: "Herr, wie du willt, so schicks mit mir / Im Leben und im Sterben! / . . . / [Tenor Recitative Follows.]

CHORUS: Allein zu dir steht mein Begier, / Herr, lass mich nicht verderben. / . . . / [Bass recitative]

CHORUS: Erhalt mich nur in deiner Huld, / Sonst wie du willt, gib mir Geduld, / Denn dein Will ist der beste. / . . . / [Soprano Recitative]

CHORUS: Herr, wie du willt, Herr, wie du willt, Herr, wie du willt."

(Lord, as Thou willst, so send it to me / In living and in dying! / . . . / My desire stands only to Thee, / Lord, let me not perish! / . . . / Only keep me in Thy favor, / Or else as Thou willst, give me patience, / For Thy will is the best. / . . . / Lord, as Thou willst, Lord, as Thou willst, Lord, as Thou willst.)

2. *Aria—tenor.* He asks that God plant the spirit of joy in his heart, because he is spiritually ill. This illness is shown by his hesitation to accept happiness and hope, while he is in his present timid mood.

This is not one of Bach's best tenor arias, but the melody is good.

3. *Recitative—bass.* This short account of our varying moods of defiance and despair, which arises from our stubborn will, diverts our thoughts from death. However, if we are Christians, we have learned to accept God's will and say [his aria follows]:

4. *Aria—bass.* The mention of death as a part of God's will provides the theme for his song. The first line of each verse returns to the initial words of the hymn, "Herr, so du willt." At the beginning of the aria, he repeats this line thrice—did Bach intend some mystical significance referring to the Trinity?

The bass depicts his own burial scene in an exceptionally moving melody. Pizzicato strings in the third verse graphically portray tolling funeral bells. His consolation is that he has met his death as God has willed it. Bach's interest in death as the entrance into the peace of heaven is well illustrated in the beauty of this aria:

"Herr, so du willt, / So presst, ihr Todesschmerzen, / Die Seufzer aus dem Herzen, / Wenn mein Gebet nur vor dir gilt.

Herr, so du willt, / So lege meine Glieder / In Staub und Asche nieder, / Dies höchst verderbte Sündenbild.

Herr, so du willt, / So schlagt, ihr Leichenglocken, / Ich folge unerschrocken, / Mein Jammer ist nunmehr gestillt."

(Lord, as Thou willst, / So press, death-pains, / The sighs from my heart, / If only my prayer is worthy before Thee.

Lord, as Thou willst, / So lay my limbs / Down in dust and ashes, / This most corrupt picture of sin.

Lord, as Thou willst, / So strike, funeral bells, / I follow unafraid, / My lament is henceforth stilled.)

5. *Chorale.* Another hymn forms the conclusion. It is also on the topic of God's influence over us through the Trinity. Therefore we must praise Him and accept His will. This chorale is based on the last stanza of L. Helmbold's hymn, "Von Gott will ich nicht lassen" (From God I Will Not Leave) (1563).

• **Nimm was dein ist, und gehe hin (Take What Is Thine, and Go Away)** (c. 1725; BWV 144).

The Gospel for Septuagesima Sunday, when this cantata was performed, is taken from Matthew 20 (1–16), the parable of the laborers in the vineyard. The text for the opening chorus is the first half of verse 14. Possibly the librettist was Picander, but this is not definite.

The main idea in each movement is that we should be content with what we have. Sufficiency (Genügsamkeit) is the keyword throughout. This thought could have been aimed at those disgruntled church-goers at St. Thomas's by the unknown librettist.

atura on "auferstanden" (arisen) especially indicates their rejoicing.

2. *Aria—tenor.* With oboe d'amore, strings and organ accompaniment, the tenor affirms that his faith leads him to believe in the Lord's Resurrection, but like Thomas, he still has doubts in his heart: "Mein Jesus ist erstanden, / Allein, was schreckt mich noch? / Mein Glaube kennt des Heilands Sieg, / Doch fühlt mein Herze Streit und Krieg, / Mein Heil, erscheine doch!" (My Jesus has arisen, / But what frightens me still? / My belief recognizes the Savior's victory, / Yet my heart feels conflict and war. / My Salvation, do appear!)

The tenor's role as Thomas, who wanted to see and touch the Lord, is dramatically brought to life in this aria-monologue scene.

3. *Recitative—alto.* She relates that Jesus is called the poison of death and a plague to hell; yet she is still troubled in her life by fear and danger. She recalls the Easter hymn of praise, which, she says, the Lord has inspired. She now introduces this hymn for the following chorale.

4. *Chorale.* This is sung with the full orchestra. It is the first verse of N. Herman's hymn, "Ershienen ist der herrlich Tag" (The Glorious Day Has Appeared), which recounts our joy over Christ's triumph. Probably the congregation sang this hymn before the church service was begun.

5. *Recitative—alto.* She continues her fearful doubting (as in her previous number) that the evil enemies, who remain on earth, will keep on harassing her. She prays to Christ to overcome her doubts through the example of His word and works.

6. *Aria—bass and Chorus (SAT).* By inserting a chorus after the single line, which the bass player sings repeatedly for his aria, Bach has created a remarkable drama. The bass plays the role of Jesus and the chorus plays the part of the disciples as a group. The tumult-motif is heard in the instrumental beginning and also every time the choir sings, but this noisy confusion is hushed when Christ speaks: "Friede sei mit euch!" (Peace be with you!) The solemnity rhythm in the flute, woodwinds and strings gives the bass voice a tone of beatific peace each time that he intrudes with his aria.

Mixed into the tumult-motif there is also the joy-motif, as the disciples behold their Lord once again: "Wohl uns! Jesus hilft uns kämpfen / . . . / Jesus holet uns zum Frieden / . . . / O Herr, hilf und lass gelingen." (Well for us! Jesus helps us fight / . . . / Jesus brings us to peace / . . . / O Lord, help and let us succeed.)

This is a truly original and masterful display of Bach's talent for dramatic music.

Schweitzer's opinion of this aria deserves to be quoted: "It is less an aria than a symphonic tone-picture. The German Bach is trying to break through the mould of the decadent Italian art. His dramatic spirit leads him to seek the way back to the larger and simpler kind of art from which he started, and to create free forms for himself." (*J.S. Bach,* Vol II, p. 192).

Bach later used this number in the *Gloria* movement of his *Short Mass in A.*

7. *Chorale.* This is the first verse of J. Ebert's "Du Friedefürst, Herr Jesu Christ" (Thou Prince of Peace, Lord Jesus Christ), accompanied by all the instruments. Its thought aptly fits the theme of the whole cantata: the praise of Christ for His gift of peace to us.

• **Du Hirte Israel, höre (Thou Shepherd of Israel, Hear)** (c. 1725; BWV 104).

The Gospel for this second Sunday after Easter is John 10 (11–16)—Christ says that He is the Good Shepherd. As well as this cantata, two other later ones were composed by Bach on this same Scriptural text: BWV 85 and BWV 112. Christian Weiss, Sr., was probably the librettist. Each movement contains the imagery of the Shepherd and His sheep.

The cantata is really a sacred pastorale, both in text and in music. Sacred and secular pastoral cantatas had been produced by Italian composers before Bach (e.g. Alessandro Scarlatti), but this work owes nothing to them.

The cantata is scored for two oboes, a taille (tenor oboe), two violins, a viola and continuo. The soli are TB with a four-part chorus.

1. *Chorus.* Psalm 80 (1) is the text for this first number, sung to the pastoral motif of the orchestral introduction. The beautiful tonal color of the oboes and strings seems to imitate the sound of bagpipes or of a shepherd's pipe with its staccato rhythm. Bach pictures the sheep as people who implore the Master to tend them.

A fugue begins with the second clause, building up to a climax at the end: "Du Hirte Israel, höre, der du Joseph hütest wie der Schafe, erscheine, der du sitzest über Cherubim." (Thou Shepherd of Israel, hear! Thou Who guardest Joseph as the sheep, appear! Thou Who sittest above the Cherubim.)

This movement should remind the listener of the pastoral sinfonia in Bach's later *Christmas Oratorio*, 1734.

2. *Recitative—tenor.* Like a worried lost sheep, the tenor expresses his fears that his shepherd may have forgotten him, although in his heart he knows that Jesus is as faithful to him as He is to His other sheep.

3. *Aria—tenor.* In deep nostalgia the tenor complains that his shepherd has been too long absent from him. We see the image of a traveler, lost in the desert, who hurried onward with ever weakening steps. (Bach illustrates this in the second and third lines by giving the oboes d'amore the step-motif.) "Verbirgt mein Hirte sich zu lange, / Macht mir die Wüste allzu bange, / Mein schwacher Tritt eilt dennoch fort." (If my shepherd hides Himself too long, / The desert makes me all too anxious. / My weak step hurries on nevertheless.)

He sounds like a lamb which has gone astray. Then, in a calmer vein, he reassures himself that when he cries out for his shepherd, His word will strengthen him in his faith.

4. *Recitative—bass.* He represents another sheep, which, with more uplifted spirits, states that he has found green pastures in the word of God, which gives him a foretaste of heaven. He entreats the Lord to guide him and the other poor and erring sheep back into His sheepfold.

5. *Aria—bass.* This is one of Bach's most beautiful arias: its pastoral serenity is reflected by the rhythm of a subdued but happy gigue. He sings the praises of the flock for their shepherd. They are now all grazing blissfully in their green meadow, reunited under His care.

The picture changes to a more somber note in the last two lines at the mention of death, which must come before the final reward for faithful sheep: "Beglückte Herde, Jesu Schafe, / Die Welt ist euch ein Himmelreich. / Hier schmeckt ihr Jesu Güte schon / Und hoffet noch des Glaubens Lohn / Nach einem sanften Todesschlafe." (Fortunate flock, Jesus' sheep, The world for you is a heavenly realm. / Here you already taste Jesus' goodness / And still hope for the reward of faith / After a soft sleep in death.)

In the quiet, solemn tone of this aria, we behold the miracle of Bach's art.

6. *Chorale.* This first stanza of Cornelius Becker's hymn, "Derr Herr ist mein getreuer Hirt" (The Lord Is My True Shepherd), retains the pastoral atmosphere of all the previous movements. It is a paraphrase of Psalm 23, in which we also find much pastoral imagery. For the text see BWV 85.

• **Wo gehest du hin? (Whither Goest Thou?)** (c. 1725; BWV 166).

This interesting cantata for the fourth Sunday after Easter is presumed to have been written by Christian Weiss, Sr., about 1725. It is unusual because it has no chorus and the third number, a chorale, is sung only by the solo soprano voice. The final chorale, however, has a four-part choir.

The Gospel is John 16 (5–15)—Jesus speaks to the disciples of His return to the Father. Verse 5 is partly quoted for the opening aria.

The soloists are SATB: the instruments are simply an oboe, strings and continuo.

1. *Aria—bass.* To just four words as given in the Scriptural verse, Bach interprets Jesus' gentle chiding of His disciples, because none of them had asked Him where He would be going. The step-motif in the oboe and string accompaniment implies also where our own wandering steps are leading us.

"Wo gehest du hin?" (Whither goest Thou?) seems a scant text on which to compose an aria, yet Bach brings out all the uncertainty in the question. He begins with an orchestral prelude and follows this with the entry of the questioning bass voice with its repeats of "wo" and "wohin."

2. *Aria—tenor.* The melody for this aria comes from Bach's *Trio in G minor for Organ* (BWV 584), which he must have composed prior to this aria. The thought expressed is that the singer asks himself where he is going, whether he moves or stands. The step-motif is continued here. His doubts concerning his destiny are reflected in the wavering tone of his singing. As a believer, he wants to think about heaven and not give his heart to the world, but he still feels like a ship without a rudder.

3. *Chorale—soprano.* This magnificent number, based on stanza three of B. Ringwaldt's "Herr Jesu Christ, ich weiss gar wohl" (Lord Jesus Christ, I Know Quite Well) (1582), has the effect of a personal prayer. The string accompaniment lends an emotionally mystical background to her appeal to Christ for spiritual guidance. This chorale setting is a masterpiece, superior to any of Bach's chorale compositions thus far in his cantatas. It would be difficult for any listener to be unmoved by it: "Ich bitte dich, Herr Jesu Christ, / Halt mich bei den Gedanken / Und lass mich ja zu keiner Frist / Von dieser Meinung wanken, / Sondern dabei verharren fest, / Bis dass die Seele aus ihrem Nest / Wird in den Himmel kommen." (I ask Thee, Lord Jesus Christ, / Keep me in Thy thoughts / And let me at no time / Waver from this resolve, / But in this remain firmly, / Until my soul from out of its nest / Will come into heaven.)

4. *Recitative—bass.* His secco declamation is very picturesque, as he denounces the transitory joys of the world: they are like rainwater which vanishes or colors that fade. Many people prize worldly fortune but do not realize that it will disappear when their last hour strikes unexpectedly. This idea leads into the next number.

5. *Aria—alto.* This has a dance-like rhythm, which may symbolize the carefree laughter of those who enjoy their good fortune. The swinging tune, played by all the instruments, gives this impression. Long runs on the verb "lacht" (laughs) in coloratura trills show Bach's ability to paint in sound an idea that even one word evokes.

In the last half of the aria, the concept that all happiness can change suddenly from morning smiles to evening sorrows does not alter the gay rhythm of the first part. Instead of the gloomy warning indicated in the text, Bach continues to paint the joy-motif. It almost seems as though he were obsessed with the verb "lacht" and wished to carry it on to the end of the aria, ignoring the meaning of the text he was setting. "Man nehme sich in acht, / Wenn das Gelücke lacht. / Denn es kann leicht auf Erden / Vor abends anders werden, / Als man am Morgen nicht gedacht." (Let one pay attention to himself, / Whenever fortune laughs. / For it can easily on earth / Become before evening otherwise / Than one didn't think in the morning.)

6. *Chorale.* This first verse of Countess Ämilia von Schwarzburg-Rudolstadt's hymn restores the serious theme of keeping in mind one's death and to prepare for it: "Wer weiss, wie nahe mein Ende, / Hin geht die Zeit, her kommt der Tod," (Who knows how near my end [is]? / Away goes time, hither comes death.)

• **Wahrlich, wahrlich, ich sage euch (Verily, Verily, I Say Unto You)** (c. 1725; BWV 86).

For Rogate Sunday, the fifth after Easter, Bach composed this cantata. The Gospel for the day is John 16 (23–30); Jesus' words in the twenty-third verse provide the text for the first number of the libretto, presumably written by Christian Weiss, Sr. Again, as in BWV 166, we find that the chorale in the middle of the work is sung by the soprano, solo, and there is no chorus movement.

The soloists are SATB, with a four-part choir for the final chorale. The orchestra is small—two oboes, two violins, a viola and continuo.

1. *Arioso—bass.* With only string accompaniment, the Biblical text is clearly and realistically dramatized by the bass in the role of Christ. There is a triple fugue in the music, which gives Christ's words to His disciples a spiritual dignity and a calm serenity. "Wahrlich, wahrlich, ich sage euch, so ihr den Vater etwas bitten werdet in meinem Namen, so wird er's euch geben." (Verily, verily, I say unto you, if you will ask the Father for anything in my Name, so He will give it to you.)

Possibly the best number in the cantata.

2. *Aria—alto.* She sings this long aria with joyous rapture because God has promised to listen to her requests and entreaties. The obbligato violin is well suited to the garden scene pictured in the first two lines—that she will pluck roses despite their pricking thorns. Perhaps the symbolism here refers to the happiness she feels in her daily life, even though it is beset with difficulties, since her thoughts are always on God's promise to hear her prayers.

3. *Chorale—soprano.* Accompanied by two oboes d'amore and continuo, she sings the sixteenth stanza of Georg Grünwald's hymn, "Komm her zu mir, spricht Gottes Sohn" (Come Here to Me, Speaks God's Són), which states that God keeps all the promises He has made. This is not as interesting as the soprano chorale in BWV 166.

4. *Recitative—tenor.* He declaims the same idea as the soprano, as if to support her preceding chorale. God keeps His word, unlike the people of this world. Knowing this, we can be joyful.

5. *Aria—tenor.* "Gott hilft gewiss" (God certainly helps) is like a motto at the beginning and end of his aria. This pleasantly light tune with strings and continuo seems to show the tenor's conviction that God has never taken His help away from him, even though sometimes he thinks that it has been postponed.

6. *Chorale.* The text is the eleventh verse of Paul Speratus's humn, "Es ist das Heil uns kommen her" (Salvation Has Come to Us). God knows what is best for us, so we should trust Him as to when He will send us help.

Somehow this work does not strike me as being one of Bach's better cantatas. It seems to lack the composer's inspiration. Was that on account of the libretto or his instrumentation?

• **Sie werden euch in den Bann tun (They Will Put You Under the Ban) I** (c. 1725; BWV 44).

For this sixth Sunday after Easter, Bach set a libretto, presumed to be by Christian Weiss, Sr., which was based on John 16 (2) for the two opening numbers. It is similar to the two previous cantatas in having its middle chorale sung by only one voice, in this case a tenor, but is unusual because it begins with a tenor-bass duet, followed by a full chorus.

The soli are SATB, with a four-part chorus. The orchestra is heavier than for BWV 86, having two oboes, a bassoon, two violins, a viola and continuo.

1. *Duet—tenor, bass.* After a brief, melancholy prelude, they sing the prophetic words of Christ to His disciples during the Last Supper—that they would be rejected from the synagogues: "Sie werden euch in den Bann tun" (They will put you under the ban.)

A gloomy mood is depicted by the music and by the soloists' emphasis on "Bann." This leads directly into the chorus, which completes the Scriptural verse.

2. *Chorus.* "Es kommt aber die Zeit, dass, wer euch tötet, wird meinen, er tue Gott einen Dienst daran." (But the time will come when whoever kills you will think he does God a service in that deed.)

This dire prophecy is illustrated by the tumult-motif in voices and instruments, as Bach imagines the scene of His disciples' coming persecution. The mob cruelty of their martyrdom is implied in the canon singing of the chorus.

3. *Aria—alto.* She transposes the idea of suffering for their faith from the disciples to all Christians, who must withstand torment, excommunication and severe pain to become true disciples of Christ.

The sad tone of the music makes this aria a lament more than a wish to imitate the disciples.

4. *Chorale—tenor.* He sings the first stanza of Martin Moller's hymn, "Ach Gott, wie manches Herzeleid" (O God, How Many Heart-Pains). To these present troubles, the rest of the verse adds the thought that his narrow way to heaven is laden with sadness. The bassoon accompaniment indicates the despondency he feels in the words of the hymn.

5. *Recitative—bass.* His description of the anti-Christ as a monster, who persecutes Christians because their teachings are against him, reveals the reason for suffering. The monster even imagines that he pleases God (as the text of the chorus in the second number suggests).

In the last two lines, the theme changes to hope that our trials will make us stronger. This is expressed by a beautiful simile: "Allein es gleichen Christen denen Palmenzweigen, Die durch die Last nur desto höher steigen." (But Christians are like those palm branches, Which through their burden only climb the higher.)

From here to the end of the cantata, the mood changes to overall joy.

6. *Aria—soprano.* The lyrical beauty of her song, with all instruments, shines forth as the highlight of the cantata. She expresses a Christian's consolation in knowing that God protects His church and that, after trouble, happiness will return to us, as sunshine after a storm. Her coloratura runs on three verbs—"wacht" (watches), "türmen" (to pile up), and "gelacht" (laughed)—impart an allegro-adagio-allegro sequence to some very colorful imagery: "Es ist und bleibt der Christen Trost, / Dass Gott für seine Kirche wacht. / Denn wenn sich gleich die Wetter türmen, / So hat doch nach dem Trübsalstürmen / Die Freudensonne bald gelacht." (It is and remains the consolation of Christians / That God watches out for His church. / For immediately when storms pile up, / So still after the trouble-storms / Has the sun of joy soon laughed.)

7. *Chorale.* This is a simple hymn, stanza fifteen of Paul Fleming's "In allen meinen Taten" (In All My Deeds). With full choir and orchestra, it expresses the soul's trust in its maker, who knows what is best for it.

• **O Ewigkeit, du Donnerwort (O Eternity, Thou Word of Thunder) I** (c. 1725; BWV 20).

Bach composed this chorale cantata from all verses of Johann Rist's hymn, "O Eternity, Thou Word of Thunder," using the original stanzas for some movements or a paraphrase for others, written, perhaps, by Picander. In 1732, Bach produced another cantata with the same title, BWV 60.

This first setting is a long cantata of two parts, performed on the first Sunday after Trinity. It was revised into its present form about 1735.

The soloists are ATB with a four-part chorus; the instruments include a trumpet, three oboes, strings and continuo.

Part I

1. *Chorale fantasia "O Ewigkeit, du Donnerwort" (O Eternity, thou word of thunder).* This opening movement sets the tone for all following numbers: the sinner's fear of everlasting damnation. Using the sweeping three-movement form of a French overture (grave-vivace-grave) with full chorus and orchestra,

Bach paints a vast panorama of the timeless duration of eternity. When an individual considers this prospect, he becomes tongue-tied with terror, as shown in the dramatic final two lines of the stanza: "Mein ganz erschrocknes Herz erbebt, / Dass mir die Zung' am Gaumen klebt." (My really frightened heart trembles, / So that my tongue sticks to my gums.) The rhythm of these lines suggests this fearful trembling. Bach's fantasia treatment of this chorale is admirably done despite its pessimistic verses. It reminds me of one of Pascal's thoughts in the previous century: "Le silence éternel de ces espaces infinis m'effraie" (The eternal silence of these infinite spaces frightens me) (*Pensées,* no. 206).

2. *Recitative—tenor.* He tries to persuade himself that perhaps there will be no lasting pain in eternity, since the duration of all earthly pain is finite. But then he recalls Jesus' words affirming that there is no limit to the tortures of hell. (Matthew 23 [33])

From this point on, in all the following numbers, eternity becomes synonymous with hell.

3. *Aria—tenor.* Continuing his thought, he sings that eternity is too long—no wonder he is anxious! Bach has painted a scene worthy of Dante's *Inferno* in this aria. The calm string accompaniment for the first three lines soon becomes agitated in the rest, which vividly describes hell: "Flammen, die auf ewig brennen, / Ist kein Feuer gleich zu nennen; / Es erschrickt und bebt mein Herz, / Wenn ich diese Pein bedenke / Und den Sinn zur Hölle lenke." (Flames, which burn forever, / No similar fire can be named; / My heart is terrified and trembles, / When I think about this pain / And turn my mind towards hell.)

The tenor's florid tone-painting in this section is excellent.

4. *Recitative—bass.* In his secco declamation, he portrays the unending pains of hell, which the damned will suffer throughout eternity.

5. *Aria—bass.* There is some relief and hope, shining through his prevailing gloom, in this aria, accompanied by two oboes. Yet it still retains an undertone of the certainty of hell for the unrepentant sinner: "Gott ist gerecht in seinen Werken: / Auf kurze Sünden dieser Welt / Hat er so lange Pein bestellt; / Ach wollte doch die Welt dies merken! / Kurz ist die Zeit, der Tod geschwind, / Bedenke dies, o Menschenkind!" (God is just in His works: / For the short sins of this world / He has ordained such long pain; / Oh, would the world notice this! / Short is time, death quick, / Consider this, O child of man!)

6. *Aria—alto.* This number is outstanding. Its solemn beauty cannot fail to stir the emotions of the listener. With most pathetic pleading, she implores us to save our souls and flee from Satan's bondage. The string accompaniment imparts a supernatural aura, as though an angel were urging us to abandon our sinning. Coloratura runs on the words "entfliehe" (escape), "plagt" (torments) and "nagt" (gnaws) make this a stupendous aria, even with the recurring portrayal of hell within it. "O Mensch, errette deine Seele, / Entfliehe Satans Sklaverei / Und mache dich von Sünden frei, / Damit in jener Schwefelhöhle / Der Tod, so die Verdammten plagt, / Nicht deine Seele ewig nagt. / O Mensch, errette deine Seele!" (O man, save thy soul, / Flee from Satan's slavery / And make thyself free from sins, / So that in that sulphur-cave, / Death, which so torments the damned, / Does not eternally gnaw thy soul. / O man, save thy soul!)

In my opinion, this aria surpasses anything else in the cantata.

7. *Chorale.* The full choir sings this pessimistic stanza. They describe the problems which man encounters to torment him on earth: cold, heat, anxiety, hunger, fear, fire and lightning—he must endure them all as long as God governs his life.

Part II

8. *Aria—bass.* Before this number, there was probably a sermon of fire and

brimstone, preached in the interval between Parts I and II. The congregation would now be roused by this sparkling aria, with obbligato trumpet and all the other instruments, representing the trumpet at the Last Judgment. We can almost visualize the rising of the dead: "Wacht auf, wacht auf, verlornen Schafe, / Ermuntert euch vom Sündenschlafe / Und bessert euer Leben bald! / Wacht auf, eh' die Posaune schallt, / Die euch mit Schrecken aus der Gruft / Zum Richter aller Welt vor das Gerichte ruft!" (Wake up, wake up, lost sheep, / Rouse yourselves from sins' sleep / And better your lives soon! / Wake up, before the trumpet sounds, / Which calls you frightened from the grave / To the Judge of the whole world before His tribunal!

9. *Recitative—alto.* With continuo only, she urges man to leave the world's vices, because he doesn't know when his time to die will come. Therefore, while he is still living, he should think about his soul and not his bodily pleasures.

10. *Duet—alto, tenor.* Again with only continuo, they denounce the world and its sin. Vice and sin can only lead man to perdition in hell, where he will hear howling and gnashing of teeth. He should remember the fate of the rich man who couldn't obtain a small drop of water to quench his thirst in his torment in hell—Luke 16 (19–31).

11. *Chorale.* This grim cantata ends in a plain setting of the opening chorale stanza (all voices and instruments), except that the last two lines are changed: "Nimm du mich, wenn es dir gefällt, / Herr Jesu, in dein Freudenzelt." (Take me, if it pleases Thee, / Lord Jesus, into Thy tabernacle of joy.)

• **Ihr Menschen, rühmet Gottes Liebe (Ye People, Vaunt God's Love)** (c. 1725; BWV 167).

The librettist for this cantata on the Feast of St. John the Baptist is unknown. The Gospel, Luke 1 (57–80)—the circumcision of John and the prophecy of his father Zacharias—is reflected in this libretto.

It is a solo cantata for SATB with clarino, oboe da caccia, strings and continuo. The music is pleasant but not outstanding, except for the final chorale.

1. *Aria—tenor.* The undulating siciliano rhythm of the strings seems to suggest the tenor's joy in knowing that Christ would soon be born. It is easy to imagine the tenor in the role of John, speaking to the people to announce the coming of the Lord and encouraging them to praise God for that. The joy-motif appears throughout the aria and its dancing, pastoral tone may have some connection with the rustic surroundings where John worked for the Lord. "Ihr Menschen, rühmet Gottes Liebe / Und preiset seine Gütigkeit! / Lobt ihn aus reinem Herzenstriebe, / Dass er uns zu bestimmter Zeit / Das Horn des Heils, den Weg zum Leben / An Jesu, seinen Sohn, gegeben." (Ye people, vaunt God's love / And praise His goodness! / Praise Him out of frank heart's impulses, / That he at the appointed time has given us / The horn of salvation, the way to life, / In Jesus, His Son.)

Note the artistic effect of his runs on "preiset."

2. *Recitative—alto.* She states that God should be praised for sending His Son as the world's redeemer. First, John is sent to prepare the way; then Jesus, to save sinners through their repentance. She expresses her last two lines in very fine arioso.

3. *Duet—soprano, alto.* Supported by oboe da caccia and continuo, they affirm that God always keeps His promises. They sing the first line simultaneously, then in canon for the rest. "Gottes Wort, das trüget nicht, / Es geschieht, was er verspricht. / Was er in dem Paradies / Und vor so hundert Jahren / Unsern Vätern schon verhiess, / Haben wir gottlob erfahren." (God's word, that doesn't deceive; / It happens as He promises. / What He in Paradise / And so many hundred years ago / Already promised to our fathers / We have experienced, praise God.) The joy-motif is apparent everywhere in this duet.

4. *Recitative—bass.* He narrates, in secco, how God has kept His promise to Abraham that He would send the Messiah. The Gospel account returns when he mentions Zacharias praising God; this leads him to the thought that we should all praise Him in the following Chorale.

5. *Chorale.* This is the high point and also the best number in the cantata. Bach treats this extended chorale with wonderful instrumentation, especially in the obbligato trumpet. It is based on stanza five of Johann Graumann's hymn, "Nun lob', mein Seel', den Herren" (Now Praise, My Soul, the Lord) (1540). This is a magnificent hymn of joyous thanksgiving and trust in God. The orchestral ostinato dance-like theme at the beginning and after each pair of lines must signify for Bach a perfect picture of heavenly bliss. "Sei Lob und Preis mit Ehren / Gott Vater, Sohn, heiligem Geist! / Der woll in uns vermehren, / Was er uns aus Gnad' verheisst, / Dass wir ihm fest vertrauen, / Gänzlich verlassn auf ihn." (Be laud and praise with honor / To God the Father, Son and Holy Spirit! / He will in us increase / What He promises us out of grace, / So that we may firmly trust Him, / Entirely rely on Him.)

• **Erforsche mich, Gott, und erfahre mein Herz (Search Me, God, and Learn of My Heart)** (c. 1725; BWV 136).

The first half of this cantata for the eighth Sunday after Trinity refers also to the first half of the Gospel for the day: Matthew 7 (15–23), Christ's warning against false prophets. The librettist may have been Christian Weiss, Sr.

There is a four-part chorus with SATB soli, and a fairly large orchestra: horn, oboe, oboe d'amore, strings and continuo; but, nevertheless, it seems that the work is lacking in musical inspiration. Perhaps Bach could find little in this text to inspire him, apart from the opening chorus.

1. *Chorus.* The four choral sections sing in canon Bach's fugal setting of this text from Psalm 139 (23). Bach may have used some previous composition for this movement, because the words sung often do not agree with the melody. Nevertheless, he used the music again for the *Cum Sancto Spiritu* of his later *Short Mass in A.* "Erforsche mich, Gott, und erfahre mein Herz, prüfe mich und erfahre, wie ich's meine." (Search me, God, and learn of my heart; test me and learn how I mean it.) This thought of sincerity towards God fits the general idea of the whole cantata, yet it seems that the music cannot bring this out.

2. *Recitative—tenor.* His rather confusing text begins by mentioning God's curse on Adam. This curse enters the soul, so that it bears sin's thorns and vice's thistles as fruit. Then he speaks of demons, who disguise themselves as angels, just as wolves pretend to be sheep. Yet he predicts that the day will come when such hypocrites will suffer unbearable terror.

3. *Aria—alto.* Accompanied by the oboe d'amore, she sings of the Judgment Day, when all secrets and hypocrisy will be exposed.—Matthew 7 (21–23): "Es kommt ein Tag, / So das Verborgne richtet, / Vor dem die Heuchelei erzittern mag. / Denn seines Eifers Grimm vernichtet, / Was Heuchelei und List erdichtet." (There comes a day, / Which judges what is hidden, / Before which hypocrisy may tremble. / For the fury of its zeal destroys / What hypocrisy and cunning connive.)

Her aria is pleasant but not exceptional.

4. *Recitative—bass.* He tries to prove that anyone may cleanse himself of sin through Christ's blood, justice and strength: if he believes in Him, the Lord's judgment will not be hard on him.

5. *Duet—tenor, bass.* This number is the most interesting in the cantata. The canon singing of the two voices with their runs on words, especially "Wunden" (wounds) and "voll" (full), is very well done. The sound of the unison violin playing is very appealing, adding to the artistic charm. "Uns treffen zwar der Sünden Flecken, / So Adams Fall auf uns

gebracht. / Allein, wer sich zu Jesu Wunden, / Dem grossen Strom voll Blut gefunden, / Wird dadurch wieder rein gemacht." (To be sure, the stains of sin hit us, / Which Adam's fall brought on us. / But whoever has found in Jesus's wounds, / The great stream full of blood, / Will thereby be made pure again.)

6. *Chorale.* This is taken from stanza nine of Johann Heermann's "Wo soll ich fliehen hin" (Whither shall I flee). All voices and instruments perform this brief stanza, which tells of the healing power of Christ's blood to save us from the devil's jaws.

• **Tue Rechnung! Donnerwort (Make a Reckoning! Thunder-Word)** (1725; BWV 168).

For the ninth Sunday after Trinity, Bach produced this cantata on a libretto by Salomo Franck. It is possible that he composed an earlier version while he was in Weimar, but this is not extant.

The Gospel for this Sunday is Luke 16 (1–9), the parable of the unjust steward. Franck's libretto is concerned with what man owes to God when the hour of judgment comes.

The soloists are SATB with a four-part chorus; the orchestra has two oboes d'amore, strings and continuo.

1. *Aria—bass.* This fine aria with string accompaniment seems to portray the bass in the role of a tax-collector, demanding us to pay God what we owe Him now. The word "Donnerwort" implies the coming Day of Judgment, which the bass repeats, for insistence on payment, at the beginning and at the end of the movement. The agitation of his urgent demand comes out well: "Tue Rechnung! Donnerwort, / Das die Felsen selbst zerspaltet, / Wort, wovon mein Blut erkaltet! / Tue Rechnung! Seele, fort! / Ach, du musst Gott wiedergeben / Seine Güter, Leib und Leben. / Tue Rechnung, Donnerwort." (Make a reckoning! Thunder-word, / That splits the rocks themselves; / Word, by which my blood runs cold! / Make a reckoning! Soul, away! / Oh, thou must give back to God / His goods, body and life. / Make a reckoning, Thunder-word.)

2. *Recitative—tenor.* With the unusual accompaniment of two oboes d'amore, he describes how everything he possesses has only been entrusted to his stewardship by God, his Master. He is overcome with fear, because his account has so many defects, caused by his callous neglect. Taking Christ's words in Luke 23 (30), he says that he wishes to hide from his Master's anger: "Wie kann ich dir, gerechter Gott, entfliehen? / Ich rufe flehentlich: / Ihr Berge fallt! ihr Hügel decket mich / Vor Gottes Zorngerichte / Und vor dem Blitz von seinem Angesichte!" (How can I flee from Thee, righteous God? / I call imploringly: / Ye mountains, fall! ye hills, cover me / From God's angry judgment / And from the lightening of His face!)

3. *Aria—tenor.* Again with the two oboes d'amore, he manages to sing a rather interesting aria, despite the dull, unpoetic text with which Bach had to cope. All his debts are inscribed in God's book: "Kapital und Interessen, / Meiner Schulden gross und klein / Müssen einst verrechnet sein. / Alles, was ich schuldig blieben, / Ist in Gottes Buch geschrieben / Als mit Stahl und Demantstein." (Capital and interest / Of my debts large and small / Must at some time be calculated. / Everything, for which I remained owing, / Is written in God's book / As with steel and diamond-stone.)

4. *Recitative—bass.* His long discourse, secco, resembles a sermon to comfort the dishonest steward and give him hope of pardon. Christ's sacrifice has effaced his debt to God, but he must strive to make good use of his worldly possessions and also help the poor to guarantee himself a place in heaven.

5. *Duet—soprano, alto.* With continuo only, they sing a delightful duet, which features an imagery of movement for the breaking of Satan's bonds throughout the whole number, even in the last half where death and the future life in heaven are depicted. This idea of

motion stems from a gently rocking rhythm as the voices sing in canon. "Herz, zerreiss des Mammons Kette, / Hände, streuet Gutes aus! / Machet sanft mein Sterbebette, / Bauet mir ein festes Haus, / Das in Himmel ewig bleibet, / Wenn der Erde Gut zerstäubet." (Heart, tear away Mammon's chain, / Hands, spread around what is good! / Make soft my death-bed; / Build for me a strong house, / That remains eternal in heaven, / When earth's possessions are turned to dust.)

The thought expressed by the text and by the music is fascinating.

6. *Chorale.* B. Ringwaldt's hymn, "Herr Jesu Christ, du höchstes Gut" (Lord Jesus Christ, Thou Highest Possession), stanza eight, is a prayer to Christ to strengthen us, so that we may join His elect in heaven.

• **Herr, gehe nicht ins Gericht (Lord, Go Not into Judgment)** (c. 1725; BWV 105).

Like the previous cantata, BWV 168, this work is for the ninth Sunday after Trinity, but which one was performed in Leipzig in 1725 is not known. The Gospel, again, is from Luke 16 (1–9), the parable of the unjust steward; the Epistle is I Corinthians 10 (6–13), St. Paul's warning against lust, pride and idolatry. Both Scriptures are used for this libretto by some unknown poet or by Christian Weiss, Sr., possibly.

Bach must have considered this text highly because it resulted in one of his real masterpieces; every number in this cantata is excellent.

The soli are SATB, with a four-part chorus. The orchestra has a horn, two oboes, two violins, a viola and continuo.

1. *Chorus.* Psalm 143 (2) provides the text for this opening chorus. The instrumental tutti prelude establishes a plaintive terror motif, which will be repeated after the chorus has sung the first sentence of the text. The choir sings their first part in adagio also, as they portray the mood of a humble penitent, whom they represent. They sing the second in canon as an allegro fugue. "Herr, gehe nicht ins Gericht mit deinem Knecht. / Denn vor dir wird kein Lebendiger gerecht." (Lord, go not into judgment with Thy servant. / For before Thee no living person becomes righteous.)

We can visualize a multitude, being dragged before their judge, in fearful expectation of certain punishment. This vocal imagery combines with the emotion felt by these penitent individuals into a highly dramatic scene.

2. *Recitative—alto.* She freely confesses her guilt to God, imploring Him not to cast her out, since she has hidden no sin from Him.

3. *Aria—soprano.* The grief-motif is apparent throughout her aria, as she depicts those trembling sinners who try to excuse their own guilt by blaming one another. The oboe and string accompaniment play a wavering melody to illustrate her song. She describes how these guilty sinners are tortured by their fearful conscience. "Wie zittern und wanken / Der Sünder Gedanken, / Indem sie sich untereinander verklagen / Und wiederum sich zu entschuldigen wagen. / So wird ein geängstigt Gewissen / Durch eigene Folter zerrissen." (How tremble and waver / The sinners' thoughts, / While they accuse among each other / And again dare to excuse themselves. / Thus is an anguished conscience / Torn apart by its own torture.) The da capo of the instrumental opening concludes the aria.

4. *Recitative—bass.* At this point, the gloomy picture of guilt changes into ecstatic hope of forgiveness. With supporting strings, the bass proclaims that Christ has removed our guilt and will Himself be our advocate to the Father. The strings play pizzicato to illustrate the arioso, in which he describes his own burial in the graveyard. The melody is not sad this time, but joyful, for by his death he may enter into heaven. Usually with Bach, pizzicato strings betoken mourning, but in this case, they signal a happy event for him. "So mag man deinen Leib, den man zum Grabe trägt, / Mit Sand und Staub beschütten, /

Dein Heiland öffnet dir die ew'gen Hütten." (So may your body, which they bear to the grave, Be sprinkled with sand and dust; Your Savior opens to you the eternal habitations.)

5. *Aria—tenor.* The exuberant joy-motif in this aria, supported by the horn and the strings, is stupendous. It resembles a victory march in its tempo; the tenor renounces Mammon and the world in order to devote himself to the cause of Christ. In my opinion, this heroic tenor aria is indeed one of Bach's greatest masterpieces in the aria genre. "Kann ich nur Jesum mir zum Freunde machen, / So gilt der Mammon nichts bei mir. / Ich finde kein Vergnügen hier / Bei dieser eitlen Welt und irdischer Sachen." (If I can just make Jesus my friend, / Then Mammon is worth nothing to me. / I find no pleasure here / In this vain world and earthly things).

6. *Chorale.* This is verse 11 of Johann Rist's "Jesu, der du meine Seele" (Jesu, Thou my Soul), with the full choir and strings. The trembling rhythm of the soprano aria (3) returns to represent the quavering soul, even though the text states that his conscience will now be calmed. Such a return to the melancholy of the first part is unusual in any of Bach's cantatas; perhaps the composer may have wished to leave the congregation thinking about their own personal sins.

• **Schauet doch und sehet, ob irgend ein Schmerz sei (Just Behold and See Whether Any Other Sorrow)** (c. 1725; BWV 46).

Up to this time of his life, Bach was aware of the ravages of war in his country, including the destruction of besieged cities. Therefore, this libretto, which may have been written by Christian Weiss, Sr., or some other unknown Leipzig clergyman, would surely fire his imagination in his setting of this work.

The Gospel for this tenth Sunday after Trinity, Luke 19 (41–48)—Christ weeps over the coming destruction of Jerusalem—also reminded the librettist of the earlier razing of that city in the time of Jeremiah. This prophet's lamentation gives the librettist his text for the opening number: Lamentations 1 (12). The first three numbers describe the scene of grief in the Old Testament account; the last three apply the lesson that Christians must improve their lives to avoid the sin which results in such destruction, sent by God as punishment.

The soli are SATB, with a four-part chorus. The orchestra is quite large: a trumpet, two transverse flutes (or recorders), two oboes da caccia, strings and continuo.

1. *Chorus.* The first sentence of this Biblical text in Bach's setting was later used for the *Qui tollis* section of his *Mass in B minor* (1733). Though the texts are different and the Mass has no orchestral introduction, the mourning theme or grief-motif is the same in both works. Bach must have thought highly of it to re-use it in his monumental masterpiece. The prelude to the entry of the chorus is marked by the tearful sobs of the flutes (or recorders). The voices then begin their tragic lament in pairs: "Schauet doch und sehet, ob irgend ein Schmerz sei wie mein Schmerz, der mich getroffen hat." (Just behold and see, whether any other sorrow is like my sorrow, which has stricken me.)

There seems to be a concerto style in this section, which comes in from the instrumental prelude, but towards the end, this is replaced by a fugue for all voices and orchestra: "Denn der Herr hat mich voll Jammers gemacht am Tage seines grimmigen Zorns." (For the Lord has made me full of lamentation on the day of His fierce anger.) The pictorial effect of this fugal part is that of a crowd, bewailing their sorrow.

2. *Recitative—tenor.* He moralizes on the fate of Jerusalem; God has punished the city, just as He did Gommorrah, for the sinful life-style of its inhabitants. A repeated grief-motif on the flutes and strings accompanies his declamation.

There is, however, a disruption in the logical sequence of the libretto: he mentions first that Jerusalem is now only a heap of stones and ashes; then says that it would be better if it were to be totally destroyed.

3. *Aria—bass.* The dramatic climax of this cantata comes now with the graphic representation of a storm of the same potency as the one which destroyed the city. Thunder and lightning are reproduced in the rumbling strings and in the blazing peals of the trumpet. This aria is another of Bach's finest. The runs on many words are impressive. The total result sounds similar to an aria from one of Haydn's *Oratorios.* "Dein Wetter zog sich auf von Weitem, / Doch dessen Strahl bricht endlich ein / Und muss dir unerträglich sein, / Da überhäufte Sünden / Der Rache Blitz entzünden / Und dir den Untergang bereiten." (Your storm comes up from afar, / Yet its flash finally breaks out / And must be unbearable for you, / Since piled-up sins / Kindle the lightning of revenge / And prepare your destruction.)

4. *Recitative—alto.* This short declamation in secco prepares the way for her following aria. A warning against sin in our own lives replaces the dreadful consequences of it we have heard up to now. She says that not only Jerusalem had sinners, but they are also present in our modern cities. If we do not improve our daily lives and keep increasing our sins, we too will be terribly punished.

5. *Aria—alto.* A very interesting aria, composed of voice, two flutes, an oboe da caccia, which makes it like a quartet, with the alto voice acting as an instrument. Bach was prone to treat voices in this manner.

The pastoral effect of his music paints an idyllic picture of Jesus, the Good Shepherd, guarding His flock, or of a mother hen protecting her chicks. This beautiful scene is disturbed only in the penultimate line by a recollection of the sinners' punishment; however, the final line restores blissful confidence in the Lord's protection of the pious. "Doch Jesus will auch bei der Strafe / Der Frommen Schild und Beistand sein, / Er sammelt sie als seine Schafe, / Als seine Küchlein liebreich ein; / Wenn Wetter der Rache die Sünder belohnen, / Hilft er, dass Fromme sicher wohnen." (Yet Jesus will also be at this punishment, / The shield and helper of the pious, / He gathers them as His sheep, / As His chickens with great love; / When storms of vengeance reward the sinners, / He helps the pious to live in safety.)

6. *Chorale.* This chorale is not set in Bach's usual four-part, simple style. Each line is followed by an interlude for two entwining flutes, playing a short stanza; a prayer to God for mercy for the sake of His Son, Who has expiated all our sins. There is an unusual ethereal effect, emanating from the repeated melody of the flutes, as though the prayer were floating heavenward.

The chorale is based on stanza nine of J.M. Meyfart's hymn, "O grosser Gott von Macht" (O Great God of Might).

• **Du sollst Gott, deinen Herren, lieben (You Should Love the Lord Your God)** (c. 1725; BWV 77).

As for the previous two cantatas, Terry suggests Christian Weiss, Sr., or someone unknown, as the librettist for this thirteenth Sunday after Trinity cantata. Bach must have found this libretto inspiring, because all the numbers are interesting.

The Gospel is Luke 10 (23–37), the parable of the Good Samaritan, from which the librettist takes verse 27 for the opening chorus.

The soli are SATB, with a four-part chorus. The male voices sing the two recitatives and the female, the two arias. The orchestra has a trumpet, two oboes, strings and continuo.

1. *Chorus with chorale.* With the chorale played by the trumpet and continuo to Luther's "Dies sind die heil'gen zehn Gebot'" (These are the holy Ten Commandments), Bach preaches his own sermon in motet style in this chorus. The overwhelming power of this combination impresses the listener, as Bach interprets in music Christ's words to His disciples: "Du sollst Gott, deinen

Herren, lieben von ganzem Herzen, von ganzer Seele, von allen Kräften und von ganzem Gemüte und deinen Nächsten als dich selbst." (You should love the Lord your God from your whole heart, from your whole soul, with all your might and all your mind, and your neighbor as yourself.)

If Bach wished to drive home the precept of brotherly love, his setting for this chorus would certainly succeed in catching the attention of the audience.

2. *Recitative—bass.* He begins, secco, by declaiming that we must give God alone all our love, to illustrate the first part of the opening chorus. Then we can be sure of His protection and benefits toward us. This theme will be continued throughout the remaining numbers, adding the idea of love for one's fellow man, as at the conclusion of the above chorus.

3. *Aria—soprano.* Accompanied by the two oboes, she sings of her heartfelt love for God, with coloratura runs on "entbrennen" (to catch fire) and "ewig" (ever). The joy-motif is present throughout. She prays that she may know the Law, so that her love for God will last forever.

4. *Recitative—tenor.* He prays that he may have the heart of a Samaritan, so that he may love his neighbor and not ignore him when he is in trouble. He will hate his own selfishness in the hope of God's mercy. The string accompaniment effectively colors his plea.

5. *Aria—alto.* This aria requires a virtuoso trumpeter as obbligato. It is a sparkling number, perhaps even too joyful for the text. She expresses the imperfection of her love for God because of her weak will. Nevertheless, the tonal colors of her voice with the sound of the trumpet make a remarkable impression. "Ach, es bleibt in meiner Liebe / Lauter Unvollkommenheit. / Hab' ich oftmals gleich den Willen, / Was Gott saget, zu erfüllen, / Fehlt mir's doch an Möglichkeit." (Ah, there remains in my love / Nothing but imperfection. / Even if I have often the will / To fulfill what God says, / The possibility still fails me.)

6. Chorale. Since Bach's manuscript omitted both the text and the instrumentation, Carl Zelter inserted verse eight of David Denicke's "Wenn einer alle Ding' verstünd'" (If One Understood All Things). This verse says that Jesus was the example of true love, which He showed to all mankind. The prayer asks that we may do likewise to our neighbor. Thus this conclusion is fitting for the theme of all the preceding movements.

• **Liebster Gott, wann werd' ich sterben? (Dearest God, When Shall I Die?)** (c. 1725; BWV 8).

This chorale cantata for the sixteenth Sunday after Trinity has its first and last numbers set directly on Caspar Neumann's hymn, which is based on a tune by Daniel Vetter, the organist at the Nicolai church in Leipzig, published just twelve years before Bach composed this cantata. The other numbers are paraphrases of the Neumann verses, possibly arranged by Picander.

The Gospel is Luke 7 (11–17)—Christ raises the son of the widow of Nain—but there is no reference to this miracle in the libretto. Instead, the text is a meditation on death as the entry to a better life in heaven. It is the epitome of Bach's philosophy on this subject, for which he composed this wonderful music for SATB soli and a four-part chorus.

The two arias are for male voices, while the females sing the two recitatives; this is the reverse of the previous cantata, BWV 77.

The orchestra includes a transverse flute, two oboes d'amore, strings, and features a horn in the continuo for the first movement.

1. *Chorus.* This is really an extended chorale, sung in chorus with all voices and instruments. Its theme of peaceful lamentation is the antithesis of the fearful animation resounding in the opening chorus of BWV 20. We can clearly visualize the timorous onlooker at a funeral, who wonders when his time of

death will come. The pizzicato strings and quavering woodwinds imitate the tolling bells, as the funeral procession moves from the church to the grave. This sound paints a tone-picture of a country graveyard in spring: "Liebster Gott, wann werd' ich sterben? / Meine Zeit läuft immer hin, / Und des alten Adams Erben, / Unter denen ich auch bin, / Haben dies zum Vaterteil, / Dass sie eine kleine Weil' / Arm und elend sind auf Erden / Und dann selber Erde werden." (Dearest God, when shall I die? / My time runs continually away, / And old Adam's heirs, / Among whom I also am, / Have this for their patrimony, / That they for a little while / Are poor and wretched on earth / And then themselves become earth.)

This theme of personal meditation on death will continue through the following two numbers.

2. *Aria—tenor.* At this point the watcher begins to think about himself. How will he face his own death? The pizzicato effect of the funeral bells is constant as he ponders over this problem. His aria seems to resemble a dramatic monologue in lyrical form. He tries to persuade himself that he has nothing to fear from death, since many thousands have already met it. His artistic vocalization with the instrumental ambience produces a fine aria.

3. *Recitative—alto.* With string accompaniment, she lists her thoughts on the aftermath of her death: where will she be buried, who will free her soul from sin, where will her belongings and her loved ones be scattered?

4. *Aria—bass.* This movement in gigue rhythm has an unrestrained joy-motif that marks the change from the former pessimism to optimistic confidence. Illustrated by its flute and string accompaniment, this pleasing, dance-like melody enhances the singer's interpretation of his lines. There is a further enchanting melody set for the last two lines; these form the climax of the whole cantata: "Doch weichet, ihr tollen, vergeblichen Sorgen! / Mich rufet mein Jesus: wer sollte nicht gehn? / Nichts, was mir gefällt, / Besitzet die Welt. / Erscheine mir, seliger, fröhlicher Morgen, / Verkläret und herrlich vor Jesu zu stehn." (Then yield, ye foolish, vain cares! / My Jesus calls me: who should not go? / Nothing that pleases me / Does the world possess. / Appear to me, blessed, happy morning, / To be standing transfigured and glorious before Jesus.)

5. *Recitative—soprano.* She says, in secco, that the world may keep her belongings; it will be enough for her to have God's spiritual blessings, which He promises to her every day, and which can never die. The happiness in her voice complements the feeling in the previous aria of the bass.

6. *Chorale.* The concluding stanza of this hymn is a magnificent prayer to God: that He grant us a good end to our lives. With Bach's setting for full chorus and instruments, it is an emotional masterpiece: "Herrscher über Tod und Leben, / Mach' einmal mein Ende gut, / Lehre mich den Geist aufgeben / Mit recht wohlgefasstem Mut. / Hilf, dass ich ein ehrlich Grab / Neben frommen Christen hab', / Und auch endlich in der Erde / Nimmermehr zuschanden werde!" (Ruler over death and life, / Make my end good some day; / Teach me to give up my spirit / With really well-seized courage. / Help, that I may have an honorable grave / Near pious Christians, / And also, that finally in the earth, / I nevermore become ashamed!)

• **Bringet dem Herrn Ehre seines Namens (Bring to the Lord the Honor of His Name)** (1725; BWV 148).

This was definitely Picander's libretto for the seventeenth Sunday after Trinity, which Bach arranged to compose this cantata. The date also may be fixed at 1725, because this was Bach's first confirmed association with Picander as his librettist.

The Gospel for the day is Luke 14 (1–11)—Christ heals the man ill with dropsy and discusses healing on the Sabbath with the Pharisees—but this observance of the Sabbath is mentioned only in passing during the two recitatives. The Epistle, Ephesians 4 (1–6), is not involved at all.

The soli are ATB, with a four-part chorus. The orchestra consists of a trumpet, three oboes, strings and organ continuo.

For its central theme, the cantata deals with the worship of God on Sunday, according to this commandment; Picander's original libretto was a satirical poem on the worldly use of the Sabbath by many people. Bach rearranged it into its present form.

1. *Chorus.* Bach called this opening movement a concerto, probably thinking that the choral voices were the concertino, and the trumpet, strings and continuo, the ripieno group. It is a blaze of tone-color in praise of God, taking its text from Psalms 29 (2) and 96 (8) in paraphrase. The harmony soars upward like a mighty summons to prayer, beginning homophonically but becoming fugal in the last half. Its magnificence is really astounding.

"Bringet dem Herrn Ehre seines Namens, betet an den Herrn im heiligen Schmuck." (Bring to the Lord the honor of His Name; pray to the Lord in holy attire.)

2. *Aria—tenor.* He sings of hastening to church to hear Christ's teachings and to hear the songs of praise of the faithful. With solo violin and continuo, the tenor interprets his text with great skill, especially in his runs on "eile" (hurry) and "Freuden" (joys): "Ich eile, die Lehren / Des Lebens zu hören, / Und suche mit Freuden das heilige Haus. / Wie rufen so schöne / Das frohe Getöne / Zum Lobe des Höchsten die Seligen aus!" (I hurry, the lessons / Of life to hear, / And joyfully seek the holy house. / How the blessed call out so beautifully / Their glad tones / In praise of the Highest!)

The joy-motif is evident throughout this excellent aria.

3. *Recitative—alto.* She begins with a paraphrase of Psalm 42 (1): "As the hart panteth after the water brooks, so panteth my soul after Thee, O God." Then she mentions the celebration of the Sabbath, where, in the congregation of the righteous, she can commune with God. Finally, she wishes that the benighted would learn of the bliss that she feels at this time. The string-only accompaniment lends a touch of beauty to her declamation.

4. *Aria—alto.* Her voice shows her joy in her complete submission to God. She hopes that He will enter her soul, so that she will find peace with Him. The text is in the form of a prayer, with the gentle, undulating rhythm of a lullaby. This is reflected in the word "Ruhebette" (bed of rest) in the last line: "Mund und Herze steht dir offen, / Höchster, senke dich hinein! / Ich in dich, und du in mich; / Glaube, Liebe, Duldung, Hoffen / Soll mein Ruhebette sein." (Mouth and heart stand open to Thee, / Highest One, sink Thyself into them! / I in Thee, and Thou in me; / Faith, love, patience, hope / Shall be my bed of rest.)

5. *Recitative—tenor.* In secco, he expresses his hope that God's Spirit will remain in him to govern his words and deeds, so that some day he may be able to celebrate the final Sabbath with God in His glory.

6. *Chorale.* As Bach provided no text for this final chorale, two have been suggested: "Amen zu aller Stund'" (Amen at All Times) as given by W. Neumann, or "Führ auch mein Herz und Sinn" (Lead Also My Heart and Mind), the eleventh verse of J. Heermann's "Wo soll ich fliehen hin" (Whither Shall I Flee). It is the latter which is heard on recordings today.

• **Alles nur nach Gottes Willen (Everything According to God's Will)** (1726; BWV 72).

Like cantata BWV 73, this work is for the third Sunday after Epiphany, but produced for the next year. The libretto was published in 1715 at Weimar by Salomo Franck in his "Evangelisches

Andachts-Opfer" (Evangelical Devotions Offering) to which Bach returned for this text.

The Gospel, Matthew 8 (1–13), describes two of Jesus' healing miracles, but these are not mentioned in the libretto, nor any idea of Jesus, the Healer. The main theme is complete submission and obedience to God's will and sublime confidence in Him.

The soli are SATB, with a four-part chorus. The instruments are two oboes, two violins, a viola and continuo—a very modest orchestra.

1. *Chorus.* There is a peculiar rhythm to the melody throughout this entire chorus, which may signify a clock ticking away the passing of time. In fact, the last word in the third line, "Zeit" (time), may have prompted Bach to use this symbolism. The stanza expresses a personal acceptance of God's will to govern one's span of life, whether in prosperity or adversity. The syncopated rhythm of the orchestra provides the background for this philosophy: "Alles nur nach Gottes Willen, / So bei Lust als Traurigkeit, / So bei gut als böser Zeit. / Gottes Wille soll mich stillen / Bei Gewölk und Sonnenschein. / Alles nur nach Gottes Willen! / Dies soll meine Losung sein." (Everything according to God's will, / So in pleasure as in sadness, / So in good as in bad times. / God's will will calm me / In clouds and sunshine. / Everything according to God's will! / This shall be my solution.

Bach later used this melody for the *Gloria* movement of his *Short Mass in G minor.*

2. *Recitative and Arioso—alto.* Franck's libretto for this number is peculiar: after a very short recitative, nine lines in succession begin with the phrase "Herr, wie du wiilt" (Lord, as Thou willst). This forms the main part of the extremely long arioso. The resulting monotony defies Bach's inventive gift for setting an interesting recitative. It seems to be less recitative than a long litany.

The last two lines of the arioso introduce her own following aria.

3. *Aria—alto.* Her aria is much more attractive, having two violins in support. She reiterates her submission to the Lord's will, although she cannot understand it sometimes. Her artistic runs and trills make this text more colorful, especially in the last two lines: "Mit allem, was ich hab' und bin, / Will ich mich Jesu lassen, / Kann gleich mein schwacher Geist und Sinn / Des Höchsten Rat nicht fassen; / Er führe mich nur immer hin / Auf Dorn-und Rosenstrassen!" (With all I have and am, / I will leave myself to Jesus, / Even if my weak spirit and mind / Do not immediately comprehend the Lord's counsel. / Whether He always may lead me away / On thorn and rose-paths!)

4. *Recitative—bass.* He states his belief in divine fatalism. When the Savior says He will do it, it is done. The Lord will strengthen the weak in their misery with His hand of mercy, for He does not disdain to enter the humble homes of the poor, when they are in distress.

5. *Aria—soprano.* With all instruments accompanying her aria, the soprano expresses in an awed tone her childlike trust and faith in Christ. The quiet and sincere feeling makes this number the best in the cantata and one of Bach's outstanding vocal gems. The dancing melody exudes a joy-motif of happiness and trust. "Mein Jesus will es tun, er will dein Kreuz versüssen, / Obgleich dein Herze liegt in viel Bekümmernissen, / Soll es doch sanft und still in seinen Armen ruhn, / Wenn es der Glaube fasst, mein Jesus will es tun!" (My Jesus will do it; He will sweeten your pain. / Although your heart lies in great trouble, / It shall yet rest softly and quietly in His arms, / If faith holds it; my Jesus will do it!)

The repetition of the first clause at the end seems to me unique for its emotional appeal.

6. *Chorale.* This is the first stanza of Markgraf Albrecht von Brandenburg-Culmbach's hymn, "Was mein Gott will, das g'scheh allzeit" (What My God Wills,

That Always Happens), with all voices and instruments. It is a fitting ending to this cantata, and Bach will use it again as the title chorus of BWV 111.

• **Es erhub sich ein Streit (There Arose a Conflict)** (1726; BWV 19).

Picander wrote the libretto for this cantata for Michaelmas in 1725. Bach revised and enlarged on it for his 1726 setting. Previously, Bach's uncle, Johann Christoph, had produced a cantata in the old style on the theme of St. Michael and the angels casting the dragon out of heaven. Bach had performed this work in Leipzig before he composed his own version in this cantata in the new operatic style.

The Gospel, Matthew 18 (1–11), does not appear in the libretto; the Epistle, Revelation 12 (7–12), is referred to in every number, paraphrased by Picander and amended by Bach.

The usual four-part chorus is used, with STB soloists.

The orchestra is lavish: three trumpets and timpani, two violins, two oboes, a viola, and a taille (a tenor oboe) in the continuo for the first and last movements.

1. *Chorus.* This is a great polyphonic fugue as background for Bach's vivid vocal fresco of the battle between the Archangel Michael and his angels and the forces of the dragon (Satan). There is no prelude; the choir and the orchestra begin immediately in a tumult-motif. Michael's victory banishes the Devil from heaven to earth, where we will now have to contend with him.

"Es erhub sich ein Streit. / Die rasende Schlange, der höllische Drache / Stürmt wider den Himmel mit wütender Rache. / Aber Michael bezwingt, / Und die Schar, die ihn umringt, / Stürzt des Satans Grausamkeit." (There arose a conflict. / The raving serpent, the hellish dragon, / Storms against heaven with furious vengeance. / But Michael conquers, / And the host, which surrounds him, / Overthrows Satan's ferocity.)

Oddly, Bach follows the da capo convention to repeat the battle scene of the first half, forgetting perhaps that Satan has been defeated! Nevertheless, this chorus is intensely dramatic.

2. *Recitative—bass.* Beginning with this number, and for all the rest of the cantata, the theme changes from the battle against evil to the mystical connection between the angels and man.

Michael has overpowered the dragon and cast him into chains. Now he will be banished from heaven. We can take comfort from the thought that we will be protected in body and soul by angels, when evil threatens us.

3. *Aria—soprano.* The first line of her text refers to Mahanaim, the place where Jacob met God's angels, Genesis 32 (1–2). The oboe d'amore obbligato engenders an intimately tender feeling in her song: "Gott schickt uns Mahanaim zu; / Wir stehen oder gehen, / So können wir in sichrer Ruh / Vor unsern Feinden stehen. / Es lagert sich, so nah als fern, / Um uns der Engel unsers Herrn / Mit Feuer, Ross und Wagen." (God send us to Mahanaim; / Whether we stand or go, / We can stand in sure calm / Before our enemies. / There is encamped, near and far, / The angel of the Lord around us / With fire, horse and chariot.)

4. *Recitative—tenor.* He continues to describe the rapport between the angels and man, contrasting the lofty state of the former with the lowliness of the latter. The accompaniment of strings seems to depict the shining angelic host, which watches over sinful mortals.

5. *Aria—tenor (with Chorale).* With strings and the trumpet softly playing the chorale tune of one of the Michaelmas hymns, the tenor sings his long aria to an adagio rhythm, which should remind the listener of the Pastoral Sinfonia in the *Christmas Oratorio,* composed ten years later. This aria, with its swinging tempo, is a tone-poem in itself. The listener can feel in this prayer to the angels all that wonderful mysticism that only Bach can infuse into a given text. This aria is in a class by itself—a first-rate masterpiece!

"Bleibt, ihr Engel, bleibt bei mir! / Führet mich auf beiden Seiten, / Dass mein Fuss nicht möge gleiten, / Aber lehrt mich auch allhier / Euer grosses Heilig singen / Und dem Höchsten Dank zu bringen!" (Stay, ye angels, stay with me! / Guide me on both sides, / So that my foot may not slip, / But teach me also here / To sing of your great holiness / And to bring thanks to the Highest!)

6. *Recitative—soprano.* This short narration, secco, exhorts us to love angels and not reject them by our sinning. They will convey us, as in a chariot, to the blessed realms of heaven, when God ordains that we bid farewell to the world.

7. *Chorale.* This is the ninth verse of an anonymous funeral hymn, "Freu' dich sehr, O meine Seels" (Rejoice Greatly, O My Soul) set for all voices and instruments. There are two Biblical references in the stanza: "Let Thy angels travel with me in Elijah's red chariot," and "Let my Soul rest in Thy bosom, as did Lazarus after death, until my body comes out of the earth to be reunited with it."

This verse summarizes the main thought very well and gives it a Scriptural context in symmetry with the opening chorus.

• **Dem Gerechten muss das Licht (On the Righteous Must the Light)** (c. 1726; BWV 195).

In its final form, this wedding cantata is dated 1737 or 1741. It has two movements that are echoed in the secular cantata "Angenehmes Wiederau" (Pleasant Wiederau), BWV 30a of 1737, but according to Terry, its original form was performed about 1726. The librettist is unknown—perhaps Bach? Bach adapted the music for it from a lost secular cantata, being in haste to have it ready for the event.

The names of the couple being married are unknown. However, Bach's grandiose setting of the text would certainly indicate that they were aristocrats or important citizens of Leipzig, whom he wished to impress.

The orchestra is sumptuous: three trumpets, timpani, two horns, two oboes, two flutes, strings and organ continuo. The cantata is divided into two parts: one before and one after the marriage ceremony.

Vor der Trauung
(Before the Marriage Service)

1. *Chorus.* Bach divides the choir into two sections, the first group acting as soloists and the second as the ripieno, in concerto style, supported by the tutti of the orchestra. In its form, this chorus is a prelude and fugue, showing that Bach was still conscious of his organ writing, even when composing for voices. This chorus would impress anyone with its grandeur.

The only Biblical text occurs in this first chorus, Psalm 97 (11, 12), which is closely paraphrased: "Dem Gerechten muss das Licht immer wieder aufgehen und Freude den frommen Herzen. / Ihr Gerechten freuet euch des Herrn und danket ihm und preiset seine Heiligkeit." (On the righteous the light must continually rise and gladness in pious hearts. / Ye righteous, rejoice in the Lord, and thank Him and praise His holiness.)

2. *Recitative—bass.* He addresses the bridal pair in his narration, stating that the light of their joy will increase as their well-being and good fortune grow. Everyone will honor their righteousness and virtue. They will find their light of happiness in each other.

3. *Aria—bass.* There is a dance-rhythm in the accompaniment, played by two oboes and strings. The tempo is also rather jerky, which would indicate that this number had its origin in a secular folksong. Bach must have been in a hurry to set this, because the text seems to be fitted to a previous melody, not really suited to a church ceremony. This aria was later imitated in BWV 30a.

Its thought continues the above recitative: that the bridal pair should praise God, because He will bless their union with ever-increasing light and joy.

4. *Recitative—soprano.* Bach must

have liked this recitative in the original cantata, as he gave it a prominent accompaniment of two flutes and two oboes. The soloist describes the blessing that the pastor will give the couple, which represents God's paternal hand joining the bride and the groom. The Lord has brought them together; therefore, they should thank Him.

5. *Chorus.* Once again, in his haste, Bach adapts this number from the unknown earlier secular work, but this time the music fits the libretto. All voices and instruments are used. The music is less complex than in the opening chorus and was used again for the final chorus of BWV 30a.

The text indicates a song a praise to God for His divine guidance and seems to be sung by the choir on behalf of the present congregation: "Wir kommen, deine Heiligkeit, / Unendlich grosser Gott, zu preisen. / Der Anfang rührt von deinen Händen, / Durch Allmacht kannst du es vollenden / Und deinen Segen kräftig weisen." (We come to praise Thy holiness, / Everlasting almighty God. / The beginning moves from Thy hands; / Through Thy omnipotence Thou canst finish it / And strongly show Thy blessing.)

The wedding ceremony followed this number.

Nach der Trauung (After the Wedding Service)

Bach's original libretto had an aria, a recitative, and a final chorus in this second part, but he replaced them later with a chorale, which is heard in modern performances. The music for the original second part has been lost.

6. *Chorale.* All voices and instruments are the same as in the opening chorus, except that two horns replace the trumpets. The hymn is the first two stanzas of Paul Gerhardt's "Nun danket all' und bringet Ehr'" (Now All Thank and Bring Honor): "Nun danket all' und bringet Ehr', / Ihr Menschen in der Welt, / Dem, dessen Lob der Engel Heer / Im Himmel stets vermeldt." (Now all thank and bring honor, / Ye men in the world, / To Him, whose praise the army of angels / Announces continually in heaven.) Bach's treatment of this chorale has a fervent, solemn overtone. Undoubtedly, the congregation attending this service would know it, but as they listened to its beautiful performance by the choir, I doubt whether they could participate in singing it this time.

• **Ich lasse dich nicht, du segnest mich denn (I Will Not Let Thee Go, Until Thou Bless Me)** (1727; BWV 157).

This is a solo cantata for tenor and bass voices, intended for the funeral of Johann Christoph von Ponickau, performed at Pomssen at a memorial service about two months after his burial. Picander's libretto has no allusions to the deceased—probably at Bach's request, since he performed this cantata in Leipzig for the Feast of the Purification on the Sunday before the memorial service.

The soli are TB, with a four-part choir for the final chorale. The orchestra comprises a transverse flute, two oboes, two violins, a violetta (viola) and continuo.

The only Biblical reference occurs in the opening duet, Genesis 32 (24–30)—Jacob wrestles with a stranger until daybreak (verse 26).

1. *Duet—tenor, bass.* The text, taken from the above verse, is now applied to all Christians, who must hold fast to the Lord in order to receive His blessing. All the following numbers will continue this theme of faithful adherence to Jesus in life and in death. "Ich lasse dich nicht, du segnest mich denn!" (I will not let Thee go, until Thou bless me!)

The voices sing in canon, perhaps to imitate the struggles of the two wrestlers, to a woodwind and string accompaniment. Their longing seems to be more for a third person than for each other, so that we may conclude that both are simply appealing to the Lord for His blessing.

2. *Aria—tenor.* He expands on the thought of the duet, with oboe d'amore and continuo accompaniment. There are

florid runs on "halte" (hold) and "Gewalt" (might), but although the aria has a certain somber quality befitting a funeral cantata, it seems to be lacking in an emphatic illustration of the text. It could be that Bach, in his haste, was undecided on how to combine the joy-motif indicated by the text with the serious tone of funeral music.

3. *Recitative—tenor.* With the aid of the strings, his declamation here is better than his above aria. He praises Jesus for the comfort He gives; the metaphor is that He is a soft bed in times of trouble. The joys of the world vanish. Without Jesus, he could depend on no one, and therefore he will never leave Him.

4. *Aria, Recitative and Arioso—bass.* The transverse flute, supported by the strings, plays continuously in a sort of rocking motto, which Schweitzer calls "a heavenly roundelay" (Vol. II, p. 202)—"Ja, ja, ich halte Jesum feste" (Yes, yes, I hold Jesus firmly).

This number resembles a scene from an opera, divided into five parts: aria, recitative secco, arioso, recitative secco and arioso. Bach had never constructed such a complex but magnificent aria.

The joy-motif is apparent throughout the song, as the bass expresses his constancy of faith in Jesus, even unto death, seen in the first recitative: "Ei, wie vergnügt / Ist mir mein Sterbekasten, / Weil Jesus mir in Armen liegt! / So kann mein Geist recht freudig rasten!" (Ah how pleasant to me is my death-casket, / because Jesus is lying in my arms! / Thus my spirit can rest quite happily.)

Three other consecutive lines in Picander's libretto are repeated, which point to the mystical union of the soul with God: "So gaeh' ich auch zum Himmel ein / wo Gott und seines Lammes Gäste / in Kronen cu der Hochzeit sein." (So I shall also enter heaven, / where God and His Lamb's guests / Are in their crowns at the wedding.)

The refrain, "Ja, ja, ich halte Jesum feste," shows how this will be possible, if he keeps the faith with Christ.

This number reveals Bach's religious thinking in the way he has interpreted the text for his musical setting.

5. *Chorale.* This is stanza six of Christian Keymann's "Meinen Jesum lass ich nicht" (I Do Not Leave My Jesus). Its simple melody, with all voices and instruments, consolidates the message conveyed in all the preceding numbers.

• **Wer da glaubet und getauft wird (Whoever Believes and Is Baptized)** (c. 1727; BWV 37).

This cantata for Ascension Day was set on the libretto of an unknown writer or of Christian Weiss, Sr. The text does not mention Christ's Resurrection, except indirectly in the bass aria. Even here, the theme is evident—the Lutheran creed that faith and baptism are more important than good works for a Christian.

The only Scriptural text occurs in the first chorus, taken from verse 16 of the Gospel for this Sunday, Mark 16 (14–20).

The soli are SATB, with a four-part chorus. The orchestra is light: two oboes d'amore, two violins, a viola and organ continuo. This seems to give the effect of a chamber cantata.

1. *Chorus.* There is a touch of nostalgia about this beautiful opening chorus. The text is Christ's last words to His disciples at His reappearance among them. Bach has recaptured the emotion of regret that we must feel at His departure. The full instrumental introduction of the theme, followed by the choir, paints a graceful picture of this longing: "Wer da gläubet und getauft wird, der wird selig werden." (Whoever believes and is baptized, he will become blessed.)

2. *Aria—tenor.* With organ continuo only, he enlarges on the merits of believing in Christ: belief is a jewel presented to us by the Lord: "Der Glaube ist das Pfand der Liebe, / Drum hat er bloss aus Liebestriebe, / Da er ins Lebensbuch mich schriebe, / Mir dieses Kleinod beigelegt." (Belief is the pledge of the love, / That Jesus cherishes for His own. / Therefore just from His impulse of love, / When He wrote my name in the book of life, / Did He bestow on me this jewel.)

3. *Chorale (Duet)—soprano, alto.* Text and tune are taken from Philipp Nicolai's fifth stanza of his hymn, "Wie schön leuchtet der Morgenstern" (How Beautifully Shines the Morning Star). The joy-motif is evident in their canonical singing of these verses, still with organ continuo only. They sing their praise of God the Father and the Son, affirming their belief in the heavenly life.

4. *Recitative—bass.* Accompanied by strings and continuo, he declaims the Lutheran doctrine that good works alone cannot replace faith; however, a Christian must practice good actions, in order to please God.

5. *Aria—bass.* Bach's tune for this aria was probably suggested by the first line, which mentions that faith gives the soul wings to soar into heaven. The oboe d'amore and strings play a joy-rhythm, representing a fluttering of wings to illustrate the text. The melodic imagery is so well done that it overshadows the Lutheran dogma in the libretto: "Der Glaube schafft der Seele Flügel, / Dass sie sich in den Himmel schwingt, / Die Taufe ist das Gnadensiegel, / Das uns den Segen Gottes bringt; / Und daher heisst ein sel'ger Christ, / Wer gläubet und getauft ist." (Belief creates the soul's wings, / So that it soars into heaven. / Baptism is the seal of mercy, / That brings us God's blessing. / And thus he is called a blessed Christian, / Whoever believes and is baptized.)

6. *Chorale.* This is stanza four of Johann Kolrose's hymn, "Ich dank' dir, lieber Herre" (I Thank Thee, Dear Lord), performed tutti. The choir asks God for belief in His Son and for forgiveness of their sins. There is no mention of baptism in this chorale stanza.

• **Lass, Fürstin, lass noch einen Strahl—Trauerode (Let, Princess, Let Another Gleam of Light—Funeral Ode)** (1727; BWV 198).

This was an occasional cantata, the libretto of which was arranged by Bach, on an ode composed by Professor Johann Christoph Gottsched of the University Church, St. Paul's, for Queen Christiane Eberhardine of Saxony and Poland, who had died 7 September 1727.

The Queen had lived apart from her husband, Augustus II, the Strong, for thirty years, because she would not convert to Roman Catholicism, as her husband had done, in order to gain the Polish crown.

She was beloved by the people for her firm adherence to the national Saxon faith, which she instilled into her son, the future Augustus III. The scandalous conduct of her husband, Augustus II, whose mistresses had hundreds of children, must have added to her martyrdom during the thirty years she lived in solitude at Pretsch, near Wittenberg.

Hans von Kirchbach, a nobleman student at the University, commissioned Gottsched to write this funeral ode and chose Bach to set the music for it, thus by-passing Görner, the director of music at St. Paul's. Kirchbach had to pay Görner twelve thalers in compensation; Bach was reprimanded but allowed to set the ode on this occasion. Bach finished the score on 15 October 1727, just two days before the funeral commemoration. He must have had little time for rehearsal!

The cantata is divided into two parts. Between these parts, von Kirchbach delivered his valedictory speech of praise and mourning.

The soloists are SATB, with a four-part chorus. The scoring is unique: two transverse flutes, two oboes d'amore, two sections of violins, violas, two violas da gamba, two lutes (used for the first time by Bach in a cantata) and continuo (both clavichord and organ). Bach probably conducted the choruses from the organ; the arias and the recitatives he directed from the clavichord.

Part I

1. *Chorus.* This majestic opening chorus, with all voices and instruments, gives the listener an impression of a large number of mourners, who cry out to the deceased Queen in heaven. The text and the rhythm of solemnity show their grief

in a motif that persists through all the following numbers. The tear-motif enters also at the last word in the third line. The quiet dignity of this chorus is fitting for an apostrophe, paying tribute to a revered monarch. "Lass, Fürstin, lass noch einen Strahl / Aus Salems Sterngewölbe schiessen, / Und sieh, mit wieviel Tränengüssen / Umringen wir dein Ehrenmal." (Let, Princess, let another gleam of light / Shoot forth from Salem's starry vault, / And see, with how many torrents of tears / We surround your memorial of honor.)

Bach borrowed this chorus, the arias and the final chorus in his *St. Mark Passion* (1731), with its libretto by Picander—lost for years, but reconstructed recently.

2. *Recitative—soprano.* With string accompaniment, she mentions all those persons and places who mourn the Queen's death: Saxony, Meissen, the populace, her husband Augustus (who had caused her much pain, but Gottsched was being diplomatic), her son, the nobility, and the middle class.

3. *Aria—soprano.* A tear-motif in the strings accompanies her singing. Nevertheless, she bids the strings be silent, because no tone can adequately reflect the country's sorrow at the loss of their mother. This is the "Schmerzenswort" (grief-word) mentioned in the text. Probably the word "Saiten" (strings) gave Bach the idea of employing them, despite the meaning of the libretto.

4. *Recitative—alto.* Flutes, oboes, strings and lute all play in quavers or pizzicato to portray the sound of bells, tolling at the Queen's funeral. Their accompaniment to the first four lines of the recitative is the best onomatopoeia that Bach ever composed: "Der Glocken bebendes Getön / Soll unsrer trüben Seelen Schrecken / Durch ihr geschwungnes Erze wecken / Und uns durch Mark und Adern gehn." (The vibrating sounds of the bells / Shall awaken the fears of our sad souls / Through their swung bronze / And go through our marrow and veins.)

She wishes that all other European countries could hear this sad clanging, which betokens Saxony's lamentation for its Queen and implies the political unrest, which has resulted under an irresponsible monarch.

5. *Aria—alto.* The violas da gamba, obbligati, with strings and lute, portray the passing of the Queen in a solemnity motif, which Schweitzer says "is like a smile of celestial serenity" (Vol. II, p. 206). This melody denotes the quivering spirit's struggle against death which triumphs in the end, as the music also dies away.

6. *Recitative—tenor.* The alto aria, above, had described the Queen as a heroine in her fight against death. The tenor now expands the idea. Her life showed us the art of dying, seen in her daily routine, withdrawn from the King and his court. Therefore, she would not shudder at confronting death, when her Creator called her.

7. *Chorus.* A beautiful four-part chorus in canon, with two fugues and an interlude between them. This stanza pays the highest homage that any queen could receive, both in its verse and in Bach's sublime setting of it: "An dir, du Vorbild grosser Frauen, / An dir, erhabne Königin, / An dir, du Glaubenspflegerin, / War dieser Grossmut Bild zu schauen." (In thee, thou example of great women, / In thee, lofty Queen, / In thee, thou guardian of the faith, / Was to be seen the picture of this magnanimity.)

Part II

8. *Aria—tenor.* In a dance-like tempo suggestive of divine felicity, Bach expresses all his innate mysticism in this aria, which has flute and oboe accompaniment. The tenor sings of the Queen, now in her celestial surroundings. All mourning for her has ceased. Bach illustrates his conception of heaven in the soothing rhythm he writes for this number: "Der Ewigkeit saphirnes Haus / Zieht, Fürstin, deine heitern Blicke / Von unsrer Niedrigkeit zurücke / Und tilgt der Erden Trugbild aus. / Ein starker Glanz von hundert Sonnen, / Der unsern Tag zu Mitternacht / Und unsre Sonne finster

macht, / Hat dein verklärtes Haupt umsponnen." (The sapphire house of eternity / Draws, Princess, thy cheerful glances / Back from our lowliness / And effaces the earth's illusion. / A strong gleam of a hundred suns, / Which makes our day become midnight / And our sun dark, / Has enveloped thy transfigured head.)

9. *Recitative-Arioso-Recitative—bass.* The first recitative, secco, praises the Queen as the model of virtue. She will now disdain her earthly crown and its vanity, because she wears the pure, pearl-white robe of innocence in her new life above.

Flutes and oboes are added for the arioso and the second recitative, which describe the grief of the inhabitants living along the Saxon and the Polish rivers. Then the towns, Torgau and Pretsch, associated with the late Queen, are personified to express their sorrow. This number is picturesque and geographically correct for this period in the eighteenth century. The arioso could stand by itself as an excellent aria.

10. *Chorus.* The unison singing of this chorus is unusual for Bach. Its pastoral style was perhaps suggested to Bach by the preceding number. It retains the solemnity rhythm befitting a royal funeral. All instruments are used as in the opening chorus. This represents the final tribute paid to the Queen by her loyal subjects, who will remember her as long as the world lasts. They will ask poets to compose in her memory, so that they can read their works during their lifetime: "Doch Königin! Du stirbest nicht, / Man weiss, was man an dir besessen; / Die Nachwelt wird dich nicht vergessen, / Bis dieser Weltbau einst zerbricht. / Ihr Dichter, schreibt, wir wollen's lesen: / Sie ist der Tugend Eigentum, / Der Untertanen Lust und Ruhm, / Der Königinnen Preis gewesen." (Yet Queen! You do not die. / They know, what they possessed in you; / Posterity will not forget you, / Until this universe some day shatters. / Ye poets, write, we want to read it: / She has been the possession of virtue, / Her subjects' delight and honor, / The glory of queens.)

There is something about this chorus which recalls the choruses we hear in Bach's *St. John* and *St. Matthew* passions.

• **Wer nur den lieben Gott lässt walten (Who Only Lets the Dear God Govern)** (1728; BWV 93).

This is, apparently, the first extant cantata by Bach, composed after the period of general mourning for Queen Christiane Eberhardine from 7 September 1727, to 6 January 1728. Bach did not have to set cantatas during this time, as none were sung.

The librettist in this case was Picander, who arranged the stanzas of Georg Neumark's hymn, of which the first stanza begins this cantata. This was Bach's second chorale cantata; his first was BWV 4 of 1724. The melody of the hymn is retained throughout all the movements. Stanzas one, four, five and seven of Neumark's hymn were kept in their original form, while stanzas two, three and six were paraphrased by Picander.

The Gospel for this fifth Sunday after Trinity, Luke 5 (1–11)—the miraculous catch of fish—is mentioned only in the tenor chorale and recitative. The main idea in the cantata, patience in suffering, is taken from the Epistle 1 Peter 3 (8–15)—unusual in a Bach libretto.

The soli are SATB, with a four-part chorus. The instruments are two oboes, two violins, a viola and continuo.

1. *Chorus.* This is a chorale fantasia in fugue, with oboes and strings playing the ritornello melody as introduction, and also before each line sung by the choir. The voices are divided into two parts SA and TB, who sing each line either in canon or in unison—first by one pair of voices and then tutti: "Wer nur den lieben Gott lässt walten / Und hoffet auf ihn allezeit, / Den wird er wunderlich erhalten / In allem Kreuz und Traurigkeit. / Wer Gott, dem Allerhöchsten,

traut, / Der hat auf keinen Sand gebaut." (Who only lets the dear God govern / And hopes in Him at all times, / Him will He wonderfully uphold / In all suffering and sadness. / Who trusts God, the All Highest, / He has not built on sand.)

Although the movement has no pictorial suggestion, the melody evokes the calm confidence one may have in God.

2. *Chorale and Recitative—bass.* With continuo only, the bass sings one line of the chorale, followed by his recitative in one, two or three lines, commenting on what he has just sung in the hymnline. It is like a dialogue in monologue form.

The chorale verses point out the futility of complaining about our pain. As Christians, we should bear our suffering with resignation.

3. *Aria—tenor.* With string accompaniment, he enlarges on the previous number, explaining that God will divert our grief, as He knows that we are His chosen children. We must, therefore, patiently await His aid.

4. *Duet and Chorale—soprano, alto.* Again with strings playing the chorale for their duet, the soprano and the alto sing this beautiful number in canon, and charmingly interpret the text in the joy-motif of the music. The thought continues that of the preceding aria: "Er kennt die rechten Freudenstunden, / Er weiss wohl, wenn es nützlich sei; / Wenn er uns nur hat treu erfunden / Und merket keine Heuchelei, / So kommt Gott, eh' wir uns versehn, / Und lässet uns viel Guts geschehn." (He knows the right hours for joy; / He well knows, when it is useful. / If He has only found us faithful / And perceives no hypocrisy, / So God comes, before we expect it, / And lets much good happen to us.)

5. *Chorale and Recitative—tenor.* This number has the same format as (2), with longer recitatives between the lines of the chorale. These recitatives give the impression of miniature sermons on trusting God to relieve our distress.

Reference is made to Peter's fishing all night in vain, until Jesus brings him success. However, this number is musically dull.

6. *Aria—soprano.* Bach's score indicated occasional use of the obbligato oboe to play the chorale melody. This is a happy song of trust in the Lord, that sparkles with its joy-motif after the lethargy of (5) above: "Ich will auf den Herren schaun / Und stets meinem Gott vertraun. / Er ist der rechte Wundersmann, / Der die Reichen arm und bloss / Und die Armen reich und gross / Nach seinem Willen machen kann." (I shall look to the Lord / And always trust my God. / He is the real magician, / Who can make the rich poor and naked / And the poor rich and great / According to His will.)

7. *Chorale.* A straightforward four-part singing of the seventh verse of the chorale, expressing trust in God's blessing for those who are faithful. It concludes with: "Denn welcher seine Zuversicht / Auf Gott setzt, den verlässt er nicht." (For whoever places his trust in God, / He will never leave him.)

• **Sehet, wir gehen hinauf gen Jerusalem (Behold, We Are Going Up to Jerusalem)** (1729; BWV 159).

Picander was the librettist for this solo cantata for Quinquagesima Sunday. It is remarkable because of Bach's setting and because it has the same feeling as the *St. Matthew Passion* which Bach was composing at that time. The bass aria reflects back to the earlier *St. John Passion,* which has the same opening words in its alto aria.

Like the 1723 cantata, BWV 22, it takes its first number from the thirty-first verse of the Gospel for this Sunday, Luke 18 (31–43).

ATB are the soloists, with a four-part chorus for the final chorale.

The instruments are an oboe, two bassoons, strings and organ continuo.

1. *Arioso and Recitative—bass, alto.* The bass voice represents Christ. He speaks to His disciples in a step-rhythm arioso accompanied by the strings: "Sehet! / Wir gehen hinauf / Gen Jeru-

salem." (Behold! / We are going up / Toward Jerusalem.)

The alto voice comments in recitative between and after these spaced lines. In this dramatic number, she plays the part of an onlooker, whose foresight of the impending tragedy makes her warn Jesus not to go. She herself will be doomed to hell, since she is afraid to follow her Master. This number again proves Bach's sense of drama in his composition.

2. *Aria and Chorale—alto, soprano.* The alto has now found the courage to follow Christ. Her aria continues the step-motif in the woodwinds and organ continuo, interspersed with the soprano, who sings stanza six of Paul Gerhardt's "O Haupt voll Blut und Wunden" (literally, "O Head Full of Blood and Wounds"; frequently translated as "O Sacred Head Now Wounded"). The texts of both parts reflect loyal following of Christ to Calvary and beyond to their own deaths. Bach creates a duet in the interplay of the two voices.

3. *Recitative—tenor.* In his secco declamation, he depicts his own grief as a spectator after the Crucifixion. He will neither seek pleasure in the world, nor long for any other friend than Jesus, until he sees Him again in His glory. His grief will be continued in the following number.

4. *Aria—bass.* The oboe and the strings impart to this aria a most poignant feeling, similar to some movements in Bach's *Passions.* The rhythm of solemnity pervades the aria both vocally and instrumentally. The bass reveals his own longing for death, in order to follow Christ in His Passion: "Es ist vollbracht, / Das Leid ist alle; / Wir sind von unserm Sündenfalle / In Gotte gerecht gemacht. / Nun will ich eilen / Und meinem Jesu Dank erteilen, / Welt, gute Nacht! / Es ist vollbracht!" (It is fulfilled, / The pain is over; / We have been made right / By God from our fall into sin. / Now I will hasten / And give thanks to my Jesus, / World, good night! / It is fulfilled!)

The majestic tempo of the music and the soloist's fine run on "eilen" produce a most impressive tone-poem of deep sorrow.

5. *Chorale.* With all voices and instruments, this thirty-third verse of Paul Stockmann's "Jesu Leiden, Pein und Tod" (Jesus' Sorrows, Pain and Death) refers to the Passion of Christ, which should give all Christians joy in the hope of being able to follow Him into heaven.

• **Ich lebe, mein Herze, zu deinem Ergötzen (I Live, My Heart, for Thy Delight)** (1729; BWV 145).

The libretto for this Easter Tuesday cantata was written by Picander, beginning at the third number, a duet for soprano and tenor. Bach may have added a chorale and a chorus for the first two numbers, because he felt that Picander's text was insufficient for such an important festival. Yet it seems strange that Bach would have set a chorus immediately after a chorale at the beginning, so we may conclude that these numbers were added by someone unknown, perhaps after Bach's death.

By these additions, there arises some confusion concerning the correct title of this cantata. The chorale begins, "Auf, mein Herz! Des Herren Tag" (Up, my heart! the day of the Lord) and the chorus "So du mit deinem Munde" (So thou with thy mouth), the latter being taken from an Easter cantata by Telemann. Since neither of these numbers was set by Bach, one must consider that the cantata begins with Picander's third number.

The Gospel, Luke 24 (36–47)—the risen Lord reappears to His disciples in Jerusalem—is referred to only indirectly in the libretto of the first two numbers.

The soli are STB with a four-voice choir for the final chorale. The orchestra consists of a trumpet, a transverse flute, two oboes d'amore, two violins and continuo.

1. *Duet—soprano, tenor.* This duet is in the form of a dialogue between Jesus, the tenor (usually a bass in Bach), and the Soul, soprano, whom Picander probably imagined from the Gospel reference to the disciples. Bach based this duet and

the subsequent aria on some since-lost music that he had composed in Cöthen.

The violin accompaniment gives the voices a dancing rhythm expressive of their joy. The Biblical reference to the laws of Moses occurs towards the end of their duet, when they both sing that the penalties have been erased by Christ's sacrifice. The secular origin of the music is obvious.

JESUS: "Ich lebe, mein Herze, zu deinem Ergötzen" (I live, my heart, for thy delight)

SEELE (SOUL): "Du lebest, mein Jesu, zu meinem Ergötzen" (Thou livest, my Jesus, for my delight)

JESUS: "Mein Leben erhebet dein Leben empor." (My Life raises up thy life.)

SEELE: "Dein Leben erhebet mein Leber empor." (Thy Life raises up my life.)

BOTH: "Die klagende Handschrift ist völlig zerrissen / Der Friede verschaffet ein ruhig Gewissen / Und öffnet den Sündern das himmlische Tor." (The complaining handwriting is completely torn up. / Peace provides a quiet conscience / And opens to sinners the heavenly gate.)

2. *Recitative—tenor.* He refers again to Moses' law, saying that Christ has pardoned him for his sins. He asks his heart to notice that he has been absolved from accusations of wrongdoing by his Savior. This leads into the following aria.

3. *Aria—bass.* The trumpet and the transverse flute really make this aria sparkle. All the instruments produce a most attractive melody in dance tempo, with the joy-motif shining through the whole number. Its gaiety seems more akin to a secular than to a sacred aria, reminding the listener of Bach's composing for the Cöthen court: "Merke, mein Herze, beständig nur dies, / Wenn du alles sonst vergisst, / Dass dein Heiland lebend ist. / Lasse dieses deinem Glauben / Einen Grund und Veste bleiben. / Auf solche besteht er gewiss. / Merke, mein Herze, nur dies!" (Notice, my heart, constantly only this, / When you forget everything else, / That your Savior is living. / Let this for your faith / Remain a base and fortress. / On such it stands certain. / Notice, my heart, only this!)

4. *Recitative—soprano.* The singer is the Soul of the opening duet. She states "Mein Jesus lebt!" (My Jesus lives!) and repeats this later in her declamation. Her faith in the Lord is such that she wishes to die, so that she may behold Him in heaven.

5. *Chorale.* This is the fourteenth verse of Nikolaus Herman's Easter hymn, "Erschienen ist der herrlich Tag" (The Glorious Day Has Appeared), plainly sung by all voices and accompanied by all instruments except the trumpet.

This is not an outstanding cantata, but Bach's borrowed numbers are splendid.

• **Gott, wie dein Name, so ist auch dein Ruhm (God, as Thy Name, So Is Thy Fame)** (1730; BWV 171).

Bach's setting for this New Year's Day cantata by Picander further reveals his self-borrowing. The Gospel, Luke 2 (21), the naming of Jesus, is only mentioned in Picander's libretto for His name, not the circumstances of His naming by the angel. Yet His name appears in every movement of the cantata.

Several years later, Bach used the music of the opening chorus for the *Patrem omnipotentem* movement of his *Mass in B minor.* He also borrowed the music of the final chorale for the final chorale of BWV 41, "Jesu, nun sei gepreiset" (Jesus, Now Be Praised), his New Year's Day cantata in 1736.

For the soprano aria in this cantata, Bach turned to the same aria in his 1725 secular composition, BWV 205, "Der zufriedengestellte Aeolus" (Aeolus Appeased), and also imitated the last part of the alto-tenor duet in that cantata.

The soli are SATB, with the usual four-part chorus. The orchestra is quite large: three trumpets, timpani, two oboes, two violins, a viola and organ continuo.

1. *Chorus.* The text for this movement

is Psalm 48 (10), omitting the last part of this verse. All voices and instruments present a sweeping fugal picture of the majesty and omnipotence of God: "Gott, wie dein Name, so ist auch dein Ruhm bis an der Welt Ende." (God, as Thy name, so is Thy fame until the end of the world.)

2. *Aria—tenor.* The two violins and organ continuo lend a floating melody to the tenor's voice. Schweitzer thinks that "the figures in the two violins . . . interlock so charmingly that we seem to see the white strips of cloud trailing across the heavens" (Vol. II, p. 233).

The text certainly inspired Bach to compose this fine musical imagery. It concludes with lines suggestive of the power of God, which moves all nations to praise Him: "Herr, so weit die Wolken gehen, / Gehet deines Namens Ruhm. / Alles, was die Lippen rührt, / Alles, was nur Odem führt, / Wird dich in der Macht erhöhen." (Lord, as far as the clouds go, / The glory of Thy Name goes. / Everything that moves its lips, / Everything that just draws breath, / Will extol Thee in Thy Might.)

Notice that this aria is addressed to the Lord and His Name.

3. *Recitative—alto.* Beginning again with a reference to Jesus' name—"Du süsser Jesus—Name, du" (Thou sweet Jesus—name, Thou)—she states, in secco, her confidence in the Lord to help her in times of trouble and danger. Therefore, He will represent her New Year's gift.

4. *Aria—soprano.* Once again the text emphasizes Jesus' name repeatedly. Picander's libretto, however, is shorter and not as picturesque as in BWV 205. Still, the beautiful effect of the obbligato violin seems to suggest the same gentle breeze wafting over her soul as it was requested by Pallas in the secular cantata: "Jesus soll mein erstes Wort / In dem neuen Jahre heissen. / Fort und fort / Lacht sein Nam' in meinem Munde, / Und in meiner letzten Stunde / Ist Jesus auch mein letztes Wort." (Jesus should be my first word / In the New Year. / Continually / His Name laughs in my mouth, / And in my last hour / Jesus is also my last word.)

5. *Recitative—bass.* With oboes and organ continuo, he recalls Christ's words in John 14 (14): "If ye ask anything in my name, I will do it." He addresses the Lord at the beginning of his declamation. Then he asks Him for protection against fire, pestilence and war and to give His blessing to the government and to the whole country. All this he asks in His name, with "Amen" repeated three times at the end.

6. *Chorale.* The full orchestra and all voices perform this third stanza of the hymn by Johannes Herman, "Jesu, nun sei gepreiset" (Jesu, Now Be Praised), in spectacular style. The trumpet fanfares after each pair of lines must have pleased Bach very much, because he reused them for the opening chorale fantasia of BWV 41 as well as for its final chorale.

• **Ich steh' mit einem Fuss im Grabe (I Stand with One Foot in the Grave)** (1730; BWV 156).

Picander's libretto for this third Sunday after Epiphany cantata was derived from the Gospel, Matthew 8 (1–13)—Jesus heals the two sick men—but Picander's poem meditates on death and accepting it as being God's will when it comes. Bach added a Sinfonia at the beginning, the adagio from his *F Minor Harpsichord Concerto* BWV 1056, transposed for oboe and strings, which he had previously composed.

Despite its lugubrious title and theme, this cantata's tragically solemn beginning changes later to a happier note of confidence in God's will.

This is a solo cantata for SATB, with a four-part chorus. The orchestra is small, but very effective: an oboe, two violins, a viola and continuo.

As a funeral cantata, this work would have been a masterpiece, but there is no evidence that Bach ever used it as such.

1. *Sinfonia.* All instruments are used for this melancholy prelude to the tenor aria. The adagio has a step-motif in its

rhythm, which suggests those steps of an ailing man approaching his death. It is a beautiful movement, reminding the listener of the quiet music in a church before a funeral service.

2. *Aria—tenor, with Chorale-soprano(s).* Picander's libretto refers to one of the sick men in the Gospel; he is now about to die, yet the meaning of the text can apply to anyone who faces the prospect of his own death.

The sopranos (plural in my recording) sing the first stanza of J.H. Schein's hymn, "Mach's mit mir, Gott, nach deiner Güt'" (Do with Me, God, According to Thy Goodness), in unison at intervals during the tenor's singing of his aria. Bach's use of strings vividly depicts the body being lowered into the grave. This melody is repeated throughout the aria. Nevertheless, its somber mood has an indescribable beauty in its pathos: "Ich steh' mit einem Fuss im Grabe, / Bald fällt der kranke Leib hinein, / Komm, lieber Gott, wenn dir's gefällt, / Ich habe schon mein Haus bestellt, / Nur lass mein Ende selig sein!" (I stand with one foot in the grave; / Soon my sick body will fall into it. / Come, dear God, when it pleases Thee; / I have already put my house in order, / Only let my end be blessed!)

This is the most impressive number in the cantata, artistically and emotionally.

3. *Recitative—bass.* In secco, he prays that God will be merciful to him and not let him suffer on his sick-bed because of his sins. He accepts God's will and is ready to die when God calls him: "Je länger hier, je später dort" (The longer here, the later there) is his conclusion in arioso.

Notice that the imagery of the leper in the Gospel appears in this sick man: "And behold, there came a leper and worshipped him, saying, Lord, if thou wilt, thou canst make me clean."—Matthew 8 (2). The latter part of this Scripture begins and concludes the following aria.

4. *Aria—alto.* In this aria, accompanied by oboe and strings, the sadness of the preceding numbers changes to joy and confidence in the Lord. Whether she represents the ailing person of the preceding movements or some other Christian, her resignation to God's will is well expressed in this prayer: "Herr, was du willt, soll mir gefallen, / Weil doch dein Rat am besten gilt. / In der Freude, / In dem Leide, / Im Sterben, in Bitten und Flehn / Lass mir allemal geschehn, / Herr, wie du willt." (Lord, what Thou willst shall please me, / Because Thy counsel is still the best. / In joy, / In sorrow, / In dying, in prayer and pleading, / Let it always happen to me, / Lord, as Thou willst.)

5. *Recitative—bass.* His secco declamation gives thanks to the Lord for keeping him in good health and hopes that his soul will also be healthy. When his body and soul weaken, he hopes for God's consolation and comfort.

6. *Chorale.* All voices and instruments perform the first verse of Kaspar Bienemann's hymn, "Herr, wie du willt, so schick's mit mir" (Lord, as Thou Willst, So Send It to Me). This chorale text has been the theme of the cantata and thus serves as a fitting conclusion.

• **Gott, man lobet dich in der Stille zu Zion (God, One Praises Thee in the Stillness of Zion)** (1730; BWV 120).

For the centenary celebration of the Augsburg Confession, 26 June 1730, Bach composed this cantata and two months later repeated it as the Ratswahl cantata. Later, in 1733, he borrowed from it for a wedding cantata, BWV 120a, "Herr Gott, Beherrscher aller Dinge" (Lord God, Ruler of All Things), which is incomplete in its music, but complete in its text.

The libretto was probably by Picander, although it could have been by Christian Weiss, Sr., according to Terry.

The beginning order is unusual for Bach: an alto aria comes first, then the chorus.

The cantata is scored for SATB soloists, a four-part chorus and a rather large orchestra of three trumpets, timpani, two oboes d'amore, strings and organ continuo.

1. *Aria—alto.* The oboes d'amore and the strings play a siciliano melody to accompany this long aria; its text is the only Biblical quotation in the cantata, Psalm 65 (1). "Gott, man lobet dich in der Stille zu Zion, und dir bezahlet man Gelübde." (God, one praises Thee in the stillness of Zion, and to Thee one pays vows.)

It is an interesting aria, giving the theme of the cantata—praise of God by the Town Council and the congregation—but it does not mpress the listener as much as he would expect in the first number. Perhaps Bach took the music from one of his earlier instrumental works (since lost) and merely superimposed the text? The coloratura treatment by the soloist of the verbs "lobet" and "bezahlet" helps to brighten the aria somewhat.

2. *Chorus.* This brilliant movement, with trumpets and percussion added to the other instruments, is a mighty song of praise, involving to the maximum both choir and listener in its terrific joy-motif. Listeners would not find it difficult to identify themselves as participants in this magnificent song of praise to God, as the chorus urges them to sing. Bach's jubilant music evokes an image of a crowd of rejoicing people. Bach must have impressed himself, for he adapted this theme for the *Et expecto* section of his *Mass in B Minor.*

Note the many runs on the first word, "Jauchzet" (rejoice): "Jauchzet, ihr erfreuten Stimmen, / Steiget bis zum Himmel 'auf! / Lobet Gott im Heiligtum / Und erhebet seinen Ruhm; / Seine Güte, / Sein erbarmendes Gemüte, / Hört zu keinen Zeiten auf!" (Rejoice, you joyful voices, / Mount up to heaven! / Praise God in His Sanctuary / And exalt His fame; / His goodness, / His pitying feeling, / Stops at no time!)

3. *Recitative—bass.* He addresses the townsfolk of Leipzig, who were proud of their linden trees, in the metaphor, "du geliebte Lindenstadt" (thou beloved linden-town). In his secco narrative, he summons them to thank God for His Fatherly protection and to fulfill their vows to Him. They should also pray that He will inspire and bless their city, their country and their newly chosen Council.

4. *Aria—soprano.* With the strings playing an adagio-cantabile melody, the soprano sings this surprisingly melancholy movement, when we would expect Bach to have written a happier tune at this point. It seems as though Bach was wishing for a more harmonious relationship with the Council, with whom he was quarreling at this time. Possibly the music reflects his pessimism. Did he think that their government could improve, to benefit himself and all the citizens of Leipzig?

The personification in the last two lines of the stanza is based on Psalm 85 (10): "Heil und Segen / Soll und muss zu aller Zeit / Sich auf unsre Obrigkeit / In erwünschter Fülle legen, / Dass sich Recht und Treue müssen / Miteinander freundlich küssen." (Salvation and blessing / Shall and must at all times / Lay themselves on our government / In desired fullness, / So that righteousness and fidelity must / Kiss each other in a friendly way.)

5. *Recitative—tenor.* Accompanied by the strings, the tenor asks the Lord to bless the new regime, so that all evil will be eliminated, and justice may thrive in our houses. Then God's pure seed and His name may be glorified among us.

6. *Chorale.* This is the fourth stanza of Luther's German version of the *Te Deum.* It is sung in straightforward fashion without any decoration in the music. The chorus prays to God to help His servants and to bless His inheritance, so that they may enter into His eternity with His saints.

In my opinion, this work does not seem to meet the same high standard as Bach's previous Ratswechsel cantatas, BWV 71, 119 and 69 (I), which have been discussed. Was this on account of the personal problems he was encountering with the local politicians at this time?

• **Ich habe meine Zuversicht (I Have [Turned] My Confidence)** (1730; BWV 188).

This cantata for the twenty-first Sunday after Trinity was based on Picander's libretto, to which Bach added as a sinfonia prelude the first movement of his *D Minor Clavier Concerto,* rearranged for organ and orchestra. It was the first of a series featuring an obbligato organ; these were all performed at the Nicolai church, because Bach wished to give the organist there, Johann Schneider, a chance to display his skill (cf. Schweitzer II, p. 237). Terry thinks that there is a possibility that Wilhelm Friedemann Bach set part of the music, but does not mention which parts. Certainly not the first two numbers, which are definitely by his father.

Neither the Epistle, Ephesians 6 (10–17), nor the Gospel, John 4 (46–54), is directly quoted in the libretto, which speaks of confidence in God's power to govern our lives. Only the Epistle, verse 10, refers to this theme: "Finally, my brethren, be strong in the Lord, and in the power of his might."

This solo work is for SATB, with the usual four-part chorus for the chorale. The orchestra consists of two oboes, two violins, a viola and obbligato organ.

1. *Sinfonia.* The first movement of a lost violin concerto became the first movement of the *D Minor Clavier Concerto,* BWV 1052, which Bach transposed for organ and orchestra here, and later used again for the Sinfonia to BWV 146. For those who know the clavier version, this organ rendition is a delight. Bach's interest in the organ must have induced him to add this number to Picander's text, even though it has nothing to do with the libretto.

2. *Aria—tenor.* Oboe and strings accompany this sincere and beautiful expression of the tenor's emotion. It is one of Bach's best tenor arias. His trust in God despite worldly difficulties is a genuine confession of faith: "Ich habe meine Zuversicht / Auf den getreuen Gott gericht, / Da ruhet meine Hoffnung feste. / Wenn alles bricht, wenn alles fällt, / Wenn niemand Treu und Glaube hält, / So ist doch Gott der allerbeste." (I have turned my confidence / To my faithful God; / There my hope rests firmly. / When everything breaks, when all falls, / When nobody keeps faith and belief, / So then is God the best of all.)

3. *Recitative—bass.* In his long secco declamation, he states that God means to do well for everyone. Even when He is angry, His anger lasts only briefly, as a passing rain cloud followed by the sunshine of His forgiving blessing. He concludes with a fine arioso, paraphrasing Genesis 32 (26): "Drum lass ich ihn nicht, er segne mich denn." (Therefore I do not leave Him, so that He may bless me then.)

4. *Aria—alto.* With cello and organ obbligato, she sings of God's moving in mysterious ways which influence our lives. Even our grief and pain can at times be in our best interest, leading us to Him. A feeling of Christian resignation to fate pervades her aria: "Unerforschlich ist die Weise, / Wie der Herr die Seinen führt. / Selber unser Keuz und Pein / Muss zu unserm Besten sein / Und zu seines Namens Preise." (Unfathomable is the way, / In which the Lord guides His own. / Even our cross and pain / Must be in our best interest / And for the praise of His Name.)

5. *Recitative—soprano.* A very short recitative with strings and organ contrasts with the previous long one for bass. She describes the swiftly passing power in the world as undependable: who can build on rank and position? Only God remains eternal. She concludes that it is well for all who trust in Him.

6. *Chorale.* This is sung by all voices in plain style. It is the first stanza of Sigismund Weingärtner's hymn beginning: "Auf meinen lieben Gott / Trau' ich in Angst und Not;" (On my dear God / I trust in worry and need;).

The rest of the stanza confirms what has been already expressed concerning God's guidance in our lives. He can rescue us from distress and help us in misfortune, since everything rests in His hands.

• **Ein feste Burg ist unser Gott (A Mighty Fortress Is Our God)** (1730; BWV 80).

For the Reformation Festival on the Two Hundredth Anniversary of the Augsburg Confession, Bach composed this outstanding chorale cantata. He returned to Salomo Franck's libretto, upon which he had set part of the cantata in 1715 for the third Sunday in Lent. This earlier version, BWV 80a, "Alles, was von Gott geboren" (Everyone Born of God) appears never to have been performed by Bach. (See [2] of this cantata.)

Franck's libretto was based on Martin Luther's hymn, concerning the casting out of a devil by Christ in Luke 11 (14–28). Bach retained these six numbers, but added the first and fifth verses of Luther's hymn, and changed Franck's last chorale to the last verse of Luther's hymn.

The soloists are SATB, with a four-part chorus. The orchestra is lavish: three trumpets, timpani, two oboes, two violins, a viola, a cello, a violone (double-bass) and organ continuo. The trumpet and timpani parts are thought to be additions by Wilhelm Friedemann Bach, which he used in one of his later Latin cantatas parodied on this work.

1. *Chorus.* This monumental opening chorus is in fugal motet style: each line of the stanza is sung in canon by the four groups of voices, accompanied and highly embellished by all instruments. Bach composed this long chorale fantasia in the Pachelbel style he had used before. Psalm 46 had inspired Luther to write this hymn, which impressed both Franck and Bach. The hymn became the battle song of the Reformation and is still included today in the Protestant hymnal.

Bach portrays the martial atmosphere of the church militant in this masterpiece of tone-painting: "Ein feste Burg ist unser Gott, / Ein gute Wehr und Waffen; / Er hilft uns frei aus aller Not, / Die uns itzt hat betroffen." (A mighty fortress is our God, / A good defense and weapon; / He helps to free us from all distress, / Which has now befallen us.)

The rest of the stanza refers to the evil enemy, Satan, whose great power and cunning make him unequalled on earth.

2. *Aria — bass, and Chorale — soprano.* This was the first number in Franck's original version. The battle motif of the first chorus is continued (less trumpets and timpani) in a different melody for the aria, while the soprano sings the second stanza of the hymn with decorated vocal effects. Note the florid runs on "(aus)erkoren" in both parts.

In the chorale stanza, the soprano declares that we can do nothing through our own might, unless Christ is our champion, who will lead us to victory over evil. The bass assures us also of the triumph of Christ's followers: "Alles, was von Gott geboren, / Ist zum Siegen auserkoren. / Wer bei Christi Blutpanier / In der Taufe Treu geschworen, / Siegt im Geiste für und für." (Everyone who is born of God, / Is chosen for conquering. / Whoever by Christ's blood-banner / Has sworn his faith in his baptism, / Conquers in his spirit forever.)

3. *Recitative — bass.* This is a very picturesque invocation to the listener that he consider himself God's child, whom Christ has enlisted in His war against Satan's army, represented by the world and its sin. He must keep his heart and soul free of Satan, painfully repent of his guilt, and then Christ's Spirit will unite with his.

4. *Aria — soprano.* Only the cello is the continuo here. She prays to ask the Lord to enter her heart and drive out Satan's influence. She longs for the renewal of Christ's image within her.

5. *Chorale.* This third stanza of Luther's hymn brings us back to the battle scenario. It is sung by all voices in unison and played by all instruments. The majesty of the music and the thought expressed make it the equal of the opening chorus: "Und wenn die Welt voll Teufel wär' / Und wollten uns verschlingen, /

So fürchten wir uns nicht so sehr, / Es soll uns doch gelingen. / Der Fürst dieser Welt, / Wie saur er sich stellt, / Tut er uns doch nichts, / Das macht, er ist gericht', / Ein Wörtlein kann ihn fällen." (And if the world were full of devils / And they wanted to devour us, / Then we are not so very much afraid, / We shall after all succeed. / The Prince of this world, / However bitter he appears, / Does nothing to us after all; / That shows he is condemned, / A little word can fell him.)

6. *Recitative—tenor.* He exhorts the listener to stand by Christ's blood-stained standard, as one would rally around a military leader. Then he must joyfully march to the war against sin. The beaten enemy will soon retreat, if he keeps God's word in his heart. The Savior will always be his shield in battle.

7. *Duet—alto, tenor.* The oboe da caccia and strings highlight their duet in canon. The textual words and phrases would indicate to Bach the joy-motif which he set for this number. Only at the end does this happiness change to a more sinister tone at the thought of inevitable death, which comes to all of us: "Wie selig sind doch die, die Gott im Munde tragen, / Doch sel'ger ist das Herz, das ihn im Glauben trägt! / Es bleibet unbesiegt und kann die Feinde schlagen / Und wird zuletzt gekrönt, wenn es den Tod erlegt." (How blessed are they, who carry God in their mouths; / Yet more blessed is the heart, which carries Him in belief! / It remains unconquered and can strike enemies / And will at last be crowned, when it overcomes death.)

8. *Chorale.* This fourth and last verse of Luther's chorale leaves the listener with the impression that all stanzas have been treated (as indeed they were). God's word will remain with us after everything else is gone; we will still have His Kingdom.

Perhaps the congregation joined in the singing of this number, since they knew Luther's hymn so well.

• **Was soll ich aus dir machen, Ephraim? (What Am I to Do with Thee, Ephraim?)** (c. 1730; BWV 89).

It was Christian Weiss, Sr., or someone unknown, who provided Bach with the libretto for this solo cantata on the twenty-second Sunday after Trinity. The parable of the unforgiving servant is taken from the Gospel for the day, Matthew 18 (23–35). This unworthy man's thoughts are expressed in all numbers except the opening bass aria in which God speaks. The theme of the cantata is God's wrath against sinners and their hope of His forgiveness, if they forgive their neighbors.

The soli are SAB, with a four-part choir for the final chorale. The orchestra includes a horn, two oboes, two violins and continuo.

We should note here that many of Bach's solo cantatas were composed because he did not have a suitable boy's voice for a part—in this case, a tenor.

1. *Aria—bass.* His text is taken from Hosea 11 (8), which shows God's anger against Ephraim and Israel on account of their sinful way of life. The bass represents God in dramatic style as he sings His denunciation. He does not wish to destroy them as He did Adama and Zeboim (two cities obliterated with Sodom and Gomorrah). His displeasure is reflected in the menacing orchestral mood-painting of the first theme. He then appears to be an angry Father, wondering how to punish His delinquent children, in the second theme. The third theme shows His decision to pardon them through His mercy: "Was soll ich aus dir machen, Ephraim? / Soll ich dich schützen, Israel? / Soll ich nicht billig ein Adama aus dir machen, / Und dich wie Zeboim zurichten? / Aber mein Herz ist andern Sinnes; / Meine Barmherzigkeit ist zu brünstig." (What am I to do with thee, Ephraim? / Am I to protect thee, Israel? / Shall I not just make an Adama of thee / And judge thee like Zeboim? / But my heart is of another mind; / My compassion is too ardent.)

2. *Recitative—alto.* Her secco narra-

tion speaks of God's vengeance on those who mock His name or those who oppress their neighbors for their debts.

3. *Aria—alto.* With organ continuo only, her aria seems to reflect the Old Testament prophets' gloomy predictions of impending doom. Bach really takes the merciless creditor to task in this number: "Ein unbarmherziges Gerichte / Wird über dich gewiss ergehen. / Die Rache fängt bei denen an, / Die nicht Barmherzigkeit getan, / Und machet sie wie Sodom ganz zunichts." (A pitiless judgment / Will certainly fall on you. / Vengeance begins with those, / Who have not shown mercy, / And quite destroys them as Sodom.)

4. *Recitative—soprano.* With organ continuo, in secco, she states that she has removed anger, quarreling and dissension from her heart and is ready to forgive her neighbor. Yet she feels still indebted to God for her sins and hopes that her contrite heart will give her absolution by her faith in Christ.

At this point the main theme turns from fear to hope.

5. *Aria—soprano.* With obbligato oboe and continuo, she sings of her faith in Christ's Blood, which will cover her sins and guilt. The joy-motif is well expressed by the combination of voice and instrumental music in canon: "Gerechter Gott, ach, rechnest du? /So werde ich zum Heil der Seelen / Die Tropfen Blut von Jesu zählen. / Ach! rechne mir die Summe zu! / Ja, weil sie niemand kann ergründen, / Bedeckt sie meine Schuld und Sünden." (Righteous God, ah, dost Thou reckon? / Then will I for the salvation of souls / Count the drops of blood from Jesus. / Ah! count up for me the total sum! / Yes, because nobody can calculate it, / It covers my guilt and sins.)

6. *Chorale.* This is verse 7 of Johann Heermann's hymn, "Wo soll ich fliehen hin?" (Whither Shall I Flee?). It is performed tutti, in simple style, expressing the thought that Christ will support me, so that I may overcome "Tod, Teufel, Höll' und Sünde" (death, devil, hell and sin).

With this optimistic thought that Christ will guide us through life, we find a happy conclusion to a despondent beginning.

• **Falsche Welt, dir trau' ich nicht (False World, I Trust You Not)** (c. 1730; BWV 52).

The opening movement of the *First Brandenburg Concerto in E Major,* BWV 1046, was used as the sinfonia prelude to this cantata for the twenty-third Sunday after Trinity. Why Bach chose this Cöthen composition to precede the vocal numbers can only be attributed to his thinking that the cantata was too short, and therefore he took a part of an existing instrumental work to supplement it.

The name of the librettist is not known. It is a solo cantata for soprano, with SATB for the final chorale.

There is no direct connection between the libretto and the Gospel for the day, Matthew 22 (15–22), unless it be the intrigue of the Pharisees as they seek to ensnare Jesus, which shows the falseness of the world.

The orchestra consists of two horns, three oboes, a bassoon, two violins, a viola, organ and continuo: a sumptuous emsemble for a solo cantata.

1. *Sinfonia.* This tutti instrumental introduction has no bearing on the vocal numbers which follow. Its brilliant allegro joy-motif seems strangely at odds with the tone of the following recitative.

2. *Recitative.* "Falsche Welt, dir trau' ich nicht!" (False world, I trust you not). She denounces the world as false and untrustworthy. It is full of scorpions and snakes among which she must live. The bassoon and organ accompaniment emphasizes her despondency over such hypocrisy and falsehood. Her text contains an Old Testament reference to Joab's murder of Abner in 2 Samuel 3 (27) as a Biblical example of treachery.

3. *Aria.* Happy relief from her sadness comes now as she consoles herself in the thought that God is her friend. Strings are added to the bassoon and organ to

brighten the picture: "Immerhin, immerhin, / Wenn ich gleich verstossen bin! / Ist die falsche Welt men Feind, / O so bleibt Gott mein Freund, / Der es redlich mit mir meint." (Always, always, / Whenever I am rejected! / [If] the false world is my enemy, / O then God remains my friend, / Who means to be honest with me.)

4. *Recitative (secco).* She states that God is faithful and repeats it three times at the end. He will not leave her in the world's madness and its snares without helping her. She will trust herself completely to Him.

5. With the charming of three oboes, the bassoon and organ continuo, she sings of her confidence in God. The middle section is almost a florid love song: "Ich halt' es mit dem lieben Gott, / Die Welt mag nur alleine bleiben. / Gott mit mir, und ich mit Gott, / Also kann ich selber Spott / Mit den falschen Zungen treiben." (I hold with my dear God; / The world may just stay alone. / God with me, and I with God, / So I myself can make fun / Of the false tongues.)

This aria seems to be the best part of the cantata for music and vocal emotion.

6. *Chorale.* This is the first stanza of Adam Reusner's hymn of the same title. "In dich hab' ich gehoffet, Herr, / Hilf, dass ich nicht zuschanden werd', / Noch ewiglich zu Spotte! / Das bitt' ich dich, / Erhalte mich / In deiner Treu', Herr Gott!" (In Thee have I hoped, Lord. / Help, that I do not come to shame, / Nor to eternal mockery! / For that I pray Thee, / Keep me in Thy faith, Lord God!) It sounds very impressive with all voices and instruments. I feel that this is one of Bach's better concluding chorales.

• **Schwingt freudig euch empor (Raise Yourselves Up Joyfully)** (1731; BWV 36).

The history of this cantata for the first Sunday in Advent is complex. Five versions exist, of which three are secular. Picander wrote the libretto for the original one, celebrating the birthday of the Princess of Anhalt-Cöthen, 30 November 1726, but the music to this is lost. In the subsequent amendments, Bach replaced Picander's recitatives by chorales.

Much has been written about Bach's transfer of secular music to religious music, but for him, all his music was to glorify God, whether in church or court. As we have seen, he sometimes had difficulties in adapting a secular text to a sacred one, yet the phenomenon of his composition is that the "Affekt" of his music suits the libretto, even if he was bored by the text he had to set or found it uninspiring.

Furthermore, there are few of Bach's cantatas which do not reflect the Gospel for the Sunday, either directly or indirectly. In this case, the jubilation at Christ's entry into Jerusalem, Matthew 21 (1–9), is indirectly referred to in all numbers, even though this Scripture is out of season as it was for BWV 61.

The soli are SATB with a four-part choir. The instruments are two oboes d'amore, a transverse flute, two violins, a viola, organ and continuo.

Part I

1. *Chorus.* Bach's enthusiasm over the coming of Christ is unrestrained in the all-pervading joy-motif of this opening chorus. Anyone who thinks that Bach's music is too often pessimistic should listen to this chorus (and indeed the rest of this cantata) to be convinced to the contrary.

We hear the same tumult-motif of the crowd in the Passions, but their soaring song of happiness contrasts with the mob's frenzy before the Crucifixion. The imagery of their jubilation, as it floats upwards from Zion (= Leipzig) to heaven, is vividly painted by Bach's brilliant melody. Equally effective is the hush in the second theme depicting the approach of the Lord, thus making a fine contrast with the first motif.

"Schwingt freudig euch empor zu den erhabnen Sternen, / Ihr Zungen, die ihr itzt in Zion fröhlich seid. / Doch haltet ein, der Schall darf sich nicht weit entfernen, / Es naht sich selbst zu euch der Herr der Herrlichkeit." (Raise yourselves up joyfully to the lofty stars, / You tongues, who are now happy in Zion. / Yet pause, the sound may not go far away; / The Lord of glory is approaching you Himself.)

2. *Chorale (Duet—soprano, alto).* As for the opening choruses in the other two cantatas for the first Sunday in Advent, BWV 61 and BWV 62, this chorale is the first verse of Luther's Christmas hymn, "Nun komm, der Heiden Heiland" (Now Come, Savior of the Heathens). The two voices present a moving scene of the wonder shown at Christ's birth. The mystical fervor in their voices is enhanced by the oboes d'amore and the organ continuo.

3. *Aria—tenor.* His text contains two remarkable figures of speech. The first is a personification of love, which Bach illustrates by a step-motif in the melody; the second is a metaphor of the soul as the bride, and Christ as the bridegroom. This latter figure becomes a simile in the last line, which describes the heart following Jesus just as a bride follows the bridegroom: "Die Liebe zieht mit sanften Schritten / Ihr Treugeliebtes allgemach. / Gleich wie es eine Braut entzücket, / Wenn sie den Bräutigam erblicket, / So folgt ein Herz auch Jesu nach." (Love draws with gentle steps / Her true love gradually to her. / Just as a bride is delighted, / When she perceives the bridegroom, / So also does a heart follow after Jesus.)

4. *Chorale.* This sixth verse of Philipp Nicolai's hymn, "Wie schön leuchtet der Morgenstern" (How Beautifully Shines the Morning Star), for all voices and orchestra, continues the thought of Christ being the bridegroom, whose coming they are celebrating in this song of joy. Its straightforward four-part delivery makes a suitable conclusion to Part I.

Part II

5. *Aria—bass.* He welcomes the Savior's birth and hopes that He will enter his heart. There is a spontaneous note of happiness in his singing, aided by the strings and the organ accompaniment.

6. *Chorale—tenor.* This is stanza six of Luther's hymn (as in 2). The oboes d'amore replace the strings in this number. The text praises Christ for His coming in the flesh to preserve our weak flesh.

7. *Aria—soprano.* The solo violin in support of her voice conjures up a light, floating atmosphere to illustrate her song of reverence for God: "Auch mit gedämpften, schwachen Stimmen / Wird Gottes Majestät verehrt. / Denn schallet nur der Geist dabei, / So ist ihm solches ein Geschrei, / Das er im Himmel selber hört." (Also with subdued, weak voices / Is God's Majesty honored. / For if the spirit only resounds in it, / Then is there to Him such a cry, / Which He Himself hears in heaven.)

The boy soprano in my recording made excellent runs on "schallet" (spirit), but in my opinion, the tempo of the whole aria seems to drag.

8. *Chorale.* This is the eighth and last stanza of Luther's hymn, having the same voices and instruments as in movement four. It is a very short praise of the Trinity and is plainly sung.

• **Ich habe genug (I Have Enough)** (c. 1731; BWV 82).

This cantata was composed for solo bass on the Feast of the Purification, 2 February 1727. Subsequently, it was performed as a solo soprano work in 1731 and 1735. Its final finished form returned as a bass solo about 1741. It is the only work which Bach designated as a "cantata" in all his church music. The librettist is unknown.

The first recitative and its following aria occur in Anna Magdalena's *Notenbüchlein* of 1725, which testifies to its use as chamber music in the Bach family. Yet it is strange that these numbers were transferred from the cantata to the clavier notebook some time after the *Notenbüchlein* was begun, not vice versa.

The Gospel for this Sunday is from Luke 2 (22–32)—the account of Simeon's recognition of Jesus in the Temple.

Simeon's thoughts as he approaches death represent those of all believers: death is a release from the misery of this world into a peaceful new life.

The orchestra for this bass version has an oboe, two violins, a viola, organ and continuo.

1. *Aria.* A beautiful string melody serves as prelude to this aria. The longing for death is depicted in the languorous rhythm of the oboe and the strings, which paint the sentimental scene as Simeon desires to join his Lord: "Ich habe genug, / Ich habe den Heiland, das Hoffen der Frommen, / Auf meine begierigen Arme genommen; / Ich habe genug! / Ich hab' ihn erblickt, / Mein Glaube hat Jesum ans Herze gedrückt; / Nun wünsch' ich noch heute mit Freuden / Von hinnen zu scheiden." (I have enough, / I have taken the Savior, the hope of the pious, / Into my eager arms; / I have enough! / I have seen Him; / My faith has pressed Jesus to my heart; / Now I wish still to die today with joy.)

The aria contains a feeling of spiritual homesickness, but the joy-motif is also mixed into it.

2. *Recitative—bass.* With organ and continuo accompaniment, he says that his only consolation will be to follow after Simeon and then be reunited with Christ. He wishes that the Lord would release him from the chains of his body, so that he may say to the world as he leaves it, "I have enough."

3. *Aria.* This is the most exquisite slumber song that Bach ever wrote in a single sacred cantata. Sleep in death is realistically described in the first two lines, gradually expanding into the calm of final peace after the misery suffered in this world. The singer's tranquil confidence is reflected in the beautiful string accompaniment: "Schlummert ein, ihr matten Augen, / Fallet sanft und selig zu! / Welt, ich bleibe nicht mehr hier, / Hab' ich doch kein Teil an dir, / Das der Seele könnte taugen. / Hier muss ich das Elend bauen, / Aber dort, dort werd' ich schauen / Süssen Friede, stille Ruh'." (Fall asleep, you weary eyes, / Close softly and blissfully! / World, I remain no more here; / I have no part in you, / Which could serve my soul. / Here I must build misery, / But there, there will I look at / Sweet peace, quiet rest.)

The tempo of the music suggests the motif of exhaustion.

4. *Recitative.* We hear a shorter number than the first recitative. He asks God when his hour of death will be, so that he can know when he can join Him. He has said his farewell to the world and awaits his burial in the sand of the cool earth, whence he will meet the Lord.

Both recitatives in this cantata were exceptionally well composed.

5. *Aria.* The joy-motif illustrates the aftermath of death, once we have left the world. The radiant vocal expression convinces the listener that death is not quite so formidable, since it means an end of suffering: "Ich freue mich auf meinen Tod, / Ach, hätt' er sich schon eingefunden. / Da entkomm' ich aller Not, / Die mich noch auf der Welt gebunden." (I rejoice at my death; / Ah, had it already taken place! / Then I escape from all suffering, / Which has still tied me to the world.) Bach's acceptance of this philosophy can be seen in the joyous tutti accompaniment which he writes for the solo bass in this number.

There is no final chorale, but this aria in itself is a marvelous ending to the cantata.

• **Ich bin vergnügt mit meinem Glücke (I Am Contented with My Good Luck)** (1731 or 1732; BWV 84).

This solo cantata for soprano, intended for Septuagesima Sunday, is definitely dated 1731 by Schweitzer, while Terry gives the above alternative dates and Neumann says about 1731. Spitta thinks that it was composed for Anna Magdalena as a part of the private religious music in the Bach household. However, since the Gospel, Matthew 20 (1–16), the parable of the laborers in the vineyard, was indicated to be read and is indirectly referred to in the libretto (contentment with one's portion), we can assume that this cantata was also performed in church.

Picander composed a poem in 1727 for the original text, which Bach revised for his setting.

The soprano plays the role of one of the laborers or that of any Christian, who is satisfied with the lot given her by God, unlike the workers in the Biblical account. There is a four-part chorale at the end.

The orchestra is light: an oboe, two violins, a viola and continuo.

1. *Aria.* The vocalist expresses her joy over the blessing that she has received from God in a fine motif of felicity. Pure contentment breathes throughout her singing: "Ich bin vergnügt mit meinem Glücke, / Das mir der liebe Gott beschert. / Soll ich nicht reiche Fülle haben, / So dank' ich ihm für kleine Gaben / Und bin nicht derselben wert." (I am contented with my good luck, / Which dear God gives to me. / If I shall not have rich fullness, / Then I thank Him for small gifts / And am not even worthy of the same.)

2. *Recitative.* In secco, she maintains that God owes her nothing; when He gives her something, it is because He loves her. What she does is only her duty and she does not expect to earn anything by that. Yet many people impatiently expect more from God than they receive. What more should they expect than to be fed, clothed, and have the promise of entry into His glory?

Her little sermon ends with the thought that it is enough for her that she does not have to go to bed hungry; this idea continues into her next aria.

3. *Aria.* Supported by the oboe and strings, the joy-motif of her aria reveals her happy philosophy, in which the true Christian should perceive the essence of his own belief: "Ich esse mit Freuden mein weniges Brot / Und gönne dem Nächsten von Herzen das Seine, / Ein ruhig Gewissen, ein fröhlicher Geist, / Ein dankbares Herze, das lobet und preist, / Vermehret den Segen, verzuckert die Not." (I joyfully eat my scanty bread / And sincerely do not begrudge my neighbor his. / A quiet conscience, a happy spirit, / A thankful heart, which lauds and praises, / Increases the blessing, sweetens the distress.) The musical quality of this number is on the same high level as the first aria.

4. *Recitative.* The didactic theme continues from the preceding recitative and aria, its first two lines referring to them: "Im Schweisse meines Angesichts / Will ich indes Brot geniessen." (In the sweat of my face / I will meanwhile enjoy my bread.)

The strings lend a solemn tone to this number. Her contentment is extended to the contemplation of her death, with which she will be also satisfied, if God rewards her with Paradise thereafter.

5. *Chorale.* This twelfth stanza of Emilie Juliane von Schwarzburg-Rudolstadt's funeral hymn, "Wer weiss, wie nahe mir mein Ende" (Who Knows, How Near to Me Is My End), expresses the contentment with God's gifts, which she has sung in each number. The four-part choir and all instruments emphasize this theme, beginning: "Ich leb' indes in dir vergnüget / Und sterb' ohn' alle Kümmernis, / Mir g'nüget, wie es mein Gott füget." (I live meanwhile content in Thee / And die without all care. / It is sufficient for me, how my God ordains.)

• **Erfreut euch, ihr Herzen (Rejoice, You Hearts)** (1731; BWV 66).

"Der Himmel dacht auf Anhalts Ruhm und Glück" (Heaven Thinks of Anhalt's Fame and Fortune) BWV 66a, was the title of the original secular cantata, composed by Bach in 1718 to celebrate the birthday of Prince Leopold of Anhalt-Cöthen. Bach borrowed from this work for BWV 66, a cantata for Easter Monday, which was first performed as a sacred cantata in 1724. The later version is the one we hear recorded today. It is interesting because two of its numbers are set in dialogue form. The name of the librettist is unknown. Terry suggests Bach.

The Gospel is Luke 24 (13–35)—Christ appears to His disciples at Emmaus—but this is only indirectly referred to in the main theme of rejoicing over the Resurrection, proper to the Easter season.

The vocalists are ATB, with a four-part chorus. The orchestra contains a trumpet, two oboes, two violins, a viola, a bassoon and continuo.

1. *Chorus.* This begins with a brilliant tutti prelude for the orchestra, followed by the chorus, singing their happiness over the Resurrection, to summon the congregation to do likewise: "Erfreut euch, ihr Herzen, / Entweichet, ihr Schmerzen, / Es lebet der Heiland und herrschet in euch!" (Rejoice, you hearts, / Vanish, you pains; / The Savior lives and rules in you!)

The tempo then changes to a slower rhythm in a duet for the altos and the basses, quickening only at the last line with a tutti return to the joy-motif: "Ihr könnet verjagen / Das Trauern, das Fürchten, das ängstliche Zagen, / Der Heiland erquicket sein geistliches Reich." (You can chase away / The mourning, the fear, the anxious trembling; / The Savior revives His spiritual Kingdom.)

The da capo of the first section, together with the orchestral ritornelli, make this a very long choral number.

2. *Recitative—bass.* Accompanied by strings and continuo, he states that our trouble has ceased with Christ's victory over the grave. Now that Christ lives, we believers have nothing to fear from necessity or death.

3. *Aria—bass.* All instruments except the trumpet support the bass as he exhorts us to praise God. The allegro melody has a dance-rhythm, which relates it to an aria in the earlier secular version.

Especially noteworthy are the runs on "ewig" and "Frieden." The orchestral ritornelli and the da capo seem to prolong the aria: "Lasset dem Höchsten ein Danklied erschallen / Für sein Erbarmen und ewige Treu. / Jesus erscheinet, uns Frieden zu geben, / Jesus beruft uns, mit ihm zu leben, / Täglich wird seine Barmherzigkeit neu." (Let a song of thanks resound to the Highest / For His pity and eternal fidelity. / Jesus appears, to give us peace, / Jesus calls us, to live with Him; / Daily His mercy becomes new.)

The music seems to contain a certain note of restraint, unusual in a Bach allegro pertaining to Easter.

4. *Recitative and Arioso (Dialogue)—alto, tenor.* An indirect allusion to the two disciples who met Jesus on the way to Emmaus is dramatized in this dialogue between Hope (tenor) and Fear (alto), which are personified.

Hope begins the recitative, commenting on his conversation with the Lord, whose words he quotes in arioso halfway through the number: "Mein Grab und Sterben bringt euch Leben, / Mein Auferstehen ist euer Trost." (My grave and death bring you life, / My Resurrection is your comfort.) Then he resumes his narrative, saying that he will continue to sing praise to Christ, thanking him for His victory over death.

The next section is a duet in canon, with very effective contrast:

HOFFNUNG (HOPE): "Mein Auge sieht den Heiland auferweckt." (My eye sees the Savior awakened.)

FURCHT (FEAR): "Kein Auge sieht den Heiland auferweckt." (No eye sees the Savior awakened.)

HOFFNUNG: "Es hält ihn nicht der Tod in Banden." (Death does not hold him in bonds.)

FURCHT: "Es hält ihn noch der Tod in Banden." (Death still holds him in bonds.)

Hereafter the recitative is resumed in dialogue form. Fear doubts that the grave will give up its dead, whereas Hope states that it cannot hold God. Fear has the last long section of recitative; she says that she partly believes in the Resurrection, but needs God's help to fully confirm her belief.

5. *Duet—alto, tenor.* With solo violin accompaniment, they begin by singing in canon almost the same text, but then change to unison for the last part:

FURCHT (FEAR): "Ich fürchte zwar des Grabes Finsternissen." (I certainly feared the grave's darkness.)

HOFFNUNG (HOPE): "Ich fürchte nicht des Grabes Finsternissen." (I did not fear the grave's darkness.)

FURCHT: "Und klagete mein Heil sei nun entrissen." (And lamented that my Savior be now torn away.)

HOFFNUNG: "Und hoffete mein Heil sei nicht entrissen." (And hoped that my Savior not be torn away.)

BEIDE (BOTH): Nun ist mein Herze voller Trost, / Und wenn sich auch ein Feind erbost, / Will ich in Gott zu siegen wissen." (Now is my heart full of comfort, / And even if an enemy becomes angry, / I will in God know how to conquer.)

6. *Chorale.* This is the third stanza of the medieval hymn for Easter "Christ ist erstanden" (Christ Is Risen). All voices sing, but no instrumentation is stated. Using the full orchestra, the short verse is very well done, especially the "Alleluja!" repeated three times at the beginning.

• **Am Abend aber desselbigen Sabbaths (On the Evening of That Same Sabbath)** (1731; BWV 42).

For the first Sunday after Easter, Bach composed this masterpiece for solo voices. The librettist is unknown, but Terry suggests Christian Weiss, Sr., and Neumann suggests Bach.

The Gospel is John 20 (19–31)—Jesus reappears to His disciples including doubting Thomas—from which the 19th verse is directly taken for the first recitative. All the other numbers are free lyrical interpretations derived from this beginning.

The soli are SATB, with a four-part chorus. The instruments are two oboes, a bassoon, two violins, a viola, organ and continuo.

1. *Sinfonia.* This is likely a movement from a previously composed instrumental concerto, which has been lost. The concerto is made up of the woodwinds as the concertino and the unison strings as the ripieno. Its tripartite form is reminiscent of a da capo aria. The soothing calm of the melody seems to paint the quiet in the countryside at twilight (cf. the arioso in the *St. Matthew Passion*): "Am Abend, da es kühle ward" (In the evening, when it became cool). This is one of Bach's most beautiful instrumental numbers.

2. *Recitative—tenor.* He narrates the miraculous event in John 20 (19), when Christ stood among His disciples in the house: "Am Abend aber desselbigen Sabbats, da die Jünger versammlet und die Türen verschlossen waren aus Furcht vor den Juden, kam Jesus und trat mitten ein." (On the evening of the same Sabbath, however, when the disciples were gathered and the doors closed out of fear of the Jews, Jesus came and stepped into their midst.)

3. *Aria—alto.* Her text begins with Matthew 18 (20), which has nothing to do with the Gospel for the day, yet continues the idea of Jesus' return to His believers. This aria is long and slow-moving despite the full orchestral accompaniment: "Wo zwei und drei versammelt sind / In Jesu teurem Namen, / Da stellt sich Jesus mitten ein / Und spricht dazu das Amen. / Denn was aus Lieb' und Not geschieht, / Das bricht des Höchsten Ordnung nicht." (Where two and three are gathered / In Jesus' dear Name, / There Jesus puts Himself in their midst / And speaks thereto the Amen. / For what happens out of love and need, / That does not break the Highest's decree.)

These last two lines seem to be irrelevant to the first part of the aria; they seem to belong to an aria in another work. Did Bach not notice this inconsistency?

4. *Duet—soprano, tenor.* Their text is stanza one of J.M. Altenburg's chorale, "Verzage nicht, O Häuflein klein" (Despair Not, O Little Flock), but takes its tune from another anonymous hymn, "Kommt her zu mir, spricht Gottes Sohn" (Come Here to Me, Says God's Son). Their canon singing gives a message of encouragement to the faithful not to despair against the enemy, as their trial will not last long.

5. *Recitative—bass.* He mentions the example of Jesus, who entered the house in which the disciples were cowering in

the shadows for fear of the Jews. The Lord allayed their fears, thus showing Himself to be the protector of His church. Therefore, let their enemies rage.

6. *Aria—bass.* Persecution is the theme portrayed in the repetition and the runs on "Verfolgung" (persecution) in the second line of the text. This contrasts with the joy-motif in the remaining lines. The calm confidence of the bass voice also contrasts with the lively, restless rhythm of the music: "Jesus ist ein Schild der Seinen, / Wenn sie die Verfolgung trifft. / Ihnen muss die Sonne scheinen / Mit der goldnen Überschrift: / Jesus ist ein Schild der Seinen, / Wenn sie die Verfolgung trifft." (Jesus is a shield to His own, / When persecution befalls them. / On them the sun must shine / With the golden superscription: / Jesus is a shield to His own, / When persecution befalls them.)

7. *Chorale.* This four-part chorale takes its first verse from stanza one of Luther's "Verleih' uns Frieden gnädiglich" (Grant Us Peace Graciously), and its second verse is a prose prayer that the princes and the government will grant us peace and good management, so that our lives may be blessed and honorable.

• **Derr Herr ist mein getreuer Hirt (The Lord Is My Faithful Shepherd)** (1731; BWV 112).

This chorale cantata for the second Sunday after Easter has all its numbers based on Wolfgang Meusel's paraphrase of the twenty-third Psalm. This fits very well into the Gospel for the day, John 10 (11–16) and the Epistle, 1 Peter 2 (21–25), where Jesus is the good shepherd. The listener should compare this libretto with the Biblical text of the twenty-third Psalm to see how closely they resemble each other.

Bach recaptures the pastoral atmosphere of the Old Testament in the astounding music he sets for this beautiful cantata.

The soli are SATB with a four-part chorus. The orchestra has two horns, two oboes d'amore, two violins, a viola and continuo.

1. *Chorus.* The melody of N. Decius's "Allein Gott in der Höh' sei Ehr'" (Only to God on High Be Honor) is used for this opening number, beginning with a short instrumental chorale fantasia, which is continued as the choir sings. There is the suggestion of a shepherd's pipe in the repeated horn flourishes within the colorful hymn-tune, which evokes a picture of the good shepherd leading His sheep into the pasture. The personification of the flock in its peaceful surroundings comes out very well in both the text and in Bach's music: "Der Herr ist mein getreuer Hirt, / Hält mich in seiner Hute, / Darum mir gar nichts mangeln wird / Irgend an einem Gute. / Er weidet mich ohn' Unterlass, / Darauf wächst das wohlschmeckend Gras / Seines heilsamen Wortes." (The Lord is my faithful shepherd, / Who holds me in His care; / Therefore nothing at all will be lacking to me / Of any kind of good thing. / He gives me pasture incessantly, / On where grows the well-tasting grass / Of His holy word.)

2. *Aria—alto.* The oboe d'amore obbligato plays in semiquavers to illustrate Bach's interpretation of running water, as she sings the first four lines of her text. The imagery of the refreshing water in the pasture continues the pastoral coloring; for us, it symbolizes the Holy Spirit: "Zum reinen Wasser er mich weist, / Das mich erquicken tue. / Das ist sein fronheiliger Geist, / Der macht mich wohlgemute. / Er führet mich auf rechter Strass' / Seiner Geboten ohn' Ablass / Von wegen seines Namens willen." (To the pure water He directs me, / That gives me refreshment. / That is His Holy Spirit, / Which makes me joyful. / He leads me on the right road / Of His commandments without ceasing / On account of His Name's sake.)

3. *Recitative—bass.* His declamation, accompanied by strings only, seems to be more arioso than recitative. We can imagine the scene as he wanders through

a gloomy, foreboding valley, which is painted by the adagio melody. Yet he will fear no misfortune, because the good shepherd will protect him from the persecution, sorrow and malice he finds in the world.

4. *Duet—soprano, tenor.* What a joyous theme in the strings after the preceding number! The soloists sing each line in turn with some overlapping; their ornate singing in the joy-motif makes this duet an exceptionally charming one: "Du bereitest vor mir einen Tisch / Vor meinen Feinden allenthalben, / Machest mein Herze unverzagt und frisch, / Mein Haupt tust du mir salben / Mit deinem Geist, der Freuden Öl, / Und schenkest voll ein meiner Seel' / Deiner geistlichen Freuden." (Thou preparest before me a table / In front of my enemies everywhere. / Thou makest my heart undismayed and fresh, / Thou dost anoint my head / With Thy Spirit, the oil of joy, / And pourest out fully to my soul / Of Thy spiritual happiness.)

5. *Chorale.* The same hymn melody, with all instruments and four-part choir, recurs as in the opening chorus: "Gutes und die Barmherzigkeit / Folgen mir nach im Leben, / Und ich werd' bleiben allezeit / Im Haus des Herren eben, / Auf Erd' in christlicher Gemein / Und nach dem Tod da werd' ich sein / Bei Christo, meinem Herren." (Goodness and mercy / Follow me in life, / And I will always remain, / Just in the house of the Lord, / On earth in the Christian community, / And after death there shall I be / With Christ, my Lord.)

• **Ich liebe den Höchsten von ganzem Gemüte (I Love the Highest with All My Might)** (1731; BWV 174).

The date of this Whit Monday solo cantata is 5 June 1729 according to the manuscript score, not 1731 as Terry gives it. Since Picander's libretto had only four numbers, Bach must have felt the need to enlarge it by adding a sinfonia as a prelude. He chose the first movement of the *Third Brandenburg Concerto,* composed while he was in Cöthen, and rescored it for the instruments listed below, which are more than the original strings.

The Gospel is John 3 (16–21)—God's love for the world—which Picander turns to a Christian's love for God.

The soli are ATB, and the final chorale has the usual four-part chorus.

The orchestra is large, as required for the sinfonia: two corni da caccia, two oboes, one tenor oboe (taille), three violins, three violas, three celli, one bassoon, one violone (double-bass) and continuo.

1. *Sinfonia.* This is a suitably happy overture to a Whitsuntide festival work, but it has no bearing on the libretto which follows. However, the number is very pleasant to hear in its new format. This shows that Bach's self-borrowings were sometimes changed for his later adaptations.

2. *Aria—alto.* The restful pace of this aria, accompanied by two oboes, contrasts with the grandiose bustle of the sinfonia. The tune is like a pastoral melody, reminding the listener of the alto aria in BWV 112 with its tranquil peace: "Ich liebe den Höchsten von ganzem Gemüte, / Er hat mich auch am höchsten lieb. / Gott allein / Soll der Schatz der Seele sein, / Da hab' ich die ewige Quelle der Gute." (I love the Highest with all my mind, / He loves me also most highly. / God alone / Shall be the treasure of my soul, / There I have the eternal source of goodness.)

3. *Recitative—tenor.* With strings and continuo, he describes how God gave His Son as a ransom for sinners. He then quotes the first line of the Gospel reading, John 3 (16), as proof of His love: "Also hat Gott die Welt geliebt!" (So God loved the world!) He asks his heart to notice this fact: before God's mighty standard, even the gates of hell tremble.

4. *Aria—bass.* Unison violins and violas lend support to the bass, whose song contains a joyful marching rhythm, symbolic of the firmness of faith expressed by the text: "Greifet zu! / Fasst das Heil, ihr Glaubenshände! / Jesus gibt sein Himmelreich / Und verlangt

nur das von euch: / Glaubt getreu bis an das Ende! (Grip fast! / Seize salvation, ye hands of faith! / Jesus gives His heavenly Kingdom / And demands only this of you: / Believe faithfully up to the end!)

This aria is the most remarkable vocal number in the cantata.

5. *Chorale.* All voices and instruments except the horns perform this first stanza of Martin Schalling's hymn (1571), "Herzlich lieb hab' ich dich, O Herr" (Heartily Do I Love Thee, O Lord). This verse praises God for the salvation He has given us through His Son, and asks that His help will continue to keep us from shame.

This is not an exceptional cantata in its vocal numbers, but the music is interesting, as we have seen.

• **Es ist das Heil uns kommen her (Salvation Has Come to Us Here)** (1731; BWV 9).

The unknown librettist for this chorale cantata on the sixth Sunday after Trinity ignored both the Epistle and the Gospel lessons, basing his libretto on Paul Speratus's hymn with the above title. He used the chorale for the first and the last verses and freely paraphrased the intervening stanzas.

Bach could hardly find the topic—the Lutheran doctrine of justification by faith rather than by works—sufficiently stimulating to fire his imagination; consequently, this cantata is not up to his usual high musical achievement. It is more a sermon on faith than a lyrical exposition of the value of faith.

The soloists are SATB, with a four-part chorus. The orchestra consists of a transverse flute, an oboe d'amore, two violins, a viola and continuo.

1. *Chorale fantasia.* This is the best movement in the cantata. The firm faith of the true Christian believer is depicted in the choral singing with its majestic instrumental accompaniment: "Es ist das Heil uns kommen her / Von Gnad' und lauter Güte. / Die Werke, die helfen nimmermehr, / Sie mögen nicht behüten. / Der Glaub' sieht Jesum, Christum an, / Der hat g'nug für uns getan, / Er ist der Mittler worden." (Salvation has come to us here / From grace and pure goodness. / Works, they never help, / They cannot possibly protect. / Faith looks towards Jesus Christ, / He has done enough for all of us; / He has become our Mediator.)

This verse summarizes the whole thought of the cantata and could stand alone without any of the following numbers.

2. *Recitative—bass.* This is the first of three secco recitatives, all given to the bass—a most unusual procedure with Bach. They might represent a preacher's sermon on theology delivered to his congregation: We were too weak to keep God's law; we should be devout, but nobody is, because each prefers to follow the wrongdoing of sin.

3. *Aria—tenor.* A fall-motif in the violin obbligato pictorially represents the despair of the sinner, as he slips into the abyss of sin and vainly searches for some hand to help him escape from the death that sin will cause. Bach paints a scene of terror through the singer's voice, as he struggles to raise himself back into life: "Wir waren schon zu tief gesunken, / Der Abgrund schluckt uns völlig ein. / Die Tiefe drohte schon den Tod, / Und dennoch konnt in solcher Not / Uns keine Hand behilflich sein." (We had already sunk too deeply, / The abyss swallowed us completely. / The depths already threatened death, / And still in such distress / No hand could be helpful to us.)

This picture of profound despair, unrelieved by any ray of hope, shows Bach's mastery of emotional word-painting, as this text indicates.

4. *Recitative—bass.* His declamation, as he continues to sermonize, changes from dejection to hope of salvation. Christ came into the world to save us. If we believe in Him, we will not be lost, but will be chosen to be with Him in heaven.

5. *Duet—soprano, alto.* Their canonic singing follows an instrumental

prelude for transverse flute and oboe d'amore. Their duet stresses the word "Glaube" (faith)—used in three successive lines of the text—the high point of the textual sermon, perhaps. "Herr, du siehest statt guter Werke / Auf des Herzens Glaubensstärke, / Nur den Glauben nimmst du an. / Nur der Glaube macht gerecht, / Alles andre scheint zu schlecht, / Als dass es uns helfen kann." (Lord, Thou lookest, instead of good works, / On the strength of the heart's belief; / Only faith dost Thou accept. / Only faith makes righteous; / Everything else seems too base, / In order that it can help us.)

6. *Recitative—bass.* His lesson continues, stating that when we recognize our sins, they strike our conscience down. Yet we can find comfort in the Gospel, which will restore our happiness and strengthen our belief in God's goodness. He will know when to help us, if we only trust in Him.

7. *Chorale.* This last stanza of Paul Speratus's hymn was also used previously to conclude BWV 155. All voices and instruments perform this plain singing of the chorale stanza, which expresses complete trust in God's providence. Our faith in Him should remove all our worries and doubts.

• **Herr, deine Augen sehen nach dem Glauben (Lord, Thine Eyes Look Towards Faith)** (1731; BWV 102).

It seems that the librettists, at this time of the year, were bent on advocating faith to cure the impenitent sinner. This cantata for the tenth Sunday after Trinity, like the previous BWV 9, points out the urgency for belief and repentance.

The librettist is unknown; Terry suggests Christian Weiss, Sr., and Neumann proposes Mariane von Ziegler.

The Gospel is Luke 19 (41–48)—Christ's announcement of the coming destruction of Jerusalem and His driving the merchants from the Temple—but this is only indirectly referred to in the libretto, which describes the day when God will vent His wrath on sinners.

The soli are ATB, with a four-part chorus. The instrumentation is light: two oboes, two violins, a viola and continuo.

Part I

1. *Chorus.* Jeremiah 5 (3) provides the text for this great fugal chorus. Bach thought enough of its music to transfer it subsequently to the *Kyrie* of his *Short Mass in G minor.* In addition, he imitated both of the following alto and tenor arias for the *Qui tollis* and the *Quoniam* movements respectively in his *Short Mass in F major.*

The chorus seems to proclaim the words of the prophet Jeremiah, as they sing his lamentation about the sins of the people: "Herr, deine Augen sehen nach dem Glauben! / Du schlägest sie, aber sie fühlen's nicht; du plagest sie, aber sie bessern sich nicht. Sie haben ein härter Angesicht denn ein Fels und wollen sich nicht bekehren." (Lord, Thine eyes look towards faith! / Thou smitest them, but they do not feel it; Thou tormentest them, but they do not improve. They have a face harder than a rock, and do not want to become converted.)

2. *Recitative—bass.* In his secco remonstrance to sinners, he asks them where is God's image that they are supposed to have, where is the strength of His word that they have forgotten? Nevertheless, God still tries through tenderness to win their stubborn hearts.

3. *Aria—alto.* The tear-motif in the oboe accompaniment and in her voice makes this number a sad lament for the stubborn soul. It loads itself with punishment, because it does not know the harm done, and thus separates itself from God's mercy.

4. *Arioso—bass.* For this number the text is Romans 2 (4, 5), which describes God's judgment on the unrepentant sinner. The marvelous harmony of the strings makes this an aria more than an arioso, but it was termed arioso, being a Scriptural quotation and to avoid having two arias in succession. With the opening chorus and the final chorale, it is the best number within the cantata.

"Verachtest du den Reichtum seiner Gnade, Geduld und Langmütigkeit? / Weissest du nicht, dass dich Gottes Güte zur Busse locket? / Du aber nach deinem verstockten und unbussfertigen Herzen häufest dir selbst den Zorn auf den Tag des Zornes und der Offenbarung des gerechten Gerichts Gottes." (Dost thou despise the riches of His grace, patience and long-suffering? / Dost thou not know, that God's goodness entices thee to repentance? / Thou, however, according to thy hardened and unready-for-repentance heart, heapest up anger for thyself on the day of wrath and of the revelation of the righteous judgment of God.)

Part II

5. *Aria—tenor.* With violin piccolo accompaniment, he paints the fear that the evildoer should feel, when he thinks he is at ease. His sins are piling up like a heavy yoke he must bear. The text has an interesting metaphor: "Die Gotteslangmut geht auf einem Fuss von Blei," (God's long-suffering goes on a foot of lead,)—i.e., God's patience will only make His anger worse when the reckoning comes.

The sermon would take place before Part II, thus separating the two arias.

6. *Recitative—alto.* Both oboes play, as the singer states that the sinner must not wait to repent. It takes only a moment to separate time and eternity, body and soul—so one must be now prepared to meet God!

7. *Chorale.* Verses six and seven of Johann Heermann's hymn, "So wahr ich lebe, spricht dein Gott" (As True as I Live, Says Thy God), with the melody of the German version of the Lord's Prayer, "Vater unser in Himmelreich" (Our Father in Heaven), makes a moving conclusion, with tutti in voices and instruments.

The sixth verse admonishes us to repent while we are still in good health. If we do not, our body and soul will burn in hell. The seventh verse is less grim: Jesus is asked to help us repent, so that we may be ready to ascend to heaven.

The melody and the way it fits the text are very appealing. This hymn is one of Bach's finest cantata chorales.

• **Geist und Seele wird verwirret (Spirit and Soul Become Confused)** (1731; BWV 35).

The obbligato organ had been used by Bach for some movements in his previous cantatas, but in this work for solo alto, he uses it in all numbers. It is most likely that Bach wrote the libretto himself, because he adapted a clavier concerto and other instrumental material for all numbers except the two recitatives, the texts of which he could have written also.

The Gospel for this twelfth Sunday after Trinity is Mark 7 (31–37), the healing of the deaf and dumb man, which Scripture Bach's text closely follows.

The orchestra has two oboes, a taille (tenor oboe), two violins, a viola, organ obbligato and continuo.

Part I

1. *Sinfonia.* This allegro movement with all the above instruments includes the only surviving fragment of the *Harpsichord concerto, BWV 1059,* which Bach has here transcribed for organ.

The following siciliano aria is the slow movement of this same work, and the Sinfonia at the beginning of Part II is the final allegro movement—this is a case where the instrumental work has been preserved by the cantata.

As an organ concerto it is delightful, but the music has no rapport with the text to be sung.

2. *Aria.* Bach was able to fit the words into this slow movement of the concerto (dating probably from his Cöthen period). With the accompanying tutti orchestra, the soloist would have to sing forte to compete—questionable in Bach's time with a boy alto, perhaps, but presenting no problem in modern performances.

The alto points out the astonishment of the people at Christ's miracle, which, conversely to the Scripture, has rendered them deaf and dumb. "Geist und Seele wird verwirret, / Wenn sie dich, mein Gott, betracht. / Denn die Wunder, so sie kennet / Und das Volk mit Jauchzen nennet, / Hat sie taub und stumm gemacht. (Spirit and soul become confused, / When they consider Thee, my God. / For the miracles, which they know / And the people name with jubilation, / Have made them deaf and dumb.)

3. *Recitative.* With organ and continuo only, she marvels at the healing miracles which Christ performed on the deaf, the dumb and the blind. Nothing can compare with these wonder-works that her reason cannot understand.

4. *Aria.* The melody is again for organ obbligato and continuo, thought to be adapted from an unidentified cello sonata. The music fits the text very well; the alto praises God for His benevolent care over us. "Gott hat alles wohl gemacht. / Seine Liebe, seine Treu' / Wird uns alle Tage neu. / Wenn uns Angst und Kummer drücket, / Hat er reichen Trost geschicket, / Weil er täglich für uns wacht." (God has done everything well. / His love, His faithfulness / Becomes new to us every day. / When anxiety and worry oppress us, / He has sent rich comfort, / Because He watches for us daily.)

Part II

5. *Sinfonia.* This is the last movement of the harpsichord concerto, with full orchestra.

6. *Recitative.* Again with organ and continuo only, she asks God to grant her soul His sweet healing power ("dein süsses Hephata"), Mark 7 (34), referring again to the Scripture for the Sunday. If He will open her ears by His touch, then her tongue will be loosened to proclaim His wonders, and she will thus prove herself to be a child and heir of God.

7. *Aria.* The full orchestra reappears to play a dance-like melody, probably derived from a lost violin concerto. Bach uses this for his concluding number instead of a chorale (assuming that he wrote the libretto, of course).

The joy-motif is evident in her singing. She wishes that Jesus would end her life of torment, so that she might join the angels in their praise of God in heaven. The music conforms very well to the text.

The happy theme of this cantata affords the soloist much scope for artistic, coloratura interpretation. It is no wonder that this is one of the most popular solo cantatas performed in Bach concerts today.

• **Es ist nichts Gesundes an meinem Leibe (There Is Nothing Healthy in My Body)** (c. 1731; BWV 25).

Picander, or some unknown librettist, composed the text for this fourteenth Sunday after Trinity cantata. Only indirect reference is made to the Gospel, Luke 17 (11–19)—the healing of the ten lepers—although the first three numbers vividly portray the afflictions of the body. Musically, the opening chorus and the soprano aria are outstanding examples of Bach's genius.

The soli are STB, with the usual four-part chorus. The instruments are a cornet, three trombones, three recorders, two oboes, two violins, a viola and continuo.

1. *Chorus (with Chorale).* The string section of the orchestra supports the four-part chorus, while the woodwinds and the brass play independently Hassler's melody for the hymn, "Ach Herr, mich armen Sünder" (Oh Lord, Me Poor Sinner). Canonical singing by the voices, divided into two sections—tenors and altos, sopranos and basses—gives the impression of a dirge, represented by the gloomy text, Psalm 38 (3). In the counterpoint for this chorus, Bach has painted an exceptionally dramatic scene, in which the singers seem to play the part of one of the lepers (or of one of us), whose infirmity is caused by his sin: "Es ist nichts Gesundes an meinem Leibe vor deinem Dräuen, und ist kein Friede in meinen Gebeinen vor meiner Sünde." (There is nothing healthy in my body before Thy threatening, and there is no peace in my bones because of my sin.)

2. *Recitative—tenor.* His in-secco listing of all the evils that have beset him has been adversely criticized by Schweitzer (Vol. II, p. 260) for the lack of good taste on the part of the librettist. Yet Picander (?) wanted to graphically illustrate in strong language both the spiritual and the bodily evils that cause degeneration of soul and body. Moreover, his equating of sin with leprosy ("Sündenaussatz"—sin's leprosy) leads him to ask where he can find a doctor to help him, and so introduces the following aria.

3. *Aria—bass.* The continuo-only accompaniment plays a step-motif, which depicts the singer dashing distractedly about, as he tries to find treatment for his malady. Both this number and the preceding recitative refer to the Biblical text, this aria adding the spiritual cure at the end. Notice the allusion to the balm of Gilead, Jeremiah 8 (22), in the libretto.

4. *Recitative—soprano.* In secco, she pleads that the Savior may cleanse her of the leprosy of her sin, as He is the doctor and the healer of all the sick. Then she will thank Him wholeheartedly for the rest of her life.

5. *Aria—soprano.* This aria is one of Bach's most beautiful compositions. In an otherwise drab and morose cantata on the state of one's health, this joyous music shines forth in radiant ecstasy. It seems that we can hear the angels singing their thanks to the Lord in this wondrous vision, evoked by her voice and by the dancing joy-motif of the orchestra. It seems as though she represents the Samaritan in the Gospel, thanking Jesu for her restoration to health. "Offne meinen schlechten Liedern, / Jesu, dein Genadenohr! / Wenn ich dort im höhern Chor / Werde mit den Engeln singen, / Soll mein Danklied besser klingen." (Open to my poor songs, / Jesu, Thy gracious ear! / When I there in the higher choir / Shall sing with the angels, / My song of thanks ought to sound better.)

The three recorders play as an independent group, contrasting with the other woodwinds and strings, thus producing an ethereal effect in the last three lines sung.

6. *Chorale.* All instruments and voices perform stanza 12 of J. Heermann's hymn, "Treuer Gott, Ich muss dir klagen" (Faithful God, I Must Complain to Thee), which Bach had used before to conclude a cantata. It speaks of the praise which they will always give God for averting their misery.

• **Wir danken dir Gott, wir danken dir (We Thank Thee, God, We Thank Thee)** (1731; BWV 29).

For this Ratswahl cantata, performed on Monday, 27 August 1731, Bach turned to some of his former instrumental works, which he altered to fit the libretto he wrote for this occasion. The obbligato organ is again featured in his lavish score: three trumpets, timpani, two oboes, strings and continuo. The soli are SATB, with a four-part chorus.

1. *Sinfonia.* Bach took the first movement of his *Suite for solo violin in E,* converting it into a tutti orchestral concerto movement in D, to preface this cantata. The festive joy-motif in the music with the obbligato organ befits the theme of gratitude towards God, with which all the following vocal numbers deal.

2. *Chorus.* Psalm 75 (1) provides the paraphrased text for this majestic and powerful choral movement, which Bach must have borrowed from some other work. The straightforward singing is unusual in an opening chorus by Bach, yet its solemnity makes it a suitable choral song of thanksgiving for this municipal festival: "Wir danken dir, Gott, wir danken dir, und verkündigen deine Wunder." (We thank Thee, God, we thank Thee, and proclaim Thy wonders.) Bach must have thought highly of it, because he transferred the melody to the *Gratias agimus* and the *Dona nobis pacem* numbers of his later *Mass in B minor.*

3. *Aria—tenor.* As we have noticed before in BWV 119, Zion in the text is

synonymous with Leipzig in Bach's mind. This aria continues the praise that the citizens of these cities should give to God for supporting them and their forefathers. The joy-motif in the rhythm, played by the solo violin obbligato, and the tenor's happy runs on "Halleluja" are fine features of this aria.

"Halleluja, Stärk' und Macht / Sei des Allerhöchsten Namen! / Zion ist noch seine Stadt, / Da er seine Wohnung hat, / Da er noch bei unserm Samen / An der Väter Bund gedacht." (Halleluja, strength and might / Be the name of the All-Highest! / Zion is still His city, / Where He has His dwelling. / There He still in our seed / Has thought about the covenant of our fathers.)

The first two lines are repeated in an aria for alto as the penultimate number of this cantata. The melody was probably taken from a movement of a violin sonata.

4. *Recitative—bass.* He tells of the confidence that citizens may have in God's protection, extending over the city and its palaces. Accordingly, they should consider themselves well-off. His text has an interesting personification: faithfulness kisses peace, Psalm 85 (10). Bach was well-versed in his Bible reading to insert this into his libretto at this point. Whether he was so sure of the last three lines of this recitative—that God is near to the people of Leipzig, because they are righteous—is questionable.

5. *Aria—soprano.* This peaceful siciliano melody for oboes, strings and organ may come from a lost violin composition. The text refers to God's guidance of Leipzig's bourgeois officials, about whom Whittaker (Vol. I, p. 256) remarks: "The association of the pompous burgomasters with a siciliano is quite humorous."

Humorous or not, this aria is a beautiful prayer, showing Bach's skill in adapting other music to a text he wants to illustrate: "Gedenk' an uns mit deiner Liebe, / Schleuss' uns in dein Erbarmen ein! / Segne die, so uns regieren, / Die uns leiten, schützen, führen, / Segne, die gehorsam sein!" (Think of us with Thy love, / Enclose us in Thy pity! / Bless those, who govern us, / Who guide, protect, lead us; / Bless those who are obedient!)

6. (a) *Recitative—alto.* She continues to pray for prosperity; then, in their prayers of thanksgiving, both the city and the country will praise God as their inhabitants say "Amen." This leads into her following aria without a break.

(b) *Aria—alto.* She repeats the first two lines of the tenor's aria (3) with organ obbligato.

7. *Chorale.* This is an additional stanza to Johann Graumann's four-verse hymn, "Nun lob', mein' Seel', den Herren" (Now Praise, My Soul, the Lord). The complete orchestra reappears with oboes and strings supporting the voices; the trumpets and drums enter at the end of the first two and the last two lines. It is a fine hymn of praise to the Trinity, showing our belief in divine guidance, and is thus in keeping with the theme of the whole cantata.

This verse was also used for the final chorale of BWV 167 and BWV 51.

• **Jauchzet Gott in allen Landen (Praise God in All Lands)** (1731 or 1732; BWV 51).

Bach was the probable librettist for this solo soprano cantata on the fifteenth Sunday after Trinity. The Gospel, Matthew 6 (23–34)—to avoid worldly worries and to seek first the Kingdom of God—has no connection with the libretto. All numbers constitute a simple song of praise to God.

On the score, Bach indicated that this work was for general use, and perhaps that is the reason why it has no bearing on the Scripture for this particular Sunday. It is the most frequently performed of Bach's solo cantatas today. Bach must have had an exceptional boy soprano in his choir for performances in his time.

The cantata is scored for trumpet, two violins, a viola and continuo (organ).

1. *Aria.* This virtuoso number brings the soprano's voice and the trumpet together in duet fashion for the first half

of the aria. A feeling of intense joy predominates throughout: "Jauchzet Gott in allen Landen! / Was der Himmel und die Welt / An Geschöpfen in sich hält, / Müssen dessen Ruhm erhöhen, / Und wir wollen unserm Gott / Gleichfalls itzt ein Opfer bringen, / Dass er uns in Kreuz und Not / Allezeit hat beigestanden." (Praise God in all lands! / What heaven and the world / Contains in itself of creatures, / Must exalt His fame, / And we want to bring to our God / Likewise now an offering, / Because He in suffering and need / Has always stood beside us.)

2. *Recitative.* This is one of Bach's best recitatives, possibly because the singer declaims it as though it were an arioso. The accompanying strings provide a beautiful effect to her singing.

The text comes from Psalm 138 (2) and Psalm 26 (8). She says that we pray in the Temple where God's honor resides, and from where His daily blessing comes to us. Even the poor efforts of our stammering mouths, which praise Him for His wonders, are pleasing to Him.

3. *Aria.* This, her second aria, with organ continuo only, is a sincere prayer to God that her thankful mind and pious way of living will make her one of God's children. The melody is very soothing, to such an extent that the audience might feel that they too are participating in her prayer: "Höchster, mache deine Güte / Ferner alle Morgen neu. / So soll für die Vatertreu' / Auch ein dankbares Gëmute / Durch ein frommes Leben weisen, / Dass wir deine Kinder heissen." (Highest One, make Thy goodness / Be further renewed every morning. / Then shall, for Thy fatherly faithfulness, / A thankful spirit also / Show through a pious life, / That we may be called Thy children.)

4. *Chorale.* Johann Graumann's additional fifth stanza to "Nun lob', mein' Seel', den Herren" (Now Praise, My Soul, the Lord), which concluded the previous cantata BWV 29, is reused here, but this time it is sung by only the soprano. Her singing runs, without pause, into a magnificent "Alleluja!" which Bach appended to it and which is as long as the chorale itself in performance.

This "Alleluja!" becomes a concerto for soprano voice and trumpet (which reenters for this ending), with the other instruments providing the accompaniment. It is a stupendous conclusion!

This cantata shows the Italian influence on Bach more than can be seen in any other cantata. Not only in his artistic treatment of the two arias and the recitative, but also in the brilliant "Alleluja," we perceive that the modern "operatic" style impressed him.

• **Wer weiss, wie nahe mir mein Ende (Who Knows, How Near to Me [Is] My End)** (1731; BWV 27).

This cantata for the sixteenth Sunday after Trinity features again an organ obbligato. The name of the librettist is unknown. The work may be classified as a chorale cantata, because there is a chorale stanza interspersed with the opening recitative as well as a chorale at the end.

The Gospel for the day narrates the story of the raising of the widow's son, Luke 7 (11–17), which is indirectly reflected in the libretto—a personal meditation on death. This is a theme in which Bach feels completely competent, as we have seen in the *Trauerode* (Funeral Ode) (BWV 198) and in the Passions.

The soli are SATB, with a four-part chorus, but for the final chorale, the sopranos divide, creating a five-part chorus—the only instance of this division in all of Bach's cantatas. The instruments are a horn, two oboes, two violins, a viola, obbligato organ and continuo.

1. *Chorale and Recitative—soprano, alto, tenor.* Stanza one of Ämilie Juliane von Schwarzburg-Rudolstadt's hymn, bearing the title of this cantata, is sung by the chorus in between the successive soli recitatives in the above-listed order. The melody of the hymn is Georg Neumark's "Wer nur den lieben Gott lässt walten," (Who Only Lets Dear God Control), which Bach arranges to suggest in its rhythm the slow passing of time, as

denoted by the swing of a clock's pendulum. There is also a grief-motif in the lamentation of the oboes and the strings. There is an extraordinary number.

CHORUS: "Wer weiss, wie nahe mir mein Ende?" (Who knows, how near to me [is] my end?)

SOPRANO: "Das weiss der liebe Gott allein, / Ob meine Wallfahrt auf der Erden / Kurz oder länger möge sein." (That dear God alone knows, / Whether my pilgrimage on earth / May be short or longer.)

CHORUS: "Hin geht die Zeit, her kommt der Tod," (Hence goes time, hither comes death,)

ALTO: "Und endlich kommt es doch so weit, / Dass sie zusammentreffen werden." (And finally it comes so far then, / That they will meet together.)

CHORUS: "Ach, wie geschwinde und behende / Kann kommen meine Todesnot!" (Oh, how quickly and nimbly / Can come the misery of my death!)

TENOR: "Wer weiss, ob heute nicht / Mein Mund die letzten Worte spricht? / Drum bet' ich alle Zeit:" (Who knows, whether not today / My mouth speaks its last words? / Therefore I pray at all times:)

CHORUS: "Mein Gott, ich bitt' durch Christi Blut, / Mach's nur mit meinem Ende gut!" (My God, I ask through Christ's blood, / Just make my end a good one!)

2. *Recitative—tenor.* In secco, he expressed his goal in life: to die blessed, so that he may inherit heaven. Therefore, he is prepared to die, knowing that a good end to his life will make it all worthwhile.

3. *Aria—alto.* Bach adapted this stanza from a text by Neumeister, but despite the accompaniment of an oboe da caccia and the obbligato organ, the alto seems to sing in a style more suited to recitative than aria. Her voice does express a joy-motif, yet it seems to lack the verve expected in the text.

She will say welcome to death when he comes to her bed and will follow him happily into her grave, taking all her troubles with her.

4. *Recitative—soprano.* She, too, states her desire to join the Lamb in the pastures of the blessed. The strings of her accompaniment flutter upward in imitation of her wish for wings, "Flügel her!" (Bring me wings!). Then at the end, she repeats the first line: "Ach, wer doch schon im Himmel wär'!" (Ah, who would be already in heaven!).

5. *Aria—bass.* Quavering strings illustrate this aria exceptionally well; the instrumental accompaniment is the same as in the previous recitative.

The mystical quality in Bach's setting for this number imparts an impression of deep sentiment in the soloist's voice during his singing. He bids farewell to the world and its tumult as he departs for heaven: "Gute Nacht, du Weltgetümmel! / Jetzt mach' ich mit dir Beschluss; / Ich steh' schon mit einem Fuss / Bei dem lieben Gott im Himmel." (Goodnight, thou worldly tumult! / Now I have done with thee; I am already standing with one foot / Near my dear God in heaven.)

6. *Chorale.* This is the first stanza of Johann Georg Albinus's hymn, "Welt, ade! ich bin dein müde," (World, Farewell! I Am Tired of Thee,) set to the melody of Johann Rosenmüller. All voices in this five-part choir and all instruments perform this fine conclusion, which contrasts the peace and joy of heaven with the war and vanity in the world.

• **Gott soll allein mein Herze haben (God Alone My Heart Shall Have)** (1731 or 1732; BWV 169).

This is the companion piece to BWV 35, set to an unknown author's libretto, again featuring the obbligato organ, and for alto solo. The first and second movements of the *E Major Harpsichord Concerto,* BWV 1053, are used for the Sinfonia and the second aria respectively, all harpsichord movements becoming organ pieces.

The Gospel, Matthew 22 (34–46)—Christ's answer to the Pharisee concerning the greatest commandment—is closely followed and freely expanded in all numbers of this cantata.

The full instrumentation for the Sinfonia and for the final Chorale (a four-part choir) includes two oboes, a tenor oboe (taille), two violins, a viola, obbligato organ and continuo.

1. *Sinfonia.* Once more, this movement has no connection with the following numbers. Still, it is a fine instrumental number, showing Bach's skill in substituting the organ for the harpsichord.

2. *Arioso and Recitative.* "Gott soll allein mein Herze haben" (God alone my heart shall have). With continuo only, her declamation emphasizes the motto which is the title of this cantata and appears in three arioso parts. This motto states that "God alone my heart shall have," because she finds in Him the highest good, whereas the world tries to win her affections by its filth. Even though some satisfaction can be found on earth, she acknowledges its imperfection, compared to God's perfect joy.

3. *Aria.* Accompanied by the organ and continuo, she sings the motto first, then the thought that she finds in Him the highest good—the same two lines as in the second arioso of the preceding number.

Her song continues with the idea that in bad times God will still love her and will refresh her with His spiritual blessings.

It may be that the melody in this aria comes from a lost instrumental work for harpsichord.

4. *Recitative.* She defines God's love, after asking the question herself. It is rest for the spirit, the delight of the senses, the soul's Paradise. It closes hell and opens heaven to us. It is Elijah's chariot, carrying us up to heaven into Abraham's bosom.

5. *Aria.* This is the high point of the cantata, played to the siciliano of the original harpsichord movement, with strings and organ. She bids farewell to the world and all its vanities. The lilting rhythm of the siciliano illustrates her departure from the world as described in the text. It is like a death lullaby, which Bach was induced to compose by the verb "Stirb" (die): "Stirb in mir, / Welt und alle deine Liebe, / Dass die Brust / Sich auf Erden für und für / In der Liebe Gottes übe; / Stirb in mir, / Hoffahrt, Reichtum, Augenlust, / Ihr verworfnen Fleischestriebe!" (Die in me, / World and all thy love, / So that my breast / Practices itself forever / In the love of God; / Die in me, / Arrogance, wealth, visual lust, / Ye depraved impulses of the flesh!)

6. *Recitative.* She recalls the two points of Christ's saying in the Scripture, concerning the greatest of the commandments: "Thou shalt love God and thy neighbor." This is the theme of the whole cantata.

7. *Chorale.* This is verse three of Luther's pre-Reformation hymn, "Nun bitten wir den heiligen Geist" (Now We Ask the Holy Spirit). All voices and instruments perform this stanza, which entreats God to love us as we love Him and each other. The "Kyrie eleis" at the end is a nice touch.

• **Man singet mit Freuden vom Sieg (One Sings with Joy of the Victory)** (1731; BWV 149).

The author who composed the text of this interesting Michaelmas libretto is unknown. The Epistle for the festival, Revelation 12 (7–12)—St. Michael and his angels conquer Satan and his dragons—has a direct brearing on the libretto (as it did in BWV 19), whereas the Gospel, Matthew 18 (1–11), is not used.

While the first two numbers refer directly to the angels' victory and the preceding battle, the rest of the text deals with the subject of when God's angels guard us, during our lifetime on earth.

The soli are SATB, with a four-part chorus. The orchestra has three trumpets, timpani, a bassoon, two violins, a violone (double-bass), a viola and continuo.

1. *Chorus.* Bach adapted the last chorus of his first secular cantata, BWV

208, "Was mir behagt, ist nur die muntre Jagd" (What Suits Me Is Only the Merry Hunt), for this opening chorus. He replaced the horns of the hunting cantata by three trumpets and drums. The text is taken from Psalm 118 (15–16) and is here applied to describe the people's rejoicing after the heavenly victory over Satan: "Man singet mit Freuden vom Sieg in den Hütten der Gerechten: / Die Rechte des Herrn behält den Sieg; die Rechte des Herrn ist erhöhet; / die Rechte des Herrn behält den Sieg." (One sings with joy of the victory in the dwellings of the righteous: / The right hand of the Lord retains the victory: the right hand of the Lord is exalted; The right hand of the Lord retains the victory.)

After the first line is sung in canon, the actual song of praise begins, with a change in the rhythm and very interesting choral treatment of the verbs "behalt" (retain) and "erhöhet" (exalt).

2. *Aria—bass.* A solo description of the struggle with Satan is his theme, accompanied only by the double-bass and continuo. There seems to be a sort of pulsating rhythm to this number, perhaps depicting the combat, or in the latter part, the outpouring of Christ's blood, which the text mentions as bringing honor and victory to the pious.

3. *Recitative—alto.* From here to the end of the solo numbers, Bach composes in free madrigal style to illustrate the proximity of angels, described in the libretto. The singer states that she does not fear a thousand enemies, because God's angels are encamped around her. How, then, would it be possible to despair, when everything collapses or breaks? God sends her, for defense, fiery steeds and chariots, together with whole hosts of angels.

4. *Aria—soprano.* Words cannot describe the beauty of this aria. The string accompaniment seems to portray the gentle, undulating motion of the guardian angels' wings, hovering over the soprano, whether she wakes or sleeps. She feels a sense of divine protection, because angels are always near to support her. Throughout this masterpiece of emotional word-painting, there is a motive of beatific peace. "Gottes Engel weichen nie, / Sie sind bei mir allerenden. / Wenn ich schlafe, wachen sie, / Wenn ich gehe, / Wenn ich stehe, / Tragen sie mich auf den Händen." (God's angels never waver, / They are near me on all sides. / When I sleep, they are awake, / When I walk, / When I stand, / They carry me in their hands.)

5. *Recitative—tenor.* In this secco narrative, he thanks God for the angels' help and asks that he may be granted the grace to regret his sins. Then his own particular angel will rejoice at his repentance and will bear him to God's bosom on the day he dies.

6. *Duet—alto, tenor.* The dark tone of the accompanying obbligato bassoon paints a sombre, late-night picture of two lonely believers, who, during their vigil, await the coming dawn, which symbolizes their reunion with God, according to the text. A feeling of awe pervades their singing, as they appeal to the angels to be alert, even if they themselves cannot sleep. "Seid wachsam, ihr heiligen Wächter, / Die Nacht ist schier dahin! / Ich sehne mich und ruhe nicht, / Bis ich vor dem Angesicht / Meines lieben Vaters bin." (Be watchful, you holy watchmen, / The night is nearly past! / I long and do not rest, / Until I am before the face / Of my dear Father.)

The syncopated rhythm in the bassoon suggests the watchful presence of angels floating above the singers.

7. *Chorale.* This is stanza three of Martin Schalling's funeral hymn, "Herzlich lieb hab' ich dich, O Herr" (Heartily Do I Love Thee, O Lord).

The full orchestra and choir perform this chorale stanza, which refers to the main theme, in wishing that angels will bear our souls to Paradise on Judgment Day. Trumpets and timpani enter only at the last word of the last line ("ewiglich")—"Ich will dich preisen ewiglich" (I Will Praise Thee Eternally), which Bach has reserved for a final flash of heavenly splendor.

• **Ich will den Kreuzstab gerne tragen (I Will Gladly Carry the Cross)** (1731 or 1732; BWV 56).

For the nineteenth Sunday after Trinity, Bach composed this solo bass cantata, which he based on an earlier Neumeister libretto. It is similar to a "Pilgrim's Progress," in its comparison of life to a sea voyage, ending in the port of heaven. After enduring the troubles of this life, the pilgrim hopes to enter the Promised Land. The text affords Bach much incentive to illustrate its nautical language, especially in the first recitative.

The Gospel, Matthew 9 (1–8), tells of Jesus as He crosses a sea by ship, and of His healing a man sick with palsy, which bears directly on the libretto.

The orchestra consists of two oboes, two violins, a bassoon, a viola and continuo. There is a four-part choir for the final chorale.

1. *Aria.* Both text and music depict a weary, sin-laden pilgrim, who is enduring his life's hardships, just as he would brave the perils of a sea-voyage, in the hope of arriving finally in a safe, sheltering harbor. The vocalist expresses his complete trust in God to help him reach his destination. Note the melancholy grief-motif throughout his aria: "Ich will den Kreuzstab gerne tragen, / Er kommt von Gottes lieber Hand, / Der führet mich nach meinen Plagen / Zu Gott, in das gelobte Land. / Da leg' ich den Kummer auf einmal ins Grab, / Da wischt mir die Tränen mein Heiland selbst ab." (I will gladly carry the cross, / It comes from God's dear hand; / It leads me after my troubles / To God, in the promised land. / There I lay my worry immediately in the grave, / There My Savior Himself wipes away my tears.)

The deep emotion in these last two lines before the da capo is beautifully conveyed by Bach's musical setting.

2. *Recitative.* The cello accompaniment plays a wave-motif throughout this number. This rhythm represents the sea-voyage amid the allegorical imagery of the stormy waves. Only at the end, when the pilgrim steps ashore into the safety of his heavenly harbor, do the raging seas subside.

He compares his wandering in the world to a trip at sea, wherein the waves represent his afflictions. His anchor, however, is God's pity, which will sustain him, until he will reach his safe port in heaven with those other righteous travelers, where all their troubles will be left behind.

3. *Aria.* Accompanied by a solo oboe, he expresses a joy-motif in his runs on the first two lines and in his wish for the bliss of heavenly happiness in the second theme. The text contains an interesting metaphor; he wishes to have the indefatigable power of an eagle to soar up from the earth. If this would happen today, he would then be free of the burden of sin that he carries.

4. *Recitative and Arioso.* With string accompaniment, the pilgrim narrates his anticipated arrival in the promised land: "Ich stehe fertig und bereit, / Das Erbe meiner Seligkeit / Mit Sehnen und Verlangen / Von Jesus Händen zu empfangen. / Wie wohl wird mir geschehn, / Wenn ich den Port der Ruhe werde sehn." (I stand ready and prepared, / To receive the inheritance of my blessing / With yearning and longing / From Jesus' hands. / How well will it happen to me, / When I shall see the port of rest.)

The arioso section now follows, repeating the last two lines of his first aria, but much more embellished and with a tear-motif. Bach has set a remarkable ending to this number by his artistic setting.

5. *Chorale.* This is the sixth verse of Johann Franck's "Du, O schönes Weltgebäude" (Thou, O Beautiful Structure of the World), set to Johann Crüger's melody, which is not found in any other Bach cantata. All voices and instruments are used.

The imagery of the sea returns in the idea of death being the helmsman, who will bring him to a safe port. The tone is hushed and solemn, befitting death as "Du Schlafes Bruder" (Thou brother of sleep), who will steer him to Jesus.

• **Ich geh' und suche mit Verlangen [Dialogus] (I Go and Seek with Longing [Dialogue])** (c. 1731; BWV 49).

This appears to be Bach's first dialogue cantata. In previous cantatas, he had used dialogue in some duets, e.g. BWV 152 and BWV 21. Now he composes music for dialogues indicated in the recitatives also. Thus we find a new genre, the dialogue cantata.

The author of the libretto for this twentieth Sunday after Trinity is unknown.

The Gospel, Matthew 22 (1–14), relates the parable of the wedding feast for the king's son, from which the librettist obtained his theme: a conversation between Christ as the Bridegroom and the Soul as the Bride.

For this solo cantata, the soli are SB, and there is no final chorale.

The instruments include an oboe d'amore, two violins, a viola, the obbligato organ and continuo. This is another work in which the obbligato organ is featured.

1. *Sinfonia.* Bach borrows the third movement of his *Harpsichord Concerto in E Major,* BWV 1053, for this introductory symphony. (He had already borrowed the first two numbers for BWV 169.) The music has no connection with the vocal numbers, but its allegro melody may symbolize the joy of a wedding feast.

2. *Aria—bass.* The obbligato organ seems to represent one of the singers in its duet with the bass voice. Throughout all numbers, the bass voice will represent Christ, while the soprano will be the Soul. The rhythm has a step-motif, indicated by the words of the text. Christ is walking in search of the Soul. "Ich geh' und suche mit Verlangen / Dich, meine Taube, schönste Braut. / Sag' an, wo bist du hingegangen, / Dass dich mein Auge nicht mehr schaut?" (I go and seek with longing / Thee, My dove, most beautiful bride. / Say where thou hast gone, / So that My eye beholds thee no more?)

The *Song of Solomon* is reflected in all numbers of this cantata.

3. Recitative—bass, soprano. With strings added to the organ, they begin the following dialogue: Jesus says that His wedding meal is ready but He cannot find the Bride. The Soul says that she is glad to hear His voice. Jesus repeats the first two lines of the preceding aria. The Soul says that she falls before His feet.

Their recitative changes now to a duet, lasting to the end of this number. They sing of their love and the sumptuous feast. They conclude by singing in unison about their haste to dress for their wedding. The drama of this love duet would fit into any opera.

4. *Aria—soprano.* Accompanied by the oboe d'amore, the violoncello piccolo and the organ, she sings a fine love song in order to entice the Bridegroom to her charms. Her wedding garment will be her Savior's justice, which she will wear when she goes to heaven.

5. *Recitative—soprano, bass.* They continue their dialogue as follows, still with obbligato organ: The Soul says that her faith has clothed her thus. Christ replies that His heart will be engaged to her throughout eternity. She adds that she is happy because the Lord has sent His servants to summon the fallen race as guests at His meal of Salvation in heaven. She wishes that she will be admitted also. Christ tells her to be faithful until death and then he will give her the crown of life.

6. *Aria—bass, and Chorale—soprano.* I think that this exquisite duet is one of Bach's happiest and most successful inspirations. The soprano sings stanza seven of Philipp Nicolai's "Wie schön leuchtet der Morgenstern" (How Beautifully Shines the Morning Star). Bach thus keeps a chorale as part of this concluding number. All instruments are used to play the two different tunes; the obbligato organ is prominent in both.

In this dialogue, the Soul as the Bride symbolizes Christ's Church as well as the individual soul which He is seeking.

JESUS: "Dich hab' ich je und je geliebet, / Und darum zieh' ich dich zu mir. / Ich komme bald, / Ich stehe vor der Tür, / Mach' auf, mein Aufenthalt! (Thee have I ever and ever loved, / And therefore I draw thee to Me. / I am coming soon, / I stand before the door, / Open, My abode!

SEELE (SOUL): Wie bin ich so herzlich froh, / Dass mein Schatz ist das A und O, / Der Anfang und das Ende. / Er wird mich doch zu seinem Preis / Aufnehmen in das Paradeis; / Des klopf' ich in die Hände. / Amen! Amen! / Komm du schöne Freudenkrone, bleib nicht lange! / Deiner wart' ich mit Verlangen." (How heartily glad am I, / That my treasure is the A and O, / The beginning and the end. / He will surely as His prize / Take me up to Paradise; / Therefore I clap my hands. / Amen! Amen! / Come Thou beautiful crown of joy, / do not remain away long! / I am waiting for Thee with longing.)

The soloists' artistic interpretation of this duet, the emotional effect of the music on the listener, and Bach's innate mysticism all combine to make a most impressive conclusion. It is one of Bach's most memorable moments.

• **Ich glaube, lieber Herr, hilf meinem Unglauben (I Believe, Dear Lord, Help My Unbelief)** (c. 1731; BWV 109).

The author of this libretto for Bach's twenty-first Sunday after Trinity cantata is unknown. The Gospel, John 4 (46–54), tells of the healing of the nobleman's sick son and of the father's consequent belief. The libretto, however, presents the opposite point of view, contrasting indecision in belief with the certainty stated in the Scripture. Indeed, the text is a dramatized sermon on unbelief versus belief: the chorus and the tenor parts represent unbelief, while the alto and the final chorale advocate belief. Thus the cantata is neatly divided into two halves.

The soloists are TA, with a four-part chorus. The instruments are a corno da caccia, two oboes, two violins, a viola and continuo.

1. *Chorus.* Only one line, from Mark 9 (24), is used as text in this number. Even with only this last part of the Biblical verse, Bach builds a monumental chorus, which, together with the final chorale, can be considered as the best movements of the cantata. The entries of the various vocal sections produce a mystic atmosphere in their group prayer for help in their unbelief: "Ich glaube, lieber Herr, hilf meinem Unglauben!" (I believe, dear Lord, help my unbelief!).

2. *Recitative—tenor.* He describes, in secco, how his faith wavers. At one moment he believes that the Lord cares about him; at another he thinks that the Lord disregards sinners. He needs the Lord's consolation and does not know how long he will have to wait for it.

3. *Aria—tenor.* There is a restlessness in the strings, as they accompany the vocalist's equally wavering interpretation of his text, which seems to confuse the listener, yet their message of doubt comes through very well: "Wie zweifelhaftig ist mein Hoffen, / Wie wanket mein geängstigt Herz! / Des Glaubens Docht glimmt kaum hervor, / Es bricht dies fast zerstossne Rohr, / Die Furcht macht stetig neuen Schmerz." (How doubting is my hoping; / How my fearful heart wavers! / Faith's wick gleams scarcely forth; / This almost broken reed is breaking; / Fear makes constantly new pain.)

Recitative—alto. Beginning with this secco number, we hear the words of comfort, which will continue to the end of the cantata. She tells the doubter to pull himself together and to remember that Jesus still works wonders. The eyes of believers should look for the Lord's salvation, even if that seems far away.

5. *Aria—alto.* The tune played by the two oboes is a kind of minuet, representing the joy-motif intended for her song. It is a pleasant aria but seems to lack that forceful persuasion for belief, which comes out only in the following chorale. Her text mentions that Christ knows His believers and will lend them His assistance to ensure that their belief will overcome their doubts.

6. *Chorale.* This extended chorale,

based on L. Spengler's hymn, "Durch Adams Fall ist ganz verderbt" (Through Adam's Fall Is All Spoiled), is the other outstanding number in this work. Its broad, spacious harmony, with all the orchestra and the four-part chorus, really persuades the listener of the value of faith in God. Bach's treatment of this chorale stanza seven is one of his best settings for any final chorale: "Wer hofft in Gott und dem vertraut, / Der wird nimmer zuschanden; / Denn wer auf diesen Felsen baut, / Ob ihm gleich geht zuhanden / Viel Unfalls hie, hab' ich doch nie / Den Menschen sehen fallen, / Der sich verlässt auf Gottes Trost; / Er hilft sein' Gläubigen allen." (Who hopes in God and trusts in Him, / He will never come to shame; / For whoever builds on this rock, / Whether to him at present occurs / Much misfortune here, I have never yet / Seen this man fall, / Who depends on God's comfort; / He helps all His believers.)

• **Ich armer Mensch, ich Sündenknecht (I Poor Man, I Servant of Sin)** (1731 or 1732; BWV 55).

This is Bach's only cantata for tenor solo. It is for the twenty-second Sunday after Trinity, the Gospel being Matthew 18 (23–35), the story of the unforgiving servant. The unknown librettist changes this Gospel account to the reverse: a guilty sinner seeking God's pardon. The pessimistic mood, which lasts until the last two numbers, makes this the least attractive of Bach's solo cantatas.

The instrumentation is very light: a transverse flute, an oboe d'amore, two violins and continuo.

1. *Aria.* All of the above instruments accompany this lamentation, as the singer, in despair, imagines himself to be approaching God's judgment seat. Bach pictures the hopelessness he feels in the wailing tones of both voice and melody: "Ich armer Mensch, ich Sündenknecht, / Ich geh' vor Gottes Angesicht / Mit Furcht und Zittern zum Gerichte. / Er ist gerecht, ich ungerecht. / Ich armer Mensch, ich Sündenknecht!" (I poor man, I servant of sin, / I am going before God's face / With fear and trembling to judgment. / He is righteous, I unrighteous, / I poor man, I servant of sin!)

2. *Recitative.* In secco, he expresses his fear of God's wrath. He says he has not followed God's plan. He wonders where he can flee to escape from God's anger: nowhere on earth, in hell or in heaven can he avoid God's judgment.

3. *Aria.* The obbligato flute accompanying his voice produces the same tear-motif found in the *St. Matthew Passion* in the alto aria, with a very similar melody. He pleads for mercy, as the flute reveals the agitation he feels in his soul. This is the most dramatic and the most impressive part of the cantata: "Erbarme dich! / Lass die Tränen dich erweichen, / Lass sie dir zu Herzen reichen; / Lass um Jesu Christi willen / Deinen Zorn des Eifers stillen! / Erbarme dich!" (Have mercy! / Let tears soften Thee, / Let them reach Thy heart; / Let for Jesus Christ's sake / Thy ardent anger be stilled! / Have mercy!)

4. *Recitative.* The strings change the tone now from despair to hope, as they accompany this declamation. He consoles himself that Christ has paid for the sins that he has committed and that God will receive him back into grace, because he will sin no more.

5. Chorale. All voices and instruments combine in the sixth verse of Johann Rist's evening hymn, "Werde munter, mein Gemüte" (Be Cheerful, My Spirit). From the quiet harmony of this number, the listener feels that the penitent has found peace through confessing his sins to God. The concluding lines of the text show this also: "Ich verleugne nicht die Schuld, / Aber deine Gnad' und Huld / Ist viel grösser als die Sünde, / Die ich stets bei mir befinde." (I do not deny my guilt, / But Thy grace and clemency / Is much greater than the sin, / Which I always find in myself.)

• **Wachet auf, ruft uns die Stimme (Wake Up, the Voice Calls to Us)** (1731; BWV 140).

This chorale cantata for the 27th Sunday after Trinity shows that Bach has returned to, and has mastered the chorale cantata format, which he will use increasingly from this date. Picander was the librettist, arranging the three stanzas of Philipp Nicolai's original hymn and its tune unchanged for the text he composed. These are the first, fourth and last numbers in this cantata.

The Gospel, Matthew 25 (1–13), the parable of the wise and the foolish virgins, is adhered to, both in the chorale verses and in Picander's recitatives and duets. Bach's musical setting does full justice to this majestic theme, with its three chorale verses standing like three sturdy columns to support the structure.

The soli are STB, with a four-part chorus. The orchestra has two oboes, taille, two violins, a violin piccolo, a viola, a horn and continuo.

1. *Chorus.* "Wachet auf, ruft uns die Stimme" (Wake up, the voice calls to us). The chorale fantasia, beginning with this line, sets the scenario for the arrival of the Bridegroom, for whom the sleeping virgins must waken. As the watchman calls midnight from his post on the battlements of Jerusalem, we hear the steady step-motif in the tempo which denotes an approaching procession. This rhythm becomes more agitated, as the sleepers wake up and prepare to meet the Bridegroom. Bach's magnificent word-painting brings this picture to life; we can visualize their consternation and also their joy, which emerges in their florid, emotional "Alleluja!" The colorful drama of this scene, and indeed in all the other numbers is worthy of Handel's best.

2. *Recitative—tenor.* In secco, he urges these maidens of Zion to come out to meet the Bridegroom, who is approaching as quickly as a deer, bringing with Him the wedding feast. The simile describes nicely the Bridegroom's youth.

3. *Duet—soprano, bass.* Their love duet, in which Jesus represents the Bridegroom and the "Seele" (Soul, the Bride) seems to refer to one of the virgins in the Scripture, who says that her lamp is burning with the oil she has provided in advance for His coming. She could thus be the chosen Bride. The violin piccolo weaves arabesques around the vocalists' exchanges in their dialogue. Note that the lines for both singers are similar:

SEELE (SOUL): "Wann kommst du, mein Heil!" (When comest Thou, my Salvation?)

JESUS: "Ich komme, dein Teil." (I am coming, thy partner.)

SEELE: "Ich warte mit brennendem Öle. / Eröffne den Saal / Zum himmlichen Mahl." (I am waiting with burning oil. / Open the hall / For the heavenly meal.)

JESUS: "Ich öffne den Saal / Zum himmlichen Mahl." (I am opening the hall for the heavenly meal.)

SEELE: "Komm, Jesu!" (Come, Jesus!)

JESUS: "Ich komme; komm liebliche Seele!" (I am coming; come lovely Soul!)

4. *Chorale—tenor.* The drama of the previous numbers is continued in this second verse of the chorale. The tenor has the role of commentator in this cantata, but his description here of the arrival of the wedding procession in front of the dining-hall is a miniature solo drama in itself. Bach's setting of this stanza with unison strings has a mystical quality about it, which enhances the tenor's singing of this verse. Note that "Zion" represents the Bride in this number.

"Zion hört die Wächter singen, / Das Herz tut ihr vor Freude springen, / Sie wachet und steht eilend auf. / Ihr Freund kommt vom Himmel prächtig, / Von Gnaden stark, von Wahrheit mächtig, / Ihr Licht wird hell, ihr Stern geht auf. / Nun komm, du werte Kron, / Herr Jesu, Gottes Sohn, / Hosianna! / Wir folgen all / Zum Freudensaal / Und halten mit das Abendmahl." (Zion hears the watchmen singing, / Her heart springs with joy, / She wakes and rises hurriedly. / Her Friend comes from heaven splendidly, / In mercy strong, in truth mighty; / Her light becomes bright, her star rises. / Now come, Thou worthy Crown, / Lord Jesus, God's Son, / Hosanna! / We are all following / To the hall of rejoicing / And are partaking of the Supper.)

5. *Recitative—bass.* All strings accompany the bass (Christ) as He sings his invitation to His Bride to come to Him within the hall. He says that He has wedded the Soul for eternity. Now the Soul can forget her pain, because she will find delight and rest with Him.

6. *Duet—soprano, bass.* A solo oboe obbligato accompanies their singing in a joy-motif, which expresses the pure bliss of their union. We can see a picture of happiness after the wedding ceremony in the rapture of their voices. The drama has here reached its climax.

SEELE: "Mein Freund ist mein!" (My Friend is mine!)

JESUS: "Und ich bin dein!" (And I am thine!)

BOTH: "Die Liebe soll nichts scheiden!" (This love nothing shall separate!)

SEELE: "Ich will mit dir / in Himmels Rosen weiden." (I wish with Thee / to pasture in heaven's roses.)

JESUS: "Du sollst mit mir / in Himmel's Rosen weiden." (Thou shalt with Me / pasture in heaven's roses.)

BOTH: "Da Freude die Fülle, da Wonne wird sein!" (There will be the fullness of joy; there will be the bliss!)

7. *Chorale.* The four-part choir and all instruments depict the supreme joy of heaven in this third and last verse of this hymn. The wedding is over and the guests are all rejoicing, in the hope that they too may have such a heavenly marriage. The joyful singing of all the participants at the feast makes this conclusion as dramatic as any of the other parts of this cantata.

Their singing of this remarkable verse paints a vision of heaven, depicted both in the text and in the music: "Gloria sei dir gesungen / Mit Menschen-und englischen Zungen, / Mit Harfen und mit Zimbeln schön. / Von zwölf Perlen sind die Pforten / An deiner Stadt; wir sind Konsorten / Der Engel hoch um deinen Thron. / Kein Aug hat je gespürt, / Kein Ohr hat je gehört / Solche Freude. / Des sind wir froh, io io, / Und singen dir / Das Halleluja für und für." (Glory be sung to Thee / With mortal and angelic tongues, / With harps and cymbals. / Of twelve pearls are the gates / Of Thy city; we are consorts / Of the angels high about Thy Throne. / No eye has ever detected, / No ear has ever heard / Such joy. / Therefore we are glad / And sing to Thee / Halleluja forever.)

• **Gelobet sei der Herr (Praised Be the Lord)** (1732; BWV 129).

This chorale cantata for Trinity Sunday was composed by Bach on the five stanzas of Johann Olearius's hymn (1665). Like BWV 4, it is a true chorale cantata; each verse of the hymn is set for chorus or aria, without recitatives. The theme is simply praise of God. Bach's setting of each number varies, though each verse begins with the same line, "Gelobet sei der Herr," the final chorale excepted. The joy-motif is apparent in all numbers.

The soli are SAB, with a four-part chorus. The orchestra has three trumpets, timpani, a transverse flute, two oboes, two violins, a viola and continuo.

1. *Chorus.* As in the previous cantata, BWV 140, Bach's embellishments on the chorale-tune show that he has developed a new type of introductory chorus—the chorale fantasia. The joy-motif bursts forth from the lively dancing rhythm, beginning with the woodwinds and the strings, and continued by the soprano voices. Trumpets and timpani play sharp fanfares at the end of each line sung. The chorale (vocal) and the hymn-tune (orchestral) are performed separately, but well synchronized.

"Gelobet sei der Herr, / Mein Gott, mein Licht, mein Leben, / Mein Schöpfer, der mir hat / Mein Leib und Seel' gegeben, / Mein Vater, der mich schützt / Von Mutterleibe an, / Der alle Augenblick / Viel Guts an mir getan." (Praised be the Lord, / My God, my Light, my Life, / My Creator, Who has given to me / My body and soul, / My Father, Who protects me / From the womb on, / Who every moment / Has done much good for me.)

2. *Aria—bass.* The continuo-only accompaniment seems to consist of organ and strings. The bass makes a long run on "Gelobet" (Praised), but the joy-motif, while present, is not as pronounced as in the other numbers.

While the opening chorale sang the praise of God, the bass sings the praise of Christ. The Son has given Himself for him, redeeming by His blood and bestowing belief, which is the highest good he can receive.

3. *Aria—soprano.* Her song is devoted to praise of the Holy Ghost. (Considered with the two preceding numbers, we thus have the Trinity in sequence for this Trinity Sunday work.) She sings that Christ has given her the Father's Holy Spirit, which strengthens her heart and provides advice, comfort and help in all her troubles. The obbligato transverse flute seems to bring an ethereal touch to her lyricism. Note her runs on "Leben" (life) and "schafft" (provides) at the end of the second and the last lines.

4. *Aria—alto.* With oboe d'amore and continuo, she sings to a pastoral melody which, with the instrumental ritornelli, makes this a long aria. Her libretto returns to the praise of all three persons of the Trinity; everything that hovers in the air of heaven magnifies Them.

5. *Chorale.* This fifth stanza of the chorale brings back the full impact of the joy-motif. Only the flute supports the voices as they sing the verse. All the other instruments play independently the tune which Bach will re-use to conclude the sixth cantata in his *Christmas Oratorio.*

All Christendom will join their voices with those of the host of angels to sing praise to God throughout eternity. This number is a fitting complement to the opening chorale fantasia: "Dem wir das Heilig itzt / Mit Freuden lassen klingen / Und mit der Engelschar / Das Heilig, heilig singen, / Den herzlich lobt und preist / Die ganze Christenheit: / Gelobet sei mein Gott / In alle Ewigkeit!" (To Whom we now the Holy / Let resound with joy, / And with the angel-host / Sing Holy, Holy; / Whom heartily lauds and praises / All Christendom: / Praised be my God / In all eternity!)

• **Brich dem Hungrigen dein Brot (Break for the Hungry Man Thy Bread)** (1732; BWV 39).

Schweitzer, Vol. II, p. 343, states that Picander wrote the libretto for this cantata on the first Sunday after Trinity. The date should be accepted as definite, because almost two thousand Protestants from Salzburg arrived then to seek refuge in the Nicolai church. They had fled from the persecution of the Archbishop of Salzburg, which was going on at this time. Bach must have noticed their pitiful state upon their arrival in Leipzig.

The Gospel for this Sunday is the story of Dives and Lazarus, Luke 16 (19–31), which applies to the charity shown by the citizens of Leipzig to these unfortunate newcomers.

The soli are SAB, with a four-part chorus. The orchestra has two recorders, two oboes, two violins, a viola and continuo.

Part I

1. *Chorus.* The text for this number comes from Isaiah 58 (7–8), which Bach sets superbly, reflecting all the meaning suggested in the phrases of the libretto. This chorus is a marvelous creation—the high point of the whole work.

The first half contains a step-motif of exhaustion, depicting the tottering, staggering steps of the poor, to whom food and shelter should be given, according to the Biblical text. The second half changes to a rapid fugue in two parts, which portrays the spiritual rewards bestowed by the Lord on the charitable. It is a movement of intense emotion and of powerful eloquence both in music and in singing.

"Brich dem Hungrigen dein Brot, und die, so in Elend sind, führe ins Haus. So du einen nacket siehest, so kleide ihn, und entzeuch dich nicht von deinem Fleisch. Alsdann wird dein Licht hervor-brechen wie die Morgenröte, und deine Besserung wird schnell wachsen. Und deine Gerechtigkeit wird vor dir hergehen, und die Herrlichkeit des Herrn wird dich zu sich nehmen." (Break for the hungry man thy bread, and those who are in misery lead into thy house. When thou seest someone naked, then clothe him, and withdraw theyself not from thy flesh. Then shall thy light break forth like the dawn, and thy improvement will quickly increase. And thy righteousness will go before thee, and the glory of the Lord will take thee unto itself.)

2. *Recitative—bass.* This rather long secco narrative appears to be a mini-sermon. He declares that God's gifts to us are only a loan. We should not keep for ourselves anything beyond our basic needs, but give the surplus of His bounty to our needy neighbors, whom we should pity. This will please Him more than any offering we make.

3. *Aria—alto.* Even with the accompaniment of a solo violin and an oboe, this aria is not very impressive. She sings of the blessing that one may receive by imitating the Creator's mercy, while one lives on earth. Note the interesting mention of harvesting in the text: "Samen" (seed), which seems to be linked to the noun "Scheuern" (barns) in the previous recitative.

Part II

4. *Arioso—bass.* This text is taken from Hebrews 13 (16). The bass voice, representing God, gives a forceful lesson on what is pleasing to Him. This number seems to summarize all of Part I: "Wohlzutun und mitzuteilen vergesset nicht; denn solche Opfer gefallen Gott wohl." (To do well and to share do not forget; for such offerings please God well.)

5. *Aria—soprano.* The unison recorders and the singing make this a very pleasant aria—the best of the three: "Höchster, was ich habe, / Ist nur deine Gabe. / Wenn vor deinem Angesicht / Ich schon mit dem Meinen / Dankbar wollt' erscheinen, / Willst du doch kein Opfer nicht." (Highest One, what I have, / Is merely Thy gift. / When before Thy face / I already with mine (my gift) / Thankfully would appear, / Thou wouldst not then desire any offering.)

6. *Recitative—alto.* With the strings for accompaniment, she asks the Lord what she can offer Him for the blessings she has received in body and soul. She says that she has nothing, except her spirit, the wish to help her neighbor, her poverty and her weak body soon to be buried. She hopes that these poor offerings will be acceptable to Him, so that she may obtain His promised bliss.

7. *Chorale.* This is the sixth stanza of David Denicke's hymn, which paraphrases the beatitudes: "Kommt, lasst euch den Herren lehren" (Come, Let the Lord Teach You). This verse speaks of the blessedness which those who pity the poor will receive. They should pray faithfully for the unfortunate, and help them in word and deed. Then they, too, will attain divine help and mercy.

• **Ich ruf' zu dir, Herr Jesu Christ (I Call to Thee, Lord Jesus Christ)** (1732; BWV 177).

Like BWV 129, this chorale cantata for the fourth Sunday after Trinity consists of only arias between the opening and the closing choral numbers. There are no recitatives. Again, this is a true chorale cantata, having all movements based on the original five stanzas of Johannes Agricola's hymn with the above title. On this Sunday, the congregation sang this chorale. Its text somewhat reflects the Gospel, Luke 6 (36–42)—be merciful and judge not—in its personal prayer for mercy and for guidance from the Lord.

The soli are SAT, with a four-part chorus. The instruments include two oboes, a violin concertante, two violins, an obbligato bassoon, a viola and continuo (organ for parts of some numbers).

1. *Chorus.* This number is a chorale fantasia for strings and oboes; it sounds like the slow movement of a violin concerto. The chorus sings a personal appeal to the Lord, representing the mental

agony of one believer who seeks spiritual help. Their prayer contains a grief-motif, which is expressed by the solo violin through its decorated playing of the hymn-tune. The emotional quality of the music makes it one of Bach's best chorale fantasias.

"Ich ruf' zu dir, Herr Jesu Christ, / Ich bitt', erhör' mein Klagen, / Verleih mir Gnad' zu dieser Frist, / Lass mich doch nicht verzagen; / Den rechten Glauben, Herr, ich mein', / Den wollest du mir geben, / Dir zu leben, / Meinem Nächsten nütz zu sein, / Dein Wort zu halten eben." (I call to Thee, Lord Jesus Christ, / I beg Thee, hear my complaint; / Grant me grace at this time, / Let me not despair; / The right faith, Lord, I mean, / Which Thou wilt give to me, / To live for Thee, / To be useful to my neighbor, / To keep Thy word exactly.)

2. *Aria—alto.* With organ continuo only, her request to the Lord is the first of those which will follow in the next two arias. Each aria is a prayer for a favor from God, sung to the chorale melody. In this case, and with a variation of the hymn-tune, she asks God not to let her be mocked, not to build all her hopes on her good acts, for these may lead her to eternal regret.

This is not one of Bach's better arias. Perhaps he was not inspired by this text.

3. *Aria—soprano.* The oboe da caccia accompaniment gives this number more interest, but it still seems to lack something. She asks God to grant her the inclination to forgive her enemies, so that He will then forgive her, too. From that time, she will have a new life, in which His Word will nourish her soul and protect her against misfortune.

4. *Aria—tenor.* A joy-motif, heard in the solo violin and in the obbligato bassoon, lifts this number well above the former arias. This is a Bach aria as it should be; probably the composer was stimulated more by this text than by the thought in the previous two numbers: "Lass mich kein Lust noch Furcht von dir / In dieser Welt abwenden. / Beständigsein ans End' gib mir, / Du hast's allein in Händen; / Und wem du's gibst, der hat's umsonst: / Es kann niemand ererben, / Noch erwerben / Durch Werke deine Gnad', / Die uns errett' vom Sterben." (Let no desire or fear / In this world turn me from Thee. / Give me constancy to the end. / Thou only hast it in Thy Hands; / And to whom Thou givest it, he has it free: / No one can inherit it, / Nor acquire / Through works Thy mercy, / Which saves us from dying.)

5. *Chorale.* All voices and instruments join in a straightforward presentation of the last verse of the hymn, which implores Christ for His help against temptation. This number is the complement to the opening chorus, both texts stressing the need for Christ's help, in order to make the individual stronger in his effort to attain faith and mercy.

• **Siehe, ich will viel Fischer aussenden (Behold, I Will Send Out Many Fishermen)** (1732; BWV 88).

This solo cantata for the fifth Sunday after Trinity refers directly to the Gospel, Luke 5 (1–11)—Simon Peter's miraculous catch of fish and his mission to catch men. The librettist is unknown; Neumann suggests Mariane von Ziegler.

Bach's superlative tone-painting in the first number makes this an outstanding movement, and the dramatic role of the bass representing Christ is exceedingly well done throughout the whole cantata.

The soli are SATB, with a four-part chorus. The orchestra has two horns, two oboes d'amore, two violins, a tenor oboe (taille) with a viola, and continuo.

Part I

1. *Aria—bass.* The text for this stupendous number is literally taken from Jeremiah 16 (16). Although it is an Old Testament quotation, Bach allots the words to the bass, as though Christ had spoken them. The oboes and strings play a wave-motif melody for the first half of the aria, to illustrate the motion of waves on the lake, whereon the fishermen are spreading their nets. In the second half,

the tempo quickens into a joy-motif, with fanfares of the horns overwhelming the strings as they depict the calls of the hunters. Bach's ability to transform the text, by his florid vocal and orchestral setting of the words, brings this picture of the hunt to realistic life. He must have remembered the hunts he witnessed during his days as court composer. This aria contains all of Bach's art: tone-painting of nature, religious drama and intense emotion, all combined into one idea. The listener will surely be impressed by this movement.

"Siehe, ich will viel Fischer aussenden, spricht der Herr, die wollen sie fischen. Und darnach will ich viel Jäger aussenden, die sollen sie fahen (fangen) auf allen Bergen und auf allen Hügeln und in allen Steinritzen." (Behold, I will send out many fishermen, saith the Lord; they shall fish for them. And thereafter I will send out many hunters; they shall catch them on all mountains and on all the hills and in all rocky crevices.)

The imagery of apostles and missionaries comes out also in this aria.

2. *Recitative—tenor.* In secco, he thinks about how the Lord could turn His mercy from us, because we are intent on separating ourselves from Him, thus causing our own ruin. He questions whether God will abandon us to the enemy's cunning and malice, since we have deserted Him. This question he answers himself in his aria which follows.

3. *Aria—tenor.* Accompanied by oboes and strings, his singing seems to reflect his wavering between doubt and faith, with confidence in God at the end of each of his doubts: "Nein, nein! Gott ist allezeit geflissen, / Uns auf gutem Weg zu wissen / Unter seiner Gnade Schein. / Ja, ja! wenn wir verirret sein / Und die rechte Bahn verlassen, / Will er uns gar suchen lassen." (No, no! God is always diligent, / To know that we are on the right way / Under the light of His mercy. / Yes, yes! when we have been erring / And have left the right road, / He will surely have us sought.)

Part II

4. *Arioso—bass.* The tenor introduces this number, which is then sung in secco by the bass. The Biblical text is Luke 5 (10), which refers to the Scripture of the opening number, but this quotation is from the New Testament. Bach's dramatic treatment of this text reappears in Christ's words to Peter—his commission to catch men's souls.

TENOR: "Jesus sprach zu Simon:" (Jesus said to Simon:)

BASS: "Fürchte dich nicht; denn von nun an / wirst du Menschen fahen." (Fear not; for from now on / thou wilt catch men.)

5. *Duet—soprano, alto.* All the violins and the oboes d'amore in unison play a pleasant melody, which seems, however, to have some difficulty in illustrating the text. The alto begins each line, followed by the soprano in canon, yet their singing of the libretto does not agree with the sound of the music. Still, this text is worth quoting for its fine religious thought: "Beruft Gott selbst, so muss der Segen / Auf allem unsern Tun / Im Übermasse ruh'n. / Stünd' uns gleich Furcht und Sorg' entgegen. / Das Pfund, so er uns ausgetan, / Will er mit Wucher wieder haben; / Wenn wir es nur nicht selbst vergraben, / So hilft er gern, damit es fruchten kann." (If God Himself calls, then must the blessing / On all our doings / Rest in overabundance, / Were fear and worry even standing against us. / The pound (talent), that He has given us, / He wants to have back with interest; / If only we ourselves do not bury it, / Then He helps gladly, so that it can bear fruit.)

6. *Recitative—soprano.* This is an interesting secco number, which has a dramatic element about it. She asks the listener why he should be afraid in his wanderings, knowing that God will protect him against all misfortune by a mere gesture of His Hand. The evils which beset him should not be too difficult to bear and will possibly be useful to him in God's plan for his life.

7. *Chorale.* The last verse of Georg Neumark's "Wer nur den lieben Gott lässt walten" (Whoever Just Lets Dear God Govern) provides the text for this closing chorale. All instruments (except the horns) and the choir perform it. They invoke us to follow God's ways, to trust in heaven's daily blessing, and to put all our hope in God, Who will never leave us.

The zeal of the missionary is reflected here as well as in all other numbers of this cantata.

• **Vergnügte Ruh', beliebte Seelenlust (Delightful Rest, Beloved Desire of the Soul)** (1732; BWV 170).

The author of this solo alto text for Bach's cantata for the sixth Sunday after Trinity is unknown. Parts of the libretto are based on the Epistle, Romans 6 (3–11), and on the Gospel, Matthew 5 (22), for this Sunday: the first aria and the first recitative respectively.

It is one of a series of solo alto cantatas with obbligato organ, which Bach composed about this time (cf. BWV 35 and BWV 169). The theme of this libretto would be very acceptable to Bach, because it derides the selfishness and the hatred, which he deplored in Leipzig society at this time. One can almost think that he wrote this libretto himself in his disgust.

The orchestra is simple: an oboe d'amore, two violins, a viola, an organ obbligato for some numbers and continuo.

1. *Aria.* Accompanied by all of the above instruments, the alto sings an exquisite slumber song. A motif of deep longing for the bliss of eternal rest after death pervades the entire number. The idea of evasion from this sinful world is an obsession; meanwhile, she will try to be virtuous until death comes: "Vergnügte Ruh', beliebte Seelenlust, / Dich kann man nicht bei Höllensünden, / Wohl aber Himmelseintracht finden; / Du stärkst allein die schwache Brust. / Drum sollen lauter Tugendgaben / In meinem Herzen Wohnung haben." (Delightful rest, beloved desire of the soul, / One cannot find thee among hell's sins, / But assuredly in the concord of heaven; / You alone strengthen the weak breast. / Therefore shall nothing but virtue's gifts / Have a dwelling-place in my heart.)

2. *Recitative.* Her secco declamation castigates the world as a house of sin. Envy and hatred that she sees about her seem to constitute a hymn of praise to Satan. People talk of vengeance (Racha) and speak venomous poison against the innocent. She appeals to God that He notice how far mankind is removed from Him by cursing and oppressing one's fellow-man. She concludes that this guilt will be difficult to pardon.

3. *Aria.* With organ obbligato and unison strings playing a tear-motif in their sobbing melody, she continues her lament over the perverted hearts seen about her. This aria is the high point of the cantata. It seems to be a kind of duet between the alto voice and the obbligato organ. It is a very demanding number for both.

"Wie jammern mich doch die verkehrten Herzen, / Die dir, mein Gott, so sehr zuwider sein; / Ich zittre recht und fühle tausend Schmerzen, / Wenn sie nur an Rach' und Hass erfreu'n. / Gerechter Gott, was magst du doch gedenken, / Wenn sie allein mit rechten Satansränken / Dein scharfes Strafgebot so frech verlacht. / Ach! ohne Zweifel hast du so gedacht: / Wie jammern mich doch die verkehrten Herzen!" (How the perverted hearts grieve me, / Which to Thee, my God, are so contrary; / I really tremble and feel a thousand pains, / When they only rejoice in revenge and hatred. / Righteous God, what mayest Thou think, / When they alone with real Satanic plots / Thus boldly scorn Thy strict punishment decree. / Ah! doubtlessly Thou hast thought thus: / How these perverted hearts grieve me!

4. *Recitative.* Accompanied by the strings, she asks who would wish to live with only hatred to return for love. Yet because she follows God's commandment

to love one's enemies as one's friends, she will turn her heart from anger. Her only wish is to live in God's perfect love; she asks when He will grant her heaven's Zion.

5. *Aria.* This is the final number, as there is no concluding chorale. All instruments support her voice in a joy-motif, probably taken from some lost instrumental work. This concerto-like theme with its dance-like melody makes this a joyous conclusion to an otherwise pessimistic cantata: "Mir ekelt mehr zu leben, / Drum nimm mich, Jesu, hin! / Mir graut vor allen Sünden, / Lass mich dies Wohnhaus finden, / Wo selbst ich ruhig bin." (It disgusts me to live longer; / Therefore take me away, Jesus! / I shudder before all sins; / Let me find this dwelling, / Where I myself am peaceful.)

• **Es wartet alles auf dich (All Things Wait for Thee)** (1732; BWV 187).

The plan for this cantata on the seventh Sunday after Trinity is the same as that for BWV 39, probably by the same anonymous librettist. Both works have Biblical quotations from the Old and the New testaments, not referring to the Scriptures for the day, but having two parts which contain identical movements.

The Gospel, Mark 8 (1–9)—Christ's miracle of feeding the four thousand—has a direct bearing on the libretto in general: the theme of thanksgiving to God for providing food for all His creatures. This may then be used as a Thanksgiving Day cantata.

The soli are SATB, with a four-part chorus. The instruments include two oboes, two violins, a viola and continuo.

Bach must have had a high opinion of this cantata, since he reused all its numbers, except the recitatives, for his *Short Mass in G minor.*

Part I

1. *Chorus.* This text is taken literally from Psalm 104 (27, 28). Bach treats these verses as a grand choral hymn of thanksgiving to God for His bounty to mankind in His total creation. The orchestra plays a pastoral theme in support of the canon singing of the chorus. A kind of staccato rhythm occurs in the second verse, after a spacious melody in the first, by which Bach may have meant to picture the work of the harvesters after their labors in the fields: "Es wartet alles auf dich, dass du ihnen Speise gebest zu seiner Zeit. Wenn du ihnen gibest, so sammeln sie; wenn du deine Hand auftust, so werden sie mit Gute gesättiget." (All things wait for Thee, that Thou mayest give to them food in its time. When Thou givest to them, then they gather; when Thou openest Thy Hand, then they are satisfied with Thy goodness.)

2. *Recitative—bass.* In secco, he ponders over the wonder that all creatures can find sustenance; he mentions the thousands of living species which inhabit the mountains, the seas and the air. No monarch with all his gold can provide them with even one single meal.

3. *Aria—alto.* She sings a sincere song of thanksgiving for the harvest which God has given them. The oboe and the strings play a joy-motif to accompany the descriptive text: "Du Herr, du krönst allein das Jahr mit deinem Gut. / Es träufet Fett und Segen / Auf deines Fusses Wegen, / Und deine Gnade ist's, die alles Gutes tut." (Thou Lord, Thou alone crownest the year with Thy goodness. / Fatness and blessing drop / On the paths of Thy foot, / And it is Thy mercy, which does all that is good.)

Part II

4. *Aria—bass.* Following the sermon, which no doubt would stress God's providence, this aria referring to Christ's teaching would have tremendous impact on the congregation. The text is taken from Matthew 6 (31, 32) and sung by the bass in the role of Christ. The forceful, dramatic style, accompanied by unison strings, is most impressive.

"Darum sollt ihr nicht sorgen noch sagen: / Was werden wir essen, was werden wir trinken, / womit werden wir uns kleiden? / Nach solchem allen trachten die Heiden. / Denn euer himmlischer Vater weiss, / dass ihr dies alles bedürfet." (Therefore you ought not to worry or say: / What shall we eat, what shall we drink, / with what shall we clothe ourselves? / After all such things the heathen strive. / For your heavenly Father knows, / that you need all these things.)

5. *Aria—soprano.* With the elaborate accompaniment of a solo oboe, she sings of her confidence that God will provide for all living creatures including herself. Accordingly, she will banish all her worries in the knowledge that she will daily receive His loving gifts.

6. *Recitative—soprano.* Accompanied by strings, she amplifies her thanks to God, knowing that she will receive His help as long as she holds to Him with childlike faith. She will accept her share of sorrow, because the Lord has accepted His. There is a feeling of fatalism in her declamation.

7. *Chorale.* "Singen wir aus Herzensgrund" (Let us sing from the depths of our heart). This beautiful, anonymous hymn is performed tutti in its fourth and sixth verses. These two verses reflect the entire thought of the cantata: God's sustenance of all living things and our thanks to Him for that. The melody and the sentiment it evokes are magnificent.

"Gott hat die Erde zugericht', / Lässt's an Nahrung mangeln nicht; / Berg und Tal, die macht er nass, / Dass dem Vieh auch wächst sein Gras; / Aus der Erden Wein und Brot / Schaffet Gott und Gibt's satt, / Dass der Mensch sein Leben hat." (God has arranged the earth, / He permits no lack of nourishment; / Mountain and valley, these He makes damp, / So that for cattle its grass also grows; / From the earth wine and bread / God creates and gives abundance of it, / So that man has his life.)

"Wir danken sehr und bitten ihn, / Dass er uns geb' des Geistes Sinn, / Dass wir solches recht verstehn, / Stets in sein' Geboten gehn, / Seinen Namen machen gross / In Christo ohn' Unterlass: / So singen wir recht das Gratias." (We very much thank and ask Him, / That He may give to us the Spirit's sense, / So that we really understand such things, / Always to walk in his laws, / To make His Name great / In Christ incessantly: / Hence we sing the Gratias.)

• **Lobe den Herren, den mächtigen König der Ehren (Praise the Lord, the Mighty King of Honors)** (1732; BWV 137).

This chorale cantata for the twelfth Sunday after Trinity is not related to the Scriptures for the day, nor is the hymn upon which the libretto was based. As in the case of BWV 69, it was also performed for the Election of Town Council during the last week in August.

The five verses of Joachim Neander's hymn all begin with the same words, "Lobe den Herren," but Bach's varied setting for each verse avoids any sense of monotony. Bach returned to the old style which he had used in BWV 4—a beginning chorus and a concluding chorale, with solo arias in between, without recitatives. The theme of the libretto is a general, personal hymn of praise to God.

The soli are SATB, with a four-part chorus. The orchestra is brilliant: three trumpets, timpani, three oboes, two violins, a viola and continuo.

1. *Chorus.* This is a chorale fantasia, featuring a joy-motif throughout, while the voice parts sing a fugue in canon. Orchestral ritornelli occur between the lines, with trumpets and drums decorating the ending of each line. The result is a magnificent portrayal of communal praise to God, in which the choir seems to encourage the congregation to join with them: "Lobe den Herren, den mächtigen König der Ehren, / Meine geliebte Seele, das ist mein Begehren. / Kommet zu Hauf, / Psalter und Harfen, wacht auf! / Lasset die Musicam hören." (Praise the Lord, the mighty King of honors, / My beloved soul, that is my desire. / Come in multitudes, / Psaltery and harps, wake up! / Let the song of praise be heard.)

2. *Aria—alto.* The solo violin accompaniment to her aria seems to evoke the sound of the eagle's wings, which are mentioned in the text. This image will be repeated in the following duet, wherein God, as the Eagle, will lead and protect His faithful. In this aria, she asks whether the listener has ever noticed how God, who governs all things so wonderfully, has preserved him as he wished.

3. *Duet—soprano, bass.* This is a fine number, sung in canon, with two oboes playing a joy-motif to illustrate the spreading of the protective Eagle wings. As the central number in the cantata and its high point, Bach infuses this verse with deeply personal emotion: "Lobe den Herren, der künstlich und fein dich bereitet, / Der dir Gesundheit verliehen, dich freundlich geleitet; / In wie viel Not / Hat nicht der gnädige Gott / Über dir Flügel gebreitet!" (Praise the Lord, Who has created you artfully and fine, / Who has granted you health, has kindly led you; / In how much trouble / Has not merciful God / Spread His wings over you!)

4. *Aria—tenor.* Continuo strings play a striking bass accompaniment to his aria and a solo trumpet illuminates his interpretation of this stanza of the chorale. His delivery has a vigor which convinces the listener of the sincerity of the text, much more than if these words were a part of a sermon, which they seem to resemble: "Lobe den Herren, der deinen Stand sichtbar gesegnet, / Der aus dem Himmel mit Strömen der Liebe geregnet; / Denke dran, / Was der Allmächtige kann, / Der dir mit Liebe begegnet." (Praise the Lord, Who has visibly blessed your station in life, / Who has rained out of heaven with streams of love; / Think about that, / Which the Almighty can do, / Who has met you with love.)

5. *Chorale.* All voices and instruments are heard in this exuberant concluding stanza. Bach's setting of the chorale tune reiterates the same group and individual praise of the opening chorus. The joy-motif recurs in full. Notice that the first part of the verse exhorts each creature which draws breath to praise the Lord, while the last lines refer to the soul. Thus body and soul will praise together, closing with "Amen."

• **Christus, der ist mein Leben (Christ, He Is My Life)** (1732; BWV 95).

This is the last of the extant cantatas for the sixteenth Sunday after Trinity (BWV 161, 8, 27), all of which are concerned with death. The Gospel is Luke 7 (11–17), the raising of the widow of Nain's son, which the libretto does not mention, but simply dwells on death as the prelude to resurrection. The unknown author of this libretto has written an unusual text, having four different chorales and only one aria, yet from these Bach could derive many images of death and resurrection and create a new form of the chorale cantata, based on several chorales rather than just one.

The soli are STB, with the usual four-part chorus. The instruments are a horn, two oboes, two violins, a viola and continuo.

1. *Chorale.* The four-part choir sings the first verse of this anonymous hymn to a full orchestral accompaniment playing Melchior Vulpius's melody, which will extend into the beginning of the following tenor recitative. The rhythm is solemnly sedate, sounding like a funeral march with its sad longing. All voices in unison make a long run on "Sterben" at the beginning of line 2: "Christus, der ist mein Leben / Sterben ist mein Gewinn; / Dem tu' ich mich ergeben, / Mit Freud' fahr' ich dahin." (Christ, He is my life; / To die is my reward. / To Him I yield myself, / With joy I travel thither.)

2. *Recitative—tenor.* This number continues without pause from the above chorale. He breaks in on the melody, which gradually dies away, leaving him to finish his recitative with continuo only. He says he will depart from the world with joy; if he is called today, he is willing and ready to return his mortal remains to the earth. He has composed his death-song and is ready to sing it.

3. *Chorale.* This is stanza one of Luther's "Nunc dimittis," sung by all voices in unison, with the horn decorating the beginning of all lines except one, "Sanft und stille" (Calmly and quietly.) This verse continues the tenor's last words in the preceding number. Oddly enough, a joy-motif shines forth in the allegro rhythm, even though it is a funeral hymn: "Mit Fried' und Freud' ich fahr' dahin, / Nach Gottes Willen, / Getrost ist mir mein Herz und Sinn, / Sanft und stille. / Wie Gott mir verheissen hat: / Der Tod ist mein Schlaf worden." (With peace and joy I travel thither, / According to God's will; / My heart and mind are comforted, / Calmly and quietly. / As God has promised me: / Death has become my sleep.)

4. *Recitative—soprano.* Accompanied by unison oboes, she bids farewell to this false world, with which she now has nothing further to do. She has put her house in order and will now rest more easily than she could by the rivers of Babylon, where she had to swallow the salt of lust and could only pick Sodom's apples.

Her number leads without pause into the next chorale, which she will sing to continue her thought, accompanied by oboes and strings.

5. *Chorale—soprano.* She sings this first stanza of Valerius Herberger's funeral hymn, again paradoxically to an exuberant joy-motif in the oboes d'amore. Note that the length of the chorale stanzas has been increasing up to this number. Bach has been experimenting with a short chorale stanza at the beginning of a cantata and then lengthening them in subsequent numbers.

"Valet will ich dir geben, / Du arge, falsche Welt, / Dein sündlich böses Leben / Durchaus mir nicht gefällt. / Im Himmel ist gut wohnen, / Hinauf steht mein Begier. / Da wird Gott ewig lohnen / Dem, der ihm dient allhier." (Farewell will I give thee, / Thou hard, false world; / Thy sinful evil life / Does not please me at all. / In heaven it is good to live; / Up there stands my desire. / There God will eternally reward / Him, who serves Him here.)

6. *Recitative—tenor.* This particular secco recitative is fortunately short; its text is simply a longing for death to come to him. Morose details, such as feeling death in his limbs and choosing death as his dowry, do not add any ray of hope. They lead into his coming aria, which likewise is pessimistic.

7. *Aria—tenor.* Throughout this number, pizzicato strings play a realistic imitation of tolling funeral bells. Yet the seeming pessimism of the text still contains a joy-motif in the tenor's singing and in the oboes d'amore. Bach's mystic philosophy of treating death as a release from worldly cares and as the gateway to Paradise is well illustrated by his pictorial music at the climax of this cantata: "Ach, schlage doch bald, sel'ge Stunde, / Den allerletzten Glockenschlag! / Komm, komm, ich reiche dir die Hände, / Komm, mache meiner Not ein Ende, / Du längst erzeufzter Sterbenstag! (Ah, strike then soon, blessed hour, / The ultimate peal of the bell! / Come, come, I reach out my hands to thee, / Come, make an end of my trouble, / Thou long sighed-for day of death!)

8. *Recitative—bass.* Whereas the two previous numbers had completely gloomy texts, the libretto now dwells more on the transition from the grave to the afterlife. His secco description of this resurrection is concluded by a brief arioso on the thought. Death is only a restful sleep before our reunion with Jesus.

9. *Chorale.* All voices and instruments portray Bach's picture of the soul about to ascend to God. This is the fourth verse of Nikolaus Herman's hymn, "Wenn mein Stündlein vorhanden ist" (When My Little Hour Is at Hand). Just as Christ has risen, so shall we. At least this conclusion ends optimistically.

• **Was Gott tut, das ist wohlgetan (What God Does, That Is Done Well) I** (1732; BWV 98).

This is the first of three chorale cantatas of the same title, based on Samuel

Rodigast's hymn. This work is for the twenty-first Sunday after Trinity, while the later ones, BWV 99 and BWV 100, are for the fifteenth. It differs from them in that it has no final chorale. This has been noted by the omission of the *Fine S.D.G.*, which Bach customarily adds at the end of a cantata. Perhaps he intended to add a chorale stanza later after the final number, a bass aria, but never did. All three cantatas begin with the first verse of Rodigast's hymn; for BWV 98 that is the only choral number. The librettist is unknown.

The Gospel for this Sunday is John 4 (46–54), Christ heals the nobleman's son, resulting in the father's belief, but this is only indirectly alluded to in the libretto. Each of the soloists expresses confidence in God's power to console him when in distress.

The soli are SATB, with the usual four-part chorus for the opening number. The instruments include two oboes, taille (a tenor oboe), two violins, a viola and continuo.

1. *Chorus (Chorale fantasia)*. This is a long chorus because of the instrumental ritornelli between each line sung by the choral groups. These orchestral interludes, however, seem to give more emphasis to the words sung, first by the sopranos, then joined by the other voices. They sing of their complete trust in God to guide them in life. It is a moving chorus in thought and music: "Was Gott tut, das ist wohlgetan, / Es bleibt gerecht sein Wille; / Wie er fängt meine Sachen an, / Will ich ihm halten stille. / Er ist mein Gott, / Der in der Not / Mich wohl weiss zu erhalten; / Drum lass ich ihn nur walten." (What God does, that is done well, / His Will remains just; / However He arranges my affairs, / I will hold to Him quietly. / He is my God, / Who in my trouble / Knows well how to sustain me; / Therefore I let only Him govern.)

2. *Recitative—tenor*. He asks God when He will save him from the torment of sorrow and anxiety he feels. Yet he tells himself that God never forsakes those who trust in His power and protection. His declamation is very convincing.

3. *Aria—soprano*. With a solo oboe to illustrate her text with a tear-motif, she begins with lamentation as did the tenor in the preceding recitative, but ends on a note of confidence just as he did, even though the da capo brings back the weeping theme in the oboe. This aria is supercharged with emotion: "Hört, ihr Augen, auf zu weinen! / Trag' ich doch / Mit Geduld mein schweres Joch. / Gott, der Vater, lebet noch, / Von den Seinen / Lässt er keinen. / Hört, ihr Augen, auf zu weinen!" (Cease, you eyes, from weeping! / I am still bearing / Patiently my heavy yoke. / God, the Father, is still living; / Of His own, / He leaves none. / Cease, you eyes, from weeping!)

4. *Recitative—alto*. This secco number shows none of the vacillation of the former movements; it is full of confidence—as is the following concluding aria. She states that God's heart is overflowing with pity for our tribulations. The Lord tells us to knock and the door of His mercy will be opened to us (Matthew 7 [7]). Therefore, when we are in deepest distress, we should lift our hearts to Him.

5. *Aria—bass*. Bach imitated a melody by Andreas Hammerschmidt, using unison violins for the accompaniment. The optimistic joy-motif continues with the idea of trust in God, Who will bless us and protect us against evil: "Meinen Jesum lass ich nicht, / Bis mich erst sein Angesicht / Wird erhören oder segnen. / Er allein / Soll mein Schutz in allem sein, / Was mir Übels kann begegnen." (I will not leave my Jesus, / Before his countenance / Will hear or bless me. / He alone / Is to be my Protector in everything / That in evil can befall me.)

• **O Ewigkeit, du Donnerwort [Dialogus] (O Eternity, Thou Word of Thunder [Dialogue] II** (1732; BWV 60).

The unknown librettist for this twenty-fourth Sunday after Trinity cantata presented Bach with a splendid opportunity to show his gift for drama. All the numbers except the final chorale are in dialogue between the personifications of Fear and Hope, the alto and the tenor respectively.

The Gospel, Matthew 9 (18–26), describes the raising of the ruler's daughter by Christ, from which miracle the librettist derived his theme on death and resurrection.

Two different chorales are used for the opening and closing numbers. Bach set this text as a solo cantata for ATB, with a four-part choir in the final chorale. It is his second composition of this cantata and is much different from the previous BWV 20.

The instrumentation includes a horn (in the opening duet), two oboes d'amore, two violins, a viola and continuo. It is an unusual work, having all its numbers in dialogue form, except the final chorale.

1. *Duet (Aria and Chorale)—alto, tenor.* This is a wonderful chorale fantasia and should be compared with the opening chorus of BWV 20. The text for the aria is the first stanza of the hymn by Johann Rist, sung by the alto (Fear). The orchestra depicts her terrified state of mind at the thought of death, playing a terror-motif of repeated quavers as she sings.

The chorale text is verse 166 of Psalm 119, "Herr, ich warte auf dein Heil" (Lord, I wait for Thy salvation), which the tenor (Hope) repeats to the end of the duet, beginning at the fourth line of the alto's aria.

FURCHT (FEAR): "O Ewigkeit, du Donnerwort, / O Schwert, das durch die Seele bohrt, / O Anfang sonder Ende! / O Ewigkeit, Zeit ohne Zeit, / Ich weiss vor grosser Traurigkeit / Nicht, wo ich mich hinwende; / Mein ganz erschrocknes Herze bebt, / Dass mir die Zung' am Gaumen klebt." (O eternity, thou word of thunder, / O sword, that pierces the soul, / O beginning without end! / O eternity, time without time. / I do not know in my great sadness / Where I should turn; / My thoroughly frightened soul trembles, / So that my tongue sticks to my gums.)

2. *Recitative—alto, tenor.* Fear and Hope alternate their comments on death, as though they were two actors, presenting opposite points of view. This will continue in the following numbers, beginning with their secco declamation here:

(FEAR: O heavy way to the last struggle and fight!)

(HOPE: My assistance is always there, / My Savior surely stands by me / With comfort at my side!)

(FEAR: The worry of death, the last pain, / Rushes up and attacks my heart / And tortures these bodily members.)

(HOPE: I place this body down as an offering before God. / If the fire of affliction is already hot, / Enough, it cleanses me for God's reward.)

(FEAR: Yet now will the great guilt of my sins / present themselves before my face!)

(HOPE: God will not pronounce any judgment of death on that account. / He gives an end to temptation's tortures, / So that one can endure them.)

3. *Duet—alto, tenor.* The same actors continue to contrast their feelings about death, supported by an oboe d'amore and a solo violin. Bach writes some fine music for them but this does not seem to illustrate their opposing sentiments. Perhaps the conflicting feelings in their short lines daunted the composer.

FURCHT (FEAR): "Main letztes Lager will mich schrecken." (My last bed will frighten me.)

HOFFNUNG (HOPE): "Mich wird des Heilands Hand bedecken." (The Savior's hand will cover me.)

FURCHT: "Des Glaubens Schwachheit sinket fast." (Faith's weakness is almost sinking.)

HOFFNUNG: "Mein Jesus trägt mit mir die Last." (My Jesus carries the burden with me.)

FURCHT: "Das offne Grab sieht greulich aus." (The open grave appears frightful.)

HOFFNUNG: "Es wird mir doch ein

Friedenshaus." (It will still be a house of peace for me.)

4. *Recitative—alto, bass.* The bass assumes the role of Christ to replace the tenor for this dialogue. Christ still represents Hope (Hoffnung) in the bass arioso replies, from Revelation 14 (13): "Blessed are the dead / which die in the Lord / from henceforth." He sings each section of the above division, repeating and adding to it a section at each reentry, to finally convince the fearful alto to hope for His paradise.

5. *Chorale.* This is stanza five of Franz Joachim Burmeister's hymn, "Es ist genug; so nimm, Herr, meinen Geist" (It Is Enough; Then Take My Spirit, Lord.) All voices and instruments give a moving interpretation of the text: it is enough to leave this world when God calls us, knowing that we will leave our earthly misery behind us for the serene peace of heaven.

• **Nun danket alle Gott (Now All Thank God)** (c. 1732; BWV 192).

This chorale cantata is very short, consisting of only three numbers, all of which are set on the original three stanzas of Martin Rinckart's hymn with the above title. Terry thinks that it is an incomplete cantata for an unknown occasion, while Whittaker assumes that it was for a Reformation Festival.

The soli are only SB in the duet. The two chorales have a four-part chorus.

The orchestra is also meager: two transverse flutes, two oboes, strings and continuo. Nevertheless, whether it is complete or incomplete, it is a beautiful and outstanding work in all its movements.

1. *Chorus.* Bach decorates in his own style the hymn-tune for this stanza, creating a marvelous chorale fantasia. The divided vocal parts sing the lines in canon and, at the end of the stanza, they repeat the first line twice in unison: "Nun danket alle Gott / Mit Herzen, Mund und Händen, / Der grosse Dinge tut / An uns und allen Enden, / Der uns von Mutterleib / Und Kindesbeinen an / Unzählig viel zugut / Und noch jetzund getan." (Now all thank God / With hearts, mouth and hands, / Who does great things / For us and all our ends, / Who for us from our mother's womb / And from infancy on / Countless much for our good / And still now has done.)

2. *Duet—soprano, bass.* They sing their lines in canon, with the bass leading in the first half of the stanza and the soprano in the last half. They are accompanied by a flute, an oboe, a violin and strings, which also play an interlude between the two halves of the stanza. This duet is a fervent song of thanks to God, who has protected us in our troubled lives and will continue to do so.

Whittaker, Vol. I, p. 459, states that "while bright and effective, the duet is not particularly notable." I would disagree with this judgment, since I feel that both the text and Bach's musical interpretation of it have a deeply emotional appeal for the listener in Bach's mystical transformation.

"Der ewig reiche Gott / Woll uns bei unserm Leben / Ein immer fröhlich Herz / Und edlen Frieden geben / Und uns in seiner Gnad' / Erhalten fort und fort / Und uns aus aller Not / Erlösen hier und dort." (May the ever rich God / Wish to give us in our life / An always joyful heart / And noble peace / And in His mercy / Sustain us continually / And from all want / Redeem us here and there.)

3. *Chorus.* This third stanza of the hymn is set to a pastoral melody, with the transverse flutes and the oboes doubling the strings in a dance-like tune. Perhaps Bach wished to paint a picture of an assembly giving joyous thanks to the Trinity. There is a joy-motif in the music which evokes an image of the Good Shepherd with His flock in their pasture, rather than merely a solemn hymn of praise suggested by the text: "Lob, Ehr' und Preis sei Gott, / Dem Vater und dem Sohne / Und dem, der beiden gleich / Im hohen Himmelsthrone, / Dem dreieinigen Gott, / Als der ursprünglich war / Und ist und bleiben wird / Jetzund und immerdar." (Laud,

honor and praise be to God, / To the Father and to the Son / And to Him, Who is equal to both / In the high throne of heaven, / To the three in one God, / As He was originally / And is now and will remain / Now and evermore.)

• **Ach Gott, wie manches Herzeleid [Dialogus] (Ah God, How Much Heart-Sorrow [Dialogue]) II** (1733; BWV 58).

This solo cantata for soprano and bass is one of two compositions by Bach with this title, although both are for different Sundays in January. It seems strange that this cantata should be termed Bach's second composition, when it was actually his first—the second was a chorale cantata about 1740, BWV 3. The numbering of the cantatas according to their publication by the editors of the Bachgessellschaft (BG) was responsible for this, even though they did give the presumed dates after each of these works.

The unknown librettist used both the Epistle, Titus 3 (4–7), justification by faith rather than by works—and the Gospel, Matthew 2 (13–15), the flight into Egypt—prescribed for this Sunday after the Circumcision.

The cantata is unusual in having its first and last numbers as chorale fantasias, which use two different hymns. The soli are SB; the soprano represents the persecuted soul (fleeing from her enemies like the Holy Family into Egypt), while the bass portrays the consoling guidance of God (the Epistle).

The orchestra consists of two oboes, taille, two violins, a viola and continuo.

1. *Chorale and Aria—soprano, bass.* The soprano sings stanza one of Martin Moller's hymn, "Ach, Gott wie manches Herzeleid" (Ah, God, How Much Heart-Sorrow) in a duet with the bass, who interjects the comforting lines of his aria as she completes each of her chorale lines. Towards the end, there is some overlapping and inversion in the sequence of the two voices. Bach's arrangement is very neatly done.

SOPRANO: "Ach Gott, wie manches Herzeleid / Begegnet mir zu dieser Zeit! / Der schmale Weg ist trübsalsvoll, / Den ich zum Himmel wandern soll." (Ah God, how much heart-sorrow / Meets me at this time! / The narrow way is full of sadness, / On which I must travel to heaven.)

BASS: "Nur Geduld, Geduld, mein Herze, / Es ist eine böse Zeit. / Doch der Gang zur Seligkeit / Führt zur Freude nach dem Schmerze." (Only patience, patience, my heart, / It is a bad time! / Yet the way to blessedness / Leads to joy after pain.)

2. *Recitative—bass.* His secco declamation offers her confidence in God's friendly protection against the harsh world and her enemies. Just as He sent His angel to warn Joseph in a dream to flee into Egypt, so He will never fail to give her His aid. His text concludes with parts of verses from Isaiah 54 (10) and Hebrews 13 (5) to illustrate this: "He says, when mountain and hill sink down, / When the flood of waters will drown you, / Then I will not leave or overlook you."

3. *Aria—soprano.* Accompanied by a solo violin obbligato, which decorates her song with a joy-motif, she affirms her renewed trust in God, in whom she will be sure of defense against all evil. Only her confidence glows in this aria: "Ich bin vergnügt in meinem Leiden, / Denn Gott ist meine Zuversicht. / Ich habe sichern Brief und Siegel, / Und dieses ist der feste Riegel, / Den bricht die Hölle selber nicht." (I am content in my sorrow, / For God is my confidence. / I have a sure charter and seal, / And this is the firm bolt, / Which even hell does not break.)

4. Recitative—soprano. Knowing that the world will persecute and hate her, she longs to see a better world, where such vices are impossible. She wishes that today she might see the Eden which God has promised her. Thus she stresses almost every word of her arioso in the last two lines: "Ach! könnt' es heute noch geschehen, / Dass ich mein Eden möchte sehen!" (Ah! could it today just happen, / That I might see my Eden!)

5. *Chorale and Aria—soprano, bass.* The soprano sings stanza two of Martin

Behm's hymn, "O Jesu Christ, mein's Lebens Licht" (O Jesus Christ, Light of My Life), to the melody of the opening number, while the bass interjects the lines of his aria as before. Bach modified the chorale tune, adapting it to a concerto movement from a lost violin concerto. A joy-motif predominates throughout, radiating happiness in both voices and in the dancing tempo. The singers follow the same order as in their first duet.

SOPRANO: Ich hab' vor mir ein' schwere Reis' / Zu dir ins Himmels Paradeis, / Da ist mein rechtes Vaterland, / Daran du dein Blut hast gewandt." (I have before me a heavy journey / To Thee in heaven's Paradise, / There is the real homeland, / For which Thou hast spent Thy Blood.)

BASS: "Nur getrost, getrost, ihr Herzen, / Hier ist Angst, dort Herrlichkeit! / Und die Freude jener Zeit / Überwieget alle Schmerzen." (Only be consoled, consoled, you hearts, / Here is worry, there glory! / And the joy of that time / Outweighs all pains.)

• **Was Gott tut, das ist wohlgetan (What God Does, That Is Done Well) II** (c. 1733; BWV 99).

For the fifteenth Sunday after Trinity, this chorale cantata was set by Bach on the original first and fifth stanzas of Samuel Rodigast's hymn, while the unknown librettist paraphrased in the intervening stanzas for the two arias and the two recitatives. "Trust in God to help us in our distress" is the theme of this cantata, reflecting the Gospel for the day, Matthew 6 (24–34).

The soli are SATB, with the usual four-part chorus. The orchestra includes a horn, a transverse flute, an oboe d'amore, two violins, a viola and continuo.

1. *Chorus (Chorale).* The text and its translation for this first stanza of Rodigast's hymn are given for BWV 98. Bach expands this chorus into a sumptuous chorale fantasia, with a lengthy orchestral introduction and long ritornelli between the vocal lines, thus producing a beautiful total effect. In fact, this orchestral part has been performed as a piece of chamber music or in a suite in recent Bach concerts (e.g. *The Wise Virgins*—ballet suite arranged from Bach by William Walton).

2. *Recitative—bass.* In secco, he affirms his trust in God's Word, on which he can depend to protect himself in times of misfortune. He will have patience in his trials, knowing that God guides his way through life. The Almighty will not allow any believer to fall or perish.

3. *Aria—tenor.* The transverse flute adorns his aria with quavering passages to illustrate the first two lines of the text, depicting the fears of the shuddering soul, but rises to a higher note of consolation in the last three lines: "Erschüttre dich nur nicht, verzagte Seele, / Wenn dir der Kreuzeskelch so bitter schmeckt! / Gott ist dein weiser Arzt und Wundermann, / Der dir kein tödlich Gift einschenken kann, / Obgleich die Süssigkeit verborgen steckt." (Do not quaver so, disheartted soul, / When your cup of sorrow tastes so bitter! / God is your wise doctor and miracle-worker, / Who can pour no deadly poison for you, / Although its sweetness remains hidden.)

4. *Recitative—alto.* She declares in this secco number that her faith is founded on the covenant, made for eternity, that God would be her light in life and in death. She will surrender herself to Him, knowing that He will rescue her from daily suffering in His own good time.

5. *Duet—soprano, alto.* Accompanied by a transverse flute and an oboe d'amore, they sing in canon of the struggle between the flesh and the spirit. The rhythm indicates a writhing to depict this contest. The spirit must endure the tortures of the flesh in order to be sanctified: "Wenn des Kreuzes Bitterkeiten / Mit des Fleisches Schwachheit streiten, / Ist es dennoch wohlgetan. / Wer das Kreuz durch falschen Wahn / Sich für unerträglich schätzet, / Wird auch künftig nicht ergötzet." (When the bitterness of pain / Struggles with the weakness of the

flesh, / It is nevertheless done well. / Whoever through false delusion / Considers his cross unbearable, / He will not be delighted in the future.)

6. *Chorale.* Lines one and eight of this final sixth stanza of the hymn are the same as the corresponding lines of the first stanza. This is a straightforward rendition of the hymn tune, sung by the four-part choir with all instruments accompanying: "Was Gott tut, das ist wohlgetan, / Dabei will ich verbleiben. / Es mag mich auf die rauhe Bahn / Not, Tod und Elend treiben, / So wird Gott mich / Ganz väterlich / In seinen Armen halten; / Drum lass' ich ihn nur walten." (What God does, that is done well, / In that I will remain. / There may drive me on the rough road / Need, death and misery; / Then God will hold me / Just as a Father / In His arms; / Therefore I just let Him rule.)

• **Gloria in excelsis Deo (Glory to God in the Highest)** (1733; BWV 191).

This is Bach's only sacred cantata with the text not in German. It has only three numbers, all of which were included when Bach expanded the work into the *Mass in B minor,* which he completed about 1747. The three movements of the cantata correspond to the opening chorus of the *Gloria,* the *Domine Deus* and the *Cum Sancto Spiritu* movements in the *B Minor Mass.*

This Missa cantata was for Christmas Day, probably 1733, following its first performance, 21 April 1733, to celebrate the new ruler, Friedrich Augustus III, on his visit to Leipzig to accept the town's oath of allegiance.

The Gospel, Luke 2 (1–14), provides the text in its fourteenth verse for the opening chorus, and the Doxology provides the remainder.

The soli are ST, with a four-part chorus. The orchestra is lavish: three trumpets, timpani, two flutes, two oboes, strings and continuo.

Since the music of the Mass is identical with that of the corresponding cantata movements, a detailed analysis should not be necessary beyond a translation of the Latin texts.

Part I

1. *Chorus.* "Gloria in excelsis Deo. Et in terra pax hominibus bonae voluntatis." (Glory to God in the highest. And on earth peace to men of good will.)

Part II

[Note that the sermon would be given after Part I.)

2. *Duet—soprano, tenor.* "Gloria Patri et Filio et Spiritui sancto." (Glory be to the Father and to the Son and to the Holy Ghost.)

3. *Chorus.* "Sicut erat in principio et nunc et semper et in saecula saeculorum. Amen." (As it was in the beginning is now and always will be in all centuries. Amen.)

• **Sei Lob und Erh' dem höchsten Gut (Be Praise and Honor to the Highest Good)** (c. 1733; BWV 117).

All nine stanzas of the hymn by Johann Jakob Schütz constitute the libretto of this chorale cantata, which is perhaps for a wedding, a Reformation festival or a thanksgiving ceremony. Unlike BWV 4, in which Bach adhered to the hymn tune with only slight variations in all movements, in this cantata he uses the hymn tune only for the opening chorus, the middle chorale and the final chorale. All the other movements are set in free madrigal style.

Bach unifies the work by giving various artistic emphases to the final motto line at the end of each stanza, "Gebt unserm Gott die Ehre!" Thus the free numbers always return to the chorale theme at the end of each of them.

As this is a fairly long cantata, the sermon was probably given after the fourth movement, the middle chorale. The theme of the work is praise to God, both in the choral and in the solo numbers.

The soli are ATB, with a four-part chorus. The instruments are two transverse flutes, two oboes, two oboes d'amore, strings and continuo.

1. *Chorus (Chorale).* This extended chorale is sung plainly, with all instruments accompanying, to the tune of the anonymous "Es ist das Heil uns kommen her" (Salvation Has Come to Us). This is congregational singing, albeit much more elaborate, with which the listeners were accustomed in singing their hymns: "Sei Lob und Ehr' dem höchsten Gut, / Dem Vater aller Güte, / Dem Gott, der alle Wunder tut, / Dem Gott, der mein Gemüte / Mit seinem reichen Trost erfüllt, / Dem Gott, der allen Jammer stillt. / Gebt unserm Gott die Ehre!" (Be praise and honor to the highest Good, / To the Father of all goodness, / To God, Who does all Wonders, / To God, Who fills my spirit / With His rich comfort, / To God, Who quietens all grief. / Give to our God the glory!)

2. *Recitative—bass.* He recounts, in secco, that all creatures praise their Creator, the King of kings; beginning with the angelic host, he mentions the inhabitants of earth, air and sea, whom God has created according to His plan. He ends with a reiterated arioso on the motto: "Gebt unserm Gott die Ehre!"

3. *Aria—tenor.* The two oboes d'amore, accompanying this number, lend a tone of confidence, which seems to color his didactic text very effectively: "Was unser Gott geschaffen hat, / Das will er auch erhalten; / Darüber will er früh und spat / Mit seiner Gnade walten. / In seinem ganzen Königreich / Ist alles recht und alles gleich. / Gebt unserm Gott die Ehre!" (What our God has created, / That will He also maintain; / Over that He will early and late / Rule with His mercy. / In His whole Kingdom / Everything is right and equal. / Give to our God the glory!)

Note that this aria has no da capo.

4. *Chorale.* The same four-part choir and the same full orchestra present this fourth verse of the hymn to the same melody. Once again, it is the group expressing their song of thanks: "Ich rief dem Herrn in meinder Not: Ach Gott, vernimm mein Schreien! / Da half mein Helfer mir vom Tod / Und liess mir Trost gedeihen. / Drum dank, ach Gott, drum dank ich dir; / Ach danket, danket Gott mit mir! / Gebt unserm Gott die Ehre!" (I cried to the Lord in my distress: / Ah God, hear my crying! / Then my Helper helped me from death / And let my comfort increase. / Therefore thanks, ah God, so I thank Thee; / Ah, thank, thank God with me! / Give to our God the glory!)

5. *Recitative—alto.* Strings accompany the first part of this number, but they are omitted in the latter part, where her arioso on the motto of the last line expresses a joy-motif. She states that the Lord is now with, and never has been separated from, His people. He remains their assurance, blessing, salvation and peace. With a mother's hands, He guides His own continually to and fro.

6. *Aria—bass.* A solo obbligato violin imparts quiet dignity to this number, as he continues the joy-motif in his singing. His personal faith in God to help him in time of trouble is beautifully expressed both in the text and in the vocal: "Wenn Trost und Hülf ermangeln muss, / Die alle Welt erzeiget, / So kommt, so hilft der Überfluss, / Der Schöpfer selbst, und neiget / Die Vateraugen denen zu, / Die sonsten nirgend finden Ruh. / Gebt unserm Gott die Ehre!" (When comfort and help must fail, / Which the whole world shows, / Then comes, then helps the abundance, / The Creator Himself, and casts / His Fatherly eyes on those, Who otherwise find rest nowhere. / Give to our God the glory!)

7. *Aria—alto.* This number is the crowning jewel of the whole cantata. It is accompanied by the strings and the transverse flutes. The melody is a very moving largo, to which the alto sings a happy hymn of devotion to God. The tune resembles a rondo with its swinging tempo in a joy-motif. This aria, in my opinion, is one of Bach's most inspired moments.

"Ich will dich all mein Leben lang, / O Gott, von nun an ehren; / Man soll, o Gott, den Lobgesang / An allen Orten hören. / Mein ganzes Herz ermuntre sich, / Mein Geist und Leib erfreue sich, / Gebt unserm Gott die Ehre!" (I will my whole life long, / O God, from now on honor Thee; / One shall, O God, Thy song of praise / Hear in all places. / Let my whole heart be encouraged, / My spirit and body rejoice; / Give to our God the glory!)

8. *Recitative—tenor.* His secco declamation repeats the motto at the end of each stanza three times within this verse. The other lines are simply an invocation to the listeners to adore only the true God: "Ihr, die ihr Christi Namen nennt, / Ihr, die ihr Gottes Macht bekennt, / Die falschen Götzen macht zu Spott, / Der Herr ist Gott, der Herr ist Gott." (You, who say Christ's Name, / You, who recognize God's power, / Mock the false idols, / The Lord is God, the Lord is God.)

9. *Chorus (Chorale).* This concluding stanza of the hymn is performed, like the opening chorus, with the same melody, but its text emphasizes the joy-motif more: "So kommet vor sein Angesicht / Mit jauchzenvollem Springen; / Bezahlt die gelobte Pflicht / Und lasst uns fröhlich singen: / Gott hat alles wohl bedacht / Und alles, alles recht gemacht. / Gebt unsrem Gott die Ehre!" (Then come before His countenance / With exultant leaping; / Pay the allegiance vowed to Him / And let us joyfully sing: / God has well thought about everything / And has done everything, everything correctly. / Give to our God the glory!)

• **In allen meinen Taten (In All My Deeds)** (1734; BWV 97).

This is another long nine-verse chorale cantata; its libretto consists of the nine stanzas of Paul Fleming's hymn, beginning with the above title. Like the previous cantata, the occasion for its performance is unknown, although Schweitzer thinks it was for a wedding. The date, however, is definitely 1734, as Bach's notation at the end of the score states.

Fleming's hymn was composed just before he set out on a journey; all stanzas reflect his prayer in the first person for God's protection on this trip and also on his journey through life.

The chorale tune is again only used in the first and last movements (cf. BWV 117). This tune has its origin in Heinrich Isaak's secular song, "Innsbruck, ich muss dich lassen" (Innsbruck, I Must Leave Thee), a well-known folk song even today.

The soli are SATB, with a four-part chorus. The instruments are two oboes, two bassoons, an obbligato violin and strings, with a cello and organ in the continuo. The organ accompanies all numbers except the recitatives.

1. *Chorus (Chorale).* This opening chorus begins with an instrumental introduction (grave), followed by a faster section (vivace), in the first two movements of a French overture. The soprano voices sing first, imitated fugally by the other vocal sections, while the instruments embellish the text with Bach's setting of it as a chorale fantasia. The voices sing in the vivace section only after the introduction. There are instrumental ritornelli interludes halfway and at the end, with a choral repeat of only the last half of the stanza (i.e., no da capo).

"In allen meinen Taten / Lass ich den Höchsten raten, / Der alles kann und hat; / Er muss zu allen Dingen, / Soll's anders wohl gelingen, / Selbst geben Rat und Tat." (In all my deeds / I let the Highest advise, / Who can do and has everything; / He must for all things, / If they are to succeed at all, / Himself give advice and action.)

2. *Aria—bass.* With continuo only, he sings this somber second verse, illustrated by a quavering melody in the accompaniment. It seems that he is involved in a weary struggle, but ends on a more confident note of resignation to God's will: "Nichts ist es spät und frühe / Um alle meine Mühe, / Mein Sorgen ist umsonst. / Er mag's mit meinen Sachen / Nach seinem Willen machen, / Ich stell's in seine Gunst." (There is nothing late and early / For all my worry, / My concern is in vain. / He may do with my

affairs / According to His Will. / I place that upon His favor.)

3. *Recitative—tenor.* With the cello and strings providing the continuo, he extends the thought of submission to God's will. He states that nothing can happen to him, other than what God has ordained for his happiness. He will accept what God has decreed for him and choose to do whatever will please Him. This idea leads into his following aria.

4. *Aria—tenor.* This is an exceptionally beautiful number. The solo obbligato violin weaves a remarkable tapestry of sound around his vocal assertion of trust in God's unfailing protection. In spite of the confident lines of the text, there seems to be an underlying grief-motif, ending the stanza in a tear-motif.

Worthy of note is the fact that in the opening chorus and in all the solo arias for the rest of this cantata, Bach divides the six-line stanzas so that the vocalists repeat only the last three lines, instead of the usual da capo. Could the length of the cantata be the reason for this? "Ich traue seiner Gnaden, / Die mich vor allem Schaden, / Vor allem Übel schützt. / Leb' ich nach seinen Gesetzen, / So wird mich nichts verletzen, / Nichts fehlen, was mir nützt." (I trust in His mercy, / Which protects me from all harm, / From all evil. / If I live according to His commandments, / Then nothing will hurt me, / Nothing will be lacking, which is useful to me.)

With his coloratura runs on "allem Schaden" and "allem Ubel," and in the generally tragic or elegiac tone of his aria, there seems to be more emphasis on his present suffering than on God's protection. However, his forceful repetition of "nichts" obviates this somewhat at the end. The solo violin playing is magnificent and could stand alone as a violin sonata movement.

5. *Recitative—alto.* This secco number is an introduction to her following aria, in the same sequence as for the tenor, above. She says that God will mercifully release her from her sins and erase her guilt. He will not immediately pronounce judgment on her wrong-doing but will be patient with her.

6. *Aria—alto.* A hauntingly beautiful melody in the strings accompanies the alto as she expresses her confidence in God's protection. Bach has infused this number with a feeling of deep emotion. It is one of his finest arias, and for me, an outstanding testimony to his musical genius.

"Leg' ich mich späte nieder, / Erwache frühe wieder, / Lieg' oder ziehe fort, / In Schwachheit und in Banden, / Und was mir stösst zuhanden, / So tröstet mich sein Wort." (If I lay myself down late, / Awaken early again, / Lie or go away, / In weakness and in bonds, / And what strikes me close at hand, / Then His Word comforts me.)

7. *Duet—soprano, bass.* This is the second of three arias in succession, a rarity in Bach's cantatas. Their singing in canon begins with the soprano for the first three lines and with the bass for the last three. They declare their acceptance of God's will, enduring the fate that He has decreed for them: "Hat er es denn beschlossen, / So will ich unverdrossen / An mein Verhängnis gehn! / Kein Unfall unter allen / Soll mir zu harte fallen, / Ich will ihn überstehn." (Has He then ordained it, / Then I will cheerfully / Go to my fate! / No misfortune at all / Shall fall on me too hard; / I will overcome it.)

This is the only da capo number in the cantata.

8. *Aria—soprano.* With the two oboes added to the string continuo, she continues the theme of the previous duet, yet her aria has more of the joy-motif in it than the two preceding numbers: "Ihm hab' ich mich ergeben / Zu sterben und zu leben, / Sobald er mir gebeut. / Es sei heut' oder morgen, / Dafür lass' ich ihn sorgen; / Er weiss die rechte Zeit." (I have surrendered myself to Him / To die and to live, / As soon as He bids me. / It may be today or tomorrow, / For that I let Him care; / He knows the right time.)

9. *Chorale.* This is an unusual concluding number, having seven voices in

the choir (as Bach marked it). Perhaps this figure has some symbolic significance, yet the chorale tune is plainly sung. This last stanza summarizes the preceding thoughts—that we should trust our Creator to determine the course of our lives: "So sei nun, Seele, seine / Und traue dem alleine, / Der dich erschaffen hat; / Es gehe, wie es gehe, / Dein Vater in der Höhe / Weiss allen Sachen Rat." (So be now, soul, His / And trust Him alone, / Who has created thee; / Let it happen, as it may happen, / Thy Father on high / Knows all things best.)

• **Widerstehe doch der Sünde (Resist Then Sin)** (1723–34; BWV 54).

The exact date of this cantata for the seventh Sunday after Trinity is very uncertain, so Terry ascribes its presentation in the above period. Bach's original setting was in Weimar in 1714 to a text composed by the Darmstadt court poet Georg Christian Lehms in 1711. It is a short solo cantata for alto of only three numbers, which makes Neumann think that it is apparently only the first half of a two-part cantata.

The Gospel for this Sunday, Mark 8 (1–9), the miracle of the feeding of the four thousand, has nothing to do with the libretto. However, the Epistle, Romans 6 (19–23), "The wages of sin is death," has a direct bearing on it. As the title suggests, the theme of the whole cantata is a musical sermon on resistance to sin.

The work is for alto solo without chorus. The orchestra is very simple: two violins and a viola, with a continuo composed of a cello, a double-bass and organ.

1. *Aria.* The admonishing tone of the text is accompanied by strings and the instruments of the continuo. The continuo depicts a trembling fear-motif together with an inexorable step-rhythm, which may represent the unrelenting onslaught of sin, resulting in death as the text states. But this rhythm could also betoken a Christian who marches steadfastly against the powers of evil: "Widerstehe doch der Sünde / Sonst ergreifet dich ihr Gift. / Lass dich nicht den Satan blenden; / Denn die Gottes Ehre schänden, / Trifft ein Fluch, der tödlich ist." (Resist then sin, / Or else its poison seizes you. / Let Satan not blind you; / For upon those who profane God's honor, / A curse falls, which is deadly.)

2. *Recitative.* With cello and organ to accompany her secco narrative, she paints a grim picture of how sin affects us. A prose translation would read: The nature of atrocious sin appears to be wonderfully beautiful from the outside, but afterwards one must experience from it much trouble with sorrow and discontent. From without, sin is gold, yet within, it shows itself to be only an empty shadow and a whitewashed grave. It is like Sodom's apples, which entice those who will never reach God's Kingdom. It is like a sharp sword, that goes through our body and soul.

3. *Aria.* A trio is formed with the voice, the violins and the viola for this final number. The harsh fugal melody conjures up a dismal vision of Satan and his sin, from whose bonds the Christian struggles to be free. This can be accomplished only through his devotion to God: "Wer Sünde tut, der ist vom Teufel, / Denn dieser hat sie aufgebracht; / Doch wenn man ihren schnöden Banden / Mit rechter Andacht widerstanden, / Hat sie sich gleich davongemacht." (Whoever commits sin, he is of the devil, / For this one has reared it; / Yet if one has withstood its vile bonds / With real devotion, / It has immediately fled.)

For me, this cantata is not very attractive. I think that Bach has set the poetry very well, despite the gloomy moralizing of the libretto, but it lacks the emotional and the picturesque qualities we have seen in other solo cantatas for one voice in this first Leipzig period, such as BWV 51 for soprano or BWV 56 for bass.

As this is the last cantata in Bach's first Leipzig period and as BWV 56 has just been mentioned, we should note that both of these compositions were two of the six extant which Bach designated as "Cantata." The other four are BWV 30, 173, 195 and 197. For all the rest, he used the terms "Concerto," "Stück," "Dialogus" and "Motetto," according to the nature of the work.

E. Composed at Leipzig (1735–1750)

For this last period of Bach's sacred cantata production, both Terry and Whittaker group these cantatas up to the end of Bach's life, although his last extant cantata is dated 1744.

Now Bach finds a new librettist in Mariane von Ziegler, the cultured widow of a Leipzig army officer, whose home was a salon for musicians and university scholars. Although she had published her poems in 1728, Bach did not use them until 1735; during that year he set ten of them in eight weeks.

Terry lists 20 cantatas produced in 1735 alone. Bach was no doubt spurred on by the success of the six cantatas comprising the *Christmas Oratorio* at the end of December 1734. As this work must have been exactly what Bach wanted to illustrate the Biblical texts for the edification of the congregation, so he hoped to continue its appeal in further cantata production in the future. Hence his feverish activity in 1735.

The most significant feature of this last period is that the number of solo cantatas diminishes and the number of chorale cantatas increases. Bach has turned his attention to the paraphrased hymn; 39 out of the 71 cantatas of this period are based on the texts of congregational hymns, amended by Bach or his librettist. Bach had experimented with the chorale cantata during his first Leipzig period but now he concentrates on it, seemingly to obtain a direct appeal to the church.

There is only one unaltered hymn used as the libretto of a cantata in this last period (BWV 100), whereas there were eight during the first Leipzig period. This must indicate that Bach had found the free, madrigal style of composing the inner movements of a chorale cantata less restrictive than the fixed verse forms with which he had had to cope before. The paraphrased setting of the hymn tune within the choruses and the chorales and the increased number of chorale fantasias, freely built on these fixed outer movements, indicate that Bach had finally reached his goal of perfect achievement in his own cantata form.

• **Lobe den Herrn, meine Seele (Praise the Lord, My Soul) II** (1735; BWV 143).

This is the second composition having the above title and it was performed on New Year's Day, 1735. Its libretto was written by an unknown poet, although both Christian Weiss, Sr., and Bach have been suggested. The text reflects the devastation caused by the War of the Polish Succession (1733 to 1738), from which most European countries had already greatly suffered. Saxony, however, had been spared much of the horror of this conflict when Augustus III entered Warsaw on 16 December 1734, and granted amnesty to the Poles. With Poland subjugated and still a part of his kingdom, his Saxon subjects celebrated him as a peacemaker.

This cantata praises God for granting the people peace through their sovereign, but the real credit is given to the Prince of Peace in the libretto.

The Biblical allusion is Psalm 146 (1, 5, 10), which is quoted directly for three of the numbers, while verses one and three of Jakob Ebert's hymn, "Du Friedefürst, Herr Jesu Christ" (Thou Prince of Peace, Lord Jesus Christ), provide the chorales.

The soli are STB, with a four-part chorus. The orchestra has three corni da caccia (hunting-horns)—the only cantata with this number of horns—timpani, a bassoon, two violins, a viola and continuo.

1. *Chorus.* This is a short, but very brilliant movement, with imposing fanfares from the horns. A striking panoply of sound is produced by the full orchestra, befitting a great ceremonial song

of praise by the chorus. Their sung text is verse one of Psalm 146: "Lobe den Herrn, meine Seele" (Praise the Lord, my soul).

2. *Chorale—soprano.* Unison violins play a gently swaying melody to accompany her singing of the first verse of the hymn. This seems to represent a motif of beatific calm, attributed to the Prince of Peace, Whom the text pictures thus: "Du Friedefürst, Herr Jesu Christ, / Wahr' Mensch und wahrer Gott, / Ein starker Nothelfer du bist / Im Leben und im Tod; / Drum wir allein / Im Namen dein / Zu deinem Vater schreien." (Thou Prince of Peace, Lord Jesus Christ, / True Man and true God, / Thou art a strong Helper in need / In life and in death; / Therefore we alone / In Thy Name / Cry to Thy Father.)

This is a really beautiful number.

3. *Recitative—tenor.* This is a very short number, quoting the fifth verse of Psalm 146. It is the only recitative in this cantata, but is effective despite its brevity. "Wohl dem, des Hilfe der Gott Jakobs ist, des Hoffnung auf dem Herrn, seinem Gott, stehet." (Well for him, whose help is the God of Jacob, whose hope stands on the Lord, his God.)

4. *Aria—tenor.* This number begins a series of three arias in succession, unusual in Bach, which he had used once before in BWV 97. What is even more rare is to find two of these three arias for tenor; the bass aria comes between them.

The text contains a contemporary historical allusion to the unhappy plight of neighboring countries which have suffered as a result of the present war. In contrast with them, the people of Saxony are enjoying now the blessing of peace, because they have put their hope in God. Strings and the bassoon accompany his aria with a rather dismal melody, expressive of unhappiness: "Tausendfaches Unglück, Schrecken, / Trübsal, Angst und schnellen Tod, / Völker, die das Land bedecken, / Sorgen und sonst noch mehr Not / Sehen andre Länder zwar, / Aber wir ein Segensjahr." (Thousandfold misfortune, fright, / Sadness, worry and sudden death / Have people, who cover the land; / Cares and yet still more distress / To be sure other countries see, / But we see a year of blessing.)

5. *Aria—bass.* The three horns, timpani, the bassoon and the continuo give his aria a dramatic quality, as he sings verse ten of the Psalm in praise of God. It is a brief aria but full of the majesty surrounding the awesome power of the Lord. Note his coloratura runs on "ewiglich" (eternally): "Der Herr ist König ewiglich, dein Gott, Zion, für und für" (The Lord is King eternally, thy God, Zion, forever and ever).

Unlike the previous aria, this and all the following numbers have a joy-motif in their melody.

6. *Aria (with Chorale)—tenor.* The strings accompany his singing with the chorale tune, as the bassoon carries on an interesting duet with the continuo in the background. The imagery of the text suggests the figure of the shepherd watching over His flock and looking down upon the strife-torn world, populated by those who do not put their trust in the God of Jacob: "Jesu, Retter deiner Herde, / Bleibe ferner unser Hort, / Dass dies Jahr uns glücklich werde, / Halte Wacht an jedem Ort, / Führ', o Jesu, deine Schar, / Bis zu jenem neuen Jahr!" (Jesus, Savior of Thy flock, / Stay longer as our refuge, / So that this year for us may become happy; / Keep watch in every place, / Guide, o Jesus, Thy flock, / Up to that [coming] new year!)

7. *Chorus and Chorale.* The lower voices of the chorus sing only one word, "Halleluja," repeatedly, while the soprano section sings the third verse of the chorale. All the instruments accompany the chorus. The "Halleluja" part seems to outweigh the sopranos, so that one must listen closely to hear all the text of this stanza of the hymn. Nevertheless, Bach has composed an astounding conclusion in his own style, which reminds the listener of Handel's great "Halleluja" chorus in *Messiah.*

"Gedenk', Herr, jetzt an dein Amt, / Dass du ein Friedfürst bist, / Und hilf uns gnädig allesamt / Jetzt und zu dieser

Frist; / Lass uns hinfort / Dein göttlich Wort / Im Fried noch länger hören." (Think, Lord, now on Thy ministry, / That Thou art a Prince of Peace, / And help us graciously altogether / Now and at this time; / Let us henceforth hear / Thy Godly Word / In peace still longer.)

• **Wär' Gott nicht mit uns diese Zeit (Were God Not With Us at This Time)** (1735; BWV 14).

This chorale cantata for the fourth Sunday after Epiphany reflects the uneasy aftermath in Saxony of the War of the Polish Succession. The unknown librettist arranged Luther's translation of Psalm 124, taking verses one and three unchanged for the opening chorus and for the final chorale; he paraphrased freely the other verses of the Psalm for the two arias and the one recitative.

The Gospel, Matthew 8 (23–27), Jesus stills the storm at sea, has no direct bearing on the libretto except in the tenor recitative and in the bass aria, where the attacks of the enemy are likened to the fury of the tempest's waves (Matthew 8 [24]).

The soli are STB, with a four-part chorus. The orchestra has a corno da caccia (hunting horn), two oboes, two violins, a viola and continuo.

1. *Chorus.* This is a movement in the style of a Pachelbel motet, sung in canon to a fugal melody without ritornelli. It is a gloomy fantasia for all instruments, while the chorus sings stanza one of Luther's Psalm 124. One would expect such a hymn of thanks for deliverance to be interpreted by a happy mood, but Bach paints a dark tone-picture for this and for the next two numbers. Despite this tone of sadness, it is a very moving number.

"Wär' Gott nicht mit uns diese Zeit, / So soll Israel sagen, / Wär' Gott nicht mit uns diese Zeit, / Wir hätten müssen verzagen, / Die so ein armes Häuflein sind, / Veracht' von so viel Menschenkind, / Die an uns setzen alle." (Were God not with us at this time, / So Israel should say, / Were God not with us at this time, / We would have had to despair, / We who are such a poor little handful, / Despised by so many children of man, / Who all set upon us.)

2. *Aria—soprano.* Accompanied by the horn and strings, she sings of the Lord's assistance, which has helped them in the conflict and without which they could not have survived. Her cheerful confidence in the Lord, expressed in a joy-motif, banishes the melancholy mood of the opening chorus: "Unsre Stärke heisst zu schwach, / Unserm Feind zu widerstehen. / Stünd' uns nicht der Höchste bei, / Würd' uns ihre Tyrannei / Bald bis an das Leben gehen." (Our strength is too weak, / To withstand our enemy. / If the Highest had not stood by us, / Their tyranny would have gone / Soon as far as to threaten our lives.)

3. *Recitative—tenor.* His secco declamation retains the despondent theme of how the enemy could have engulfed them, if God had permitted it. His description is very picturesque: "Ja, hätt' es Gott nur zugegeben, / Wir wären längst nicht mehr am Leben; / Sie rissen uns aus Rachgier hin, / So zornig ist auf uns ihr Sinn. / Es hätt' uns ihre Wut / Wie eine wilde Flut / Und als beschäumte Wasser überschwemmet, / Und niemand hätte die Gewalt gehemmet." (Yes, if God had allowed it, / We would have been long ago dead; / They would tear us away vindictively, / So angry at us is their mind. / Their rage would have submerged us / Like a wild flood / And as foaming water, / And nobody would have restrained their force.)

4. *Aria—bass.* With oboes and continuo, he sings of the relief from the enemy which everyone feels. Through God's strong protection, we are free of their menace. When they oppose us angrily like wild waves, God's hands support us.

Although the text changes from gloom to rejoicing, the listener can discern little of the joy-motif in the melody. It appears that Bach reserved that for the following final chorale.

5. *Chorale.* All voices and the full orchestra are used to interpret this third verse of Luther's translation of the Psalm. There is an innate feeling of joy underlying a tone of reverence in it. It is a moving song of thanksgiving to God for victory: "Gott Lob und Dank, der nicht zugab, / Dass ihr Schlund uns möcht' fangen. / Wie ein Vogel des Stricks kömmt ab, / Ist unsre Seel' entgangen: / Strick ist entzwei, und wir sind frei; / Des Herren Name steht uns bei, / Des Gottes Himmels und Erden." (Praise and thanks to God, Who did not allow / That their gorge might catch us. / As a bird escapes from the net, / Our soul has gone away: / The net is broken, and we are free; / The Lord's Name stands by us, [who are] / Of God's heaven and earth.)

• **Ich bin ein guter Hirt (I Am a Good Shepherd)** (1735; BWV 85).

This is Bach's second composition on the theme of the Good Shepherd (the first was BWV 104). Musically, it has everything the listener expects, and it is a masterpiece. The librettist was Mariane von Ziegler, who based her text on the Gospel for this Misericordias Domini Sunday, i.e., the second Sunday after Easter, John 10 (11–16), and also employed in it two different chorales, freely paraphrasing the rest of this Gospel for the other numbers. Bach's cantata resembles a miniature pastoral symphony in five movements—much shorter than Beethoven's *Symphony No. 6,* yet also entrancing.

As the chorales occur in the middle and at the end, rather than at the beginning and at the end as is usually the case with chorales in Bach's cantatas, this work is considered to be a solo cantata for SATB, with a four-part chorus.

In the orchestral score, the instruments indicated are two oboes, a violoncello piccolo, two violins, a viola and continuo.

1. *Arioso—bass.* His text is John 10 (11), which he sings in the role of Christ. The oboes and strings play an exquisitely plaintive melody to accompany him. The listener can clearly visualize the presence of the Lord saying: "Ich bin ein guter Hirt; ein guter Hirt lässt sein Leben für die Schafe." (I am a Good Shepherd; a good shepherd lays down his life for the sheep.)

There is a mood of foreboding in Bach's setting of these words, which points ahead to the Sacrifice that the Lord will make. Bach paints an ominous picture of an impending storm, looming up just beyond the horizon, with its thundercloud over the landscape, similar to Beethoven's in the later *Pastorale (Symphony No. 6).*

2. *Aria—alto.* The menacing cloud vanishes in this happy pastoral melody for oboe, violoncello piccolo and strings. A note of confidence is apparent in the joy-motif of the music and in her runs on "rauben" (rob).

She expresses the trust that the sheep have in their Shepherd; nobody can steal them from Him, while they are in their pleasant pasture. Bach's lilting melody evokes the imagery of their contentment: "Jesus ist ein guter Hirt; / Denn er hat bereits sein Leben / Für die Schafe hingegeben, / Die ihm niemand rauben wird. / Jesus ist ein guter Hirt. (Jesus is a good Shepherd; / For He has already given / His life for the sheep, / Of which nobody will rob Him. / Jesus is a good Shepherd.)

3. *Chorale—soprano.* She sings stanza one of Cornelius Becker's hymn "Derr Herr ist mein getreuer Hirt" (The Lord Is My Faithful Shepherd), which paraphrases the first three verses of the twenty-third Psalm. Two oboes and the continuo support her with the tune of Nikolaus Decius's "Allein Gott in der Höh' sei Ehr'" (To God Alone on High Be Glory). This is the same stanza that was used for the concluding chorale of BWV 104, but now it is sung by a solo soprano voice: "Der Herr ist mein getreuer Hirt, / Dem ich mich ganz vertraue; / Zur Weid, er mich, sein Schäflein, führt, / Auf schöner grüner Aue; / Zum frischen Wasser leit' er mich, / Mein' Seel' zu laben kräftiglich / Durchs

sel'ge Wort der Gnaden." (The Lord is my faithful Shepherd, / In Whom I completely trust; / To the pasture He leads me, His lamb, / On the beautiful green meadow; / To the cool water He leads me, / To refresh my soul strongly / Through the blessed word of grace.)

The calm serenity of her declamation maintains the pastoral mood, which was also found in the final chorale of BWV 104.

4. *Recitative—tenor.* With strings for accompaniment, he describes how the Good Shepherd would avert any danger which might threaten His flock. The tone throughout this monologue is exceptionally dramatic, while retaining a continued pastoral ambience.

When the hirelings sleep, then this Shepherd watches over His sheep, so that each can enjoy in desired rest the pasture in which the streams of life flow. Then, if the wolf of hell seeks entry to devour the sheep, this Shepherd will hold its jaws shut.

5. *Aria—tenor.* The sheer beauty of this number is astounding. With unison strings to accompany him, his singing has a fervently mystical tone about it, which increases as he refers to the Crucifixion at the end. Bach prepares for this mystical touch in repeating thrice the first word in this text, "Seht" (See)—a reference to the Trinity? The da capo reinforces this impression.

"Seht, was die Liebe tut. / Mein Jesus hält in zarter Hut / Die Seinen feste eingeschlossen / Und hat am Kreuzesstamm vergossen / Für sie sein teures Blut." (See what love does. / My Jesus keeps in tender care / His own firmly enclosed, / And on the tree of the Cross has poured out / For them His precious blood.)

6. *Chorale.* This tutti conclusion is supercharged with intense emotion. Confidence in God's protection against all enemies is expressed by all the believers in the congregation (all the sheep in the flock). The fourth stanza of Ernst Christoph Homburg's hymn "Ist Gott mein Schild und Helfersmann" (If God Is My Shield and Helper), still retains the idea of the Good Shepherd in its deeply moving harmony.

"Ist Gott mein Schutz und treuer Hirt, / Kein Unglück mich berühren wird: / Weicht, alle meine Feinde, / Die ihr mir stiftet Angst und Pein, / Es wird zu eurem Schaden sein, / Ich habe Gott zum Freunde." (If God is my protection and true Shepherd, / No misfortune will touch me: / Retreat, all my enemies, / Who cause me anxiety and pain; / It will be to your harm, [since] / I have God for my friend.)

• **Ihr werdet weinen und heulen (You Will Weep and Howl)** (1735; BWV 103).

The libretto for this cantata on the third Sunday after Easter (Jubilate) was written by Mariane von Ziegler in her poetry collection of 1728. Bach emended the text with the help of either Picander or Christian Weiss, Jr. This Sunday's Gospel is John 16 (16–23), the twentieth verse of which is used for the opening chorus.

The theme follows Bach's usual overall pattern in many of his cantatas, beginning with a sadness-motif in the first four numbers, and then changing to a joy-motif in the last two. The first chorus seems to represent the scheme of the whole cantata, because its initial tone of grief turns to rejoicing at the end of the movement.

The soli are ATB, with a four-part chorus. The orchestra is quite large: a trumpet, a piccolo flute, a transverse flute, two oboes d'amore, two violins, a viola and continuo.

1. *Chorus and solo basses.* Christ's prophecy to His disciples of their coming affliction in the world and how it will be changed into joy is well interpreted by Bach's fugal setting of the Scriptural text. Christians will weep and grieve, while the world mocks them in malicious glee. Bach paints a fresco of these two emotions in the first sentence until the basses, solo, representing Christ, enter to sing His message of hope in the last two sentences. The last sentence is repeated

in another fugue with ritornello by the chorus. This is a very powerful movement, showing how Bach's skillful artistry can combine two themes in one: "Ihr werdet weinen und heulen, aber die Welt wird sich freuen. / Ihr aber werdet traurig sein. Doch eure Traurigkeit soll in Freude verkehret werden." (You will weep and howl, but the world will rejoice. / You, however, will be sad. Yet your sadness shall be changed into joy.)

2. *Recitative—tenor.* His secco number is very short, resuming the lamentation over the Lord's departure. He asks who should not sink in mourning when their Beloved is torn away from them. The Salvation of their souls and hearts will not now be present to heal their pains.

3. *Aria—alto.* Her text begins with a paraphrase of Jeremiah 8 (22), continuing the lamentation of the tenor: "Kein Arzt ist ausser dir zu finden. / Ich suche durch ganz Gilead. / Wer heilt die Wunden meiner Sünden, / Weil man hier kein Balsam hat?" (No doctor is to be found except Thee; / I am searching through all Gilead. / Who heals the wounds of my sins, / Because here they have no balm?)

The remainder of her aria implores the Savior's pity to save her from the death which His absence will cause her. Her grieving tone is well depicted by the transverse flute, but it seems that her declamation is more like a recitative than an aria.

4. *Recitative—alto.* Bach shortened Mariane von Ziegler's text for this number to make it balance with the previous tenor recitative. Here, however, the theme changes from lamentation to joy.

She says that the Lord will turn her anguish and sorrow into happiness just as He promised. She will therefore prepare herself for His return, which she anticipates with a bright run on "Freude" (joy).

5. *Aria—tenor.* Trumpet, oboes and strings accompany the singer's telling of his joy at seeing Jesus again. All the clouds of sadness have disappeared; the ailing Christian has found his health again from the balm provided by his Savior. A dancing melody gives a joy-rhythm both in the vocal and in the instrumental accompaniment. The aria is like a burst of sunshine after dismal weather.

"Erholet euch, betrübte Sinnen, / Ihr tut euch selber allzu weh. / Lasst von dem traurigen Beginnen, / Eh' ich in Tränen untergeh', / Mein Jesus lässt sich wieder sehen, / O Freude, der nichts gleichen kann! / Wie wohl ist mir dadurch geschehen, / Nimm, nimm mein Herz zum Opfer an!" (Recover yourselves, troubled minds, / You make yourselves all too sorrowful. / Leave the sad beginning, / Before I sink in tears. / My Jesus lets Himself be seen again; / O joy, which nothing can equal! / How well it has thus happened to me; / Take, take my heart as an offering!)

6. *Chorale.* This ninth stanza of Paul Gerhardt's hymn, "Barmherz'er Vater, höchster Gott" (Merciful Father, Highest God), performed by all voices and instruments, brings this cantata to a happy, confident close and refers to the Biblical text of the opening chorus: "Ich hab' dich einen Augenblick, / O liebes Kind, verlassen; / Sieh aber, sieh, mit grossem Glück / Und Trost ohn' alle Massen / Will ich dir schon die Freudenkron', / Aufsetzen und verehren; / Dein kurzes Leid soll sich in Freud' / Und ewig Wohl verkehren." (I have left you for a moment, / O dear child; / But see, see, with great good luck / And comfort without measure / I will set on you / the crown of joy and honor; / Your short sorrow shall change to joy / And eternal well-being.)

• **Es ist euch gut, dass ich hingehe (It Is Good for You, That I Go Away)** (1735; BWV 108).

Mariane von Ziegler's libretto for this cantata on the fourth Sunday (Cantate) after Easter was another of her poems emended by Bach. Two quotations from the Gospel, John 16 (5–15), are used in two movements, while another of Paul Gerhardt's hymns forms the final chorale verse.

The subject of this cantata is the Holy Ghost, whom Christ promises to send to His disciples and to all believers after His departure from the world. The arias and the recitatives are freely composed on this theme as it is expressed in the Gospel quotations.

The soli are ATB, with a four-part chorus. The orchestra is smaller, consisting of two oboes d'amore, two violins, a viola and continuo.

1. *Arioso—bass.* This number is really an aria, but as the bass represents Christ speaking, Bach calls it an arioso as he always does in this case. The text is taken from John 16 (7); the words suggest a step-motif, which Bach illustrates very well. A staccato rhythm, played by the oboe d'amore and the strings, portrays both the Lord's steps as He leaves His disciples, and those of the Comforter as He approaches them: "Es ist euch gut, dass ich hingehe; denn so ich nicht hingehe, kommt der Tröster nicht zu euch. So ich aber gehe, will ich ihn zu euch senden." (It is good for you, that I go away; for if I do not go away, the Comforter will not come to you. Then if I go, I will send Him to you.)

2. *Aria—tenor.* Representing a disciple or a believer, the tenor replies to the Lord, saying that no doubts will hinder his belief, even though Christ has departed. His trust in the Lord will console him in the knowledge that his faith will lead him to peace among other redeemed Christians. A solo violin adds a beautiful effect to his vocal delivery.

"Mich kann kein Zweifel stören, / Auf dein Wort, Herr, zu hören. / Ich glaube, gehst du fort, / So kann ich mich trösten, / Dass ich zu den Erlösten / Komm' an erwünschten Port." (No doubt can disturb me, / From listening, Lord, to Thy Word; / I believe, if Thou goest away, / Then I can console myself / That I may come to the redeemed / At the wished-for port.)

3. *Recitative—tenor.* This short declamation marks the transition from the theme of the Lord's departure to that of the arrival of the Holy Spirit. The rest of the cantata will deal with how the Holy Ghost influences us.

Here he says that the Lord's Spirit will so direct him that he will go on the right way. Then he asks a rhetorical question, anxiously wondering if the Spirit sent by Christ is not already here with him.

4. *Chorus.* All voices and instruments produce this monumental motet movement, which consists of three separate fugues. It seems that Bach is trying to show the power of the Holy Ghost through the energetic and forceful canonical choral singing. The voices are doubled by the oboes and strings in a joy-motif, which makes one of the most brilliant choruses that Bach ever composed. The text is taken from John 16 (13): "Wenn aber jener, der Geist der Wahrheit, kommen wird, der wird euch in alle Wahrheit leiten. Denn er wird nicht von ihm selber reden, sondern was er hören wird, das wird er reden, und was zukünftig ist, wird er verkündigen." (When that one, however, the Spirit of truth will come, He will lead you into all truth. For He will not speak of Himself, but what He will hear, that will He speak, and what is to come will He proclaim.)

5. *Aria—alto.* There is a feeling of intense longing in the exquisite melody which combines with a joy-motif at the end. Only strings and continuo are used to paint a scene of beatific peace which the Holy Spirit imparts. The smooth serenity of this aria makes the listener feel the flow of grace from the Holy Spirit: "Was mein Herz von dir begehrt, / Ach, das wird mir wohl gewährt. / Überschütte mich mit Segen, / Führe mich auf deinen Wegen, / Dass ich in der Ewigkeit / Schaue deine Herrlichkeit!" (What my heart desires of Thee, / Ah, that will be certainly granted to me. / Pour over me Thy blessings, / Lead me on Thy ways, / So that in eternity / I may look upon Thy glory!)

6. *Chorale.* Tutti forces perform verse

10 of Paul Gerhardt's hymn "Gott Vater, sende deinen Geist" (God the Father, Send Thy Spirit). This verse describes the guiding power of the Holy Ghost to direct our steps into God's grace. As a concluding chorale, it summarizes admirably the theme of this cantata.

• **Bisher habt ihr nichts gebeten in meinem Namen (Hitherto You Have Prayed for Nothing in My Name)** (1735; BWV 87).

Another of Mariane von Ziegler's poems from her 1728 collection entitled "Versuch in gebundener Schreibart" (Attempt in the Art of Metrical Writing) provides the text, emended by Bach, for this solo cantata on the fifth Sunday (Rogate) after Easter. The poetess blended both the Gospel, John 16 (23–30), and the Epistle, James 1 (22–27), in her libretto: we should call upon the Lord for help in our prayers and we should be doers of the word, not hearers only.

The soli are ATB, with a four-part chorus. The instruments are two oboes, an oboe da caccia, two violins, a viola and continuo.

1. *Arioso—bass.* All instruments accompany him as he sings the first part of the Gospel verse, John 16 (24). The dramatic quality of his singing the role of Christ as He speaks to His disciples arrests the listener's attention immediately. As in the opening arioso of BWV 108, this is an aria more than an arioso because of the repetition of its sections and the soloist's artistic interpretation. Bach gives a stern tone to the melody for his setting of Jesus' reproving words to His disciples: "Bisher habt ihr nichts gebeten in meinem Namen" (Hitherto you have prayed for nothing in my Name).

2. *Recitative—alto.* The Epistle, exhorting us to be doers of the word, seems to weigh upon her conscience in this secco declamation to all those who have not actively followed God's law. They must immediately pray to the Lord in repentance and reverence.

3. *Aria—alto.* This number is a prayer of the guilty soul to God, supplicating Him to have patience with us and to forgive our trespasses. The accompanying oboes da caccia convey a tone of true humility as she implores forgiveness and help against further transgressions. The Gospel text, John 16 (25), recurs when she asks the Lord to speak no more in proverbs as He states in this verse. The da capo reinforces her contrition.

4. *Recitative—tenor.* Bach added this number to the libretto to avoid having three successive arias and to introduce the following arioso. It is impressive though short, being accompanied by strings, and itself concluding in a fine arioso: "Wenn unsre Schuld bis an den Himmel steigt, / Du siehst und kennest ja mein Herz, das nichts vor dir verschweigt, / Drum suche mich zu trösten." (When our guilt mounts up to heaven, / Thou surely seest and knowest my heart, that conceals nothing from Thee. / Therefore seek to comfort me.)

5. *Arioso—bass.* Again speaking as Christ, he sings the last part of John 16 (33) in the same dramatic style as in the opening arioso, but accompanied by only the continuo this time. Christ restores hope to the sinner in this arioso, which again more resembles an aria: "In der Welt habt ihr Angst, aber seid getrost, ich habe die Welt überwunden." (In the world you have tribulation, but be consoled, I have overcome the world.)

6. *Aria—tenor.* A beautiful siciliano melody is played by the strings as he sings of his confidence in the help that Jesus will give him. He will suffer without complaint, being sure of Christ's consolation. This aria is striking because it combines a grief-motif with a joy-motif. The undulating tempo throughout seems to represent the peaceful, soothing effect of the comfort he finds in Jesus. The expression of his inner emotion is marvelous—an outstanding example of Bach's ability to draw feeling from the words of the text. This is a trait of Bach's art—that he looks inward (while Handel looks outward).

"Ich will leiden, ich will schweigen, / Jesus wird mir Hilf' erzeigen, / Denn er tröst' mich nach dem Schmerz. / Weicht, ihr Sorgen, Trauer, Klagen, / Denn warum sollt' ich verzagen? / Fasse dich, betrübtes Herz!" (I will suffer, I will be silent, / Jesus will show me help, / For He comforts me after my pain. / Begone, you cares, mourning, laments, / For why should I despair? / Compose yourself, troubled heart!)

Note his coloratura treatment of "Weicht" and "verzagen."

7. *Chorale.* This is a straightforward tutti performance of the ninth verse of Heinrich Müller's "Selig ist die Seele" (Blessed Is the Soul). Hopeful trust in Jesus to banish all our sorrows and pain brings the cantata to an optimistic end: "Muss ich sein betrübt? / So mich Jesus liebt, / Ist mir aller Schmerz / Über Honig süsse, / . . . / Seine Liebe macht zur Freuden / Auch das bittre Leiden." (Must I be sad? / If Jesus loves me, / All sorrow is for me / Sweeter than honey, / . . . / His love changes to joy / Even bitter sorrow.)

• **Gott fähret auf mit Jauchzen (God Goes Up with Rejoicing)** (1735; BWV 43).

It is probable that the librettist for this Ascension Day cantata was the same unknown poet who had been writing libretti for Bach's cousin, composer Johann Ludwig Bach of Meiningen. The work is long, having two parts with a total of nine solo numbers, of which Bach himself is thought to have written two (numbers two and three). Because its length might go beyond the time allowed for performance (30 minutes), Bach set all the arias without da capo.

The Gospel for Ascension Day is Mark 16 (14–20), of which the nineteenth verse is quoted in a soprano recitative. All the other numbers reflect on this last appearance of Christ and His Ascension. After this soprano recitative (number four), all of the six following arias and recitatives are taken completely from an anonymous hymn," (Mein Jesus hat nunmehr" (My Jesus Has Now). This use of an entire hymn within a cantata's inner movements is unique in Bach's cantata production.

The soli are SATB, with a four-part chorus. There is a brilliant orchestra with three trumpets, timpani, two oboes, two violins, a viola and continuo.

Part I

1. *Chorus.* The oboes and strings play a short but evocative introductory adagio into which the trumpets break forth in a joyous motif. The basses begin to sing a fugue, followed by the other voices during the first sentence. Then we hear another fugue for the second sentence. Both of these fugal sections of the text, Psalm 47 (5–6), Bach interprets in resounding music to paint a scene of intense rejoicing: "Gott fähret auf mit Jauchzen, und der Herr mit heller Posaune. / Lobsinget, lobsinget Gott: lobsinget, lobsinget unserm König." (God goes up with rejoicing, and the Lord with a resounding trumpet. / Sing praises, sing praises to God: sing praises, sing praises to our King.)

2. *Recitative—tenor.* With continuo only, he describes how the heavenly host will celebrate Christ's victory. Psalm 68 (18) is mentioned, wherein Christ has led captivity captive. He says that God's army will sing Halleluja eternally to Him for the honor, salvation, praise, kingdom, power and might signified by His Name.

3. *Aria—tenor.* Unison violins play a rising and falling theme which at first suggests the undulating host that ministers to God (Daniel 7 [10]), and then symbolizes the movement of earth and heaven under Him according to the text: "Ja tausendmal tausend begleiten den Wagen, / Dem König der Kön'ge lobsingend zu sagen, / Dass Erde und Himmel sich unter ihm schmiegt, / Und was er bezwungen, nun gänzlich erliegt." (Yes, a thousand times a thousand accompany the chariot, / To tell the King of Kings in songs of praise, / That earth and heaven bends beneath Him, / And what He has conquered, now yields completely.)

4. *Recitative—soprano.* With con-

tinuo only in secco, she quotes the Gospel verse, Mark 16 [19], describing the Ascension: "Und der Herr, nachdem er mit ihnen geredet hatte, ward er aufgehoben gen Himmel und sitzet zur rechten Hand Gottes." (And the Lord, after He had spoken with them, was raised up to heaven and sits at the right hand of God.)

5. *Aria—soprano.* This number is the first of six successive verses of the anonymous hymn. Oboes and strings accompany her with a step-motif representing the Lord's return to His Father. This march-like tempo illustrates the text very well: "Mein Jesus hat nunmehr / Das Heilandwerk vollendet / Und nimmt die Wiederkehr / Zu dem, der ihn gesendet. / Er schliesst der Erde Lauf, / Ihr Himmel, öffnet euch / Und nehmt ihn wieder auf!" (My Jesus has now / Completed His Savior's work / And makes His return / To Him, Who sent Him. / He finishes His journey on earth; / Ye heavens, open / And take Him up again!)

Although this verse and also the next verse of recitative may seem to be in an illogical sequence after the preceding soprano recitative, one can only think that this happened because Bach did not want to break up the six stanzas of the hymn, except by the sermon, which comes at the end of this number.

Part II

6. *Recitative—bass.* In a dramatic tone, he describes Christ's triumph over Satan and the forces of evil. The tremulous motif, played by the accompanying strings, depicts the fear that Christ strikes into them.

7. *Aria—bass.* With only trumpet accompaniment, he begins on a joyful note which then changes to a grief-motif but finally returns to the joy-motif at the end of the aria; each of the three melodies reflects the words as he sings this stanza. The image of the wine-press (Isaiah 63 [3]) comes out well in the stamping rhythm of the first and last motives, with a quiet, bewailing section between them: "Er ist's, der ganz allein / Die Kelter hat getreten, / Voll Schmerzen, Qual und Pein, / Verlorne zu erretten / Durch einen teuren Kauf. / Ihr Throne, mühet euch / Und setzt ihm Kränze auf!" (It is He, Who quite alone / Has trodden the wine-press, / Full of pain, torture and affliction, / To save the lost / Through an expensive purchase. / Ye Thrones, take pains / And place garlands upon Him!)

This is the best aria in the cantata, both vocally and instrumentally.

8. *Recitative—alto.* She narrates the scene of the Father crowning the Son, which was mentioned at the end of the preceding aria. Her joy at beholding this vision is reflected in her last two lines: "Ich stehe hier am Weg / Und schau'ihm freudig nach." (I stand here on the way / And gaze joyfully after Him.) These same two lines will be repeated at the end of the next two numbers, changing only the final adverb to indicate the speaker's mood.

9. *Aria—alto.* Two oboes give a melancholy tone to this aria. She sees a vision of the Lord sitting at God's right hand as He smites His enemies in order to help His servants in their distress. She herself presents a picture of a Christian gazing up to heaven and yearning to be with Christ: "Ich sehe schon im Geist, / Wie er zu Gottes Rechten / Auf seine Feinde schmeisst, / Zu helfen seinen Knechten / Aus Jammer, Not und Schmach; / Ich stehe hier am Weg / Und schau' ihm sehnlich nach." (I already see in my spirit, / How at God's right hand / He smites His enemies, / To help His servants / Out of their lamentation, distress and shame; / I stand here on the way / And gaze longingly after Him.)

10. *Recitative—soprano.* In this secco number she mentions the dwelling that the Lord will prepare for her, so that she can be eternally at His side, free of woe and anguish. Therefore she stands on the way and calls thankfully after Him. This number concludes the six consecutive verses of the anonymous hymn.

11. *Chorale.* The text for this hymn is the first and thirteenth verses of Johann

Rist's "Du Lebensfürst, Herr Jesu Christ" (Thou Prince of Life, Lord Jesus Christ). All voices and instruments give a straightforward performance. The first verse mentions Christ's Ascension into heaven and His victory for which we should praise Him. The thirteenth verse entreats Him to bring us to join Him in paradise, so that we may then stand before Him and see His face. These two verses summarize the thoughts expressed in Part I and Part II, respectively.

• **Lobet Gott in seinen Reichen (Praise God in His Kingdoms)** (c. 1735; BWV 11).

Bach termed this remarkable composition for Ascension Day "Oratorium Festo Ascensionis Christi," known as the "Oratorium auf Himmelfahrt" today in the subtitle of Neumann's text. This was Bach's second oratorio, the first being the *Christmas Oratorio* (1734), and the third the *Easter Oratorio* (1736). This work could have been performed on the same date as BWV 43 since Bach sometimes composed two different cantatas for important church festival days, one for the St. Thomas Church and one for the St. Nicholas Church. However, Terry ascribes only an approximate date, whereas Dürr gives 1735 definitely but states that BWV 43 was performed in 1726. It should be noted that Dürr dates most of Bach's sacred cantatas of the last Leipzig period back to the first period, 1723 to 1730.

The difference between an oratorio and a cantata is that in the former there is an Evangelist who narrates a Biblical story, interspersed with free arias and recitatives which comment on the events narrated, whereas in the latter, there is no story told in dramatic form but merely Biblical quotations, arias and recitatives, which illustrate and comment on the theme without any plot. As this cantata is a dramatic representation of the Ascension, with the tenor Evangelist narrating the action, Bach was justified in calling it an oratorio, even though it is on a smaller scale than his *Passions* or the *Christmas Oratorio*.

Both the Epistle, Acts 1 (11–12), and the Gospel, Mark 16 (19), appear in the libretto, plus Luke 24 (50–52). These three Scriptural quotations comprise the three recitatives for the tenor Evangelist. The author of the libretto is unknown.

The soli are SATB, with a four-part chorus. The orchestra has three trumpets, timpani, two flutes, two oboes, unison violins and violas, and continuo.

In my opinion, this work is Bach's supreme achievement in all his cantatas. The religious fervor of the vocal expression and the musical splendor in every number, especially in the choral movements, make this composition an enduring monument to the greatest church composer that the world has ever seen.

1. *Chorus.* This brilliant tutti opening movement is like a prayer of invocation, exhorting all Christians to praise God. It seems to resemble the function of the chorus in a Greek drama, which prepares the audience for the coming action. Both Terry and Neumann attribute this movement to the opening aria of Bach's secular cantata "Froher Tag, verlangte Stunden" (Happy Day, Longed For Hours), performed 5 June 1732, of which the music is lost. Whatever its origin, the impact of the two themes is stunning.

"Lobet Gott in seinen Reichen, / Preiset ihn in seinen Ehren, / Rühmet ihn in seiner Pracht; / Sucht sein Lob recht zu vergleichen, / Wenn ihr mit gesamten Chören / Ihn ein Lied zu Ehren macht." (Praise God in His kingdoms, / Praise Him in His glory, / Magnify Him in His splendor; / Seek to rightly equal His praise, / When you with collected choruses / Make a song to honor Him.)

2. *Recitative—tenor.* This is the first of the Evangelist's recitatives with continuo only, upon which each of the following recitatives, arias or chorales will comment, until the Evangelist speaks again. With this number, the scenario of the oratorio begins: "Der Herr Jesus hub seine Hände auf und segnete seine Jünger, und es geschah, da er sie segnete,

schied er von ihnen." (Lord Jesus raised His hands and blessed His disciples, and it happened, as He blessed them, He departed from them.)

3. *Recitative—bass.* Two transverse flutes accompany his commentary on this sad event—sad for him in the role of one of the disciples. He asks the Lord if the hour has come when He must depart from them. He mentions the warm tears flowing down the disciples' cheeks as they long for Him. Now all their comfort is almost gone. He implores the Lord that He should not yet leave them.

4. *Aria—alto.* Bach reused the melody for this aria in the *Agnus Dei* movement of his later completed *Mass in B minor,* where it is shortened by about one half. A grief-motif is expressed by the sobbing rhythm of the unison violins, as she pleads "Ach bleibe doch" (Ah, do stay) at the beginning of her aria, expanding the longing of the previous bass recitative. The painful sorrow she feels comes out very well in the second subject of her number. It seems that she is playing the part of one of the disciples in this highly emotional and dramatic monologue.

5. *Recitative—tenor.* He resumes the Biblical narrative: "Und ward aufgehoben zusehens und fuhr auf gen Himmel, eine Wolke nahm ihn weg vor ihren Augen, und er sitzet zur rechten Hand Gottes." (And He was visibly raised up and went up toward heaven; a cloud took Him away before their eyes, and He sits at the right hand of God.)

6. *Chorale.* All voices and instruments harmonize to perform stanza four of the Ascension hymn "Du Lebensfürst, Herr Jesu Christ" (Thou Prince of Life, Lord Jesus Christ) by Johann Rist. It is an exceptionally moving number and seems to conclude the first section of the cantata, although no part divisions are indicated in the libretto.

"Nun lieget alles unter dir, / Dich selbst nur ausgenommen; / Die Engel müssen für und für / Dir aufzuwarten kommen. / Die Fürsten stehn auch auf der Bahn / Und sind dir willig untertan; / Luft, Wasser, Feuer, Erden / Muss dir zu Dienste werden." (Now everything lies beneath Thee, / Only with the exception of Thyself; / The angels must ever and ever / Come to wait upon Thee. / Princes also stand on the way / And willingly submit to Thee; / Air, water, fire, earth / Must become Thy servants.)

7. *Recitative—tenor, bass.* The tenor Evangelist begins in a step-rhythm which leads into an arioso duet for himself with the bass. The duet has unison singing for the first sentence and canonical singing with an animated joy-motif for the second. The Gospel texts are quoted in both parts.

TENOR: "Und da sie ihm nachsahen gen Himmel fahren, siehe, da stunden bei ihnen zwei Männer in weissen Kleidern, welche auch sagten:" (And as they watched Him going heavenwards, behold, there stood beside them two men in white clothing, who also said:)

TENOR AND BASS: "Ihr Männer von Galiläa, was stehet ihr und sehet gen Himmel? Dieser Jesus, welcher von euch ist aufgenommen gen Himmel, wird kommen, wie ihr ihn gesehen habt gen Himmel fahren." (You men of Galilee, why do you stand and look up toward heaven? This Jesus, who is taken from you up into heaven, will come, as you have seen Him going up to heaven.)

8. *Recitative—alto.* She sings a short declamation of four lines, in which she entreats the Lord to return to eradicate her sadness or else she will hate every moment of her monotonous life.

9. *Recitative—tenor.* The Evangelist continues the Gospel narrative: "Sie aber beteten ihn an, wandten um gen Jerusalem von dem Berge, der da heisset der Olberg, welcher ist nahe bei Jerusalem und liegt einen Sabbater-Weg davon, und sie kehreten wieder gen Jerusalem mit grosser Freude." (They however worshipped Him, turned around towards Jerusalem from the mount, which is called the Mount of Olives, which is near Jerusalem and lies a Sabbath-Day's journey from there, and returned to Jerusalem with great joy.)

10. *Aria—soprano.* Bach paints a beautiful vision of the Lord floating in the ethereal realms as the soprano sings the words of the text that suggested this image to him. Two unison flutes with an oboe and strings also in unison give an impression of airy lightness and lofty grandeur: "Jesu, deine Gnadenblicke / Kann ich doch beständig sehen. / Deine Liebe bleibt zurücke, / Dass ich mich hier in der Zeit / An der künft'gen Herrlichkeit / Schon voraus im Geist erquicke, / Wenn wir einst dort vor dir stehen." (Jesu, Thy looks of mercy / I can see continually. / Thy love remains behind, / So that I may in time / Refresh myself in the future glory / Which I already in advance feel in spirit, / When we stand one day there before Thee.)

11. *Chorale.* This seventh stanza of Gottfried Wilhelm Sacer's Ascension hymn "Gott fähret auf gen Himmel" (God Ascends into Heaven) is performed by all voices and instruments with regal splendor. Bach makes this an extended chorale by using an instrumental interlude in canon as well as canon playing throughout. It is a wonderful chorale fantasia, full of Bach's personal longing and mysticism, which transports the listener so much that he can identify with the composer's emotion. This single chorale alone enables the listener to comprehend Bach better than any other movement in any other of his cantatas. It is a key to his innate religious convictions, which are expressed by an exuberant, bouncing tempo.

"Wann soll es doch geschehen, / Wann kömmt die liebe Zeit, / Dass ich ihn werde sehen, / In seiner Herrlichkeit? / Du Tag, wann wirst du sein, / Dass wir den Heiland grüssen, / Dass wir Heiland küssen? / Komm, stelle dich doch ein! (When is it then to happen, / When will come that dear time, / That I will see Him, / In His glory? / Thou Day, when wilt thou be, / That we greet the Savior, / That we kiss the Savior? / Come, appear then!)

• **Auf Christi Himmelfahrt allein (On Christ's Journey to Heaven Alone)** (1735; BWV 128).

This is the third cantata for Ascension Day, given the date of 1735 by Whittaker, Neumann and Terry but dated 1725 by Dürr. Schweitzer notes (Vol. II, p. 336, footnote) that "for feast days Bach needed two cantatas, as the evening service also had to be musical." So it is not impossible that Bach performed three different cantatas on this day: BWV 43, 11 and 128—two in the main churches at the principal service, and the third in one of these churches (St. Thomas's or St. Nicholas's) for the evening service.

Mariane von Ziegler was the poet for this smaller Ascension cantata, the libretto of which Bach emended for his setting. The text reflects on the meaning of Christ's Ascension for the believer, without any direct quotation from either the Gospel or the Epistle for the day.

The soli are ATB, with a four-part chorus. The orchestra consists of a trumpet, two horns, two oboes, two violins, an oboe da caccia, a viola and continuo.

1. *Chorus.* Actually, this is an extended chorale fantasia rather than a straight chorus. Since it has another chorale to end the work, this cantata should be classed as a chorale cantata. The chorale in this first chorus is stanza one of Josua Wegelin's hymn with the above cantata title, set to the tune of Nikolaus Decius's "Allein Gott in der Höh sei Ehr'" (To God, Alone on High, Be Glory).

A stupendous joy-motif pervades the whole chorus in combination with a rhythm of felicity that the tutti instrumentation plays most impressively. It is one of the best numbers in this cantata: "Auf Christi Himmelfahrt allein / Ich meine Nachfahrt gründe / Und allen Zweifel, Angst und Pein / Hiermit stets überwinde; / Denn weil das Haupt im Himmel ist, / Wird seine Glieder Jesus Christ / Zu rechter Zeit nachholen." (On Christ's journey to heaven alone / I base my own following journey. / And all doubt, anxiety and pain / With this I always overcome: / For since the Head is in heaven, / Jesus Christ will bring His members / After Him at the right time.)

The remarkable tone-painting in this movement enables the listener to visualize the splendor of heaven which awaits him.

2. *Recitative—tenor.* He declares, secco, that he is ready for Jesus to call him from the misery of the world to Salem's tent (paradise), where he will be transfigured. His last two lines paraphrase 1 Corinthians 13 (12): then he will see God face to face as promised in the Scripture.

3. *Aria and Recitative—bass.* This is the other outstanding number in this cantata. Amid the strings which accompany him, trumpet fanfares are featured in the first section to portray a majestic picture of the Son sitting at the right hand of the Father. This aria then becomes a piano recitative, with strings only in a hushed tone, to depict the awesome mystery of our own transition from earth to heaven.

The first aria section contains a lively joy-rhythm, while the second recitative part has a subdued serenity-motif befitting the text.

ARIA: "Auf auf, mit hellem Schall / Verkündigt überall: / Mein Jesus sitzt zur Rechten! / Wer sucht mich anzufechten? / Ist er von mir genommen, / Ich werd' einst dahin kommen," (Up up, with bright sound / Proclaim everywhere: / My Jesus sits at the right hand! / Who seeks to attack me? / He is taken from me; / I will one day come there,)

RECITATIVE: "Wo mein Erlöser lebt. / Mein Augen werden ihn in grösster Klarheit schauen. / O könnt' ich im voraus mir eine Hütte bauen! / Wohin? Vergebner Wünsch! / Er wohnt nicht auf Berg und Tal, / Sein Allmacht zeigt sich überall: / So schweig, verwegner Mund, / Und suche nicht dieselbe zu ergründen!" (Where my Redeemer lives. / My eyes will behold Him most clearly. / O could I in advance build myself a hut! / Where? Vain wish! / He does not live in mountain and valley; / His omnipotence shows itself everywhere: / So be quiet, rash mouth, / And do not seek to get to the bottom of it!"

4. *Duet—alto, tenor.* With oboe d'amore and continuo accompaniment, they sing, first in canon and later in unison, this commentary on the end of the previous recitative. Nobody can fathom God's power; therefore they too will keep silent and not try to understand the source of His power. They are content to gaze through the stars to see Christ sitting at the right hand of God.

The da capo reinforces their acceptance of this mystery, but in general this duet is not very interesting.

5. *Chorale.* All voices and instruments are used for this fourth stanza of Matthäus Avenarius's hymn "O Jesu, meine Lust" (O Jesu, My Joy). This text pleads for a merciful judgment for us, so that we too may be placed to the right of God and behold His glory forever. Horn fanfares return to paint a scene of joyous splendor—the Father and the Son together on their thrones.

• **Sie werden euch in den Bann tun (They Will Put You Under the Ban) II** (1735; BWV 183).

Mariane von Ziegler composed the libretto for this cantata for the Sunday after Ascension. Like BWV 44 for the same day, it takes its text for the opening number from the Gospel for the day, John 16 (2), but this time for a bass recitative instead of a choral duet. All numbers reflect on the persecution which the disciples and their followers will have to undergo, according to Christ's prophetic words.

Bach emended the libretto and also used the unusual combination of four oboes (two oboes d'amore and two oboes da caccia) for his instrumental setting, which he never did again in any of his other sacred cantatas.

The soli are SATB, with a four-part chorus for the final chorale. The orchestra has the four oboes mentioned, a violoncello piccolo, two violins, a viola and a continuo of both harpsichord and organ.

1. *Recitative — bass.* Accompanied by all four oboes and continuo, he declaims Christ's words to His Apostles. In the role of Christ, the bass gives a very dramatic opening to this work which is itself a miniature drama. All the following numbers will be sung by soloists who play the part of disciples or believers, and who join together to sing the final chorale.

"Sie werden euch in den Bann tun, es kömmt aber die Zeit, dass, wer euch tötet, wird meinen, er tue Gott einen Dienst daran." (They will put you under the ban, but there comes the time, that, whoever kills you, will think, he does God a service in that.)

2. *Aria — tenor.* With violoncello and organ continuo, he sings of his defiance to his rejection by the world and even to death which threatens him. This first part refers to the Gospel quoted above, but he adds that Christ's protective arm will cover him in such circumstances. This aria has an interesting melody, but it seems to be lacking in the emotion that the words call for.

3. *Recitative — alto.* The four oboes and the strings accompany her short declamation, as she states that she is ready to give her blood and her life to her Savior. She will dedicate herself to Him and consoles herself that His Spirit will stand by her, should too much happen to her.

4. *Aria — soprano.* The two oboes da caccia and the strings play an introduction to her aria and then accompany her throughout. The melody is very beautiful as she appeals to the Holy Ghost for His guidance. This is the finest number in this cantata: "Höchster Tröster, heiliger Geist, / Der du mir die Wege weist, / Darauf ich wandeln soll, / Hilf meine Schwachheit mit vertreten, / Denn von mir selbst kann ich nicht beten, / Ich weiss: du sorgest für mein Wohl." (Highest Comforter, Holy Ghost, / You, Who show me the ways, / On which I should wander, / Help my weakness by interceding, / For of myself I cannot pray. / I know: Thou carest for my well-being.)

5. *Chorale.* All voices and instruments are used in this fifth verse of Paul Gerhardt's Whitsunday hymn "Zeuch ein zu deinen Toren" (Move in to Thy Gates).

The text of this stanza changes the thought of not being able to pray, as at the end of the previous aria, to the capability for prayer which the Holy Spirit will teach us. These prayers and our songs of praise will bring us the Lord's help in times of trial and trouble.

• **Wer mich liebet, der wird mein Wort halten (Whoever Loves Me Will Keep My Word) II** (1735; BWV 74).

For the first two numbers of this Whitsunday cantata, Bach borrowed the first and the last movements of his earlier Weimar cantata with the same title, BWV 59. Mariane von Ziegler wrote the libretto for this second version.

The Gospel, John 14 (23–31), is quoted literally for verses 23, the opening chorus, and 28, the bass aria. Romans 8 (1) is also quoted for the bass recitative; both bass numbers are sung by the soloist in the role of Christ. Unlike BWV 59, which gives the impression of being incomplete, this cantata has a closing chorale and so is definitely complete.

The soli are SATB, with a four-part chorus. The orchestra has three trumpets, timpani, two oboes, an oboe da caccia, two violins, a viola and continuo.

1. *Chorus.* Exactly the same spirited tune is used by Bach for this number as he used for the opening duet of BWV 59, but he has enlarged it now for full orchestra and chorus. Bach divides the voices into three groups for canonical singing: SA, TB and AT; the result is very impressive and stirring.

For a translation of this text see BWV 59.

2. *Aria — soprano.* Bach adapted this second number also from the earlier version's last number, changing it from a bass to a soprano aria, and adding an oboe da caccia obbligato. Bach did not heed the self-borrowing, it seems, because the emotions expressed by the

two texts are different: praise of God's glory which we hope to attain, in the earlier work, and an appeal to Him to enter our hearts, in this one.

3. *Recitative—alto.* Once again the listener can perceive the miniature drama presented by all numbers in this cantata (each soloist appears as a disciple or a believer, who comments after each Gospel quotation delivered by the bass). In secco, she repeats the previous thought in the soprano's aria, that her heart is open to God and that she hopes that He will never leave her.

4. *Aria—bass.* With continuo only playing a step-motif to illustrate his arioso text by a rhythm first ascending and then descending, the bass sings Christ's words in verse 28 of the Gospel: "Ich gehe hin und komme wieder zu euch. Hättet ihr mich lieb, so würdet ihr euch freuen." (I go away and come again to you. If you loved Me, then you would rejoice.) The coloratura run on "freuen" at the end is splendid. The aria has no da capo and the step-rhythm is continued throughout.

5. *Aria—tenor.* A resounding joy-motif, in both his voice and in the string accompaniment, is featured in this "actor's" response to Christ's words. The second part of his aria illustrates his unshaken faith in the Lord, despite Satan's attempts to divert him from it: "Kommt, eilet, stimmet Sait' und Lieder / In muntern und erfreuten Ton. / Geht er gleich weg, so kömmt er wieder, / Der hochgelobte Gottessohn. / Der Satan wird indes versuchen, / Den Deinigen gar sehr zu fluchen. / Ist er mir hinderlich, / So glaub' ich, Herr, an dich." (Come, hurry, tune strings and songs / In a merry and joyous tone. / If He now goes away, then He comes again, / The highly-praised Son of God. / Satan will try meanwhile, / To strongly curse Thy servant. / He is behind me, / Therefore I believe, Lord, in Thee.)

The da capo of this aria repeats the happy faith of the believer.

6. *Recitative—bass.* All three oboes lend a sombre tone to this quotation from Romans 8 (1), imagined by Bach as spoken by Christ but actually the words of the Apostle Paul: "Es ist nichts Verdammliches an denen, die in Christo Jesu sind." (There is nothing damnable in them who are in Christ Jesus.)

7. *Aria—alto.* Like the tenor aria, this number has a da capo, and is of even superior quality. All oboes and strings realistically portray the rattling of hell's chains, which the words of the text suggested to Bach. An image of the chains breaking occurs in the second half of the aria, where the forte tempo changes to piano at the mention of Christ's suffering. A joy-motif comes in the last line as he derides Satan's fury. The da capo brings back the picture of the writhing struggle against hell's bonds, which are broken by Christ's sacrifice.

"Nichts kann mich erretten / Von höllischen Ketten / Als, Jesu. dein Blut! / Dein Leiden, dein Sterben / Macht mich ja zum Erben: / Ich lache der Wut." (Nothing can save me / From hellish chains / Than, Jesus, Thy Blood! / Thy suffering, Thy death / Make me indeed Thy heir: / I laugh at the rage.)

The realistic drama in this number is enhanced by runs on the words "erretten" (save) and "Ketten" (chains). It is an example of Bach's tone-painting in his own inimitable style. This is a magnificent aria in every respect.

8. *Chorale.* This is stanza two of Paul Gerhardt's hymn, "Gott Vater, sende deinen Geist" (God our Father, send Thy Spirit). It is performed in unadorned style by all voices and instruments. The idea of the descent of the Holy Ghost upon us conforms with the Whitsunday Scripture: we are not worthy of receiving this gift, but Christ has won it for us by His sacrificial atonement for our sins.

• **Also hat Gott die Welt geliebet (God So Loved the World)** (1735; BWV 68).

For Whit Monday Bach set another of Mariane von Ziegler's poems, making a few changes in her text which closely adheres to the Gospel for the day, John 3 (16–21). Verses 16 and 18 are quoted for the opening and the closing choruses, respectively.

The librettist designated the first chorus as a chorale for which Bach took stanza one of Salomo Liscow's hymn with the above title. Yet this is not a chorale cantata because the chorale does not appear in any other number and there is no final chorale.

Bach borrowed the melody for the two arias from his 1716 Weimar secular hunting cantata, BWV 208, "Was mir behagt" (What Suits Me); whether he was in a hurry to compose this work or whether these past melodies pleased him, we do not know.

The soli are SB, with a four-part chorus. The orchestra has three trumpets, three trombones, two oboes, taille (a tenor oboe), a horn, two violins, a violoncello piccolo, a viola and continuo.

1. *Chorus (Chorale).* This is an extended chorale in siciliano rhythm, supported by the horn in the continuo. With their siciliano introduction, the oboes and violins establish a mood of lulling peace, which is then developed by the voices gently symbolizing the grace which emanates from the Father through the Holy Ghost. It is a fine, evocative movement of blissful serenity: "Also hat Gott die Welt geliebt, / Dass er uns seinen Sohn gegeben. / Wer sich im Glauben ihm ergibt, / Der soll dort ewig bei ihm leben. / Wer glaubt, dass Jesus ihm geboren, / Der bleibet ewig unverloren, / Und ist kein Leid, das den betrübt, / Den Gott und auch sein Jesus liebt." (God so loved the world, / That He gave us His Son. / Whoever gives himself in faith to Him, / He shall live there with Him eternally. / Whoever believes that Jesus was born for him, / He remains forever saved, / And there is no sorrow which troubles him, / Whom God and also his Jesus loves.)

2. *Aria—soprano.* Bach added a violoncello piccolo to the oboe, violin and continuo accompaniment of the soprano aria sung by Pales in BWV 208 when he imitated this melody. The joy-motif is the same as in its secular counterpart, and serves equally well to praise the Lord as it did originally to flatter Duke Christian von Sachsen-Weissenfels: "Mein gläubiges Herze, / Frohlocke, sing, scherze, / Dein Jesus ist da! / Weg Jammer, weg Klagen, / Ich will euch nur sagen: / Mein Jesus ist nah." (My believing heart, / Rejoice, sing, be merry, / Your Jesus is there! / Away lamentation, away mourning, / I will only say to you: / My Jesus is near.)

Bach expanded the original length of this aria, which has become one of his most popular numbers in concerts today.

3. *Recitative—bass.* The first line of this secco declamation refers to the Epistle, Acts 10 (42–48), the descent of the Holy Ghost on Peter's company and on Cornelius. He states that he is also a man like Peter (God accepts all men in every nation) and hopes to find joy, because Christ does not forget him. The Lord did not come into the world to judge, but to be the Mediator between man's guilt and God.

4. *Aria—bass.* This number is the second borrowing from the hunting cantata, also a bass aria. Pan sings about himself as a pagan deity in the secular work to the same tune as the Christian believer sings to Christ in this one. There is nothing shocking about the melody fitting both texts equally well. All music was religious in Bach's compositions.

"Du bist geboren mir zugute, / Das glaub' ich, mir ist wohl zumute, / Weil du für mich genug getan. / Das Rund der Erde mag gleich brechen, / Will mir der Satan widersprechen, / So bet' ich dich, mein Heiland, an." (Thou hast been born for my well-being; / That, I believe, makes me feel well, / Because Thou hast done enough for me. / The earth's sphere may immediately break, / And even if Satan wants to oppose me, / Then I worship Thee, my Savior.)

Bach makes both of these arias da capo (two and four), although they are not da capo in Mariane von Ziegler's libretto.

5. *Chorus.* The Biblical text quoted is John 3 (18). All voices, divided into four parts, sing this melody in canon to a

fugue played by all instruments. It is an unusual conclusion, because Bach generally concludes on an optimistic theme, whereas here the mood is threatening for the unbeliever, in sharp contrast to the joy-motif in the opening chorus. Nevertheless, this chorus in its motet form presents a moving panorama of the Last Judgment. The overwhelming power of Bach's orchestration emphasizes the text, so that we can feel God's compassion for His believers and His wrath for unbelievers in this marvelous musical tableau: "Wer an ihn glaubet, der wird nicht gerichtet, wer aber nicht glaubet, der ist schon gerichtet, denn er glaubet nicht an den Namen des eingebornen Sohn Gottes." (Who believes in Him, he is not judged, but who does not believe, he is already judged, for he does not believe in the name of the only begotten Son of God.)

• **Er rufet seinen Schafen mit Namen (He Calls His Sheep by Name)** (1735; BWV 175).

This cantata for Whit Tuesday continues the series of Mariane von Ziegler's libretti that Bach chose at this time. The Gospel for the day is John 10 (1–11), from which parts of verses three and six are quoted in two of the three recitatives. The other numbers all reflect on this Gospel. Bach made extensive changes to Mariane von Ziegler's text and also borrowed the melody for the tenor aria from the bass in his earlier 1717 secular cantata "Durchlauchtster Leopold" (Most Serene Highness Leopold), BWV 173a.

The soli are ATB, with a four-part chorus for the final chorale. The instruments used are three recorders, two trumpets, a violoncello piccolo, two violins, a viola and continuo.

1. *Recitative—tenor.* For this number and the following aria, the three recorders give a pastoral ambience suitable for the words of the texts. Here the tenor recites the second part of verse three in the Gospel with a step-motif for illustration: "Er rufet seinen Schafen mit Namen und führet sie hinaus." (He calls His sheep by name and leads them out.)

2. *Aria—alto.* The three recorders illustrate the obedient following of the sheep through the green meadow after their Shepherd and also their longing to be there with Him always. The beautiful melody evokes this pastoral scene: "Komm, leite mich, / Es sehnet sich / Mein Geist auf grüner Weide. / Mein Herze schmacht, / Ächzt Tag und Nacht, / Mein Hirte, meine Freude! (Come, lead me, / My spirit longs / For green pastures. / My heart languishes, / It groans day and night, / My Shepherd, my joy!)

3. *Recitative—tenor.* In secco, he narrates his feeling of longing to find his Shepherd, just as the alto did in her previous aria. It seems that each vocalist in this dramatic cantata represents a lost sheep or believer trying to find the Lord. His hope will be realized at the wished-for dawn, symbolic of the Lord's appearance.

4. *Aria—tenor.* Accompanied by a violin and the violoncello piccolo obbligato playing a tripping step-motif to illustrate the text, he sings of the approach of the Shepherd. However, the lightness of the secular borrowed number does not accord with the seriousness of the last part of this text, which Bach expanded from its original form: "Es dünket mich, ich seh' dich kommen, / Du gehst zur rechten Türe ein. / Du wirst im Glauben aufgenommen / Und musst der wahre Hirte sein. / Ich kenne deine holde Stimme, / Die voller Lieb' und Sanftmut ist, / Dass ich im Geist darob ergrimme, / Wer zweifelt, dass du Heiland seist." (It seems to me, I see Thee coming, / Thou goest in by the right door. / Thou art received in faith / And must be the true Shepherd. / I know Thy charming voice, / Which is full of love and gentleness, / So that I become angry in my spirit / At whoever doubts that Thou art the Savior.)

5. *Recitative—alto, bass.* Strings accompany this number, which is divided into two parts. The alto gives the last part

of verse six of the Gospel: "Sie vernahmen aber nicht, was es war, das er zu ihnen gesaget hatte." (They did not comprehend, however, what it was that He had said to them.) Then the bass comments on this with his own declamation. He says that we are men whose blinded reason, like that of the dumb, prevents their comprehension. In his arioso of the last two lines, he apostrophizes "Vernunft" (reason), saying that when Jesus speaks to her, that happens for her salvation.

6. *Aria—bass.* In the first part, brilliant fanfares of the two trumpets punctuate the step-motif of the continuo, which suggest that the spiritually deaf should open their ears. At the end of the third line the trumpets cease, after they have signaled Christ's victory over the devil and death.

The second part is accompanied by continuo only; it quietly speaks of the full life to be had by a Christian who follows Christ and bears His Cross.

This is the outstanding number in this cantata because of Bach's skillful contrast of forte and piano in the two parts of his interpretation of the text: "Öffnet euch, ihr beiden Ohren, / Jesus hat euch geschworen, / Dass er Teufel, Tod erlegt. / Gnade, G'nüge, volles Leben / Will er allen Christen geben, / Wer im folgt, sein Kreuz nachträgt." (Open your two ears, / Jesus has sworn to you, / That He has laid low devil and death. / Mercy, abundance, a full life / Will He give to all Christians. / Who follows Him, bears His Cross after.)

7. *Chorale.* All instruments and the four-art choir perform this ninth stanza of Johann Rist's "O Gottes Geist, mein Trost und Rat" (O God's Spirit, My Comfort and Counsel). This fits perfectly the Whitsuntide theme of heeding the Holy Ghost which was advocated in all numbers from four to six. God's word, compared to the morning star, seems to be connected with Christ's appearance at the end of number three—the tenor recitative. Bach added "Alleluja" twice at the end of this stanza.

• **Es ist ein trotzig und verzagt Ding (There Is a Defiant and Despondent Thing)** (1735; BWV 176).

This cantata for Trinity Sunday is the last of Mariane von Ziegler's texts emended and set by Bach. The Gospel, John 3 (1–15)—Nicodemus comes to speak to Jesus at night—is referred to in the second number, an alto recitative. The cantata is highly dramatic in portraying this nocturnal visit. The main idea of this cantata is the stubborn opposition in men's hearts against seeing the light because they prefer evil's darkness. Yet their obstinacy is contrasted with their timidity before God.

The soli are SAB, with the four-part chorus. The instruments include two oboes, an oboe da caccia, two violins, a viola and continuo.

1. *Chorus.* This text is based on Jeremiah 17 (9), which the four-part choir begins to sing immediately in a fugue played tutti by the instruments. They sing a vehement denunciation of mankind's heart in a tumultuous and pessimistic tone, reminiscent of the tumult-motif in Bach's *Passions.*

"Es ist ein trotzig und verzagt Ding um aller Menschen Herze." (There is a defiant and despondent thing about all men's hearts.)

2. *Recitative—alto.* In secco, she compares Joshua's wish for the sun to remain still with Nicodemus's desire for night to fall, so that each might attain his purpose. She picks up the word "verzagt" (discouraged) to begin her exposition: "Ich meine, recht verzagt, / Dass Nikodemus sich bei Tag nicht, / Bei Nacht zu Jesu wagt. / Die Sonne musste dort bei Josua so lange stille steh'n, / So lange bis der Sieg vollkommen war gescheh'n: / Hier aber wünschet Nikodem: O säh ich sie zu Rüste geh'n!" (I think, really timid, / That Nicodemus dares not go by day / But by night to Jesus. / The sun had to stand still so long there with Joshua, / So long until the victory had happened completely: / Here, however, Nicodemus wishes: O if I might see it go to rest!)

3. *Aria—soprano.* Bach illustrates the words of her text by a lively gavotte in a march-rhythm, incorporating a joy-motif in the accompanying strings. The soprano assumes the role of Nicodemus as he speaks these words to himself on his way to meet Jesus that night. This follows the idea of the previous recitative, where Nicodemus is waiting for nightfall before going to visit Jesus. It is the most interesting number in this cantata for thought and musical expression.

"Dein sonst hell beliebter Schein / Soll für mich umnebelt sein. / Wenn ich nach dem Meister frage, / Denn ich scheue mich bei Tage. / Niemand kann die Wunder tun, / Denn sein Allmacht und sein Wesen, / Scheint, ist göttlich auserlesen, / Gottes Geist muss auf ihm ruh'n." (Thy usual bright, beloved gleaming / Shall be fog-enshrouded for me. / When I ask about the Master, / For I am fearful by day, / Nobody can perform the miracles, / Except His omnipotence and His being. / It seems, He is divinely chosen; / God's Spirit must rest on Him.)

4. *Recitative—bass.* Nicodemus has now arrived with Christ and is speaking to Him. He asks Jesus not to wonder why he has come at night. He explains that his own weakness prevents him from approaching Christ by day. Yet he says that he feels consoled, because Jesus receives his heart and his spirit in his new life. Bach added a final arioso line at the end, paraphrasing verse 15 of the Gospel, to show Nicodemus's profession of faith: "Weil alle, die nur an dich glauben, nicht verloren werden." (Because all, who only believe in Thee, are not lost.)

5. *Aria—alto.* The two oboes and the oboe da caccia in unison provide the obbligato melody for her aria. It seems that the text rebukes Nicodemus for his hesitation, compared to her own trusting faith; Bach illustrates this by giving an elegiac tone to the first part and then changing to a brighter rhythm in the second part: "Ermuntert euch, furchtsam und schüchterne Sinne, / Erholet euch, höret, was Jesus verspricht: / Dass ich durch den Glauben den Himmel gewinne, / Wenn die Verheissung erfüllend geschieht, / Werd' ich dort oben / Mit Danken und Loben / Vater, Sohn und heiligen Geist / Preisen, der dreieinig heisst." (Cheer up, fearful and timid minds, / Recover, hear what Jesus promises: / That I through faith win heaven. / When the fulfilled promise happens, / I shall up there praise / With thanks and praising / Father, Son and Holy Ghost / Who are called the Three-in-One.)

6. *Chorale.* This fine tutti number is stanza eight of Paul Gerhardt's Trinity hymn "Was alle Weisheit in der Welt" (What All Wisdom in the World). It is an unadorned song of praise to the Trinity for being our Protector and Savior.

• **Was willst du dich betrüben (Why Wilt Thou Be Troubled)** (1735; BWV 107).

With this chorale cantata for the seventh Sunday after Trinity, Bach began a series in the chorale genre which continued until 1744, the date of his last extant cantata. In this type of cantata, the librettists are the hymn writers (with sometimes additional verses by other poets) whose chorales Bach set for almost all of his cantatas during this last period.

Why Bach turned to the chorale cantata almost exclusively at this time might be attributed to his wish to compose a "purer" church music than he had found in the free poetry of his previous librettists, or perhaps there was no suitable new librettist available to him.

The Gospel for this Sunday is Mark 8 (1–9), the miracle of the feeding of the four thousand; the doubts of the disciples and their subsequent confidence in Jesus are only indirectly referred to in Johann Heermann's hymn with the above title. All six stanzas of this hymn are set by Bach, followed by stanza 14 of another hymn by David Denicke, "Ich will zu aller Stunde" (I Will at Every Hour), for the final chorale.

The plan used by Bach is unusual: only one recitative, which is followed by four arias in succession (the first time Bach has placed four arias together); yet these arias are different from each other and thus hold the listener's interest.

The soli are STB, with a four-part chorus. The orchestra has a corno da caccia, two transverse flutes, two oboes d'amore, two violins, a viola, organ and continuo.

1. *Chorus.* With all voices and instruments, the comforting words of the first stanza of Heermann's hymn are presented. The effect of the sung text is heightened by the beautiful melody, independently played and featuring the flute. The choir sings an extended chorale but not a chorale fantasia. It seems that the chorus reflects the calm trust which the disciples had in their Lord and which the individual Christian should have today: "Was willst du dich betrüben, / O meine liebe Seel', / Ergib dich, den zu lieben, / Der heisst Immanuel. / Vertraue ihm allein; / Er wird gut alles machen / Und fördern deine Sachen, / Wie dir's wird selig sein." (Why wilt thou be troubled, / O my dear soul? / Give thyself to love Him, / Who is called Immanuel. / Trust Him alone; / He will do everything well / And promote thy affairs, / So it will be blessed for thee.)

2. *Recitative—bass.* This seems to be the only number unsuited to the verse form of the chorale stanza, even though he is accompanied by the two oboes d'amore, the organ and the continuo.

He reminds his soul that God never leaves those who trust in Him. For any believer in distress, the Lord will perform a miracle to rescue him from his fearful oppression.

3. *Aria—bass.* The imagery of the hunt occurs in this vivace aria. Bach illustrates the text with his setting for strings and organ, but unaccountably without a horn, to express the pursuit of what is useful and good, with God's help. Bach blends this vision of the chase very artistically into the quiet confidence of the latter part of the aria.

"Auf ihn magst du es wagen / Mit unerschrocknem Mut; / Du wirst mit ihm erjagen, / Was dir ist nütz und gut. / Was Gott beschlossen hat, / Das kann niemand hindern / Bei allen Menschenkindern; / Es geht nach seinem Rat. (With Him you may attempt it / With fearless courage; / You will pursue with Him, / What is useful and good for you. / What God has decided, / That can nobody hinder / Among all the children of men; / It goes according to His counsel.)

4. *Aria—tenor.* This is the first cantata with two arias for the same voice (number six will be the second tenor aria). Organ and continuo here depict the rolling contortions of the dragon (Satan) for which the libretto calls. The imagery changes at the last line to a picture of quiet assurance in the verse, "Denn dein Werk fördert Gott." (For God furthers your work.)

5. *Aria—soprano.* The two oboes d'amore play a duet accompaniment to emphasize God's guiding of our lives, a predestination which nobody can avoid. The chorale tune reappears in this number, while the high soprano illustrates God's lofty grandeur, before she summarizes in the last line: "Was Gott will, das geschieht" (What God wishes, that happens).

6. *Aria—tenor.* The two transverse flutes and the pizzicato continuo give to this number a joy-motif befitting its text—the antithesis of his former aria. Complete trust and happiness are expressed both in his text and in the melody: "Drum ich mich ihm ergebe, / Ihm sei es heimgestellt; / Nach nichts ich sonst mehr strebe, / Denn nur was ihm gefällt. / Drauf wart'ich und bin still / Sein Will', der ist der beste, / Das glaub'ich steif und feste, / Gott mach'es, wie er will!" (Therefore I surrender myself to Him, / To Him be it left; / For nothing else do I strive any more, / Than for only what is pleasing to Him. / For that I wait and am quiet; / His will is the best, / I believe that strongly and firmly; / God does as He wishes!)

7. *Chorale.* Bach composed a stunning

siciliano for all voices and instruments for this fourteenth verse of David Denicke's hymn. The graceful tune presents a joyous picture of a fervent group prayer to the Trinity for protection against evil. It is a splendid conclusion to a marvelous cantata: "Herr, gib, dass ich dein Ehre / Ja all mein Leben lang / Von Herzengrund vermehre, / Dir sage Lob und Dank. / O Vater, Sohn und Geist, / Der du aus lauter Gnaden / Abwendest Not und Schaden, / Sei immerdar gepreist!" (Lord, grant, that I Thy honor / All my life long / May increase from the depths of my heart. / To Thee I say thanks and praise. / O Father, Son and Spirit, / Thou, Who out of pure mercy / Turnest away distress and harm, / Be forever praised!)

• **Was frag' ich nach der Welt (What Do I Ask of the World)** (1735; BWV 94).

For the ninth Sunday after Trinity, in this cantata, Bach retained the chorale cantata form but added recitatives and arias written by an unknown librettist. It seems, however, that he was experimenting with a new type of recitative, inasmuch as he interpolated sections of the chorale into the two long recitatives in this work. Both of these numbers are sung by a soloist. The result is not a very happy one. The opening chorus and the tenor aria are the only noteworthy numbers in this cantata.

The Gospel, Luke 16 (1–9), the parable of the unjust steward, is not reflected in the text directly, but perhaps indirectly in that the theme is on the vanity of the world and its riches.

The soli are SATB, with a four-part chorus. The orchestra has a transverse flute, two oboes, two violins, a viola, an organ and continuo.

1. *Chorus.* This is a beautiful fantasia based on the first stanza of a hymn by Georg Michael Pfefferkorn, accompanied by all voices and instruments. The spacious, floating melody seems to represent the transitory nature of worldly things and still, at the same time, the elevated permanence of the spiritual life to come.

The movement resembles a concerto for flute; beginning with an orchestral introduction, the transverse flute continues to embellish the choral singing, which is accompanied throughout by the oboes and the strings. It is not difficult for the listener to visualize the choir in heaven with Jesus, as they sing this mystical number which summarizes the thought of the whole cantata: "Was frag'ich nach der Welt / Und allen ihren Schätzen, / Wenn ich mich nur an dir, / Mein Jesu, kann ergötzen! / Dich hab'ich einzig mir / Zur Wollust vorgestellt, / Du, du bist meine Ruh: / Was frag'ich nach der Welt!" (What do I ask of the world / And all its treasures, / When I can delight, / My Jesus, only in Thee! / Only Thee have I placed / Before myself for my pleasure, / Thou, Thou art my rest: / What do I ask of the world!)

2. *Aria—bass.* In secco, he attempts to illustrate the image of the world's disintegration as stated in the text, but the result is not too convincing. At the end he repeats the first line of the chorale—the motto line.

Schweitzer (Vol. II, p. 77) sees tone-painting of clouds in this aria, but the tumbling rhythm makes this difficult to imagine.

3. *Chorale and Recitative—tenor.* The next verse of the chorale is sung arioso at intervals in the recitative. The two oboes accompany the chorale sections in a duet, while the longer declamation parts are sung in secco.

The tenor reproaches the proud and the rich for their vain ambition, which will be obliterated at their death. He, however, as a Christian, will place no importance on the wealth of the world but rather on the spiritual blessings of living with Christ. Two lines of the chorale stanza begin this number, and the motto "Was frag' ich nach der Welt!" ends it.

4. *Aria—alto.* If any images of floating clouds occur in this cantata, it is certainly in the obbligato transverse flute accompaniment to this aria that they appear. The vanities of this world seem to float away like clouds, leaving Jesus as the

only permanent possession at the end of her aria: "Betörte Welt, betörte Welt! / Auch dein Reichtum, Gut und Geld / Ist Betrug und falscher Schein. / Du magst den eitlen Mammon zählen, / Ich will dafür mir Jesum wählen; / Jesus, Jesus soll allein / Meiner Seele Reichtum sein. / Betörte Welt, betörte Welt!" (Deluded world, duped world! / Even thy wealth, goods and money / Are deception and false appearance. / Thou may count vain Mammon; / Instead of that I will choose Jesus for me. / Jesus, Jesus shall alone / Be the wealth of my soul. / Deluded world, duped world!)

5. *Chorale and Recitative — bass.* Here the same procedure is used as before in the tenor chorale and recitative. This time the chorale lines are played adagio with only secco accompaniment for the whole number.

His text continues the theme on the sham of this world; the last lines of the chorale verse being: "Wenn mich mein Jesus ehrt: / Was frag' ich nach der Welt!" (If my Jesus honors me: / What do I ask of the world!)

This number is not at all successful in its appeal to the listener.

6. *Aria — tenor.* A swinging gigue melody, in the accompaniment of strings, organ and continuo, makes this the most outstanding number in this cantata. Bach's setting elevates the music high above the banal imagery of the text in the last part where the mole is depicted. Despite the poor poetry, this is a fine aria: "Die Welt kann ihre Lust und Freud', / Das Blendwerk schnöder Eitelkeit, / Nicht hoch genug erhöhen. / Sie wühlt, nur gelben Kot zu finden, / Gleich einem Maulwurf in den Gründen / Und lässt dafür den Himmel stehen." (The world its desire and joy, / The dazzle of mean vanity, / Can not raise high enough. / It grubs, to find only yellow filth, / Like a mole in the ground / And for that leaves heaven waiting.)

7. *Aria — soprano.* Again, Bach rises above the mediocre poetry of this verse with the charming solo oboe accompaniment for this number. Quiet peace and joy permeates her song, but it lacks the forceful emotion in the previous tenor aria.

Note that there are two arias in succession at this point, neither one referring directly to the chorale.

"Es halt' es mit der blinden Welt, / Wer nichts auf seine Seele hält, / Mir ekelt vor der Erden. / Ich will nur meinen Jesum lieben / Und mich in Buss und Glauben üben, / So kann ich reich und selig werden." (Let him hold with the blind world, / Who places no importance on his soul. / I am disgusted with the world. / I will love only my Jesus / And practice repentance and belief. / Then I can become rich and blessed.)

8. *Chorale.* All voices and instruments are used for verses seven and eight of the original chorale, with each verse beginning and ending with the motto line. These stanzas repeat the idea that death will wipe away all earthly joys and possessions and only Jesus will remain as our eternal treasure.

• **Ich freue mich in dir (I Rejoice in Thee)** (1735 or 1737; BWV 133).

Both Spitta and Terry date this cantata for the Tuesday after Christmas, 1735, while Neumann gives about 1737, also Terry's alternative date. It is a chorale cantata based on Kaspar Ziegler's Christmas hymn with this title. The librettist is unknown or may have been Christian Weiss, Jr., according to Terry. Bach set this arrangement with stanzas one and four in their original form as the first and the last choruses, and the intervening stanzas paraphrased in the arias and in the recitatives.

The Gospel for the day is John 1 (1–14), the fourteenth verse — "And the Word was made flesh and dwelt among us" — being reflected throughout the libretto.

The soli are SATB, with a four-part chorus. The orchestra has a cornetto, two oboes d'amore, two violins, a viola and continuo.

1. *Chorus.* All instruments play a dancing joy-motif at the beginning, which is continued after each line sung,

to produce a chorale fantasia full of supreme happiness. If the orchestral ritornelli were played alone, they could create a separate sinfonia. In the last three lines, the tone of reverence seems to evoke the scene in the manger in Bethlehem.

"Ich freue mich in dir / Und heisse dich willkommen, / Mein liebes Jesulein! / Du hast dir vorgenommen, / Mein Brüderlein zu sein. / Ach, wie ein süsser Ton! / Wie freundlich sieht er aus, / Der grosse Gottessohn!" (I rejoice in Thee / And bid Thee welcome, / My dear little Jesus! / Thou hast undertaken, / To be my little Brother. / Ah, how sweet a sound! / How friendly He looks, / The great Son of God!)

2. *Aria—alto.* The words of her aria refer to the fourteenth verse of John 1, "The Word became flesh." The accompanying oboes d'amore play a joy-motif at first, which changes into a mystical mood in the second half, when she says that she has seen God face to face and now her soul will be healed. Bach interprets the mystery of this Birth with motives of first joy, and then of awe.

"Getrost! es fasst ein heiliger Leib / Des Höchsten unbegreiflichs Wesen. / Ich habe Gott—wie wohl ist mir geschehen!— / Von Angesicht zu Angesicht gesehen. / Ach! meine Seele muss genesen." (Be comforted! A holy body / Enfolds the incomprehensible Highest's being. / I have seen God—how well it has / happened to me—face to face. / Ah! my soul must be healed.

3. *Recitative—tenor.* His secco declamation begins with a reference to Adam's hiding himself from God, Genesis 3 (8), which he says that he will not do, because he knows God's merciful nature. His final arioso lines state that God has become a little child, Jesus, who has a personal relationship with him.

4. *Aria—soprano.* The marvel of the Lord's birth is the "sweet sound" mentioned in the first stanza of the chorale. The accompanying strings realistically depict the merry ringing of the bells in a joy-motif which announces this wonderful news.

In the first part of her aria, the strings give an echo effect to her singing, as though her words are being repeated by angels hovering over the manger. From the middle to the end, the tempo changes to largo in a grief-motif for those hard hearts who do not acknowledge Jesus.

"Wie lieblich klingt es in den Ohren, / Dies Wort: mein Jesus ist geboren, / Wie dringt es in das Herz hinein! / Wer Jesu Namen nicht versteht, / Und wem es nicht durch's Herze geht, / Der muss ein harter Felsen sein." (How lovely it rings in my ears, / This word: my Jesus is born, / How it presses into my heart! / Whoever does not understand Jesus' Name, / And whose heart it does not enter, / He must be a hard rock.)

Bach has here created one of his most exquisite arias by combining two different lyrical themes with amazing skill.

5. *Recitative—bass.* In secco, he says that he will not now be afraid of death and its pain, because Jesus will be with him even to his grave. His final arioso is sung as a prayer: "Wer Jesum recht erkennt, / Der stirbt nicht, wenn er stirbt, / Sobald er Jesum nennt." (Whoever truly recognizes Jesus, / He does not die, when he dies, / As long as he names Jesus.)

6. *Chorale.* This is the sixth and last verse of the chorale, sung in plain style and with the full orchestra. The thought is that the believer will remain faithful to Jesus and live for Him, even though the world disintegrates. Then at the last, he will fall asleep in Him.

• **Was Gott tut, das ist wohlgetan (What God Does, That Is Done Well) III** (1735; BWV 100).

This is Bach's third and last setting of Samuel Rodigast's hymn, this time for the fifteenth Sunday after Trinity, as was BWV 99 (c. 1733). BWV 98, the first, was composed c. 1732 for another Sunday.

Both of these earlier compositions had their middle stanzas arranged as free paraphrases, but for this last setting, Bach retains all six stanzas of the hymn without alteration. There are no recitatives; the intervening numbers are a duet and three arias. Each stanza of the hymn begins with the motto line, the title of the cantata.

The libretto has no connection with the Gospel for this Sunday; it is simply a hymn of praise and submission to God. As each stanza is set differently, there is no monotony in this fascinating cantata.

The soli are SATB, with a four-part chorus. The orchestra is very large: two horns, timpani, a transverse flute, an oboe d'amore, two violins, a violoncello, a violone, a viola, organ and continuo.

1. *Chorus.* The melody of the chorale is completely heard only in this number and in the final chorale stanza, although its tune pervades all the other movements. For this and the last movement, Bach returned to borrowing from his previous settings, but made this opening the most lavish and festive of them all. Here the orchestra plays a concerto for flute, oboe d'amore and violin, enriched by the two horns and the drums. All voices sing in unison to this accompaniment. The result is as magnificent as any occasional outdoor piece by Handel or Telemann.

For the text and its translation, see BWV 98, p. 131.

2. *Duet—alto, tenor.* With organ and continuo only, they sing in canonic imitation the second stanza, which has a step-motif expressing their confidence in God. It is fairly interesting but lacks the force of the opening movement—probably intentionally, to give variety. Their text reveals their patient trust in God to guide them on the right path and to turn misfortune from them.

3. *Aria—soprano.* Supported by the transverse flute and organ-continuo, she sings that God is the miraculous physician who can heal her soul by his Divine magic. Bach illustrates this by the rapid high notes of the flute, which seem to represent the healing medicine flowing from God to her.

"Was Gott tut, das ist wohlgetan, / Er wird mich wohl bedenken; / Er, als mein Arzt und Wundermann, / Wird mir nicht Gift einschenken / Für Arzenei. / Gott ist getreu, / Drum will ich auf ihn bauen / Und seiner Gnade trauen." (What God does, that is done well. / He will certainly remember me; / He, as my Doctor and Miracle-worker, / Will not pour out poison for me / As medicine. / God is faithful. / Therefore I will build on Him / And trust in His mercy.)

4. *Aria—bass.* All strings which accompany him give this aria a joy-motif, in contrast with the preceding one. His brilliant runs on the words italicized below and the syncopated melody make this a noteworthy aria.

"Was Gott tut, das ist wohlgetan, / Er ist mein Licht, mein *Leben,* / Der mir nichts Böses gönnen kann, / Ich will mich ihm *ergeben* / In *Freud'* und Leid! / Es kommt die Zeit, / Da öffentlich *erscheinet,* / Wie *treulich* er es meinet." (What God does, that is done well. / He is my light, my *life,* / Who can bestow on me nothing evil, / I will *surrender* myself to Him / In *joy* and sorrow! / There is coming the time, / When it will openly *appear,* / How *faithfully* He means it.)

5. *Aria—alto.* The tone now changes to pathos as the text indicates. The oboe d'amore obbligato is prominent, with the violoncello, violone and organ aiding this sad but beautiful melody. Her aria begins with a grief-motif, becoming a joy-motif in the last half.

"Was Gott tut, das ist wohlgetan, / Muss ich den Kelch gleich schmecken, / Der bitter ist nach meinem Wahn, / Lass' ich mich doch nicht schrecken, / Weil doch zuletzt / Ich werd' ergötzt / Mit süssem Trost im Herzen; / Da weichen alle Schmerzen." (What God does, that is done well. / Must I now taste the cup, / Which is bitter according to my delusion; / Still I do not let myself be afraid, / Because in the end / I will be delighted / With sweet comfort in my heart. / Then all pains will vanish.)

6. This sixth and last verse of the chorale was used by Bach to conclude his first Leipzig cantata, BWV 75, "Die Elenden sollen essen" (The Miserable

Shall Eat) and also for BWV 99, but never before with such resounding éclat as in this number. The horns and timpani, which he added, really make this conclusion sparkle. In fact, both this and the opening chorus are so imposing, that with the splendid aria arrangement of the chorale verses between them, one might judge this work to be one of Bach's highest achievements in the chorale cantata genre.

For a translation of this stanza, see BWV 99, pp. 135–136.

• **Wo soll ich fliehen hin (Whither Shall I Flee)** (1735; BWV 5).

In spite of his desire to adhere to the chorale throughout a chorale cantata, Bach still required a librettist to paraphrase the inner verses, arias and recitatives, which would give him more freedom for composition than he would find in continuous chorale verses. This chorale cantata for the nineteenth Sunday after Trinity is an example of this method; Picander is presumed to be its librettist.

Johann Heermann's hymn with the above title was chosen for verses one and eleven to provide the opening chorus and the concluding chorale. The Gospel, Matthew 9 (1–8), Christ heals the palsied man through forgiveness of his sins, is reflected in the arias and recitatives.

The soli are SATB, with a four-part chorus. The instruments comprise a slide trumpet, two oboes, two violins, a viola and continuo.

1. *Chorus.* This is a chorale fantasia on the first verse of the hymn, performed by all voices and instruments. It conveys the impression, made by a grand fresco, of doubt and confusion in its step-motif. We can perceive the uncertain steps of the singers as they search for relief from their present afflictions: "Wo soll ich fliehen hin, / Weil ich beschweret bin / Mit viel und grossen Sünden? / Wo soll ich Rettung finden? / Wenn alle Welt herkäme, / Mein Angst sie nicht wegnähme." (Whither shall I flee, / Because I am oppressed / With many heavy sins? / Where shall I find relief? / If the whole world should come, / It would not take away my anguish.)

2. *Recitative—bass.* The usual secco declamation states that the filth of sin has stained his soul so that he is separated from God. Still the blood of Jesus will wash these spots of sin from him, and thus he will not remain rejected by God.

3. *Aria—tenor.* This is the only occasion in Bach's sacred cantatas in which a solo viola obbligato accompanies an aria. It plays a flowing wave-motif, suggesting the descent of Christ's Blood on him to purify him of sin. Runs on the words "walle" (pour), "Strömen" (streams) and "wäschet" (wash) reinforce the water imagery. In the sublime dignity of the melody there is also a joy-motif.

"Ergiesse dich reichlich, du göttliche Quelle, / Ach, walle mit blutigen Strömen auf mich! / Es fühlet mein Herze die tröstliche Stunde, / Nun sinken die drückenden Lasten zu Grunde, / Es wäschet die sündlichen Flecken von sich." (Pour out richly, Thou divine source, / Ah, pour on me with streams of Blood! / My heart feels the comforting hour, / Now the oppressive burdens sink down. / The sinful spots wash themselves off.)

4. *Recitative (with Chorale)—alto.* A solo oboe plays the chorale melody independently throughout her declamation. She says that she is comforted by the knowledge that her sins are buried in her Savior's grave. When the faithful seek refuge with Him, their anguish and pain will disappear. They will overcome the devil, death and sin through the protection of Christ's priceless Blood.

5. *Aria—bass.* This number is the high point of the cantata. The trumpet and unison strings imitate the sound of battle with the host of Satan, mentioned in the previous number. The first part of his aria, with ritornello, shows his defiance of Satan's demons; the second part subsides into a quiet joy-motif to represent the victory of Christ's Blood. The da capo repeats the theme of conflict with sin.

"Verstumme, Höllenheer, / Du machst mich nicht verzagt! / Ich darf dies Blut dir zeigen, / So musst du plötzlich schweigen, / Es ist in Gott gewagt!" (Be silent, army of hell, / You do not make me despair! / I may show you this Blood; / Then you must suddenly be silent. / It is dared in God!)

6. *Recitative—soprano.* She states, in secco, that she is the smallest part of the world, but hopes that even the smallest drop of Christ's blood will wash her clean of sin, since it can cleanse the whole world.

7. *Chorale.* This is stanza 11 of Heermann's chorale, performed tutti in plain style. Bach used this same verse previously in 1715 to conclude BWV 163:

"Führ auch mein Herz und Sinn / Durch deinen Geist dahin, / Dass ich mög' alles meiden, / Was mich und dich kann scheiden, / Und ich an deinem Leibe / Ein Gliedmass ewig bleibe." (Lead also my heart and mind / Along through Thy Spirit, / So that I may avoid everything, / Which can part Thee and me, / And I may, on Thy Body, / Ever remain a member.)

• **Gott, der Herr, ist Sonn und Schild (God, the Lord Is Sun and Shield)** (1735; BWV 79).

For the Reformation Festival, on 30 October 1735, according to Spitta, Bach composed this rousing cantata on a text by an unknown librettist. He later imitated the music of three numbers for three movements in his *Short Masses.* This is not a chorale cantata, since the first movement is not a chorale stanza, but Bach uses two different chorales in the middle and at the end.

The political context is apparent in the libretto, which reflects the victory of the national religion at this time during the War of the Polish Succession. Bach's martial music in the opening chorus and in the first chorale number testifies to this.

The Scriptures for the day, Revelation 14 (6–8) and Thessalonians 2 (3–8), have no direct bearing on the libretto.

The soli are SATB, with the usual four-part chorus. The orchestra has two horns, timpani, two transverse flutes, two oboes, two violins, a viola and continuo.

1. *Chorus.* Psalm 84 (11) is quoted literally for this first number: "Gott, der Herr, ist Sonn und Schild. Der Herr gibt Gnade und Ehre; er wird kein Gutes mangeln lassen den Frommen." (God, the Lord is sun and shield. The Lord gives mercy and honor; He will let no good thing be lacking to the pious.) The instruments paint a scene of glittering military triumph in the first theme, wherein the rhythm suggests the tramping of an armed host. The chorus, with entries of its four parts in succession, sings the second theme in fugue, independent of the orchestra. In the last clause of this vast chorus, the voices combine and unite with the instruments.

Schweitzer describes the movement thus: "The chorus is one of the most impressive ever written by Bach. A positively blinding radiance gleams from it; it is as if we were looking at a victorious battle in the rays of morning." (*J.S. Bach,* Vol. II, p. 331).

2. *Aria—alto.* The obbligato transverse flute makes a tranquil contrast with the boisterous opening chorus. Her first line is a paraphrase of the first sentence of the Psalm, which then develops into a peaceful song of praise to God for His protection against our enemies: "Gott ist unsre Sonn und Schild! / Drum rühmet dessen Güte / Unser dankbares Gemüte, / Die er für sein Häuflein hegt. / Denn er will uns ferner schützen, / Ob die Feinde Pfeile schnitzen / Und ein Lästerhund gleich billt." (God is our sun and shield! / Whose goodness, therefore, / Our thankful mind praises, / Which He cherishes for His little flock. / For He will protect us further, / Whether our enemies carve arrows / And a blasphemous dog even barks.)

3. *Chorale.* The same tutti choir and orchestra as in the opening chorus perform plainly the first stanza of Martin Rinckart's chorale, upon which Bach had set his earlier chorale cantata, "Nun

danket alle Gott" (Now All Thank God), BWV 192. (See p. 133 for a translation of this verse.)

The step-motif of the bass continuo suggests again the victorious march of the Lord's army, greeted by the shouts of thanksgiving of the multitude, which the choir represents. Fanfares of the horns with timpani repeat the martial atmosphere of the opening chorus.

4. *Recitative—bass.* He narrates, in secco, his thanks to God for having delivered them from a foreign yoke. The political overtones of Augustus III's claim to the throne of Catholic Poland appear in his text. He hopes that God will be the Mediator and show His way to the blind populace of Poland and of Saxony.

5. *Duet—soprano, bass.* Unison strings in this accompaniment give their duet a cheerful sprightliness, even though the soloists produce a tumult-motif as they sing in canon. They pray that God will never abandon them in any further conflicts they may have. Bach's melody makes their prayer one of deep emotional appeal: "Gott, ach Gott, verlass die Deinen / Nimmermehr! / Lass dein Wort uns helle scheinen; / Obgleich sehr / Wider uns die Feinde toben, / So soll unser Mund dich loben." (God, ah God, leave Thy people / Nevermore! / Let Thy Word shine brightly on us, / Although sorely / The enemies rage against us. / Then our mouth shall praise Thee.)

6. *Chorale.* This is the eighth stanza of Ludwig Helmboldt's hymn, "Nun lasst uns Gott dem Herren" (Now Let Us to God the Lord), set to an anonymous melody which Bach harmonized for all voices and instruments here. Although short, it is an effective conclusion, being in itself a prayer: "Erhalt uns in der Wahrheit, / Gib ewigliche Freiheit, / Zu preisen deinen Namen / Durch Jesum Christum, Amen!" (Keep us in the truth, / Give everlasting freedom, / To praise Thy Name / Through Jesus Christ, Amen!)

• **Jesu, nun sei gepreiset (Jesus, Now Be Praised)** (1736; BWV 41).

This chorale cantata for New Year's Day takes stanzas one and three of the hymn by Johannes Herman, beginning with the above title. The librettist for the intervening numbers is unknown. Stanza two of the hymn is freely paraphrased for these arias and recitatives, which reflect the feeling of the Saxon nation's thanksgiving over the ending of the War of the Polish Succession, just concluded.

Neither the Gospel, Luke 2 (21), nor the Epistle, Galatians 3 (23–29), has any bearing on the libretto, which is, in all its numbers, simply a song of grateful praise and a prayer for God's continued blessing in the New Year.

The soli are SATB, with a four-part chorus. The orchestra has three trumpets, timpani, three oboes, two violins, a violoncello piccolo, a viola, organ and continuo.

1. *Chorus.* Bach set this first verse of the chorale in two parts: the first, following the instrumental introduction, contains a tremendous joy-motif; the second turns to a pensive adagio ending in a lively fugue. This is the longest chorale fantasia that Bach has written in any of his cantatas thus far. It is a stupendous movement.

"Jesu, nun sei gepreiset / Zu diesem neuen Jahr / Für dein Güt, uns beweiset / In aller Not und Gefahr, / Dass wir haben erlebet / Die neu fröhliche Zeit, / Die voller Gnade schwebet / Und ewiger Seligkeit; / Dass wir in guter Stille / Das alte Jahr haben erfüllet. / Wir wollen uns dir ergeben / Jetzund und immerdar, / Behüte Leib, Seel' und Leben / Hinfort durch's ganze Jahr." (Jesus, now be praised / On this New Year / For Thy goodness, shown to us / In all trouble and danger, / That we have survived to / The new happy time, / Which hovers full of grace / And eternal blessing; / That we in good peace / Have fulfilled the old year. / We wish to devote ourselves to Thee / Now and forever. / Protect body, soul and life / Henceforth through the whole year.)

2. *Aria—soprano.* Both arias in this cantata are exceptionally beautiful. This one has a flowing pastoral melody, played by the three oboes, to introduce the vocalist and sustain her throughout the aria. The tempo changes after the second line, developing into a joy-motif and ending with "Halleluja" in the last line.

The first part is a prayer for a happy year and the second, her present rejoicing that this may be fulfilled: "Lass uns, o höchster Gott, das Jahr vollbringen, / Damit das Ende so, wie dessen Anfang sei. / Es stehe deine Hand uns bei, / Dass künftig bei des Jahres Schluss / Wir bei des Segens Überfluss / Wie jetzt ein Halleluja singen." (Let us, O highest God, finish the year, / So that the end may be like the start. / May Thy hand stand by us, / So that in future at the year's end, / We, at the overflow of blessing, / As now, may sing a Halleluja.)

3. *Recitative—alto.* With organ and continuo to accompany her, she states that the days of our lives lie in God's hand. His eye sees both the welfare and the suffering in our city and in our country; she wishes both, however, according to His wise mercy.

4. *Aria—tenor.* The solo violoncello piccolo in the accompaniment lends a mystical tone to the prayer of his text. An adagio melody reinforces his plea that God will give peace, if people accept His Word: "Woferne du den edlen Frieden / Für unsern Leib und Stand beschieden, / So lass der Seele doch dein seligmachend Wort! / Wenn uns dies Heil begegnet, / So sind wir hier gesegnet / Und Auserwählte dort." (As far as Thou hast decided noble peace / For our body and position, / So leave to our soul Thy blessed Word! / When this salvation meets us, / Then we are blessed here, / And the Elected ones there.)

5. *Recitative and Chorus—bass and four-part choral intonation.* Accompanied by the organ and continuo, the bass warns us that the enemy (Satan) tries to disturb our rest by day and night. He asks God to hear our communal prayer, a line of the Lutheran litany, "Den Satan unter unsre Füsse treten" (To tread Satan under our feet), which the four-part chorus intones, before he resumes his narrative. This dramatic interruption adds unexpected force to this number. He concludes that we will then remain God's chosen, entering heaven after our suffering and sorrows here on earth. The political connotation of the text in the worldly enemies of Saxony is apparent.

6. *Chorale.* This is the sixth and last verse of J. Herman's hymn, brilliantly supported by the fanfare motif of the obbligato trumpets and timpani, which was heard in the opening chorus. All voices and instruments combine in this rousing finale: "Dein ist allein die Ehre, / Dein ist allein der Ruhm. / Geduld im Kreuz uns lehre, / Regier all unser Tun, / Bis wir fröhlich abscheiden / Ins ewig' Himmelreich, / Zum wahren Fried und Freuden, / Den Heil'gen Gottes gleich. / Indes mach's mit uns allen / Nach deinem Wohlgefallen! / Solchs singet heut' ohn' Scherzen / Die christgläubige Schar / Und wünscht mit Mund und Herzen / Ein selig's neues Jahr." (Thine is alone the honor. / Thine is alone the glory. / Teach us patience in suffering, / Govern all our doings, / Until we happily depart / Into the eternal Kingdom of Heaven, / To true peace and joy, / Like the Saints of God. / Meanwhile do with us all / According to Thy pleasure! / So sings seriously today / The faithful Christian flock / And wishes with mouth and heart / A blessed New Year.)

• **Meine Seufzer, meine Tränen (My Sighs, My Tears)** (1736; BWV 13).

Bach's interpretation of his libretti, in this case a very gloomy text, is evident in the music he set in this cantata for the second Sunday after Epiphany. The author of this poem was the Darmstadt court librarian, Georg Christian Lehms. It is not a chorale cantata, but two different chorales are used, one in the third movement and one at the end.

The soprano recitative has the only one slight reference to the Gospel, John 2

(1–11), Christ's first miracle of turning water into wine at the wedding in Cana. Whereas we would expect to hear a happy theme for this event, there is only despondent sadness for the whole cantata; yet Bach would like this text, because he had a predilection for such topics and because he could find scope for free composition therein. The grief of the sinner and his desire for help from Jesus are a subject in which Bach reveled.

The soli are SATB, with the usual four-part chorus. The orchestra has two recorders, an oboe da caccia, two violins, a viola and continuo.

1. *Aria—tenor.* The lamentation of the vocalist is accompanied by a grief-motif played by a quartet of the two recorders, the oboe da caccia and the continuo. Sighs and tears are depicted in this instrumental coloring, which paints a picture of deep personal melancholy: "Meine Seufzer, meine Tränen / Können nicht zu zählen sein. / Wenn sich täglich Wehmut findet / Und der Jammer nicht verschwindet, / Ach! so muss uns diese Pein / Schon den Weg zum Tode bahnen." (My sighs, my tears / Cannot be counted. / When melancholy occurs daily / And lamentation does not disappear, / Ah! then must this pain for us / Already be paving the way to death.)

2. *Recitative—alto.* With secco accompaniment, she states that God has not heeded her weeping nor offered any comfort to her. The hour for His help is still far away and, in the meantime, she pleads in vain.

3. *Chorale—alto.* The full orchestra plays the delightful melody of Louis Bougeois's "Ainsi qu' on oit le cerf" (As One Hears the Stag) as she sings stanza two of Johann Heermann's hymn "Zion klagt mit Angst und Schmerzen" (Zion Laments with Fear and Pain). This and the final chorale verse are the only bright numbers of confidence in the cantata, even though this chorale fantasia also contains a rhythm of noble grief. Its dancing melody, which entrances the listener, makes it the most impressive number in the cantata.

"Der Gott, der mir hat versprochen / Seinen Beistand jederzeit, / Der lässt sich vergebens suchen / Jetzt in meiner Traurigkeit. / Ach! Will er denn für und für / Grausam zürnen über mir, / Kann und will er sich der Armen / Jetzt nicht wie vorhin erbarmen?" (God, Who has promised me / His assistance at all times, / He lets Himself be sought in vain / Now in my mourning. / Ah! Will He then for ever and ever / Cruelly rage over me; / Can and will He on the poor / Not have pity now as heretofore?)

4. *Recitative—soprano.* In secco, she returns to the theme of despair, with the only Gospel reference in her last two lines, stating that God can change her melancholy into the wine of joy.

5. *Aria—bass.* A solo violin and unison recorders accompany him in the first two lines with a sobbing rhythm and a tear-motif, which contrast with the hopeful confidence of the rest of his text. However, the da capo brings back the sadness of the first part before the final chorale, so that the overall impression of suffering is evident: "Achzen und erbärmlich Weinen / Hilft der Sorgen Krankheit nicht; / Aber wer gen Himmel siehet / Und sich da um Trost bemühet, / Dem kann leicht ein Freudenlicht / In der Trauerbrust erscheinen." (Groaning and piteous weeping / Does not help the illness of cares; / But whoever looks toward heaven / And concerns himself there for comfort, / For him a light of joy can easily / Appear in his mourning breast.)

6. *Chorale.* All voices and instruments give a straightforward performance of the fifteenth stanza of Paul Flemming's hymn "In allen meinen Taten" (In All My Deeds). Confidence in God returns, but not enough to convince the listener after the gloomy mood of the previous aria.

Bach used this same chorale stanza at the end of BWV 44 and BWV 97. For a translation of the text, see p. 138.

• **Kommt, eilet und laufet [Osteroratorium] (Come, Hurry and Run [Easter Oratorio])** (1736; BWV 249).

Bach's oratorios for Christmas, Easter and Ascension resemble his own cantatas more than the oratorios of Handel, because their shorter form stresses emotional reactions rather than dramatic narrative. This does not mean, however, that Bach lacks a sense of drama in his oratorios; for him the action is internal, lying in the feelings expressed by the soloists and the choruses and not in the development of a story. Bach's *Christmas Oratorio* consists of six separate cantatas, while the Easter and the Ascension works are single cantatas, even though Bach called them oratorios and named the Biblical characters beside each number in this one.

The music of two previously composed secular cantatas was imitated by Bach in the oratorio: BWV 217 (249a), 1725, "Entfliehet, verschwindet, entweichet, ihr Sorgen" (Flee, Disappear, Yield, Ye Cares), to celebrate the birthday of Duke Christian von Sachsen-Weissenfels, and BWV 249b, 1726, "Verjaget, zerstreuet, zerrüttet, ihr Sterne" (Dispel, Scatter, Disarrange, Ye Stars), to honor the birthday of the commandant of Leipzig, Count Joachim Friedrich Flemming.

The librettist for the earlier cantata texts was Picander, whom Terry suggests as the writer of the oratorio text also, because of its similar free madrigal style. He follows the Gospel, Mark 16 (1–8), the Resurrection, very closely in his poetic paraphrasing.

This *Easter Oratorio* is one of Bach's masterpieces and must have been one of his favorite compositions, since he repeated its performance even into the 1740s.

The soli are SATB, with a four-part chorus. The festive orchestra includes three trumpets, timpani, two oboes, an oboe d'amore, a bassoon, two recorders, a transverse flute, violins and basso continuo. It is the largest orchestra since that used for the *Christmas Oratorio* and the *Mass in B minor.*

1. *Sinfonia.* This instrumental overture is divided into two parts: the first an allegro tutti featuring the trumpets and the drums, the second an adagio with woodwinds and strings. These movements depict the joy at the Resurrection and its melancholy aftermath, respectively. If we consider the following allegro vocal number as a part of these movements, we see that Bach has composed a complete instrumental concerto—fast, slow, fast.

Probably this sinfonia originated in a lost concerto from Bach's Cöthen period. It reminds the listener of the sinfonia preceding his Easter cantata, BWV 31, but it is much longer.

2. *Duet and Chorus—tenor, bass.* Bach added a chorus to the opening duet in the two earlier secular versions, probably because he felt that a chorus was necessary to open a religious drama. An exuberant joy-motif runs throughout this number, in which the tempo depicts the hastening of John, Peter, Mary Magdalene and Mary the mother of Jesus to the sepulcher wherein Jesus was buried. The animated step-motif of the opening rhythm leads us to imagine the little group of the two disciples and the two women running there.

The chorus sings the first two lines (repeated in the da capo), accompanied by trumpets, drums, oboes and strings. Then the duet for tenor and bass follows with only the oboes and strings. Bach has here painted a most brilliant picture in the two contrasting sections.

JOHANNES (JOHN): "Kommt, eilet und laufet, ihr flüchtigen Füsse" (Come, hurry and run, you fleeting feet)

PETRUS (PETER): "Erreichet die Höhle, die Jesum bedeckt! / Lachen und Scherzen / Begleitet die Herzen, / Denn unser Heil ist auferweckt." (Reach the tomb, which encloses Jesus! / May laughter and joy / Accompany our hearts, / For our Salvation has awakened.)

3. *Recitative—alto, soprano, tenor, bass.* This is a most unusual recitative. Each of the Biblical characters comments in turn, the number ending with unison

singing by both men, followed by both women. Even with only the continuo in support, it is very melodious.

For this and the following numbers, it will be necessary to quote all texts to relate them with the actors or actor involved.

MARIA MAGDALENA (MARY MAGDALENE): "O kalter Männer Sinn! / Wo ist die Liebe hin, / Die ihr dem Heiland schuldig seid?" (O cold mind of men! / Where has the love gone, / Which you owe to the Savior?)

MARIA JACOBI (MARY THE MOTHER OF JESUS): "Ein schwaches Weib muss euch beschämen!" (A weak woman must shame you!)

PETRUS (PETER): "Ach, ein betrübtes Grämen" (Ah, a sad grieving)

JOHANNES (JOHN): "Und banges Herzeleid" (And anxious sorrow)

BEIDE MÄNNER (BOTH MEN): "Hat mit gesalznen Tränen / Und wehmutsvollem Sehnen / Ihm eine Salbung zugedacht," (Has with salty tears / And melancholy longing / Intended for Him an anointment,)

BEIDE FRAUEN (BOTH WOMEN): "Die ihr, wie wir, umsonst gemacht." (Which you, as we, have done in vain.)

4. *Aria—soprano.* The reference to the embalming of Jesus in the previous recitative no doubt caused the librettist to include this thought in the text of this aria. Here, however, it seems that she is referring more to her own soul than to Jesus.

The airy melody played by the transverse flute adds to the ethereal tone of the vocal, thus painting a beautiful picture of the bliss of heaven.

MARIA JACOBI (MARY THE MOTHER OF JESUS): "Seele, deine Spezereien / Sollen nicht mehr Myrrhen sein. / Denn allein / Mit dem Lorbeerkranze prangen, / Stillt dein ängstliches Verlangen." (Soul, thy spices / Shall no more be myrrh. / For only / With the laurel wreath sparkling, / Is thy anxious longing stilled.)

5. *Recitative—tenor, bass, alto.* As in the previous recitative, the actors return to converse with each other, thus presenting another short drama based on the Gospel story.

PETRUS (PETER): "Hier ist die Gruft," (Here is the vault,)

JOHANNES (JOHN): "Und hier der Stein, / Der solche zugedeckt. / Wo aber wird mein Heiland sein?" (And here the stone, / That enclosed such a place. / But where will my Savior be?)

MARIA MAGDALENA (MARY MAGDALENE): "Er ist vom Tode auferweckt! / Wir trafen einen Engel an, / Der uns solches kundgetan." (He is awakened from death! / We met an angel, / Who has informed us of it.)

PETRUS (PETER): "Hier seh' ich mit Vergnügen / Das Schweisstuch abgewickelt liegen." (Here I see with pleasure / His sweat-cloth lying unwound.)

Note that the word "Schweisstuch" also leads into the following aria—another descriptive detail of the scene of Christ's burial.

6. *Aria—tenor.* As in the pastoral aria "Schafe können sicher weiden" (Sheep May Safely Graze) of his earlier secular cantata BWV 208, composed for Duke Christian von Sachsen-Weissenfels, Bach paints a picture of rustic peace with recorders and strings. There is a lulling dream-like quality in the tune of the first part, which presents us with a vista of the serene fields of heaven. The second half changes to a more confident tone, expressed with a joy-motif. This is an exceptional aria, despite adverse criticism of the word "Schweisstuch," repeated so often as the key-word of the aria.

PETRUS (PETER): Sanfte soll mein Todeskummer / Nur ein Schlummer, / Jesu, durch dein Schweisstuch sein. / Ja, das wird mich dort erfrischen / Und die Zähren meiner Pein / Von den Wangen tröstlich wischen." (Soft shall be my troubles in death, / Only a slumber, / Jesus, through Thy sweat-cloth. / Yes, that will refresh me there / And the tears of my pain / It will wipe comfortingly from my cheeks.)

7. *Recitative and Arioso—soprano, alto.* Both women sing, first in unison, then in canon, the four lines of this

number. It adds little to the dramatic action, except to show their reaction at finding the tomb empty.

BEIDE FRAUEN (BOTH WOMEN): "Indessen seufzen wir / Mit brennender Begier: / Ach, könnt' es doch nur bald geschehen, / Den Heiland selbst zu sehen!" (Meanwhile we sigh / With burning desire: / Ah, could it only soon happen / To see the Savior Himself!)

8. *Aria—alto.* The oboe d'amore and strings accompany her as she interprets the sad words of yearning of her text. Bach has, however, set a lively joy-motif first, which only becomes a grief-motif in the second half. The da capo then restores the bouncy joviality of the beginning, which prepares for the joy in the last two numbers. This aria resembles a personal monologue in a play.

MARIA MAGDALENA (MARY MAGDALENE): "Saget, saget mir geschwinde, / Saget, wo ich Jesum finde, / Welchen meine Seele liebt! / Komm doch, komm, umfasse mich; / Denn mein Herz ist ohne dich / Ganz verwaiset und betrübt." (Tell then, tell me quickly, / Say where I may find Jesus, / Whom my soul loves! / Come then, come, embrace me; / For my heart is, without Thee, / Completely desolate and sad.)

9. *Recitative—bass.* It seems that Bach favored John as the male protagonist in this drama, because he assigns this last commentary to him. Yet Bach had given Peter the only solo male aria in this work, probably because he wanted a high voice there.

JOHANNES (JOHN): "Wir sind erfreut, / Dass unser Jesus wieder lebt, / Und unser Herz, / So erst in Traurigkeit zerflossen und geschwebt, / Vergisst den Schmerz / Und sinnt auf Freudenlieder; / Denn unser Heiland lebet wieder." (We are glad, / That our Jesus lives again, / And our heart, / Just now melted and wavering in sadness, / Forgets its pain / And thinks about songs of joy; / For our Savior lives again.)

10. *Chorus.* This tutti final chorus resembles the first two movements of a French overture—slow, fast, slow. The four-part chorus plays this role in the concluding dramatic scene—probably to represent the reaction of modern witnesses to this divine mystery.

The fast section in the last two lines is very brief and ends abruptly; probably it was Bach's intention to emphasize Christ's victory over death.

"Preis und Dank / Bleibe, Herr, dein Lobgesang. / Höll' und Teufel sind bezwungen, / Ihre Pforte sind zerstört. / Jauchzet, ihr erlösten Zungen, / Dass man es im Himmel hört. / Eröffnet, ihr Himmel, die prächtigen Bogen, / Der Löwe von Juda kommt siegend gezogen!" (Praise and thanks / Remain, Lord, Thy song of praise. / Hell and the devil are overcome; / Their gates are destroyed. / Rejoice, ye redeemed tongues, / So that it is heard in heaven. / Open, ye heavens, thy splendid arches; / The Lion of Judah comes triumphantly!)

• **Bleib' bei uns, denn es will Abend werden (Abide with Us, For It Will Become Evening)** (1736; BWV 6).

The Gospel for Easter Monday, Luke 24 (13–35), Christ appears to two of His disciples as they walk towards the village of Emmaus, inspired the unknown librettist of this cantata. His poem adheres closely to the Gospel; the text for the opening chorus is a quotation from the twenty-ninth verse.

Bach's tone-painting derived from this libretto is remarkable, especially the first two numbers, which suggest twilight and the gentle approach of night with astonishing realism. Throughout the cantata, the dramatic context reflects the thoughts of the disciples or of modern believers. It is a charming and very beautiful work.

The soli are SATB, with a four-part chorus. The orchestra has two oboes, an oboe da caccia, a violoncello piccolo, two violins, a viola and continuo.

1. *Chorus.* Woodwinds and strings paint a scene of the haunting beauty of twilight, as the chorus of disciples pleads with Jesus to stay with them. The gloomy tone of their voices gives the impression that night is weighing heavily upon

them. They repeat their plea, "Bleib bei uns," seven times first, and then seven times more in a double fugue with a grief-motif after the ritornello: "Bleib bei uns, denn es will Abend werden, und der Tag hat sich geneiget." (Abide with us, for it will become evening, and the day has bent to a close.)

Bach has here produced a masterpiece of art, interpreting his text with a musical painting in dark hues.

2. *Aria—alto.* Bach borrowed the music for this number from the first aria in his 1734 secular cantata "Thomana sass annoch betrübt" (Thomana Sat Still Saddened), performed by the students of the Thomasschule to celebrate the appointment of the new rector, Johann August Ernesti. The text for this cantata remains, but its music has been lost.

The beautiful imagery of the sad night scene is evoked by the obbligato oboe da caccia accompaniment, thus continuing the impression of the opening chorus: "Hochgelobter Gottessohn, / Lass es dir nicht sein entgegen, / Dass wir itzt vor deinem Thron / Eine Bitte niederlegen: / Bleib, ach bleibe unser Licht, / Weil die Finsternis einbricht!" (Highly praised Son of God, / Let it not be contrary to Thee, / That we now before Thy throne / Lay down a request: / Stay, ah stay, our Light, / Because the darkness is beginning!)

3. *Chorale—soprano.* The light tone of the soprano with her violoncello accompaniment alleviates the gloom. The first and second stanzas of Nikolaus Selnecker's hymn "Ach bleib bei uns, Herr Jesu Christ" (Ah, Stay with Us, Lord Jesu Christ) are quoted. These verses implore the Lord to remain with us, just as the opening Biblical quotation did.

4. *Recitative—bass.* Despair returns in this secco number. He states that in many places darkness has prevailed, because great and small people have not done their Christian duty. His last line paraphrases a part of Revelation 2 (5): "Drum hast du auch den Leuchter umgestossen." (Therefore hast Thou pushed over their candlestick also.)

5. *Aria—tenor.* The brightness of Christ's word, mentioned in the text, is translated by the strings which accompany his more optimistic aria. His prayer, however, still retains dark overtones in the third line at the thought of the ways of sin; this is suggested by a stumbling and sinking rhythm. Then the last part restores the theme of confidence. It is a very moving number: "Jesu, lass uns auf dich sehen, / Dass wir nicht / Auf den Sündenwegen gehen. / Lass das Licht / Deines Worts uns heller scheinen / Und dich jederzeit treu meinen." (Jesus, let us look to Thee, / So that we do not go / On the way of sins. / Let the light / Of Thy Word shine more brightly on us / And truly signify Thee always.)

6. *Chorale.* This tutti final chorale is the second stanza of Luther's hymn "Erhalt' uns, Herr, bei deinem Wort" (Keep Us, Lord, in Thy Word). The chorus prays that Christ will show His power and protect His "poor Christendom," so that all Christians will eternally praise Him.

• **Gottlob! nun geht das Jahr zu Ende (Thank God! Now the Year Goes to Its End)** (1736 or 1725–27; BWV 28).

Terry and Neumann give the date of this cantata as 1736 but Spitta and Dürr choose the earlier times. All numbers praise God and look forward to the coming year. Yet in its prayer for peace in the final chorale, this cantata may have been performed in 1736 after the recent end of the War of the Polish Succession.

It seems strange that Bach should turn back to this libretto by Erdmann Neumeister, published in 1716, and even stranger that the poem has nothing to do with either the Gospel or the Epistle for this Sunday after Christmas. Even the format is unusual, for Bach's setting begins with an aria, which is followed by a chorus, instead of the reverse order.

The soli are SATB, with a four-part chorus. The orchestra has a cornetto (horn), taille (a tenor oboe), three trombones, two oboes, two violins, a viola and continuo.

1. *Aria—soprano.* Oboes and strings accompany her song of praise to God, because the old year has ended and she hopes for God's favor in this new one. The melody flows along like a happy stream, supporting her song of rejoicing with a swinging joy-motif, which is reminiscent of ballet rhythm. It is a beautiful introduction: "Gottlob! nun geht das Jahr zu Ende, / Das neue rücket schon heran. / Gedenke, meine Seele, dran, / Wieviel dir deines Gottes Hände / Im alten Jahre Guts getan! / Stimm' ihm ein frohes Danklied an; / So wird er ferner dein gedenken / Und mehr zum neuen Jahre schenken." (Thank God! now the year goes to its end, / The new one moves already here. / Think about it, my soul, / How much good thy God's hands / Have done for thee in the old year! / Strike up for Him a happy song of thanks, / So that He will think further on thee / And present more for the New Year.)

2. *Chorus.* This is a great motet-like chorale fantasia for all voices and instruments, which overpowers all the other numbers in its majesty. Bach probably composed it first and then set the rest of this work. It is a tremendous achievement of 174 bars, which Bach noted at the end. The text is the first stanza of Johann Graumann's hymn: "Nun lob', mein' Seel', den Herren, / Was in mir ist, den Namen sein! / Sein Wohltat tut er mehren, / Vergiss es nicht, o Herze mein! / Hat dir dein' Sünd' vergeben / Und heilt dein' Schwachheit gross, / Errett' dein armes Leben, / Nimmt dich in seinen Schoss. / Mit reichem Trost beschüttet, / Verjüngt, dem Adler gleich. / Der Kön'g schafft Recht, behütet, / Die leid'n in seinem Reich." (Now praise, my soul, the Lord, / What is in me, His Name! / He does increase His benefit, / Do not forget it, o my heart! / He has forgiven thee thy sin / And heals thy great weakness; / He saves thy poor life, / Takes thee into His bosom. / Endows with rich comfort, / Rejuvenates, like the eagle. / The King does right, cares for / Those who suffer in His kingdom.)

3. *Recitative (Arioso)—bass.* This secco number contrasts with the majestic might of the preceding chorus. The vocalist sings a very fine arioso on this quotation from Jeremiah 32 (41): "So spricht der Herr: Es soll mir eine Lust sein, dass ich ihnen Gutes tun soll, und ich will sie in diesem Lande pflanzen treulich, von ganzem Herzen und von ganzer Seele." (Thus speaks the Lord: It shall be a joy to Me, that I shall do good for them, and I will plant them faithfully in this land, with My whole heart and with My whole soul.)

4. *Recitative—tenor.* It is again unusual that Bach would set two successive recitatives, but this one is different, with its string accompaniment. The tenor's first four lines describe God as a spring from which only goodness flows, a light where only grace shines, a treasure wherein there is only blessing, a Lord who means to be true and sincere. Whoever loves Him, believing as a child, hearing His Word and turning from his evil ways, God will give to him Himself with all His gifts. Whoever has God, he must have everything.

5. *Duet—alto, tenor.* Although this duet is accompanied only by the continuo, the voices create an attractive joy-motif in their imitative singing: "Gott hat uns im heurigen Jahre gesegnet, / Dass Wohltun und Wohlsein einander begegnet. / Wir loben ihn herzlich und bitten daneben, / Er woll' auch ein glückliches neues Jahr geben. / Wir hoffen's von seiner beharrlichen Güte / Und preisen's im voraus mit dankbar'm Gemüte." (God has blessed us in the new year, / So that well-doing and well-being met each other. / We praise Him heartily and pray besides, / He will also give a happy new year. / We hope it from His constant goodness / And praise it in advance with a thankful mind.)

6. *Chorale.* All voices and instruments are used in this sixth and last stanza of Paul Eber's hymn "Helft mir Gottes Güte preisen" (Help Me Praise God's Goodness), which Bach had set in 1724 for the concluding chorale of BWV 16 (cf. p.

46). This is perhaps one reason why Spitta moved the date of this cantata back ten years.

The text of the stanza praises God and Christ and asks for peace in the New Year, which could apply to any time, but would be especially fitting at the beginning of 1736, when peace had returned to Poland and Saxony.

• **Wer Dank opfert, der preiset mich (Whoso Offers Thanks, He Praises Me)** (1737; BWV 17).

The librettist for this cantata on the fourteenth Sunday after Trinity is unknown, although Neumann suggests Bach or Mariane von Ziegler. The Gospel, Luke 17 (11–19), Jesus heals the ten lepers in Samaria, is partly quoted but thoroughly reflected in the libretto. Although it is not long, the cantata is in two parts, the sermon coming between them. The two arias are especially attractive in thought and musical setting.

The soli are SATB, with the usual four-part chorus. The instrumentation is light but effective: two oboes, two violins, a viola and continuo.

Part I

This part deals with praise and thanks to God on a general level.

1. *Chorus.* Bach imitated the music for this number for the *Cum sancto Spiritu* section of his *Short Mass in G major.* The text quotes Psalm 50 (23), alluding to the one Samaritan leper who thanked Jesus for healing him. There is a step-motif, probably suggested to Bach by the words "der Weg" (the way), in the vocal fugue begun after the first ritornello of oboes and strings. An intense feeling of joy lies in the melody. "Wer Dank opfert, der preiset mich, und das ist der Weg, dass ich ihm zeige das Heil Gottes." (Whoso offers thanks, he praises Me, and that is the way, that I show him the salvation of God.)

2. *Recitative—alto.* This declamation is interesting, even with continuo only. Her voice rises or falls, as does Bach's music, according to the meaning of the words in her text (e.g. "Luft" [air]—high, "Wasser" [water]—low).

She states that the whole world is a silent witness to God's majesty; air, water, the firmament and the earth—all nature praises God, as do all living creatures which draw breath. The tongues of the latter resemble wings, rising in praise of His glory.

3. *Aria—soprano.* The first two lines paraphrase Psalm 57 (10), sung with violin and continuo accompaniment. Bach's floating melody paints a scene of clouds moving across the sky, derived from these lines of the text. This imagery continues the description of nature in the previous recitative. The last line of her aria ties up with the thought of the way to God's salvation in the opening chorus; the words "den Weg des Heils" (the way of salvation) recur here. It is a charmingly picturesque aria: "Herr, deine Güte reicht, so weit der Himmel ist, / Und deine Wahrheit langt, so weit die Wolken gehen. / Wüsst' ich gleich sonsten nicht, wie herrlich gross du bist, / So könnt' ich es gar leicht aus deinen Werken sehen. / Wie sollt' man dich mit Dank dafür nicht stetig preisen? / Da du uns willst den Weg des Heils hingegen weisen." (Lord, Thy goodness reaches as far as heaven extends, / And Thy truth stretches as far as the clouds go. / Even if I did not know otherwise, how gloriously great Thou art, / Then I could quite easily see it from Thy works. / How should one not continually praise Thee with thanks for that? / Since Thou wishest to show us the way towards salvation.)

Part II

This part treats the specific incident of the Samaritan in dramatic form.

4. *Recitative—tenor.* He quotes Luke 17 (15, 16), which shows the Samaritan's gratitude to Jesus for healing him: "Einer aber unter ihnen, da er sahe, dass er gesund worden war, kehrete um und preisete Gott mit lauter Stimme und fiel auf sein Angesicht zu seinen Füssen und dankete ihm; und das war ein Samariter."

(One of them, however, as he saw that he had become healthy, turned back and praised God with a loud voice and fell on his face at His feet and thanked Him; and he was a Samaritan.)

5. *Aria—tenor.* The accompanying strings play a dancing, folk-tune melody to illustrate the Samaritan's joyful, dramatic monologue, in which he seems to be dancing with happiness after the miracle of his healing. Bach sketches this scene with fine imagery, just as he did in the previous soprano aria. There is no da capo to this number, which is surprising for such blissful enchantment: "Welch Ubermass der Güte / Schenkst du mir! / Doch was gibt mein Gemüte / Dir dafür? / Herr, ich weiss sonst nichts zu bringen, / Als dir Dank und Lob zu singen." (What abundance of goodness / Dost Thou present to me! / Yet what does my mind give / To Thee for it? / Lord, I know nothing else to bring, / Than to sing thanks and praise to Thee.)

6. *Recitative—bass.* In secco, the Samaritan lists all the benefits God has given him: body, life, intelligence, health, strength and mind—streams of grace, which lead him to love, peace, justice and joy in God's Spirit. He hopes that God has planned a complete healing of his body and soul in his coming heavenly life.

7. *Chorale.* This is the third stanza of Johann Graumann's hymn "Nun lob', mein' Seel', den Herren" (Now Praise, My Soul, the Lord), which paraphrases Psalm 103 (13–16). It is performed plainly and tutti; it should be quoted because its first part bears on the thought of this cantata, and because the remainder recalls a similarity with the *German Requiem* of Brahms: "Wie sich ein Vat'r erbarmet / Ub'r seine junge Kindlein klein, / So tut der Herr uns Armen, / So wir ihn kindlich fürchten rein. / Er kennt das arm' Gemächte, / Gott weiss, wir sind nur Staub, / Gleich wie das Gras vom Rechen, / Ein' Blum' und fallendes Laub, / Der Wind nur drüber wehet, / So ist es nimmer da: / Also der Mensch vergehet, / Sein End', das ist ihm nah." (As a father pities / His small children, / So does the Lord us poor ones, / Provided that we fear Him purely and childishly. / He knows the poor creature, / God knows, we are only dust, / Like the grass from the rake, / A flower and falling foliage; / The wind only blows over it, / Then it is never there: / So man passes. / His end, that is near to him.)

• **Gott ist unsre Zuversicht (God Is Our Confidence)** (1737; BWV 197).

For Christmas Day 1728, Bach had composed a cantata, "Ehre sei Gott in der Höhe" (Glory to God in the highest), BWV 197a, of which the music has been lost except for two of the arias in this present cantata which borrow from those original arias. Picander wrote that original libretto, which is still available.

This is a wedding cantata on a grand scale, celebrating the marriage of two unknown but very important people. Bach himself was probably the librettist of this long but brilliant work, which is divided into two parts: before the wedding service and after it ("Vor der Trauung" and "Nach der Trauung").

The soli are SAB (no tenor soloist), with a large four-part chorus.

The instruments employed are three trumpets, timpani, two oboes, an oboe d'amore, two transverse flutes, two bassoons, strings and continuo—all used in the first sumptuous chorus but not in the two chorales, as Bach did not specify the instruments to be used in them.

Vor der Trauung

1. *Chorus.* The fugal theme, played tutti by the orchestra, is an imposing prelude to this solemn ceremony and continues to accompany the choir in the first two lines. There is the suggestion of a step-motif in the repeated beats of the melody throughout the movement. The rest of the stanza is sung in canon by the sopranos and the altos.

This is the most impressive number in the cantata. The listener feels drawn into this magnificent hymn of praise, as though he too were present in the church on this occasion: "Gott ist unsre Zuversicht, / Wir vertrauen seinen Händen. / Wie er unsre Wege führt, / Wie er unser Herz regiert, / Da ist Segen allerenden." (God is our confidence, / We trust His hands. / As He guides our ways, / As He rules our heart, / There is blessing everywhere.)

2. *Recitative—bass.* Throughout this cantata, strings as well as the continuo accompany the recitatives. He states that God is the best provider, who wonderfully and joyfully governs our actions, even when they are not planned or reasoned. God has written with His hand the happiness of His children from their youth onward.

3. *Aria—alto.* Bach borrowed the melody for this aria from the identical tune in the alto aria of BWV 217 (249a), the secular cantata which he had composed in 1725. It is accompanied by oboes and strings and has three themes: the first is in the tempo of a lullaby, the second more animated, and the third reveals a tone of confidence which the words of the text indicated to Bach for his word-painting. This aria is a good example of the attention paid to the words in his text: "Schläfert allen Sorgenkummer / In den Schlummer / Kindlichen Vertrauens ein! / Gottes Augen, welche wachen / Und die unser Leitstern sein, / Werden alles selber machen." (Put to sleep all worrisome cares / In the slumber / Of child-like trust! / God's eyes, which watch / And are our guiding-star, / Will themselves do everything.)

4. *Recitative—bass.* Strings play throughout, as he narrates this text. He says that we should therefore follow God's urging, which is the right way to lead us through danger and finally into Canaan. God binds our hearts together through His proved love and His holy altar. The singer prays that the Lord Himself will be in these loving flames, uniting the bridal pair.

5. *Chorale.* This is stanza three of Luther's "Nun bitten wir den heiligen Geist" (Now We Ask the Holy Spirit), which concludes BWV 169 also: "Du süsse Lieb', schenk' uns deine Gunst, / Lass uns empfinden der Liebe Brunst, / Dass wir uns von Herzen einander lieben / Und in Fried auf einem Sinne bleiben. / Kyrie eleis!" (Thou sweet love, give us thy favor, / Let us feel the warmth of love, / So that we love one another from our hearts / And remain in peace with one mind. / Kyrie eleison!

Nach der Trauung

6. *Aria—bass.* Oboes, strings and the bassoon play a rocking tune that Bach rearranged from the alto aria in BWV 197a. In this original version, it was a cradle-song for the infant Jesus, yet Bach's adaptation fits beautifully the text addressed to the newly wedded couple: "O du angenehmes Paar! / Dir wird eitel Heil begegnen, / Gott wird dich aus Zion segnen / Und dich leiten immerdar. / O du angenehmes Paar!" (O thou pleasing couple! / Nothing but salvation will meet thee, / God will bless thee from Zion / And lead thee forever. / O thou pleasing couple!)

7. *Recitative—soprano.* At first with strings, but ending in a secco arioso, she declares that God has been true and paternal towards the couple from their childhood and will remain their best Friend until the end. They can believe with certainty that they will never lack for anything good, resulting from the sweat and toil of their hands. Her last arioso line states: "Wohl dir! dein Glück ist nicht zu zählen." (Well for thee! Thy good-luck is not to be counted.)

8. *Aria—soprano.* This melody for oboes and strings is again borrowed from BWV 197a, wherein it is used as in a bass aria. Its joy-motif seems to resemble the gay rhythm of a German country-dance or Ländler to illustrate the happiness that she had mentioned in her above recitative. The light tone of the soprano voice adds to the joyful impression made by music and text: "Vergnügen und Lust, / Gedeihen und Heil / Wird wachsen und stärken und laben. / Das Auge, die Brust / Wird ewig sein Teil / An süsser Zufriedenheit haben." (Delight and

pleasure, / Prosperity and salvation / Will grow and strengthen and revive. / The eye, the breast / Will always have its share / Of sweet contentment.)

9. *Recitative—bass.* Oboes and strings support him in this short number, which sounds like the message in a wedding card: "Und dieser frohe Lebenslauf / Wird bis in späte Jahre währen. / Denn Gottes Güte hat kein Ziel, / Die schenkt dir viel, / Ja mehr, als selbst das Herze kann begehren. / Verlasse dich gewiss darauf!" (And this happy course of life / Will last into late years. / For God's goodness has no limit; / It gives you much, / Yes more, than even the heart can desire. / Depend certainly on that!)

10. *Chorale.* This is a paraphrase of stanza seven of Georg Neumark's hymn "Wer nur den lieben Gott lässt walten" (Who Only Lets the Dear God Rule) which also concluded BWV 93, the cantata with that title, and BWV 88 (cf. pp. 88 and 126).

The first four lines of the original stanza are changed to: " So wandelt froh auf Gottes Wegen, / Und was ihr tut, das tut getreu! / Verdienet eures Gottes Segen, / Denn der ist alle Morgen neu;" (So walk happily on God's ways, / And what you do, that do faithfully! / Earn your God's blessing, / For that is new every morning;)

• **Freue dich, erlöste Schar (Rejoice, Redeemed Flock)** (1738; BWV 30).

For the Festival of St. John the Baptist, 24 June 1738, Bach borrowed from and reconstructed his secular homage cantata "Angenehmes Wiederau" (Pleasant Wiederau), BWV 30a, performed 28 September 1737. Picander was the librettist for the earlier work, by which he hoped to curry favor from Johann Christian von Hennicke, whom this "Dramma per Musica" honored. This latter had been a lackey who had risen to the nobility; the acquisition of his estate at Wiederau in Saxony was the occasion for the work. It is likely that Bach, with Picander's help, restructured the recitatives and added a chorale stanza for this sacred version.

The Gospel for Johannistag (St. John's Day), Luke 1 (57–80), the birth of John and the song of praise of his father Zacharias, is referred to throughout the libretto, but without any direct quotations. The vocalists' praise of God is identified with that of Zacharias or of his son, especially in the choruses and arias, thus making this cantata highly dramatic.

Although Bach inserted his ready-made music into the new libretto, instead of deriving his setting from the words of the text as he usually did, he was still able to create a masterpiece in this sacred adaptation. For him, all his music was religious, dedicated to the glory of God. Both Schweitzer (Vol. II, p. 289) and Whittaker (Vol. II, p. 89), however, deplore Bach's unheedful application of secular music to sacred arias in this particular cantata. Nevertheless, I feel that this long cantata in two parts is one of his finest vocal compositions.

The soli are SATB, with a four-part chorus. The orchestra is large and festive: three trumpets, timpani, two transverse flutes, two oboes, an oboe d'amore, two violins, a viola with organ and continuo.

Part I

1. *Chorus.* Without any introduction, the full choir and all instruments launch into a spectacular opening chorus, which will be repeated as the final number of the cantata. Brilliant playing of the three trumpets in unison, with winds and strings doubling the voices, lend dazzling color to this outstanding number. The chorus is divided into two sections, which are very dramatic, as though Zacharias himself were speaking: "Freue dich, erlöste Schar, / Freue dich in Sions Hütten. / Dein Gedeihen hat itzund / Einen rechten festen Grund, / Dich mit Wohl zu überschütten." (Rejoice, redeemed flock, / Rejoice in Zion's dwellings. / Thy thriving has now / A really firm basis / For pouring well-being on thee.)

Such a dramatic beginning will be extended into all following numbers.

2. *Recitative—bass.* All recitatives are

secco in this first part of the cantata and keep to the same pattern of recitative—aria for the same soloist, except the tenor's recitative. This is the first of two such double numbers for the bass, who appears to play the role of Zacharias, addressing the assembled Israelites in both. Here he tells the people that they may now have undisturbed rest, for which their forefathers had often longed and hoped. The burden of the law is removed. Therefore they should unite in a song of praise to God.

3. *Aria—bass.* Strings, organ and continuo accompany his own song of praise to God for his son, as indicated in the Biblical text.

Whittaker thinks that the florid triplet theme "is scarcely in keeping with the austere figure of John the Baptist" (Vol. II, p. 91), but in my opinion, the music's joy-motif represents Zacharias's happiness at his son's birth: "Gelobet sei Gott, gelobet sein Name, / Der treulich gehalten Versprechen und Eid! / Sein treuer Diener ist geboren, / Der längstens darzu auserkoren, / Dass er den Weg dem Herrn bereit'." (Praised be God, praised His Name, / Who faithfully has kept promise and oath! / His true servant has been born, / Who for very long has been chosen, / That he prepare the way of the Lord.)

4. *Recitative—alto.* She is identified as John, playing this part here and in her subsequent aria. John announces the King, to Whom the people must hasten, for His words will show them light and the way to the blessed meadows of heaven.

5. *Aria—alto.* Her text is an appeal to sinners to approach Jesus to obtain forgiveness. This can readily be associated with the preaching of John. Even though a gavotte tune is played by the obbligato transverse flute with strings and organ continuo, which indicate the secular origin of this aria, the syncopated step-motif does fit the new text. This blissful melody paints a picture of the peace offered by the Savior: "Kommt, ihr angefochtnen Sünder, / Eilt und lauft, ihr Adamskinder, / Euer Heiland ruft und schreit! / Kommet, ihr verirrten Schafe, / Stehet auf vom Sündenschlafe, / Denn itzt ist die Gnadenzeit!" (Come, you tempted sinners, / Hasten and run, you children of Adam, / Your Savior calls and cries! / Come, you lost sheep, / Rise up from the sleep of sin, / For now is the time of mercy!)

6. *Chorale.* With the exception of the trumpets and the drums, all voices and instruments perform in simple style stanza three of Johann Olearius's hymn for St. John's Day, "Tröstet, tröstet, meine Liebe" (Comfort, Comfort, My Love). This verse makes a fitting conclusion to Part I, inasmuch as it describes John's preaching in the wilderness to prepare the way for the Lord.

Part II

7. *Recitative—bass.* Zacharias now reappears for his second recitative and aria. Oboes, strings, organ and continuo are used in both numbers. He asks the Lord to remember the covenant made with their forefathers: that He would keep faith with them and rule them with mercy. In return, he will strive to live in holiness and in fear of God. His text refers again to the Gospel, Luke 1 (73–75).

8. *Aria—bass.* This is a poetic monologue which shows that Zacharias intends to please God and hate what displeases Him. The above accompaniment plays a graceful melody adapted from the secular version of the aria.

"Ich will nun hassen / Und alles lassen, / Was dir, mein Gott, zuwider ist. / Ich will dich nicht betrüben, / Hingegen herzlich lieben, / Weil du mir so genädig bist." (I will now hate / And leave everything, / That is repugnant to Thee, my God. / I will not grieve Thee, / But on the contrary heartily love Thee, / Because Thou art so merciful to me.)

9. *Recitative—soprano.* This begins another recitative-aria coupling for the same voice. Although she might play the role of Zacharias or of John, it seems more likely that here she is an Israelite who has been listening to either of them.

She asserts that her faith will remain steadfast from day to day. Despite man's weak nature, she will praise God for the covenant that He has made with her.

10. *Aria—soprano.* Strings accompany this charming aria, in which she emphasizes her longing to enter heaven and to remain thankful to the Lord. The meadows of Wiederau in the original text are transformed into the meadows of heaven in this. There is a Biblical reference to Psalm 120 (5), where she says that she will build an altar to God in the tents of Kedar. The tempo implies hurried movement.

"Eilt, ihr Stunden, kommt herbei, / Bringt mich bald in jene Auen! / Ich will mit der heil'gen Schar / Meinem Gott ein'n Dankaltar / In den Hütten Kedar bauen, / Bis ich ewig dankbar sei." (Hasten, ye hours, come along, / Bring me soon into those meadows! / I will with the holy flock / Build to my God an altar of thanks / In the dwellings of Kedar, / So that I may be ever thankful.)

11. *Recitative—tenor.* It is difficult to identify the tenor with any definite Biblical individual, but he might be another Israelite (to maintain the drama of the previous numbers). His text is a message of consolation, such as might be preached in a sermon: death will free him from the imperfections of his earthly life.

12. *Chorus.* As in the opening and closing choruses of BWV 30a, the full orchestra and choir returns to repeat the same melody, with a slightly different text for the final chorus. The choir could again represent Zacharias, speaking to the congregation: "Freue dich, geheil'gte Schar, / Freue dich in Sions Auen! / Deiner Freude Herrlichkeit, / Deiner Selbstzufriedenheit / Wird die Zeit kein Ende schauen." (Rejoice, holy flock, / Rejoice in Zion's meadows! / Of the splendor of thy joy, / Of thy self-contentment, / Time will see no end.)

• **Liebster Immanuel, Herzog der Frommen (Dearest Immanuel, Lord of the Righteous)** (c. 1740; BWV 123).

This chorale cantata for Epiphany is based on a hymn by Ahasverus Fritsch, the first and the sixth stanzas being quoted for its opening and final numbers, and the intervening stanzas being paraphrased for the arias and recitatives. The libretto has no connection with the Gospel or the Epistle for the Feast of the Epiphany, and the name of the librettist is unknown.

From this date (about 1740) until 1744, Bach's attention was concentrated on the chorale cantata, set or based on only one hymn. There are a few regular choral works in this, his last, great period of cantata production, but his preoccupation was definitely with the setting of the single chorale type.

The soli in this work are ATB, with a four-part chorus. The instruments are two transverse flutes, two oboes d'amore, two violins, a viola and continuo.

1. *Chorus.* This is a magnificent chorale fantasia for full chorus and orchestra on the first verse of the hymn. Its tune is a French dance, a courante, which Bach uses only once here in all his cantatas. The unison flutes are especially picturesque, evoking a blissful picture of the Savior in heavenly glory. The melody is full of devout longing; the instrumental introduction, followed by its ritornelli, adds an aura of mysticism to the voices of the choir. The text suggests a crowd, appealing to Jesus to come to them: "Liebster Immanuel, Herzog der Frommen, / Du, meiner Seele Heil, komm, komm nur bald! / Du hast mir, höchster Schatz, mein Herz genommen, / So ganz vor Liebe brennt und nach dir wallt, / Nichts kann auf Erden / Mir liebers werden, / Als wenn ich meinen Jesum stets behalt." (Dearest Immanuel, Lord of the righteous, / Thou, Savior of my soul, come, only come soon! / Thou, Highest Treasure, hast taken my heart from me, / Which is all burning with love and flows toward Thee. / Nothing on earth can / Be dearer to me, / Than when I constantly hold my Jesus.)

2. *Recitative—alto.* Her secco narration tells of how much joy she feels at being one of the elect. When she speaks

Jesus' Name, her heart is refreshed by His manna, just as dew revives dry land. Even in danger and pain, her heart is gladdened by His strength.

3. *Aria—tenor.* Three changes of tempo by the accompanying oboes d'amore and continuo mark the three different states of mind in the tenor's text. He appears to be a traveler through life who struggles along under his burden (lento), who confronts storms periodically (allegro), but who finally receives light and salvation from Jesus (adagio).

"Auch die harte Kreuzesreise / Und der Tränen bittre Speise / Schreckt mich nicht. / Wenn die Ungewitter toben, / Sendet Jesus mir von oben / Heil und Licht." (Even the hard journey of the Cross / and the bitter food of tears / Do not frighten me. / When the storms rage, / Jesus sends to me from above / Salvation and light.)

4. *Recitative—bass.* This secco number relates his confidence in Jesus. No hellish enemy can devour him, since now his crying conscience is silent. Why should the host of the enemy encircle him? Even death itself has no power over him. He is destined for victory because Jesus is his Helper.

5. *Aria—bass.* He begins on a pessimistic note that reflects his loneliness because the world despises him. His mood then changes to a joy-motif at the thought that Jesus is always near him. The da capo, however, brings him back to his misery. The continuo, only, accompanies his first sadness; a transverse flute illustrates his turn to joy: "Lass, o Welt, mich aus Verachtung / In betrübter Einsamkeit! / Jesus, der ins Fleisch gekommen / Und mein Opfer angenommen, / Bleibet bei mir allezeit." (O world, leave me in contempt, / In sad loneliness! / Jesus, Who has come in the flesh / And has accepted my offering, / Remains beside me always.)

6. *Chorale.* This is stanza six of the hymn, performed tutti and plainly in a very slow tempo. It is as impressive as the opening chorus; they are the best numbers in this cantata. The last three lines are repeated, piano, to interpret the peace implied in these significant words, descriptive of a burial scene. The courante rhythm of the opening chorus returns in this concluding number.

"Drum fahrt nur immer hin, ihr Eitelkeiten, / Du, Jesu, du bist mein, und ich bin dein. / Ich will mich von der Welt zu dir bereiten. / Du sollst in meinem Herz und Munde sein. / Mein ganzes Leben / Sei dir ergeben, / Bis man mich einsten legt ins Grab hinein." (Therefore always depart, you vanities. / Thou, Jesus, Thou art mine and I am Thine. / I will prepare myself from the world for Thee. / Thou shalt be in my heart and mouth, / My whole life / Shall be devoted to Thee, / Until at some time they lay me in the grave.)

• **Liebster Jesu, mein Verlangen [Dialogus] (Dearest Jesu, My Longing [Dialogue])** (1738–40; BWV 32).

This cantata, in dialogue format, was for the first Sunday after Epiphany. Bach had composed two other cantatas in dialogue before (BWV 60 and BWV 58), and had used dialogues in some recitatives and of course in all duets of his previous settings.

It is obvious that Bach had a keen sense of drama and was aware of this as he studied the libretto for his composition. These texts, moreover, were marked sometimes with the names of the actors (singers for Bach) for recitatives and duets. Here, as in BWV 60 and BWV 249 (the Easter Oratorio), the names are indicated opposite numbers or parts of numbers.

The Gospel for this Sunday, Luke 2 (41–52), the incident of the lost boy Jesus, found by his parents as He was questioning the doctors in the temple, enters only in the first recitative (verse 49) and does not inspire the whole text, as was the case with the 1724 cantata for this same Sunday, BWV 154. The librettist for this work is unknown.

The soli are SB, with a four-part chorus for the final chorale. The soprano represents the Soul and the bass, Jesus. The instrumentation is light: an oboe, two violins, a viola and continuo.

1. *Aria—soprano.* Accompanied by all instruments, she sings of her longing for Jesus in a duet with the oboe. This dramatic opening might represent her as Mary, seeking her lost Son, especially if one considers it in conjunction with the following bass recitative and aria in which He replies. However, the remaining numbers make it clear that it is the Soul and Jesus conversing throughout.

She begins with a tear-motif, indicative of her worried agitation over the absence of Jesus, but concludes with a joy-motif at the prospect of finding Him again: "Liebster Jesu, mein Verlangen, / Sage mir, wo find' ich dich? / Soll ich dich so bald verlieren / Und nicht ferner bei mir spüren? / Ach! mein Hort, erfreue mich, / Lass dich höchst vergnügt umfangen. (Dearest Jesu, my longing, / Tell me, where do I find Thee? / Shall I so soon lose Thee / And feel Thee no longer beside me? / Ah! my refuge, make me glad; / Let Thyself be embraced with utmost delight.)

2. *Recitative—bass.* In the role of Jesus, he answers with continuo only in a paraphrase of verse 49 of the Gospel: "Was ist's, dass du mich gesuchet? Weisst du nicht, dass ich sein muss in dem, das meines Vaters ist?" (Why is it that you have sought me? Do you not know, that I must be about that which concerns my Father?)

3. *Aria—bass.* The solo violin obbligato plays a beautiful melody which depicts Christ dwelling in heaven, as stated in the text. It seems that this aria points forward to the main duet which will follow (5): It is a very dramatic monologue in itself: "Hier, in meines Vaters Stätte, / Find't mich ein betrübter Geist. / Da kannst du mich sicher finden, / Und dein Herz mit mir verbinden, / Weil dies meine Wohnung heisst." (Here, in my Father's abode, / A sad spirit finds me. / There thou canst surely find me, / And bind thy heart to me, / Because this is called my dwelling.)

4. *Recitative (Dialogue)—soprano, bass.* For this number and the following duet, the sections sung by the Soul and by Jesus are indicated in the margin of the text. The string accompaniment and the dramatic vocal exchanges make this a superior recitative to the usual.

The Soul asks Jesus for consolation and help. He replies that she must curse earthly sham in order to enter His dwelling. She asserts that she will love only Him, after she has praised His dwelling in a quotation from Psalm 84 (1, 2). Jesus says that she can be happy, if her heart and spirit love Him. She concludes the dialogue, saying that His word takes her heart away from Babel's borders and that she will devoutly keep it in her soul.

5. *Duet—soprano, bass.* All instruments play a motif of supreme joy, while the voices in canon express their own unrestrained happiness. The tempo depicts a merry dance, as Christ and the Soul sing together in delight. Bach must have deeply felt the radiant bliss of heaven in this text when he bestowed such a joyful melody upon it.

BEIDE (BOTH): "Nun verschwinden alle Plagen, / Nun verschwindet Ach und Schmerz." (Now all troubles disappear, / Now groaning and pain have gone.)

SEELE (SOUL): "Nun will ich nicht von dir lassen," (Now I will not leave Thee,)

JESUS: "Und ich dich stets umfassen." (And I will always embrace thee.)

SEELE: "Nun vergnüget sich mein Herz" (Now my heart is delighted)

JESUS: "Und kann voller Freude sagen:" (And full of joy can say:)

BEIDE: "Nun verschwinden alle Plagen, / Nun verschwindet Ach und Schmerz!" (Now all troubles disappear, / Now groaning and pain have vanished!)

6. *Chorale.* This is stanza 12 of Paul Gerhardt's hymn "Weg, mein Herz, mit den Gedanken" (Away, My Heart, with the Thoughts), which is performed tutti. It is plainly sung, the text asking God to open the gates of heaven for "me," to love and to guide me, so that I may embrace Him and no more grieve Him.

• **Meinen Jesum lass' ich nicht (My Jesus I Do Not Leave)** (1735–44; BWV 124).

Christian Keymann's hymn with this title must have been one of Bach's favorites, for he had already set its sixth stanza as the final chorale in two previous cantatas, BWV 154 and BWV 157. Now he sets a complete chorale cantata for the first Sunday after Epiphany based on Keymann's entire hymn. His unknown librettist retained the first and sixth stanzas, while paraphrasing the intervening ones.

The text has no direct connection with the Gospel, Luke 2 (41–52); still the joy of Mary and Joseph at finding Jesus in the temple might be seen in the personal tone of the libretto. The main idea, however, is more general—that we will cling to Jesus in spite of our worldly troubles.

The soli are SATB, with a four-part chorus. The orchestra requires a horn, a concertante oboe d'amore, two violins, a viola and continuo with organ and strings.

1. *Chorus.* The concertante oboe d'amore is featured in the melody, which portrays the choir's confident joy at never leaving Christ. There is a fine touch of imagery in this first stanza: the simile of the sticking burr to illustrate adherence to Christ.

"Meinen Jesum lass' ich nicht, / Weil er sich für mich gegeben, / So erfordert meine Pflicht, / Klettenweis' an ihm zu kleben. / Er ist meines Lebens Licht, / Meinen Jesum lass' ich nicht." (My Jesus I do not leave, / Because He has given Himself for me; / So my duty requires, / Like a burr to cling to Him. / He is the light of my life; / I do not leave my Jesus.)

2. *Recitative—tenor.* He states that as long as a drop of blood moves in his heart and veins, only Jesus will be his life and his all. As Jesus has done such wonderful things for him, he will offer to Him his body and his life as a gift.

3. *Aria—tenor.* This is an exceptionally beautiful number, accompanied by the oboe d'amore and the strings. It begins with a slight terror-motif in the quavering strings but concludes in a tone of confidence with the motto of the hymn: "Ich lasse meinen Jesum nicht" (I do not leave my Jesus). Both melodies illustrate the text very well: "Und wenn der harte Todesschlag / Die Sinnen schwächt, die Glieder rühret, / Wenn der dem Fleisch verhasste Tag / Nur Furcht und Schrecken mit sich führet / Doch tröstet sich die Zuversicht: / Ich lasse meinen Jesum nicht." (And when the hard stroke of death / Weakens the senses, touches the limbs, / When the day hated by the flesh / Brings with itself only fear and terror, / Yet this confidence comforts: / I do not leave my Jesus.)

4. *Recitative—bass.* As in the preceding tenor aria, the bass begins in a tone of woe, but ends on a note of hope. His secco declamation speaks of the discomfort he feels in his soul because of the loss of Jesus, but turns to hope at the prospect of embracing the Savior after he has run his course on earth.

5. *Duet—soprano, alto.* The organ is prominent in the continuo accompaniment of this brilliant number. An unrestrained joy-motif throughout interprets the theme of escape from the world into the presence of Jesus: "Entziehe dich eilends, mein Herze, der Welt, / Du findest im Himmel dein wahres Vergnügen. / Wenn künftig dein Auge den Heiland erblickt, / So wird erst dein sehnendes Herze erquickt, / So wird es in Jesu zufriedengestellt." (Withdraw quickly, my heart, from the world; / You will find in heaven your true delight. / When in future your eye perceives the Savior, / Only then will your longing heart be refreshed; / Then will it be made content in Jesus.)

6. *Chorale.* A beautiful tutti performance of this sixth stanza of Keymann's hymn closes the cantata (cf. BWV 154 and BWV 157): "Jesum lass' ich nicht von mir, / Geh' ihm ewig an der Seiten; / Christus lässt mich für und für / Zu den Lebensbächlein leiten. / Selig, der mit mir so spricht: / Meinen Jesum lass' ich nicht." (I do not leave Jesus from me, /

I go always at His side; / Christ lets me forever / Be led to the little brooks of life. / Blessed is he who speaks thus with me: / My Jesus I do not leave.)

• **Ach Gott, wie manches Herzeleid (Ah God, How Much Heart-Sorrow) I** (1735–44; BWV 3).

According to the Bach-Gesellschaft's numbering, this BWV 3 number places this cantata ahead of BWV 58, the other cantata with this title, whereas in date sequence, it follows BWV 58 according to Neumann and Terry. It is a chorale cantata for the second Sunday after Epiphany, based on one long hymn by Martin Moller and arranged by an unknown librettist. Verses one, two and eighteen are quoted for the first, second and sixth numbers, while verses four to six, nine and ten are paraphrased for the other three numbers of this cantata. The first verse of the hymn was also used in BWV 44 as well as in BWV 58.

Neither the Gospel nor the Epistle for this Sunday has any bearing on its text. Its theme is the change from earthly pain to heavenly joy, which results from Jesus' help and through faith in Him.

The soli are SATB, with a four-part choir. The orchestra has two oboes d'amore, two violins, a viola and a horn and a trombone in the basso continuo.

1. *Chorus.* This is a chorale fantasia, begun by the basses with the trombone and continuo, and then joined by the altos, tenors and sopranos in that order. The adagio rhythm expresses a dragging grief-motif, continuing to the end of this number. Bach's tone-painting here presents a scene of complex group lamentation by all voices and all instruments. For a translation of this verse, see p. 134.

2. *Chorale and Recitative – tenor, alto, soprano, bass.* The choir sings the second stanza of the chorale with intervals between the lines, during which the soloists' recitatives enter in the above order. They are accompanied by the continuo only. Like the above chorus, it is a complex number: "Wie schwerlich lässt sich Fleisch und Blut / Zwingen zu dem ewigen Gut. / Wo soll ich mich denn wenden hin? / Zu dir, o Jesu, steht mein Sinn." (How difficult does flesh and blood / Allow itself to be forced to eternal good. / Where then shall I turn? / To Thee, o Jesus, stands my thought.)

The tenor comments on the first line: flesh and blood is only concerned with earthly, vain things and heeds neither God nor heaven.

The alto comments after the second line: Jesus is her all and yet her flesh is so contrary.

The soprano remarks after the third line: her flesh is weak, but her spirit is willing; she asks Jesus to help her, since He knows her heart.

The bass concludes after the fourth line: whoever trusts in the Lord's advice and help will receive His friendship and goodness.

3. *Aria – bass.* Again with only continuo accompaniment, this aria begins with a grief-motif, changing to a joy-motif in the third line. Bach has the tenor make repeated long runs on the word "Freudenhimmel" (heaven of joy) where this change occurs in the text: "Empfind' ich Höllenangst und Pein, / Doch muss beständig in dem Herzen / Ein rechter Freudenhimmel sein. / Ich darf nur Jesu Namen nennen, / Der kann auch unermessne Schmerzen / Als einen leichten Nebel trennen." (If I feel hell's anguish and pain, / Still there must constantly be in my heart / A real heaven of joy. / I need only mention the name of Jesus, / Which can disperse even immeasurable pains / Like a light mist.)

4. *Recitative – tenor.* He declaims, in secco, that his body and soul are less important to him than his love of Jesus. Fear of death and the grave, as well as distress and need, are insignificant compared to the rich treasure he finds in Jesus.

5. *Duet – soprano, alto.* This is one of Bach's best duets and the gem in this cantata. The oboes d'amore and the strings provide an entrancing melody to introduce and accompany the soloists throughout. Contrast is shown in the grief-motif that Bach set for the first line

and the joy-motif he set for the rest of the number. The soloists sing in canon for each line, the soprano following the alto: "Wenn Sorgen auf mich dringen, / Will ich in Freudigkeit / Zu meinem Jesu singen. / Mein Kreuz hilft Jesus tragen, / Drum will ich gläubig sagen: / Es dient zum besten allezeit." (When cares press upon me, / I will in joy / Sing to my Jesus. / Jesus helps to carry my cross; / Therefore will I say in my belief: / It serves always for the best.)

6. *Chorale.* The horn replaces the trombone in the instrumental tutti of this final eighteenth stanza of the chorale: "Erhalt' mein Herz im Glauben rein, / So leb' und sterb' ich dir allein, / Jesu, mein Trost, hör' mein Begier, / O mein Heiland, wär' ich bei dir." (Keep my heart pure in faith, / So that I may live and die for Thee alone. / Jesus, my comfort, hear my desire, / O my Savior, were I with Thee.)

Apart from the exceptional duet, this cantata is not especially noteworthy. The complexity of the first two numbers may indicate that Bach was experimenting with his setting of them, but the total result does not seem to be up to his usual quality.

• **Was mein Gott will, das g'scheh allzeit (What My God Wills, That Happens Always)** (1735–44; BWV 111).

This chorale cantata for the third Sunday after Epiphany is not connected with either the Epistle or the Gospel for this Sunday. Markgraf Albrecht von Brandenburg-Culmbach's hymn with the above title was arranged in a poem by an unknown librettist. In this cantata, the first verse of the chorale is quoted unchanged; this had been set for the concluding verse of the chorale in both BWV 72 and BWV 144. The fourth verse is now being used for the final chorale, the second and the third stanzas being paraphrased for the arias and recitatives.

The subject of the cantata is submission to God's will and trust in Him.

The vocalists are SATB, with a four-part chorus. The instruments are few: two oboes, two violins, a viola and continuo.

1. *Chorus.* In spite of the small number of instruments he used, Bach composed a chorale fantasia which is a masterpiece. The joy-motif, developed by the various vocal parts, is most impressive and far superior to the choral presentation at the end of BWV 72 and BWV 144.

"Was mein Gott will, das g'scheh allzeit, / Sein Will', der ist der beste; / Zu helfen den'n er ist bereit, / Die an ihn gläuben feste. / Er hilft aus Not, der fromme Gott, / Und züchtiget mit Massen: / Wer Gott vertraut, fest auf ihn baut, / Den will er nicht verlassen." (What my God wills, that happens always, / His will, that is the best; / He is ready to help those, / Who firmly believe in Him. / He helps out of trouble, our righteous God, / And chastises with moderation: / Who trusts God, firmly builds on Him, / Him will He not leave.)

2. *Aria—bass.* Confident trust in God for comfort and assurance is the theme of this number, accompanied only by the continuo. There is a long run on the last word "widerstreben" to emphasize the futility of man's opposition to God's will.

"Entsetze dich, mein Herze, nicht, / Gott ist dein Trost und Zuversicht / Und deiner Seele Leben. / Ja, was sein weiser Rat bedacht, / Dem kann die Welt und Menschenmacht / Unmöglich widerstreben." (Do not be afraid, my heart, / God is thy comfort and confidence / And the life of thy soul. / Yes, what His wise advice provides, / Against that can the world and human power / Impossibly strive.)

2. *Recitative—alto.* She describes, in secco, the foolish person, who like Jonah (Jonah 1 [3]), wishes to flee from God. Does he not know that his thoughts are known to God, who has even counted the hairs of his head? Only he is well-off who has chosen God's protection and who patiently awaits His decision to determine his actions.

4. *Duet—alto, tenor.* The fascinating

melody of this number comes from a combination of a joy-motif and a step-motif. The voices sing in canon and reproduce a scene of two trusting believers who, like carefree children, confidently tread along life's path even though they know that its end is death. God knows when they will die, but He will be there to comfort them then. The sentiment expressed in the text and Bach's marvelous interpretation of it in the music make this duet outstanding: "So geh' ich mit beherzten Schritten, / Auch wenn mich Gott zum Grabe führt. / Gott hat die Tage aufgeschrieben, / So wird, wenn seine Hand mich rührt, / Des Todes Bitterkeit vertrieben." (So I go with encouraged steps, / Even if God leads me to the grave. / God has written down the days, / So when His hand touches me, / The bitterness of death will be driven away.)

5. *Recitative—soprano.* The oboes accompany her imagined description of the circumstances of her death. She prays that God will receive her spirit after her death-bed struggle, and she asks Him to help her faith in Him conquer the devil, death and sin.

6. *Chorale.* The fourth and last stanza of the same hymn is quoted in its original form. All voices and instruments unite in this final plea to God for protection and guidance.

• **Ich hab' in Gottes Herz und Sinn (I Have into God's Heart and Mind)** (1735–44; BWV 92).

This chorale cantata is longer than average and is again based on only one hymn, Paul Gerhardt's with the above title. The hymn has twelve stanzas, which the unknown librettist contracted into nine numbers: stanzas one, two, five, ten and twelve are in their original form and the others are paraphrased. Neither the Gospel or the Epistle for this Septuagesima Sunday is mentioned in the libretto, which is simply a confession of faith in every number.

The soli are SATB, with the usual four-part chorus. The orchestra consists of two oboes d'amore, two violins, a viola and continuo—again very simple, yet with it Bach does wonders.

1. *Chorus.* This majestic chorale fantasia impresses the listener with its feeling of complete confidence in God. The first verse of the hymn is sung and played tutti, the sopranos carrying the canto fermo of the chorale melody. It is a magnificent opening number: "Ich hab' in Gottes Herz und Sinn / Mein Herz und Sinn ergeben, / Was böse scheint, ist mein Gewinn, / Der Tod selbst ist mein Leben. / Ich bin ein Sohn des, der den Thron / Des Himmels aufgezogen; / Ob er gleich schlägt und Kreuz auflegt, / Bleibt doch sein Herz gewogen." (I have into God's heart and mind / Surrendered my heart and mind. / What appears evil is my winning; / Death itself is my life. / I am a son of Him, Who ascended / The throne of heaven; / Whether He strikes and imposes suffering, / Yet His heart remains inclined toward me.)

2. *Chorale and Recitative—bass.* The second verse of the chorale is sung at intervals by the bass alone, interspersed with sections of his recitative. Continuo only accompanies both parts of this strange and unwieldy number, which, apart from the joy-motif in the chorale lines, seems to have little musical merit. Bach must have been puzzled by how he should set it.

The thought of the recitatives is very confused, yet related to each line of the chorale: (a) Though mountains and hills collapse, (b) the Savior will not fail to protect me with His precious blood. (c) Even if I should be thrown into the sea, I would not drown. (d) I would think of Jonah and Peter who turned to Him, and He will strengthen my faith and watch over my soul. (f) Nothing equals in constancy His goodness. (g) Until my final day, my foot shall stand firm on this rock. (h) I will let myself be found in my belief as firm as a rock. (i) I will know at the right time the hand that He offers me.

The chorale lines preceding each of the above sections are: (a) "Es kann mir fehlen nimmermehr!" (It can never fail me!) (b) "Mein Vater muss mich lieben." (My Father must love me.) (c) "Wenn er mich auch gleich wirft ins Meer," (Even if He throws me into the sea,) (d) "So will er mich nur üben," (Then He only wants to try me,) (e) "Und mein Gemüt," (And my mind,) (f) "in seiner Güt," (in His goodness,) (g) "Gewöhnen, fest zu stehen." (To accustom to stand fast.) (h) "Halt' ich denn stand," (Then I hold my position,) (i) "weiss seine Hand," (and know His hand) (j) "Mich wieder zu erhöhen." (Will be raising me again.)

The Baroque complexity of this disturbing movement makes the listener marvel that Bach could do as well with it as he did!

3. *Aria—tenor.* This aria paraphrases stanzas three and four of the hymn. It is a graphic picture of the destruction of everything not upheld by God. The accompanying strings depict the stormy wrath of God against Satan and his supporters. As in a painting, we can see Satan, raging as he sinks back into the abyss, through the verbs "wüten" (to rage), "rasen" (to rave) and "krachen" (to crash), which are given emphatic runs. This is contrasted with God's conquering strength in the other lines. It is a miniature battle-scene, reminiscent of the opening chorus of BWV 80.

4. *Chorale—alto.* The oboes d'amore accompany her straightforward singing of stanza five, which presents the thought that God knows all our joys and pains and that we can depend on Him, even though our present state is sad.

5. *Recitative—tenor.* This secco narration paraphrases stanzas six to eight of the hymn. It is the only single recitative in this cantata. The tenor says that we Christians should not be fearful of anguish and pain, since Jesus Himself endured much more of them. We must be patient and trust God. He ends with an arioso on the word "Geduld!" (Patience!)

6. *Aria—bass.* Continuo only accompanies this paraphrase of stanza nine. The text conjures up the imagery of a windstorm beating over a grain-field; Bach's melody suggests a parallel in the stormy violence of the scene at Golgotha. Just as the wind produces a better crop, so His sacrifice will bear fruit in the soul of a Christian, who also endures the discipline of pain.

7. *Chorale and Recitative—bass, tenor, alto, soprano.* Stanza 10 is sung with interpolations of the soloists, each giving his recitative in the above order. This is a better arrangement than number two, because the choir's lines are not interrupted for so long by the soloists' following comments. Their theme is submission to God's will and praise of Him and His Son.

8. *Aria—Soprano.* Bach's setting for this aria uses the oboe d'amore and pizzicato strings, which produce a magic touch of pastoral charm. The oboe seems to sing in duet with the soprano throughout, making this the most appealing number in the cantata.

"Meinem Hirten bleib' ich treu, / Will er mir den Kreuzkelch füllen, / Ruh' ich ganz in seinem Willen, / Er steht mir im Leiden bei. / Es wird dennoch, nach dem Weinen, / Jesu Sonne wieder scheinen. / Jesu leb' ich, der wird walten, / Freu' dich, Herz, du sollst erkalten, / Jesus hat genug getan. / Amen; Vater, nimm mich an!" (To my Shepherd I remain faithful, / Even if He will fill my cup of suffering; / I rest completely in His will, / He stands by me in suffering. / There will, nevertheless, after weeping, / Shine the sun of Jesus again. / For Jesus I live, He will govern, / Rejoice, my heart, you will grow cold. / Jesus has done enough. / Amen; Father, receive me!)

9. *Chorale.* All voices and instruments combine in this twelfth stanza of the hymn. Acceptance of our suffering and trust in the Lord as our Shepherd are the themes of this last verse, thereby summarizing the thought in all the previous numbers.

• **Mit Fried' und Freud' ich fahr' dahin (With Peace and Joy I Travel Thither)** (1735–44; BWV 125).

Another unknown librettist arranged

Luther's hymn with the above title as Bach's text for the Feast of the Purification of the Blessed Virgin Mary. Luther's poem directly reflects the Gospel, Luke 2 (22–32), which includes the *Nunc Dimittis* of Simeon. Verses one, two and four of the hymn become numbers one, three and six of the cantata, and the other verses are freely paraphrased.

Bach had already set the first verse on the tune attributed to Luther also in BWV 106 and BWV 95; he had also used the direct Scriptural quotation for the bass Intonation and Recitative in BWV 83. Like this cantata, BWV 83 closes with the same fourth stanza of the hymn.

The soli are ATB, with a four-part chorus. The orchestra has a transverse flute, an oboe d'amore, two violins, a viola, and a horn in the continuo of the opening chorus.

1. *Chorus.* Bach's own mystical interpretation of death pervades the melody that he wrote for this awe-inspiring chorale fantasia. He combines a hesitant step-motif with a motif of exhaustion to depict a gradual sinking forward into the beatific peace of death suggested by the lines sung. The flute is prominent during this intensely moving scene; it seems to superimpose a joy-motif on this solemn moment, especially during the first three lines. For Bach, the hour of death should symbolize joy at the prospect of meeting God.

For the text and the translation of this stanza, see BWV 95, p. 130.

2. *Aria—alto.* The funereal mood is here continued, but now without any trace of joy to alleviate its grief-motif. The melody is sorrowful throughout, even though the text expresses the idea of Jesus giving comfort at its end. The transverse flute and the oboe d'amore obbligati play short, sobbing dissonances to emphasize the end of life in the body. The expression, which Bach derived from the text, probably makes this the most extraordinary aria that he ever composed.

"Ich will auch mit gebrochnen Augen / Nach dir, mein treuer Heiland, seh'n. / Wenn gleich des Leibes Bau zerbricht, / Doch fällt mein Herz und Hoffen nicht. / Mein Jesus sieht auf mich im Sterben / Und lässet mir kein Leid gescheh'n." (I will even with dimmed eyes / Look to Thee, my dear Savior. / Although the body's frame breaks up, / Yet my heart and hoping does not fall. / My Jesus looks on me as I die / And lets no harm happen to me.)

3. *Recitative and Chorale—bass.* Again, as in some of his previous cantatas, and noticeably at this period, Bach combines a chorale stanza with a recitative for one voice. In this case, the commentary precedes each chorale line. This seems to have a better result than in the previous cantata, BWV 92 (number two, also for bass solo). Perhaps the accompanying strings and a clearer text account for this.

The declamatory sections are interpreted in order, each followed by the quoted lines of the chorale stanza:

He says that it is a wonder that the heart is not terrified by the grave and by the pain of death.

"Das macht Christus, wahr' Gottes Sohn, / Der treue Heiland," (Christ, the true Son of God does that, / The faithful Savior,)

He delights the spirit with the sweetness of heaven already on our death-bed.

"Den du mich, Herr, hast sehen lahn," (Which Thou, Lord, hast let me see,)

When in fulfilled time an arm of faith may embrace the salvation of the Lord;

"Und machst bekannt" (And makest known)

From the exalted God, the Creator of all things,

"Dass er sei das Leben und Heil," (That He is life and salvation,)

He is the comfort and portion of men, / Their rescuer from ruin

"Im Tod und auch im Sterben." (In death and also in dying.)

4. *Duet—tenor, bass.* A flood of joyous light, after the blackness of what has been portrayed, bursts forth in the joy-motif of the violins. The first line of this stanza is a paraphrase of Luke 2 (32), and

the remaining lines expand on this theme of joy. After the gloom of death, this duet shines with the radiant light of hope.

"Ein unbegreiflich Licht erfüllt den ganzen Kreis der Erden. / Es schallet kräftig fort und fort / Ein höchst erwünscht Verheissungswort: / Wer glaubt, soll selig werden." (A mystic light fills the whole sphere of the earth. / There resounds loudly on and on / A most wished-for word of promise: / Whoever believes shall become blessed.)

5. *Recitative—alto.* Her secco declamation describes the inexhaustible treasure in God's goodness, which He has reserved for us. Instead of the anger and curse that we have piled upon ourselves, we will be loaded with mercy, if we believe in Him.

6. *Chorale.* All voices and instruments unite in praise of God, which this fourth and last stanza of Luther's hymn expresses: "Er ist das Heil und selig Licht / Für die Heiden, / Zu erleuchten, die dich kenne nicht, / Und zu weiden. / Er ist deins Volks Israel / Der Preis, Ehr', Freud' und Wonne." (He is the salvation and blessed light / for the heathen, / To enlighten those, who do not know Thee, / And to feed them. / He is of Thy people Israel / The praise, honor, joy and bliss.)

• **Erhalt' uns, Herr, bei deinem Wort (Keep Us, Lord, in Thy Word)** (1735–44; BWV 126).

This rousing chorale cantata for Sexagesima Sunday was arranged by an unknown librettist on Luther's hymn of three stanzas with the above title. Its text does refer to the Gospel for the day, Luke 8 (4–15): the parable of the sower, especially verse 11, "The seed is the word of God." However, the other Biblical verses were changed by Luther and the librettist into a prayer for victory over our enemies, both temporal and spiritual, and a final prayer for peace under good government.

Stanzas one and three and another hymn by Luther, "Verleih' uns Frieden gnädiglich"(Graciously Grant Us Peace) are set in their original form. The second stanza is freely paraphrased for numbers two, four and five of the cantata.

The soli are ATB, with a four-part chorus. The orchestra has a trumpet, two oboes, two violins, a viola and continuo.

1. *Chorus.* Bach's blaring trumpet sounds the charge in this battle-scene for full choir and orchestra. Luther wrote the hymn at the time of the war against the Turks and while his struggle against the Pope was at its height. These thoughts occur also in Luther's Litany, which Bach had expressed in his 1714 cantata for the same Sunday, BWV 18, as well as here.

This chorale fantasia presents a wonderful panorama of an advancing army. A rhythm of joy is used by Bach to express its elation in victory. It reminds the listener of the similar opening choruses in BWV 19 and BWV 79. The first line seems to refer to the fifteenth verse of this Gospel for the day: "Erhalt' uns, Herr, bei deinem Wort, / Und steur' des Papsts und Türken Mord, / Die Jesum Christum, deinen Sohn, / Stürzen wollen von seinem Thron." (Keep us, Lord, in Thy word, / And stop the murder by the Pope and Turks, / Who, Jesus Christ, Thy Son, / Wish to throw down from His throne.)

2. *Aria—tenor.* The two obbligato oboes play in duet to a spiritual melody which enhances the tenor's prayer to God for His aid against their enemies. The church militant needs His help. Coloratura runs on the verbs "erfreuen" and "zerstreuen" add a personal, intimate touch to his fervent prayer: "Sende deine Macht von oben, / Herr der Herren, starker Gott! / Deine Kirche zu erfreuen / Und der Feinde bittern Spott / Augenblicklich zu zerstreuen." (Send Thy might from above, / Lord of Lords, powerful God! / To gladden Thy church / And the enemies' bitter mockery / To disperse in a moment.)

3. *Chorale and Recitative—alto, tenor.* This is another of Bach's experimental combinations of chorale with recitative. It seems that he was

experimenting with this method in all the chorale cantatas of this last period. Both soloists sing the chorale lines together and then alternate for the narrative sections. They state that false Christian brethren are a danger to Christian unity, and pray for the Lord's help to protect their faith.

This number is well done but not exceptionally impressive.

4. *Aria—bass.* With continuo only, his declamation is like a fiery sermon against the forces of evil. The rhythm illustrates the motion of the fall of arrogant evil-doers and their vain attempts to rise again from the abyss into which they have been hurled back. The bass paints a picture of the triumph of God in a denouncing climax: "Stürze zu Boden schwülstige Stolze! / Mache zunichte, was sie erdacht! / Lass sie den Abgrund plötzlich verschlingen, / Wehre dem Toben feindlicher Macht, / Lass ihr Verlangen nimmer gelingen!" (Throw to the ground swollen proud ones! / Bring to nothing what they have planned! / Let the abyss suddenly devour them. / Check the raging of their hostile might. / Let their longing never succeed!)

5. *Recitative—tenor.* Peace returns with this calm assurance that God watches over His church and that His blessing and help will be granted to us. His word and truth will be enshrined in the teaching which we have received from Him.

6. *Chorale.* This tutti, two-stanza addition to Luther's first chorale is a prayer for peace and good government. Its quiet beauty contrasts with the preceding aria and it ends with a fine "Amen."

"Verleih' uns Frieden gnädiglich, / Herr Gott, zu unsern Zeiten; / Es ist doch ja kein andrer nicht, / Der für uns könnte streiten, / Denn du, unser Gott, alleine. / Gib unsern Fürst'n und aller Obrigkeit / Fried' und gut Regiment, / Dass wir unter ihnen / Ein geruh'g und stilles Leben führen mögen / In aller Gottseligkeit und Ehrbarkeit. / Amen." (Graciously grant us peace, / Lord God, in our time; / There is surely no other, / Who could fight for us, / Than Thou, our God, alone. / Give to our princes and to all authority / Peace and good government, / So that we under them / May lead a calm and quiet life / In all godliness and uprightness. Amen.)

• **Herr Jesu Christ, wahr' Mensch und Gott (Lord Jesus Christ, True Man and God)** (1735–44; BWV 127).

This chorale cantata for Quinquagesima Sunday is based on Paul Eber's hymn entirely. Verses one and eight are verbally retained for the opening chorus and for the final chorale; the other intervening stanzas are paraphrased for the recitatives and the arias.

The librettist is unknown; possibly Picander could have arranged the text that Bach used. The text has only one reference to the Gospel for that Sunday, Luke 18 (31–43), the opening chorus alluding to the thirty-second verse.

In this magnificent and outstanding work, Bach has achieved his aim of composing a perfect chorale cantata, which is the first of many more to come, though not all will be of this high caliber.

The soli are STB, with a four-part chorus. The orchestra has a trumpet, an oboe, two flutes, two violins, a viola and continuo.

1. *Chorus.* This chorale fantasia presents a picture of Christ's humiliation before His crucifixion. A rhythm of solemnity in the accompanying strings and woodwinds dominates throughout the movement. A tone of profound respect for the Lord in His suffering reminds the listener of similar passages in Bach's *Passions:* "Herr Jesu Christ, wahr' Mensch und Gott, / Der du littst Marter, Angst und Spott, / Für mich am Kreuz auch endlich starbst / Und mir deins Vaters Huld erwarbst, / Ich bitt' durchs bittre Leiden dein: / Du wollst mir Sünder gnädig sein." (Lord Jesus Christ, true man and God, / Thou Who suffered martyrdom, anguish and scorn, / For me also died finally on the Cross, / And for me won Thy Father's favor, / I beg through Thy bitter suffering: / Thou wilt be merciful to me, a sinner.)

2. *Recitative—tenor.* He expresses, in secco, his confidence that Jesus will stand by him when the hour of his own death comes. The Lord has shown him His own patience in suffering and his faith will likewise support him at this time.

3. *Aria—soprano.* The woodwinds and the strings, pizzicato, illustrate the sadness of this death-scene with a tear-motif. The quiet serenity of her passing is marked by the plucked strings and by staccato quavers of the flutes and oboes, all in imitation of tolling bells. Her text mentions that she is unafraid, although the melody seems to indicate the reverse. It is a superlative aria, nevertheless, for its realistic imagery and personal emotion: "Die Seele ruht in Jesu Händen, / Wenn Erde diesen Leib bedeckt. / Ach ruft mich bald, ihr Sterbeglocken, / Ich bin zum Sterben unerschrocken, / Weil mich mein Jesus wieder weckt." (The soul rests in Jesus' hands, / When earth covers this body. / Ah call me soon, ye death-bells; / I am unafraid of dying, / Because my Jesus wakes me again.)

4. *Recitative and Aria—bass.* Bach's past experiments with inserting the chorale tune into a recitative finally succeed perfectly in this amazing combination. There are seven different tempi in the music, all depicting the Judgment Day. The trumpet adds colorful peals throughout, adding to the awesome scene suggested by the quavering strings. Four lines are Biblical quotations, unrelated to the Gospel for the day, but pertaining to the Last Day.

The bass sings the recitative section first, then switching dramatically into the role of Christ for his aria part. The hymn-tune is apparent more in the recitative than in the aria section. The recitative vividly describes the scene when the world will be destroyed when the trumpet sounds. He imagines himself standing before God's judgment seat with Jesus beside him as his advocate. Then, without pause, he begins his dramatic monologue with himself in the role of Jesus: "Fürwahr, fürwahr, euch sage ich: / Wenn Himmel und Erde im Feuer vergehen, / So soll doch ein Gläubiger ewig bestehen. / Er wird nicht kommen ins Gericht / Und den Tod ewig schmecken nicht. / Nur halte dich, / Mein Kind, an mich: / Ich breche mit starker und helfender Hand / Des Todes gewaltig geschlossenes Band." (Verily, verily, I say to you: / When heaven and earth vanish in fire, / Then shall a believer eternally last. / He will not come into judgment / And will not taste death forever. / Only hold thyself, / My child, to Me: / I break with a strong helping hand / Death's forcefully locked bond.)

5. *Chorale.* Stanza eight of Eber's hymn, performed tutti except for the trumpet, closes this admirable chorale cantata which is perfect in every respect—thought, emotion, imagery and Bach's musical interpretation of the text to bring these qualities out: "Ach, Herr, vergib all unser Schuld, / Hilf, dass wir warten mit Geduld, / Bis unser Stündlein kömmt herbei, / Auch unser Glaub' stets wacker sei, / Dein'm Wort zu trauen festiglich, / Bis wir einschlafen seliglich." (Ah, Lord, forgive all our guilt, / Help us to wait with patience, / Until our death-hour comes along. / Also may our faith be always brave, / To trust in Thy word steadfastly, / Until we blessedly fall asleep.)

• **Wie schön leuchtet der Morgenstern (How Beautifully Gleams the Morning Star)** (c. 1740; BWV 1).

For those who think Bach's sacred cantatas are full of gloom, this chorale cantata for the Annunciation of the Blessed Virgin Mary will be a revelation. It is happy, with a joy-motif shining in every number. Bach's use of the orchestra to provide the imagery of local color is equal to that of his 1724 Epiphany cantata BWV 65 in their opening choruses.

Stanzas one and seven of Philipp Nicolai's hymn of the above title were set in their original form for the first and the last numbers, the intervening stanzas being paraphrased for the arias and recitatives by someone unknown, possibly Picander.

Both the Old Testament lesson, Isaiah 7 (10–15), and the Gospel, Luke 1 (26–38), are reflected in the libretto; both Scriptures foretell Christ's birth.

The soli are STB, with a four-part chorus. The orchestra is brilliant: two horns, two oboi da caccia, two concertante violins, two ripieno violins, a viola and continuo.

1. *Chorus.* The two concertante violins begin the melody, which is then repeated by the horns and the rest of the instruments, before the choir begins to sing. There is a step-motif in this wonderul chorale fantasia, giving us a picture of the slowly moving caravan of the Magi who are following the morning star to Bethlehem. This morning star symbolizes Jesus in the text. The horns denote royalty, both in the procession of the Wise Men, as they pass through the desert, and in the significance of the star. This movement presents an unforgettable cameo of this nocturnal scene, combined with a feeling of profound reverence in the Wise Men and also in the congregation, expressed by the choir on their behalf.

Variations in the vocal and the instrumental treatment hold the listener fascinated, even though it is a long number. The embellishments on the chorale melody create a mystical joy-motif, and yet the total result is simple and realistic: "Wie schön leuchtet der Morgenstern / Voll Gnad' und Wahrheit von dem Herrn, / Die süsse Wurzel Jesse! / Du Sohn Davids aus Jakobs Stamm, / Mein König und mein Bräutigam, / Hast mir mein Herz besessen, / Liebreich, / Freundlich, / Schön und herrlich, gross und ehrlich, reich von Gaben, / Hoch und sehr prächtig erhaben." (How beautifully gleams the Morning Star / Full of grace and truth from the Lord, / The sweet root of Jesse! / Thou Son of David from Jacob's line, / My King and my Bridegroom, / Thou hast taken my heart, / Lovely, Friendly, / Beautiful and glorious, great and honest, rich in gifts, / Highly and very splendidly exalted.)

2. *Recitative—tenor.* A dramatic touch comes in his secco declamation, as though he were addressing the Lord, either as one of the Wise Men or as a modern believer. The text resembles a short prayer of thanks to Jesus for His coming into the world to bring us the "bread of heaven" in His word, which neither the grave nor danger can tear from our hearts. Gabriel's announcement to Mary is mentioned in his text.

3. *Aria—soprano.* An obbligato oboe da caccia twists and turns to illustrate the dancing flames of divine love which are mentioned in her text. The strings of the continuo play pizzicato as the background for her joyful song, which is as simple and direct as the other numbers in this cantata. Like the previous recitative, it is a prayer for heavenly love: "Erfüllet, ihr himmlischen göttlichen Flammen, / Die nach euch verlangende gläubige Brust! / Die Seelen empfinden die kräftigsten Triebe / Der brünstigsten Liebe / Und schmecken auf Erden die himmlische Lust." (Fill, ye heavenly divine flames, / The believing breast longing for you! / Our souls feel the strongest drives / Of most ardent love, / And on earth taste the pleasure of heaven.)

4. *Recitative—bass.* He states, in secco, that his soul is not moved by any earthly light, which cannot compare with that spiritual light, emitted by the Savior's star. The star symbolizes the Lord's flesh and blood; this gives him refreshing blessing. For this, he should offer thanks and praise to the Lord, and this thought leads into the following aria.

5. *Aria—tenor.* The joy-motif emerges in full force in his vocal expression and in the two groups of strings: two solo concertante and two ripieno violins. The effect is like that of a small concerto movement, supporting the tenor's joyful allegro. The melody is captivatingly graceful with many instrumental echo effects: "Unser Mund und Ton der Saiten / Sollen dir / Für und für / Dank und Opfer zubereiten. / Herz und Sinnen sind erhoben, / Lebenslang / Mit Gesang,

Grosser König, dich zu loben." (Our mouth and sound of the strings / Shall for Thee / Forever / Prepare thanks and offerings. / Heart and mind are uplifted, / All our lives / With song, / Great King, to praise Thee.)

6. *Chorale.* All voices and instruments, with the horns being in the continuo, render the seventh stanza of Nicolai's hymn, which Bach had previously set for the concluding chorale for soprano only in BWV 49. To compare Bach's elaborate full choir treatment here with the duet at the end of BWV 49, the reader should refer to pages 117–118, where a text and its translation are given. The laudatory comments made there apply equally well to Bach's setting here.

• **Wir müssen durch viel Trübsal in das Reich Gottes eingehen (We Must Through Much Tribulation Enter the Kingdom of God)** (c. 1740; BWV 146).

The Gospel for the third Sunday after Easter (Jubilate) is John 16 (16–23), man's sorrows in the world which will thereafter turn to joy. The message is well presented in the libretto of this cantata. The librettist is unknown, although Schweitzer names Picander (Vol. II, p. 343).

Bach's abiding interest in the organ had induced him to introduce it into some of his previous cantatas. In this work, he borrows again the organ transcription of his *D Minor Clavier Concerto,* BWV 1052, for the first two movements. In 1731, he had used the first movement as the sinfonia for BWV 188. It is probable that Bach himself was the organist when he conducted the first performance of BWV 146.

The soli are SATB, with a four-part chorus. The instruments included are a transverse flute, taille, two oboi d'amore, two violins, a viola, the organ and continuo.

1. *Sinfonia.* It seems to me that Bach chose this allegro for organ solo and orchestra because its joyous mood suited the thought of the following numbers, and not because he was pleased by his transcription and wanted to hear it again, as some theorists have suggested. Its melody gives the impression of the gradual triumph of happiness over sorrow, which is the theme of this cantata.

2. *Chorus.* By adding the slow adagio movement of his transcribed clavier work, Bach has created the first two movements of an organ concerto. Handel's organ concerti come to mind, except that this is vocal as well as instrumental. A deeply moving grief-motif is evident as the choir sings its text, a part of Acts 14 (22). This is one of Bach's most solemn choruses: "Wir müssen durch viel Trübsal in das Reich Gottes eingehen." (We must through much tribulation enter the kingdom of God.)

3. *Aria—alto.* Accompanied by a solo violin and continuo, her long da capo aria contains a feeling of ecstatic joy over leaving the wickedness of Sodom in this world: "Ich will nach dem Himmel zu, / Schnödes Sodom, ich und du / Sind nunmehr geschieden. / Meines Bleibens ist nicht hier, / Denn ich lebe doch bei dir / Nimmermehr in Frieden." (I wish to go to heaven, / Evil Sodom, I and you / Are henceforth separated. / My remaining is not here, / For I do not live with you / Ever in peace.)

4. *Recitative—soprano.* The recitatives in this cantata are very long. This one complains about the singer's miserable state in this evil world in comparison with the bliss of those in heaven. The accompanying strings help to maintain interest during this long number. She longs to be with Jesus and continues this wish in her following aria.

5. *Aria—soprano.* Bach's setting is remarkable in that he retains one melancholy theme throughout, even though the text indicates a change to joy at the end. The transverse flute and the two oboi d'amore accompany her song with tear-motifs to illustrate her lines. This is a very long da capo aria, but Bach infuses it with artistry and feeling: "Ich säe meine Zähren / Mit bangem Herzen aus. / Jedoch mein Herzeleid / Wird mir die Herrlichkeit / Am Tage der seligen Ernte gebären." (I sow my tears / With an

anxious heart. / Yet the sorrow of my heart / Will bear me glory / On the day of the blessed harvest.)

6. *Recitative—tenor.* In secco, he declares that he will patiently bear his cross, because his present sufferings are not worth the splendor that awaits him. To deserve his crown, he must fight against the enemies and the evils which oppress him. This long narration leads into the following duet.

7. *Duet—tenor, bass.* Their rapturous singing in canon banishes all the previous gloom. A rollicking joy-motif shines forth in both the vocal dialogue and in the oboi d'amore and strings. It is one of Bach's most joyous duets, with its dancing tempo and florid vocal passages: "Wie will ich mich freuen, wie will ich mich laben, / Wenn alle vergängliche Trübsal vorbei! / Da glänz ich wie Sterne und leuchte wie Sonne, / Da störet die himmlische selige Wonne / Kein Trauern, Heulen und Geschrei." (How I will rejoice, how I will be refreshed, / When all passing afflictions are over! / Then I shall gleam like stars and shine like the sun; / Then the heavenly blessed bliss / No mourning, howling and shouting will disturb.)

8. *Chorale.* Bach did not indicate either the text or the orchestration for this final chorale, so Johann Schop's hymn-tune to Gregorius Richter's hymn, stanza nine, "Lasset ab von euren Tränen" (Leave off your tears) is substituted, according to Neumann.

• **O ewiges Feuer, O Ursprung der Liebe (O Eternal Fire, O Source of Love)** (c. 1740–41; BWV 34).

This cantata for Whitsunday was arranged by Bach from his own previously composed wedding cantata of 1726 for a ceremony in Leipzig. The music for this earlier work (BWV 34a) is incomplete, but the libretto for it is complete.

The librettist of the original version is unknown; Bach himself probably wrote the text of this second cantata, reducing the numbers from seven to five. Movements one, three and five conform with the first version in words and music.

Both cantatas appear to be connected more with the Epistle, Acts 2 (1–12)—the descent of the Holy Spirit in tongues of fire—than with the Gospel, John 14 (23–31), which also mentions the arrival of the Comforter.

The soli are ATB, with a four-part chorus. The orchestra is sumptuous: three trumpets, timpani, two oboes, two transverse flutes, two violins, a viola and continuo.

1. *Chorus.* This is divided into two sections, the first beginning in a blaze of orchestral color with a tutti joy-motif, and the second in a calmer, beseeching tone. The canon singing increases the symbolic mysticism of both sections, which signifies the descent of the Holy Ghost. This is a splendid example of Bach's expertise in bringing his text to life through evocative music: "O ewiges Feuer, O Ursprung der Liebe, / Entzünde die Herzen und weihe sie ein! / Lass himmlische Flammen durchdringen und wallen, / Wir wünschen, o Höchster, dein Tempel zu sein. / Ach lass dir die Seelen im Glauben gefallen!" (O eternal fire, o source of love, / Kindle our hearts and consecrate them! / Let heavenly flames penetrate and undulate; / We wish, o Highest, to be Thy temple. / Ah, let our souls in faith please Thee!)

2. *Recitative—tenor.* He asserts, in secco, that our hearts keep the words of the Lord's Gospel (John 14 [23]) and therefore his heart is ready to receive Him.

3. *Aria—alto.* The ethereal tone of the accompanying transverse flutes and strings presents a serene picture of heaven's repose. Their pulsating melody suggests the quiet flutter of angelic wings to enhance her tender slumber-song. This has been considered to be one of Bach's most beautiful arias: "Wohl euch, ihr auserwählten Seelen, / Die Gott zur Wohnung auserlesen. / Wer kann ein grösser Heil erwählen? / Wer kann des Segens Menge zählen? / Und dieses ist vom Herrn geschehen." (Well for you,

you chosen souls, / Whom God has elected for His dwelling. / Who can choose a greater salvation? / Who can count the multitude of blessing? / And this has happened by the Lord.)

4. *Recitative—bass.* This short, secco number continues without pause into the final chorus. He says that God chooses His own holy dwellings into which He puts salvation and blessing. Then He calls over this consecrated house (the heart) His word of blessing.

5. *Chorus.* All voices and instruments used in the opening chorus perform this equally magnificent conclusion. The text is based on Psalm 122 (6), which becomes a motto, "Peace over Israel," in vocal repetition: "Friede über Israel! / Dankt den höchsten Wunderhänden, / Dankt, Gott hat an euch gedacht. / Ja, sein Segen wirkt mit Macht, / Friede über Israel, / Friede über euch zu senden." (Peace over Israel! / Thank the highest wonder-hands, / Thank, that God has thought of you. / Yes, His blessing works with might, / Peace over Israel, / Peace to send over you!)

• **Ach Gott, vom Himmel sieh' darein (Ah God, from Heaven Look Into It)** (c. 1740; BWV 2).

With this composition for the second Sunday after Trinity, Bach returns to the chorale cantata, his main preoccupation during this last period. The previous two works were of the regular type.

Luther's hymn upon which this libretto is based is a paraphrase of Psalm 12. Picander was probably the librettist. Stanzas one and six are retained for the first and the last numbers, the intervening stanzas being paraphrased for the arias and recitatives. Luther's hymn refers more to the Epistle, 1 John 3 (13–18), concerning brotherly love, than to the Gospel for the day, Luke 14 (16–24).

The soli are ATB, with the four-part chorus. The orchestra has four trombones, two violins, two oboes, a viola and continuo.

1. *Chorus.* This tutti is a chorale fantasia in the archaic motet style of Pachelbel, with canon singing by the various entries of the choir. It sounds like a lament to God over man's lack of faith and failure to keep His word. The gloomy severity of this number does not make it very attactive: "Ach Gott, vom Himmel sieh' darein / Und lass dich's doch erbarmen! / Wie wenig sind der Heil'gen dein, / Verlassen sind wir Armen; / Dein Wort man nicht lässt haben wahr, / Der Glaub' ist auch verloschen gar / Bei allen Menschenkindern." (Ah God, from heaven look into it / And let Thyself pity it! / How few are Thy saints, / Forsaken are we poor people; / Thy word is not taken as true, / Faith is also quite extinguished / Among all the children of man.)

2. *Recitative—tenor.* He continues this complaint, in secco, by saying that men teach empty, false deceit against God and His truth. They offend the church with their wit and replace the Bible with their foolish reason. They are like dead men's graves, appearing beautiful from without, but containing stench and decay within.

3. *Aria—alto.* This is her personal prayer to God to eradicate their false teachings. A solo violin with the continuo adds to her vehemence: "Tilg', o Gott, die Lehren, / So dein Wort verkehren! / Wehre doch der Ketzerei / Und allen Rottengeistern; / Denn sie sprechen ohne Scheu: / Trotz dem, der uns will meistern!" (Erase, o God, the teachings, / Which pervert Thy word! / Check the heresy / And all plotting minds; / For they say without fear: / Defiance to him, who wants to master us!)

4. *Recitative—bass.* Strings accompany his description of how God decides to help poor people in their confusion. God's words are spoken in arioso during the last half of this number.

5. *Aria—tenor.* The smooth flow of the melody played by the oboes and strings seems to portray the smelting of silver as stated in the text. This imagery and the idea of a Christian's purification through suffering make this the best

number in the cantata. However, the dark color-tones of the music persist in the tragic mood as in all the other movements of this cantata: "Durch's Feuer wird das Silber rein, / Durch's Kreuz das Wort bewährt erfunden. / Drum soll ein Christ zu allen Stunden / Im Kreuz und Not geduldig sein." (Through fire silver becomes pure, / Through the Cross is founded the kept word. / Therefore should a Christian every hour / Be patient in suffering and distress.)

6. *Chorale.* This sixth verse of Luther's hymn is performed tutti as was the opening chorus and, like all the previous numbers, concludes with the same appeal to God for His help against the ungodly: "Das woll'st du Gott bewahren rein / Vor diesem arg'n Geschlechte; / Und lass uns dir befohlen sein, / Dass sich's in uns nicht flechte. / Der gottlos Hauf sich umher find't, / Wo solche lose Leute sind / In deinem Volk erhaben." (That Thou wilt keep pure / From this wicked race; / And let us be commended to Thee, / So that it may not fasten itself in us. / The godless band is located around us, / Where such loose people are / In among Thy exalted folk.)

This is an unusual cantata, because it contains just one melancholy theme throughout, without any uplifting ray of hope which Bach usually puts at the end of his cantatas. It is not one of Bach's best chorale cantatas. Perhaps the tone of lamentation and moralizing overpowers any musical beauty that Bach could draw from such a libretto.

• **Ach Herr, mich armen Sünder (Ah Lord, Me Poor Sinner)** (c. 1740; BWV 135).

Bach's usual setting of sadness becoming joy returns in this chorale cantata for the third Sunday after Trinity. An unknown librettist arranged the verses of a hymn by Cyriakus Schneegass with the above title, based on Psalm 6. Stanzas one and six of this hymn are set in their original form and the intervening stanzas are paraphrased for the arias and the recitatives.

The libretto refers indirectly to the parable of the lost sheep in the Gospel for the day, Luke 15 (1–10), and to the Epistle, 1 Peter 5 (6–11), but the poem is a free interpretation of the thoughts of a repentant sinner. It is a superb work in its emotional content and in its music.

The soli are ATB, with a four-part chorus. The instruments are two oboes, two violins, a viola and a trombone in the continuo of the opening chorus, with a horn in the closing chorale.

1. *Chorus.* All instruments play the melody of H.L. Hassler's "Herzlich tut mir verlangen" (Heartily I Long For), into which successive voices enter with wonderful effect. Each line of the chorale is preceded by the instrumental ritornelli to create a unique chorale fantasia. Thus Bach has painted a beautiful tone-poem on the emotions of a repentant sinner: "Ach Herr, mich armen Sünder / Straf' nicht in deinem Zorn, / Dein' ernsten Grimm doch linder, / Sonst ist's mit mir verlor'n. / Ach Herr, wollst mir vergeben / Mein' Sünd' und gnädig sein, / Dass ich mag ewig leben, / Entflieh'n der Höllenpein." (Ah Lord, me poor sinner / Do not punish in Thy anger; / Moderate Thy stern wrath, / Otherwise I am lost. / Ah Lord, Thou wilt forgive me / My sin and be merciful, / So that I may ever live / To escape from the torment of hell.)

2. *Recitative—tenor.* This secco, personal appeal to Jesus for relief from his misery describes in detail the suffering of a guilty soul. Jesus is the only physician who can cure his fears and dry his tears. His regret has wasted him physically, and he asks the Lord why He is so long in coming to him.

3. *Aria—tenor.* He now expresses his desperate need for help, supported by two oboes. Only at the end is his poignant pleading touched by a note of hope: "Tröste mir, Jesu, mein Gemüte, / Sonst versink' ich in den Tod, / Hilf mir, hilf mir durch deine Güte / Aus der grossen Seelennot! / Denn im Tod ist alles stille, / Da gedenkt man deiner nicht. / Liebster Jesu, ist's dein Wille, / So erfreu' mein Angesicht!" (Comfort for

me, Jesus, my mind, / Or else I am sinking into death. / Help me, help me through Thy goodness / Out of my soul's great distress! / For in death everything is still; / There one does not think of Thee. / Dearest Jesus, if it is Thy will, / Then make my countenance glad!)

4. *Recitative—alto.* Pessimism returns in this secco number. She states that she is tired through grieving. Her soul knows no peace the whole night long, as she lies sweating and weeping. She has become old because of mourning and anxiety.

5. *Aria—bass.* The mood changes to hopeful confidence now, with string accompaniment. The lost sheep has been found and now defies those evil-doers who have led him astray. The music maintains a step-motif to suggest his hastening away from them: "Weicht, all ihr Übeltäter, / Mein Jesus tröstet mich! / Er lässt nach Tränen und nach Weinen / Die Freudensonne wieder scheinen; / Das Trübsalswetter ändert sich, / Die Feinde müssen plötzlich fallen / Und ihre Pfeile rückwärts prallen." (Begone, all you evil-doers, / My Jesus comforts me! / He lets, after tears and weeping, / The sun of joy shine again; / The gloomy weather changes, / Our enemies must suddenly fall / And their arrows ricochet backwards.)

6. *Chorale.* This doxology for the concluding tutti praises the Trinity, giving joyous thanks for the everlasting blessing that we have received. Its total joy-motif makes it a fitting ending to a magnificent work.

• **Christ, unser Herr, zum Jordan kam (Christ, Our Lord, Came to the Jordan)** (c. 1740; BWV 7).

For the Feast of St. John the Baptist, Bach set this chorale cantata on an arrangement of Luther's hymn by an unknown librettist. Verses one and seven are quoted for the first and seventh stanzas of his text and the intermediate verses are paraphrased. No allusion is made to either the Epistle or the Gospel for the day; the poem is based only on Luther's hymn, which describes the work of John the Baptist. Yet there are references to the New Testament in this libretto.

Bach's setting is full of pictorial realism in both choral numbers; the recitatives are dramatic and the arias are melodious, even though didactic. It has its own particular beauty, which distinguishes it from his other cantatas. All numbers are joyfully optimistic, unlike BWV 2, where the opposite is the case.

The soli are ATB, with the usual four-part chorus. The instruments include two oboi d'amore, two violins, a concertante violin, a viola and continuo partly with organ.

1. *Chorus.* The imagery in this chorale fantasia is complex. A rhythm of solemnity is expressed in J. Walther's melody for this number, which Bach assigns to the tenor section, followed by the other voices. At the same time, the instruments play a wave-motif to depict the slight motion of small waves and the strong rolling of larger ones. These motives combine into a beautiful scene, which represents Christ receiving His baptism from John at the river Jordan: "Christ, unser Herr, zum Jordan kam / Nach seines Vaters Willen, / Von Sankt Johanns die Taufe nahm, / Sein Werk und Amt zu erfüllen; / Da wollt' er stiften uns ein Bad, / Zu waschen uns von Sünden, / Ersäufen auch den bittern Tod / Durch sein selbst Blut und Wunden; / Es galt ein neues Leben." (Christ, our Lord, came to the Jordan / According to His Father's will. / From St. John He took baptism / To fulfill His work and ministry. / There He wanted to establish a bath for us, / To wash us from sins, / Also to drown bitter death / Through His own blood and wounds; / It was worth a new life.)

2. *Aria—bass.* Accompanied by string continuo only, the bass assumes the role of a preacher who stresses the importance of baptism. There is much repetition of his first two lines including the da capo repeats. Then his theme changes to depict the outpouring of baptismal water. A step-motif indicates this act of faith: "Merkt und hört, ihr Menschenkinder, /

Was Gott selbst die Taufe heisst. / Es muss zwar hier Wasser sein, / Doch schlecht Wasser nicht allein. / Gottes Wort und Gottes Geist / Tauft und reiniget die Sünder." (Note and hear, you children of men, / What God Himself calls baptism. / There must certainly be water there, / Yet not only plain water; / God's word and God's Spirit / Baptizes and cleanses sinners.)

3. *Recitative—tenor.* His secco narration recounts dramatically God's presence at Christ's baptism in the voice from heaven saying, "This is my beloved Son, in whom I am well pleased" (Matthew 3 [17]). We should therefore accept Him as our Savior and hear His teaching.

4. *Aria—tenor.* Two concertante violins accompany him with an ethereal melody, symbolically suggestive of the fluttering of a dove, to represent the descent of the Holy Spirit: "Des Vaters Stimme liess sich hören, / Der Sohn, der uns mit Blut erkauft, / Ward als ein wahrer Mensch getauft. / Der Geist erschien im Bild der Tauben, / Damit wir ohne Zweifel glauben, / Es habe die Dreifaltigkeit / Uns selbst die Taufe zubereit'." (The Father's voice let itself be heard; / The Son, who redeemed us with blood, / Was baptized as a real man. / The Spirit appeared in the form of doves, / So that we believe without doubt, / The Trinity itself / Prepared the baptism for us.)

The didactic strain in this text is softened in the beauty of Bach's melody.

5. *Recitative—bass.* Drama infuses the arioso on Christ's words to His disciples, as the bass interprets the role of the Lord. Strings enhance his declamation, in which he quotes Matthew 28 (19) and Mark 16 (16)—the command to teach the heathen and to impart knowledge of the saving grace of faith and baptism.

6. *Aria—alto.* By adding the oboe d'amore and strings to the continuo, Bach sets a beautiful melody which again overshadows the didacticism of her text. It is the most impressive of the three arias in this cantata: "Menschen, glaubt doch dieser Gnade, / Dass ihr nicht in Sünden sterbt, Noch im Höllenpfuhl verderbt! / Menschenwerk und Heiligkeit / Gilt vor Gott zu keiner Zeit. / Sünden sind uns angeboren, / Wir sind von Natur verloren; / Glaub' und Taufe macht sie rein, / Dass sie nicht verdammlich sein." (Mankind, believe then in this grace, / So that you do not die in sin, / Nor perish in the pool of hell! / Man's work and holiness / Avail at no time before God. / Sins are born in us, / We are lost by nature; / Faith and baptism make them clean, / So that they are not damnable.)

7. *Chorale.* All voices and instruments perform this seventh stanza of Luther's hymn, in which the melody again evokes the imagery of Jordan's waves. Like all previous numbers, it reflects mankind's joyful hope in the redemption of baptism and Christ's sacrifice.

• **Meine Seel' erhebt den Herren (My Soul Magnifies the Lord)** (c. 1740; BWV 10).

For the Visitation of the Blessed Virgin Mary, Bach set this chorale cantata, based directly on the Gospel, Luke 1 (46–55). Verses 46–48 and 54 are quoted and the other verses are paraphrased by the unknown librettist.

In 1723 Bach had composed the first version of his *Magnificat* in Latin for the evening service on Christmas Day in St. Thomas's. This later form is completely in German, taking only the opening chorus and the duet from the Gospel, but giving the doxology for the concluding chorale in the vernacular, as it was in Latin in the last movement of the *Magnificat.*

The soli are SATB, with a four-part chorus. The orchestra consists of a trumpet, two oboes, two violins, a viola and continuo.

1. *Chorus.* Reinforced by the trumpet, the plainchant melody (Tonus Peregrinus) to which this hymn is customarily sung is used in this chorus and in the final chorale. An exuberant joy-motif infuses the entire number in a

tumult of rejoicing by the voices and the instruments: "Meine Seel' erhebt den Herren, und mein Geist freuet sich Gottes, mein Heilandes; denn er hat seine elende Magd angesehen. Siehe, von nun an werden mich selig preisen alle Kindeskind." (My soul magnifies the Lord, and my spirit rejoices in God, my Savior; for He has regarded His poor maiden. Behold, from now on, all children's children will praise me as blessed.)

2. *Aria—soprano.* Strings and unison oboes accompany her aria, at first forte and then quietly, after the first line repeating the word "Herr." She sings a beautiful prayer of thanks to God for having chosen her out of all women as the Mother of Christ: "Herr, der du stark und mächtig bist, / Gott, dessen Name heilig ist, / Wie wunderbar sind deine Werke! / Du siehest mich Elenden an, / Du hast an mir so viel getan, / Dass ich nicht alles zähl' und merke." (Lord, Thou who art strong and mighty, / God, whose Name is holy, / How wonderful are Thy works! / Thou lookest upon me, wretched one; / Thou hast done so much for me, / That I do not count and notice everything.)

3. *Recitative—tenor.* His secco narrative is a dramatic description of how God grants His faith and His goodness daily to those who fear Him and look to Him for help. On the other hand, He scatters the proud in their arrogance, like chaff.

4. *Aria—bass.* Only the continuo accompanies the bass in this paraphrase of the movement "Deposuit potentes de sede" of the Latin *Magnificat.* Thus he has full vocal scope to develop the description of the fate that awaits the lowly and the mighty: "Gewaltige stösst Gott vom Stuhl / Hinunter in den Schwefelpfuhl; / Die Niedern pflegt Gott zu erhöhen, / Dass sie wie Stern' am Himmel stehen. / Die Reichen lässt Gott bloss und leer, / Die Hungrigen füllt er mit Gaben, / Dass sie auf seinem Gnadenmeer / Stets Reichtum und die Fülle haben." (God pushes the powerful from their seat / Down into the brimstone-pool; / The lowly, God is accustomed to raise up, / So that they stand like stars in the sky. / The rich, God leaves destitute and empty. / The hungry he fills with gifts, / So that they, on His ocean of mercy, / Always have riches and abundance.)

5. *Duet—alto, tenor.* As in Bach's *Magnificat* for this number, the trumpet and unison oboes play the Tonus Peregrinus melody to accompany the vocalists. This is the high point of this cantata. The singers' voices are both in imitation of each other and in unison: "Er denket der Barmherzigkeit und hilft seinem Diener Israel auf." (He thinks of mercy and helps up His servant Israel.)

6. *Recitative—tenor.* He begins, in secco, with a paraphrase of verse 55 of the Gospel, "As he spake to our fathers, to Abraham, and to his seed for ever," but in the last half, the strings seem to portray calmly lapping waves. This imagery comes from the text, which mentions Abraham's descendants to be as numerous as the sands of the seashore. Christ brought the grace and truth of God's word to rescue them from Satan.

7. *Chorale.* A tutti performance of the doxology with the plainchant melody concludes this cantata. It has the same noble dignity as the final chorus of the *Magnificat* and adds a prolonged "Amen" at the end: "Lob und Preis sei Gott dem Vater und dem Sohn und dem heiligen Geiste, wie es war im Anfang, jetzt und immerdar und von Ewigkeit zu Ewigkeit, Amen." (Praise and honor be to God the Father and to the Son and to the Holy Ghost, as it was in the beginning, now and evermore and from eternity to eternity. Amen.)

• **Es ist dir gesagt, Mensch, was gut ist (It Has Been Told to Thee, Man, What Is Good)** (1732–40; BWV 45).

This cantata for the eighth Sundy after Trinity is of the free madrigal type, which makes Schweitzer think that the librettist was Picander (cf. Vol. II, p. 343). Terry suggests Christian Weiss, Sr.; Neumann and Whittaker say that he was someone unknown. Even the dating is very vague. Dürr's modern research places it back to 1726.

The text bears directly on the Gospel, Matthew 7 (15–23), a warning against false prophets and workers of iniquity, with the twenty-second and twenty-third verses being quoted for the bass Arioso of Part II.

Although the main thought of all numbers is on righteous conduct, Bach was able to alleviate their didactic texts with enchanting melodies. There is also a strong feeling for the dramatic in the arias, especially in the Arioso. However, Bach cannot derive any imagery from this preaching libretto.

The soli are ATB, with a four-part chorus. The instruments are two transverse flutes, two oboes, two violins, a viola and continuo with organ included.

Part I

1. *Chorus.* The Biblical text for this tutti opening is Micah 6 (8). The orchestra plays the first melody before the voices enter; they sing in imitation according to their parts, with much repetition of the first words, "Es ist dir gesagt." The second part develops into a fugue for voices and instruments.

"Es ist dir gesagt, Mensch, was gut ist und was der Herr von dir fordert, nämlich Gottes Wort halten und Liebe üben und demütig sein vor deinem Gott." (It has been told to thee, man, what is good and what the Lord demands of thee, namely, to keep God's word and practice love and be humble before thy God.)

The deep emotion that Bach has drawn out of this text is surprising.

2. *Recitative—tenor.* He states, secco, that the Lord's will lets him know what will please Him. God's will is the plumbline of his conduct, to which he would adhere with humility and love. Thus he will prove his obedience as a true servant should.

3. *Aria—tenor.* As a soliloquy on his previous recitative, Bach brings this number to dramatic life in an agreeable melody for strings as accompaniment: "Weiss ich Gottes Rechte, / Was ist's, das mir helfen kann, / Wenn er mir als seinem Knechte / Fordert scharfe Rechnung an. / Seele, denke dich zu retten; / Auf Gehorsam folget Lohn, / Qual und Hohn / Drohet deinem Übertreten." (I know God's justice, / What it is that can help me, / When He from me as His servant / Demands sharp reckoning. / Soul, think about saving thyself; / On obedience follows reward, / Torment and scorn / Threaten thy transgression.)

Part II

4. *Arioso—bass.* This is the most dramatic number in this cantata. The bass assumes the role of Christ to declaim the two quotations from Matthew 7 (22–23). It is more aria than arioso with its string accompaniment such as Bach had used before in the bass aria of BWV 187 (cf. pp. 127–128): "Es werden viele zu mir sagen an jenem Tage: Herr, haben wir nicht in deinem Namen geweissaget, haben wir nicht in deinem Namen Teufel ausgetrieben, haben wir nicht in deinem Namen viel Taten getan? Dann werde ich ihnen bekennen: ich habe euch noch nie erkannt; weichet alle von mir, ihr Übeltäter!" (There will be many who say to me on that day: Lord, have we not in Thy name prophesied, have we not in Thy name driven out devils, have we not in Thy name done many deeds? Then will I make known to them: I have not ever recognized you; begone from Me, ye evil-doers!)

5. *Aria—alto.* An obbligato transverse flute accompanies her with a joy-motif to denote the ethereal favor bestowed on believers. This aria is one of Bach's masterly works of art, transforming the text into a mystical alto rhapsody. The first part of the text is based on Matthew 10 (32): "Wer Gott bekennt / Aus wahrem Herzensgrund, / Den will er auch bekennen. / Denn der muss ewig brennen, / Der einzig mit dem Mund / Ihn Herren nennt." (Whoever acknowledges God / Out of the true depths of his heart, / Him will He also acknowledge.

For he must forever burn, / Who simply with his mouth / Calls him Lord.)

6. *Recitative—alto.* This secco number follows the thought of her previous aria; her heart and mouth will be her judge. God will reward her according to her attitude; if she does not follow His word, she harms her soul. Yet if she believes in Him, His help is assured and He will accomplish His will through her.

7. *Chorale.* This is stanza two of Johann Heermann's hymn, "O Gott, du frommer Gott" (O God, Thou pious God), performed tutti but plainly. It is a prayer for God's help in doing what is right and a wish that they may succeed in doing it well.

This cantata has some very fine numbers, but it is not an outstanding work. Perhaps the didactic cast of the text impeded Bach's endeavors.

• **Wo Gott, der Herr, nicht bei uns hält (If God, the Lord, Does Not Hold with Us)** (1735–40; BWV 178).

This is another cantata for the eighth Sunday after Trinity, a chorale cantata based on only one hymn. Stanzas one, two, four, five, seven and eight of the hymn by Justus Jonas are set in their original form, while the other stanzas are paraphrased for the arias. The libretto deals again with the false prophets of Matthew 7 (15–23), but the name of the librettist is unknown.

It is interesting to note that this hymn was not prescribed in Leipzig churches on this Sunday, but was in other towns such as Augsburg, Darmstadt and Frankfurt. So one would wonder why Bach selected it for this particular cantata.

The soli are ATB, with a four-part chorus. The orchestra consists of two oboes, two oboi d'amore, a viola and a horn in the soprano continuo.

1. *Chorus.* Psalm 124 provides the text for this opening chorale fantasia; all instruments play a spirited call to battle against false prophets. Their orchestral introduction is a prelude to the entry of the choir, whose parts are sung in syncopated imitation: "Wo Gott, der Herr, nicht bei uns hält, / Wenn unsre Feinde toben, / Und er unsrer Sach' nicht zufällt / Im Himmel hoch dort oben, / Wo er Israels Schutz nicht ist / Und selber bricht der Feinde List, / So ist's mit uns verloren." (If God, the Lord, does not hold with us, / When our enemies rage, / And He does not agree with our cause / There in heaven high above, / If He is not Israel's protection / And Himself breaks the enemies' guile, / Then it is lost with us.)

2. *Chorale and Recitative—alto.* The recitative lines are interpolated into the seven lines of the chorale's second stanza, all intended by Bach to be sung by the alto solo, but the chorale lines are sung by the high voices in modern performances, it seems. The alto's solo comments follow each choral section. She states that man's strength and wit do not frighten His believers, who know that He will never leave them. God will not allow the "snake-like" cunning of the perverted to prevail.

3. *Aria—bass.* Accompanied by unison violins, the bass depicts a storm at sea in which the enemy, metaphorically the waves, seeks to shatter Christ's little ship. Bach's ability to paint a realistic picture in sound is well demonstrated in this number: "Gleichwie die wilden Meereswellen / Mit Ungestüm ein Schiff zerschellen, / So raset auch der Feinde Wut / Und raubt das beste Seelengut. / Sie wollen Satans Reich erweitern, / Und Christi Schifflein soll zerscheitern." (Just as the wild sea-waves / With violence dash a ship to pieces, / So does the fury of the enemies' rage / And robs us of our best soul-goodness. / They want to extend Satan's kingdom, / And Christ's little ship is to be completely wrecked.)

4. *Chorale.* The two oboi d'amore accompany his singing of this corresponding stanza of the chorale, all in straightforward style. This verse states that our enemies declare us to be heretics and therefore seek our blood. Yet they boast that they are also Christians, greatly esteemed by God. But God's name will cover their roguishness when He awakens to it.

5. *Chorale and Recitative—bass, tenor, alto.* As for number two, the chorale lines of this stanza are interspersed with the soloists' comments, beginning and ending with the bass. This alternation makes this number very dramatic, and each soloist has vivid description in his text. They say that foolish, false prophets may be compared to lions which open their jaws to devour true believers. But God will destroy them in their heresy by the fire of His wrath.

6. *Aria—tenor.* The melody of the accompanying strings has a broken cadence to illustrate staggering reason, as indicated in the first line of his text. His apostrophe to reason, the adversary of faith, presents a musical image of a tottering old man who should hold his tongue: "Schweig', schweig' nur, taumelnde Vernunft! / Sprich nicht: die Frommen sind verlor'n, / Das Kreuz hat sie nur neu gebor'n. / Denn denen, die auf Jesum hoffen, / Steht stets die Tür der Gnade offen; / Und wenn sie Kreuz und Trübsal drückt, / So werden sie mit Trost erquickt." (Be silent, just be silent, staggering reason! / Do not say: the pious are lost; / Only recently the Cross has reborn them. / For to them, who hope in Jesus, / Stands the door of mercy always open, / And when misery and sadness oppress them, / Then they are revived with comfort.)

7. *Chorale.* This is a straightforward, tutti performance of the hymn's seventh and eighth stanzas. It summarizes all the ideas expressed and amplified in the preceding text: God knows how reason plots against faith; He will console us so that we do not waver in our belief. Accordingly, we can let the world murmur as it will.

• **Nimm von uns, Herr, du treuer Gott (Take from Us, Lord, Thou True God)** (c. 1740; BWV 101).

Although Dürr dates this chorale cantata as far back as 1724 and Whittaker, following Terry, gives the date as late as 1745, when Frederick the Great's second invasion of Saxony occurred, the libretto does stress the scourge of war as well as the time of plague in 1584, when Martin Moller wrote this hymn.

The unknown librettist—Schweitzer names Picander (Vol. II, p. 375)—arranged stanzas one, three and five in their original form and paraphrased the other stanzas, which Bach set as arias. All verses of the poem reflect upon the sadness caused by war and plague; Bach illustrates their theme of lamentation with deep emotional appeal.

For this tenth Sunday after Trinity, the Gospel is Luke 19 (41–48); the libretto reflects verses 41 to 44—Christ's prediction of the destruction of Jerusalem. This Scripture would have great significance for Bach and the congregation so soon after the latest war, because Leipzig was the modern Jerusalem in their opinion.

The soli are SATB, with a four-part chorus. The orchestra has a transverse flute, two oboes, taille, two violins, a viola and continuo which includes a horn, three trombones as well as strings.

1. *Chorus.* This chorale fantasia is unlike any other movement in any of Bach's cantatas. All the above instruments are involved in a grief-motif, which begins as a prelude before the voices of the choir enter, and is then developed in the ritornelli. This theme of intense mourning has a beauty all its own in the style of a Pachelbel motet or one of Buxtehude's choruses. The solemn, march-like rhythm impresses the listener with its austere dignity. Its mysterious grandeur is irresistible: "Nimm von uns, Herr, du treuer Gott, / Die schwere Straf' und grosse Not, / Die wir mit Sünden ohne Zahl / Verdienet haben allzumal. / Behüt' vor Krieg und teuer Zeit, / Vor Seuchen, Feu'r und grossem Leid." (Take from us, Lord, Thou true God, / The heavy punishment and great distress, / Which we with countless sins / Have deserved all too often. / Protect from war and famine, / From pestilences, fire and great sorrow.)

2. *Aria—tenor.* A solo obbligato violin brightens this number considerably after the complex melancholy heard in

the above chorus, yet his text is still a prayer for God's protection: "Handle nicht nach deinem Rechten / Mit uns bösen Sündenknechten, / Lass das Schwert der Feinde ruh'n! / Höchster, höre unser Flehen, / Dass wir nicht durch sündlich Tun / Wie Jerusalem vergehen!" (Do not deal according to Thy law / With us evil servants of sin. / Let the sword of our enemies rest! / Highest, hear our beseeching, / So that we, through sinful doing, / Do not perish like Jerusalem!)

3. *Recitative and Chorale—soprano.* The organ in the continuo carries the chorale lines, which alternate with recitative passages, both parts being sung by only the soprano in a rhythm of felicity. Her theme is a further prayer that God may give their country peace and protection from the enemy. The people will strive to do what is good and thus deserve His bounty, not His anger.

4. *Aria with Chorale—bass.* This is a strange setting of the librettist's equally strange text. Only the first line of the chorale stanza is given; the remaining lines are paraphrased but retain the chorale tune of the beginning line. The woodwinds illustrate the menace of God's wrath on sinners, mentioned in the text. This number is another prayer that God will cease punishing us and have patience with our weak flesh.

5. *Chorale and Recitative—tenor.* It will be noticed that the chorale tune and parts of its verses have been used in all numbers from three to five. This will continue to the end of the work, indicating Bach's desire to maintain the one chorale throughout all numbers and to apply the hymn in his own innovative style. Here, the secco lines of the chorale stanza alternate with sections of free recitative, as in number three above. The tenor also prays to God to strengthen them in their weakness so that they may resist evil.

6. *Duet—soprano, alto.* Two lines of the chorale stanza occur in the middle of this text; the rest is a free paraphrase. It seems that this movement resembles more an elaborate quintet for transverse flute, oboe, continuo, soprano and alto than a vocal duet.

Schweitzer points out that the theme is similar to the sobbing, sighing melody in the aria "Erbarme dich" (Have pity) of the *St. Matthew Passion* (Vol. II, p. 376). Both numbers have a similarity in their beautiful plea for God's mercy: "Gedenk' an Jesu bittern Tod! / Nimm, Vater, deines Sohnes Schmerzen / Und seiner Wunden Pein zu Herzen, / Die sind ja für die ganze Welt / Die Zahlung und das Lösegeld; / Erzeig' auch mir zu aller Zeit, / Barmherz'ger Gott, Barmherzigkeit! / Ich seufze stets in meiner Not: / Gedenk' an Jesu bittern Tod!" (Think about Jesus' bitter death! / Take, Father, Thy Son's sufferings / And the pain of His wounds to Thy heart; / Those are indeed for the whole world / The payment and the ransom money; / Show to me too at all times, / Merciful God, mercy! / I sigh constantly in my distress: / Think about Jesus' bitter death!)

7. *Chorale.* This last stanza of Moller's chorale is a prayer for God's protection and guidance. The solemnity of its tutti performance makes the entire cantata a tragic but beautiful composition. Bach will use it again to conclude BWV 90.

"Leit' uns mit deiner rechten Hand / Und segne unser Stadt und Land; / Gib uns allzeit dein heil'ges Wort, / Behüt' vors Teufels List und Mord; / Verleih' ein seligs Stündelein, / Auf dass wir ewig bei dir sein." (Lead us with Thy right hand / And bless our city and country. / Give us always Thy holy word; / Protect us from the devil's cunning and murder. / Grant us a blessed last hour, / So that we may be eternally with Thee.)

• **Herr Jesu Christ, du höchstes Gut (Lord Jesus Christ, Thou Highest Good)** (c. 1740; BWV 113).

For the eleventh Sunday after Trinity, Bach set this highly emotional chorale cantata, arranged on Bartholomäus Ringwaldt's hymn by an unknown librettist, who wrote stanzas one, two, four and eight in their original form and paraphrased the remainder.

The Gospel for the day, Luke 18 (9–14), the parable of the Pharisee and the publican, is mentioned only in the tenor recitative. The tenth verse of the Epistle, 1 Corinthians 15 (1–10), God's redeeming grace, suggested the main theme of penitence. The intense, personal emotion of this subject inspired Bach to compose a masterpiece in this cantata.

The soli are SATB, with a four-part chorus. The instruments are a transverse flute, two oboes, two oboi d'amore, two violins, a viola and continuo.

1. *Chorus.* The decorated melody of this fantasia seems to represent water welling from a spring, as the beginning lines suggest, and then to depict waves of comfort on a tortured conscience in the remainder. The chorale melody will appear entirely or partly in every number in this cantata. The choir sings in simple harmony without imitation in their parts: "Herr Jesu Christ, du höchstes Gut, / Du Brunnquell aller Gnaden, / Sieh' doch, wie ich in meinem Mut / Mit Schmerzen bin beladen / Und in mir hab' der Pfeile viel, / Die im Gewissen ohne Ziel / Mich armen Sünder drücken." (Lord Jesus Christ, Thou highest good, / Thou source of all mercy, / See then, how I in my mind / Am laden with pain / And have in me many arrows, / Which in my conscience endlessly / Oppress me poor sinner.)

2. *Chorale—alto.* This second chorale verse, a prayer for pity, is accompanied by the strings in an exceptionally beautiful setting. More than in any other number in this cantata, Bach's musical treatment of this verse is a pleasure to hear: "Erbarm' dich mein in solcher Last, / Nimm sie aus meinem Herzen, / Dieweil du sie gebüsset hast / Am Holz mit Todesschmerzen, / Auf dass ich nicht vor grossem Weh / In meinen Sünden untergeh', / Noch ewiglich verzage." (Pity me with such a burden. / Take it out of my heart, / Because Thou hast atoned for it / On the Cross with pains of death, / So that I do not from great woe / Perish in my sins, / Nor eternally despair.)

3. *Aria—bass.* Accompanied by the two oboes d'amore, he sings the first line of the hymn's third stanza, which is paraphrased for the remainder. The tone of this aria is more declamatory in its self-reproach than lyrical: "Fürwahr, wenn mir das kommet ein, / Dass ich nicht recht vor Gott gewandelt / Und täglich wider ihn misshandelt, / So quält mich Zittern, Furcht und Pein. / Ich weiss, dass mir das Herze bräche, / Wenn mir dein Wort nicht Trost verspräche." (Truly, when that occurs to me, / That I have not walked rightly before God / And have daily acted wrongly against Him, / Then trembling, fear and pain torment me. / I know that my heart would break, / If Thy word should not promise me comfort.)

4. *Chorale and Recitative—bass.* Once again, as in some previous chorale cantatas, the chorale lines are interspersed with lines of recitative. The former are sung to the chorale melody, while the latter are declaimed; the whole number has only secco accompaniment. His thought is that the sweet singing of Christ's word gives him such comfort that his conscience no longer torments him.

5. *Aria—tenor.* The obbligato flute's joy-motif illustrates the happiness he feels in Christ's word of forgiveness. Its lovely melody makes this number the only bright sport in the whole cantata: "Jesus nimmt die Sünder an: / Süsses Wort voll Trost und Leben! / Er schenkt die wahre Seelenruh / Und rufet jedem tröstlich zu: / Dein' Sünd' ist dir vergeben." (Jesus accepts sinners: / Sweet word full of comfort and life! / He presents true peace in the soul / And calls to each person comfortingly: / Thy sin is forgiven thee.)

6. *Recitative—tenor.* This is in the usual plain declamatory style, with strings accompanying. There are references to the contrite publican of the Gospel and to the penitent David and Manasseh in the Old Testament. He wishes that the Lord will likewise accept him.

7. *Duet—soprano, alto.* Again quoting

only the first line of this hymn stanza, Bach continues to use parts of the chorale melody for the paraphrased remainder of this text. The soloists sing the lines in imitation, with very long, florid runs on the verbs "erreget" (aroused), "auferleget" (laid), "gebe" (give or produce—here used in an idiom, "sich zufrieden geben," to be content) and "lebe" (live) which occur at the end of lines. Their shaking semiquavers are played also by the accompanying continuo. It seems that Bach is trying to convey an impression of God's anger thereby: "Ach, Herr, mein Gott, vergib mir's doch, / Womit ich deinen Zorn erreget, / Zerbrich das schwere Sündenjoch, / Das mir der Satan auferleget, / Dass sich mein Herz zufrieden gebe / Und dir zum Preis und Ruhm hinfort / Nach deinem Wort / In kindlichem Gehorsam lebe." (Ah, Lord, my God, forgive me then, / That I have aroused Thy anger. / Shatter the heavy yoke of sin, / That Satan has laid upon me, / So that my heart may be content / And for Thy praise and honor henceforth, / According to Thy word, / May live in childlike obedience.)

8. *Chorale.* No instruments are stated for the plain rendering of this last stanza of the hymn. The choir asks the Lord to strengthen them, to heal them with His wounds, and to abide with them at their hour of death. Then their faith will enable them to join His elect.

• **Ihr Tore zu Zion (Ye Gates in Zion)** (c. 1740; BWV 193).

The librettist of this truly magnificent Ratswechsel cantata is unknown. However, Picander wrote the libretto for Bach's 1727 secular homage cantata, BWV 193a, "Ihr Häuser des Himmels" (Ye houses of heaven), which celebrates the name-day of Augustus II. Three movements are borrowed from this work, of which only the text survives, to permit a reconstruction in this sacred cantata. Even the sacred version is incomplete, because Bach noted that a recitative was omitted before the final chorus, itself a repeat of the opening chorus. This note in the score may indicate that Bach had a part in the composition of the text, which is original throughout and based on four different Psalms, referred to in the first four numbers.

The soli are only SA, with a four-part chorus. The orchestra is brilliant as befits the occasion: three trumpets, timpani, two oboes, an oboe d'amore, a bassoon, unison violins, a violoncello, a viola, organ and continuo.

1. *Chorus.* A stunning tutti produces a panoply of majestic music, with trumpet fanfares to honor the presence of royalty in the case of the secular cantata. Here the homage is being paid to God. Zion represents Leipzig as its modern counterpart; Bach's music fits this religious text equally well as it does the opening secular text. This same chorus will be repeated at the end of the cantata as Bach indicated *(Chorus ab initio repetatur).*

The first line is based on Psalm 87 (2). The noun "Tore" (gates) was later changed to "Pforten" (portals), so that now this cantata may have two titles.

"Ihr Tore zu Zion, ihr Wohnungen Jakobs, freuet euch! / Gott ist unsers Herzens Freude, / Wir sind Völker seiner Weide, / Ewig ist sein Königreich." (Ye gates in Zion, ye dwellings of Jacob, rejoice! / God is the joy of our heart, / We are people of His pasture, / Eternal is His kingdom.)

2. *Recitative—soprano.* In secco, she declaims Psalm 121 (4) in her first line, followed by her own thoughts on this. A summary would be: the Guardian of Israel does not fall asleep or slumber. His countenance is the shadow of our right hand. The whole country has increased in its abundance. Who can exalt Thee enough for that, Lord?

3. *Aria—soprano.* An oboe and strings accompany her fervent prayer of thanks to God, which is also a plea to Him that He pardon our transgressions. Her text is well interpreted by a rhythm of solemnity throughout. There is a beautiful reverence in this melody. The last line of her text refers to Psalm 65 (2): "O

thou that hearest prayer, unto thee shall all flesh come."

"Gott, wir danken deiner Güte, / Denn dein väterlich Gemüte / Währet ewig für und für. / Du vergibst das Übertreten, / Du erhörest, wenn wir beten, / Drum kömmt alles Fleisch zu dir." (God, we thank Thy goodness, / For Thy fatherly disposition / Lasts eternally forever and ever. / Thou forgivest transgression. / Thou hearest, when we pray. / Therefore all flesh comes to Thee.)

4. *Recitative—alto.* This secco number begins by apostrophizing Leipzig as the present Jerusalem and then compares these earthly cities with the heavenly one. Leipzig should be delighted to hold such a municipal festival as this, having peace within its walls and justice in its lawcourts and palaces. She prays that its fame and light may continually endure. The third line refers to Psalm 9 (7): "He hath prepared his throne for judgment."

5. *Aria—alto.* A solo oboe d'amore obbligato with the continuo produces an enchanting melody to accompany her prayer that the Lord send us His blessing. This tune evokes imagery of a bud (the blessing) bursting into blossom: "Sende, Herr, den Segen ein, / Lass die wachsen und erhalten, / Die für dich das Recht verwalten / Und ein Schutz der Armen sein! / Sende, Herr, den Segen ein!" (Send in, Lord, Thy blessing. / Let those persons increase and maintain, / Who for Thee administer justice / And who are a protection for the poor! / Send in, Lord, Thy blessing!)

6. *Chorus.* The initial tutti chorus is repeated, leaving the listener enthralled by its grandeur. It is one of Bach's most fascinating choruses; its repetition does not detract from the total grand impression of the work.

• **Allein zu dir, Herr Jesu Christ (Only in Thee, Lord Jesus Christ)** (c. 1740; BWV 33).

This chorale cantata for the thirteenth Sunday after Trinity was composed by an unknown librettist on a hymn with this title by either Johannes Schneesing or Konrad Hubert. Stanzas one and four are set in their original form for the opening chorus and the final chorale; the intervening stanzas are freely paraphrased.

The Epistle, Galatians 3 (15–22)—Christ fulfills the promise of the law—is reflected in the inner numbers; the Gospel, Luke 10 (23–37)—the parable of the good Samaritan—is mentioned only in the tenor-bass duet.

The soli are ATB, with a four-part chorus. The orchestra consists of two oboes, two violins, a viola, organ and continuo.

1. *Chorus.* A joy-motif predominates in this chorale fantasia, while the instruments play in a step-rhythm, symbolic of steadfast faith, both in the orchestral introduction and in the ritornelli after each line sung by the choir of their prayer to Christ: "Allein zu dir, Herr Jesu Christ, / Mein' Hoffnung steht auf Erden; / Ich weiss, dass eu mein Tröster bist, / Kein Trost mag mir sonst werden. / Von Anbeginn ist nichts erkor'n, / Auf Erden war kein Mensch gebor'n, / Der mir aus Nöten helfen kann. / Ich ruf' dich an, / Zu dem ich mein Vertrauen hab'." (Only in Thee, Lord Jesus Christ, / My hope remains on earth. / I know that Thou art my Comforter; / There will be no comfort for me otherwise. / From the beginning nothing is ordained. / On earth no man was born, / Who can help me out of troubles. / I call to Thee, / In Whom I have my trust.)

The fifth line affirms the Lutheran doctrine of free-will against predestination.

2. *Recitative—bass.* Organ and continuo accompany his statement of personal guilt. This contrasts with the joy found in the opening chorus. He addresses God to state that his conscience will make him unable to answer any questions on the law. Yet, because he sincerely regrets his sins, he hopes that God will forgive them.

3. *Aria—alto.* Bach depicts the sinner's wavering steps in the beginning of this text by a step-motif for pizzicato strings above the continuo accompaniment with organ. This march-like melody

continues throughout the aria, even when the latter part of the text states that Christ's comforting words have done enough for her. It is an aria of great beauty, but seems, perhaps, too long with its slow tempo and da capo: "Wie furchtsam wankten meine Schritte, / Doch Jesus hört auf meine Bitte / Und zeigt mich seinem Vater an. / Mich drückten Sündenlasten nieder, / Doch hilft mir Jesu Trostwort wieder; / Dass er für mich genug getan." (How fearful were my faltering steps, / Yet Jesus listens to my prayer / And shows me to His Father. / Sins' burdens pressed me down, / Yet Jesus' word of comfort helps me again, / So that He has done enough for me.)

4. *Recitative—tenor.* He implores God not to reject him, even though daily he violates His commandments. He prays for Christ's assistance in the struggle with his conscience. May God pity him and give him true Christian faith to make him active in his love for others. Organ and continuo accompany his narrative.

5. *Duet—tenor, bass.* Two oboes support their prayer to God that He will fill their spirits with love for their neighbor, as in the case of the good Samaritan. If enemies should disturb their good intentions, they pray that God will help them to achieve their works of love. They sing each pair of lines in imitation but conclude them in unison. Bach's setting is unusually artful, but the overall result is not too noteworthy, as the parts do not blend very well.

"Gott, der du die Liebe heisst, / Ach, entzünde meinen Geist, / Lass zu dir vor allen Dingen / Meine Liebe kräftig dringen. / Gib, dass ich aus reinem Triebe / Als mich selbst den Nächsten liebe; / Stören Feinde meine Ruh', / Sende du mir Hilfe zu!" (God, Thou who art called love, / Ah, kindle my spirit, / Let before all things / My love strongly impress Thee. / Grant, that I out of pure impulse / Love my neighbor as myself. / Should enemies disturb my peace, / Send me Thy help!)

6. *Chorale.* This plain, tutti performance of the fourth verse of the hymn gives praise to the Trinity, and asks God to always help us, so that we may please Him, here in this life, and in eternity.

• **Jesu, der du meine Seele (Jesus, Thou Who My Soul)** (1735–44; BWV 78).

For the fourteenth Sunday after Trinity, this chorale cantata is a perfect example of Bach's achievement in this type. Johann Rist's hymn provides the basis for the whole work: stanzas one and twelve are set in the original text for the opening and the concluding numbers; two lines of stanza three begin the tenor recitative; four lines of stanza ten are placed at the end of the bass recitative; the remaining stanzas are paraphrased by the unknown librettist for the other numbers.

The Gospel for the day, Luke 17 (11–19), the healing of the ten lepers, is reflected in all verses of the hymn by the thought that sin is a leprosy that blights the conscience and the soul.

The soli are SATB, with a four-part chorus. The orchestra consists of a transverse flute, two oboes, two violins, a cello, a violone, a viola and continuo with organ. There is also a horn in the continuo for the opening chorus.

1. *Chorus.* The sopranos carry the chorale melody, while the other vocal parts enter in imitation for each line. The horn and the flute double the melody an octave above. After a short instrumental introduction, the voices begin with a grief-motif, which turns into a joy-motif at the end. The anguish of the sin-tormented conscience becomes a joyful confidence in its fervent appeal to God for help: "Jesu, der du meine Seele / Hast durch deinen bittern Tod / Aus des Teufels finstrer Höhle / Und der schweren Seelennot / Kräftiglich herausgerissen / Und mich solches lassen wissen / Durch dein angenehmes Wort, / Sei doch itzt, o Gott, mein Hort!" (Jesus, Thou who my soul / Hast through Thy bitter death / Powerfully torn out of the devil's dark cave / And my deep distress of soul, / And hast let me know so / Through Thy pleasing word, / Be then now, O God, my refuge!)

This fantasia is an outstanding example of the magical power of Bach's art to bring out all the nuances of the hymn-text in sound and feeling.

2. *Duet—soprano, alto.* Organ, cello, and violone accompany this number with a gay, skipping theme, its hurried step-motif realistic in its interpretation of the text. The voices sing the first two lines in canon, uniting at the end in happy repetitions of "zu dir"; they then continue with the brilliant joy-motif of the rest of the aria, culminating with runs on the last word "erfreulich." The melody of the first two lines charmingly reproduces the hastening of eager feet towards Jesus: "Wir eilen mit schwachen, doch emsigen Schritten, / O Jesu, o Meister, zu helfen zu dir. / Du suchest die Kranken und Irrenden treulich. / Ach höre, wie wir / Die Stimmen erheben, um Hilfe zu bitten! / Es sei uns dein gnädiges Antlitz erfreulich!" (We hurry with weak, yet eager steps, / O Jesus, O Master, to Thee for help. / Faithfully Thou seekest the sick and wayward. / Ah hear, as we / Raise our voices to pray for help! / May Thy gracious countenance be joyful toward us!)

3. *Recitative—tenor.* He confesses that he is a child of sin which, like leprosy, will not leave him. His will makes him want to choose evil, and he feels powerless to compel it to do right. His conscience is burdened by the unbearable pain of his sinning. He begs the Lord not to count his misconduct which has angered Him.

4. *Aria—tenor.* Hope of forgiveness and Christ's aid to help him resist future sins are the ideas in his text. The supporting transverse flute and the pizzicato violone play a joy-motif in the last half of the aria; their melody enhances his declaration of confidence in Jesus for his fight against evil: "Das Blut, so meine Schuld durchstreicht, / Macht mir das Herze wieder leicht / Und spricht mich frei. / Ruft mich der Hölle Heer zum Streite, / So stehet Jesus mir zur Seite, / Dass ich beherzt und sieghaft sei." (Thy Blood, which cancels my guilt, / Makes my heart light again / And makes me free. / If the army of hell calls me to combat, / Then Jesus stands at my side, / So that I am courageous and triumphant.)

5. *Recitative—bass.* Strings accompany his long declamation (the tenor recitative was long also, but only secco) on his own contrite emotions, as he remembers the Lord's sacrifice for his sins. He will offer his sorrowful heart for the blood that Jesus shed for him. This last thought is expressed by his moving arioso in the last four lines, which are quoted from stanza ten of the hymn.

6. *Aria—bass.* An oboe is featured, above the tutti string accompaniment, in a motif of beatific peace which his words suggest. This beautiful aria shows his complete trust in Christ to still his conscience and give him hope: "Nun du wirst mein Gewissen stillen, / So wider mich um Rache schreit; / Ja, deine Treue wird's erfüllen, / Weil mir dein Wort die Hoffnung beut, / Wenn Christen an dich glauben, / Wird sie kein Feind in Ewigkeit / Aus deinen Händen rauben." (Now Thou wilt quieten my conscience, / Which cries against me for vengeance. / Yes, Thy faith will fulfill it, / Because Thy word offers me hope. / If Christians believe in Thee, / No enemy in eternity will steal them / Out of Thy hands.)

7. *Chorale.* All voices and instruments join in a joyous affirmation of faith in God, as stated in this twelfth verse of the hymn. The choir asks for God's help to strengthen them against sin and death, so that they will not despair. They will trust in Him until they meet Him in eternity after their earthly strife—a fitting concluding thought.

This is an excellent chorale cantata in every respect.

• **Warum betrübst du dich, mein Herz (Why Art Thou Sad, My Heart?)** (c. 1740; BWV 138).

The hymn upon which this chorale cantata for the fifteenth Sunday after Trinity is based is conjectured to be composed by Hans Sachs and set to an anonymous melody. Schweitzer thinks that Picander was the librettist for Bach's setting, and Neumann places the date about 1732. This date is probably correct, although the experimental aspect of Bach's format might indicate Terry's vague date, c. 1740, for these later chorale cantatas.

The Gospel, Matthew 6 (24–34), has its thirty-fourth verse, ". . . Sufficient unto the day is the evil thereof," reflected throughout this libretto. Stanzas one, two and three of the hymn are set in their original form; however, one and two are broken by the insertion of recitatives after their third line in numbers one and three of the cantata. Especially for an opening number, this procedure is most unusual and must have given Bach scope for experimentation.

The soli are ATB, with a four-part chorus. The instruments are two oboi d'amore, two violins, a viola and continuo—much lighter than usual.

1. *Chorale and Recitative—alto.* The melody of the first part of this chorale stanza contains a grief-motif. After the alto recitative portion, the tune has a more optimistic note of confidence. The fantasia in the choral section represents the querulous thoughts of an individual, and the intervening solo alto section gives the replies of the heart, so that this number is really a dialogue between them. Bach uses this same experimental method in number three of this cantata, with the same dramatic effect.

"Warum betrübst du dich, mein Herz? / Bekümmerst dich und trägest Schmerz / Nur um das zeitliche Gut?" (Why art thou sad, my heart? / Art thou worried and bearest pain / Only for temporal good?)

The alto's (heart's) answer is that she is poor and oppressed by heavy cares. From evening until morning she feels deep distress. Who will release her from this evil world? She wishes to be dead.

The chorale verse continues: "Vertrau' du deinem Herren Gott, / Der alle Ding' erschaffen hat." (Trust in thy Lord God, / Who has created all things.)

2. *Recitative—bass.* His lamentation is a development of the alto's recitative. He feels that the Lord despises him in His anger. Consequently he has lost all confidence in himself, because his sighs and tears interfere with his work performance.

This number runs into the next without any pause.

3. *Chorale and Recitative—soprano, alto.* The choir sings the second chorale stanza, repeating its last two lines after the soprano and the alto recitatives. "Er kann und will dich lassen nicht, / Er weiss gar wohl, was dir gebricht, / Himmel und Erd' ist sein!" (He can and will not leave thee, / He knows quite well thy needs. / Heaven and earth is His!)

The soprano's text (the reply of the heart) refers to verse 26 of the Gospel, which states that God cares for cattle and birds, but she is unsure of His providing for her.

The last two lines of the chorale stanza are now sung by the choir: "Dein Vater und dein Herre Gott, / Der dir besteht in aller Not." (Thy Father and thy Lord God, / Who supports thee in all need.)

The alto continues with the heart's reply: she feels forsaken and hated by God because of her poverty. Even if God means well by her, her financial worries oppress her every day. Who will then stand by her?

The answer comes in the choir's repetition of the above last two lines; at this point the dialogue finishes.

4. *Recitative—tenor.* The morose theme of the previous numbers now changes to joyous faith, which continues throughout the rest of the cantata. In secco, he states that he finds comfort only if God will not leave or neglect him. The world may hate him, but he will cast his cares on the Lord; He will help him, if not today, then tomorrow. So he will lay his worries under his pillow, knowing that God will sustain him (as the bass will sing in the following aria.)

5. *Aria—bass.* This aria, accompanied by strings, follows the preceding recitative without break. It is the only aria in this cantata and, considered with the concluding chorale, one of its two best

numbers: "Auf Gott steht meine Zuversicht, / Mein Glaube lässt ihn walten. / Nun kann mich keine Sorge nagen, / Nun kann mich auch kein Armut plagen. / Auch mitten in dem grössten Leide / Bleibt er mein Vater, meine Freude, / Er will mich wunderlich erhalten." (On God stands my confidence; / My faith lets Him rule. / Now no care can gnaw me, / Now, too, can no poverty torment me. / Even in the midst of the greatest pain, / He remains my Father, my joy. / He will sustain me wonderfully.)

Bach used the melody of this aria also in the *Gratias agimus* movement of his *Short Mass in G major.*

6. *Recitative—alto.* This is a very short, secco number, in which she bids farewell to all her cares and may now live in peace, as though she were in heaven.

7. *Chorale.* This tutti performance of the third stanza of the hymn is the highlight of this cantata, of a quality to make the listener regret that it is so short. Absolute trust in God to comfort us in our misery on earth is beautifully expressed in words and sound: "Weil du mein Gott und Vater bist, / Dein Kind wirst du verlassen nicht, / Du väterliches Herz! / Ich bin ein armer Erdenkloss, / Auf Erden weiss ich keinen Trost." (Because Thou art my God and Father, / Thou wilt not leave Thy child, / Thou Fatherly heart! / I am a poor clod of earth; / On earth I know no comfort.)

Apart from the merit of the splendid bass aria and the impressive final chorale, this cantata has little to recommend it. The experiment of mixing parts of chorale verses with recitative as a form of dialogue does not give the listener a clear impression of the cantata as a whole. The lengthy recitatives and the scarcity of arias also detract from the work.

• **Ach, lieben Christen, seid getrost (Ah, Dear Christians, Be Comforted)** (c. 1740; BWV 114).

An unknown librettist arranged this hymn by Johannes Gigas for Bach's chorale cantata on the seventeenth Sunday after Trinity. Verses one, three and six are set in their original form for numbers one, four and seven of the cantata, and the other verses are paraphrased for the intervening numbers. The poem has no direct connection with the Scriptures prescribed for this Sunday, apart from a Gospel reference in the bass recitative. It simply admonishes the Christian for his sins and advises him to patiently bear the punishment they bring, so that Christ will redeem him now and console him in his hour of death.

Bach's music draws deep emotion and some picturesque imagery from this text. The result is a very fine cantata.

The soli are SATB, with a four-part chorus. The instruments are two oboes, a flute, two violins, a viola and continuo in which a horn is added for the first and last numbers.

1. *Chorus.* A striking joy-motif permeates this chorale fantasia, based on the melody of the anonymous "Wo Gott der Herr nicht bei uns hält" (Where God, the Lord, Does Not Hold with Us). The orchestral prelude, repeated in the ritornelli, sets the scene for the vocal entries singing the lines in imitation. There is a tear-motif on "verzagen" (despair), but otherwise only joyful encouragement in their voices and their accompaniment: "Ach, lieben Christen, seid getrost, / Wie tut ihr so verzagen! / Weil uns der Herr heimsuchen tut, / Lasst uns von Herzen sagen: / Die Straf' wir wohl verdienet han, / Solchs muss bekennen jedermann, / Niemand darf sich ausschliessen." (Ah, dear Christians, be comforted, / How you do so despair! / Because the Lord punishes us, / Let us say from our heart: / We have well deserved the punishment, / Such must everyone admit; / Nobody may exclude himself.)

This is an outstanding chorale fantasia.

2. *Aria—tenor.* The solo transverse flute obbligato contrasts the emotions felt by a pilgrim in the two parts of the text. First he is wandering in weary disconsolation through a gloomy valley, and then he turns to Jesus for comfort,

his grief-motif changing to a joy-motif. His repetition of the last four words, "weder aus noch ein" (an idiom for "which way to turn"—literally, neither out nor in) marks his bewilderment at the beginning and leads back to the da capo.

"Wo wird in diesem Jammertale / Für meinen Geist die Zuflucht sein? / Allein zu Jesu Vaterhänden / Will ich mich in der Schwachheit wenden; / Sonst weiss ich weder aus noch ein." (Where will be in this valley of lament / The refuge for my soul? / Only to the Father-hands of Jesus / Will I turn in my weakness. / Otherwise I don't know which way to turn.)

3. *Recitative—bass.* His secco narration mentions how Christ healed the man sick with dropsy, Luke 14 (1–4), in the Gospel for this Sunday. The librettist, however, refers to this illness as the dropsy of sin. To be cured, the sinner must bear his guilt with patience and prepare himself for death, when his innocence will be restored.

4. *Chorale—soprano.* She sings this third verse of the hymn accompanied by continuo only. The transformation of our body through death is metaphorically compared to the sprouting of grains of wheat when they are buried in the earth (John 12 [24]). Bach's short, quavering rhythm in the continuo portrays the action of sowing wheat throughout the number: "Kein Frucht das Weizenkörnlein bringt, / Es fall denn in die Erden; / So muss auch unser irdischer Leib / Zu Staub und Aschen werden, / Eh' er kömmet zu der Herrlichkeit, / Die du, Herr Christ, uns hast bereit' / Durch deinen Gang zum Vater." (The little grain of wheat brings no fruit, / Unless it falls into the earth; / So, too, must our earthly body / Become dust and ashes, / Before it comes to the glory, / That Thou, Lord Christ, hast prepared for us / Through Thy going to the Father.)

5. *Aria—alto.* This splendid aria, joyfully accompanied by an oboe and strings, radiates confidence in our transfiguration through death. The last three words, "verklärt und rein," (transfigured and pure), summarize the perfection that awaits us after inevitable death. This aria and the opening chorus contain profound emotion. Bach's mysticism is involved in the musical setting of this aria, which contrasts with the pictorial quality of the preceding number: "Du machst, o Tod, mir nicht ferner bange, / Wenn ich durch die Freiheit nur erlange, / Es muss ja so einmal gestorben sein. / Mit Simeon will ich in Friede fahren, / Mein Heiland will mich in der Gruft bewahren / Und ruft mich einst zu sich verklärt und rein." (Thou, O death, makest me no longer anxious, / If only I attain my freedom through thee. / One must certainly die some day. / With Simeon I will go in peace. / My Savior will preserve me in the vault / And call me to Himself one day, transfigured and pure.)

6. *Recitative—tenor.* This short, secco recitative advises us to think about our soul, which we will return to God, together with our body. God will care for us, watch over us and give us His love all our lives and even after we die.

7. *Chorale.* It seems that all Christians express their confidence in this tutti performance of the hymn's sixth stanza, which is plainly sung, but with the same sincere emotion as in the other numbers: "Wir wachen oder schlafen ein, / So sind wir doch des Herren; / Auf Christum wir getaufet sein, / Der kann dem Satan wehren, / Durch Adam auf uns kömmt der Tod, / Christus hilft uns aus aller Not, / Drum loben wir den Herren." (Whether we wake or fall asleep, / So we are still the Lord's. / In Christ we are baptized. / He can protect us from Satan. / Through Adam, death comes upon us. / Christ helps us out of all distress. / Therefore we praise the Lord.)

This is an excellent cantata. Bach's musical settings fit the thought of both punishment for sin and consolation in the redemption following atonement.

• **Herr Christ, der ein'ge Gottessohn (Lord Christ, the Only Son of God)** (c. 1740; BWV 96).

Elisabeth Kreuziger was the poet for the hymn, upon which the libretto for this eighteenth Sunday after Trinity was arranged for Bach's chorale cantata. Stanzas one and five are set in their original form for the opening chorus and the concluding chorale verse, respectively. The other verses are paraphrased by the unknown poet for the recitativi and arias.

Matthew 22 (34–46) is referred to in the first recitative for alto: Christ confuses the Pharisees by calling Himself the Son of David (verses 41–46).

The cantata's main thought is that Christ is the only Son of God, whose love will enter our souls to guide us; we may then return His love and thus gain entry into heaven.

The soli are SATB, with a four-part chorus. The orchestra has a transverse flute, a piccolo flute, a piccolo violin, two oboes, two violins, with a horn and a trombone in the continuo.

1. *Chorus.* This must surely be one of the most beautiful fantasias that Bach ever wrote. Unison playing of the piccolo flute and piccolo violin in semiquavers persists throughout, with charming flourishes after each line sung by the choir. The altos have the cantus firmus, preceding the imitative entry of the other vocal parts.

From its ethereal melody in the orchestral prelude to its radiant conclusion in the soprano voices at the end, this exquisite number gives a vision of celestial beauty with the imagery of Christ as the morning star. Words cannot adequately describe the wonder of this mystic moment with Bach, as he portrays his Savior: "Herr Christ, der ein'ge Gottessohn, / Vaters in Ewigkeit, / Aus seinem Herzen entsprossen, / Gleichwie geschrieben steht. / Er ist der Morgensterne, / Sein' Glanz streckt er so ferne / Vor andern Sternen klar." (Lord Christ, the only Son of God, / Of the Father in eternity, / Sprung from His heart, / Just as it stands written. / He is the Morning Star, / He extends His gleam so far / As to be clear from other stars.)

The piccolo instruments, imitating the tune of shepherds' pipes, endow this pastoral melody with enchanting realism.

2. *Recitative—alto.* Her secco narrative describes the power of God's love in sending His Son to bless us, to open heaven and close hell for us. Her text refers to the Gospel when she mentions that David in his spirit had already honored Christ. God had chosen a chaste woman to be His mother.

3. *Aria—tenor.* The obbligato solo transverse flute seems to depict a motion of pulling that the first line suggested to Bach. In the rest of the aria, its semiquavers play a joy-motif representing the "holy flames" of love as stated in the text: "Ach ziehe die Seele mit Seilen der Liebe, / O Jesu, ach zeige dich kräftig in ihr! / Erleuchte sie, dass sie dich gläubig erkenne, / Gib, dass sie mit heiligen Flammen entbrenne, / Ach wirke ein gläubiges Dürsten nach dir!" (Ah, draw the soul with cords of love, / O Jesus, ah, show Thyself strong in it! / Illuminate it, to recognize Thee in faith, / Grant it to be consumed with holy flames, / Ah, create a believing thirst for Thee!)

4. *Recitative—soprano.* This secco number is a prayer to God to guide her in the right way, because she is unenlightened in her soul and therefore errs often in her flesh. If He will go by her side, her way will certainly lead her to heaven.

5. *Aria—bass.* Oboes and strings play a wavering melody that the first two lines of this text suggested to Bach. His irresolution is painted in very picturesque imagery in the step-motif of the rhythm. Then the pictorial idea changes to one of confident trust in the Lord's leadership, whereupon the instrumental melody conforms but maintains the step-motif, now with a feeling of decided confidence: "Bald zur Rechten, bald zur Linken / Lenkt sich mein verirrter Schritt. / Gehe doch, mein Heiland, mit, / Lass mich in Gefahr nicht sinken, / Lass mich ja dein weises Führen / Bis zur Himmelspforte spüren!" (Now to the right, now to the left, / My erring step turns.

Go then, my Savior, with me. / Let me not sink into danger; / Let me follow Thy wise leading / Up to the portal of heaven!)

6. *Chorale.* All voices with strings sing a simple version of this fifth verse of the chorale. Bach had previously set an ornate version of this for the conclusion of BWV 22, and plainly as here for BWV 132 and BWV 164. In all cases it fits the ideas expressed in the preceding numbers of each work. See p. 30 for a translation of the first four lines of this verse. The remaining three lines are: "Wohl hier auf dieser Erden, / Den Sinn und all Begierden / Und G'danken hab'n zu dir." ([May the new man live] Well here on this earth, / And have his mind and all desires / And thoughts turned to Thee.)

• **Herr Gott, dich loben alle wir (Lord God, We All Praise Thee)** (c. 1740; BWV 130).

For the Feast of St. Michael, this is Bach's last complete extant cantata. It follows BWV 19 and BWV 149 in having its libretto derived from Revelation 12 (7–12)—Michael vanquishes Satan and his hosts and casts them out of heaven. The unknown librettist took Paul Eber's hymn for this Sunday, retained verses one, eleven and twelve for the opening and closing chorales, and paraphrased the other verses for his poem.

This chorale cantata praises God for creating angels to protect us from the wiles of Satan.

The soli are SATB, with a four-part chorus. The orchestra has three trumpets, timpani, a transverse flute, three oboes, two violins, a viola and continuo.

1. *Chorale.* This choral and instrumental fantasia resembles a song of thanksgiving to God after a victory, yet has a superimposed theme which depicts the battle itself in the melody. Sparkling trumpet flourishes and the rhythmic boom of drums portray a triumphant march after the battle. All instruments play this theme as a prelude and after the choir has completely sung the stanza, as well as in the ritornelli after each line. The cantus firmus is given to the sopranos, while the other parts enter in imitation for each line: "Herr Gott, dich loben alle wir / Und sollen billig danken dir / Für dein Geschöpf der Engel schon, / Die um dich schweb'n um deinen Thron." (Lord God, we all praise Thee / And should justly thank Thee / For Thy creation of angels, / Who hover around Thee and around Thy throne.)

2. *Recitative—alto.* She describes the angels as heroes, sent by God to protect the poor little flock of believers from Satan's fury, just as they protected Christ.

3. *Aria—bass.* The three trumpets and timpani support his vocal lines without obscuring them. Bach thus produces a vivid tone-painting of Satan at work. The rhythm in the vocal delivery and in the melody represents the incessant battle against the plots of the devil: "Der alte Drache brennt vor Neid / Und dichtet stets auf neues Leid, / Dass er das kleine Häuflein trennet. / Er tilgte gern, was Gottes ist, / Bald braucht er List, / Weil er nicht Rast noch Ruhe kennet." (The old dragon burns with envy / And always invents new misery, / To separate the little flock. / He would gladly erase what is God's. / He soon uses cunning, / Because he does not know rest or repose.)

4. *Recitative (Duet)—soprano, tenor.* This is the first time in his extant cantatas that Bach has set a recitative for duet, and he does it very well, with the two voices singing in beautiful imitation. The protective role of the angels is mentioned in their text—two parts of the Old Testament, Daniel 6 (16) and 3 (1–30): "Wohl aber uns, dass Tag und Nacht / Die Schar der Engel wacht, / Des Satans Anschlag zu zerstören! / Ein Daniel, so unter Löwen sitzt, / Erfährt, wie ihn die Hand des Engels schützt. / Wenn dort die Glut / In Babels Ofen keinen Schaden tut, / So lassen Gläubige ein Danklied hören. / So stellt sich in Gefahr / Noch jetzt der Engel Hilfe dar." (Well

for us, that day and night / The host of angels watches, / To destroy Satan's attack! / A Daniel, who sits among lions, / Experiences how the angel's hand protects him. / When the glow there / In Babylon's furnace does him no harm, / So let believers hear a song of thanks. / Thus is shown in danger / Even now the help of angels.)

5. *Aria—tenor.* The accompanying transverse flute obbligato plays a gavotte-like tune with a joy-motif reminiscent of the pastoral fields of heaven. We can imagine the Prince of angels surrounded by the angelic host and wish that we too, as believers, may likewise be conveyed to Him by the chariot of Elias: "Lass, o Fürst der Cherubinen, / Dieser Helden hohe Schar / Immerdar / Deine Gläubigen bedienen; / Lass sie auf Elias Wagen / Sie zu dir gen Himmel tragen!" (Let, O Prince of the Cherubim, / The high host of these heroes / Always / Serve Thy believers; / Let them [the angels] in Elias's chariot / Carry them [the believers] up to Thee in heaven!)

6. *Chorale.* Stanzas 11 and 12 of the chorale are performed tutti, with trumpet flourishes at the end of each line sung. The eleventh stanza praises and thanks God for the assistance given us by the angels. The twelfth stanza prays that He may always be ready to bid His angels protect His flock, so that they will realize the value of His promised word.

• **Ich elender Mensch, wer wird mich erlösen (I Wretched Man, Who Will Deliver Me)** (c. 1740; BWV 48).

It seems that Bach paused in composing chorale cantatas on a single hymn when he set this cantata for the nineteenth Sunday after Trinity. Neumann gives its date about 1732, and Terry suggests that the unknown librettist could have been Picander.

The Gospel for this Sunday is Matthew 9 (1–8), Jesus heals the palsy-afflicted man by forgiving him his sins. From this Scripture is derived the message of this libretto: that Christ's forgiveness for our sins will heal us in body and in soul.

Bach sets two different hymns: one for the opening and closing numbers, and the other quoted for the third movement.

There are only two soloists, AT, but there is the usual four-part chorus.

The orchestra has a trumpet, two oboes, two violins, a viola and continuo.

1. *Chorus with Chorale.* The chorale tune, "Herr Jesu Christ, ich schrei' zu dir" (Lord Jesus Christ, I Cry to Thee), is played by strings only for the opening ritornello, into which the trumpet and unison oboes enter in canon as the sopranos and altos begin to sing, also in canon. Bach gives their voices a tear-motif suited to their text, Romans 7 (24), which is quoted. The whole choir voices the lament of the palsy-stricken man, who represents all mankind suffering with disease of body or soul: "Ich elender Mensch, wer wird mich erlösen vom Leibe dieses Todes?" (I wretched man, who will deliver me from the body of this death?)

Bach creates a stupendous chorus even out of such a short verse.

2. *Recitative—alto.* The accompanying strings lend an atmosphere of gloom to this description of her suffering. She complains about her bodily pain caused by her sins. The world for her has become a house of sickness and death; her body must carry its torment to the grave. Yet her soul, feeling the strongest poison, will utter a burning sigh at the hour of her death.

3. *Chorale.* Repentance and atonement are advised in this fourth stanza of the hymn, "Ach Gott und Herr" (Ah, God and Lord) by Martin Rutilius, sung by all voices to an anonymous tune. Their text seems to fit the thoughts of the palsied man at the moment of his being restored to health, or those of the congregation listening: "Soll's ja so sein, / Dass Straf' und Pein / Auf Sünde folgen müssen, / So fahr' hie fort / Und schone dort / Und lass mich hie wohl büssen." (It should certainly be so, / That punishment and pain / Must follow after sin. /

So continue here / And spare there / And let me here well atone.)

4. *Aria—alto.* A solo oboe plays a joy-motif to illustrate the happiness of the new person after the cure. Her soul has been cleansed and is now ready for a new, holy life: "Ach lege das Sodom der sündlichen Glieder, / Wofern es dein Wille, zerstöret darnieder! / Nur schone der Seele und mache sie rein, / Um vor dir ein heiliges Zion zu sein." (Ah lay down the Sodom of sinful limbs, / As Thou wilt, destroyed down there! / Only spare the soul and make it clean, / In order that it be a holy Zion for Thee.)

5. *Recitative—tenor.* He describes, in secco, the Savior's power to heal even among the dead. Although our souls and bodies appear dead, He can revive them through His wondrous strength.

6. *Aria—tenor.* This magnificent aria, featuring a violin and oboe in unison with string accompaniment, is the most melodious and emotionally charged number in this cantata. It has a beautiful joy-motif in its swinging dance-like rhythm that enhances the fervent feeling of his text. We see an image of his soul dancing in ecstasy after it has been freed from sin: "Vergibt mir Jesus meine Sünden, / So wird mir Leib und Seel' gesund. / Er kann die Toten lebend machen / Und zeigt sich kräftig in den Schwachen. / Er hält den längst geschlossnen Bund, / Dass wir im Glauben Hilfe finden." (If Jesus forgives me my sins, / Then my body and soul become healthy. / He can make the dead living / And shows Himself powerful in the weak. / He keeps the long-concluded bond, / That we find help in faith.)

7. *Chorale.* Stanza 12 of the chorale for the opening chorus is now performed tutti, whereas before, it was played only by the instruments as the cantus firmus. This verse is a prayer to Christ that He will end the pain in our hearts, and to God that He will do with us as He pleases, since we are and will remain His.

• **Schmücke dich, o liebe Seele (Adorn Thyself, O Dear Soul)** (c. 1740; BWV 180).

This chorale cantata for the twentieth Sunday after Trinity is based on a hymn by Johann Franck, arranged by an unknown librettist. The hymn and his poem reflect the Gospel for this Sunday, Matthew 22 (1–14), the parable of the wedding of the king's son, but emphasize the sacrament of communion derived from the Scripture used for this particular libretto.

No fears, warnings or threats of pain and punishment occur; every number expresses the divine serenity of the Eucharist and its symbolic significance. Bach's setting contains all the mystical joy that he feels when he associates his soul with Christ, the Bridegroom, at the heavenly banquet.

Stanzas one, four and nine of the hymn are retained unchanged for numbers one, three and seven; the others are paraphrased.

The soli are SATB, with a four-part chorus. The instruments are two recorders, two transverse flutes, an oboe, an oboe da caccia (English horn), a violoncello piccolo, two violins, a viola and continuo.

1. *Chorus.* Bach's fantasia on the first verse of this hymn has a melody of a pastoral lullaby, played by the recorders, oboes and strings. Its sedate beauty begins with the orchestral introduction, repeated in the ritornello at the end. When the voices enter, the sopranos carry the cantus firmus, while the other parts sing the lines in imitation.

We can visualize the happiness of the soul as she joins the Bridegroom in mystic union. She will be beautifully dressed, now that she has shed the darkness of sin: "Schmücke dich, o liebe Seele, / Lass die dunkle Sündenhöhle, / Komm ans helle Licht gegangen, / Fange herrlich an zu prangen; / Denn der Herr voll Heil und Gnaden / Lässt dich itzt zu Gaste laden. / Der den Himmel kann verwalten, / Will selbst Herberg' in dir halten." (Adorn thyself, oh dear soul. /

Leave the dark hole of sin, / Come into the bright light, / Begin to sparkle splendidly; / For the Lord, full of salvation and mercy, / Has you now invited as a guest. / He, who can rule heaven, / Wants Himself to take lodging in you.)

2. *Aria—tenor.* The obbligato transverse flute provides a joyful sparkle to this aria, which encourages the soul to admit the Lord into itself. Here her emotions are described, whereas it was her raiment in the opening chorus. There is also a feeling of excited anticipation in the joy-motif of voice and melody: "Ermuntre dich, dein Heiland klopft, / Ach, öffne bald die Herzenspforte! / Ob du gleich in entzückter Lust / Nur halb gebrochne Freudenworte / Zu deinem Jesu sagen musst." (Arouse thyself: thy Savior knocks, / Ah, open soon the gates of thy heart! / Whether thou immediately in delighted joy / Only half broken words of happiness / Must say to thy Jesus.)

3. *Recitative and Arioso—soprano.* Before she sings the chorale verse, she gives her recitative in secco, which compares the precious gifts of the heavenly meal with the useless trifles offered by the world. She says that a child of God will want His treasure and will say (this arioso is the fourth verse of the chorale): "Ach, wie hungert mein Gemüte, / Menschenfreund, nach deiner Güte! / Ach, wie pfleg' ich oft mit Tränen / Mich nach dieser Kost zu sehnen! / Ach, wie pfleget mich zu dürsten / Nach dem Trank des Lebensfürsten! / Wünsche stets, dass mein' Gebeine / Sich durch Gott mit Gott vereine." (Ah, how my mind hungers, / Friend of man, for Thy goodness! / Ah, how often with tears am I accustomed / To long for this food! / Ah, how I am used to thirst / For the drink of the Prince of life! / I constantly wish that my bones / May join through God with God.)

This arioso is accompanied by the violoncello piccolo to illustrate the longing she expresses.

4. *Recitative—alto.* The two transverse flutes denote the joy-motif indicated by the text, at first moderately because it is tinged with fear, then growing in intensity for the last half of her narration. She declares that her heart feels fear when it considers the secret of God's work, which her reason cannot explain. Our belief in God's word, however, will strengthen the joy in our soul when we perceive how great is the love for us in the Savior's heart.

5. *Aria—soprano.* Bach's setting of this aria is extraordinary. All the instruments used in the opening chorus, except one oboe and the viola, support her song. He has not done this for any aria heretofore, thus showing the importance he placed on it. As the instruments play this superlative joy-motif, they inject little shafts of light to illustrate her song. The first two lines of her text must have really inspired Bach, as this wonderful composition testifies with its da capo. The second part has a change of melody to suit the fervent prayer that she expresses: "Lebens Sonne, Licht der Sinnen, / Herr, der du mein alles bist! / Du wirst meine Treue sehen / Und den Glauben nicht verschmähen / Der noch schwach und furchtsam ist." (Sun of life, Light of the senses, / Lord, Thou who art my all! / Thou wilt see my fidelity / And not disdain my belief / Which is still weak and fearful.)

This aria is second to none in all of Bach's sacred cantatas.

6. *Recitative—bass.* This is a further prayer, in secco, to Christ, asking that the love which caused Him to come from heaven to earth be not bestowed upon him in vain. May the Lord kindle a similar love in his spirit in return.

7. *Chorale.* The instrumentation is not stated for this quoted ninth stanza of the hymn. Accordingly, it is sung tutti by the choir in the plain version with which the whole congregation was familiar. This is usual for the last chorale stanza in Bach's chorale cantatas. It is a beautiful Communion prayer: "Jesu, wahres Brot des Lebens, / Hilf, dass ich doch nicht vergebens / Oder mir vielleicht zum Schaden / Sei zu deinem Tisch geladen.

Lass mich durch dies Seelenessen / Deine Liebe recht ermessen / Dass ich auch, itzt auf Erden, / Mög' ein Gast im Himmel werden." (Jesus, true Bread of life, / Help that I not in vain / Or perhaps to my harm / Be invited to Thy table. / Let me through this meal of the soul / Rightly measure Thy love / So that I too, now on earth, / May become a guest in heaven.)

• **Aus tiefer Not schrei ich zu dir (Out of Deep Distress I Cry to Thee)** (c. 1740; BWV 38).

This chorale cantata for the twenty-first Sunday after Trinity has its libretto based on Luther's hymn of this title, which was sung at Luther's funeral—Psalm 130, *De Profundis,* in his German translation.

The unknown librettist refers to the Gospel, John 4 (47–54)—Jesus heals a nobleman's son—in the fourth number but quotes the first and the fifth stanzas of Luther's hymn for the opening chorus and for the final chorale. All the intervening stanzas are paraphrased.

The soli are SATB, with a four-part chorus. The orchestra consists of four trombones, two oboes, two violins, a viola and basso continuo which includes a bassoon, a violoncello, a violone and organ.

1. *Chorus.* Bach sets this melody in the style of a Pachelbel motet, which would be familiar to his Lutheran congregation. Without any instrumental prelude, the basses begin to sing a fugue accompanied by the full orchestra. The other voices follow in turn to begin each of the following lines in canon. The rhythm of solemnity portrays a serious mood, appropriate for the supplication in the text.

This chorale fantasia, with its direct appeal for God's help in times of distress, sets the emotional stage for all subsequent numbers: "Aus tiefer Not schrei' ich zu dir, / Herr Gott, erhör' mein Rufen; / Dein gnädig Ohr neig' her zu mir / Und meiner Bitt' sie öffne! / Denn so du willt das sehen an, / Was Sünd' und Unrecht ist getan, / Wer kann, Herr, vor dir bleiben?" (Out of deep distress I cry to Thee. / Lord God, hear my calling; / Thy gracious ear turn to me / And open them to my pleading! / For as Thou wilt perceive / What sin and wrong is done, / Who can, Lord, remain before Thee?)

2. *Recitative—alto.* The violoncello and organ continuo support her explanation that comfort and forgiveness can only come from the Savior's mercy. Satan's deceit and cunning afflict the whole life of man. Our prayers will bring spiritual joys only if we believe in the wonderful works of Jesus.

3. *Aria—tenor.* The two oboes accompany this aria, the only one in the cantata. It is thought that Bach borrowed its melody from another unknown aria, because the declamation does not always conform with the tune: "Ich höre mitten in den Leiden / Ein Trostwort, so mein Jesus spricht. / Drum, o geängstigtes Gemüte, / Vertraue deines Gottes Güte, / Sein Wort besteht und fehlet nicht, / Sein Trost wird niemals von dir scheiden!" (I hear in the midst of sufferings / A word of comfort that my Jesus speaks. / Therefore, o anguished mind, / Trust in God's goodness. / His word remains and does not fail; / His comfort will never depart from thee!)

4. *Recitative with Chorale—soprano.* The chorale melody is played "a battuta" (in tempo) by the violoncello and the organ of the continuo during her declamation. This is the sole instance in any recitative where Bach uses this method. She laments that her belief is so weak that she feels it is built on damp ground. How can she not know her Helper, who rescues her from her misery, even though her faith is weak? She says that she must trust His almighty hand and the truth He speaks.

5. *Terzett (Trio)—soprano, alto, bass.* The only earlier trio in any cantata occurred in BWV 150, but Bach will use it again in BWV 122 and BWV 116 during this last period of cantata composition. As in the previous recitatives, this

number is accompanied only by the continuo's violoncello and organ, thus leaving the voices paramount in their singing. Its melody has a fine joy-motif which, with the canon singing of the trio, produces a miniature motet: "Wenn meine Trübsal als mit Ketten / Ein Unglück an dem andern hält, / So wird mich doch mein Heil erretten, / Dass alles plötzlich von mir fällt. / Wie bald erscheint des Trostes Morgen / Auf diese Nacht der Not und Sorgen!" (When my trouble as with chains / Holds one misfortune to the next, / Then my Savior will still rescue me, / So that everything falls suddenly from me. / How soon appears the morning of comfort / After this night of distress and worries!)

6. *Chorale.* The fifth stanza of Luther's chorale is here performed tutti, with the rhythm of solemnity as in the opening chorus, but ending on a note of confidence in the Lord's redeeming power: "Ob bei uns ist der Sünden viel, / Bei Gott ist viel mehr Gnade; / Sein' Hand zu helfen hat kein Ziel, / Wie gross auch sei der Schade. / Er ist allein der gute Hirt, / Der Israel erlösen wird / Aus seinen Sünden allen." (Whether there is much sinning with us, / With God is much more mercy; / His helping hand has no limit, / However great the harm may be. / He alone is the Good Shepherd, / Who will redeem Israel / From all its sins.)

• **Mache dich, mein Geist, bereit (Make Thyself, My Spirit, Ready)** (c. 1740; BWV 115).

For the twenty-second Sunday after Trinity, this chorale cantata's libretto abridges the ten stanzas of Johann Burchard Freystein's hymn into six numbers. Stanzas one and ten are set in their original form at the beginning and the end; the other stanzas are paraphrased with the exception of two lines of stanza seven quoted at the beginning of the soprano aria, number four.

The Gospel for this Sunday, Matthew 18 (23–35), the parable of the unforgiving servant, is not directly connected with the libretto, which deals more with the punishment for yielding to Satan.

The soli are SATB, with a four-part chorus. The orchestra has a transverse flute, an oboe d'amore, two violins, a viola, a violoncello piccolo, and continuo including a horn in the chorale numbers.

1. *Chorus.* The joy-motif in this tutti fantasia on an anonymous melody expresses determination to resist Satan's temptations. It has a surprisingly modern dance-like tempo that reminds the listener of a waltz. Beautiful trills by the transverse flute at the end of each line add a charming touch, even though the text is very serious: "Mache dich, mein Geist, bereit, / Wache, fleh' und bete, / Dass dich nicht die böse Zeit / Unverhofft betrete; / Denn es ist / Satans List / Über viele Frommen / Zur Versuchung kommen." (Make thyself, my spirit, ready, / Watch, beseech and pray, / That the evil time / Does not unexpectedly surprise thee; / For it is / Satan's cunning / Coming over many pious people / For their temptation.)

2. *Aria—alto.* The oboe d'amore, strings and continuo accompany this interesting aria, which depicts the deep sleep of the slumbering soul (adagio), then its waking for punishment (allegro), and finally its return to its ultimate sleep in death. The tempi for her voice and the instruments conform to the lines of her text. Bach uses very picturesque imagery to set these lines with realism: "Ach schläfrige Seele, wie? ruhest du noch? / Ermuntre dich doch! / Es möchte die Strafe dich plötzlich erwecken / Und, wo du nicht wachest, / Im Schlafe des ewigen Todes bedecken." (Ah sleepy soul, what? art thou resting still? / Rouse thyself then! / The punishment might suddenly wake thee / And, when thou art not watching, / Cover thee in the sleep of eternal death.)

3. *Recitative—bass.* In this long secco number, he states that God abhors the darkness of sin and will send His light of mercy to us, if our spirits will see it. Satan's guile is limitless when he plots to ensnare sinners, so if you break God's

mercy-pact, you cannot receive His help. The whole world and its inhabitants are false brothers, who wish to flatter themselves at the price of your flesh and blood.

4. *Aria—soprano.* The transverse flute, the violoncello piccolo and the continuo play a multo adagio tempo to accompany this beautiful number. Whereas the watch against sin has been the thought until now, here it is a prayer for God's patience and His pardon for past sins. As indicated above, the first two lines quote from the seventh stanza of the hymn, neatly connecting the ideas of praying and watching: "Bete aber auch dabei / Mitten in dem Wachen! / Bitte bei der grossen Schuld / Deinen Richter um Geduld, / Soll er dich von Sünden frei / Und gereinigt machen!" (But pray too therewith / In the midst of watching! / Ask, in your great guilt, / Your Judge for patience, / That He make you free of sins / And purified!)

5. *Recitative—tenor.* His shorter secco number describes God's response to our prayers. He listens to our crying and gives us His strength to sustain us when our enemies rejoice. His Son, through whom we pray, will come to us as our Helper, giving us courage and strength. He declaims the last line as arioso.

6. *Chorale* This tenth and last stanza of the hymn is plainly sung in Bach's usual setting of a straightforward presentation, familiar to the congregation. The thought expressed is that we should watch and pray because the time is near when God will destroy the world and judge us.

This is an excellent cantata despite the admonitions heard in every number. Bach's masterful settings make the listener forget the grim tone of the libretto.

• **Wohl dem, der sich auf seinen Gott (Well for Him, Who on His God)** c. 1740; BWV 139).

The unknown librettist for this chorale cantata on the twenty-third Sunday after Trinity based his poem on Johann Christoph Rübe's hymn of this title, but it has no allusion to either the Epistle or the Gospel for the day. He quoted stanzas one and five for the opening and the closing numbers, and paraphrased the others.

From Rübe's chorale, the librettist derived the thought of his poem: that we should seek God's friendship to obtain comfort and help in resisting Satan's sins.

The soli are SATB, with a four-part chorus. The instruments are two oboi d'amore, two violins, a viola, organ and continuo.

1. *Chorus.* The melody for this fantasia and for the final chorale stanza is Johann Hermann Schein's "Mach's mit mir, Gott, nach deiner Güt'" (Do with Me, God, According to Thy Goodness), which Bach decorates in his usual way with interesting instrumental combinations and canon singing by the choir. The sopranos begin the verse and the other parts follow each line in imitation: "Wohl dem, der sich auf seinen Gott / Recht kindlich kann verlassen! / Den mag gleich Sünde, Welt und Tod / Und alle Teufel hassen, / So bleibt er dennoch wohlvergnügt, / Wenn er nur Gott zum Freunde kriegt." (Well for him, who on his God / Can rely really childlike! / Him may even sin, world and death / And all devils hate. / Nevertheless, he remains well contented, / If he only obtains God as his friend.)

2. *Aria—tenor.* A solo violin concertante and organ continuo accompany his dramatic assertion that God is his friend (repeated emphatically at the beginning and in the da capo). Now he can defy the envy, hatred and mockery of his enemies: "Gott ist mein Freund; was hilft das Toben, / So wider mich ein Feind erhoben! / Ich bin getrost bei Neid und Hass. / Ja, redet nur die Wahrheit spärlich, / Seid immer falsch, was tut mir das? / Ihr Spötter seid mir ungefährlich." (God is my friend; what does rage help, / That an enemy has raised against me! / I am comforted in envy and hatred. / Yes, speak the truth only sparingly, / Be always false, what does that do to me? / You mockers are not dangerous to me.)

This aria is not exceptional; perhaps

because it is more declamatory than tuneful.

3. *Recitative—alto.* The only Biblical reference in this cantata, Matthew 10 (16), occurs in the first two lines of this secco number, where she says that the Lord sends His own into the midst of ravenous wolves. Around Him the horde of evil-doers are cunningly placed to harm and mock Him. Yet the Lord's mouth utters such a wise decision that He protects "me," too, from the world.

4. *Aria—bass.* Bach's mastery at setting aria texts is really evident in this number, accompanied by the two oboi d'amore, a violin and organ continuo. Bach creates a highly dramatic scene, as the soloist describes his misfortunes and how God helps him, by changing the tempo from tristezza to vivace and finally to andante, thus illustrating the successive grief- and joy-motives of the text. The first theme symbolizes his depression, the second (the third line) the helping hand of the Lord, and the third God's consoling light. The interplay of these three themes, with the da capo of the first two, analyzes his emotions in an impressive and picturesque style: "Das Unglück schlägt auf allen Seiten / Um mich ein zentnerschweres Band. / Doch plötzlich erscheinet die helfende Hand. / Mir scheint des Trostes Licht von weiten; / Da lern' ich erst, dass Gott allein / Der Menschen bester Freund muss sein." (Misfortune strikes on all sides / Around me a very heavy bond. / Yet suddenly appears the helping hand. / The light of comfort shines on me afar. / Only then I learn that God alone / Must be the best friend of man.)

5. *Recitative—soprano.* Strings and organ continuo accompany this statement of confidence in God as her friend. Even though she bears a heavy burden of sin within herself, her Savior will let her find rest. She will give her innermost soul to God; then, if He accepts it, the guilt of her sins and Satan's cunning will fall away from her.

6. *Chorale.* This is the fifth and last stanza of the chorale, simply performed tutti, with woodwinds and a violin doubling the soprano. The last line refers back to the beginning of the first chorale stanza and summarizes the thought of the preceding numbers: "Dahero Trotz der Höllen Heer! / Trotz auch des Todes Rachen! / Trotz aller Welt! mich kann nicht mehr / Ihr Pochen traurig machen! / Gott ist mein Schutz, mein' Hilf' und Rat; / Wohl dem, der Gott zum Freunde hat!" (Therefore, defiance to hell's army! / Defiance also to the jaws of death! / Defiance to all the world! their boasting / Can no more make me sad! / God is my Protector, my help and counsel; / Well for him, who has God for his friend!)

• **Ach wie flüchtig (Ah How Fleeting)** (c. 1740; BWV 26).

Many of Bach's chorale cantatas had their opening fantasias set on the organ preludes that he had previously composed. This one is derived from the same prelude in his *Orgelbüchlein,* composed about twenty years earlier.

Michael Franck was the author of this hymn for the twenty-fourth Sunday after Trinity, but the librettist for Bach's cantata is unknown. Stanzas one and thirteen are quoted for the outer numbers, while the others are paraphrased for the four inner numbers. There is no direct connection with the Epistle or the Gospel for this Sunday, but the thought may have been suggested by the Gospel, Matthew 9 (18–26), the raising to life of the ruler's daughter.

The libretto deals with the transitory nature of all earthly things and this subject is very agreeable to Bach, affording him scope for musical settings with splendid imagery.

The soli are SATB, with a four-part chorus. The orchestra consists of a transverse flute, three oboes, two violins, a viola and continuo including organ and a horn.

1. *Chorus.* Bach's fantasia paints a symbolic picture of mists drifting and dissolving like clouds in a valley, representing the brief life-span of man. A similar image of clouds, sailing across the

sky more majestically, is conjured up by the opening movement of his *Fourth Orchestral Suite,* which Bach will again use for the chorale fantasia which begins cantata BWV 110. Both of these cantata movements are marvelous examples of Bach's ability to create tone-poems.

"Ach wie flüchtig, ach wie nichtig / Ist der Menschen Leben! / Wie ein Nebel bald entstehet / Und auch wieder bald vergehet, / So ist unser Leben, sehet!" (Ah how fleeting, ah how transitory / Is man's life! / As a mist soon arises / And again soon disappears, / So is our life, behold!)

The choir sings the lines in unison, with imitation of their parts only in the second line.

2. *Aria—tenor.* Accompanied by the transverse flute and a solo violin, the tenor depicts the hasty flow of gushing water, which breaks over rocks before vanishing into the earth. This metaphor shows the rapid passing of our lives. Great virtuosity is demanded of the singer to cope with the speedy tempo of the first two lines. The remainder slows to represent the water drops, like time, running away: "So schnell ein rauschend Wasser schiesst, / So eilen unsers Lebens Tage. / Die Zeit vergeht, die Stunden eilen, / Wie sich die Tropfen plötzlich teilen, / Wenn alles in den Abgrund schiesst." (As quickly as rushing water shoots out, / So hasten the days of our life. / Time passes by, hours hurry along, / Just as drops suddenly divide, / When everything shoots into the abyss.)

3. *Recitative—alto.* The imagery continues, chiefly through contrast in the juxtaposed words in each line, italicized here. Organ and the continuo accompany her picturesque narrative: "Die *Freude* wird zur *Traurigkeit,* / Die *Schönheit* fällt als eine *Blume,* / Die grösste *Stärke* wird *geschwächt,* / Es *ändert sich* das *Glücke* mit der Zeit, / Bald *ist es aus* mit *Ehr' und Ruhme,* / Die *Wissenschaft,* und *was ein Mensche dichtet,* / Wird endlich durch das *Grab vernichtet.*" (*Joy* becomes *sadness.* / *Beauty* falls like a *flower.* / The greatest *strength* becomes *weakened.* / *Luck changes* with time. / Soon *it is over* with *honor and fame.* / *Knowledge* and *what a man invents,* / Is finally *exterminated* by the *grave.*)

4. *Aria—bass.* With unison oboes and organ continuo, he interprets the continuing visual details in this text remarkably well, especially those in the last three lines—"verzehrende Gluten," "wallenden Fluten," "in Trümmern zerfällt." Bach's melody has a pomposity reminiscent of some of Handel's arias, but there is no evidence of borrowing or imitating. Bach was merely illustrating the world's pomp and vanity as stated in the text: "An irdische Schätze das Herze zu hängen, / Ist eine Verführung der törichten Welt. / Wie leichtlich entstehen verzehrende Gluten, / Wie rauschen und reissen die wallenden Fluten, / Bis alles zerschmettert in Trümmern zerfällt." (To hang the heart on earthly treasures / Is a temptation of the foolish world. / How easily arise consuming flames, / How roar and tear boiling floods, / Until all is smashed and falls in ruins.)

5. *Recitative—soprano.* As in the alto recitative, this text also has a tendency to contrast ideas, but now in each pair of lines, instead of in each separate line. Accompanied by organ and continuo, she declaims the following thoughts in each pair of lines: (a) the highest splendor is enveloped finally by death's night; (b) whoever has sat like a god does not escape dust and ashes; (c) when his last hour strikes and he is carried to the earth, (d) and the foundation of his greatness breaks, he will be quite forgotten.

6. *Chorale.* This is a straightforward, tutti performance of the thirteenth and last stanza of the hymn, which reiterates the message expressed throughout the cantata and concludes on a note of hope: "Ach wie flüchtig, ach wie nichtig / Sind der Menschen Sachen! / Alles, alles, was wir sehen, / Das muss fallen und vergehen; / Wer Gott fürcht', bleibt ewig stehen." (Ah how fleeting, ah how invalid / Are the affairs of men! / All, all, that we see, / That must fall and

disappear; / Whoever fears God remains standing forever.)

Note that even this final number shows contrast between what and who will disappear and endure.

• Es reifet euch ein schrecklich Ende (There Ripens for You a Dreadful End) (c. 1740; BWV 90).

This solo cantata for the twenty-fifth Sunday after Trinity is by an unknown librettist who added other Biblical allusions to his text, which already reflects both this Sunday's Epistle and Gospel. The Epistle is 1 Thessalonians 4 (13–18), the resurrection of the living and the dead on Judgment Day; the Gospel is Matthew 24 (15–28), Jesus predicts the end of the world.

Before Bach, both Carissimi and Marc-Antoine Charpentier had composed cantatas on this awesome topic, and in Germany, Dietrich Buxtehude's oratorio consisting of five cantatas, *Das jüngste Gericht* (The Last Judgment), had appeared at the beginning of the eighteenth century. One might wonder whether Bach had heard this work in the Marienkirche in Lübeck as part of Buxtehude's *Abendmusik* during the time that he overstayed his leave from his position as organist in Arnstadt from October 1705 to February 1706. Certainly Bach's shorter cantata has all the forceful drama of the concluding cantata in Buxtehude's oratorio, although naturally in his own style.

The soli are ATB, with a four-part chorus for the final chorale. The instruments consist of a trumpet (only for the bass aria), two violins, a viola and continuo of violoncello, violone and organ.

1. *Aria—tenor.* Strings and continuo play a short prelude, before accompanying his denunciation of sinners in this dramatic number. The quavering melody depicts the sinners' fearful shuddering as they confront the wrath of their Judge whom they have forgotten. The da capo reinforces the impression of God's anger towards them.

It seems strange that the vocalist on my recording pronounces the verb in the first line, "reifet" (ripens), as "reisset" (pulls), just because modern libretto texts show this latter verb. Neumann suggests that "raffet" (sweeps away) was probably meant by the librettist, although he gives "reifet" as the verb in his own text too. But "hin" (motion)? Could this have been a printer's error?

"Es reifet [reisset] euch ein schrecklich Ende, / Ihr sündlichen Verächter, hin. / Der Sünden Mass ist voll gemessen, / Doch euer ganz verstockter Sinn / Hat seines Richters ganz vergessen." (There ripens [pulls you] for you a dreadful end, / You sinful scorners, there [thither]. / The measure of your sins is fully weighed; / Yet your very insensible mind / Has quite forgotten its Judge.)

2. *Recitative—alto.* She says that ingratitude for God's goodness towards us is a sin, which will lead to our perdition. Then she gives a paraphrase of Romans 2 (4): "Or despisest thou the riches of his goodness and forbearance and longsuffering; not knowing that the goodness of God leadeth thee to repentance?" God's innumerable good deeds can be seen in the erection of temples which spread the manna of His word. Our wickedness makes His benefits useless to us.

3. *Aria—bass.* The alto's didactic theme is continued in his declamation, portraying dramatically God's anger. Trumpet fanfares illustrate the two added paraphrases of Scripture denoting God's ire on Judgment Day: Revelation 2 (5) and Luke 19 (46): "So löschet im Eifer der rächende Richter / Den Leuchter des Wortes zur Strafe doch aus. / Ihr müsset, o Sünder, durch euer Verschulden / Den Greuel an heiliger Stätte erdulden, / Ihr machet aus Tempeln ein mörderisch Haus." (So the avenging Judge extinguishes in His zeal / The light of His word as a punishment. / You must, o sinners, through your guilt / Suffer for outraging the holy place. / You make of temples a murderous house.)

This aria paints a magnificent panorama of the terror on the Last Day.

4. *Recitative—tenor.* He imparts a ray of hope to the elect, whom Jesus will protect in that fateful day and also through their lives before that time. This is the only glimmer of light in this stern cantata. His secco declamation retains the dramatic tone of all the previous numbers. God's eye watches over His chosen and the Hero of Israel will help them resist their countless foes. The strength of His word becomes more evident in times of danger.

5. *Chorale.* This is stanza seven of Martin Moller's hymn, "Nimm von uns, Herr, du treuer Gott" (Take from Us, Lord, Thou True God), which is also the title of chorale cantata BWV 101. This number is set to the melody of Luther's German version of the Lord's Prayer; it is plainly sung, although the instrumentation is not stated. See p. 204 for a translation of this verse.

This is a grim cantata in its thought, but Bach's excellent musical setting focuses our attention on the sound rather than the dire message.

• **Nun komm, der Heiden Heiland (Now Come, Savior of the Heathen) II** (c. 1736–40; BWV 62).

Bach composed his first cantata, BWV 61, on this Advent hymn by Martin Luther at Weimar in 1714. This second chorale version, like its predecessor, also only indirectly refers to the Gospel for the first Sunday in Advent, Matthew 21 (1–9)—Christ's triumphal entry into Jerusalem on Palm Sunday—again out of season. The libretti of both cantatas are concerned with personal reflections on the meaning of the approaching birth of the Savior (cf. pp. 11–12).

The librettist is unknown, but it might have been Picander. Stanzas one and eight are quoted for the opening and closing numbers, and the intervening stanzas are paraphrased.

The soli are SATB, with a four-part chorus. The instruments are two oboes, two violins, a viola, and a horn in the continuo.

1. *Chorus.* There is an aura of mystery in this fantasia, intentionally painted by Bach's setting, to evoke the circumstances pertaining to the Virgin Birth. After the orchestral introduction, the sopranos begin to sing the melody, and the other parts follow each line in canon, with an angel-motif in the basses. The melody gives an impression of hushed reverence and a vision of eternal space, both associated with this miraculous event. This number is the best in the cantata.

For the text and a translation of this first verse of Luther's hymn, see p. 11.

2. *Aria—tenor.* All instruments except the horn accompany his exhortation that we should revere this Immaculate Conception. Mankind's quiet joy, upon beholding this wonder, is expressed by the rhythm. Bach maintains the tone of mystery in his setting of this text: "Bewundert, o Menschen, dies grosse Geheimnis: / Der höchste Beherrscher erscheinet der Welt. / Hier werden die Schätze des Himmels entdecket, / Hier wird uns ein göttliches Manna bestellt, / O Wunder! die Keuschheit wird gar nicht beflecket." (Marvel, o men, at this great mystery: / The highest Ruler appears to the world. / Here are revealed heaven's treasures. / Here is arranged divine manna for us. / O wonder! chastity is not at all tarnished.)

3. *Recitative—bass.* In secco, he describes Christ's mission to redeem us. God sends His only begotten Son to be the Hero of Judah by saving those who have fallen through sin. His last line is an arioso on the wondrous blessing that mankind receives thereby.

4. *Aria—bass.* Unison strings reinforce the idea of strength indicated by his text, which compares the strong Hero with the weakness of men. It is a prayer for Christ's leadership and His power to give us strength: "Streite, siege, starker Held! / Sei für uns im Fleische kräftig. / Sei geschäftig, / Das Vermögen in uns Schwachen / Stark zu machen!" (Fight, conquer, strong Hero! / Be for us mighty in the flesh. / Be active, / The capacity in us weak ones / To make strong!)

5. *Recitative (Duet)—soprano, alto.* Strings accompany their unison singing of each line in this unusual setting by Bach. The number is more duet than recitative, even though it lacks a da capo. It seems to be a song sung by two angels or by two children, as they behold the Infant in the manger. It is a beautiful Christmas carol: "Wir ehren diese Herrlichkeit / Und nahen nun zu deiner Krippen / Und preisen mit erfreuten Lippen, / Was du uns zubereit'; / Die Dunkelheit verstört' uns nicht / Wir sehen dein unendlich Licht." (We honor this glory, / And now come near Thy cradle, / And praise with joyful lips / What Thou hast prepared for us. / Darkness does not disturb us. / We see Thy unending light.)

6. *Chorale.* All voices and instruments perform this eighth stanza of Luther's hymn, the doxology: "Lob sei Gott, dem Vater, g'ton, / Lot sei Gott, sein'm ein'gen Sohn, / Lob sei Gott, dem heil'gen Geist, / Immer und in Ewigkeit." (Praise be done to God, the Father, / Praise be to God, His only Son, / Praise be to God, the Holy Ghost, / Always and in eternity.)

• **Gelobet seist du, Jesu Christ (Praised Be Thou, Jesus Christ)** (c. 1735–40; BWV 91).

This chorale cantata for Christmas Day could well have been the first of a series for Christmas week, all dating about this time. These are BWV 91, 57, 121, 151 and 122. If they are all in the same year, we would be reminded of the six cantatas that compose the *Christmas Oratorio* of 1734.

Luther's hymn of the above title was used by the unknown librettist (likely Picander). In his poem he quotes the first, second and seventh stanzas for the first, second and sixth numbers, and paraphrases the intervening ones.

Bach's setting for each number brings out all the joy of Christmas Day implied in Luther's hymn. The music is exceptionally beautiful.

The soli are SATB, with a four-part chorus. The orchestra consists of two horns, timpani, three oboes, two violins, a viola and continuo.

1. *Chorus.* This chorale fantasia gives the impression of regal majesty combined with great rejoicing. Horns and timpani accompany the melody, which the oboes and strings play in imitation of each other as the sopranos sing each line, also imitated by the other vocal parts. All lines are followed by instrumental ritornelli; the rhythm in the continuo indicates the Trinity for each line. It is a grand opening movement: "Gelobet seist du, Jesu Christ, / Dass du Mensch geboren bist / Von einer Jungfrau, das ist wahr, / Des freuet sich der Engel Schar. / Kyrie eleis!" (Praised be Thou, Jesus Christ, / That Thou hast been born Man / Of a Virgin; that is true. / Therefore the host of angels rejoices. / Kyrie eleis! [Lord, have mercy!])

2. *Chorale and Recitative—soprano.* Her narration is interspersed with the choir's singing of the second stanza of the hymn. Bach has used this alternating method before, not always successfully, but here it is well done.

She states, secco, that God has chosen the time and the place for the Birth of His Son.

The choir interpolates: The eternal Father's only Child.

She continues, saying that He is born as the eternal Light from Light.

CHORALE: Whom one now finds in the cradle.

SOPRANO: O men, see what the power of love has done,

CHORALE: In our poor flesh and blood.

SOPRANO: And was this then not accursed, condemned, lost?

CHORALE: Eternal goodness is hidden;

SOPRANO: Thus it is chosen as our blessing.

3. *Aria—tenor.* The three oboes accompany him with a rhythm of quiet solemnity, that gives his voice the tone of a soothing lullaby in the first half of his aria. The second part, however, has a touch of the didactic about it, before the cradle-song imagery returns in the da

capo: "Gott, dem der Erdenkreis zu klein, / Den weder Welt noch Himmel fassen, / Will in der engen Krippe sein. / Erscheinet uns dies ew'ge Licht, / So wird hinfüro Gott uns nicht / Als dieses Lichtes Kinder hassen." (God, for whom the earth's orbit is too small, / Whom neither world nor heaven contains, / Wishes to be in the narrow cradle. / If this eternal light appears to us, / Then henceforth God will not / Hate us as children of this light.)

4. *Recitative—bass.* Strings with the continuo accompany his apostrophe to Christendom. He asks us to be ready to receive our Creator. God's Son comes to us as a guest, showing His love, which we should reciprocate. He concludes with an arioso, stating that Christ comes to us for the purpose of leading us through this vale of tears to His throne.

5. *Duet—soprano, alto.* The dotted rhythm of solemnity recurs in the unison violin melody that accompanies their singing. This melody has a sort of echo effect in the first section, which beautifully depicts two angels singing in imitation of each other. Their imitative style continues in the second section, as they depict Christ's tribulations on earth, but this changes to a unison, florid joy-motif finally, to illustrate their text: "Die Armut, so Gott auf sich nimmt, / Hat uns ein ewig Heil bestimmt, / Den Uberfluss an Himmelsschätzen. / Sein menschlich Wesen machet euch / Den Engels-Herrlichkeiten gleich, / Euch zu der Engel Chor zu setzen." (The poverty that God assumes, / Has intended for us eternal salvation, / The over-abundance of heaven's treasures. / His human condition makes you / Equal to angels' glories, / To set you in the choir of angels.)

This is a memorable duo because of its exalted thought and artistic charm.

6. *Chorale.* This tutti performance of the last verse of Luther's hymn has the same royal splendor as the opening chorale fantasia, although it is shorter. Bach had previously used this same verse for the second number of BWV 64 (cf. p. 45), but there not with such lavish instrumentation: "Das hat er alles uns getan, / Sein' gross' Lieb' zu zeigen an. / Des freu' sich alle Christenheit / Und dank' ihm des in Ewigkeit. / Kyrieleis!" (All that He has done for us, / To show His great love. / For that may all Christendom rejoice / And thank Him for that in eternity. / Kyrie eleis! [Lord, have mercy!])

This is a wonderful chorale cantata, well balanced and with deep emotional impact. It is one of Bach's masterpieces.

• **Unser Mund sei voll Lachens (May Our Mouth Be Full of Laughter)** (1734–40; BWV 110).

It is difficult to determine the year in which this solo cantata for Christmas Day was composed. Terry gives about 1740; Whittaker says after 1734; Neumann hesitates between 1725 and 1731; Dürr states 1735 according to his later chronological research. Since we are following Terry's original order, the above date given by Whittaker seems probable.

The name of the librettist is unknown; both Christian Weiss, Sr., and Picander (see Schweitzer, Vol. II, p. 343) are suggested, as well as Bach himself.

Unlike BWV 91, the libretto does have a direct reference to the Gospel for Christmas Day, Luke 2 (1–14); verse 14 is quoted for the soprano-tenor duet. There are two other Biblical quotations used, apart from the Gospel.

Only one recitative appears; like all the other numbers except the alto aria, it is infused with the joy of Christmas and trust in God. Were it not for the unconforming aria, Bach's composition would be a magnificent tone-poem combining brilliant orchestral adaptation with vocal virtuosity.

The soli are SATB, with a four-part chorus. The orchestra is astounding: three trumpets, timpani, two transverse flutes, three oboes, a bassoon, two violins, a viola, organ and continuo.

1. *Chorus.* Bach's skill in adapting the entire first movement of his *4th D major Orchestral Suite (Overture),* BWV 1069, must be admired. This is a French-style

overture, with grave-allegro-grave sections; the choir sings only during the second allegro section, into which Bach fits their text most adroitly.

Like the opening chorus of BWV 26, the slow outer movements of this number seem to paint a picture of clouds floating serenely across the sky. This must be the composer's way of showing the atmosphere of majestic calm before and at the manger scene in Bethlehem. This repeated impression surrounds the outburst of unrestrained joy in the vocal allegro and sets a jubilant tone for the two following numbers. The melody of the second part fits the text of Psalm 126 (2, 3) perfectly, and the voices realistically depict merry laughter: "Unser Mund sei voll Lachens, und unsre Zunge voll Rühmens. Denn der Herr hat Grosses an uns getan." (May our mouth be full of laughter, and our tongue full of praising. For the Lord hath done great things for us.)

This outstanding chorus is in a class by itself among Bach's great achievements.

2. *Aria—tenor.* Flutes, bassoon, organ and continuo accompany his own expression of happiness, as he encourages his listeners to also appreciate God's gift of His Son to us. The joy-motif in his song and in the accompanying transverse flutes and bassoon is a fine interpretation of his text: "Ihr Gedanken und ihr Sinnen, / Schwinget euch anitzt von hinnen! / Steiget schleunig himmelan / Und bedenkt, was Gott getan! / Er wird Mensch, und dies allein, / Dass wir Himmelskinder sein." (You thoughts and meditations, / Lift yourselves now up from here! / Climb quickly heavenward / And consider what God has done! / He becomes Man, and this alone, / So that we may be children of heaven.)

3. *Recitative—bass.* Strings, with the organ and continuo, accompany his short prayer to the Lord, quoting Jeremiah 10 (6) and maintaining the joy-motif throughout: "Dir, Herr, ist niemand gleich, du bist gross, und dein Name ist gross, und kannst's mit der Tat beweisen." (Nobody is like unto Thee, Lord; Thou art great, and Thy name is great, and Thou canst prove it with Thy deed.)

4. *Aria—alto.* It seems strange that such a verse was written in an otherwise joyful libretto. Bach must have been puzzled as to how he should set it; the resultant music proves his dilemma in its varying tempi. The obbligato oboe d'amore plays a wailing melody during the first part, seemingly to depict the writhings of the worm as the text indicates. Only in the last two lines do we hear a slight tone of hope in the organ and continuo, but hardly in the vocal. As an aria, this number is uninspiring, and even the thought is confused at the end of this very peculiar text: "Ach Herr, was ist ein Menschenkind, / Dass du sein Heil so schmerzlich suchest? / Ein Wurm, den du verfluchest, / Wenn Höll' und Satan um ihn sind; / Doch auch dein Sohn, den (=wenn?) Seel' und Geist / Aus Liebe seinen Erben heisst." (Ah Lord, what is a child of man, / That Thou so painfully seekest his saving? / A worm, which Thou cursest, / When hell and Satan are around him, / But also Thy son, whom [when?] soul and spirit / Call [themselves?] His heir out of love.)

5. *Duet—soprano, tenor.* Bach borrowed the tune for this number from the interpolated section "Virga Jesse floruit" of his original *Magnificat* (BWV 243), transposing the bass voice to tenor. Their text is Luke 2 (14), dramatically sung as a dialogue by two angels instead of by the multitude of "a heavenly host" as the thirteenth verse states. Bach brings this angelic scene to life through their singing in canon with brilliant runs on "Friede" (peace) and "Wohlgefallen" (goodwill). Only organ and continuo accompany them: "Ehre sei Gott in der Höhe und Friede auf Erden und den Menschen ein Wohlgefallen!" (Glory be to God on high and peace on earth and good-will to men!)

6. *Aria—bass.* This stirring number begins with rousing trumpet flourishes in order to embellish the first melody, played by the woodwinds and the strings.

In the second half, the trumpet and oboes are silent because the soloist is addressing the strings. One can see how closely Bach was influenced by his text, as in this instance. Yet Bach retains the joy-motif of the first part throughout the aria: "Wacht auf! ihr Adern und ihr Glieder, / Und singt dergleichen Freudenlieder, / Die unserm Gott gefällig sein. / Und ihr, ihr andachtsvollen Saiten, / Sollt ihm ein solches Lob bereiten, / Dabei sich Herz und Geist erfreu'n." (Wake up! you veins and limbs, / And sing the same songs of joy, / That are pleasing to our God. / And you, you devout strings, / Should prepare for Him such praise, / In which heart and spirit rejoice.)

7. *Chorale.* A plain, tutti performance of Kaspar Füger's fifth stanza of his hymn "Wir Christenleut'" (We Christianfolk) provides a joyous, though brief, conclusion. The choir praises God for the joy He has given at the Nativity, which we will remember at all times.

• **Selig ist der Mann [Dialogus] (Blessed Is the Man [Dialogue])** (c. 1740; BWV 57).

For the Feast of St. Stephen, 26 December, Bach turned back to the solo dialogue cantata form, which he had not set for some time. Perhaps this was because the St. Thomas choir had been deteriorating during the six years after the *Christmas Oratorio* (see Whittaker, Vol. II, p. 153), so that Bach did not have the necessary choral forces available when he opted for this dialogue libretto.

The Epistle for the day, Acts 7 (54–59), the martyrdom of Stephen, is referred to in the text of the opening number quoting James 1 (12), and in the third recitative. The unknown librettist (possibly Picander) makes his text dramatic enough through dialogue between Jesus and the Soul, but it is difficult to see why Bach called his setting a "Concerto in Dialogo" in the score, unless he meant the concerto aspect of the vocal parts with the instruments as the ripieno—no different from any other of his cantatas. Yet it might be because of the alternating arias.

The moralizing tone is out of keeping with the joyous spirit of Christmas, but its music is very attractive nonetheless.

The soli are SB, with a four-part chorus. The orchestra has two oboes, a tenor oboe (taille), two violins, a viola, organ and continuo.

1. *Aria—bass* (JESUS). The bass plays the role of Jesus, and the soprano that of the Soul, throughout all numbers except the final chorale verse. Drama begins immediately in this lovely, profoundly moving aria, in which Christ utters the words of James 1 (12) pertaining to St. Stephen, the first Christian martyr. His accompaniment is unusual in that all instruments play; their melody begins with a tone of pathos, representing earthly suffering, and ends with a theme of assurance: "Selig ist der Mann, der die Anfechtung erduldet; denn, nachdem er bewähret ist, wird er die Krone des Lebens empfahen." (Blessed is the man, who endures temptation; for, after he is tried, he will receive the crown of life.)

2. *Recitative—soprano* (SOUL). She enumerates the troubles that beset her heart, if she does not find comfort in Jesus. This secco, picturesque narrative describes her pain as a worm in her blood; she must live as a sheep among a thousand wolves, submitting herself to their cruelty like Abel (cf. Matthew 23 [35]). Her heart would break if she had no comfort from Jesus, and she would say (her following aria):

3. *Aria—soprano.* Strings and continuo play a tear-motif to illustrate the pathos of her first two lines. This motif recurs in the second part to show her longing for His comfort, but now with a different melody, still with a grief theme: "Ich wünschte mir den Tod, / Wenn du, mein Jesu, mich nicht liebtest. / Ja wenn du mich annoch betrübtest, / So hätt' ich mehr als Höllennot." (I would wish death for myself, / If Thou, my Jesus, didst not love me. / Yes, if Thou saddened me still, / Then I would have more than hell's misery.)

4. *Recitative—soprano, bass.* This secco dialogue is composed of two statements: Jesus says that He will give her His comfort; she answers that she will accept His pledge of love, knowing that it will defend her against her enemies.

5. *Aria—bass.* It is unusual that Bach should have the same accompaniment for two consecutive arias—like number three, this aria has strings and continuo. The thought follows upon the end of the preceding recitative, assuring her of Jesus' support and comfort. Beginning with an emphatic outburst of defiance against His enemies, which the melody illustrates, the aria turns to beautiful vocal imagery to depict His consolation, breaking like the sun through dark clouds. This is an excellent aria because of its contrast of mood and melody in both parts: "Ja, ja, ich kann die Feinde schlagen, / Die dich nur stets bei mir verklagen, / Drum fasse dich, bedrängter Geist. / Bedrängter Geist, hör' auf zu weinen, / Die Sonne wird noch helle scheinen, / Die dir itzt Kummerwolken weist." (Yes, yes, I can strike enemies, / Who always accuse you to Me. / Therefore compose yourself, oppressed spirit. / Oppressed spirit, cease your weeping; / The sun will yet shine brightly, / Which now shows you clouds of worry.)

6. *Recitative (Dialogue—soprano, bass).* In this secco number, the first two lines are spoken by Jesus, and the remainder by the Soul. Jesus says that she will find rest in His bosom. She replies that she would like to be in her coffin, so that she could enter heaven like Stephen and be with her Lord.

7. *Aria—soprano.* Continuing her above wish for death to release her soul, she sings blissfully of her coming reunion with Christ. A solo violin obbligato with organ and continuo suggests a fluttering bird (the soul) as it wings its way up into Jesus' bosom. There is a constant joy-motif in both parts of the aria to depict this happy flight. There are no regrets or sadness in her desire for death; her flowery runs on "Freuden" (joy) and "Begier" (eagerness) emphasize this.

"Ich ende behende mein irdisches Leben, / Mit Freuden zu scheiden verlang' ich itzt eben. / Mein Heiland, ich sterbe mit höchster Begier, / Hier hast du die Seele, was schenkest du mir?" (I end swiftly my earthly life; / With joy to depart I desire right now. / My Savior, I die most eagerly; / Here Thou hast the soul, what givest Thou to me?)

Notice the peculiar repetition of "was" (what) in the last line.

8. *Chorale.* This tutti conclusion is stanza six of Ahasuerus Fritsch's hymn "Hast du denn, Jesu, dein Angesicht" (Hast Thou Then, Jesus, Thy Countenance). It seems that the choir is expressing Jesus' final reply to the Soul, thus keeping the dialogue effect even at the end of the cantata: "Richte dich, Liebste, nach meinem Gefallen und gläube, / Dass ich dein Seelenfreund immer und ewig verbleibe, / Der dich ergötzt / Und in den Himmel versetzt / Aus dem gemarterten Leibe." (Direct thyself, dearest, according to My pleasure and believe / That I remain thy soul's Friend always and eternally, / Who delights thee / And transfers thee into heaven / From thy tortured body.)

The spiritual love expressed by the words and music of this work is sure to captivate the listener. It is a love that transcends the grave and reveals Bach's own personal mysticism even more than one can perceive in his previous dialogue cantatas.

• **Christum wir sollen loben schon (Christ We Should Certainly Praise)** (c. 1735–40; BWV 121).

This chorale cantata was performed in 1735 according to Spitta, although both Whittaker and Terry say about 1740 and Dürr goes back to 1724. Irrespective of the exact date, it seems to belong to the period of Bach's mature style.

Like BWV 57, it is for the second day of Christmas, St. Stephen's Day, but is based on Luther's hymn of this title rather than on either the Epistle or Gospel for the day. Stanzas one and eight of the hymn are quoted by Picander, presumably the librettist, and the other verses are paraphrased for his poem. It is a magnificent setting by Bach, reflecting the joy of Christmas in every number. The opening chorus and the bass aria are outstanding.

The soli are SATB, with a four-part chorus as usual. The orchestra, however, is unusually impressive: a horn, an oboe d'amore, three trombones, two violins, a viola and continuo with organ therein.

1. *Chorus.* The melody for this excellent fantasia is adapted from the Latin Christmas hymn of Coelius Sedulius (c. 450), "A solis ortus cardine," which Bach sets in the Pachelbel motet style of the seventeenth century. All instruments are used to double the vocal parts. The horn and the trombones play in a rhythm of solemnity, while the voices in imitation sing each line of this majestic hymn of praise.

"Christum wir sollen loben schon, / Der reinen Magd Marien Sohn, / So weit die liebe Sonne leucht / Und an aller Welt Ende reicht." (Christ we should certainly praise, / Son of the pure Maid Mary, / As far as the dear sun shines / And reaches to the end of the whole world.)

2. *Aria—tenor.* This is a very tuneful number, accompanied by the oboe d'amore and continuo, but it seems that Bach applied its melody from another unknown aria to these words, because the declamation appears to be stilted. Also the melody is not that of the chorale tune.

"O du von Gott erhöhte Kreatur, / Begreife nicht, nein, nein, bewundre nur: / Gott will durch Fleisch des Fleisches Heil erwerben. / Wie gross ist doch der Schöpfer aller Dinge, / Und wie bist du verachtet und geringe, / Um dich dadurch zu retten vom Verderben." (O thou creature exalted by God, / Do not understand; no, no, just admire: / God will win salvation of the flesh through flesh. / How great is then the Creator of all things, / And how despised and worthless thou art, / To thereby save thyself from ruin.)

3. *Recitative—alto.* Her secco narrative expresses wonder that God has chosen a chaste body for His temple. Our understanding cannot comprehend this mystery, done on our behalf.

4. *Aria—bass.* This is one of Bach's most stunning arias. Strings accompany the bass, playing a joy-motif to evoke the image of the babe leaping in Elisabeth's womb when Mary greeted her (Luke 1 [41–45]). Bach's uncanny ability to bring this scene to realistic life through his musical setting is astounding.

"Johannis freudenvolles Springen / Erkannte dich, mein Jesu, schon. / Nun da ein Glaubensarm dich hält, / So will mein Herze von der Welt / Zu deiner Krippe brünstig dringen." (John's joyful leaping / Recognized Thee, my Jesus, already. / Now since an arm of faith holds Thee, / So will my heart press fervently / From the world to Thy crib.)

5. *Recitative—soprano.* In secco, she imagines herself to be present at the manger, as she adores the Child and offers Him her thanksgiving. She wonders why God, in all His power, should assume the form of a humble servant, living in poverty. For His association with the common people, she wishes to sing a song of praise and thanks amidst the chorus of angels. This thought leads into the final chorale.

6. *Chorale.* This is verse eight of Luther's hymn, plainly sung by all voices and accompanied by all instruments. The chorale tune is now heard unadorned and easily recognized by the congregation: "Lob, Ehr' und Dank sei dir gesagt, / Christ, gebor'n von der reinen Magd, / Samt Vater und dem heil'gen Geist / Von nun an bis in Ewigkeit." (Praise, honor and thanks be said to Thee, / Christ, born of the pure Maid, / Together with the Father and the Holy Ghost / From now on until eternity.)

This is a spectacular chorale cantata, well balanced, and with great musical imagery.

• **Süsser Trost, mein Jesus kommt (Sweet Comfort, My Jesus Comes)** (c. 1740; BWV 151).

For the third day of Christmas, Bach set this solo cantata on the text of an unknown librettist, who derived it from the Epistle for this same Sunday, St. John the Evangelist's Day. This Epistle is Hebrews 1 (1–14): Christ is higher than the angels. The libretto, however, stresses Jesus' presence on earth, in order to comfort and redeem mankind, rather than His exalted position in heaven.

The intimate, personal tone of this cantata reminds the listener of the solo soprano cantata BWV 199, although its theme is one of joy rather than of repentance. Both cantatas have exceptionally beautiful solo soprano arias.

The soli are SATB, with a four-part chorus. The instrumentation is simple: a transverse flute, an oboe d'amore, two violins, a viola and continuo.

1. *Aria—soprano.* In the first section of her aria, the transverse flute plays charming arabesques over the pastoral melody of all the other instruments. The molto adagio rhythm seems like a gentle lullaby which gives an impression of the melting tenderness in the comfort that Jesus brings to us. The second section has a livelier joy-rhythm to denote the happiness she feels when Jesus is near her.

This aria is one of Bach's greatest compositions for the solo soprano voice.

"Süsser Trost, mein Jesus kömmt, / Jesus wird anitzt (= uns jetzt) geboren! / Herz und Seele freuet sich, / Denn mein liebster Gott hat mich / Nun zum Himmel auserkoren." (Sweet comfort, my Jesus comes. / Jesus is now born to us! / Heart and soul rejoices, / For my dearest God has / Chosen me now for heaven.)

2. *Recitative—bass.* In secco, he tells his heart to rejoice because God has sent His dear Son to free the world from its chains of slavery and its servitude. God has become a man, even more lowly and poorer than we. This thought is developed in the following alto aria.

3. *Aria—alto.* The oboe d'amore and the strings play a beautiful but somber andante melody, in which the rhythmic beat seems to indicate humility as it sinks, rises, and sinks again. The second section becomes more animated, as she sings of the blessings that Jesus brings to her, despite His poverty: "In Jesu Demut kann ich Trost, / In seiner Armut Reichtum finden. / Mir macht desselben schlechter Stand / Nur lauter Heil und Wohl bekannt, / Ja seine wundervolle Hand / Will mir nur Segenskränze winden." (In Jesus' humility I can find comfort, / In His poverty riches. / His wretched state makes known to me / Only pure salvation and well-being. / Yes, His wondrous hand / Will only weave for me garlands of blessing.)

4. *Recitative—tenor.* He describes, in secco, what these blessings are: Christ's lowliness among men has enabled them to see the light of His salvation, whereby heaven will be opened to them. He has left heaven and His Father, in order to show mankind His love as one of the poorest; therefore our hearts will be devoted to Him.

5. *Chorale.* Stanza eight of Nikolaus Herman's Christmas hymn, "Lobt Gott, ihr Christen allzugleich" (Praise God, ye Christians altogether) (1560), is harmonized tutti to close this cantata. Its plain performance makes an impressive conclusion, even though it is brief: "Heut' schleusst er wieder auf die Tür / Zum schönen Paradeis, / Der Cherub steht nicht mehr dafür, / Gott sei Lob, Ehr' und Preis." (Today He reopens the door / To beautiful Paradise; / The Cherub stands no more before it. / To God be laud, honor and praise.)

• **Das neugebor'ne Kindelein (The Newborn Little Child)** (c. 1742; BWV 122).

This is a chorale cantata for the Sunday after Christmas, based on the hymn by Cyriakus Schneegass with the above title. Verses one, three and four of the hymn are quoted for numbers one, four and six of the cantata, and verse two is paraphrased for the second and third numbers. There is no reference to either the Epistle or the Gospel for this Sunday.

The unknown librettist was probably Bach himself.

The soli are SATB, with a four-part chorus. The instruments include three transverse flutes, an oboe da caccia, two oboes, a bassoon, two violins, a viola and continuo with organ.

1. *Chorus.* A swinging joy-motif in the oboes and strings gives the melody a cheerful lilt, repeated in the ritornelli after each line sung. The sopranos carry the cantus firmus, followed by the other parts in imitation with flowing runs. Entrancing lyricism is the result: "Das neugebor'ne Kindelein, / Das herzeliche Jesulein / Bringt abermal ein neues Jahr / Der auserwählten Christenschar." (The new-born little Child, / The dearly beloved little Jesus, / Brings again a New Year / To the chosen Christian flock.)

2. *Aria—bass.* Only the continuo accompanies his exhortation to men that they should appreciate the birth of their Redeemer, who will deliver them from their sins. They should heed the angels' joyful shouts, which announce that God is reconciled with them now: "O Menschen, die ihr täglich sündigt, / Ihr sollt der Engel Freude sein. / Ihr jubilierendes Geschrei, / Dass Gott mit euch versöhnet sei, / Hat euch den süssen Trost verkündigt." (O men, you who daily sin, / You should be the joy of angels. / Their jubilant cry, / That God is reconciled with you, / Has announced to you sweet comfort.)

3. *Recitative (with Chorale)—soprano.* This is the only number in which we hear the three transverse flutes. It seems that these represent the angelic chorus, as they play the chorale tune above her declamation from the third line on. She states that the angels, who previously avoided sinners as cursed, now rejoice over their salvation. God, who has rejected us from the society of angels, has now come to earth to give us his blessing. So we should thank Him for the long-awaited new covenant.

4. *Chorale and Aria (Duet)—alto and soprano, tenor.* This number is actually a trio. The soprano and the tenor sing a duet, interspersed with the alto's singing of the third verse of the hymn. The lines are sung alternately, beginning with the chorale. Each text complements the other, and the whole is accompanied by unison strings, playing a siciliano melody.

This duet-chorale combination is a new experiment with Bach and, although not outstanding, still has much musical merit. Accordingly, I cannot agree with Whittaker's comment, "The elements promise well but the number is totally devoid of inspiration" (Vol. II, p. 260).

CHORALE: "Ist Gott versöhnt und unser Freund, / Was kann uns tun der arge Feind? / Trotz Teufel und der Höllen Pfort, / Das Jesulein ist unser Hort." (If God is reconciled and our friend, / What can the harsh enemy do to us? / In spite of the devil and the gate of hell, / Dear Jesus is our refuge.)

DUET: "O wohl uns, die wir an ihn glauben, / Sein Grimm kann unsern Trost nicht rauben; / Ihr Wüten wird sie wenig nützen, / Gott ist mit uns und will uns schützen." (O well for us, who believe in Him, / His rage cannot steal our comfort; / Their fury will be of little use to them. / God is with us and will protect us.)

5. *Recitative—bass.* Strings accompany this number, which begins with a quotation from Psalm 118 (24): "This is the day which the Lord hath made." On this day He brought His Son into the world.

The bass then lists the happy fulfillment of expectant waiting for this blessed time, the faithful hope, the belief, the love, and the joy which pierces sadness. A joy-rhythm appears in the last two lines at the mention of "Freudigkeit" (joy).

6. *Chorale.* All voices and instruments of number one harmonize in a plain presentation of the sixth stanza of the chorale: "Es bringt das rechte Jubeljahr, / Was trauern wir denn immerdar? / Frisch auf! itzt ist es Singenszeit, / Das Jesulein wendt alles Leid." (The Christ-

Child brings the year of real jubilee. / Why then do we mourn continually? / Awake! now it is singing-time; / Little Jesus turns all sorrow away.)

• **Du Friedefürst, Herr Jesu Christ (Thou Prince of Peace, Lord Jesus Christ)** (1744; BWV 116).

This chorale cantata for the twenty-fifth Sunday after Trinity is the last of Bach's extant church cantatas, although Terry subsequently changed his mind about its chronological order, placing BWV 101 one year after it, in 1745. The unknown librettist's text reflects Frederick the Great's invasion of Saxony in the autumn of 1744 and is based on both Scriptural passages for this Sunday. Both the Epistle, 1 Thessalonians 4 (13–18), and the Gospel, Matthew 24 (15–28), deal with the second coming of Christ and are timely for the political situation.

Stanzas one and seven of Jakob Ebert's hymn are quoted for the opening and closing chorale numbers, the intervening stanzas being paraphrased for the other numbers. The theme is an eloquent appeal to the Prince of Peace to deliver His people from the scourge of war and to show them mercy for their sins.

The soli are SATB, with a four-part chorus. The orchestra has two oboi d'amore, two violins, a viola and continuo with a horn added for the two chorale numbers.

1. *Chorus.* This tutti fantasia begins with the orchestral ritornello as an introduction. Then the voices enter, singing each line in imitation, and followed by the ritornello. The first section has a joy-rhythm which changes to a grief-motif in the second, depicting both the confidence and terror of the text. The vocal parts are full of dramatic emotion: "Du Friedefürst, Herr Jesu Christ, / Wahr Mensch und wahrer Gott, / Ein starker Nothelfer du bist / Im Leben und im Tod. / Drum wir allein / Im Namen dein / Zu deinem Vater schreien." (Thou Prince of Peace, Lord Jesus Christ, / True Man and true God, / Thou art a strong Helper in need, / In life and in death. / Therefore we, alone, / In Thy Name / Cry to Thy Father.)

2. *Aria—alto.* The drama continues here in her pessimistic dejection over the prospect of being judged by God. The obbligato oboe d'amore and the continuo play a grief-motif, which Bach has patterned on the words of her text: "Ach, unaussprechlich ist die Not / Und des erzünten Richters Dräuen! / Kaum, dass wir noch in dieser Angst, / Wie du, o Jesu, selbst verlangst, / Zu Gott in deinem Namen schreien." (Ah, unspeakable is the misery / And the threatening of the angered Judge! / It is scarcely that we, in this anguish, / As Thou, o Jesus, Thyself longeth / To cry to God in Thy Name.)

Note that the verb "schreien" (cry) appears at the end of the last line in both of the above numbers, their last two lines expressing a similar thought.

3. *Recitative—tenor.* In this short, secco number, he asks Christ to remember that He is the Prince of Peace, sending us His word of love. Would He suddenly turn His heart from us, after giving us usually so much help?

4. *Terzett (Trio)—soprano, tenor, bass.* The grief-motif continues in this dramatic interplay of voices, accompanied by only the continuo to make the vocal part predominant. This trio has the same tone of penitence that was so moving in the soprano aria of BWV 199, "Tief gebückt und voller Reue" (Deeply Bowed and Full of Remorse). Both these numbers are charged with beautiful emotion, making them unique in all of Bach's sacred solo compositions.

"Ach, wir bekennen unsre Schuld / Und bitten nichts als um Geduld / Und um dein unermesslich Lieben. / Es brach ja dein erbarmend Herz, / Als der Gefallnen Schmerz / Dich zu uns in die Welt getrieben." (Ah, we confess our guilt / And ask for nothing than patience / And Thy immeasurable loving. / Thy pitying heart broke, / When the pain of those fallen / Drove Thee to us in the world.)

5. *Recitative—alto.* Strings and the continuo accompany her plea that Christ end their suffering and restore peace to their country. This number definitely refers to the sorrows caused by the present war. It is one of Bach's best recitatives.

6. *Chorale.* Stanza seven of the hymn is plainly performed, tutti, as a prayer for Christ to enlighten men's minds so that peace may be restored: "Erleucht' auch unsern Sinn und Herz / Durch den Geist deiner Gnad', / Dass wir nicht treiben draus ein Scherz, / Der unsrer Seelen schad'. / O Jesu Christ, / Allein du bist, / Der solch's wohl kann ausrichten." (Enlighten also our mind and heart / Through the Spirit of Thy mercy, / So that we do not make a joke of that / Which may harm our souls. / O Jesus Christ, / Thou art alone, / The One who can arrange such things.)

• **Nun ist das Heil und die Kraft (Now Is the Salvation and the Strength)** (c. 1740; BWV 50).

All that remains of this Michaelmas cantata is its first double chorus. This is the only eight-part chorus in any of Bach's sacred cantatas. It is very difficult to imagine what the remainder of the cantata would have been like after this stupendous chorus. Its text is quoted from the Epistle for St. Michael's Day, Revelation 12 (10).

The orchestra is as grandiose as the choir: three trumpets, timpani, three oboes, strings, organ and continuo.

A joy-motif is combined with a motif of strength in the rhythm, which represents the defeat of Satan. The sopranos and the basses of choir I begin the fugal theme, imitated by the other voices. Choir II bursts in with great force upon their fugue. In the second section, the fugue is altered by the two choirs tossing fragments of their declamation back and forth between their sections. The two choirs unite finally to bring the movement to an impressive climax.

This is a masterpiece of Bach's mature chorale writing in motet style. There is a feeling of mystic power that makes it more than a hymn of triumph over the forces of evil. It seems to be Bach's personal faith in God's supremacy.

"Nun ist das Heil und die Kraft und das Reich und die Macht unsers Gottes seines Christus worden, weil der verworfen ist, der sie (uns) verklagete Tag und Nacht vor Gott." (Now is the salvation and the strength and the kingdom and the might of our God become His Christ's, because he is cast out, who accused them (us) day and night before God.)

• **O Jesu Christ, mein's Lebens Licht (O Jesus Christ, Light of My Life)** (1737–40; BWV 118).

This is another chorus, the first movement of a funeral cantata which was performed at the grave-side ceremony for Count Friedrich von Flemming, 11 October 1740. It is the only extant part of the original cantata, which Bach probably composed about three years before this burial. Like BWV 50, it is a chorus in motet style but with only one four-part choir.

Stanza one of Martin Behm's hymn is its text; the exclusive brass and woodwind accompaniment suggests that the performance was in the open air at the cemetery. Two litui (bass cornetti), one cornetto (horn), three trombones and organ continuo compose the orchestra. No strings are indicated for the original or organ performance—the only time that this has happened in any of Bach's extant cantatas, except for the chorale part of the opening chorus of BWV 25. (The organ would not have been used at the grave-side ceremony, but only in later indoor performances. [Ed.])

Such instrumentation and the serious declamation of the choir produce a motif of deep solemnity, reminiscent of some of the choral writings of Heinrich Schütz in the 17th century. The movement has a straightforward simplicity befitting the ceremony for which it was intended. The upper voices begin to sing the melody of each line, which is then repeated by the lower voices. This is one of the most moving chorale settings that Bach ever composed. It has a melancholy beauty all its own.

"O Jesu Christ, mein's Lebens Licht, / Mein Hort, mein Trost, mein Zuversicht! / Auf Erden bin ich nur ein Gast, / Und drückt mich sehr der Sünden Last." (O Jesus Christ, Light of my life, / My Refuge, my Comfort, my Assurance! / On earth I am only a guest, / And the burden of sins oppresses me greatly.)

• **Bekennen will ich seinen Namen (I Will Acknowledge His Name)** (c. 1740; BWV 200).

Another surviving part of a cantata occurs in this alto aria; the cantata is designated for the Sunday of the Purification of the Virgin Mary. The text by an unknown librettist reflects the Gospel, Luke 2 (22–32), in verses 29–32. It must have been part of a complete cantata because the score pages do not have Bach's inscriptions J.J. and S.D. Gl. before and after the work as usual. Furthermore, the light instrumental accompaniment—two violins, a cello and bass continuo—could indicate an aria within a cantata where the alto voice would not be obscured by heavy instrumentation.

A short instrumental introduction gives the melody for her song, repeated at the end as a postlude. Her text is a confession of faith in Jesus. The result is an exceptionally beautiful hymn, expressing her personal conviction in the power of the Lord to redeem and bless all nations including herself.

The listener can well imagine that he is sitting in the peaceful serenity of a church, as he hears the alto's awe-inspiring song, full of Bach's own mysticism.

Aria—alto. "Bekennen will ich seinen Namen, / Er ist der Herr, er ist der Christ, / In welchem aller Völker Samen / Gesegnet und erlöset ist. / Kein Tod raubt mir die Zuversicht: / Der Herr ist meines Lebens Licht." (I will acknowledge His Name, / He is the Lord; He is Christ, / In Whom the seed of all nations / Is blessed and redeemed. / No death robs me of my confidence: / The Lord is the Light of my life.)

II. The Secular Cantatas

Bach's non-religious cantatas are less important than his sacred ones and fewer in number but some of them are directly related to his church cantatas. Beginning with a few occasional compositions for his ducal employers in Weimar and in Cöthen, Bach's genius in this genre reached its full development during his Leipzig years as Cantor of St. Thomas's. His former position as Hofkapellmeister to Leopold's court in Cöthen may have induced him to set *pièces de circonstance* to prove that he could do more than produce yearly cycles of religious cantatas as Leipzig's Cantor.

These profane cantatas were mostly intended to entertain and flatter the princes and electors with whom he hoped to gain favor. Some were written for Bach's friends or associates, including two cantatas in Italian to prove that he could deal with the current European model. Weddings, birthdays, anniversaries and homage ceremonies for royal visits are the subjects of these works. From some of them, Bach borrowed movements for his sacred cantatas, as has been previously indicated where this has occurred.

At first these presentations were held indoors—in a hunting lodge near Weimar, or in the Cöthen ducal court and later in Leipzig in Zimmermann's Coffee House where Bach directed the Collegium Musicum. But in fine weather, these cantatas were played outdoors, either on Leipzig's market square or in Zimmermann's garden outside town.

Bach's secular cantatas are really miniature operas (although Bach took no interest in this genre) without costumes and stage settings. The vocalists play the part of characters from Greek mythology in highly dramatic scenes. This was conventional in European dramatic and musical spectacles of the seventeenth and eighteenth centuries, yet some of Bach's secular works have modern personages as actors playing a burlesque role: the *Peasant Cantata* and the *Coffee Cantata* (BWV 212 and BWV 211).

Picander was Bach's librettist for the Leipzig works; his texts gave Bach much imagery for musical setting. Hence the pictorial aspect of Bach's music is exceptionally charming, evoking realistic pictures for the listener. Also the emotions or affections expressed by the music made it easy for Bach to transfer themes from some of these profane works into sacred ones (including the *Christmas Oratorio*). Bach knew that all his music had religious undertones.

A. Composed at Weimar

• **Amore traditore (Love, You Traitor)** (date ?; BWV 203).

Both the date and the place of performance of this solo Italian cantata for bass are unknown. The name of its librettist is also unknown. It seems likely that Bach composed the work as an experiment in the Italian-style cantata, which was in fashion in the early eighteenth century and produced by such composers as Handel and Alessandro Scarlatti. Bach's cantata has no pastoral setting as in some of their works, but it is similar in the emotions expressed and in the light instrumental accompaniment.

There are only three numbers in this solo bass cantata; the only instrument is a harpsichord. The vocalist expresses his feelings on love, after suffering from unrequited love. This is the sole theme of the cantata.

1. *Aria.* He expresses his firm decision to separate himself from love, because it brings him only torment. The melody does not emphasize his resentment, implied in the text, but is gentle in tone; this is unusual in Bach's interpretation of a text!

"Amore traditore / Tu non m'inganni più. / Non voglio più catene. / Non voglio affanni, pene, / Cordoglio e servitù." (Love, you traitor / You deceive me no more. / I want no more chains. / I wish no sorrow, pain, / Heart-grief and slavery.)

2. *Recitative.* This monologue continues to give his reasons for avoiding love: "Voglio provar, / Se posso sanar / L'anima mia dalla piaga fatale, / E viver si può senza il tuo strale; / Non sia più la speranza / Lusinga del dolore, / E la gioja nel core, / Più tuo scherzo sarà nella mia costanza." (I wish to prove, / If I can heal / My soul of the fatal wound, / And live, if I can, without your arrow; / Let there be no more / The flattering hope of pain / And joy in my heart; / No more your joking will be my constancy.)

3. *Aria.* This last number summarizes his philosophy on the futility of loving; he has experienced too much anguish from love. Bach's flowing keyboard melody contains a joy-motif, which reveals very well the happiness he feels at being freed from the bondage of love: "Chi in amore ha nemica la sorte, / E follia, se non lascia d'amar, / Sprezzi l'alma la crude ritorte, / Se non trova mercede al penar." (Whoever in love has fate as an enemy, / It is folly, if he does not give up loving; / The soul despises the cruel bonds, / If it does not find reward in its suffering.)

This is probably Bach's first attempt at composing in the Italian manner. One would wonder why this and the other Italian cantata, BWV 209, were his only works in this genre, since he must have heard others in the Saxon courts where he was employed. Perhaps he did not consider them as anything more than a diversion, like the tunes he heard at the Dresden Opera.

• **Non sa che sia dolore (He Does Not Know What Pain Is)** (1714; BWV 209).

The reason for this other Italian cantata has never been explained clearly. Until recently it was thought to be a cantata marking the departure of Bach's friend, the Rector J.M. Gesner, from Leipzig on his posting to Ansbach in 1729, but this date conflicts with the early date of the cantata. Today nobody knows for whom or by whom the poem was written. All that can be learned from the text is that some clever Italian youth must return to his homeland for military service. His German friends grieve as he is about to depart on his voyage by sea. The solo soprano voice represents their sentiments, accompanied by a transverse flute, strings and continuo.

1. *Sinfonia.* It is unusual that Bach would compose such a fine and lengthy da capo overture for such a simple solo cantata. This instrumental number resembles a concerto movement. It seems to set the tone for the grief-motives in the two following movements, yet still contains a rhythm of confident joy throughout.

2. *Recitative.* Strings accompany her feelings of sorrow at losing a friend. It is the same regret we all feel at such a time: "Non sa che sia dolore / Chi dall' amico suo parte e non more. / Il fanciullin' che plora e geme / Ed allor che più ei teme, / Vien la madre a consolar. / Va dunque a cenni del cielo, / Adempi or di Minerva il zelo." (He does not know what his pain is / Who departs from his friend and does not die. / A child who weeps and groans / And then when he fears more, / His mother comes to comfort him. / Go therefore at the sign of heaven, / To fill yourself with Minerva's zeal.)

3. *Aria.* The transverse flute is added to the strings for this aria. There is a grief-motif in the first two lines, which changes to a wave-motif to imply the coming sea-

voyage—both themes derived from the text: "Parti pur e con dolore / Lasci a noi dolente il core. / La patria goderai, / A dover la servirai; / Varchi or di sponda in sponda, / Propizi vedi il vento e l'onda." (Go then and with pain / Leave to us our suffering heart. / You will gladden your country, / In having to serve it. / Now set out from shore to shore; / May you see the wind and wave propitious.)

4. *Recitative.* Her short, secco narrative describes the glory that awaits the voyager in Italy: "Tuo saver al tempo e l'età contrasta, / Virtù e valor solo a vincer basta; / Ma chi gran ti farà più non fusti / Ansbaca, piena di tanti Augusti." (Your knowledge is contrasted with your time and age. / Your virtue and valor are alone enough for conquering. / But who will make you greater than you were / In Ansbach, full of so many patrons?)

5. *Aria.* All instruments play a joy-motif to depict the happiness he will feel as he makes the homeward voyage. The text compares the voyager to a sailor, who sings confidently once the sea has become calm. This metaphor may symbolize the despondent mood of the Italian as he departs from his friends, later changing to confidence when he has settled in his native land: "Ricetti gramezza e pavento, / Qual nocchier, placato il vento, / Più non teme o si scolora, / Ma contento in su la prora / Va cantando in faccia al mar." (Hide anxiety and fear, / What sailor, once the wind is stilled, / Does no more fear or become pale, / But stands contented on his prow / And goes singing into the face of the sea.)

This cantata is Bach's closest approach to opera. It is unlikely that he produced any other cantatas of this type, even in the works that have been lost, because his abiding interest was in sacred vocal music for his Church, itself a religion for him.

• **Was mir behagt [Jagdkantate] (What Suits Me [Hunting Cantata])** (1716; BWV 208).

After Bach had experimented with the Italian cantata in Weimar about 1714–15, he composed this Hunting Cantata, his first secular work in German. Its libretto is by Salomo Franck. Bach's employer in Weimar, Duke Wilhelm Ernst, was invited to a hunting party given by Duke Christian von Sachsen-Weissenfels, who was celebrating his fifty-third birthday on 23 February 1716 in this manner. Bach composed a birthday ode for this occasion, which would be Duke Wilhelm Ernst's birthday gift and a surprise for Duke Christian. It was performed as *Tafelmusik* (table music) during the feast in the hunting lodge after the chase.

The soloists are two sopranos, a tenor and a bass, with this quartet forming the chorus. They represent the actors in this neo-classical Greek drama, in fact a miniature opera: Diana, Pales, Endymion and Pan, respectively. Diana is the goddess of the hunt, Endymion a shepherd and her wooer, Pales the goddess of flocks, and Pan the god of shepherds.

The orchestra has three hunting horns, two oboes, a bassoon, two recorders, strings, and a cello in the continuo.

Diana tells Endymion that she has no time for his love today, because she must join in the hunt which honors Duke Christian's birthday. Endymion wishes also to participate, while Pales and Pan want to sing their tribute of praise to Christian. For Duke Christian is the ideal ruler, giving his domain peace and prosperity in a Saxony torn by intermittent wars—this is the hopeful message of the cantata.

Bach's word-painting and tonal Affekt make this first secular cantata an artistic masterpiece, which impressed Bach himself so much that he repeated it in April of the same year for Ernst August, nephew of Ernst Wilhelm, and again at Weissenfels in 1729, and in Leipzig about 1735 for royal events. Parts were incorporated into Bach's sacred cantatas: BWV 149, the opening chorus from the final one here; for BWV 68, the hunting aria and two other arias were transferred from this cantata.

1. *Recitative—soprano 1* (DIANA): "Was mir behagt, ist nur die muntre Jagd!" (What suits me is only the merry hunt!) In secco, Diana states that her only delight is in hunting. Even before dawn, her arrow has felled acceptable game.

Bach brings each actor on stage in turn, each beginning with a recitative followed by an aria in the first half of the cantata.

2. *Aria—soprano 1* (DIANA). The accompanying hunting music is vividly portrayed by two hunting horns above the continuo to paint a picture of the actual hunt. It is not a long aria (to avoid boring the noble guests?), but it is very realistic.

"Jagen ist die Lust der Götter, / Jagen steht den Helden an. / Weichet, meiner Nymphen Spötter, / Weichet von Dianen Bahn!" (Hunting is the pleasure of gods, / Hunting becomes heroes. / Begone, mockers of my nymphs, / Begone from Diana's path!)

3. *Recitative—tenor* (ENDYMION). The continuo, only, accompanies his exclamation of surprise that Diana would rather hunt than devote herself to him on this day.

4. *Aria—tenor* (ENDYMION). He sings in a caressing tone, pleading for her love, accompanied again by only the continuo. The melody is a soothing lullaby.

"Willst du dich nicht mehr ergötzen / An den Netzen, / Die der Amor legt? / Wo man auch, wenn man gefangen, / Nach Verlangen / Lust und Lieb' in Banden pflegt." (Wilt thou no more delight / In the nets, / That Amor [Love] lays? / Where one also, when one is caught, / After longing, / Is accustomed to the bonds of desire and love.)

5. *Recitative—soprano 1, tenor* (DIANA, ENDYMION). This is a dialogue between Diana and Endymion, ending in a brilliant arioso. Diana says that she loves him nevertheless, but Christian, who is the Pan of the forest, must have his birthday celebration. Then Endymion asks permission to join her, so that they may present their "joy-offering" to Christian together. They will both carry their torches to the feast. Bach has created a small opera scene in this number.

6. *Recitative—bass* (PAN). The entry of the god Pan here is quite dramatic. Pan acknowledges his namesake, Christian, and says that he will lay down his shepherd's staff before Christian's scepter, because Christian governs his country so well that even the forest and the fields seem to laugh with joy.

7. *Aria—bass* (PAN). Two oboes and the bassoon give this aria a tone of royal pomp and dignity, befitting the god of shepherds. Here Pan eulogizes Christian. This is one of the arias adapted for BWV 68 about twenty years later.

"Ein Fürst ist seines Landes Pan, / Gleichwie der Körper ohne Seele / Nicht leben, noch sich regen kann, / So ist das Land die Totenhöhle, / Das sonder Haupt und Fürsten ist, / Und so das beste Teil vermisst." (A prince is the Pan of his country, / Just as the body without a soul / Can neither live nor move, / So is that country a cave of death, / That is without a head and princes, / And so lacks its best part.)

8. *Recitative—soprano 2* (PALES). The goddess of flocks, Pales, now appears on stage to add her praises of Christian to those of the whole country. This leads to one of Bach's most undying arias.

9. *Recitative—soprano 2* (PALES). Two recorders give a touch of magic to this exceptional pastoral melody. If Bach had composed only this one number, it alone would have brought him immortality. We have the proof of this in its many instrumental performances for modern concerts or solemn occasions.

The melody evokes a feeling of heavenly peace and a visual panorama of shepherds quietly tending their flocks. In the second part of her aria, this becomes a comparison with wise rulers, who bring peace and happiness to their people. It is like a cameo, engraved with a picture of the ideal life that all people seek on earth. This is Bach's word-painting at its best, a scene of peace on earth, worthy of the angels' song at Christmas.

"Schafe können sicher weiden, / Wo ein guter Hirte wacht. / Wo Regenten wohl regieren, / Kann man Ruh' und Friede spüren / Und was Länder glücklich macht." (Sheep can safely graze, / Where a good shepherd watches. / Where rulers govern well, / One can feel rest and peace / And what makes countries happy.)

10. *Recitative—soprano 1* (DIANA). This is only two lines, in secco, as Diana urges the group to join their voices in festive song, which will be the following chorus.

11. *Chorus (Aria à 4).* A resounding joy-motif for the quartet singing in canon is supported by the hunting horns, oboes, the bassoon and the strings (their first appearance). A fugal melody with a swinging rhythm recalls the atmosphere of the hunt through its flowing strides amid horn calls. Diana has resumed her leadership as the chorus extols the sun, which represents Duke Christian in this number: "Lebe, Sonne dieser Erden, / Weil Diana bei der Nacht / An der Burg des Himmels wacht, / Weil die Wälder grünen werden, / Lebe, Sonne dieser Erden!" (Live, Sun of this earth, / Because Diana at night / Watches in the fortress of the sky, / Because the woods become green, / Live, Sun of this earth!)

12. *Duet—soprano 1, tenor* (DIANA, ENDYMION). A solo violin accompanies their duet; this time they address the sun's rays which brighten their lives and cause plant life to grow. There is a peaceful and gracious charm in the continuo only accompaniment, enhanced by a rocking rhythm and quavers in the solo violin.

"Entzücket uns beide, / Ihr Strahlen der Freude, / Und zieret den Himmel mit Demantgeschmeide, / Fürst Christian weide / Auf lieblichsten Rosen, befreiet vom Leide!" (Delight us both, / You rays of joy, / And adorn the sky with diamond jewels. / May Prince Christian pasture / On loveliest roses, freed from sorrow!)

13. *Aria—soprano 2* (PALES).This is the other aria borrowed for BWV 68. Pales expresses her appreciation for the protection given to her flocks by the "Saxon hero," Christian, and wishes him a long life: "Weil die wollenreichen Herden / Durch dies weitgepries'ne Feld / Lustig ausgetrieben werden, / Lebe dieser Sachsenheld!" (Because the wool-rich herds / Are merrily driven out / Through this widely-praised field, / May this Saxon hero live!)

14. *Aria—bass* (PAN). To a lilting gigue played by only the continuo, Pan summons the fields and the meadows to wish Christian a long life, so that they too may thrive. We can almost see Pan dancing with glee, as he sings in this exuberant joy-motif: "Ihr Felder und Auen, / Lasst grünend euch schauen, / Ruft Vivat itzt zu! / Es lebe der Herzog in Segen und Ruh'." (You fields and meadows, / Let yourselves be seen turning green. / Cry out "May he live" now! / Long live the Duke in blessing and peace.)

15. *Chorus.* This tutti final number, four voices and all instruments, was adapted for the opening chorus of BWV 149 about fifteen years later. It is a magnificent ending, uniting all actors and instrumentalists in a final paean of well-wishing to Christian: "Ihr lieblichste Blicke, / Ihr freudige Stunden, / Euch bleibe das Glücke / Auf ewig verbunden! / Euch kröne der Himmel mit süssester Lust! / Fürst Christian lebe! Ihm bleibe bewusst, / Was Herzen vergnüget, / Was Trauern besieget!" (You most lovely views, / You joyful hours, / May good luck remain with you / Forever united! / May heaven crown you with sweetest joy! / Long live Prince Christian! May he stay aware of / What delights hearts, / What conquers sorrow!)

B. Composed at Cöthen

• **Durchlauchtster Leopold (Most Serene Leopold)** (1717; BWV 173a).

Although this serenade, termed *Serenada* in the original score, for the birthday of Bach's patron, Prince Leopold of Anhalt-Cöthen, is never performed today, its flattering text deserves examination for comparison with the later sacred cantata, BWV 173, which was based on it, and for references often made to it. With the exception of the last two arias, omitted in the religious version, the movements and their music are the same. Even the final (omitted) bass aria in Leopold's *Serenata* was to be transferred to the tenor aria in the sacred cantata of later date, BWV 175, *Er rufet seinen Schafen mit Namen (He Calls His Sheep by Name)*. Such exact borrowing gives the impression that Bach prized this work highly, despite the passing nature of its single performance.

Bach was probably the librettist of this work paying homage to his prince, who then became his firm friend and godfather to one of his children in 1718.

The cantata has only two soloists: a soprano and a bass. Its orchestration is also light: two transverse flutes, a bassoon and a quartet of strings with harpsichord continuo. Its chamber-music quality might indicate the style of music-making that Bach found upon his arrival at the Cöthen court, where Leopold himself played various stringed instruments and could sing bass.

1. *Recitative—soprano.* Her invocation to Leopold here sounds like a birthday-card message. It is a prelude to all the following numbers praising him: "Durchlauchtster Leopold, / Es singet Anhalts Welt / Von neuem mit Vergnügen. / Dein Köthen sich dir stellt, / Um sich vor dir zu biegen, / Durchlauchtster Leopold." (Most serene Leopold! / So sings Anhalt's world / Anew with pleasure. / Your Cöthen presents itself to you, / In order to bow before you. / Most serene Leopold!)

2. *Aria—soprano.* Two flutes, strings and continuo accompany this first aria. "Güldner Sonnen frohe Stunden, / Die der Himmel selbst gebunden, / sich von neuem eingefunden, / Rühmet, singet, stimmt die Saiten, / Seinen Nachruhm auszubreiten!" (Happy hours of golden suns, / Which heaven itself has ordained, / Appear anew. / Praise, sing, tune the strings, / To spread abroad his fame hereafter!)

3. *Aria—bass.* With the accompaniment of strings and continuo, he continues the eulogy: "Leopolds Vortrefflichkeiten / Machen uns itzt viel zu tun. / Mund und Herze, Ohr und Blicke / Können nicht bei seinem Glücke, / Das ihm billig folget, ruhn." (Leopold's excellences / Make for us now much to do. / Mouth and heart, ear and vision / Cannot rest at his good-fortune / That justly follows him.)

4. *Aria—soprano, bass.* This tripartite movement has two single arias, beginning with the bass, and concluding with a duet. The two flutes return above the accompanying strings.

BASS: "Unter seinem Purpursaum / Ist die Freude / Nach dem Leide, / Jedem schenkt er weiten Raum, / Gnadengaben zu geniessen, / Die wie reiche Ströme fliessen." (Beneath his purple hem / Is joy / After sorrow. / To each he gives ample space / To enjoy his gifts of favor, / Which flow like rich streams.)

SOPRANO: "Nach landesväterlicher Art / Er ernähret, / Unfall wehret: / Drum sich nun die Hoffnung paart, / Dass er werde Anhalts Lande / Setzen in beglückten Stande." (In his paternal way / He nourishes, / Diverts misfortune: / Now therefore hope pairs itself, / That he will put Anhalt's country / In a fortunate position.)

BASS AND SOPRANO: "Doch wir lassen unsre Pflicht / Froher Sinnen / Itzt nicht rinnen, / Heute, da des Himmels Licht / Seine Knechte fröhlich machet / Und auf seinem Szepter lachet." (Yet we do not let our duty, / With happy minds, / Now run away / Today, as the light of heaven / Makes his servants happy / And laughs upon his scepter.)

5. *Recitative (Duet)—soprano, bass.* They begin this number together as a recitative, but break into canon singing in arioso after the first line: "Durchlauchtigster, den Anhalt Vater nennt, / Wir wollen dann das Herz zum Opfer

bringen; / Aus unsrer Brust, die ganz vor Andacht brennt, / Soll sich der Seufzer Glut zum Himmel schwingen." (Most serene one, whom Anhalt calls father, / We want then to bring our hearts as an offering. / Out of our breast, which burns entirely with devotion, / Shall the glow of our sighs mount to heaven.)

6. *Aria—soprano.* The two flutes and strings accompany the happy prediction of her text with the dancing joy-motif of a bourrée: "So schau dies holden Tages Licht / Noch viele, viele Zeiten; / Und wie es itzt begleiten / Hohes Wohlsein und Gelücke, / So wisse es, wenn es anbricht / Ins Künftige, von Kummer nicht." (Thus the light of this charming day / Still many, many ages will behold, / And as it now accompanies / Great well-being and good-fortune, / So may it know, when it breaks forth / In the future, nothing of sorrow.)

7. *Aria—bass.* Supported by the cello and the bassoon as obbligato, he continues the soprano's joyful prophecy: "Dein Name gleich der Sonnen geh, / Stets während bei den Sternen steh! / Leopold in Anhalts Grenzen / Wird im Fürstenruhme glänzen." (May your name go like suns, / While always standing near the stars! / Leopold, in Anhalt's boundaries, / Will gleam in the fame of princes.)

8. *Chorus (Duet)—soprano, bass.* For this secular cantata, this number is a duet more than a chorus, although it is marked "chorus" on Bach's original score. It is a fine tutti number; there is little wonder that Bach used it again in the later sacred version.

"Nimm auch, grosser Fürst, uns auf, / Und die sich zu deinen Ehren / Untertänigst lassen hören! / Glücklich sei dein Lebenslauf, / Sei dem Volke solcher Segen, / Den auf deinem Haupt wir legen!" (Take us up also, great prince, / And those who, to your honor, / Let themselves be heard most submissively! / May your course through life be happy; / May you be to your people such a blessing / As we lay on your head!)

• **Weichet nur, betrübte Schatten (Just Begone, Sad Shadows)** (1717–23; BWV 202).

In one of the years in which Bach was *Hofkapellmeister* (Court Concert Master) to Prince Leopold of Anhalt-Cöthen, this solo soprano wedding cantata was performed. The librettist is unknown. Bach composed it as *Tafelmusik* (table-music), probably sung by Anna Magdalena with the accompaniment of Cöthen court musicians, but where or for whose wedding is also unknown. The cantata would have been lost, had not a music student, Rinck, copied the score in 1730.

The wedding must have taken place in the spring, because the text refers to this season throughout. If the cantata had not been intended for a wedding, one could consider it to be an ode to spring, for it is a tone-poem on nature waking to life after winter. Such a description occupies the first half of the cantata, leading into the themes of love and marriage in the second part. The allusions are taken from Roman classical mythology: Phoebus (the sun god), Amor (the god of love), and Flora (the goddess of flowers)—which indicates that this wedding was for, and attended by, aristocrats.

The instruments are simply an oboe and strings with harpsichord and basso continuo. There is a chamber music quality about the work, which recalls the type of music that Bach was constrained to compose in Cöthen, and with which he was familiar. All numbers are for a solo soprano voice.

1. *Aria.* An adagio melody in the first two lines paints a picture of slowly rising mists and vanishing shadows as the cold dampness of winter departs. Arpeggios of the strings and the languorous tone of the oboe symbolize in word-pictures a changing landscape.

In the latter part, her aria becomes infused with a joy-motif, with the soloist and the oboe performing in canon over the allegro melody. One can almost visualize the blossoming spring flowers as one listens to this part. The exquisite beauty of this aria is unique.

"Weichet nur, betrübte Schatten, / Frost und Winde, geht zur Ruh'! / Florens Lust / Will der Brust / Nichts als frohes Glück verstatten, / Denn sie träget Blumen zu." (Just begone, sad shadows; / Frost and winds, go to your rest! / Flora's pleasure / Will to the breast / Grant nothing but happy good-luck, / For she brings forth flowers.)

2. *Recitative.* Her very short arioso describes the charming renewal of life on mountains and in valleys, now that the day is free of cold. The attractive picture has become doubly beautiful.

3. *Aria.* Harpsichord continuo, only, accompanies her as she sings the picturesque imagery of her text: the prancing steeds of Phoebus conducting his chariot across the sky. Her runs on "eilt" (hurries) indicate his haste as a lover wooing earth (as the metaphor in the text states). The melody has a persistent step-motif to illustrate this idea, thus introducing the courtship and marriage themes to follow into the already established nature-setting.

"Phoebus eilt mit schnellen Pferden / Durch die neugeborne Welt. / Ja, weil sie ihm wohlgefällt, / Will er selbst ein Bühler werden." (Phoebus hurries with swift horses / Through the new-born world. / Yes, because she pleases him well, / He wishes himself to become a wooer.)

4. *Recitative.* The arioso style predominates in this declamation. It is a wonderful blend of natural color and emotional imagery. Amor delights to be active when the purple shades of evening fall over meadows, when then their flowers are most beautiful. So then, as these flowers appeal to the affections, he will contrive to attract lovers' hearts to each other.

5. *Aria.* The cameo-like image of Amor at work continues in this allegro melody, accompanied by a solo violin. The words and music evoke a pastoral atmosphere, in keeping with the scene of two lovers. Details of this natural setting are well expressed as she sings the first two lines.

"Wenn die Frühlingslüfte streichen / Und durch bunte Felder weh'n, / Pflegt auch Amor auszuschleichen, / Um nach seinem Schmuck zu seh'n, / Welcher, glaubt man, dieser ist, / Dass ein Herz das andre küsst." (When the spring-breezes stroke / And waft through brightly-colored fields, / Cupid is also accustomed to steal out, / To see to his adornment, / Which, one believes, is this / That one heart kisses the other.)

6. *Recitative.* The adornment or jewel that Amor seeks is the happiness that a favorable destiny has given two souls, as she explains in this number.

7. *Aria.* The first part is accompanied by a joy-motif in the solo oboe, which continues in the second part, where the rhythm depicts a wave-motif superimposed. The aria has a joyful bounce—Bach's way of denoting the happiness that one finds in love. Perhaps he was thinking of his own personal experiences when he composed this tune. Certainly his love affairs and his home-life were happy.

"Sich üben im Lieben, / Im Scherzen sich herzen / Ist besser als Florens vergängliche Lust. / Hier quellen die Wellen, / Hier lachen und wachen / Die siegenden Palmen auf Lippen und Brust." (To practice loving, / To enhearten oneself in joking, / Is better than Flora's passing pleasure. / Here the waves spring forth; / Here laugh and awaken / The conquering palms on lips and breast.)

8. *Recitative.* She addresses the bridal pair, wishing that their bond of chaste love be free of the uncertainty of change. May no sudden falling away or clap of thunder perturb their love impulses.

9. *Gavotte (Aria).* This concluding tutti dance melody may have been taken from one of Bach's unknown Cöthen suites. It is a marvelous parting wish for the happiness of the newlyweds, as they joyfully dance their way together into their future life: "Sehet in Zufriedenheit / Tausend helle Wohlfahrtstage, / Dass bald bei der Folgezeit / Eure Liebe Blumen trage!" (See in contentment / A thousand bright days of well-being, / So

that soon in the time to follow / Your love may bear blossoms!)

C. *Composed at Leipzig*

• **Entfliehet, verschwindet, entweichet, ihr Sorgen (Flee, Disappear, Give Way, Ye Cares)** (1725; BWV 249a).

This secular cantata was the original version of the *Easter Oratorio,* BWV 249, composed and performed in Weissenfels before the sacred work in Leipzig. Picander was its librettist, and like the later sacred version, it has ten numbers with only the recitatives differing.

In 1716 Bach had composed his Hunting Cantata (Jagdkantate), BWV 208, to honor the birthday of Duke Christian of Sachsen-Weissenfels. So nine years later he collaborated with Picander to pay homage to this nobleman on his birthday, 23 February 1725, because Bach had become Court Composer to Weissenfels shortly before he obtained employment as Cantor in St. Thomas's.

Like the earlier work, this Shepherd Cantata was also presented as "table-music," having mythological characters to sing their roles in another "dramma per musica." For this performance at the Weissenfels Court, the instrumentation would have been the same as for the later *Easter Oratorio;* likewise the vocalists were again SATB, except that there was no chorus.

The "actors" in this drama are two shepherds, Damoetas (bass) and Menalcus (tenor), with two shepherdesses, Doris (soprano) and Sylvia (alto). The pastoral atmosphere is well depicted in both the text and the music.

1. *Sinfonia.* This overture resembles the first two movements of a concerto. The allegro features trumpets, woodwinds and strings, while the following adagio section is confined to oboes and strings. Unlike the same sinfonia as played to introduce the *Easter Oratorio,* the adagio section here seems to be out of place, because of its sadness motif, in view of what follows in the remainder of the cantata. Perhaps Bach had adapted this fast-slow movement from one of his Cöthen concerti and was unwilling to omit the slow section.

2. *Duet (double)—bass, tenor / soprano, alto.* The melody of the above allegro is repeated by the orchestra to accompany both groups of male and female singers, as in turn they interpret the exuberant joy-motif of their lines. The shepherds' runs on "Lachen" (laughing) and "Scherzen" (joking) emphasize the banishment of their care, and also that of the shepherdesses, who interrupt them by repeating their first lines in the second duet. The effect of this second duet is delightful to hear.

DAMOETAS, MENALCAS: "Entfliehet, verschwindet, entweichet, ihr Sorgen, / Verwirret die lustigen Regungen nicht! / Lachen und Scherzen / Erfüllet die Herzen, / Die Freude malet das Gesicht." (Flee, disappear, give way, ye cares, / Do not confuse our happy emotions! / Laughing and joking / Fills our hearts; / Joy paints our faces.)

DORIS, SYLVIA: "Entfliehet, verschwindet, entweichet, ihr Sorgen; / Verwirret die lustigen Regungen nicht!" (Flee, disappear, give way, ye cares; / Do not confuse our happy emotions!)

3. *Recitative—bass, tenor, alto, soprano.* The shepherds ask who interrupts their singing. The shepherdesses reply that they, too, wish to participate in such bliss and ask to know why they should not join in the rejoicing.

4. *Aria—soprano* (DORIS). Accompanied by the obbligato flute, she expresses her heart-felt joy in an ethereal da capo song. As yet we do not know the cause of her rapture, but we will surely learn as the drama unfolds.

"Hunderttausend Schmeicheleien / Wallen jetzt in meiner Brust; / Und die Lust, / So die Zärtlichkeiten zeigen, / Kann die Zunge nicht verschweigen." (A hundred thousand flatteries / Now well up in my breast, / And the pleasure, / That my affections show, / My tongue cannot conceal.)

5. *Recitative—bass, soprano, tenor,*

alto. This number appears to be a conference of all four actors on their plans for the day. Doris has the most to say. Replying to Damoetas's question about what she plans to do and where she wishes to go, she says to seek the flower goddess near beeches, oaks or lindens, in order to bind a wreath for their dear Christian, whose birthday celebration is now beginning.

Menalcas says that the shepherdesses may accompany Damoetas and himself, since they are also going on the same road to meet Christian at his Court.

Sylvia wonders who will tend the sheep in their absence.

6. *Aria—tenor* (MENALCAS). This is another remarkable aria in which Bach depicts the pastoral scene of two shepherds playing their pipes amid their flocks. He creates this image by using two recorders while, at the same time, the undulating rhythm of the strings presents an exquisitely charming lullaby. Here there is no problem with the text (cf. the word "Schweisstuch" (sweatcloth) in the tenor aria of the *Easter Oratorio*). We can visualize only the serene picture of placidly grazing sheep as they eat their fill and sleep. It may be more than coincidence that Bach composed this number following the second soprano's aria, "Schafe können sicher weiden" (Sheep May Safely Graze), in BWV 208, also dedicated to the same Duke Christian.

"Wieget euch, ihr satten Schafe, / In dem Schlafe / Unterdessen selber ein! / Dort in jenen tiefen Gründen, / Wo schon junge Rasen sein, / Wollen wir euch wiederfinden." (Rock yourselves, you contented sheep, / In sleep / Meanwhile! / There in those deep valleys, / Where there is already young grass, / We will find you again.)

7. *Recitative—bass*. (DAMOETAS), *alto* (SYLVIA). In this dialogue Damoetas tells Sylvia that the shepherdesses may go with Menalcas and himself to the court, but he wonders where they can find flowers for their wreaths in this cold month of the year.

She replies that she cannot see any flowers yet, but wishes that her efforts might bring some forth from their cold grave, even before their time.

8. *Aria—alto* (SYLVIA). Accordingly, she appeals to Flora, the goddess of flowers, to bring an early spring, so that flowers may appear for them. Bach uses oboes and strings to produce a movement motif, illustrating the imagined response to her entreaty as stated in the text: "Komm doch, Flora, komm geschwinde, / Hauche mit dem Westenwinde / Unsre Felder lieblich an, / Dass ein treuer Untertan / Seinem milden Christian / Pflicht und Schuld bezahlen kann." (Come then, Flora, come quickly, / Breathe with your west-wind / Delightfully over our fields, / So that a faithful subject / Can pay his duty and obligation / To his gentle Christian.)

9. *Recitative—bass* (DAMOETAS). He asks his companions why they should be concerned that Duke Christian would wish flowers for his birthday. He thinks that Christian would prefer to hear their expression of fidelity and love for him. Therefore, they should stand before him and sing their songs of praise, accompanied by drums (the full orchestra for Bach!). This leads into the final number.

10. *Quartet—soprano, alto, tenor, bass*. This resounding closing became a chorus in the last number of the *Easter Oratorio*. It was no doubt performed more as a quartet in the original presentation, although the grandiose effect would have been probably the same. Each group in turn pays homage to Christian, repeating the lines in imitation, with an orchestral interlude after the first two lines. The tempo accelerates into a short fugue for the last two lines.

"Glück und Heil / Bleibe dein beständig Teil! / Grosser Herzog, dein Vergnügen / Müsse wie die Palmen stehn, / Die sich niemals niederbiegen, / Sondern bis zu Wolken gehn! / So werden sich künftig bei stetem Gedeihen / Die Deinen mit Lachen und Scherzen erfreuen." (May good luck and prosperity / Remain your constant lot! / Great Duke, your contentment / Must stand as the palm-trees, / Which never bend down / But go up to the clouds! / So shall your subjects rejoice in future / With constant thriving and laughter and merriment.)

• **Schwingt freudig euch empor (Swing Up Joyfully)** (1725; BWV 36c).

No other cantata in Bach's total production was borrowed from by him more than this one: there are three secular versions besides the sacred one of about 1730. This is the first version, presumed to celebrate the birthday of Johann Matthias Gesner, who was Rector of the Thomasschule from 1730 to 1734, but more probably that of his predecessor, Johann Heinrich Ernesti, because of the earlier date of this cantata. The other versions include a birthday cantata for the Princess of Anhalt-Cöthen of 1726 (BWV 36a), the sacred version of about 1730 (BWV 36), and a birthday cantata for the Leipzig University professor Johann Florens Rivinus of about 1733 (BWV 36b).

The unknown librettist of this work may have been Picander, since he or Bach revised the texts for the later adaptations. The religious overtones in this work raise it above the level of a congratulatory birthday wish. Both the text and Bach's interpretation of it show a mystical affinity between respect for learning and reverence for God. This cantata offers the best proof that Bach unites the secular with the sacred in many of his nonreligious textual interpretations.

The only other secular cantata expressing Christian thought in its text is BWV 204, *Ich bin in mir vergnügt* (I am content with my lot). Like this work, it has a light chamber-music style: it was performed in Bach's family circle, and possibly BWV 36c was also presented in the Thomasschule, where both the Rector and Bach had their living quarters and a music room.

The soloists are STB, with a four-part chorus. The instruments employed are an oboe d'amore, a viola d'amore, strings and harpsichord continuo.

1. *Chorus.* The joy-motif of the first two lines contrasts with the subdued tone of the last pair. Our heart-felt feelings may go up to God, but they are earth-bound also in paying our respect to our honored teacher: "Schwingt freudig euch empor und dringt bis an die Sternen, / Ihr Wünsche, bis euch Gott vor seinem Throne sieht! / Doch, haltet ein! ein Herz darf sich nicht weit entfernen, / Das Dankbarkeit und Pflicht zu seinem Lehrer zieht." (Swing up joyfully and press on to the stars, / You wishes, until God sees you before His throne! / But wait! A heart may not go far away / That draws thanks and obligation to its teacher.)

Each soloist in turn will now have a recitative and an aria.

2. *Recitative—tenor.* His accompanied declamation gives an analysis of the heart's sentiments. A heart experiences many thousand joys, but cannot find contentment in them, because it always hopes to discover more. Its burning devotion is like a bright light rising up to God. Yet the fame of its dear teacher acts as the pole to attract its wishing and longing like a magnet.

3. *Aria—tenor.* Bach illustrates the beginning of this number with a dancing step-motif, suggested to him by the text's personification of love. The obbligato oboe d'amore gives the impression of running throughout the aria: "Die Liebe führt mit sanften Schritten / Ein Herz, das seinen Lehrer liebt. / Wo andre auszuschweifen pflegen, / Wird dies behutsam sich bewegen, / Weil ihm die Ehrfurcht Grenzen gibt." (Love, with soft steps, leads / A heart that loves its teacher. / Where others are accustomed to wander, / This one will move carefully, / Because respect gives him limits.)

4. *Recitative—bass.* With this number, we come to the direct address of the honored gentleman, which will continue in all numbers to the end of the cantata. He says that the teacher is a highly deserving man, whose constant teaching has brought him the highest honor and also his grey hair. Having their gratitude,

respect and his own fame, he will not condemn their happy testimony that he must guide their hearts as their light and leader.

5. *Aria—bass.* All strings accompany this fervent expression of appreciation for the birth of the Rector. The joy-motif moves to a surprising climax at the Biblical quotation in the last line—a marvelous compliment to the teacher on his birthday.

"Der Tag, der dich vor dem gebar, / Stellt sich vor uns so heilsam dar / Als jener, da der Schöpfer spricht: / Es werde Licht!" (The day, upon which you were born, / Presents itself to us as beneficial / As that when the Creator speaks: / Let there be light!)

6. Recitative—soprano. She states that there is only one thing to worry about—that this offering is too imperfect. Yet if their dear teacher will kindly accept it, then its poor worth will climb as high as their devoted thoughts could wish.

7. *Aria—soprano.* The viola d'amore is featured above the accompanying strings in this artistic solo. Bach has contrived another contrast between the first two lines (a motif of exhaustion) and the last three lines (a motif of felicity) which contain very expressive runs on the verb "schallet" (resounds): "Auch mit gedämpften, schwachen Stimmen / Verkündigt man des Lehrers Preis. / Es schallet kräftig in der Brust, / Ob man gleich die empfundne Lust / Nicht völlig auszudrücken weiss." (Also with subdued, weak voices / The teacher's praise is announced. / It resounds strongly in the breast, / Whether one does not know right away / How to express his felt joy fully.)

8. *Recitative—tenor.* This very short number leads into the final movement. He says that in such joyful hours the aim of our wish is found. This pertains to nothing else than the teacher's life.

9. *Chorus and Recitatives—tenor, bass, soprano.* Bach experimented successfully here in combining the choral lines with soloist recitative. The result is a charming conclusion to the cantata. Each soloist, in the above order, alternates with the chorus. The tenor and the soprano voices are accompanied, while the bass is secco. The chorus sings to the rhythm of a bourrée, played by all instruments and reminiscent of Bach's instrumental suites of the Cöthen period.

CHORUS: "Wie die Jahre sich verneuen, / So verneue sich dein Ruhm!" (As the years renew themselves, / So may your fame renew itself!)

TENOR: "Jedoch, was wünschen wir, / Da dieses von sich selbst geschieht, / Und da man deinen Preis, / Den unser Helicon am besten weiss, / Auch ausser dessen Grenzen sieht?" (However, for what we are wishing, / Since this happens by itself, / And since your praise, / Which our Helicon knows best, / Is also seen beyond its borders?)

CHORUS: "Dein Verdienst recht auszulegen, / Fordert mehr als wir vermögen." (To rightly explain your merit, / Demands more than we are able.)

BASS: "Drum schweigen wir / Und zeigen dadurch dir, / Dass unser Dank zwar mit dem Munde nicht, / Doch desto mehr mit unserm Herzen spricht." (Therefore we are silent, / And thereby show you / That our thanks does not speak out of our mouths, / But all the more out of our hearts.)

CHORUS: "Deines Lebens Heiligtum / Kann vollkommen uns erfreuen." (The sanctity of your life / Can make us completely glad.)

SOPRANO: "So öffnet sich der Mund zum Danken / Denn jedes Glied nimmt an der Freude teil; / Das Auge dringt aus den gewohnten Schranken / Und sieht dein künftig Glück und Heil." (So our mouths open in thanks, / For every member participates in this joy; / Our eyes emerge from their usual limitation / To see your coming good-luck and well-being.)

CHORUS: "Wie die Jahre sich verneuen, / So verneue sich dein Ruhm!" (As the years renew themselves, / So may your fame renew itself!)

The repetition of these opening choral

lines rounds off nicely this final number with a sort of motto that one would be pleased to read on a birthday card.

It is interesting to compare this cantata with BWV 207 of the following year, Bach's other congratulatory cantata to a professor, to observe the differences in the way he treats the given text.

• **Der zufriedengestellte Aeolus (Aeolus Appeased)** (1725; BWV 205).

Although Bach desired European recognition as a composer, unlike Handel and Mozart he was never attracted to the opera as a means of gaining international renown. He was content, as he is said to have remarked to his son Wilhelm Friedemann, to go with the boy to visit the Dresden opera "to hear the pretty little Dresden songs." However, the Italian opera, which influenced the operatic productions of Hasse in Dresden and Handel in Hamburg, must have impressed Bach. The format and the dramatic aspect of Bach's cantatas show that this genre was derived from the opera.

Beginning with this cantata, Bach calls all his major secular cantatas musical dramas, adding the sub-title for each "Dramma per Musica" (Drama in music) because he designates the actor-singers and has a large orchestration in opera style.

This first Dramma per Musica was composed for the birthday on August 3, 1725, of August Friedrich Müller, a Professor at Leipzig University, on a libretto by Picander. Bach's motive for setting the cantata was to impress the University Council, who had deprived him of what he considered to be his right—to have jurisdiction over the music in the University Church as well as in the other Leipzig churches.

The actors in this neo-classical Greek production (it resembles a stage play without costumes) are Pallas, the goddess of wisdom (soprano); Pomona, the goddess of fruit (alto); Zephyrus, the god of gentle breezes (tenor); and Aeolus, the god of winds (bass). A four-part chorus represents a chorus of the winds in the opening number and closes the cantata with a birthday wish for Professor Müller. The orchestra has one of the largest groups of instruments assembled by Bach for any of his cantatas: three trumpets, two horns, timpani, two transverse flutes, two oboes, an oboe d'amore, a viola d'amore, a viola da gamba, two violas, eight violins, two violoncelli, a violone, a bassoon and continuo including a cembalo and organ.

We may assume that this lavish production took place in the open Market Place with members of the student body as performers.

1. *Chorus of the Winds.* All instruments except the oboe d'amore, the viola d'amore and the viola da gamba play a melody with a brilliant and vivacious rhythm to illustrate the power of the imprisoned winds and the derangement in nature that they will cause, once they break out of their confinement. The vocal parts sing explosive repetitions of the first verbs, "Zerreisset, zersprenget," followed by a united repetition of the first two lines, and unison singing for the rest of the chorus.

Bach's tone-painting for this chorus is amazing: the winds become alive as they describe the havoc they will wreak: "Zerreisset, zersprenget, zertrümmert die Gruft, / Die unserm Wüten Grenze gibt! / Durchbrechet die Luft, / Dass selber die Sonne zur Finsternis werde, / Durchschneidet die Fluten, durchwühlet die Erde, / Dass sich der Himmel selbst betrübt!" (Tear up, blow up, shatter the cave, / Which gives a limit to our raging! / Break through the air, / So that even the sun becomes darkness. / Cut through the floods, upturn the earth, / So that heaven itself grieves!)

2. *Recitative—bass* (AEOLUS). Aeolus promises the winds that they will soon be released from their vault now that summer is drawing to a close. Thrice he sings, "Ich geb' euch Macht" (I give you power): first to vent their wrath of cold, frost and snow on flowers, leaves and clover; then to rend cedars and mountain-tops; and finally to extinguish the

stars' fire by blowing up tempestuous seas.

3. *Aria—bass* (AEOLUS). A motif of tremendous joy is expressed in this aria, accompanied by an oboe and strings. It reminds the listener of Handel's aria, "Haste thee, nymph, and bring with thee," in *L'Allegro.* Both arias express realistic laughter: Bach's is of the Schadenfreude (joy in hurting) type, according to Aeolus's character, while Handel's is just unbridled merriment. Bach enhances the joy-motif by giving Aeolus realistic runs on "lachen" and "krachen." His number precedes Handel's by fifteen years.

"Wie will ich lustig lachen, / Wenn alles durcheinandergeht, / Wenn selbst der Fels nicht sicher steht, / Und wenn die Dächer krachen, / So will ich lustig lachen!" (How merrily will I laugh, / When everything is in confusion, / When even the rock does not stand firm. / And when the roofs crack, / Then will I merrily laugh!)

4. *Recitative—tenor* (ZEPHYRUS). Now a series of pleas by the other actors that Aeolus delay release of the winds. The contrast between the gentle Zephyrus and the arrogant Aeolus is an example of Bach's masterful characterization. In secco, he begs Aeolus to defer his decision as a favor to him as one of his winds.

5. *Aria—tenor* (ZEPHYRUS). Accompanied by the viola da gamba and the viola d'amore, the tenor's song is full of regret that he and the summer foliage will disappear. The melody paints a tone-picture of the melancholy of autumn: "Frische Schatten, meine Freude, / Sehet, wie ich schmerzlich scheide, / Kommt, bedauert meine Schmach! / Windet euch, verwaiste Zweige, / Ach! ich schweige, / Sehet mir nur jammernd nach!" (Cool shadows, my joy, / See how painfully I depart. / Come, pity my disgrace! / Entwine yourselves, orphaned branches. / Ah! I am silent, / Look upon me only with pity!)

6. *Recitative—bass* (AEOLUS). Aeolus answers, in secco, that Zephyrus almost moves him, but seeing Pomona and Pallas, he wonders why they are approaching him.

7. *Aria—alto* (POMONA). Bach has reserved the other accompanying instrument, the oboe d'amore, for this very beautiful lament over the impending blight of her fruit tress, caused by the untimely arrival of the winds. The tempo of the melody evokes the imagery of leaves falling listlessly from the trees: "Können nicht die roten Wangen, / Womit meine Früchte prangen, / Dein ergrimmtes Herze fangen, / Ach, so sage, kannst du seh'n, / Wie die Blätter von den Zweigen / Sich betrübt zur Erden beugen, / Um ihr Elend abzuneigen, / Das an ihnen soll gescheh'n." (Cannot the red cheeks, / With which my fruits glow, / Catch thy angered heart? / Ah, then speak, canst thou see / How the leaves of the branches / Bend sadly to the earth / To avert their misery, / That is to happen to them.)

8. *Recitative—alto, soprano* (POMONA, PALLAS). Pomona begins this secco number by asking Aeolus if he will remain rock-hard against her request. Pallas says that perhaps she can influence Aeolus. A short duet occurs in the last line as they sing that Aeolus may soon show himself kinder towards them.

9. *Aria—soprano* (PALLAS). A solo violin obbligato accompanies her smoothly flowing address, first to Zephyrus and then to Aeolus. The same lines are repeated for both of them. Bach's melody suggests a picture of trees and grass bending under the gentle breezes of Zephyrus: "Angenehmer Zephyrus, / Dein von Bisam reicher Kuss / Und dein lauschend Kühlen / Soll auf meinen Höhen spielen. / Grosser König Aeolus, / Sage doch dem Zephyrus, / Dass sein bisamreicher Kuss / Und sein lauschend Kühlen / Soll auf meinen Höhen spielen." (Pleasant Zephyrus, / Thy musk-rich kiss / and thy drowsy coolness / Shall play on my heights. / Great king Aeolus, / Say then to Zephyrus, / That his musk-rich kiss / And his drowsy coolness / Shall play on my heights.)

Bach borrowed this number for the soprano aria in his later BWV 171.

10. *Recitative—soprano, bass* (PALLAS, AEOLUS). The two transverse flutes appear in the last part of the continuo accompanying this dialogue, in which Pallus gives the reason why the winds should be still restrained. She and her muses wish to celebrate August Müller's birthday on Helicon. Although the tyrannical Aeolus does not like a woman interfering in his will, he agrees to withhold his winds during this festivity. Aeolus's exclamations of surprise at hearing Müller's name add a fine dramatic touch to this number.

11. *Aria—bass* (AEOLUS). This is a splendid aria for all brass and percussion, with forceful vocal runs on "zurücke" (back) and "wehet" (blow) to show Aeolus's command over the winds. It is one of Bach's most impressive coloratura arias in highly dramatic style.

"Zurücke, zurücke, geflügelten Winde, / Besänftiget euch! / Doch wehet ihr gleich, / So wehet doch itzund nur gelinde! (Back, back winged winds, / Calm yourselves! / Yet if you blow, / Then blow now only gently!)

12. *Recitative—soprano, alto, tenor* (PALLAS, POMONA, ZEPHYRUS). This trio expresses, with continuo only, the joy felt by each of the deities over the fulfillment of their wishes. There is a unison declamation between their individual exclamations, and a duet for Pomona and Zephyrus at the end, as they agree to join the festivity of Pallas on Helicon.

13. *Duet—alto, tenor* (POMONA, ZEPHYRUS). The two transverse flutes play an accompanying joy-motif as they sing of the birthday gifts that they will bring to August Müller at his party.

POMONA: "Zweig' und Äste / Zollen dir zu deinem Feste / Ihrer Gaben Überfluss." (Twigs and boughs / pay thee for thy feast / With the abundance of their gifts.)

ZEPHYRUS: "Und mein Scherzen soll und muss, / Deinen August zu verehren, / Dieses Tages Lust vermehren." (And my jesting shall and must, / To honor thy August, / Increase the joy of this day.)

POMONA: "Ich bringe die Früchte mit Freuden herbei," (I bring the fruits with joy here,)

ZEPHYRUS: "Ich bringe mein Lispeln mit Freuden herbei" (My rustling)

BOTH: "Dass alles zum Scherzen vollkommener sei." (So that everything may be more perfect in jollity.)

14. *Recitative—soprano* (PALLAS). In secco, Pallas invites all to come to the festivity on her heights, where all the muses are eagerly waiting for them to begin the celebration. Pallas asks them to join the chorus of August's well-wishers as they hasten to the party, thus introducing the final chorus.

15. *Chorus.* The melody of this concluding tutti number resembles a march or the processional music of an academic song-fest. Since the University students must have formed this particular choir, they would be familiar with this serenade style. Their song is a tremendous compliment to their Professor; the instrumental color of trumpets, horns and drums is a tribute worthy of royalty!

"Vivat August, August vivat! / Sei beglückt, gelehrter Mann! / Dein Vergnügen müsse blühen, / Dass dein Lehren, dein Bemühen / Möge solche Pflanzen ziehen, / Womit ein Land sich einstens schmücken kann." (Long live August, long live August! / Be fortunate, learned man! / Your satisfaction must blossom, / In that your teaching, your caring, / May raise such plants, / With which a country can adorn itself some day.)

• **Vereinigte Zwietracht der wechselnden Saiten (United Discord of the Varying Strings)** (1726; BWV 207).

This is Bach's second "Dramma per Musica," again composed in honor of a member of the teaching faculty of Leipzig University, Gottlieb Kortte, on his appointment as Professor of Roman Law, December 11, 1726. This date seems to indicate that it was performed in the main hall of the University rather than out of doors; also the cantata proper is preceded by a march for three trumpets, timpani and strings, usual for an academic indoor procession.

The characters in this drama are personifications of Glück (Fortune), soprano; Dankbarkeit (Gratitude), alto; Fleiss (Diligence), tenor; and Ehre (Fame), bass. It is not known who the librettist was. There is no plot in the cantata; it consists of a series of numbers praising Kortte and encouraging students to emulate him. The four-part choruses and the arias are very impressive, but the recitatives are too long and boring because of their pedantic preaching to the students.

The instruments are three trumpets, timpani, two transverse flutes, two oboes d'amore, a tenor oboe (taille), a bassoon, strings and continuo.

1. *Chorus.* After a colorful introductory march, the orchestra plays the second Allegro movement of the *First Brandenburg Concerto,* adapted by Bach for the ritornello of this chorus. The choir sings the lines, sometimes in unison and sometimes in imitation by parts. The drums illustrate their second line very effectively. Bach's concerto movement fits the text exactly, but the text is unusual because it is the only instance, after BWV 172, where the orchestral sections are addressed directly, until BWV 214: "Vereinigte Zwietracht der wechselnden Saiten, / Der rollenden Pauken durchdringender Knall! / Locket den lüsternen Hörer herbei, / Saget mit euren frohlockenden Tönen / Und doppelt vermehrtem Schall / Denen mir emsig ergebenen Söhnen, / Was hier der Lohn der Tugend sei!" (United discord of the varying strings, / The penetrating rumble of rolling drums, / Attract the desirous listener to you. / Tell with your rejoicing tones / And doubly increased sound / To my busily devoted sons, / What the reward of virtue is here!)

2. *Recitative—tenor* (FLEISS) (DILIGENCE). As one would expect, Diligence exhorts these youthful students to work hard to reach their goals, so that they may enjoy their old age in the rest that a "sour sweat" has sweetened for them.

3. *Aria—tenor* (FLEISS) (DILIGENCE). An oboe d'amore and a violin play a very attractive joy-motif throughout, depicting the reward that Diligence offers. Bach illustrates the words "Fuss" (Foot), "Schritte" (Steps), and "Tritte" (Paces) with a dancing step-rhythm for the lines where they occur. We see the image of a confident, carefree student as he strides along the road that Diligence has set for him, until he reaches the end, where he will find his reward. Perhaps Bach was thinking of his own persistent efforts to improve himself by study, when he composed this fine aria.

"Zieht euren Fuss nicht zurücke, / Ihr, die ihr meinen Weg erwählt! / Das Glücke / Merket eure Schritte, / Die Ehre zählt die sauern Tritte, / Damit, dass nach vollbrachter Strasse / Euch werd' in gleichem Übermasse / Der Lohn von ihnen zugezählt." (Do not turn your foot back, / You who choose my way! / Good luck / Marks your steps, / Honor counts the difficult paces, / So that, after your completed journey, / To you will be counted back / The reward from them in equal abundance.)

4. *Recitative—bass, soprano* (EHRE, GLUCK) (FAME, FORTUNE). In the above order, each states the nature of the reward he will give. Fame will bestow his laurel wreath on those "sons" of Diligence who have shunned worldly voluptuousness. Fortune affirms that her favor depends also on the individual student. Her recitative is not as clearly expressed and is more long-winded than his.

5. *Duet—bass, soprano* (EHRE, GLUCK) (FAME, FORTUNE). Although this libretto contains only moralizing preaching on students' efforts, Bach's spirited melody and artistic setting for the vocalists monopolize the listener's attention. Yet the figurative language of the text is very fine also.

EHRE: "Den soll mein Lorbeer schützend decken" (FAME: Him shall my laurel cover protectingly)

GLUCK: "Der soll die Frucht des Segens schmecken" (FORTUNE: He shall taste the fruit of blessing)

(BOTH): "Der durch den Fleiss zu Sternen steigt." (Who by diligence climbs to the stars.)

EHRE: "Benetzt des Schweisses Tau die Glieder, / So fällt er in die Muscheln nieder, / Wo er der Ehre Perlen zeugt." (FAME: If the dew of sweat dampens limbs, / Then it drops down into shells, / Where it produces pearls of glory.)

GLUCK: "Wo die erhitzten Tropfen fliessen, / Da wird ein Strom daraus entspriessen, / Der denen Segensbächen gleicht." (FORTUNE: Where the heated drops flow, / From there will a stream spring forth, / Which is like those brooks of blessing.)

This duet is followed by an orchestral interlude, the final movement of the *First Brandenburg Concerto.* Like the opening piece, it appears to be a march. These are the only instrumental numbers in the secular cantatas, apart from the sinfonias in BWV 212 and BWV 209.

6. *Recitative—alto* (DANKBARKEIT) (GRATITUDE). Gratitude brings the thought of their teacher as an example to the listening student body. Through his scholarship, he has attained his chair, in spite of those who envy him. Therefore our well-wishes should sincerely spring from our hearts, as the flames spring from lighted candles.

7. *Aria—alto* (DANKBARKEIT) (GRATITUDE). Gratitude would like to carve Kortte's image in marble to make him immortal, but she realizes that stone will crumble in time and therefore his students' deeds will be a more perpetual memorial to a model teacher. Bach seizes on the first line, from which he paints a realistic and vivid tone-picture, with the two transverse flutes and continuo playing a dotted rhythm. We can hear the stone-masons at work as they chisel the teacher's memorial! This rhythm continues throughout the aria; Bach has composed a unique way of expanding the imagery to express the toil of students. For Bach himself knew the perseverance required for success in learning.

"Ätzet dieses Angedenken in den härt'sten Marmor ein! / Doch die Zeit verdirbt den Stein. / Lasst vielmehr aus euren Taten / Eures Lehrers Tun erraten! / Kann man aus den Früchten lesen, / Wie die Wurzel sei gewesen, / Muss sie unvergänglich sein." (Engrave this memorial in hardest marble! / Yet time corrodes stone. / Rather let your deeds from / Your teacher's doing be guessed! / If one can read from the fruits, / How the root has been, / It must be imperishable.)

8. *Recitative—tenor, bass, soprano, alto* (FLEISS, EHRE, GLUCK, DANKBARKEIT) (DILIGENCE, FAME, FORTUNE, GRATITUDE). Each character in this order praises Kortte as the ideal scholar. Fleiss addresses the sleepy idlers of the University to imitate Kortte's industry. Even Augustus II has recognized this professor and has named him as his teacher. Whether the librettist knew that this was true is questionable in view of the Elector's other activities, good and bad. Ehre states that he has given Kortte many laurels and will continue to do so, since the Monarch still protects him.

Glück speaks of the favors she bestows on Kortte, which make him happy. Dankbarkeit says that the students have not appreciated Kortte enough, because they have failed in their duty to him. Now she asks them to join in his praise by singing the following chorus.

9. *Chorus.* This final tutti number suggests a march, similar to the orchestral prelude, as the students' procession moves through the hall. After the first line, which is all that the choir sings, each of the soloists sings a line in succession and ending in unison. The rapid tempo of their development astounds the listener, until the choir returns to sing the da capo of the thunderous first line. Bach has certainly composed a most novel chorus here: "Kortte lebe, Kortte blühe! / Den mein Lorbeer unterstützt, / Der mir selbst im Schosse sitzt, / Der durch mich stets höher steigt, / Der die Herzen zu sich neigt, / Muss in ungezählten Jahren / Stets geehrt in Segen steh'n, / Und zwar wohl der Neider Scharen, / Aber nicht der Feinde seh'n." (Long live Kortte, may Kortte flourish! / Whom my

laurel supports, / Who himself sits in my bosom, / Who through me always climbs higher, / Who inclines hearts to himself, / Must in countless years / Stand always honored in blessing, / And surely see the hosts of the envious, / But not those of enemies.)

On 3 August 1734, Bach adapted this cantata as a birthday cantata entitled *Auf, Schmetternde Töne* (Up, Resounding Tones), BWV 207a, in honor of Augustus III. All he had to do was change the libretto to fit the royal occasion, since the music is identical for all numbers. But who the librettist was for this borrowed work is also unknown.

• **Auf, schmetternde Töne (Up, Resounding Tones)** (3 August 1734; BWV 207a).

Whittaker states that Picander was the librettist for this royal birthday cantata as well as for the 1726 original version (Vol. II, p. 654). It would seem that the learned classical allusions in the text would indicate Picander as its author. This later version in honor of the Elector Augustus III's birthday reveals Bach's most complete borrowing from any of his previously composed cantatas. The music for each number was simply applied to the new work—an unusual procedure for a composer who normally drew his inspiration from the text he set. Perhaps Bach thought that his Leipzig audience would not remember his cantata of eight years before!

Bach conducted the performance by his Collegium Musicum in Zimmermann's Garden, apparently in the evening, because the Leipzig newspaper announcements for this coming event mentioned illuminations. Augustus III was not present, being in Poland at the time, but many Leipzig dignitaries attended and thus the King would be informed of this tribute to him.

The lavish orchestra with choir and vocalists was identical with that which Bach had used in BWV 207 in praise of Professor Kortte.

Although this later version is seldom performed today, its libretto should be examined as a part of Bach's complete vocal cantata production.

1. *Chorus.* After the same orchestral march as in the original, the chorus begins to sing. Their text addresses the instruments of the orchestra as it had in the earlier version and in BWV 214 of the previous year: "Auf, schmetternde Töne der muntern Trompeten; / Ihr donnernden Pauken, erhebet den Knall! / Reizende Saiten, ergötzet das Ohr; / Suchet auf Flöten das Schönste zu finden; / Erfüllet mit lieblichem Schall / Unsre so süsse als grünende Linden / Und unser frohes Musenchor!" (Up, resounding tones of merry trumpets; / You thundering drums, raise thunder! / Charming strings, delight the ear; / Try to find the greatest beauty on flutes; / Fill with lovely sound / Our just as sweet as greening lindens / And our happy chorus of muses!)

2. *Recitative—tenor.* The poetic ability of the librettist (Picander?) is at its best in this picture of nature along Leipzig's Pleisse River. But Bach's adapted music paints no visual imagery of this landscape.

"Die stille Pleisse spielt / Mit ihren kleinen Wellen. / Das grüne Ufer fühlt / Itzt gleichsam neue Kräfte / Und doppelt innre, rege Säfte. / Es prangt mit weichem Moos und Klee; / Dort blühet manche schöne Blume. / Hier hebt zur Flora grossem Ruhme / Sich eine Pflanze in der Höh / Und will ihr Wachstum zeigen. / Der Pallas holder Hain / Sucht sich in Schmuck und Schimmer zu erneu'n; / Die Castalinnen singen Lieder; / Die Nymphen gehen hin und wider / Und wollen hier und dort bei unsern Linden / Und was? den angenehmen Ort / Ihres schönsten Gegenstandes finden. / Denn dieser Tag bringt allen Lust; / Doch in der Sachsen Brust / Geht diese Lust am allerstärksten fort." (The calm Pleisse plays / With her little waves. / The green shore feels / Now likewise new strength / And doubles her inner, active sap. / It sparkles with soft moss and clover; / There many a pretty flower blooms. / Here to Flora's great glory / A plant raises itself up / And wants to show its growth / The charming grove of Pallas / Tries to renew itself in ornament and glitter; / The Castalians (nymphs of Parnassus) sing songs; / Nymphs go hither and thither / And wish here and there near our lindens / And for what? To find the pleasant spot / Of their prettiest object. / For this day brings joy to all; / Yet in the breast of Saxons / This joy goes along most strongly.)

3. *Aria—tenor.* Extravagant praise of Augustus personally and for his protection of Saxony is the theme of each number from this point to the end of the libretto: "Augustus' Namenstages Schimmer / Verklärt der Sachsen Angesicht. / Gott schützt die frommen Sachsen immer, / Denn unsers Landesvaters Zimmer / Prangt heut in neuen Glückes Strahlen, / Die soll itzt unsere Ehrfurcht malen / Bei dem erwünschten Namenslicht." (The splendor of August's birthday / Transfigures the face of Saxons. / God protects pious Saxons always, / For our sovereign's room / Shines today in the rays of new good-luck, / Which shall now portray our respect / For the wished-for light of his name.)

4. *Recitative—soprano, bass.* Vividly descriptive local color pertaining to Leipzig and the lively dialogue between the soloists make this number's text particularly attractive.

SOPRANO: "Augustus' Wohl / Ist der treuen Sachsen Wohlergehn." (August's welfare / Is the well-being of faithful Saxons.)

BASS: "Augustus' Arm beschützt / Der Sachsen grüne Weiden." (August's arm protects / Saxons' green meadows.)

SOPRANO: "Die Elbe nützt / Dem Kaufmann mit so vielen Freuden." (The Elbe is useful / To the merchant with its so many joys.)

BASS: "Des Hofes Pracht und Flor / Stellt uns Augustus' Glücke vor." (The court's splendor and prosperity / Presents to us August's good fortune.)

SOPRANO: "Die Untertanen sehn / An jedem Ort ihr Wohlergehn." (His subjects see / In every place their well-being.)

BASS: "Des Mavors heller Stahl muss alle Feinde schrecken, / Um uns vor allem Unglück zu bedecken." (Mars' bright steel must frighten all enemies, / In order to protect us from all misfortune.)

SOPRANO: "Drum freut sich heute der Merkur / Mit seinen weisen Söhnen / Und findt bei diesen Freudentönen / Der ersten güldnen Zeiten Spur." (Therefore Mercury rejoices today / With his wise sons / And finds in these joyful tones / The trace of the first golden times.)

BASS: "Augustus mehrt das Reich. (Augustus increases the kingdom.)

SOPRANO: Irenens Lorbeer wird nie bleich." Irene's laurel never becomes pale.)

SOPRANO AND BASS: "Die Linden wollen schöner grünen, / Um uns mit ihrem Flor bei diesem hohen Namenstag zu dienen." (The lindens wish to turn more beautifully green, / In order to serve us with their blooming on this high birthday.)

5. *Aria (Duet)—bass, soprano.* Peace and prosperity make Saxony the ideal country in which to live.

BASS: "Mich kann die süsse Ruhe laben;" (Sweet rest can refresh me;)

SOPRANO: "Ich kann hier mein Vergnügen haben." (I can here have my pleasure.)

SOPRANO AND BASS: "Wir beide stehn hier hiochst beglückt." (We both stand here most lucky.)

BASS: "Denn unsre fette Saaten lachen / Und können viel Vergnügen machen, / Weil sie kein Feind noch Wetter drückt." (For our plump seeds laugh / And can make much delight, / Because no enemy or bad weather oppresses them.)

SOPRANO: "Wo solche holde Stunden kommen, / Da hat das Glücke zugenommen, / Das uns der heitre Himmel schickt." (Where such charming hours come, / There has good fortune increased, / Which the cheerful sky sends to us.)

6. *Recitative—alto.* Although he takes pleasure in the royal sport of hunting, as an enlightened ruler, Augustus will not let his people starve: "Augustus schützt die frohen Felder, / Augustus liebt die grünen Walder, / Wenn sein erhabner Mut / Im Jagen niemals eher ruht, / Bis er ein schönes Tier gefället. / Der Landmann sieht mit Lust / Auf seinem Acker schöne Garben. / Ihm ist stets wohlbewusst, / Wie keiner darf in Sachsen darben. / Wer sich nur in sein Glücke findt / Und seine Kräfte recht ergründt." (Augustus protects the happy fields; / Augustus loves the green forests, / When his sublime courage / In hunting never rests / Until he has felled a fine animal. / The peasant sees with joy / Beautiful sheaves on his field. / He is always well aware / That nobody in Saxony may be in want. / Whoever he may be who just finds himself in his good fortune / And rightly establishes his powers.)

7. *Aria—alto.* "Preiset, späte Folgezeiten, / Nebst dem gütigen Geschick / Des Augustus grosses Glück! / Denn in des Monarchen Taten / Könnt ihr Sachsens Wohl erraten; / Man kann aus dem Schimmer lesen, / Wer Augustus sei gewesen." (Praise, late posterity, / Besides favorable fate / The great good fortune of Augustus! / For in the monarch's deeds / You can guess Saxony's welfare; / One can read from the splendor / Who Augustus has been.)

8. *Recitative—tenor, bass, soprano, alto.* Flattery for Augustus by each soloist in turn makes this number exceedingly tedious.

TENOR: "Ihr Fröhlichen, herbei! / Erblickt, ihr Sachsen und ihr grosse Staaten, / Aus Augustus' holden Taten, / Was Weisheit und auch Stärke sei! / Sein allzeit starker Arm schützt teils Sarmatien, / Teils auch der Sachsen Wohlergehn. / Wir sehen als getreue Untertanen / Durch Weisheit die für uns erlangte Friedensfahne. / Wie sehr er uns geliebt, / Wie mächtig er die Sachsen stets geschützet, / Zeigt dessen Säbels Stahl, der vor uns Sachsen blitzet. / Wir können unsern Landesvater / Als einen Held und Siegesrater / In dem grossmächtigsten August / Mit heisser Ehrfurcht itzt verehren / Und unsre Wünsche mehren." (You happy ones, come here! / Notice, you Saxons and you great states, / From the gracious deeds of Augustus / What wisdom and strength too is! / His constantly strong arm protects partly Poland, / And partly also Saxons' well-being. / We see as loyal subjects / The flag of peace, attained for us through wisdom. / How very much he has loved us, / How mightily he has always protected Saxons, / Shows his saber's steel, which shines before us Saxons. / We can honor the father of our country / As a hero and victory-counselor / In this most powerful August / With warm respect now / And increase our wishes.)

BASS: "Ja, ja, ihr starken Helden, seht der Sachsen unerschöpfte Kräfte / Und ihren hohen Schutzgott an und Sachsens Rautensäfte! / Itzt soll der Saiten Ton / Die frohe Lust ausdrücken, / Denn des Augustus fester Thron / Muss uns allzeit beglücken." (Yes, yes, you strong heroes, look at the inexhaustible power of Saxons / And their high protecting god and Saxony's rue-sap! [The rue is in the Saxon coat of arms.] / Now shall the tone of strings / Express happy joy, / For the firm throne of Augustus / Must always bring us good fortune.)

SOPRANO: "Augustus gibt uns steten Schatten, / Der aller Sachsen und Sarmaten Glück erhält, / Der stete Augenmark der Welt / Den alle Augen hatten." (Augustus gives us constant protection. / He holds the fortune of all Saxons and Poles, / The constant point of view of the world / For whom all had eyes.)

ALTO: "O heitres, hohes Namenslicht! / O Name, der die Freude mehrt! / O allerwünschtes Angedenken, / Wie stärkst du unsre Pflicht! / Ihr frohe Wünsche und ihr starke Freuden, / Die Pleisse sucht durch ihr Bezeigen / Die Linden in so jungen Zweigen / Der schönen Stunden Lust und Wohl zu krön'n / Und zu erhöhn." (Oh, glad, high name of light! / Oh, name which increases joy! / Oh, all-to-be-wished for memory, / How you strengthen our duty! / You happy wishes and you strong joys, arise! / The Pleisse strives though her showing / The lindens in such young branches / To crown and enhance the joy and well-being of these fine hours.)

9. *Chorus.* "August lebe! / Lebe König! / O Augustus, unser Schutz, / Sei der starren Feinde Trutz, / Lebe lange deinem Land, / Gott schützt deinen Geist und Hand. / So muss durch Augustus' Leben / Unsers Sachsens Wohl bestehen; / So darf sich kein Feind erheben / Wider unser Wohlergehn." (Long live August! / Long may you live, King! / Oh Augustus, our guardian, / Be the defiance of our obstinate enemies; / Live long for your country; / God protects your spirit and hand. / Therefore through August's life / Our Saxony's welfare must continue. / Therefore no enemy may arise / Against our well-being.)

• **Ich bin in mir vergnügt [Von der Vergnügsamkeit] (I Am Content in Myself [On Contentment])** (c. 1728; BWV 204).

This solo cantata for soprano was probably first sung by Anna Magdalena in Bach's family circle during the mourning interval for Queen Christiane Eberhardine (see BWV 198) when Bach could not compose church cantatas. The reason for its performance on any other occasion is not known. The recitatives are all very long and complex, which would make one wonder about its suitability for domestic use. On the other hand, the arias are short and tuneful; the final one is the gem of the whole work, another of Bach's outstanding soprano solo arias with intense emotional beauty. The instrumentation is very simple: two oboes, a transverse flute, two violins and continuo.

1. *Recitative.* She begins with a statement of the theme: "Ich bin in mir vergnügt, ein andrer mache Grillen, / Er wird doch nicht damit den Sack noch Magen füllen!" (I am content in myself, another may have fancies; / He will still not fill his purse or stomach with them!)

Each line of this number is broken into two halves, each half contrasting with the other as the above lines illustrate. The unknown librettist was very skillful in this arrangement.

2. *Aria.* The two oboes and the continuo accompany her further comparison of those who find satisfaction within themselves and those who seek it in the world but never find it there: "Ruhig und in sich zufrieden / Ist der grösste Schatz der Welt. / Nichts geniesset, der geniesset, / Was der Erden Kreis umschliesset, / Der ein armes Herz behält." (To be at peace and satisfied within oneself / Is the greatest treasure of the world. / He enjoys nothing, who enjoys / What the earth's sphere encloses, / That person has a poor heart.)

Bach adorns these last lines with a tear-motif.

3. *Recitative.* Strings accompany her denunciation of those who misguidedly seek property and wealth, which vanish like dust. Money, pleasure and honor are likewise to be despised as a source of contentment.

4. *Aria.* As she sings of where true riches may be found, a solo violin accompanies her with a melody that is charmingly persuasive: "Die Schätzbarkeit der weiten Erden / Lass' meine Seele ruhig sein. / Bei dem kehrt stets der Himmel ein, / Der in der Armut reich kann werden." (The treasure of the wide world, / May it leave my soul in peace. / Heaven always comes to him, / Who can become rich in his poverty.)

5. *Recitative.* This secco number contains several interesting metaphors: comparing discontent and worries to hundred-weights created by our fancies, comparing the contentment sent from heaven to the pearls in oyster-shells or to a jewel that is unobtainable in all of earth's treasures.

6. *Aria.* Beautiful imagery is woven by a transverse flute that plays a sparkling melody, depicting the shining pearls of content in the last line. The bliss she

feels in her own peace of mind is well expressed by her song: "Meine Seele sei vergnügt, / Wie es Gott auch immer fügt. / Dieses Weltmeer zu ergründen / Ist Gefahr und Eitelkeit, / In sich selber muss man finden / Perlen der Zufriedenheit." (May my soul be contented, / However God decrees it to be. / To fathom the sea of this world / Is danger and vanity. / In oneself must one find / Pearls of satisfaction.)

7. *Recitative and Arioso.* With these two secco parts almost equally divided, she begins the recitative section by comparing a noble person to a pearl-shell—smug in the knowledge of the wealth it contains. But in conclusion, she states that she prefers God's favor to earthly riches.

In her arioso section, she mentions how vain it is to depend on friends for help when one is in trouble. If she makes desire her aim in life, she will only cause herself anxiety and sorrow, because everything temporal comes to an end.

8. *Aria.* Oboes and strings play the basic joy-motif for this aria, while the transverse flute plays its own happy melody above theirs. The emotional Affekt of this combination with her voice is stupendous; this aria has a mystical appeal that would qualify it for a place in any of Bach's sacred cantatas. It is one of Bach's divine inspirations.

"Himmlische Vergnügsamkeit, / Welches Herz sich dir ergibet, / Lebet allzeit unbetrübet / Und geniesst der güldnen Zeit. / Göttliche Vergnügsamkeit, / Du, du machst die Armen reich / Und dieselben Fürsten gleich. / Meine Brust bleibt dir geweiht." (Heavenly contentment, / Whatever heart gives itself to thee, / Lives always without sadness / And enjoys the golden time. / Divine contentment, / Thou, thou makest the poor rich / And like those same princes. / My heart remains devoted to thee.)

• **Geschwinde, geschwinde, ihr wirbelnden Winde [Der Streit zwischen Phoebus und Pan] (Quickly, Quickly, You Whirling Winds [The Contention between Phoebus and Pan])** (1731; BWV 201).

Bach had been directing the Leipzig Collegium Musicum since 1729 when he composed the music for this satirical "Dramma per Musica" in the summer of 1731. This cantata was likely presented in Zimmermann's Garden near the Grimm Gate, where this group of students from the University gave open-air concerts.

Bach must have collaborated very closely with Picander for this libretto, which ridicules those opposed to his music. The work is aimed especially at the Hamburg music critic Johann Adolf Scheibe, represented by Midas in the cantata. Scheibe had criticized Bach's vocal music as being artificial, tedious and too learned. It seems that his enmity resulted from being rejected by Bach for the position as organist in St. Thomas's in 1729.

Picander takes his story from Ovid—the singing contest between Phoebus (Apollo), bass 1, and Pan, bass 2, respectively the gods of wisdom and of the woods, and adds four other characters to his drama: Momus (the god of mockery), soprano; Mercury (the god of commerce), alto; Tmolus (the Lydian god who judged the contest), tenor 1; and Midas (the Phrygian king and also reputed to be a judge), tenor 2.

The orchestra consists of three trumpets, timpani, two transverse flutes, two oboi d'amore, two violins, a viola and continuo. There is a four-part chorus.

1. *Chorus.* As with BWV 205, this opening chorus is addressed to the winds. On this occasion, however, they are commanded to retreat into their cave in order to leave the air free for the coming song-contest. Bach's melodic setting of the first part portrays the haste of the whirling winds as they sweep back into their confinement; his second theme interprets the echo effect of the singing that will result from the quiet in the air after their departure. In the first section, the voices enter in succession, demonstrating their power, whereas in the second, they sing

with frequent breaks in the lines, as if waiting to hear their own echo. Bach has illustrated this text exceptionally well: "Geschwinde, geschwinde, / Ihr wirbelnden Winde, / Auf einmal zusammen zur Höhle hinein! / Dass das Hin- und Widerschallen / Selbst dem Echo mag gefallen, / Und den Lüften lieblich sein." (Quickly, quickly, / You whirling winds, / At once together into the cave, / So that the reverberations / May please even Echo, / And be delightful to the airs.)

2. *Recitative—bass 1* (PHOEBUS), *bass 2* (PAN), *soprano* (MOMUS). The two contestants, Phoebus and Pan, hold a dialogue on their respective expertise in singing, which concludes with a scornful comment against Pan by Momus.

Phoebus asks Pan how he can be so unashamed in believing that his singing is superior to that of the god of poetry and music. Pan replies that the woods applaud his musical ability, and that even the choirs of nymphs dance to the music he plays on his reed-pipe. Phoebus sayst that may please nymphs but not gods; Pan answers that his melody can charm all nature, and even birds want to learn to sing from him. Phoebus represents Bach's conception of music and Pan, Scheibe's.

Momus derides Pan as the great mastersinger.

3. *Aria—soprano* (MOMUS). This aria, accompanied by continuo only, resembles a number from comic opera. Momus scoffs at Pan's boasting, calling it empty wind to his master Phoebus. He states "Das macht der Wind" (That, the Wind Does) to a different tune after each line: (1) That one boasts and has no money, (2) That one takes all he sees for truth, (3) That fools are wise, (4) That luck itself is blind.

4. *Recitative—alto* (MERCURIUS), *bass 1* (PHOEBUS), *bass 2* (PAN). Mercury says that they need not quarrel, but that each should choose a judge. Phoebus selects Tmolus and Pan takes Midas. Mercury summons the audience to listen and decide who is the better singer.

5. *Aria—bass 1* (PHOEBUS). Phoebus expresses his languishing yearning for the youth Hyacinthus as the subject of his beautiful song. Bach's own artistic view on singing is expressed in this moving declamation, aided by a transverse flute, an oboe d'amore and strings which play a bewitching and gentle melody. This is Bach's art at its best.

"Mit Verlangen / Drück' ich deine zarten Wangen, / Holder, schöner Hyazinth. / Und dein' Augen küss' ich gerne, / Weil sie meine Morgensterne / Und der Seele Sonne sind." (With longing / I press your tender cheeks, / Charming, beautiful Hyacinth. / And I like to kiss your eyes, / Because they are my morning-stars / And the sun of my soul.)

6. *Recitative—soprano* (MOMUS), *bass 2* (PAN). A very short number: Momus calls on Pan to sing his aria, and he answers that he will surpass Phoebus.

7. *Aria—bass 2* (PAN). The violins play a joyful tune as they accompany Pan's song; this lampoons Scheibe's "natural" style by its comical broken runs on "wackelt" (trembles) in the first line. In the remainder, Bach is either contrasting this plain manner with his own learned style or with the over-affected singing of some operatic soloists. Such an opera buffa number must have given his student-audience much amusement.

"Zu Tanze, zu Sprunge, so wackelt das Herz. / Wenn der Ton zu mühsam klingt, / Und der Mund gebunden singt, / So erweckt es keinen Scherz." (For dancing, for leaping, so trembles the heart. / If the tone sounds too labored, / And the mouth sings tightly, / Then it arouses no fun.)

8. *Recitative—alto* (MERCURIUS), *tenor 1* (TMOLUS). Mercury calls the judges for their verdict. Tmolus now makes his entry in the comedy. He decides that Phoebus has won, because Pan's song can only charm nymphs and is not comparable with that of Phoebus.

9. *Aria—tenor* (TMOLUS). Over the placid continuo melody, an obbligato oboe d'amore supports his enthusiasm

for Apollo's entrancing vocal prowess. This is true art for him: "Phoebus, deine Melodei / Hat die Anmut selbst geboren. / Aber wer die Kunst versteht, / Wie dein Ton verwundernd geht, / Wird dabei aus sich verloren." (Phoebus, your melody / Has given birth to charm itself. / But whoever understands art, / How your tone goes admirably, / Is lost out of himself by it.)

10. *Recitative—bass 2* (PAN), *tenor 2* (MIDAS). Now Pan asks his referee, Midas, for his opinion. Midas supports him, of course, and states that he is so impressed that he will teach Pan's "natural" style to the trees. He thinks that Phoebus sings too artificially.

11. *Aria—tenor 2* (MIDAS). The joy-motif in the accompanying strings denotes Midas's feeling of victory for Pan. In the second part, however, both the violins and the continuo depict the braying of an ass, which Midas is made to resemble for his judgment. The symbolic irony in Bach's setting would not be lost on the audience.

"Pan ist Meister, lasst ihn geh'n! / Phoebus hat das Spiel verloren, / Denn nach meinen Beiden Ohren / Singt er unvergleichlich schön." (Pan is master, let him go! / Phoebus has lost the game, / For according to both my ears / He sings with incomparable beauty.)

12. *Recitative—all soloists in this order: soprano, alto, tenor 1, bass 1, tenor 2, bass 2.* To the dismay of Midas and Pan, each actor comments adversely on Midas's poor judgment. Phoebus even tells him that he has donkey's ears.

13. *Aria—alto* (MERCURIUS). Mercury sings this fine aria, accompanied by flutes and strings, to bring the contest and opinions on it to an end. The melody even depicts the ringing of bells on a fool's cap, as Mercury points out the danger of thoughtless judgment, using the metaphor of drowning when a ship sinks: "Aufgeblasne Hitze, / Aber wenig Grütze / Kriegt die Schellenmütze / Endlich aufgesetzt. / Wer das Schiffen nicht versteht / Und doch an das Ruder geht, / Ertrinket mit Schaden und Schanden zuletzt." (Inflated ardor, / But few brains / Gets the cap of bells / Finally placed upon him. / Whoever does not understand navigation / And still goes to the rudder, / Drowns finally with harm and shame.)

14. *Recitative—soprano* (MOMUS). Momus cannot refrain from giving Midas a parting gibe, saying that there are others who are equally thoughtless in their judgment. Bach must have been thinking of his Leipzig critics when he set this number. Momus asks Phoebus to now take up his lyre, as his songs are the loveliest.

15. *Chorus.* The idea of the strings in Phoebus's lyre recurs in the first line of this tutti conclusion. It seems that the chorus confirms the triumph not only of Phoebus but also of Bach himself over his detractors: "Labt das Herz, ihr holden Saiten, / Stimmet Kunst und Anmut an! / Lasst euch meistern, lasst euch höhnen, / Sind doch euren süssen Tönen / Selbst die Götter zugetan." (Refresh the heart, you charming strings, / Harmonize art and gracefulness! / Let yourselves be mastered, scorned; / Yet to your sweet tones / Even the gods are devoted.)

• **Schweigt stille, plaudert nicht [Kaffee-Kantate] (Be Silent, Do Not Chat [Coffee Cantata])** (c. 1732; BWV 211).

Picander wrote this libretto as a satire on the influence of coffee-drinking on the inhabitants of Leipzig, which had spread from the city's coffee-shops into some private homes. Bach was probably the librettist for the last two numbers, which were not in Picander's poem.

These coffee-dispensing establishments had increased so much at this time that the Leipzig Council had imposed a tax on them. This tax is still in effect on coffee purchases in Germany today. Zimmermann's Coffee House would be affected by this tariff; it was here that Bach performed his comic cantata by the Collegium Musicum under his direction.

The plot is very simple: Schlendrian insists that his daughter, Lieschen, must give up coffee-drinking or he will not find a suitable husband for her. Since she wants both, Lieschen will acquiesce in her father's wish, but will have her marriage contract state that she may brew coffee whenever she pleases.

The soli are a narrator (tenor), Lieschen (soprano), and Schlendrian (bass). The instruments are a transverse flute, two violins, a viola and harpsichord continuo.

1. *Recitative—tenor:* "Schweigt stille, plaudert nicht" (Be silent, do not chat). The narrator introduces the comedy by asking the audience to be silent and listen to Herr Schlendrian's complaints about his daughter when both appear on stage. All the recitatives in this cantata are secco.

2. *Aria—bass.* Schlendrian typifies the grumpy father whose children never listen to him. A syncopated rhythm in Bach's musical accompaniment illustrates his suppressed fury, already mentioned by the narrator as making his humor bear-like: "Hat man nicht mit seinen Kindern / Hunderttausend Hudelei! / Was ich immer alle Tage / Meiner Tochter Lieschen sage, / Geht ohne Frucht vorbei." (Does not one have with his children / A hundred-thousand vexations! / What I always say every day / To my daughter Lieschen / Goes past without bearing fruit.)

3. *Recitative—bass, soprano.* This dialogue, in which the father states his will and the daughter her reason why she must have coffee thrice daily, will be followed by two further recitatives with arias separating them. Lieschen says that without coffee, she will become dried up like a roasted goat.

4. *Aria—soprano.* With an obbligato transverse flute, Bach's melody lifts Lieschen's praise of coffee well above the banality of Picander's text. As in all the other arias in this cantata, Bach's musical setting portrays the character of the soloist very distinctly. Coffee is Lieschen's weakness here, as she herself confesses: "Ei! wie schmeckt der Kaffee süsse, / Lieblicher als tausend Küsse, / Milder als Muskatenwein. / Kaffee, Kaffee muss ich haben; / Und wenn jemand mich will laben, / Ach, so schenkt mir Kaffee ein!" (Oh! how sweet coffee tastes, / Nicer than a thousand kisses, / Milder than muscatel wine. / Coffee, coffee I must have; / And if anyone wants to refresh me, / Ah, then he pours out coffee for me!)

5. *Recitative—bass, soprano.* In dramatic fashion, their dialogue continues. Schlendrian threatens to keep Lieschen indoors and not buy her fashionable clothing, unless she consents to give up coffee. But Lieschen still insists on her favorite beverage.

6. *Aria—bass.* With only continuo accompaniment, old Schlendrian first bewails the stubborn attitude of girls, but changes to a more confident tone in the last two lines, because he believes that he can persuade Lieschen by his final argument: give up coffee and she will have a husband: "Mädchen, die von harten Sinnen, / Sind nicht leichte zu gewinnen. / Doch trifft man den rechten Ort: / O! so kömmt man glücklich fort." (Girls, who are of hard disposition, / Are not easy to win. / Yet if one hits the right spot: / Oh! then one comes away happy.)

7. *Recitative—bass, soprano.* Their discussion resumes. Schlendrian says that Lieschen must obey him; she says that she will, but not in regard to coffee. Then he says that she will not have a husband; thereupon, she declares that she will forsake coffee. As Schlendrian listens to her following aria, he thinks that he has won.

8. *Aria—soprano.* The beautiful, sweeping grace of this aria makes it the best number in the cantata. It would not be difficult to imagine that it would fit into one of Bach's sacred cantatas, because Lieschen's emotional longing for a husband has the same Affekt as the soul's longing for Christ. The transverse flute and strings give a brilliant interpretation of Picander's text, which is not on a par with Bach's setting: "Heute noch, / Lieber Vater, tut es doch! / Ach, ein Mann! / Wahrlich, dieser steht mir an! / Wenn es sich doch balde fügte, / Dass ich endlich für Kaffee, /Eh' ich

noch zu Bette geh', / Einen wackern Liebsten kriegte!" (Today then, / Dear father, do it! / Ah, a husband! / Truly, this one suits me! / If it soon happened, / That I finally for coffee, / Before I go to bed, / Should get a brave lover!)

This number ended Picander's libretto. It is thought that Bach added the rest.

9. *Recitative—tenor.* The narrator recounts how Schlendrian goes in search of a husband for Lieschen, but that she lets it be secretly known that no suitor may woo her, unless he promises to have it written in their marriage-contract that she may brew coffee when she wishes. Thus Lieschen intends to dupe her father and her future husband.

10. *Chorus.* The three soloists and all instruments perform this trio with all the usual joy of a concluding number in Italian comic-opera. Even Schlendrian joins in singing the moral of this play: coffee is too strong a temptation for womenfolk, who must have their own way, just as Lieschen had hers!

"Die Katze lässt das Mausen nicht, / Die Jungfern bleiben Kaffeeschwestern. / Die Mutter liebt den Kaffeebrauch, / Die Grossmama trank solchen auch, / Wer will nun auf die Töchter lästern!" (The cat does not leave mousing; / Maidens remain coffee-sisters. / Mother loves the coffee-habit, / Grandma drank such too. / Who will now revile the daughters?)

• **Lasst uns sorgen, lasst uns wachen [Die Wahl des Herkules] (Let Us Take Care, Let Us Watch [The Choice of Hercules])** (1733; BWV 213).

This is the first of three cantatas addressed to the royalty of Saxony; this "Dramma per Musica" honors the birthday of the eleven-year-old Crown Prince, Friedrich Christian. It was performed at the summer meeting of the Collegium Musicum in Zimmermann's Garden, September 5, 1733, but unattended by any of the royal family. It seems that both the librettist, Picander, and Bach hoped to gain royal favor when the news of its performance reached Dresden.

It is interesting to note that Handel composed a one-act opera in English with the same title and plot in 1751, eighteen years after Bach's cantata. Picander's original title was "Herkules auf dem Scheide-Wege" (Hercules at the Crossroads). The characters in both works are identical, except that Bach has a recitative for Mercury instead of Handel's aria for an Attendant on Pleasure.

From this royal "Dramma per Musica" and the two subsequent ones, BWV 214 and 215, Bach borrowed movements for his *Christmas Oratorio,* performed at the end of December 1734 and the beginning of January 1735. Excepting the final chorus, taken from BWV 184, all the principal numbers of this cantata were incorporated in the *Christmas Oratorio.*

Picander takes his subject from classical mythology. Hercules (alto) must make a choice between Pleasure (soprano) and Virtue (tenor) as his guide through life. In his first aria, he asks Echo to help him decide and, following her advice, chooses Virtue. Of course, Hercules is the Crown Prince, whose choice will make him a virtuous ruler. Mercury (bass) enters only for the final recitative.

The orchestra includes two horns, an oboe d'amore, an oboe, two violins, a bassoon, two violas and continuo. There is a four-part chorus for the opening and closing numbers.

1. *Chorus (Resolution of the gods).* That Bach could easily transform the sentiment expressed by this council of pagan deities into the devotional Christian hymn that begins Part IV (36) of the *Christmas Oratorio* testifies to his ability of making any secular text religious. The two horns, two oboes and strings produce a rhythm of solemnity, similar to that of the processional music in the opening choruses of BWV 1 and BWV 65.

Here the gods declare their intention of watching over their son Hercules (Prince Friedrich) so that he may become the most perfect ruler on earth: "Lasst uns sorgen, lasst uns wachen / Über unsern Göttersohn! / Unser Thron / Wird auf Erden / Herrlich und verkläret werden, / Unser Thron / Wird aus ihm ein Wunder machen." (Let us take care, let us watch / Over our son of the gods! / Our throne / Will become on earth / Glorious and transfigured; / Our throne / Will make a wonder out of him.)

2. *Recitative—alto* (HERCULES). Hercules has come to the crossroads and cannot decide which path he should follow to reach virtue and fame. His reason requires him to choose the right way; in his perplexity, he calls on the tree branches to indicate the way he should go.

3. *Aria—soprano* (PLEASURE). Pleasure entices him with her charms, as she sings the slumber-song so well known in Part II (19) of the *Christmas Oratorio;* here she is accompanied only by strings, but what a difference there is in the thought expressed in the two versions! "Schlafe, mein Liebster und pflege der Ruh, / Folge der Lockung entbrannter Gedanken! / Schmecke die Lust / Der lüsternen Brust, / Und erkenne keine Schranken!" (Sleep, my beloved and care for your rest, / Follow the lure of passionate thoughts! / Taste the delight / Of the lustful heart, / And recognize no limits!)

Was Picander satirizing the life-style of Friedrich's grandfather, Augustus the Strong, when he wrote this text?

4. *Recitative—soprano* (PLEASURE), *tenor* (VIRTUE). Pleasure begins this dialogue with Virtue, as each propounds the reason why Hercules should choose between them. Pleasure tells Hercules to follow her path, which is carefree and spread with roses of delight. Virtue states that Hercules will require care and diligence to raise his mind to attain noble goals. His path offers that.

Pleasure asks who would choose to sweat when he can find ease and satisfaction by choosing her way to true welfare. Virtue retorts that she means to ruin his true welfare.

5. *Aria—alto* (HERCULES). Pizzicato continuo and obbligato oboe support his voice in this echo aria, in which Echo persuades Hercules (really he persuades himself) to refuse Pleasure and accept Virtue. Bach borrowed this aria for Part IV (39) of the *Christmas Oratorio* without any change in the instrumentation or the echo effect.

"Treues Echo dieser Orten, / Sollt' ich bei den Schmeichelworten / Süsser Leitung irrig sein? / Gib mir deine Antwort: Nein! [Nein!]" (Faithful Echo of these places, / Should I by the flattering words / Of sweet guidance go astray? / Give me your answer: No! [No!])

"Oder sollte das Ermahnen, / Das so mancher Arbeit nah, / Mir die Wege besser bahnen? / Ach, so sage lieber: Ja! [Ja!]" (Or should the warning / Of so much approaching work, / Pave the ways better for me? / Ah, then rather say: Yes! [Yes!])

6. *Recitative—tenor* (VIRTUE): With this number leading into his following aria, Virtue asks Hercules to take his hand and he will show him the way to attain his ancestors' fame and deeds. Virtue calls him his true son.

7. *Aria—tenor* (VIRTUE). Bach uses a fugal melody for this aria, in which an oboe, a solo violin, continuo and voice enter in succession, almost like a quartet. The same tenor aria will be borrowed for Part IV (41) in the *Christmas Oratorio.* Bach's soaring theme for the first part is derived from the text, describing the flight of an eagle. The second section paints a tranquil scene as the eagle hovers, after reaching its desired height: "Auf meinen Flügeln sollst du schweben, / Auf meinem Fittich steigest du / Den Sternen wie ein Adler zu. / Und durch mich / Soll dein Glanz und Schimmer sich / Zur Vollkommenheit erheben." (On my wings you shall soar, / On my pinion you climb / To the stars like an eagle. / And through me / Shall your splendor and gleaming / Rise to perfection.)

8. *Recitative—tenor* (VIRTUE). It is unusual that Bach should set three numbers in succession for the tenor voice here, but apparently Picander's text required a further comment by Virtue: that Pleasure is a seductress for heroes, and therefore the gods have rejected her.

9. *Aria—alto* (HERCULES). The youthful Hercules now dismisses Pleasure

and recalls his feat of destroying the serpents which sought his death while he was still in his cradle. Bach will transfer this same aria to Part I (4) of the *Christmas Oratorio,* adding an oboe to the obbligato violin and strings that accompany this version: "Ich will (mag) dich nicht hören, ich will dich nicht wissen, / Verworfene Wollust, ich kenne dich nicht. / Denn die Schlangen, / So mich wollten wiegend fangen, / Hab' ich schon lange zermalmet, zerrissen." (I will [may] not hear you, I will not know you, / Infamous Pleasure, I do not recognize you. / For the snakes, / Which wanted to catch me in my cradle, / I have already long ago crushed, torn apart.)

10. *Recitative—alto* (HERCULES), *tenor* (VIRTUE). Hercules says that only Virtue will be his constant guide from now on. Virtue adds that they will be so closely associated that nobody will be able to tell them apart. Then they both sing the final line: "Wer will ein solches Bündnis trennen?" (Who will break such a union?)

11. *Duet—alto* (HERCULES), *tenor* (VIRTUE). This love-scene between two masculine characters, especially as they are related to each other, seems peculiar, but both Picander and Bach had to show their mutual joy over such an alliance in words and in music. In Bach's transfer of this duet to Part III (29) of the *Christmas Oratorio,* the spiritual rapture of this secular duet is lost.

HERCULES: "Ich bin dein." (I am yours.)

VIRTUE: "Du bist meine." (You are mine.)

BOTH: "Küsse mich! / Ich küsse dich. / Wie Verliebte sich verbinden, / Wie die Lust, die sie empfinden, / Treu und zart und eifrig, / So bin ich." (Kiss me! / I kiss you. / As betrothed unite, / As the joy they feel, / Faithful and tender and eager, / So am I.)

12. *Recitative—bass* (MERCURY). Mercury requests all the other gods to behold this picture of Friedrich, Saxony's Crown Prince, as personified by Hercules. He says that the whole country is full of joyous expectation, awaiting the marvels achieved by the young Prince. Now they should listen to the tribute paid to Friedrich by a chorus of muses.

13. *Chorus* (CHORUS OF MUSES). The last chorus of BWV 184 is the origin of this tutti in gavotte tempo. Bach had composed it for the Cöthen court during his first years in Leipzig. Mercury sings the last part solo, interpolated between the two opening lines and its da capo: "Lust der Völker, Lust der Deinen, / Blühe, holder Friederich!" (Joy of the people, joy of your own, / Flourish, charming Frederick!)

MERCURY: "Deiner Tugend Würdigkeit / Stehet schon der Glanz bereit, / Und die Zeit / Ist begierig zu erscheinen; / Eile, mein Friedrich, sie wartet auf dich!" (For the worthiness of your virtue / Your glory already stands ready, / And time / Is eager to appear; / Hurry, my Frederick, it waits for you!)

• **Tönet, ihr Pauken! Erschallet, Trompeten (Sound, You Drums! Resound, Trumpets)** (1733; BWV 214).

On December 8, 1733, Bach performed this "Dramma per Musica," only completed the night before, to celebrate the birthday of Queen Maria Josepha, Consort of Augustus III. Bach himself was the librettist, because the initials J.S.B. appear on the libretto as well as J.J. (Jesu Juva—Jesus help) at the beginning and SDGl (Soli Deo Gloria—To God alone the glory) at the end. Almost invariably, Bach inscribed his sacred cantatas thus. This is further proof that the sacred and the secular merged in his music; indeed, he transferred two choruses and two arias from this cantata into the *Christmas Oratorio.*

The performance probably took place in Zimmermann's Coffee House with Bach directing the Collegium Musicum; as with BWV 213, none of the Royal Family was in the audience, but news of the event would certainly reach the Dresden court. This is the second cantata by which Bach hoped to support his application for the position of Court Composer in Dresden.

Like Picander, Bach takes his characters from classical mythology: Irene (tenor), one of the three Horae goddesses who controlled the seasons and representing peace; Bellona (soprano), goddess of war; Pallas (alto), goddess of wisdom; and Fama (bass), fame—all feminine deities, although two soloists are male! There is no plot to this drama; all characters simply praise the Queen on her birthday.

The orchestra is large for an indoor festive work: three trumpets, timpani, two transverse flutes, two oboes, strings and a continuo with organ and bassoon. There is the usual four-part chorus.

1. *Chorus.* This is the same as the opening number of the *Christmas Oratorio,* Part I (1). As in BWV 207, Bach's text has the choir address the instruments and voices before expressing their birthday wish to the Queen: "Tönet, ihr Pauken! Erschallet, Trompeten! / Klingende Saiten, erfüllet die Luft! / Singet itzt Lieder, ihr muntren Poeten! / Königin lebe! wird fröhlich geruft. / Königin lebe! dies wünschet der Sachse. / Königin lebe und blühe und wachse." (Sound, you drums! Resound, trumpets! / Resonant strings, fill the air! / Sing songs now, you cheerful poets! / May the Queen live! is happily cried. / May the Queen live! this the Saxon wishes. / May the Queen live and flourish and grow!)

2. *Recitative—tenor* (IRENE). The goddess of peace states that this is the day when Poles and Saxons may rejoice together over their Queen's birthday. Her olive-tree is symbolically flourishing; she is not afraid that stormy weather will disrupt this happy event.

3. *Aria—soprano* (BELLONA). The two transverse flutes with pizzicato continuo accompany her song of joy over the triumph of the Queen's husband, Elector Augustus III, over his rival, Sanislaus Lesczynski, aided by France in his claim to the Polish throne. Bach derives this joy-motif from his text; there are no martial overtones, however.

"Blast die wohlgegriffnen Flöten, / Dass Feind, Lilien, Mond erröten, / Schallt mit jauchzendem Gesang! / Tönt mit eurem Waffenklang! / Dieses Fest erfordert Freuden, / Die so Geist als Sinnen weiden." (Blow the well-held flutes, / So that the enemy, lilies and moon blush; / Resound with rejoicing song! / Sound with the clangor of your arms! / This festival demands joys, / Which nourish spirit as well as minds.)

4. *Recitative—soprano* (BELLONA). Bellona refers to her instruments of war, which have made Saxony victorious: the crashing metal of her cannon, her gleaming muskets and the tread of her heroic sons. Their triumph should increase the joy that Saxons feel on this day.

5. *Aria—alto* (PALLAS). Two unison oboes accompany her as she calls upon her Muses to cease their writing and to join in the new songs of this birthday celebration. Bach adapted this number for Part II (15) of the *Christmas Oratorio,* there using transverse flutes instead of oboes.

"Fromme Musen! Meine Glieder! / Singt nicht längst bekannte Lieder! / Dieser Tag sei eure Lust! / Füllt mit Freuden eure Brust! / Werft so Kiel als Schriften nieder / Und erfreut euch dreimal wieder!" (Pious Muses! My associates! / Do not sing long-known songs! / May this day be your delight! / Fill your breast with joys! / Throw quill and writing down / And rejoice again three times!)

6. *Recitative—alto* (PALLAS). She states that heaven has sent the Queen to comfort and protect her Muses, who revere her and wish her a long life to give them joy.

7. *Aria—bass* (FAMA). Fame now pays tribute to the Royal Consort, accompanied by an appropriate melody of trumpet and strings. This aria will become Part I (8) of the *Christmas Oratorio.*

"Kron' und Preis gekrönter Damen, / Königin! mit deinem Namen / Füll' ich diesen Kreis der Welt. / Was der Tugend stets gefällt / Und was nur Heldinnen haben, / Sei'n dir angeborne Gaben!" (Crown and prize of crowned ladies, /

Queen! with your name / I fill this orbit of the world. / What always pleases virtue / And what only heroines have, / Are for you born gifts!)

8. *Recitative – bass* (FAMA). Unison transverse flutes and oboes illustrate Fame's continued praise of the Queen, which will be spread throughout the world and even to the stars of heaven. Both Saxons and Poles will derive benefit from her authority, because she is under the protection of heaven. May she stay with us long and only return late to the stars.

9. *Chorus.* Afterwards transferred to Part III (24) of the *Christmas Oratorio,* this tutti number begins with separate entries by Irene, Bellona and Pallas, followed by a choral presentation of the last three lines. Its arrangement is unique in Bach's choruses.

IRENE: "Blühet, ihr Linden in Sachsen, wie Zedern!" (Bloom, ye lindens in Saxony, like cedars!)

BELLONA: "Schallet mit Waffen und Wagen und Rädern!" (Resound with weapons and chariots and wheels!)

PALLAS: "Singet, ihr Musen, mit völligem Klang!" (Sing, ye Muses, with full tone!)

ALL: "Fröhliche Stunden, ihr freudigen Zeiten! / Gönnt uns noch öfters die güldenen Freuden: / Königin, lebe, ja lebe noch lang." (Happy hours, ye joyful times! / Do not often begrudge us golden joys: / Queen, live, yes live still long.)

• **Preise dein Glücke, gesegnetes Sachsen (Praise Your Good Luck, Blessed Saxony)** (1734; BWV 215).

On October 5, 1733, Augustus III had been crowned King of Poland in Cracow; a year later, he came with his Consort and the Crown Prince to Apel's House in Leipzig, arriving there on October 2, 1734, in order to be present for the town's celebration of his birthday on October 7. For this momentous event all Leipzig had prepared and Bach had already composed a cantata, "Schleicht, spielende Wellen" (Glide, Playing Waves), BWV 206, to be performed on that day. But since the royal party would be present for the first anniversary of the Elector's coronation, Bach felt obliged to hastily provide another cantata to mark this earlier event. Despite the short notice, he produced this royal cantata, BWV 215, in about three days.

His librettist was a Leipzig schoolmaster, Johann Christian Clauder. Members of the Collegium Musicum, which Bach directed, performed the work on the Market Place before the windows of the royal family at about nine o'clock. A ceremonial procession, headed by four counts with students bearing torches, preceded the cantata presentation. The noblemen were allowed to kiss the King's hands as part of the ceremony that, with Bach's cantata, resembled a gala serenade to honor their King.

The soli are STB, with an eight-part double chorus, arranged in two choirs for the opening movement, and a four-part choir for the conclusion. The brilliant orchestra comprises three trumpets, timpani, two transverse flutes, two oboes d'amore, two violins, a viola, a cello, a bassoon and continuo.

The Stadtpfeifer, Gottfried Reiche, who was Bach's first trumpeter in the cantata, died the next day because of overexertion and smoke inhalation.

1. *Chorus.* Bach had previously used this melody for the opening chorus of another secular cantata, "Es lebe der König, der Vater im Lande" (Long Live the King, the Father of the Country), BWV Anh. 11, to celebrate in this "Dramma per Musica" the name-day of Augustus the Strong, August 3, 1732. But since the music for this work is lost, only a conjectured analogy has been found. What is certain, however, is Bach's use of this movement for the "Osanna" number of his later completed *Mass in B minor.*

Throughout all of Clauder's libretto, the religious significance of the unification of the Crowns of Saxony and Poland is apparent – God protects Augustus III. This is the theme of the entire cantata.

It is not a "Dramma per Musica" at all since there are no characters or plot, but simply numbers praising Saxon royalty. Yet it was entitled originally, "Dramma per Musica overo Cantata gratulatoria."

"Preise dein Glücke, gesegnetes Sachsen, / Weil Gott den Thron deines Königs erhält. / Fröhliches Land, / Danke dem Himmel und küsse die Hand, / Die deine Wohlfahrt noch täglich lässt wachsen / Und deine Bürger in Sicherheit stellt." (Praise your good luck, blessed Saxony, / Because God maintains your King's throne. / Happy country, / thank heaven and kiss the hand, / That lets your welfare daily increase / And puts your citizens in safety.)

Note that the four counts were permitted to kiss the Sovereign's hand in token of their allegiance before the cantata was sung.

2. *Recitative—tenor.* Each soloist has a recitative followed by an aria. Then all combine in a final recitative before the final chorus. Here the tenor flatters Augustus, telling him that his paternal hand brings blessings from heaven on their country. He is the image of his great father and his deeds deserve the homage of our respect, fidelity and love. The two oboes d'amore accompany his declamation, to which are added strings in his following aria.

3. *Aria—tenor.* Defiance of the King's enemies and praise of his rule over his own people are the themes of this aria: "Freilich trotzt Augustus' Name, / Ein so edler Götter Same, / Aller Macht der Sterblichkeit. / Und die Bürger der Provinzen / Solcher tugendhafte Prinzen / Leben in der güldnen Zeit." (Certainly Augustus's name, / One of such a noble godly seed, / Defies all mortal might. / And the citizens of the provinces / Of such virtuous princes / Live in the golden age.)

4. *Recitative—bass.* In his long secco number, the flattery continues. He asks Sarmatia (Poland) what inspired her to take the Saxon Piast, Augustus III (Piasts were the rulers in Silesia until 1675), to sit on her throne. He answers his own question by saying that it was the virtue of the worthy son of great Augustus the Strong which determined their choice, despite many Poles who curse him. Yet their curse will turn to their own blessing when they realize the good fortune that he will bring to them.

5. *Aria—bass.* With this accompaniment for oboe and strings, Bach realistically interprets his text denouncing the Polish and French enemies of Augustus. They buzz like a swarm of noisome flies: "Rase nur, verwegner Schwarm, / In dein eignes Eingeweide! / Wasche nur den frechen Arm / Voller Wut / In unschuld'ger Brüder Blut / Uns zum Abscheu, dir zum Leide, / Weil das Gift / Und der Grimm von deinem Neide / Dich mehr als Augustum trifft!" (Rage then, insolent swarm, / In your own entrails! / Just wash your impertinent arm, / Full of fury / In innocent brothers' blood, / For our abhorrence, for your harm, / Because the poison / And the fierceness of your envy / Strikes you more than it does Augustus!)

6. *Recitative—soprano.* The two transverse flutes accompany her affirmation that God helps and protects Augustus's throne in allowing Danzig, at the mouth of the Vistula, to fall to his besieging forces. Now Augustus will show his conquered Polish subjects more favor than severity.

7. *Aria—soprano.* The flutes are joined by the strings to play the melody that Bach will borrow for the bass aria of Part V (47) of the *Christmas Oratorio.* The enlightenment of the soul so that it commits no evil, in the *Oratorio* text, has a parallel in this, describing the clemency of Augustus towards his vanquished foes. Hence in both arias, the transverse flutes play a peace-motif.

"Durch die von Eifer entflammten Waffen / Feinde bestrafen / Bringt zwar manchem Ehr' und Ruhm; / Aber die Bosheit mit Wohltat vergelten, / Ist nur der Helden, / Ist Augustus' Eigentum." (Through weapons inflamed by zeal / To punish enemies / Surely brings to many honor and fame. / But to repay evil with well-doing, / Is only for heroes, / Is the prerogative of Augustus.)

8. *Recitative and Arioso—tenor, bass, soprano.* Each soloist gives his recitative in the above order and then all join in a trio arioso at the end. The tenor asks Augustus to permit the Muses to sing his praise for becoming King of Poland. The bass thanks Augustus because he has protected their city of lindens, Leipzig, from threatened occupation by the French, and thanks the Queen for the comfort and happiness she has given her subjects. The soprano calls Leipzig the ancient Greek town of Pindus, both marked by their state of well-being.

In their trio in arioso, they ask heaven to let their welfare be spread in many thousand branches, in defiance of others who envy them.

9. *Chorus.* This tutti final movement is the best number in the cantata and also one of Bach's most impressive choruses. Its straightforward prayer to God would qualify its place in any of Bach's sacred cantatas. The choir sings the text homophonically. It is a most moving and reverent final tribute to Augustus on his first anniversary as King of Poland: "Stifter der Reiche, Beherrscher der Kronen, / Baue den Thron, den Augustus besitzt! / Ziere sein Haus / Mit unvergänglichem Wohlergehen aus, / Lass uns die Länder in Friede bewohnen, / Die er mit Recht und mit Gnade beschützt!" (Founder of empires, Ruler of crowns, / Build up the throne, that Augustus owns! / Adorn his house / With undying prosperity. / Let us inhabit his lands in peace, / Which he protects with justice and with mercy!)

• **Schleicht, spielende Wellen (Glide, Playing Waves)** (1734; BWV 206).

This "Dramma per Musica" was the second to be performed before the royal presence, this time on Augustus III's birthday, October 7, 1734, two days after BWV 215 was presented. The Elector and his Consort were still in residence in the merchant Apel's House on the Market Place. Here they heard the celebrations of the Leipzig citizens, including Bach's cantata, in the gala ceremony before their windows.

Picander was the librettist, presumably, for this royal ode. Bach must have had a high opinion of the original music that he composed for it, because he never borrowed from it for subsequent cantatas and repeated its performance, unchanged, for the Elector's birthday in 1736. Members of Bach's Collegium Musicum under his direction performed the work on both occasions.

The actors were four allegorical characters, representing the rivers that flow through Saxony and Poland: the Vistula (bass), the Elbe (tenor), the Danube (alto) and the Pleisse (soprano). With a recitative followed by an aria, each river in turn proclaims its reason to swear allegiance to him. This cleverly designed format for the inner numbers is contained between two stupendous four-part choruses.

Picander's libretto gave Bach much scope for word tone-painting of nature, as almost every number has its own distinctive wave motif; the text also stresses the geographical-political significance of each river.

The orchestra is as lavish as it was in the other royal cantatas: three trumpets, timpani, two oboes d'amore, three transverse flutes, strings and a continuo of a cello and a double-bass.

1. *Chorus.* This opening tutti number, addressed to all four rivers, paints a picture of their natures in the calm, violence and joy of three different wave motives. Bach's ability to bring their waves to life in sound is amazing. He changes the tempo according to the thought of the text: "Schleicht, spielende Wellen, und murmelt gelinde, / Nein, rauschet geschwinde, / Dass Ufer und Klippe zum öftern erklingt! / Die Freude, die unsere Fluten erreget, / Die jegliche Welle zum Rauschen beweget, / Durchreisset die Dämme, / Worein sie Verwundrung und Schüchternheit zwingt." (Glide, playing waves, and murmur gently. / No, rush quickly, / So

that shore and cliff often resound! / The joy, that arouses our floods, / Which moves every wave to rushing, / Breaks through the dams, / By which it constrains their astonishment and shyness.)

2. *Recitative—bass* (VISTULA). His gruesome recollection of the slaughter caused by the fighting along his shores is accompanied secco. Picander mentions the disposal of the dead with their now rusting weapons in these Polish waters which have witnessed the recent battles, and compares the Vistula to Cocytus, the river of the underworld in classical mythology. Picander was adept at inserting classical allusions into his libretti to demonstrate his learning; there are more in this cantata, proving that he was its librettist. The bass continues his narrative, saying that Augustus has brought this carnage to an end and the water is now fit to drink. He asks all Poles to acknowledge the sovereignty of Augustus with him, as he sings his following aria.

3. *Aria—bass* (VISTULA). Strings accompany him, with a rhythm of solemnity, as he sings of his fidelity to Augustus. A dancing wave motif is apparent in this melody. The ancient Greek custom of keeping the doors of the temple of Janus open in time of war, and closing them in peace, begins this number's text: "Schleuss des Janustempels Türen, / Unsre Herzen öffnen wir! / Nächst den dir getanen Schwüren / Treibt allein, Herr, deine Güte / Unser kindliches Gemüte / Zum Gehorsam gegen dir." (Close the doors of Janus's temple, / We are opening our hearts! / After the vows that we have made to you, / Your goodness alone, Lord, urges / Our child-like mind / To obedience towards you.)

4. *Recitative and Arioso—tenor* (ELBE). The main river of Saxony agrees with Vistula's praise in this secco narrative, adding that Augustus has his father's noble, conqueror-like appearance. The Elbe says that he has only loaned Augustus to Poland and will not allow him to be torn from his bosom.

His arioso, accompanied by a solo violin obbligato, paints a picturesque and melodious picture of what he would rather do than give up Augustus: to have his waters mix with those of the Ganges and allow a Hindu to fish in them.

5. *Aria—tenor* (ELBE). The solo violin obbligato depicts a gently rocking panorama of the Elbe's waves, as the Tritons beneath the surface witness their blissful applause of Augustus. The serenity in the melody of this aria well describes the Elbe, as it meanders on its course through Germany: "Jede Woge meiner Wellen / Ruft das goldne Wort August! / Seht, Tritonen, muntre Söhne, / Wie vor nie gespürter Lust / Meines Reiches Fluten schwellen, / Wenn in dem Zurückeprallen / Dieses Namens süsse Töne / Hundertfältig widerschallen." (Every billow of my waves / Calls out the golden word Augustus! / See, Tritons, cheerful sons, / How with never-felt delight / The floods of my kingdom swell, / When in the echo / Of this name's sweet sounds / They resound a hundredfold.)

6. *Recitative—alto* (DANUBE). She states, in secco, that she, too, rejoices with the "father of many rivers" (the Elbe) over the hero (Augustus). The Danube symbolizes the origin of Maria Josepha, the Austrian Consort of Augustus, and the daughter of the Austrian Emperor, Karl VI.

7. *Aria—alto* (DANUBE). The two oboes d'amore accompany her praise for the Queen with a joy-motif that includes a lightly rolling wave rhythm in its melody. This may also suggest the Queen's affection for her husband, and the Danube's wish that they will have many children: "Reis, von Habsburgs hohem Stamme, / Deiner Tugend helle Flamme / Kennt, bewundert, rühmt mein Strand. / Du stammst von den Lorbeerzweigen, / Drum muss deiner Ehe Band / Auch den fruchtbar'n Lorbeern gleichen." (Scion, of Hapsburg's lofty family-tree, / The bright flame of your virtue / My shore knows, admires, praises. / You spring from the laurel branches, / Therefore must the bond of your marriage / Also be like the fruitful laurel.)

8. *Recitative—soprano* (PLEISSE). Leipzig's small river now interrupts the oratory of these "mossy heads of strong streams" to say that they must content themselves with alternately sharing the affection of the royal pair, because she is closest to them, while they reside in her town.

9. *Aria—soprano* (PLEISSE). The three transverse flutes, symbolic of the three rivers that she is addressing, play the melody of a gavotte to accompany her. The tune suggests the gentle lapping of the waves in these rivers: "Hört doch! der sanften Flöten Chor / Erfreut die Brust, ergötzt das Ohr. / Der unzertrennten Eintracht Stärke / Macht diese nette Harmonie / Und tut noch grössre Wunderwerke, / Dies merkt, und stimmt doch auch wie sie!" (Hear then! the choir of gentle flutes / Gladdens the breast, delights the ear. / The strength of undivided concord / Makes this neat harmony / And does still greater wonderworks. / Note this, and tune together as they!)

10. *Recitative—bass, tenor, alto, soprano.* The Vistula, Elbe and Danube agree to be united in their obedience to Augustus as their little sister advised. Pleisse applauds their decision, which will bring joy to all people living in their territories. Picander makes another reference to classical mythology in her text: on the shores of these rivers, altars will be built and naiads will dance around them.

Pleisse then invites her sisters to join with her in singing the final chorus.

11. *Chorus.* This spectacular tutti number, with its charming pastoral melody in the form of a rondo dance, is the ultimate of all of Bach's secular final choruses. The overpowering majesty of the choral singing and the dancing wave-motif of the rhythm touch the listener like a magic spell. Perhaps Bach was so inspired by the prayer to God for long life wished for Augustus that he made this chorus of the rivers a religious as well as a secular tribute in its music: "Die himmlische Vorsicht der ewigen Güte / Beschirme dein Leben, durchlauchter August! / So viel sich nur Tropfen in heutigen Stunden / In unsern bemoosten Kanälen befunden, / Umfange beständig dein hohes Gemüte / Vergnügen und Lust!" (The heavenly foresight of eternal goodness / May it protect your life, serene Augustus! / As many as the drops in today's hours / Are found in our mossy canals, / So may your lofty mind constantly / Embrace delight and pleasure!)

• **Angenehmes Wiederau, freue dich (Pleasant Wiederau, Rejoice)** (1737; BWV 30a).

The libretto of this "Dramma per Musica" was written by Picander, who hoped thereby to obtain favor with the powerful Count Brühl of Dresden. The occasion was the acquisition of a manor and estate at Wiederau by Johann Christian von Hennicke, a protégé of Count Brühl, for whom Picander also worked as a government official. Picander asked Bach to set the music for this cantata as part of the homage celebration at Wiederau for Hennicke.

The following year, Picander rearranged his libretto to suit BWV 30, the church cantata, in which he reduced the numbers from 13 to 12. Bach adapted his music to fit all these new verses. This is the most complete instance of Bach's self-borrowing for any of his single cantatas. Did Bach wish to prove a point about how his music was always religious, or was this simply a hurried adaptation?

Allegorical characters, as in BWV 207, are the actors in this secular drama: soprano—Zeit (time), alto—Glück (Good Luck), tenor—Elster (name of a local river), bass—Schicksal (Fate), and a four-part chorus. The sequence of entries for each soloist is dramatically striking, for each gives a recitative followed by an aria as the next number, the bass being given two such entries.

The festive orchestra is the same as that for the religious version a year later: three trumpets, timpani, two transverse flutes, two oboes, an oboe d'amore, two violins, a viola, with organ and continuo.

1. *Chorus.* This opening number, with all voices and instruments, will be repeated at the end of the cantata (only the text will be changed). Whittaker's evaluation of this chorus is worth noting: "The opening chorus is one of the finest that he ever wrote, pulsating with abounding life, massive, brilliant, and effective. It fits the church text as well as, or even better than the secular one, except for details here and there. The rejoicing is too tremendous for such an insignificant place as Wiederau, it is more appropriate to the hosts of heaven" (Vol. II, p. 89).

In both versions of this cantata there are powerful runs on "freue dich" (rejoice)—an unlimited motif of unrestrained joy.

"Angenehmes Wiederau, / Freue dich in deinen Auen! / Das Gedeihen legt itzund / Einen neuen festen Grund, / Wie ein Eden dich zu bauen." (Pleasant Wiederau, / Rejoice in your meadows! / Prosperity now lays / A new, firm foundation, / As if to build you into an Eden.)

2. *Recitative—bass.* Schicksal (Fate) states that he and his companions, Time, Good Fortune, and the Elster (River), have moved into the manor and the precincts of Wiederau and that nothing will move them away from there. The others interrupt his praise of the locale to assert, in unison, that Wiederau's name should be changed to "Hennicke's Rest." Then Fate concludes, saying that the lord's subjects should accept him joyfully, thus leading into his following aria.

3. *Aria—bass.* With string accompaniment and in Italian aria style, he makes long, florid runs on "Freuden" (joys), "Heil" (prosperity), "segnen" (to bless) and "Allmacht" (omnipotence).

SCHICKSAL: "Willkommen im Heil, willkommen in Freuden, / Wir segnen die Ankunft, wir segnen das Haus! / Sei stets wie unsre Auen munter, / Dir breiten sich die Herzen unter, / Die Allmacht aber Flügel aus." (FATE: Welcome in prosperity, welcome in joys, / We bless your arrival; we bless the house! / Be always cheerful as our meadows; / Hearts spread themselves beneath you. / Omnipotence, however, spreads out wings over you.)

4. *Recitative—alto.* Glück (Good Luck) asserts that, just as Hennicke's Wiederau is pledged to him, so she will be also faithful. He will always find her unchanged and unwavering at his side. This declamation leads into her aria.

5. *Aria—alto.* Good Luck sings this number to the rhythm of a gavotte, which the orchestra plays with an instrumental introduction. This feature may indicate that the tune came from some lost orchestral suite, since no other aria by Bach is similar.

GLUCK: "Was die Seele kann ergötzen, / Was vergnügt und hoch zu schätzen, / Soll dir Lehn und erblich sein. / Meine Fülle soll nichts sparen / Und dir reichlich offenbaren, / Dass mein ganzer Vorrat dein." (GOOD LUCK: What can delight the soul, / What is pleasing and highly to be prized, / Shall be a loan, heritable to you. / My abundance shall spare nothing / And richly reveal to you / That my whole store is yours.)

6. *Recitative—bass.* Fate declares that he has considered taking Hennicke under his protection, because he is worthy of it. Furthermore, he will not cease to watch over him, in order to make his glory more wide-spread and flourishing.

7. *Aria—bass.* Fate now expands on his recitative, accompanied by the oboe d'amore, a solo violin and strings.

SCHICKSAL: "Ich will dich halten, / Und mit dir walten, / Wie man ein Auge zärtlich hält. / Ich habe dein Erhöhen, / Dein Heil und Wohlergehen / Auf Marmorsäulen aufgestellt." (FATE: I will hold you, / And rule with you, / As an eye is kept tenderly [on you]. / I have put your rising, / Your prosperity and well-being, / Up on pillars of marble.)

8. *Recitative—soprano.* Zeit (Time) now begins her eulogy of Hennicke by promising to increase his welfare from day to day. She will bear him on her wings until she, herself, is limited by

eternity. She expands this thought in her following aria.

9. *Aria—soprano.* ZEIT: "Eilt, ihr Stunden, wie ihr wollt, / Rottet aus und stosst zurücke! / Aber merket das allein, / Dass ihr diesen Schmuck und Schein, / Dass ihr Hennicks Ruhm und Glücke / Allezeit verschonen sollt!" (TIME: Hasten, you hours, as you wish, / Root out and push back! / But only notice this, / That you should always spare / This jewel and splendor, / Hennicke's fame and fortune!)

10. *Recitative—tenor.* The River Elster comments now, saying that he concedes his meadow to Fate, Good Luck and Time. They should build their dwellings firmly here, not forgetting to pour out their gifts on these meadows.

11. *Aria—tenor.* Bach did not transfer this number to BWV 30. Yet he imitated it in the penultimate soprano aria of his later wedding cantata, BWV 210.

ELSTER: "So wie ich die Tropfen zolle, / Dass mein Wiederau grünen solle, / So fügt auch euern Segen bei! / Pfleget sorgsam Frucht und Samen, / Zeiget, dass euch Hennicks Namen / Ein ganz besondres Kleinod sei!" (ELSTER: So just as I pay duty on the drops, / So that my Wiederau should become green, / Then also add your blessing! / Carefully tend to fruit and seed; / Show that for you Hennicke's name / May be a quite special jewel!)

12. *Recitative—soprano, bass, alto.* Each soloist, in the above order, adds remarks on what has been sung. This trio concludes the last three lines in unison.

ZEIT: "Drum, angenehmes Wiederau, / Soll dich kein Blitz, kein Feuerstrahl, / Kein ungesunder Tau, / Kein Misswachs, kein Verderben schrecken!" (TIME: Therefore, pleasant Wiederau, / No lightning, no flash of fire, / No unhealthful dew, / No misgrowth, no spoiling should frighten you!)

SCHICKSAL: "Dein Haupt, den teuren Hennicke / Will ich mit Ruhm und Wonne decken." (FATE: Your head, dear Hennicke, / I will cover with fame and bliss.)

GLUCK: "Dem wertesten Gemahl / Will ich kein Heil und keinen Wunsch versagen." (GOOD LUCK: To your most worthy consort / I will refuse no happiness nor wish.)

ALLE: "Und beider Lust, / Den einigen und liebsten Stamm, August, / Will ich auf meinem Schosse tragen." (ALL: And for the joy of both of you, / I will bear the only and dearest family, August, / On my bosom.)

13. *Chorus.* This is identical with the opening number, all voices and instruments being used. The resounding impact of the music makes a spectacular conclusion.

"Angenehmes Wiederau, / Prange nun in deinen Auen. / Deines Wachstums Herrlichkeit, / Deiner Selbstzufriedenheit / Soll die Zeit kein Ende schauen!" (Pleasant Wiederau, / Sparkle now in your meadows. / Of the splendor of your growth, / Of your self-satisfaction / Time should see no end!)

• **Mer hahn en neue Oberkeet [Bauernkantate] (We Have a New Overlord [Peasant Cantata])** (1742; BWV 212).

That Bach had a sense of dramatic comedy was shown in the *Coffee Cantata,* BWV 211, in which he painted the manners and customs of the bourgeoisie. Now he furthers the picture of contemporary society with this burlesque portrayal of the peasants of Saxony. Thanks to his contact with common people as well as with aristocrats, he could accurately mirror in his music their thoughts and emotions. Picander's text gave him the opportunity to use folk-music and folk-dance tunes in the movements, just as Telemann had done in his works.

The occasion for the performance of this cantata was the acquisition of an estate, Klein-Zschocher, near Leipzig, by Carl Heinrich von Dieskau. He was the inspector of land, liquor and income taxes and Picander's superior; Picander was the local receiver of land and liquor taxes. This cantata was part of the homage celebrations whereby the villagers honored their new Lord of the

Manor. A holiday was declared, August 30, 1742, for this event, and it seems likely that Bach came from Leipzig with his Collegium Musicum to perform the cantata before the manor.

The plot is very simple: two peasants, Mieke (soprano) and her unnamed lover (bass), discuss their new master and his wife, tease each other, relate the gossip of the region, complain about taxes and finally go to the inn for free beer, courtesy of (landlord) Gutsherr Dieskau. There is no chorus; their dialogue occurs in the recitatives and arias. The instruments are a transverse flute, a horn, two violins, a viola and continuo.

1. *Sinfonia.* This orchestral number for strings and continuo introduces the vocal numbers like the overture to a play. Several folk-melodies or Ländler, similar to the tunes played by a village band, create a suitable country atmosphere for the drama.

2. *Duet—soprano, bass.* Picander's text, for this number only, is in the dialect of Upper Saxony, where Kleinzschocher was located. Picander writes in the vernacular for this verse alone, although he tries to maintain the local color with a few slang expressions in the remainder of his libretto: "Mer hahn en neue Oberkeet / An unsern Kammerherrn. / Ha gibt uns Bier, das steigt ins Heet, / Das ist der klare Kern. / Der Pfarr mag immer büse tun; / Ihr Speelleut' halt euch flink! / Der Kittel wackelt Mieken schun, / Das klene luse Ding." (We have a new overlord / In our chamberlain. / He gives us beer that goes to the head; / That is the clear grain. / The parson may always be angry; / You musicians strike up quickly! / The itch [to begin] shakes Mieke already, / The giddy little thing.)

3. *Recitative (Dialogue)—soprano, bass.* This exchange must have amused the audience with its opera buffa flavor and the slang words in its text (indicated in brackets here). The peasant asks Mieke to give him her mouth [Guschel] to kiss. She replies that she would not refuse if that were all, but he is a lout [Bärenhäuter] and will always want more. Besides, the new lord will see them. The peasant remarks that the lord likes to do a little dallying [Dahlen] himself.

4. *Aria—soprano.* A graceful polonaise melody of strings and continuo accompanies this rather coarse text, as she describes her feelings during her lovemaking. Apparently Mieke has had some previous experience in this regard, which has not been disagreeable!

"Ach, es schmeckt doch gar zu gut, / Wenn ein Paar recht freundlich tut; / Ei, da braust es in dem Ranzen, / Als wenn eitel Flöh' und Wanzen / Und ein tolles Wespenheer / Miteinander zänkisch wär'." (Ah, it tastes really very good, / When a couple are right friendly. / Hey, it blusters in the belly, / As if only fleas and bugs / And a furious army of wasps / Were quarreling with each other.)

5. *Recitative—bass.* He turns the discussion to the tax-collector, who has a sulphurous temperament and punishes poor folks with additional taxes when they have barely paid the last.

6. *Aria—bass.* This is another polonaise for strings, in which the peasant pleads with the tax-collector to leave the poor at least something on which to live. It would seem that the weight of taxation on the common people was even heavier in the eighteenth century than in our own!

"Ach Herr Schösser, geht nicht gar zu schlimm / Mit uns armen Bauersleuten üm! / Schont nur unsrer Haut; / Fresst ihr gleich das Kraut / Wie die Raupen bis zum kahlen Strunk, / Habt nur genung!" (Ah Mr. Tax-collector, deal not too badly / With us poor peasant folk! / Only spare our hide; / Eat the plant leaves / Like caterpillars to the bare stalk. / Only be satisfied!)

7. *Recitative—soprano.* She changes the topic to a discussion of Dieskau, the new lord, whom she describes as the best, even if he has no bag of pennies for gratuities for them.

8. *Aria—soprano.* Bach composed a sarabande tune for this aria, based on Corelli's "Les Folies d'Espagne," which

Bach had probably known years before, when he was a violinist at the Celle court with its Lully-type French music. Strings and the continuo accompany her in this dance tune: "Unser trefflicher / Lieber Kammerherr / Ist ein kumpabler Mann, / Den niemand tadeln kann." (Our excellent / Dear chamberlain / Is a capable man, / Whom nobody can criticize.)

9. *Recitative (Dialogue)—soprano, bass.* First the bass states that the new lord has helped old and young; he has recently protected their village against the recruiting drive for men. Then Mieke adds that their new master has intervened in the peasants' interest when the tax-collector has been active.

10. *Aria—soprano.* She sings another song in praise of Dieskau's protection, comparing their happy state with that of two neighboring villages, Knauthain and Cospuden. / Her joy-motif over avoiding the "crazy" taxes is enhanced by a peasant dance-tune played by the strings: "Das ist galant, / Es spricht niemand / Von den caducken Schocken. / Niemand redt ein stummes Wort, / Knauthain und Cospuden dort / Hat selber Werg (Werk) am Rocken." (That is polite; / No one speaks / Of the crazy taxes. / Nobody utters a mute word. / Knauthain and Cospuden there / Have themselves work on their distaffs.) (to avoid them?)

11. *Recitative—bass.* He speaks of the Lady of the Manor; she has no conceit and associates with the peasants as one of them. She is pious, thrifty, and has even contributed many dollars to her lord from the sale of a bat!

12. *Aria—bass.* Despite his praise of the lady, the peasant implies that the villagers have had to contribute fifty dollars towards this feast, without any aid from her. So their celebration will not be lavish and they will have to save to replace this spent money. He sings his aria to a mazurka melody played by the strings.

13. *Recitative—soprano.* Now Mieke returns to praising the lord and his lady before she will consent to go to the inn for dancing. Her following aria describes her feelings.

14. *Aria—soprano.* This beautiful number is accompanied by the transverse flute and strings. The melody has a rhythm of solemnity, often used by Bach for serious movements: "Klein-Zschocher müsse / So zart und süsse / Wie lauter Mandelkerne sein. / In unsere Gemeine / Zieh' heute ganz alleine / Der Überfluss des Segens ein." (Klein-Zschocher must be / As tender and sweet / As pure almond-kernels. / In our community / May there, quite alone today, / Enter the abundance of blessing.)

15. Recitative—bass. Mieke's pretentious aria does not impress her companion. He tells her that he will now sing an aria more typical of country-folk.

16. *Aria—bass.* The horn is added to the strings to play a vivacious hunting-tune, which was also a well-known folk-melody in Saxony at this time: "Es nehme zehntausend Dukaten / Der Kammerherr alle Tag' ein! / Er trink' ein gutes Gläschen Wein / Und lass' es ihm bekommen sein!" (May the chamberlain take in / Ten thousand ducats every day! / May he drink a good little glass of wine / And let it be agreeable to him!)

17. *Recitative—soprano.* She observes that the fine people present will laugh at such a song, so she will try an old-fashioned folk-song. This has the same horn and string accompaniment as in the peasant's aria.

18. *Aria—soprano.* She addresses her song to Frau von Dieskau, who had had only daughters thus far in her marriage: "Gib, Schöne, / Viel Söhne / Von art'ger Gestalt, / Und zieh' sie fein alt, / Das wünschet sich Zschocher und Knauthain fein bald!" (Give, fair one, / Many sons / Of fine form, / And bring them up to a fine age. / That is desired by Zschocher and Knauthain very soon!)

19. *Recitative—bass.* He agrees with Mieke's opinion that his previous aria sounded too common compared with hers. Therefore, he will now sing another in a more cultivated town style.

20. *Aria—bass.* His "learned" song is

none other than Pan's aria in BWV 201, "Zu Tanze, zu Sprunge, so wackelt das Herz" (For Dancing, for Leaping, So Trembles the Heart) in which Bach had satirized the "natural" style advocated by his critic Scheibe. Bach borrowed this number to show that the peasant cannot differentiate between a formal and a rustic melody, as he addresses the lady: "Dein Wachstum sei feste / Und lache vor Lust! / Deines Herzens Trefflinchkeit / Hat dir selbst das Feld bereit', / Auf dem du blühen musst." (May your increase be sure / And may you laugh with joy! / The excellence of your heart / Has itself prepared the field for you, / On which you must thrive.)

21. *Recitative (Dialogue)—soprano, bass.* Mieke says that they have paid enough compliments in their singing. Her lover replies that they must now depart for dancing at the inn. The girl knows that his real reason is to drink there, and her remark leads into her last aria.

22. *Aria—soprano.* The tune for this number is a country-dance, taken from a students' drinking song, which Bach applies to Picander's text. The strings play a joy-motif to support her vocal lines: "Und dass ihr's alle wisst, / Es ist nunmehr die Frist / Zu trinken. / Wer durstig ist, mag winken. / Versagt's die rechte Hand, / So dreht euch unverwandt / Zur linken!" (And so that you all know, / It is now the time / For drinking. / Whoever is thirsty may beckon. / If the right hand refuses, / Then turn unmoved / To your left!)

23. *Recitative (Dialogue)—soprano, bass.* The countryman says that Mieke has guessed rightly in her aria. She replies that they will "waddle" on their way together to the inn; Bach uses a step-motif to illustrate the words of the text. The man adds that unfortunately both the village policeman, Herr Ludwig, and the tax-collector must also be there.

24. *Duet (Chorus).* This is not a chorus, as indicated in the libretto, but simply a duet accompanied by strings. The melody is a bourrée in folk-tune style. Bach illustrates the mention of bagpipes in the first two lines through imitative rhythm in voices and instruments. The remaining lines express their good wishes to Herr Dieskau, as they drink his beer and dance: "Wir gehn nun, wo der Dudelsack / In unsrer Schenke brummt; / Und rufen dabei fröhlich aus; / Es lebe Dieskau und sein Haus, / Ihm sei beschert, / Was er begehrt, / Und was er sich selbst wünschen mag!" (We are now going where the bagpipe / Hums in our inn. / And we call out happily with it; / Long live Dieskau and his house. / To him be granted, / What he desires, / And what he may wish for himself!)

In addition to its fine melodies, this cantata deserves a place in our modern light-opera repertoire, because it has much human interest, reaching from the eighteenth century into our own. Moreover, the weaknesses in society then were the same as those we find today: unjust taxation, flattery for patronage and self-interest.

• **O holder Tag, erwünschte Zeit (O Charming Day, Wished-for Time)** (c. 1741–44; BWV 210).

This secular cantata for soprano solo was for an unknown wedding. The bridegroom must have been an important patron of music, according to the text of the libretto. But this cantata is more than a wedding compliment; it is also Bach's defense of his music against the criticism of his Rector, J.A. Ernesti, in the St. Thomas Church, and that of Rector Biedermann of Freiberg. Both of these clergymen opposed music for its tendency (in their opinion) to corrupt students.

It is likely that Picander was the librettist for this cantata, as well as for the later imitation in BWV 210a "O, angenehme Melodei" (O, Pleasant Melody), c. 1749, which pays homage to Count Flemming, who was the Prime Minister of Saxony and a patron of the arts at the height of the Biedermann controversy.

BWV 210 was performed as table-music at the wedding feast after the ceremony. Therefore it is probable that the soprano soloist was an adult (Anna Magdalena?), as the work was sung outside the church. The instruments are a transverse flute, an oboe d'amore, strings and harpsichord continuo.

1. *Recitative.* Addressing the guests with the words "O holder Tag, erwünschte Zeit" (O charming day, wished-for time), she says that they should forget their melancholy on this happy day that God has arranged for them. This opening narrative emphasizes also the importance of music to bring joy to this festive occasion. In fact, all of the following libretto deals with the pros and cons of music's place in any wedding.

2. *Aria.* The oboe d'amore and the strings play a suave melody to illustrate the first three lines, becoming more animated in the last two. The emotional effect of music on the wedding guests is well described: "Spielet, ihr beseelten Lieder, / Werfet die entzückte Brust / In die Ohnmacht sanfte nieder! / Aber durch Saiten Lust / Stärket und erholt sie wieder!" (Play, soul-inspired songs; / Cast the delighted breast / Gently down into unconsciousness! / But through the joy of the strings / Strengthen and revive it again!)

3. *Recitative.* This number and the following aria argue against the role of music at a wedding. Both are accompanied by the oboe d'amore and the strings. She says that the bridal pair should have quiet for the prayer they offer at the altar of their hearts.

4. *Aria.* She sings a charming slumber-song with a sleep-motif in the accompaniment. Bach even contrives to show the appeal of music while she declaims against it: "Ruhet hie, matte Töne, / Matte Töne, ruhet hie! / Eure zarte Harmonie / Ist vor die beglückte Eh' / Nicht die wahre Panacee." (Rest here, languid tones, / Languid tones, rest here! / Your tender harmony / Is for the happy marriage / Not the true panacea.)

5.*Recitative.* This, her first long secco monologue, is in favor of music for joyous events, such as the present wedding, as well as for sad occasions such as death. Both high patrons of music and common people appreciate its value in their lives. The last two lines introduce her following aria.

6. *Aria.* She reverts to her argument against music in this number, which sounds like a funeral-motif, and has nothing to do with the wedding festivity. The obbligato transverse flute illustrates the elegiac meaning of her text. As in the previous aria, Bach's andante melody favors music in spite of the text. It is a hauntingly beautiful aria: "Schweigt, ihr Flöten, schweigt, ihr Töne, / Denn ihr klingt dem Neid nicht schöne, / Eilt durch die geschwärzte Luft, / Bis man euch zu Grabe ruft!" (Be silent, flutes, be silent, tones, / For you do not sound beautiful to the envious. / Hasten through the darkened air, / Until you are called to the grave!)

7. *Recitative.* She gives another long secco declamation to encourage music to defy its detractors. Music is the child of heaven; its critics are the envious brood of hell—perhaps referring to Ernesti and Biedermann. But heaven will protect music through great patrons, such as the present bridegroom. She will therefore honor him (in her following aria).

8. *Aria.* Bach borrowed this number from his secular cantata "Angenehmes Wiederau" (Pleasant Wiederau), BWV 30a, a happy transposition with oboe d'amore and string accompaniment. Its melody has a spacious grace, combined with a motif of solemnity to make it very effective: "Grosser Gönner, dein Vergnügen / Muss auch unsern Klang besiegen, / Denn du verehrst uns deine Gunst. / Unter deinen Weisheitsschätzen / Kann dich nichts so sehr ergötzen / Als der süssen Töne Kunst." (Great patron, your pleasure / Must overcome even our sound, / For you honor us by your favor. / Among the treasures of your wisdom / Nothing can delight you so much / As the art of sweet tones.)

9. *Recitative.* All instruments accompany both this number, addressed to the

worthy bridegroom, and the following final aria. She says that noble harmony will banish sadness from his life, and that his name will become famous throughout the world as a protector of music. Meanwhile, will he permit her to sing her wish for his future happiness in his married life?

10. *Aria.* The religious significance of this text must have induced Bach to compose such an inspired joy-motif to accompany her magnificent compliment to the newlyweds: "Seid beglückt, edle Beide, / Edle Beide, seid beglückt! / Beständige Lust / Erfülle die Wohnung, vergnüge die Brust, / Bis dass euch die Hochzeit des Lammes erquickt!" (Be fortunate, noble pair, / Noble pair, be fortunate! / May constant joy / Fill your dwelling, delight your breast, / Until the wedding of the Lamb revives you!)

III. The Christmas Oratorio (Weihnachts-Oratorium)

(1734–35; BWV 248)

This work, consisting of six separate, yet interlinked cantatas, was Bach's first attempt at oratorio composition. He followed this work with the *Ascension Oratorio* (BWV 11) in 1735 and the *Easter Oratorio* (BWV 249) in 1736.

Why Bach decided to refer to the Christmas cantatas as oratorios can only be conjectured. Did he wish to imitate the popular Dresden oratorio of this time, or to preserve the outstanding parts of some of his previous secular cantatas that, after their single performance, he thought would be lost? What is certain is that his oratorios, like others of the period, stress the dramatic action more than is apparent in religious cantatas.

Biblical characters are featured in each of the Christmas oratorios together with angels, shepherds, witnesses to the event and also an Evangelist who narrates the Gospel story in his recitative. Thus the dramatic aspect is emphasized more than it is in Bach's single cantatas. Even with this difference, however, Bach's oratorios still retain the choruses, arias and recitatives of the cantata form.

The *Christmas Oratorio* and the *Mass in B minor* are the two greatest achievements in all of Bach's religious music. The *Christmas Oratorio* shines forth as the culmination of all his efforts to develop the cantata for the church.

Each of its cantatas was first performed on the six consecutive feast days of the Christmas season of 1734 to 1735, being later combined into the *Oratorio* as we know it today.

I. Jauchzet, frohlocket! Auf, preiset die Tage! (Shout, Rejoice! Up, Praise the Days) (Weihnachts-Oratorium, Part 1—for Christmas Day 1734).

It is fitting that Bach should choose a stupendous joy-motif to begin the story of Christ's birth, the theme of the entire work. From his secular, royal cantata, *Tönet, ihr Pauken!*, BWV 214, in honor of the birthday of the reigning Queen Maria Josepha on December 8, 1733, he borrowed the first chorus and adapted it to his new text. Both libretti express rejoicing over the birth of royalty—the consort of Friedrich Augustus III and the Holy Infant Jesus.

This first cantata was presented twice on Christmas Day 1734: in the morning at the St. Nicholas and in the afternoon at the St. Thomas Church, according to the original printed title preceding each cantata.

The large instrumentation—three trumpets, timpani, two transverse flutes, two oboes d'amore, two oboes da caccia, two horns, a cello, a double-bass, strings, a bassoon and organ continuo—might make this number seem unusual for indoor performance (the same orchestra was used for the indoor [?] performance of BWV 214's opening chorus). Yet Bach has made all voices of the choir clearly distinct in his arrangement.

The soloists are the usual SATB with the tenor also singing the part of the Evangelist. His recitatives are quotations from Luke 2 (1–7) in this cantata. The movements throughout the *Oratorio* will be numbered consecutively.

1. *Chorus.* This opening is unique in Bach's religious work, being the only time that a sacred cantata begins with a solo for drums, followed immediately by trumpet fanfares. However, Bach had used the same accompaniment for the opening chorus of BWV 214, so it was quite appropriate to transfer music from terrestrial to celestial royalty.

It is a tribute to Bach that he could adapt the joy-motif of his secular text to this religious one. His musical interpretation of the nouns and verbs (italicized) would make any listener believe that this is an original chorus: "*Jauchzet, frohlocket!* auf, *preiset* die *Tage,* / *Rühmet,* was heute der *Höchste* getan! / *Lasset* das *Zagen, verbannet* die *Klage,* / Stimmet voll *Jauchzen* und *Fröhlichkeit* an! / Dienet dem Höchsten mit herrlichen Chören, / Lass uns den Namen des Herrschers verehren!" (*Shout, rejoice!* up, *praise* the *days,* / *Boast of* what today the *Highest* did! / *Leave hesitation, banish complaint,* / Raise your voices full of *shouting* and *happiness!* / Serve the Highest with glorious choruses, / Let us honor the Name of the Lord!)

Instruments and voices in their parts follow each other in imitation in these lines. The piano hush of the last two lines provides a very effective contrast before the da capo.

2. *Recitative—tenor (Evangelist).* In this and all his subsequent recitatives, he is accompanied by the cello, the double-bass and the organ. He begins the narrative of the Christmas story by quoting Luke 2 (1–6). His serious declamation of the circumstances under which Mary and Joseph came to Bethlehem contrasts with the joy of the opening chorus.

3. *Recitative—alto.* The two oboes d'amore are added to the continuo as the alto, playing the part of the Virgin Mary throughout the *Oratorio,* comments on how Christ's birth will influence the welfare of her people. She urges all Israel to pay homage to Jesus, her new-born Babe and its Bridegroom. This thought is amplified in her following aria.

4. *Aria—alto.* This beautiful number was borrowed from the alto aria (9) of BWV 213, *Die Wahl des Herkules* (The Choice of Hercules), the royal secular cantata. Here, however, the oboe d'amore and strings betray nothing of the foreboding snake imagery evoked in the earlier cantata for the Crown Prince. Rather the joy-motif predominates; the lilting charm of the melody coincides with the message of the text. Bach has very cleverly adapted this to Mary's apostrophe to Zion to welcome the Infant-Bridegroom: "Bereite dich, Zion, mit zärtlichen Trieben, / Den Schönsten, den Liebsten bald bei dir zu sehn! / Deine Wangen / Müssen heut viel schöner prangen, / Eile, den Bräutigam sehnlichst zu lieben!" (Prepare thyself, Zion, with tenderness, / To see with you soon the Most Beautiful, the Dearest One! / Thy cheeks / Must today sparkle much more beautifully. / Hurry to love the Bridegroom most longingly!)

5. *Chorale.* This is the first stanza of Paul Gerhardt's 1653 hymn "Wie soll ich dich empfangen" (How Shall I Receive Thee), plainly sung in unison by the choir with two transverse flutes, two oboes d'amore, strings and organ. This well-known Christmas hymn would impress the congregation because of its thought on how they, too, can fittingly greet Jesus.

6. *Recitative—tenor (Evangelist).* With the accompaniment noted in his first recitative (2 above), he quotes Luke 2 (7) in Luther's translation of the Bible: "Und sie gebar ihren ersten Sohn, und wickelte ihn in Windeln, und legte ihn in eine Krippe, denn sie hatten sonst keinen Raum in der Herberge." (And she bore her first Son, and wrapped Him in swaddling clothes and laid Him in a manger, for they had otherwise no room in the inn.)

7. *Chorale and Recitative—soprano and bass.* The two oboes d'amore with strings and organ continuo give this chorale the enchantment of a carol sung at a candlelight service. While the soprano sings this sixth stanza of Martin Luther's hymn "Gelobet seist du, Jesus

Christ" (Praised Be Thou, Jesus Christ), the bass interpolates his narrative comments between each of her lines. Bach had used this method of setting recitatives in some of his previous cantatas.

SOPRANO: "Er ist auf Erden kommen arm." (He has come to earth poor.)

BASS: "Wer kann die Liebe recht erhöhen, / Die unser Heiland für uns hegt?" (Who can really estimate the love, / That our Savior cherishes for us?)

SOPRANO: "Dass er unser sich erbarm." (So that He has pity on us.)

BASS: "Ja, wer vermag es einzusehen / Wie ihn der Menschen Leid bewegt?" (Yes, who may perceive / How men's sorrow moves Him?)

SOPRANO: "Und in dem Himmel mache reich" (And that it may make [us] rich in heaven)

BASS: "Des Höchsten Sohn kömmt in die Welt, / Weil ihm ihr Heil so wohl gefällt." (The Son of the Highest comes into the world, / Because its salvation pleases Him so well.)

SOPRANO: "Und seinen lieben Engeln gleich" (And likewise His dear angels)

BASS: "So will er selbst als Mensch geboren werden." (So He Himself wishes to be born as a Man.)

SOPRANO: "Kyrieleis!" (God, have mercy!)

8. *Aria—bass.* Bach borrowed this number intact from the bass aria for Fame (7) in BWV 214. The scoring is identical: a trumpet, a transverse flute, strings, bassoon and organ continuo, skillfully conforming to this new text. Praise for the Queen Electress has now become tribute to the Holy Child in His humility: "Grosser Herr, o starker König, / Liebster Heiland, o wie wenig / Achtest du der Erden Pracht! / Der die ganze Welt erhält, / Ihre Pracht und Zier erschaffen, / Muss in harten Krippen schlafen." (Great Lord, o strong King, / Dearest Savior, o how little / Dost Thou heed earth's splendor! / He, Who holds the whole world in His hands, / [And Who] has created its splendor and ornament, / Must sleep in a hard manger.)

9. *Chorale.* The full choir and orchestra perform this brief thirteenth stanza of Martin Luther's 1535 hymn "Vom Himmel hoch, da komm ich her" (From Heaven Above, I Come Here), which refers to Christmastide. This makes a seasonable conclusion for Bach's cantata for Christmas Day: "Ach, mein herzliches Jesulein! / Mach dir ein rein sanft Bettelein, / Zu ruhn in meines Herzens Schrein, / Dass ich nimmer vergesse dein." (Ah, my heart-beloved little Jesus! / Make Thyself a pure, soft, little bed, / In which to rest in my heart's shrine, / So that I may never forget Thee.)

II. Und es waren Hirten in derselben Gegend (And There Were Shepherds in the Same Region) (Weihnachts-Oratorium, Part 2—for St. Stephen's Day [Boxing Day] 1734).

Apparently services were held in the Leipzig Lutheran churches on each of the two days after Christmas Day. Accordingly Bach composed a cantata for each of these saints' days: St. Stephen's and St. John the Evangelist's. Thus he was able to continue the Christmas story begun the day before.

The Gospel for this second day of Christmas is Luke 2 (15–20), but Bach's text is based on verses eight to fourteen for the Evangelist's recitatives. He retains the vocal and the instrumental forces that he used in Part 1.

This time the morning performance took place in St. Thomas's and the afternoon repeat in St. Nicholas's, according to the original text.

10. *Sinfonia.* Bach uses all woodwinds, strings and organ for this symphonic masterpiece. It is quite different from the pastorale symphony in Handel's *Messiah,* because it has a feeling of restlessness or anticipation amid the calm serenity befitting "shepherds watching over their flocks by night."

Bach divides his orchestra into two parts: one to be played by the two transverse flutes, the bassoon and the organ continuo to symbolize the angels' music, and the other played by the four oboes and the strings to represent the shepherds' pipe melody. Although these two parts are independent, they blend in a very picturesque evocation of nature. One might compare this tone-painting with the first two movements of Beethoven's *Sixth Symphony*. Bach's is, of course, much shorter. Yet both symphonies have the same aura of calm mixed with uneasiness.

Spitta's opinion on this magnificent movement is worthy of note: "a combination of opposite factors . . . of the grace of the Eastern idyl with the severity of the starlit boreal winter's night, gave the fundamental feeling of this symphony. . . . The romantic feeling for nature, which so unmistakably breathes from it, also pervades the magnificent chorus of angels (21) *Glory to God in the highest* where the sparkling accompaniment makes us feel as if we are gazing into the vault of stars" (Spitta II, p. 581).

11. *Recitative—tenor* (EVANGELIST). He resumes the narrative from Luke 2 (8–9) which he had ended at verse 6 in Part 1. This quotation is clearly linked with the wonderful tone-painting heard in the Sinfonia: "Und es waren Hirten in derselben Gegend auf dem Felde bei den Hürden, die hüteten des Nachts ihre Herde. Und siehe, des Herren Engel trat zu ihnen, und die Klarheit des Herrn leuchtet um sie, und sie furchten sich sehr." (And there were shepherds in the same country on the field near their sheep-pens, who were watching over their flocks by night. And behold, the angel of the Lord came up to them, and the glory of the Lord shone around them, and they were very much afraid.)

12. *Chorale.* As in a classical Greek dramatic chorus, the choir sings the ninth stanza of Johann Rist's 1641 hymn "Ermuntre dich, mein schwacher Geist" (Take Courage, My Weak Spirit). This is a verse of consolation to allay the shepherd's fears, as expressed in the Evangelist's preceding Biblical quotation.

"Brich an, du schönes Morgenlicht, / Und lass den Himmel tagen! / Du Hirtenvolk, erschrecke nicht, / Weil dir die Engel sagen: / Dass dieses schwache Knäbelein / Soll unser Trost und Freude sein, / Dazu den Satan zwingen / Und letztlich Friede bringen." (Break forth, thou beautiful morning-light, / And let the sky become day! / You shepherd-folk, do not be afraid, / Because the angels say to you / That this weak little boy / Is to be our consolation and joy, / In that He will overcome Satan / And finally bring peace.)

13. *Recitative—tenor* (EVANGELIST), *soprano* (THE ANGEL). Luke 2 (10–11) provides the text for this number. In true oratorio style, Bach arranges this quotation as a dramatic dialogue. He will use this method again in number 20 of this cantata and in some of the recitatives in the rest of the work.

EVANGELIST: "Und der Engel sprach zu ihnen:" (And the angel spoke to them:)

THE ANGEL: "Fürchtet euch nicht, siehe, / Ich verkündige euch grosse Freude, / Die allem Volk widerfahren wird. / Denn euch ist heute der Heiland geboren, / Welcher ist Christus, der Herr / In der Stadt David." (Fear not, behold, / I announce to you great joy, / Which will come to all people. / For to you is born today the Savior, / Who is Christ, the Lord, / In the city of David.)

14. *Recitative—bass.* Bach's sense of drama is further revealed when he gives the bass three solo recitatives in this cantata, of which this is the first. This soloist-actor may represent the emotional reaction of a spectator or a member of the congregation, according to this and his subsequent remarks in dramatic monologues, which show their importance in Bach's thinking by the accompaniment he gives to them: four oboes, the cello, the double-bass, the bassoon and the organ.

He states that what God has promised to Abraham, He now lets be fulfilled. A shepherd must have heard all that before and another shepherd must know now that His promise has come to pass.

15. *Aria—tenor.* Bach transfers this number from the alto aria in BWV 214

(5) without any loss of meaning, fitting the melody of one transverse flute, cello and organ continuo into the new text. Both words and music suit this further commentary exhorting the shepherds to visit the Christ-Child in the manger: "Frohe Hirten, eilt, ach eilet, / Eh ihr euch zu lang verweilet, / Eilt, das holde Kind zu sehn! / Geht, die Freude heisst zu schön, / Sucht die Anmut zu gewinnen, / Geht und labet Herz und Sinnen!" (Happy shepherds, hurry, ah hurry, / Before you delay too long; / Hasten to see the charming Child! / Go, the joy is too fine. / Seek to obtain the sweetness; / Go and refresh your heart and mind!)

16. *Recitative—tenor* (EVANGELIST). He continues the narrative from Luke 2 (12) in which the Angel speaks to the shepherds: "And this you will have for a sign: you will find the Child wrapped in swaddling clothes and lying in a manger."

17. *Chorale.* The choir sings stanza eight of Paul Gerhardt's 1667 hymn "Schaut, schaut, was ist für Wunder dar" (See, See, What Kind of Wonder Is There). This verse must have been chosen by Bach himself to follow the preceding recitative. He uses the same instruments that he had used in the Sinfonia (10).

"Schaut hin! dort liegt im finstern Stall, / Des Herrschaft gehet über all, / Da Speise vormals sucht ein Rind, / Da ruhet jetzt der Jungfrau'n Kind." (Look there! there lies in the dark stable, / He whose power goes over all. / There, before, an ox sought food; / There rests now the Virgin's Child.)

18. *Recitative—bass.* He continues in his role as a spectator/commentator for this second dramatic monologue, accompanied by the same instruments as in number 14 above.

Urging the shepherds to go to see the Son of the Highest in His crib, he adds that they should also sing a cradle-song to Him in chorus, as they stand before the manger. This anticipates the next aria.

19. *Aria—alto.* Once again Bach uses a previous aria from BWV 213 (3). There it was sung by a soprano acting Wollust (Pleasure), but here by an alto (the Virgin Mary). Why Bach chose an alto rather than a soprano voice to represent Mary is difficult to say, but the beauty of this exquisitely tender lullaby is beyond description. Lasting more than ten minutes, it is also the longest number in the *Oratorio.* The four oboes, one transverse flute, with the usual cello, double-bass and organ play an entrancing melodic accompaniment. This aria is one of the most appealing that Bach ever composed. He must have intended it to be, since it features the Holy Mother on his stage: "Schlafe, mein Liebster, geniesse der Ruh, / Wache nach diesem für aller Gedeihen! / Labe die Brust, / Empfinde die Lust, / Wo wir unser Herz erfreuen!" (Sleep, my Dearest, enjoy Thy rest. / Wake hereafter for the welfare of all! / Refresh Thy breast, / Perceive the pleasure, / In which our heart rejoices!)

It seems that Bach had no problem in adapting the secular tone to this one. Anyone who listens to this aria will be deeply moved, whether he knows the corresponding number in BWV 213 or not.

20.–21. *Recitative—tenor* (EVANGELIST) *and Chorus.* These numbers are taken together, because they depend on each other. The tenor begins by quoting Luke 2 (13) in his recitative, and the chorus, representing the full choir of angels, sings the fourteenth verse immediately after. This chorus has the same instrumental accompaniment as in the Sinfonia (10). It presents an amazing panorama of angels singing God's praise in the heavens above the manger scene. Such drama really brings this Biblical verse to life through Bach's audiovisual ability to create it. This is a moment in Bach that the listener will never forget.

EVANGELIST: "Und alsobald war bei dem Engel die Menge der himmlischen Herrscharen, die lobten Gott und sprachen:" (And suddenly there was with the Angels the multitude of the heavenly host, who praised God and said:)

THE ANGELS: "Ehre sei Gott in der Höhe, und Friede auf Erden, und den Menschen ein Wohlgefallen." (Glory be to God on high, and peace on earth, and to men goodwill.)

22. *Recitative—bass.* He makes a short, unaccompanied comment on the chorus of angels which will lead into the following final chorale. Remarking on the angels' jubilation, he requests the congregation to raise their voices likewise in joyous song.

23. *Chorale.* Again accompanied by the instruments of the Sinfonia (10), the choir sings stanza two of Paul Gerhardt's 1653 hymn "Wir singen dir, Immanuel" (We Sing to Thee, Immanuel), with which the audience would be acquainted at Christmas. Could they not have also sung this verse with the choir at the original Leipzig performances?

"Wir singen dir in deinem Heer / Aus aller Kraft Lob, Preis und Ehr, / Dass du o langgewünschter Gast, / Dich nunmehr eingestellet hast." (We sing to Thee in Thy army / With all our strength laud, praise and honor, / That Thou, o long-wished Guest, / Hast now Thyself appeared.)

III. Herrscher des Himmels, erhöre das Lallen (Ruler of Heaven, Hear the Stammering) (Weihnachts-Oratorium, Part 3—for St. John the Evangelist's Day 1734).

The title of the original text of this cantata for the third day of Christmas states that it was performed only in the St. Nicholas Church. It seems strange that there was no repeat in St. Thomas's.

Bach uses the same chorus for both the opening and concluding numbers. Such repetition of a movement within the same cantata is unusual in his composition. This is the last chorus of his previous secular cantata, BWV 214, altered to fit the new text. The full orchestra and choir of the *Oratorio*'s opening movement (1) reappear for these two mighty identical numbers.

24. *Chorus.* This majestic opening number is well suited to greet royalty. Here it is the Christ Child, whereas before it was Queen Maria Josepha (BWV 214 [9]). Bach's musical setting has all the panache of the occasion. It is a tremendous prayer of thanksgiving that must have pleased him so much that he decided to re-use it in the final chorus instead of the usual chorale: "Herrscher des Himmels, erhöre das Lallen, / Lass dir die matten Gesänge gefallen, / Wenn dich dein Zion mit Psalmen erhöht. / Höre der Herzen frohlockendes Preisen, / Wenn wir dir jetzo die Ehrfurcht erweisen, / Weil unsre Wohlfahrt befestiget steht." (Ruler of Heaven, hear the stammering, / Let these weak songs please Thee, / When Thy Zion extols Thee with psalms. / Hear the rejoicing praise of our hearts, / When we now show Thee our reverence, / Because our welfare stands confirmed.)

25.–26. *Recitative—tenor* (EVANGELIST) *and Chorus.* Here again, as in numbers 20–21 of Part 2, we have two interrelated numbers. Dramatic action resumes in this quotation from Luke 2 (15): the Evangelist quotes the first part of this verse, followed by the chorus of shepherds, who are accompanied by the flutes, oboes, strings, bassoon and the organ.

EVANGELIST: "Und da die Engel von ihnen gen Himmel fuhren, sprachen die Hirten untereinander:" (And as the angels went from them towards Heaven, the shepherds spoke among themselves:)

DIE HIRTEN: "Lasset uns nun gehen gen Bethlehem und die Geschichte sehen, die da geschehen ist, die uns der Herr kundgetan hat." (THE SHEPHERDS: Let us now go toward Bethlehem and see the story, which has happened there, which the Lord has made known to us.)

27. *Recitative—bass.* He is the same actor/commentator of Part 2, reappearing here to remark on the previous number. The two transverse flutes, the cello, the double-bass, the bassoon and the organ accompany him.

He states that God has comforted and redeemed Israel, thus ending its suffering. Therefore the shepherds should go to Bethlehem, since they, too, are Israelites and must be concerned.

28. *Chorale.* Two oboes and strings are added to the previous accompaniment in number 27, as the choir sings stanza seven of Martin Luther's hymn "Gelobet seist du, Jesu Christ" (Praised be Thou, Jesus Christ), following stanza six in Part 1 (7). The thought of thanksgiving is now applied to the congregation: "Dies hat er alles uns getan, / Sein gross LIeb zu zeigen an; / Des freu sich alle Christenheit, / Und dank ihm des in Ewigkeit. / Kyrieleis!" (All this He has done for us, / To show His great love. / For this may all Christendom rejoice, / And thank Him for that eternally. / Lord, have mercy!)

29. *Aria (Duet)—soprano, bass.* The lyricism shown in the arias of all six cantatas of this work is stunning. They could even be grouped together for the program of a Bach concert. Their emotional appeal is, I believe, the heart of this *Oratorio.* I do not agree with Schweitzer (II, p. 308) and footnote) that "for a popular performance in church we can safely cut out almost all the arias without any risk of leaving a mere torso; as a matter of fact by so doing we shall make the action all the clearer and more beautiful." On the contrary, these arias form an integral part of the whole, and should therefore be retained in any full or partial performance of the work.

This particular duet is a heartfelt prayer of devotion offered by two believers. It features two oboes d'amore with the usual continuo accompaniment and is a borrowing of the duet for alto and tenor (Virtue and Hercules) in BWV 213 (11).

"Herr, dein Mitleid, dein Erbarmen / Tröstet uns und macht uns frei. / Deine holde Gunst und Liebe, / Deine wundersamen Triebe / Machen deine Vatertreu / Wieder neu." (Lord, Thy compassion, Thy pity / Comforts us and makes us free. / Thy charming favor and love, / Thy wonderful workings / Make Thy Fatherly faithfulness / New again.)

30. *Recitative—tenor* (EVANGELIST). Luke 2 (16–19) continues his narrative from where he left off in movements 25 and 26 concerning the shepherds: "Und sie kamen eilend und fanden beide, Mariam und Joseph, dazu das Kind in der Krippe liegend. Da sie es aber gesehen hatten, breiteten sie das Wort aus, welches zu ihnen von diesem Kind gesaget war. Und alle, vor die es kam, wunderten sich der Rede, die ihnen die Hirten gesaget hatten. Maria aber behielt alle diese Worte und bewegte sie in ihrem Herzen." (And they came hastening and found both Mary and Joseph, and with them the Babe lying in the manger. And when they had seen Him, they spread the word out which was spoken to them about this Child. And all, before whom their word came, marvelled at the report which the shepherds had told them. But Mary kept all these words and pondered them in her heart.)

31. *Aria—alto.* Resulting from the end of this recitative, Mary sings her second poignant aria, which, like her cradlesong (number 19), I find indispensable in this *Oratorio.*

A solo violin, added to the continuo instruments, enhances the moving sentiment expressed by her text. Such personal appeal to her heart and its belief would not be out of place in any opera of this period: "Schliesse, mein Herze, dies selige Wunder / Fest in deinem Glauben ein! / Lasse dies Wunder der göttlichen Werke / Immer zur Stärke / Deines schwachen Glaubens sein!" (Enclose, my heart, this blessed wonder / Firmly in your faith! / Let this marvel of Godly works / Be always for the strength / Of your weak faith!)

32. *Recitative—alto.* Mary asserts that she will keep the certain evidence of her Child's divinity, that she has learned at this time, in the sure confines of her heart.

This short number is supported by the two transverse flutes as well as the continuo.

33. *Chorale.* The librettist probably chose this chorale because it reiterates the

idea of Mary's devotion as expressed in the previous two numbers. Bach adds two oboes to the two transverse flutes to accompany this plain rendition of stanza 15 of Paul Gerhardt's 1653 hymn "Fröhlich soll mein Herze springen" (Joyfully Shall My Heart Leap): "Ich will dich mit Fleiss bewahren, / Ich will dir / Leben hier, / Dir will ich abfahren, / Mit dir will ich endlich schweben / Voller Freud / Ohne Zeit / Dort im andern Leben." (I will keep Thee with diligence; / I will for Thee / Live here; / To Thee will I depart. / With Thee will I finally soar / Full of joy, / Timelessly, / There in the other life.)

34. *Recitative—tenor* EVANGELIST. This is his final Gospel quotation in this cantata: Luke 2 (20): "Und die Hirten kehrten wieder um, preiseten und lobten Gott um alles, das sie gesehen und gehöret hatten, wie denn zu ihnen gesaget war." (And the shepherds returned, glorified and praised God for everything that they had seen and heard, as it had been told to them.)

35. *Chorale.* With the same instrumentation as in number 33, the choir sings stanza four of Christoph Runge's 1653 hymn "Lasst Furcht und Pein" (Leave Fear and Pain). As this title suggests, the choir (and presumably the congregation) show forth the same joyous praise as the Evangelist had just noted among the shepherds: "Seid froh dieweil, / Dass euer Heil / Ist hie ein Gott und auch ein Mensch geboren; / Der, welcher ist / Der Herr und Christ / In Davids Stadt, von vielen auserkoren." (Be glad the while, / That your Savior / Has been born God and also Man here; / He who is / The Lord and Christ / In David's city, chosen from many.)

24(b). *Chorus.* This repeats the same splendid chorus (number 24) that began this cantata.

IV. Fallt mit Danken, fallt mit Loben (Fall with Thanks, Fall with Praise) (Weihnachts-Oratorium, Part 4—for New Year's Day [The Feast of the Circumcision] 1735).

Beginning with this cantata, up to the end of the *Oratorio,* the predominant mood reflects lyrical rejoicing and praise to God over Christ's birth. Of course, the dramatic and narrative movements are still present to motivate these melodic arias, choruses and chorales.

For this cantata, Bach borrows three of its seven numbers from BWV 213, his secular cantata, *Die Wahl des Herkules* (The Choice of Hercules)—the opening chorus (1) and the two arias (5, 7). The title above the original printed text states that it was performed on this date first in the morning at St. Thomas's, and then in the afternoon at St. Nicholas's.

36. *Chorus.* Instead of trumpets and timpani, Bach used two horns, plus two oboes, strings, bassoon and organ, for this opening number. The text of this religious version is much more impressive than its corresponding secular one, indicating devotion to God rather than to the Crown Prince: "Fallt mit Danken, fallt mit Loben / Vor des Höchsten Gnaden—Thron! / Gottes Sohn / Will der Erden / Heiland und Erlöser werden. / Gottes Sohn / Dämpft der Feinde Wut und Toben." (Fall with thanks, fall with praising / Before the throne of mercy of the Highest! / God's Son / Will of the earth / Become its Savior and Redeemer. / God's Son / Quells the rage and fury of our enemies.)

37. *Recitative—tenor* (EVANGELIST). He quotes Luke 2 (21), which is the Gospel for this day: "Und da acht Tage um waren, dass das Kind beschnitten würde, da ward sein Name genennet Jesus, welcher genennet war von dem Engel, ehe denn er im Mutterleibe empfangen ward." (And as eight days were past, so that the Child would be circumcised, then was His name called Jesus, who was named by the angel, before He was conceived in the womb.)

38. *Recitative—bass and Duet—soprano, bass.* Again the spectator actors, played by the bass and the soprano, appear, in order to add their comments on the above Biblical narrative.

The bass begins his declamation by

expressing his devotion to Jesus. In the middle section of this number the soprano joins him in a lovely duet, each singing alternate lines. Her text is part of stanza one of Johann Rist's 1642 hymn "Jesu, du mein liebstes Leben" (Jesus, Thou My Dearest Life). Strings as well as organ continuo accompany their duet.

Then the bass concludes his recitative with a fine arioso section that expresses his faithful love for Jesus even until the hour of his own death.

39. *Aria—soprano.* This is the famous echo aria for alto from BWV 213 (5), which Bach transcribed here for soprano. Now the echo is the answer to her rhetorical questions on fear and death rather than on the choice between Pleasure and Virtue. Note the vocal echo effect of *nein* (no) and *ja* (yes) at the end of each half of this aria. One oboe, the bassoon, the double-bass and the organ also produce similar echo effects throughout.

"Flösst mein Heiland, flösst dein Namen / Auch den allerkleinsten Samen / Jenes strengen Schreckens ein? / Nein, du sagst ja selber nein. [Nein.] / Sollt ich nun das Sterben scheuen? / Nein, dein süsses Wort ist da! / Oder sollt ich mich erfreuen? / Ja, du Heiland sprichst selbst ja. [Ja.]" (Does Thy Name, my Savior, instil / Even the tiniest seed / Of that dread fear? / No, Thou Thyself sayest no. [No.] / Should I now shun death? / No, Thy sweet word is there! / Or should I rejoice? / Yes, Thou Thyself, my Savior, sayest yes. [Yes.])

40. *Recitative—bass and Chorale—soprano.* He continues to pledge his fidelity to God in his heart and asks Him how he can express his thanks. Interwoven with his declamation, the soprano sings the second part of stanza one of Johann Rist's hymn that she had begun during his former recitative (number 38). The thought in both of their texts coincides. Strings and the organ accompany them.

41. *Aria—tenor.* This is Bach's third borrowing from BWV 213 (7) in this cantata. It is a great aria in both versions, but this version lacks the imagery of soaring heavenward on eagle's wings that the secular text expressed. Two solo violins are featured.

"Ich will nur dir zu Ehren leben, / Mein Heiland, gib mir Kraft und Mut, / Dass es mein Herz recht eifrig tut! / Stärke mich, / Deine Gnade würdiglich / Und mit Danken zu erheben!" (I will only live to honor Thee. / My Savior, give me strength and courage, / So that my heart responds quite eagerly! / Strengthen me, / To extol Thy graciousness worthily / And with thanks!)

42. *Chorale.* Bach must have been impressed by the chorales of Johann Rist, because he uses them throughout this cantata. We hear now stanza 15 of Rist's 1642 hymn "Hilf, Herr Jesu, lass gelingen" (Help, Lord Jesus, Let It Succeed). With the same instruments used in the first chorus (36), the choir sings a personal prayer to Jesus to guide each of us in our daily lives. This is one of Bach's outstanding interpretations of a chorale text. We can even imagine that Bach himself is praying here: "Jesus richte mein Beginnen, / Jesus bleibe stets bei mir! / Jesus zäume mir die Sinnen, / Jesus sei nur mein Begier. / Jesus sei mir in Gedanken, / Jesu, lass mich nicht wanken!" (Jesus, direct my beginning. / Jesus, stay always with me. / Jesus, restrain my senses. / Jesus, be my only desire. / Jesus, be in my thoughts. / Jesus, let me not waver!)

V. Ehre sei dir, Gott gesungen (May Honor Be Sung to Thee, God) (Weihnachts-Oratorium, Part 5—for the Sunday after New Year's Day 1735).

The original text states that this cantata was intended for performance in the St. Nicholas Church. As with Part 3, no mention is made of a repeat in St. Thomas's.

Bach's text does not follow the Gospel for this Sunday, Matthew 2 (13–23), but rather that of the Epiphany Sunday Gospel, Matthew 2 (1–6). In this libretto, Biblical quotations occur more frequently than in Part 4, where there is only one.

Bach's self-borrowing is restricted here to only the bass aria, transposed from the soprano aria in BWV 215 (7), the homage cantata to Friedrich August III that was performed only three months before.

43. *Chorus.* Accompanied by the two oboes d'amore, strings, the bassoon and the organ, this opening chorus is a resounding hymn of praise to the Almighty. The majestic melody must have been suggested to Bach by each of the nouns and their associated verbs (italicized) in this text. We hear more than a song of thanksgiving—we can visualize the vastness of God's beneficence on His world. This chorus overflows with the boundless joy motif of its text and is certainly one of Bach's supreme compositions: "*Ehre sei* dir, *Gott, gesungen* / Dir *sei Lob* und *Dank bereit'.* / *Dich erhebet alle Welt,* / Weil dir *unser Wohl gefällt,* Weil anheut / Unser aller *Wunsch gelungen,* / Weil uns *dein Segen* so herrlich *erfreut.*" (*May honor be sung* to Thee, *God,* / For Thee *may praise* and *thanks be ready.* / *All the world exalts* Thee, / Because *our welfare pleases* Thee, / Because this day / Our every *wish is fulfilled,* / Because *Thy blessing gladdens* us so.)

44. *Recitative—tenor* (EVANGELIST). Matthew 2 (1) is quoted now to continue the narrative: "Da Jesus geboren war zu Bethlehem im jüdischen Lande, zur Zeit des Königes Herodis, siehe, da kamen die Weisen vom Morgenlande gen Jerusalem und sprachen:" (When Jesus was born in Bethlehem in Judea, at the time of King Herod, behold, there came the wise men from the east to Jerusalem and they said:)

45. *Chorus and Recitative—alto.* Bach comes forth again as a dramatist in this number. The wise men quote Matthew 2 (2). They are the chorus, accompanied by the same instruments as in the opening chorus (43); the alto interpolates her recitative-commentary between their lines.

DIE WEISEN: "Wo ist der neugeborne König der Jüden?" (THE WISE MEN: Where is the new-born King of the Jews?)

MARIA: "Sucht ihn in meiner Brust, / Hier wohnt er, mir und ihm zur Lust." (MARY: Seek Him in my breast, / Here He dwells, to my and His joy.)

DIE WEISEN: "Wir haben seinen Stern gesehen im Morgenlande und sind kommen, ihn anzubeten." (THE WISE MEN: We have seen His star in the east and have come to worship Him.)

Mary ends her recitative now by saying that the light of the star signifies the light shining from her Son. Even though the heathen (including the wise men) do not know Him, His light will shine upon them so that they will want to worship Him.

46. *Chorale.* Following Mary's thought and with the same instrumental accompaniment as in the preceding movement, the choir sings stanza five of Georg Weissel's 1642 hymn "Nun, liebe Seel, nun ist es Zeit" (Now, Dear Soul, It Is Time). This verse states that the light of the Lord's countenance will dispel all our gloom.

47. *Aria—bass.* Transposed by Bach from the soprano aria in BWV 215 (7), the text for this aria is much clearer and therefore the singer's personality is better expressed. He is the same actor as in Part 4. He offers here his own votive prayer, accompanied by one oboe d'amore and the organ: "Erleucht auch meine finstre Sinnen, / Erleuchte mein Herze / Durch der Strahlen klaren Schein! / Dein Wort soll mir die hellste Kerze / In allen meinen Werken sein; / Dies lässet die Seele nichts Böses beginnen." (Enlighten also my dark senses, / Light up my heart / By the clear shine of Thy radiance! / Thy Word shall be my brightest candle / In all my actions; / This lets the soul undertake no evil.)

48. *Recitative—tenor* (EVANGELIST): Matthew 2 (3) continues his narrative: "Da das der König Herodes hörte, erschrak er und mit ihm das ganze Jerusalem." (When King Herod heard that, he was frightened and with him all Jerusalem.)

49. *Recitative—alto.* Strings and the organ accompany the response of Mary to

the above quotation: Why should you be terrified by the presence of Jesus? Should you not rather rejoice because He promises to renew the welfare of mankind?

50. *Recitative—tenor* (EVANGELIST): He quotes Matthew 2 (4–6) which describes Herod's questioning of the high priests and the scribes about where Jesus was to be born. Herod hears the answer, including the prophet's saying that He would be the Lord over Israel.

The tenor sings the last part of this number as an arioso.

51. *Aria (Trio)—soprano, alto, tenor.* A solo violin, playing over the cello, double-bass and organ continuo, produces an impression of mystical longing, as the soloists sing their lines in imitation of each other. At first, the soprano and the tenor appear to be a duet, with the alto singing her line separately. Then in the da capo, all three voices exchange their lines to create a real trio. This trio is a miniature musical drama.

SOPRANO: "Ach, wann wird die Zeit erscheinen?" (Ah, when will the time appear?)

TENOR: "Ach, wann kommt der Trost der Seinen?" (Ah, when will the Consoler of His people come?)

ALTO: "Schweigt, er ist schon wirklich hier!" (Be quiet, He is already really here!)

SOPRANO AND TENOR: "Jesu, ach so komm zu mir!" (Jesu, ah! then come to me!)

Notice how Mary expresses her confidence in the third line.

52. *Recitative—alto.* The two oboes d'amore are here added to the continuo instruments.

Following her part in the trio, Mary reaffirms that her Child is already ruling over our hearts and making them His throne. This assurance is a nice touch.

53. *Chorale.* With the same instrumentation as in the opening chorus (43), the choir sings stanza nine of Johann Franck's 1655 hymn "Ihr Gestirn, ihr hohen Lüfte" (You Stars, You High Airs). Its reference to Jesus entering our heart fits well into Mary's recitative (52) above: "Zwar ist solche Herzensstube, / Wohl kein schöner Fürstensaal, / Sondern eine finstre Grube; / Doch sobald dein Gnadenstrahl / In denselben nur wird blinken, / Wird es voller Sonnen dünken." (Certainly such a room for the heart / Is no beautiful princely hall, / But rather a dark cavity; / Yet as soon as Thy ray of grace / Therein will only sparkle, / It will appear to be full of suns.)

VI. Herr, wenn die stolzen Feinde schnauben (Lord, When Our Proud Enemies Pant) (Weihnachts—Oratorium, Part 6—for Epiphany Sunday 1735).

The title of the original printing of this final cantata reads: "Am Feste der Offenbahrung Christi. Frühe zu St. Thomae. Nachmittag zu St. Nicolai." (On the Feast of the Revelation of Christ. In the morning at St. Thomas's. In the afternoon at St. Nicholas's.) This is the reverse order of presentation from Part 1.

Six of the eleven numbers in this cantata are recitatives, Biblical or freely composed, indicating that Picander and Bach wished to stress the story content. This is not to say, however, that the lyricism of the solo and choral numbers is at all inferior to those of the previous cantatas in the work. After all, they do evolve from the recitatives and add to the dramatic action.

54. *Chorus.* Bach returns to his full orchestra (except the two transverse flutes) that he had used for the opening choruses of Parts 1 and 3. Neumann (*Kentatentexte,* note on page 482) presumes that this chorus was borrowed from BWV Anh. 10 (1) beginning "So kämpfet nun, ihr muntern Töne" (Then Struggle Now, Ye Merry Tones), a secular birthday cantata (1731) to Count Flemming, of which the text survives but not the music.

Whatever the source of this rousing movement, it is another magnificent example of Bach's expertise in choral composition: "Herr, wenn die stolzen Feinde schnauben, / So gib, dass wir im festen Glauben / Nach deiner Macht und Hilfe sehn. / Wir wollen dir allein vertrauen, / So können wir den scharfen Klauen / Des Feindes unversehrt entgehn." (Lord, when our proud enemies pant, / Then grant, that we in firm belief / Look to Thy might and help. / We want to trust in Thee alone, / Then we can escape unharmed / From the sharp claws of our enemy.)

This text presents Bach with the imagery of the Devil and his minions as being bloodthirsty monsters, yet Bach's melody does not bring this out, except in the first line, perhaps. This might be a sure indication that this chorus was borrowed from another of his cantatas. The martial tone recalls the first chorus in BWV 80.

These creatures are symbolic of Herod and his murderers who seek to slay the newborn child. The Gospel for Epiphany, however, is limited to Matthew 2 (1–12)—the visit of the wise men whom Herod sends to find Jesus. The Evanglist's recitatives follow these verses, but all the other numbers reflect on the flight of the Holy Family into Egypt, frustrating Herod as described in the remaining verses of Matthew 2.

55. *Recitative—tenor* (EVANGELIST) *and bass* (HEROD). This is an interesting though short dialogue in which Herod makes a dramatic appearance.

EVANGELIST: "Da berief Herodes die Weisen heimlich und erlernet mit Fleiss von ihnen, wann der Stern erschienen wäre. Und weiset sie gen Bethlehem und sprach:" (Then Herod called the wise men secretly and learned diligently from them when the star would appear. And he directed them toward Bethlehem and said:)

HERODES: "Ziehet hin und forschet fleissig nach dem Kindlein, und wenn ihrs findet, / sagt mirs wieder, dass ich auch komme und es anbete." (Go there and seek diligently the little child, and when you have found Him, tell it to me again, so that I may come also and worship Him.) [Matthew 2 (7–8).]

56. *Recitative—soprano.* Proceeding from the previous number, she comments on Herod's villainy, with strings and organ accompaniment. Her declamation is very dramatic as she accuses Herod of falsehood. Let him try to ensnare Jesus; he will not succeed, because his evil intentions are known to the Father, who will protect His Son.

57. *Aria—soprano.* Her confidence in God is expressed beautifully in this aria, accompanied by an oboe d'amore, strings, the bassoon and the organ. This aria and the Virgin's lullaby (19) are the best solo numbers in the whole *Oratorio,* and both are indispensable for any performance of this work. Once again it seems that Bach was motivated by the nouns in this text (italicized) when he composed the musical tonality within and surrounding each of these words. The resultant emotional effect on the listener is tremendous.

"Nun ein *Wink* von seinen *Händen* / Stürzt *ohnmächtger Menschen Macht.* / Hier wird alle *Kraft* verlacht! / Spricht *der Höchste* nur *ein Wort,* / Seiner *Feinde Stolz* zu enden, / O, so müssen sich *sofort* / *Sterblicher Gedanken* wenden." (Only a *gesture* from *His Hands* / Overthrows the *might of powerless men.* / Here all *strength* is laughed to scorn! / If *the Highest* speaks only *one word.* / To end the *pride of His enemies,* / O, then must *immediately* / *Mortal thoughts* be turned aside.)

58. *Recitative—tenor* (EVANGELIST). He continues the story, quoting Matthew 2 (9–11), of the visit of the wise men to the manger, where they worshipped the babe and offered their symbolic gifts of gold, frankincense and myrrh.

59. *Chorale.* This is the first stanza of Paul Gerhardt's Christmas hymn (1653). It is plainly sung, accompanied by two oboes, strings, the bassoon and the organ. One can visualize the wise men, as they offer their presents, and at the same time the congregation, as they dedicate their lives to Jesus: "Ich steh an deiner Krippen hier, / O Jesulein, mein Leben. / Ich komme, bring und schenke dir, / Was du mir hast gegeben. / Nimm hin, es ist mein Geist und Sinn, / Herz, Seel

und Mut, nimm alles hin / Und lass dirs wohlgefallen!" / (I stand here at Thy crib, / O little Jesu, my life. / I come, bring and present to Thee / What Thou hast given me. / Take it; it is my spirit and mind, / Heart, soul and disposition; take it all / And let it please Thee well!)

60. *Recitative—tenor* (EVANGELIST). With this number, he ends his reading of the Christmas story. He quotes Matthew 2 (12), which tells how God warned the wise men in a dream not to return to Herod, so that they "departed into their own country another way."

61. *Recitative—tenor.* Bach sets this longer recitative and the following aria with the same accompaniment: two oboes d'amore, the cello, the double-bass, the bassoon and the organ. The tenor bids the wise men depart, but says that Jesus will remain with him. He will devote himself to serving Him and to returning His love. No enemy can interfere with his good luck in having Jesus for his Friend, because when he calls on Him for help, he can count on receiving it from Him.

62. *Aria—tenor.* This is the final aria in the cantata and in the whole *Oratorio.* The tenor sings his defiance to his arrogant foe (Satan and company), for he knows that his Savior will defend him. This bravura aria, after his previous recitative, is well suited as a final solo number: "Nun mögt ihr stolzen Feinde schrecken; / Was könnt ihr mir für Furcht erwecken? / Mein Schatz, mein Hort ist hier bei mir. / Ihr mögt euch noch so grimmig stellen, / Droht nur, mich ganz und gar zu fällen, / Doch seht! mein Heiland wohnet hier." (Now you proud foes may be afraid; / What kind of fear can you awaken in me? / My Treasure, my Protector is here by me. / You may appear ever so grim, / And just threaten to fell me completely, / But see, my Savior dwells here!)

63. *Recitative (Quartet)—soprano, alto, tenor, bass.* Although very short, this arioso quartet has remarkable impact on the listener just before he hears the final chorale. It seems that each soloist individually expresses his or her own confidence through repetition of the first two lines, before they all join in unison to sing the last third line: "Was will der Hölle Schrecken nun, / Was will uns Welt und Sünde tun, / Da wir in Jesu Händen ruhn?" (What will the terrors of hell do now, / What will the world and sin do to us, / Since we rest in the hands of Jesus?)

64. *Chorale.* With the same instrumental accompaniment as in the opening chorus (54), the choir sings stanza four of Georg Werner's 1648 hymn "Ihr Christen auserkoren" (Ye Chosen Christians). This particular stanza makes a fitting conclusion to this cantata and to the entire work—namely, that Christ's triumph over the evil that besets man will enable him to reach Heaven in the end: "Nun seid ihr wohl gerochen / An euer Feinde Schar, / Denn Christus hat zerbrochen / Was euch zuwider war. / Tod, Teufel, Sünd und Hölle / Sind ganz und gar geschwächt; / Bei Gott hat seine Stelle / Das menschliche Geschlecht." (Now you are well avenged / Upon the host of your enemies, / For Christ has broken apart / That which was against you. / Death, the Devil, sin and hell / Are weakened totally; / With God has its place / The human race.)

There can be no doubt that Bach agreed with the thought of this stanza.

Appendix A: The Sacred Cantatas by Type

1. Free

All Bach cantatas except those listed below are of the free type.

2. Solo:

BWV	p.
189	3
199	10
161	15
162	16
163	17
132	18
152	19
155	20
59	20
158	24
173	25
134	27
22	29
23	30
24	35
164	37
153	47
154	49
81	50
83	51
184	56
165	57
181	63
166	66
86	67
44	68
167	71
168	73
157	83
159	88
145	89
120	92

3. Chorale:

BWV	p.
16	46
153	47
4	52
73	61
20	69
8	77
93	87
112	104
9	106
27	112
140	119
129	121
177	123
137	128
95	129
98	130
60	131
192	133
99	135
117	136
97	138
143	141
14	143
128	153
107	160
94	162
133	163
100	164
5	166
41	168
28	174
123	181

4. Single Chorale:

BWV	p.
4	52
20	69
8	77
93	87
80	95
112	104
140	119
129	121
177	123
137	128
98	130
192	133
99	135
117	136
97	138
14	143
94	162
133	163
100	164
5	166
41	168
123	181
124	184
3	185
111	186
92	187
125	188
126	190
127	191
1	192
2	196
135	197

2. Solo:

BWV	p.
188	94
89	96
52	97
82	99
84	100
42	103
174	105
35	108
51	111
27	112
169	113
56	116
49	117
55	119
88	124
170	126
60	131
58	134
54	140
85	144
108	146
87	148
183	154
175	158
13	169
32	182
90	223
110	226
57	228
151	231

3. Chorale:

BWV	p.
124	184
3	185
111	186
92	187
125	188
126	190
127	191
1	192
2	196
135	197
7	198
10	199
178	202
101	203
113	204
33	207
78	208
138	209
114	211
96	212
130	214
48	215
180	216
38	218
115	219
139	220
26	221
62	224
91	225
121	229
122	231
116	233

4. Single Chorale:

BWV	p.
7	198
10	199
178	202
101	203
113	204
33	207
78	208
138	209
114	211
96	212
130	214
180	216
38	218
115	219
139	220
26	221
62	224
91	225
121	229
122	231
116	233

Appendix B: Cantatas by BWV Number

BWV No.		Page
1	Wie schön leuchtet der Morgenstern	192
2	Ach Gott, vom Himmel sieh' darein	196
3	Ach Gott, wie manches Herzeleid I	185
4	Christ lag in Todesbanden	52
5	Wo soll ich fliehen hin	166
6	Bleib' bei uns, denn es will Abend werden	173
7	Christ, unser Herr, zum Jordan kam	198
8	Liebster Gott, wann werd' ich sterben?	77
9	Es ist das Heil uns kommen her	106
10	Meine Seel' erhebt den Herren	199
11	Lobet Gott in seinen Reichen (Himmelfahrtsoratorium)	151
12	Weinen, Klagen, Sorgen, Zagen	54
13	Meine Seufzer, meine Tränen	169
14	Wär' Gott nicht mit uns diese Zeit	143
15	*Demonstrated not to be the work of Bach.*	
16	Herr Gott, dich loben wir	46
17	Wer Dank opfert, der preiset mich	176
18	Gleichwie der Regen und Schnee vom Himmel fällt	7
19	Es erhub sich ein Streit	31
20	O Ewigkeit, du Donnerwort I	69
21	Ich hatte viel Bekümmernis	8
22	Jesus nahm zu sich die Zwölfe	29
23	Du wahrer Gott und Davids Sohn	30
24	Ein ungefärbt Gemüthe	35
25	Es ist nichts Gesundes an meinem Leibe	109
26	Ach wie flüchtig	221
27	Wer weiss, wie nahe mir mein Ende	112
28	Gottlob! nun geht das Jahr zu Ende	174
29	Wir danken dir Gott, wir danken dir	110
30	Freue dich, erlöste Schar	179
30a	Angenehmes Wiederau, freue dich	269
31	Der Himmel lacht, die Erde jubilieret	13
32	Liebster Jesu, mein Verlangen (Dialogus)	182
33	Allein zu dir, Herr Jesu Christ	207
34	O Ewiges Feuer, O Ursprung der Liebe	195
35	Geist und Seele wird verwirret	108
36	Schwingt freudig euch empor	98
36c	Schwingt freudig euch empor	246
37	Wer da glaubet und getauft wird	84
38	Aus tiefer Not schrei ich zu dir	218
39	Brich dem Hungrigen dein Brot	122
40	Dazu ist erschienen der Sohn Gottes	43

BWV No.		Page
41	Jesu, nun sei gepreiset	168
42	Am Abend aber desselbigen Sabbaths	103
43	Gott fähret auf mit Jauchzen	149
44	Sie werden euch in den Bann tun I	68
45	Es ist dir gesagt, Mensch, was gut ist	200
46	Schauet doch und sehet, ob irgend ein Schmerz sei	75
47	Wer sich selbst erhöhet, der soll erniedrigt werden	27
48	Ich elender Mensch, wer wird mich erlösen	215
49	Ich geh' und suche mit Verlangen	117
50	Nun ist das Heil und die Kraft	234
51	Jauchzet Gott in allen Landen	111
52	Falsche Welt, dir trau' ich nicht	97
53	*Demonstrated not to be the work of Bach.*	
54	Widerstehe doch der Sünde	140
55	Ich armer Mensch, ich Sündenknecht	119
56	Ich will den Kreuzstab gerne tragen	116
57	Selig ist der Mann (Dialogus)	228
58	Ach Gott, wie manches Herzeleid II (Dialogus)	134
59	Wer mich liebet, der wird mein Wort halten I	20
60	O Ewigkeit, du Donnerwort II (Dialogus)	131
61	Nun komm, der Heiden Heiland I	11
62	Nun komm, der Heiden Heiland II	224
63	Christen, ätzet diesen Tag	42
64	Sehet, welch eine Liebe hat uns der Vater erzeiget	44
65	Sie werden aus Saba alle kommen	48
66	Erfreut euch, ihr Herzen	101
67	Halt im Gedächtnis Jesum Christ	64
68	Also hat Gott die Welt geliebet	156
69	Lobe den Herrn, meine Seele I	59
70	Wachet! betet! betet! wachet!	21
71	Gott ist mein König	2
72	Alles nur nach Gottes Willen	79
73	Herr, wie du willst, so schick's mit mir	61
74	Wer mich liebet, der wird mein Wort halten II	155
75	Die Elenden sollen essen	31
76	Die Himmel erzählen die Ehre Gottes	33
77	Du sollst Gott, deinen Herren, lieben	76
78	Jesu, der du meine Seele	208
79	Gott, der Herr, ist Sonn' und Schild	167
80	Ein feste Burg ist unser Gott	95
81	Jesus schläft, was soll ich hoffen?	50
82	Ich habe genug	99
83	Erfreute Zeit im neuen Bunde	51
84	Ich bin vergnügt mit meinem Glücke	100
85	Ich bin ein guter Hirt	144
86	Wahrlich, wahrlich, ich sage euch	67
87	Bisher habt ihr nichts gebeten in meinem Namen	148
88	Siehe, ich will viel Fischer aussenden	124
89	Was soll ich aus dir machen, Ephraim?	96
90	Es reifet euch ein schrecklich Ende	223
91	Gelobet seist du, Jesu Christ	225

BWV No.		Page
92	Ich hab' in Gottes Herz und Sinn	187
93	Wer nur den lieben Gott lässt walten	87
94	Was frag' ich nach der Welt	162
95	Christus, der ist mein Leben	129
96	Herr Christ, der ein'ge Gottessohn	212
97	In allen meinen Taten	138
98	Was Gott tut, das ist wohlgetan I	130
99	Was Gott tut, das ist wohlgetan II	135
100	Was Gott tut, das ist wohlgetan III	164
101	Nimm von uns, Herr, du treuer Gott	203
102	Herr, deine Augen sehen nach dem Glauben	107
103	Ihr werdet weinen und heulen	145
104	Du Hirte Israel, höre	65
105	Herr, gehe nicht ins Gericht	74
106	Gottes Zeit ist die allerbeste Zeit (Actus tragicus)	5
107	Was willst du dich betrüben	160
108	Es ist euch gut, dass ich hingehe	146
109	Ich glaube, lieber Herr, hilf meinem Unglauben	118
110	Unser Mund sei voll Lachens	226
111	Was mein Gott will, das g'scheh allzeit	186
112	Der Herr ist mein getreuer Hirt	104
113	Herr Jesu Christ, du höchtes Gut	204
114	Ach, lieben Christen, seid getrost	211
115	Mache dich, mein Geist, bereit	219
116	Du Friedefürst, Herr Jesu Christ	233
117	Sei Lob und Ehr' dem höchsten Gut	136
118	O Jesu Christ, mein's Lebens Licht	234
119	Preise, Jerusalem, den Herrn	38
120	Gott, man lobet dich in der Stille zu Zion	92
121	Christum wir sollen loben schon	229
122	Das neugebor'ne Kindelein	231
123	Liebster Immanuel, Herzog der Frommen	181
124	Meinen Jesum lass' ich nicht	184
125	Mit Fried' und Freud' ich fahr' dahin	188
126	Erhalt' uns, Herr, bei deinem Wort	190
127	Herr Jesu Christ, wahr' Mensch und Gott	191
128	Auf Christi Himmelfahrt allein	153
129	Gelobet sei der Herr	121
130	Herr Gott, dich loben alle wir	214
131	Aus der Tiefe rufe ich, Herr, zu dir	1
132	Bereitet die Wege, bereitet die Bahn	18
133	Ich freue mich in dir	163
134	Ein Herz, das seinen Jesum lebend weiss	27
135	Ach Herr, mich armen Sünder	197
136	Erforsche mich, Gott, und erfahre mein Herz	72
137	Lobe den Herren, den mächtigen König der Ehren	128
138	Warum betrübst du dich, mein Herz	209
139	Wohl dem, der sich auf seinen Gott	220
140	Wachet auf, ruft uns die Stimme	119
141	*Demonstrated not to be the work of Bach.*	
142	*Demonstrated not to be the work of Bach.*	

BWV No.		Page
143	Lobe den Herrn, meine Seele II	141
144	Nimm was dein ist, und gehe hin	62
145	Ich lebe, mein Herze, zu deinem Ergötzen	89
146	Wir müssen durch viel Trübsal in das Reich Gottes eingehen	194
147	Herz und Mund und Tat und Leben	23
148	Bringet dem Herrn Ehre seines Namens	78
149	Man singet mit Freuden vom Sieg	114
150	Nach dir, Herr, verlanget mich	4
151	Süsser Trost, mein Jesus kommt	231
152	Tritt auf die Glaubensbahn	19
153	Schau', lieber Gott, wie meine Feind'	47
154	Mein liebster Jesus ist verloren	49
155	Mein Gott, wie lang', ach lange	20
156	Ich steh' mit einem Fuss im Grabe	91
157	Ich lasse dich nicht, du segnest mich denn	83
158	Der Freide sei mit dir	24
159	Sehet, wir gehen hinauf gen Jerusalem	88
160	*Demonstrated not to be the work of Bach.*	
161	Komm, du süsse Todesstunde	15
162	Ach, ich sehe, jetzt da ich zur Hochzeit gehe	16
163	Nur jedem das Seine	17
164	Ihr, die ihr euch von Christo nennet	37
165	O heiliges Geist-und Wasserbad	57
166	Wo gehest du hin?	66
167	Ihr Menschen, rühmet Gottes Liebe	71
168	Tue Rechnung! Donnerwort	73
169	Gott soll allein mein Herze haben	113
170	Vergnügte Ruh', beliebte Seelenlust	126
171	Gott, wie dein Name, so ist auch dein Ruhm	90
172	Erschallet ihr Lieder	53
173	Erhöhtes Fleisch und Blut	25
173a	Durchlauchtster Leopold	240
174	Ich liebe den Höchsten von ganzen Gemüte	105
175	Er rufet seinen Schafen mit Namen	158
176	Es ist ein trotzig und verzagt Ding	159
177	Ich ruf' zu dir, Herr Jesu Christ	123
178	Wo Gott, der Herr, nicht bei uns hält	202
179	Siehe zu, dass deine Gottesfurcht nicht Heuchelei sei	58
180	Schmücke dich, o liebe Seele	216
181	Leichtgesinnte Flattergeister	63
182	Himmelskönig, sei willkommen	12
183	Sie werden euch in den Bann tun II	154
184	Erwünschtes Freudenlicht	56
185	Barmherziges Herze der ewigen Liebe	14
186	Ärgre dich, O Seele, nicht	36
187	Es wartet alles auf dich	127
188	Ich habe meine Zuversicht	94
189	Meine Seele rühmt und preist	3
190	Singet dem Herrn ein neues Lied	60
191	Gloria in excelsis Deo	136

BWV No.		Page
192	Nun danket alle Gott	133
193	Ihr Tore zu Zion	206
194	Höchsterwünschtes Freudenfest	40
195	Dem Gerechten muss das Licht	82
196	Der Herr denkt an uns	3
197	Gott ist unsre Zuversicht	177
198	Lass, Fürstin, lass noch einen Strahl (Trauerode)	85
199	Mein Herze schwimmt im Blut	10
200	Bekennen will ich seinen Namen	235
201	Geschwinde, geschwinde, ihr wirbelnden Winde	257
202	Weichet nur, betrübte Schatten	242
203	Amore traditore	236
204	Ich bin in mir vergnügt	256
205	Der zufriedengestellte Aeolus	248
206	Schleicht, spielende Wellen	267
207	Vereinigte Zwietracht der wechselnden Saiten	250
207a	Auf, schmetternde Töne	253
208	Was mir behagt, ist nur die muntre Jagd (Hunting Cantata)	238
209	Non sa che sia dolore	237
210	O holder Tag, erwünschte Zeit	274
211	Schweiget stille, plaudert nicht (Coffee Cantata)	259
212	Mer hahn en neue Oberkeet (Peasant Cantata)	271
213	Lasst uns sorgen, lasst uns wachen (Die Wahl des Herkules)	261
214	Tönet, ihr Pauken! Erschallet, Trompeten!	263
215	Preise dein Glücke, gesegnetes Sachsen	265
248	Weihnachts-Oratorium	277
249	Kommt, eilet und laufet (Osteroratorium)	171
249a	Entfliehet, verschwindet, entweichet, ihr Sorgen	244

Bibliography

Arnold, Denis. *Bach.* O.U.P., 1984.

Boyd, Malcolm. *Bach.* J.M. Dent, 1983.

Daw, Stephen. *The Music of Johann Sebastian Bach: The Choral Works.* Fairleigh Dickinson University Press, 1981.

Day, James. *The Literary Background to Bach's Cantatas.* Dobson, 1961.

Forkel, J. *J.S. Bach.* C.S. Terry, trans., 1920. With notes and appendices by Charles Sanford Terry (reprint Da Capo 1970).

Geiringer, Karl. *Johann Sebastian Bach, the Culmination of an Era.* O.U.P., 1966.

Grew, Eva and Sydney. *Bach.* Dent, 1947 (paperback 1972).

Pirro, André. *J.S. Bach.* M. Savill, trans. Orion Press (Crown Publishers), 1957.

Robertson, Alec. *The Church Cantatas of J.S. Bach.* Cassell, 1972.

Schrade, Leo. *Bach: The Conflict Between the Sacred and the Secular.* Da Capo, 1973 (reprint of Merlin Press edition, 1955).

Schweitzer, A. *J.S. Bach.* E. Newman, trans. 2 vols. Black, 1955.

Smend, Friedrich. *Back in Köthen.* John Page, trans. Stephen Daw, ed. Concordia Publishing, 1985.

Spitta, P. *J.S. Bach.* 2 vols. Dover, 1952.

Terry, Charles S. *The Music of Bach, an Introduction.* Dover, 1963.

Westrup, J.A. *Bach Cantatas.* B.B.C., 1966.

Whittaker, W.G. *The Cantatas of Johann Sebastian Bach, Sacred and Secular.* 2 vols. O.U.P., 1959.

In German:

Dürr, Alfred. *Die Kantaten von Johann Sebastian Bach.* 2 vols. Bärenreiter, Kassel, 1971.

Neumann, W. *Johann Sebastian Bach—Sämtliche Kantaten Texte.* 1956.

Schulze, Hans-Joachim. *Johann Sebastian Bach, Leben und Werke in Dokumenten.* 1975.

Schulze, Walther Siegmund. *Johann Sebastian Bach.* 1976.

Index

Abendmusik 223
Adama 96
Agricola, Johann (1492–1566) 123
Albinus, Johann Georg (1624–1679) 16, 26, 113
Albrecht, Markgraf von Brandenburg-Ansbach (1490–1568) 63, 80, 186
allegorical characters 214, 251, 253, 261–63, 263–65, 267–71
Ämilie Juliane von Schwarzburg-Rudolstadt (1637–1706) 67, 101, 112
angel/angels 214, 215, 226, 227, 232, 281, 282
Anhalt-Cöthen 25, 98, 101
Ansbach 237
Apel, Andreas Dietrich (1666–1718) 265
Arnstadt 7, 223
Augsburg 202
Augsburg Confession 60, 92, 95
August II (The Strong), Elector of Saxony (1670–1733) 40, 85, 206, 252, 262, 265, 266
August III, Elector of Saxony (1696–1763) 85, 136, 141, 168, 253, 264–69
Avenarius, Matthäus (1625–1692) 154

Bach, Anna Magdalene (née Wilcke) (1701–1760) 37, 40, 100, 242, 256, 275
Bach, Johann Christoph (1671–1721) 81
Bach, Johann Ludwig (1677–1731) 149
Bach, Johann Sebastian (1685–1750): (a) career: as cantor in Leipzig 29, 31, 244, as court composer to Dresden 263, as court composer to Weissenfels 244, as court concertmaster in Weimar 7, as dramatist 21, 25, 38, 43, 49, 50, 51, 55, 64, 65, 109, 119, 151, 169, 171, 201, 203, 248–63, 267–69, 271–74, as librettist 2, 4, 21, 23–26, 28, 40, 43, 46–49, 56, 82, 103, 105, 107, 108, 110, 111, 113, 141, 148, 158, 176, 177, 195, 206, 226, 241, 259, 261, 263, 287, as organist 40, as organist, concertmaster in Weimar 7, as organist in Mühlhausen 1, as preacher 14, 15, 17, 18, 35–38, 40, 41, 56, 59, 75, 76, 97, 101, 106, 123, 127, 140, 251, 252, 275, as religious thinker 30, 37, 38, 41, 43, 77, 84, 130, 148, 153, 194, 196, 220, 285; (b) instrumental pieces borrowed for cantatas: Brandenburg Concerti 25, 28, 97, 105, 222, 251, 252, concerti 25, 52, 57, 58, 112, 123, 228, 244, dance tunes 40, 61, 90, 102, 175, French danses: (a) bourrée 242, 247, 274, (b) chaconne 5, 7, (c) contre-danse (country-dance) 56, 178, 274, (d) courante 181, (e) gavotte 41, 57, 160, 180, 215, 263, 269, 270, (f) gigue 11, 37, 41, 52, 55, 78, 163, 240, (g) loure 19, (h) mazurka 273, (i) minuet 26, 28, 29, 41, 118, (j) passacaglio 54, (k) passepied 28, (l) polonaise 272, (m) rondeau 30, 84, 137, 269, (n) sarabande 272, Harpsichord Concerto in D minor (BWV 1052) 94, 194, Harpsichord Concerto in E major (BWV 1053) 113, 117, Harpsichord Concerto in F minor (BWV 1056) 91, Harpsichord Concerto (fragment) (BWV 1059) 108, interludes for orchestra 252, *Notenbüchlein* 99, oratorios 225, 244, 245, 261–266, organ 82, 94, *Orgelbüchlein* 221, overtures (French) 11, 19, 39, 40, 69, 138, 173, 226, sinfonias 1, 3, 4, 7, 8, 32, 34, 53, 54, 66, 81, 91, 97, 103, 105, 108–10, 114, 117, 171, 226, 237, 244, 252, 272, 279, sonata/sonatina 6, 12, 13, 25, Suite in E major for solo violin 110, suites (unknown) 243, 247, 270, Trio in G minor for organ 67; (c) style and personal theory: addressing instruments as persons (textual) 55, 86, 228, 253, 259, 264, Affekt theory xiii, 14, 98, 211, 236, 238, 257, 260, cantata and oratorio, difference between 277, cantatas termed otherwise 240, 242, chamber music effect 241, 242, 246, chorale treatment 217, 220, 221, chorus treatment 248, 257 (winds), 261, (pagan gods), 263 (muses), coloratura runs on words 4, 14, 15, 17, 18, 20, 22, 24, 32, 44, 45, 57, 63,

(Bach, Johann Sebastian, cont.) 65, 67, 69, 70–72, 77, 79, 84, 89, 93, 95, 99, 102, 122, 123, 139, 142, 156, 165, 186, 188, 190, 227, 243, 244, 249, 250, 258, 270, combination of themes 88, 91, 96, 148, 150, 164, 187, contrast 9, 32, 50, 81, 118, 158, 159, 165, 171, 185, 189, 212, 222, 278, folk music adapted 271–74, personal religious inscriptions 235, 263, secular cantatas, religious feeling in 29, 98, 179, 236, 246, 260, 261, 263, 267, 269, 270, 276, 278, 284, self-borrowing 29, 56, 82, 83, 90, 98, 101, 105, 114, 155, 157, 158, 174, 177–79, 239, 241, 244, 246, 249, 253, 261–65, 269, 271, 277–88, settings (experiments with) 19, 20, 36, 39, 41–43, 45, 46, 50, 52, 57, 59–61, 64–66, 68, 84, 106, 112, 113, 117, 121, 123, 129, 130, 134, 136, 139, 142, 146, 149, 154, 160–62, 174, 186, 189, 191, 204, 205, 210, 211, 214, 218, 221, 225, 227, 234, 247, 252, style: (a) concerto 42, 43, 75, 79, 108, 162, 165, 171, 193, 194, 228, 237, 244, (b) Italian 7, 18, 27, 52, 112, 236, 237, 248, 261, (c) mature 8, 141, 166, 181, 208, 227, 229, 234, (d) motet 62, 76, 143, 147, 158, 175, 196, 203, 218, 230, 234, views on singing 237–59, voices treated as instruments 76, 82, 126, 140, weddings, role of music at 274–76, word illustration by sound 9, 17, 18, 22, 28, 41, 42, 44, 52, 53, 58, 68, 106, 108, 115, 116, 120, 125, 127, 135, 139, 172, 176, 181, 182, 190, 192, 198, 222, 229, 233, 238, 239, 243, 245, 259, 267, 286, 288; (d) other works borrowed from or influenced by cantatas: *Magnificat* (BWV 243) 199, 200, 227, Mass in B minor (BWV 232) 75, 90, 110, 136, 152, 171, 265, 277, Passions 98, 112, 151, 159, 191, *St. John Passion* (BWV 245) 30, 31, 87, 88, 89, *St. Mark Passion* (BWV 247) 86, 89, *St. Matthew Passion* (BWV 244) 87, 88, 89, 103, 119, 204, *Short Mass in F major* (BWV 233) 43, 107, *Short Mass in A major* (BWV 234) 59, 65, 72, *Short Mass in G minor* (BWV 235) 80, 107, 127, *Short Mass in G major* (BWV 236) 58, 59, 176, 211, *Short Masses* 167

Bach, Maria Barbara (1684–1720) 3, 25

Bach, Wilhelm Friedemann (1710–1784) 37, 94, 95, 248

B.G. (Bachgesellschaft) = Bach Society xvi, 3, 134, 185

baptism 57, 58, 84, 198, 199

Becker, Cornelius (1561–1604) 66, 144

Beethoven, Ludwig van (1770–1827) 144, 280

Behm, Martin (1557–1622) 135, 234

belief (faith) 9, 11, 41, 52, 66, 80, 84, 85, 96, 97, 99, 101, 106, 107, 118, 119, 123, 156–58, 160, 161, 185, 190, 192, 199, 203, 207, 217, 234

Bethlehem 227

Biedermann, Johann Gottlieb (1705–1772) 274

Bienemann, Kaspar (1540–1591) 61, 92

Bourgeois, Louis (c. 1510–c. 1561) 170

Brahms, Johannes (1833–1897) 177

Brühl, Graf Heinrich von (1700–1763) 269

burlesque 236, 271

Burmeister, Franz Joachim (1633–1672) 133

Buxtehude, Dietrich (c. 1637–1707) 1, 2, 5, 53, 203, 223

BWV (Bach-Werke-Verzeichnis) = Catalog of Bach's works by Wolfgang Schmieder (1950) xv

cameo 239, 243

cantata, as termed by Bach 99, 141

cantatas: chorale 141, 160; dates of 31, 78; dialogue 117, 132; incomplete 60, 80, 131, 133, 195, 206, 234, 235; lost 64, 82, 151

Carissimi, Giacomo (1605–1674) 223

Celle 11, 39, 273

Charpentier, Marc-Antoine (1634–1704) 223

Christ, the Bridegroom 216

Christian, Duke of Saxe-Weissenfels (1682–1736) 171, 172, 238–40, 244, 245

Christian, Friedrich, Prince (1722–1763) 261, 265

Christian conduct, thinking 8, 14, 35, 38, 61, 64, 67–70, 73, 94, 101, 122, 123, 174, 191, 196, 197, 201, 207, 246, 256

Christmas: carol 48, 225, 239, 278; hymns 230, 278, 279; later cantatas for 225, 226, 228, 229, 231

church, dedication of 40

Clauder, Johann Christian (1701–1779) 265

coffee shops 259

collegium musicum 31, 236, 253, 257, 259, 261, 263, 265, 267, 272

color tones 13, 32, 45, 70, 80, 174, 250

comedy 258–60

comic opera 258–61, 271–74

Communion 11, 16, 216–218

confession (affirmation) of faith 187, 198, 209, 235

confidence (trust) in God/Jesus 9, 91, 92, 94, 97, 107, 125, 128, 131, 134, 139, 143–45, 155, 165, 170, 177–79, 186, 187, 192, 202, 208, 209, 211, 219, 221

conscience 101, 207–09
contentment 256
Corelli, Arcangelo (1653–1713) 272
Cöthen 25, 61, 90, 97, 108, 171, 236, 242–44, 247, 263
Cruciger (= Kreuziger) Elisabeth (c. 1500–1535) 18, 29, 38, 213
Crüger, Johann (c. 1624) 116

Dante Alighieri (1265–1321) 70
Danube 267–69
Danzig 266
Darmstadt 29, 169, 202
Decius, Nicolaus (d. 1541) 104, 144, 153
Denicke, David (1603–1680) 47, 77, 160, 162
dialogue 9, 19, 21, 28, 41, 55, 88, 89, 102, 117, 120, 132, 134, 182, 211, 254, 259–61, 279, 280, 282, 286, 288
didactic texts 201, 202, 225, 227, 228, 239, 271–74
Dieskau, Carl Heinrich von (c. 1742) 271
Dornheim 3
doxology 136, 198, 199, 225
dramatic action scenes xv, 9, 16, 20, 29, 30, 34, 38, 41, 49–51, 55, 56, 63, 65, 68, 71, 74, 75, 88, 89, 101, 102, 109, 119, 120, 124, 125, 132, 144, 147, 152, 155, 156, 171, 177, 179–83, 221, 223, 224, 227, 228, 233, 236, 238–40, 244, 245, 248, 250, 251, 258, 263–65, 267–69, 277, 281, 282, 287
dramma per musica 179, 248, 257, 261–71
Dresden 40, 248, 261, 263, 269, 277
duets, later forms of 232, 240–42, 244, 254, 263, 283
Dürr, Alfred 151, 153, 174, 201, 203, 226, 229

Eber, Paul (1511–1569) 46, 175, 191, 192, 214
Eberhardine, Christiane, Electress of Saxony (1671–1727) 31, 85–87, 256
Ebert, Jakob (1549–1615) 65, 141, 233
echo, effects of 164, 226, 262, 285
Eilmar, Georg Christian (1665–1715) xiv, 1, 2, 5
Elbe 267–69
elegy 5, 15, 85, 139, 204, 275
Elster (River) 269
Ephraim 96
Ernesti, Johann August (1707–1781) 174, 274
Ernesti, Johann Heinrich (1652–1729) 246
Ernst August, Duke of Saxe-Weimar (1688–1748) 238

fantasia (chorale) 12, 36, 53, 60, 61, 69, 89, 104, 106, 120, 123, 128, 131, 132, 134, 138, 143, 164, 166, 168, 175, 181, 185–87, 189–91, 193, 196–98, 203, 205, 207, 209–11, 213–16, 218–22, 230, 233
fatalism/destiny (Christian concept) 6, 61, 80, 94, 100, 101, 125, 126, 128, 161, 169, 186
figurative/descriptive language 5, 9, 13, 15, 16, 20, 27, 33, 40, 44, 47, 50, 53, 56, 58, 63, 67, 69, 85, 99, 104, 116, 132, 140, 158, 172, 175, 187, 215, 226, 228, 238, 243, 251, 256, 262, 264
flattery of royalty/nobility 241, 253–56, 261–69, 274, 275
Fleming, Paul (1609–1640) 69, 138, 170
Flemming, Joachim Friedrich von (1667–1728) 171, 234, 274
folk-song 82, 138, 177
forgiveness 18, 205, 207, 209, 215, 218
Forkel, Johann Nikolaus (1729–1818) 31
Franck, Johann (1618–1677) 45, 51, 116, 216, 287
Franck, Michael (1609–1667) 221
Franck, Salomo (1659–1725) xiv, 5, 7, 8, 12–15, 17–21, 23, 24, 31, 36, 37, 54, 55, 57, 73, 79, 95, 238
Frankfurt 202
Frederick the Great (1712–1786) 203, 233
Freystein, Johann Burchard (1671–1718) 219
friendship (toward man and God) 74, 76, 77, 97, 121, 122, 163, 220, 237, 256, 289
Fritsch, Ahasverus (1629–1701) 181, 229
Füger, Kaspar (1521–1592) 44
fugue 6, 10, 23, 27, 32, 33, 35, 36, 39, 45, 57–60, 63, 68, 72, 75, 81, 87, 128, 146, 147, 168, 201, 218, 234, 240, 245
Fullen, Statz Hilmor von (1691–1751) 40
funeral, references to 5, 15, 62, 74, 78, 82, 83, 91, 130, 189, 234

Gerhardt, Paul (1607–1676) 42, 44, 47, 49, 83, 89, 146–48, 155, 156, 160, 183, 187, 281, 282, 284, 288
"German Requiem" 177
Gesner, J. Matthias (1691–1761) 237, 246
Gigas, Johannes (1514–1581) 211
Görner, J. Gottlieb (1697–1778) 85
Gottsched, J. Christoph (1700–1766) 85
Graumann (Poliander), Johann (1487–1541)

72, 111, 175, 177
Graupner, Christoph (1683–1760) 10, 29
Greek drama 151, 238, 248, 280
Grimm Gate 257
Grossgebauer, Philipp (d. 1711) 5
Grünwaldt, Georg (d. 1530) 68
guilt 207

Halle 7, 40, 42
Hamburg 27, 40, 51, 248
Hammerschmidt, Andreas (1611/12–1675) 131
Handel, George Frideric (1685–1759) 2, 3, 10, 22, 142, 148, 171, 194, 222, 236, 248, 249, 261
Harnoncourt, Nikolaus xv
Hasse, J. Adolf (1699–1783) 248
Hassler, Hans Leo (1564–1612) 109, 197
Haydn, Joseph (1732–1809) 76
Heermann, Johann (1585–1647) 10, 18, 40, 73, 79, 97, 108, 110, 166, 167, 170, 202
Heineccius, Johann Michael (1674–1722) 42
Helbig, Johann Friedrich (c. 1720) xiv, 27
Helicon 250
Helmboldt, Ludwig (1532–1598) 58, 62, 168
Hennicke, Graf Johann Christian von (1681–1752) 179, 269–71
Henrici, Christian Friedrich (1700–1764) *see* Picander
Herberger, Valerius (1562–1627) 130
Herman, Johannes (1548–1563) 61, 91, 168, 169
Herman, Nikolaus (c. 1480–1561) 13, 65, 90, 231
Hildebrand, Zacharias (1688–1757) 40
Himmelsburg 5, 6
Holy Spirit 55, 57, 104, 122, 130, 147, 155–57, 195, 199, 225
homage 265, 266, 271, 274
Homburg, Ernst Christoph (1605–1681) 145
Hubert (Huber), Konrad (1507–1577) 207
Hyacinthus 258
hymns, treatment of 124, 136, 140, 165, 235, 278, 286
hypocrisy 36, 58, 88, 201

illness 215
imagery evoked by sound 3, 8, 9, 11, 14, 30, 33, 38, 41, 44, 48, 54, 71, 76, 104, 115, 116, 120, 122, 127, 129, 133, 142, 149, 154, 156, 158, 161, 162, 168, 182, 184, 185, 191, 193, 195, 196, 202, 205, 207, 211, 213, 215, 216, 222, 227, 243, 245, 249, 251, 252, 287
immaculate conception 224, 225, 230
instrumentation 19, 39, 55, 59, 67, 68, 72, 75, 81, 85, 107, 108, 153, 167, 235, 250, 287
Isaak, Heinrich (c. 1450–1517) 138

Jahn, Martin (c. 1620–1682) 23, 49
Janus 268
Jeremiah 75, 107, 110, 124
Jerusalem 11, 29, 38, 49, 120, 153, 203, 207, 224
Joseph I, Emperor, (1678–1711) 2, 3
Josepha, Maria, Electress of Saxony (1699–1757) 263–65, 268, 277
Judgment Day 21, 71–73, 115, 119, 158, 192, 223

Karl VI, Emperor of Austria (1685–1740) 268
Keymann (Keimann), Christian (1607–1662) 18, 21, 23, 44, 50, 84, 184
Kirchbach, Hans Carl von (1704–1753) 85
Knoll, Christoph (1563–1621) 15
Kolrose, Johann (d. 1558) 85
Kortte, Gottlieb (1698–1731) 250
Kuhnau, Johann (1660–1722) 29, 53

Lämmerhirt, Tobias (1639–1707) 5
Lehms, Georg Christian (1684–1717) 140, 169
Leipzig 10, 38, 62, 98, 203, 206, 207, 236, 259
Leipzig churches 202, 248, 279
Leipzig Consistory 38
Leipzig Market Place 248, 265, 267
Leipzig Town Council 38, 50, 52, 59, 93, 259
Leipzig University 250
Leipzig University Church 20, 248
Leipzig University Council 29, 248
Leipzig University faculty 248, 250
Leipzig University students 250, 252, 257, 263
Leopold, Prince of Anhalt-Cöthen (1694–1728) 25, 27, 236, 241, 242
Lesczynski, Stanislaus, King of Poland (reigned 1704–1709, 1733–1734) 264
libretto texts 223

linden trees 39, 93, 254, 265, 267
Liscow, Salomo (1640–1689) 157
litui 234
local color 39, 48, 192, 254, 259, 265, 268, 269, 271
longing: for death 14, 16, 37, 52, 62, 78, 100, 112; for God/Jesus 5, 16, 30, 71, 84, 114, 116, 127, 147, 158, 181, 183, 184, 194, 217, 228; for heaven 14, 21, 45, 116, 126, 134, 194; for a person 14, 30
Lübeck 51
Lubeck City 223
lullaby or slumber-song 60, 63, 79, 100, 114, 126, 178, 195, 216, 225, 231, 239, 245, 275, 281, 283, 288
Lully, Jean-Baptiste (1632–1687) 273
Luther, Martin (1483–1546) xiv, 6, 11, 21, 23, 25, 34, 35, 38, 39, 45, 46, 52, 53, 60, 76, 93, 95, 99, 104, 114, 130, 143, 174, 178, 189, 190, 191, 196, 197, 199, 218, 219, 224–26, 229, 230, 278, 279, 283
Lutheran doctrine 85, 169, 190, 207

Magnificat 3, 23, 42
marches 15, 48, 105, 160, 203, 207, 214, 250–52
Marienkirche 223
Mattheson, Johann (1681–1764) 8
medieval hymns 103
medieval mystery plays 34
Meissen 86
Meusel, Wolfgang (1497–1563) 104
Meyfart, Johann Matthäus (1590–1642) 76
Moller, Martin (1547–1606) 69, 134, 185, 203, 204, 224
monologue/soliloquy 65, 78, 145, 152, 177, 183, 192, 201, 237, 280, 281
motifs (ideas evoked by the rhythm): angel 224; anger 223, 234, 260; battle 81, 95, 167, 190, 214; dance 216, 219, 240, 243, 251, 273; exhaustion 100, 189; fall 106; fear 73, 140, 184; grief 9, 10, 20, 49, 53, 74, 75, 85, 86, 113, 116, 119, 124, 139, 152, 170, 185, 194, 203, 208, 210, 212, 228, 233, 237; joy (felicity) 8–10, 12, 13, 16, 20, 23, 26, 28, 32, 33, 37, 39, 42–44, 46, 48, 49, 52–56, 60, 61, 64, 65, 67, 68, 71, 77–80, 84, 85, 90, 96–98, 100–02, 105, 109, 113, 115, 118, 121, 122, 124, 125, 128–30, 135, 137–39, 142–44, 146, 147, 153, 154, 156, 160, 169, 175, 182–86, 193–95, 199, 201, 204, 208, 211–13, 215–17, 219, 226–28, 230–34, 237, 238, 240, 242–44, 246, 247, 249, 250, 257, 264, 270, 273, 274, 276–78; motion 33, 73, 74, 209, 213, 245; peace 115, 266; sadness/regret 8, 15, 84, 93, 96, 142, 143, 145, 170, 182, 194, 231, 244, 249, 275; serenity/calm 23, 25, 31, 34, 60, 63, 65, 68, 86, 89, 141, 154, 209; sleep 219, 275; solemnity 10, 12, 13, 39, 66, 85, 86, 89, 206, 234, 268; step 19, 29, 33, 37, 54, 64, 67, 89, 91, 99, 117, 120, 122, 140, 147, 156, 158, 166, 168, 176, 177, 180, 189, 193, 198, 207, 209, 213, 243, 246, 251; storm 76; tear 85, 86, 107, 116, 126, 131, 139, 159, 170, 183, 192, 215, 228, 256; tumult 22, 23, 25, 50, 65, 69, 81, 93, 159, 163; wave/water 8, 18, 33, 36, 50, 116, 124, 198, 200, 202, 238, 243, 267–69
motto 68, 114, 136, 137, 162, 163, 165, 184, 196, 248
Mozart, Wolfgang Amadeus (1756–1791) 248
Mühlhausen 1, 2, 5
Müller, August Friedrich (1684–1761) 248, 250
Müller, Heinrich (1631–1675) 149
mysticism 6, 11, 21, 26, 29, 32, 43, 45, 70, 81, 84, 86, 99, 113, 118, 130, 133, 145, 153, 162, 164, 169, 181, 189, 193, 195, 201, 212, 213, 229, 235, 257
mythology (Greek/Roman) 236, 238, 242, 257, 261, 264, 268, 269

Neander (Neumann), Joachim (1650–1680) 128
Neumann, Caspar (1648–1715) 77
Neumann, Werner 50, 79, 100, 103, 107, 124, 140, 151, 153, 163, 174, 176, 185, 195, 200, 210, 215, 223, 226, 287
Neumark, Georg (1621–1681) 9, 59, 87, 112, 126, 179
Neumeister, Erdmann (1671–1756) xiv, 5, 7, 10, 21, 31, 35, 50, 116, 174
Nicolai, Philipp (1556–1608) 11, 56, 85, 99, 117, 120, 192
Nicolaikirche (St. Nicholas's Church) 31, 38, 42, 94, 122, 151, 153, 277, 279, 282, 284, 285, 287

Olearius, Johann (1611–1684 121, 180
opera 9, 81, 84, 112, 117, 236–39, 248, 283
oratorios 43, 76, 81, 122, 151, 171, 223, 225, 244, 245, *compare* Bach, Johann Sebastian, instrumental pieces borrowed for cantatas: oratorios

organ obbligato 108, 110, 112, 113, 117, 126
organs 40
Ovid, Publius Ovidius Naso (43 B.C.–A.D. 17 ?) 257

Pachelbel, Johann (1653–1706) 53, 143, 196, 203, 218, 230
pardon 206
parody *see* Bach, Johann Sebastian, style and personal theory: self-borrowing
Pascal, Blaise (1623–1662) 70
pastoral themes/pastorales 16, 38, 40, 56, 65, 66, 71, 76, 87, 104, 105, 122, 133, 144, 145, 158, 169, 172, 188, 213, 215, 231, 239, 243–45, 264
penitence/repentance 27, 71, 74, 97, 107, 108, 148, 205, 212, 215, 223
persecution 7, 8, 104
personification 116, 132, 159, 216, 246, 248, 257, 261–63, 265; *see also* figurative/descriptive language
Pfefferkorn, Georg Michael (1646–1731) 45, 162
Piast 266
Picander (= Henrici, Christian Friedrich, 1700–1764) xiv, 31, 38, 60, 62, 63, 69, 77, 78, 81, 83, 87–90, 92, 93, 98, 101, 105, 109, 110, 120, 166, 171, 177, 179, 192, 194, 196, 200, 203, 206, 210, 215, 224, 226, 228, 229, 236, 248, 253, 257, 259–62, 267–69, 271, 274, 287
pictorial evocations 5, 8, 12, 13, 15, 18, 19, 32, 38, 39, 42–45, 48, 50, 53, 56, 58, 61, 64, 66, 69, 70, 74, 75, 81, 83, 86, 91, 95 99, 115, 116, 171, 188, 190, 198, 212, 216, 217, 221, 223, 227, 230, 236, 252, 288
Pietism 21, 26
pilgrim 116, 211
Pindus (River) 267
pizzicato 11, 12, 16, 62, 74, 78, 86, 130, 161, 188, 192, 193, 207, 209, 264
plague 203
Pleisse (River) 253, 267–69
Pomssen 83
Ponikau, Johann Christoph von (d. 1726) 83
praise of God/Jesus 2, 39, 46, 60, 79, 91, 93, 95, 110, 112, 128, 129, 136, 137, 141, 151, 157, 165, 168, 177, 179–81, 193, 199, 200, 224, 227, 284, 286
prayer 31, 34, 43, 76, 78, 79, 111, 112, 124, 148, 162, 169, 191, 193, 195, 196, 204–08, 213, 216, 217, 220, 224, 227, 283, 286
prayer book (Lutheran) 31, 108
predestination 32, 161, 207, 208
Pretsch 85, 87
Probestück, (test piece) 29, 30
prophets 201–03
punishment 211

Ratswahl (town council election) 2, 38, 59, 92, 93, 110, 128, 206
realism 227, 230, 236, 239, 252, 268
reason 158, 203
redemption 216
Reiche, Gottfried (1667–1734) 265
renunciation, of the world 45, 56, 73, 75
Resurrection 13, 23, 24, 53, 64, 101, 102, 130, 171–73
Reusner, Adam (1496–c. 1575) 5, 98
rhapsody 201
Richter, Gregorius (1598–1649) 133, 167
Rilling, Helmuth xv
Rinckart, Martin (1598–1649) 133, 167
Ringwaldt, Bartholomäus (1530–1599) 1, 74, 204
Rist, Johann (1607–1667) 23, 49, 69, 75, 119, 132, 151, 152, 159, 208, 280, 285
Rivinus, Johann Florens (1701–1761) 246
Robertson, Alec 50
Rodigast, Samuel (1649–1708) 32, 54, 131, 135, 164
Rosenmüller, Johann (c. 1620–1684) 17, 25, 113
Rube, Johann Christoph (1665–1746) 220
Runge, Christoph (1619–1681) 284
Rutilius, Martin (1551–1618) 215

Sacer, Gottfried Wilhelm (1635–1699) 153
Sachs, Hans (1494–1576) 27, 209
Salzburg 122
Samaritan 38, 76, 77, 176, 208
satire 257, 259, 262, 274
Scarlatti, Alessandro (1660–1725) 18, 66, 236
Schalling, Martin (1532–1608) 106, 115
Scheibe, Johann Adolf (1708–1776) 257, 258
Schein, Johann Hermann (1586–1630) 92, 220
Schneegass, Cyriakus (1546–1597) 197, 231
Schneesing, Johannes (d. 1567) 207
Schneider, Johann (1702–1788) 94
Schop, Johann (d.c. 1665) 195
Schütz, Heinrich (1585–1672) 234
Schütz, Johann Jakob (1640–1690) 136
Schweitzer, Albert (1875–1965) xiii, 8, 17, 84, 86, 91, 94, 100, 109, 122, 138, 162,

167, 174, 179, 200, 203, 204, 209, 226, 283
Second Silesian War 203
Selnecker, Nikolaus (1530–1592) 174
serenade 25, 240, 241, 250, 265
siciliano 71, 93, 108, 111, 114, 148, 157, 232
Silbermann, Gottfried (1683–1753) 40
sins and sinners 7, 18, 36, 40, 44, 50, 57–59, 71, 72, 74–76, 97, 105–08, 119, 126, 140, 148, 156, 166, 180, 191, 197, 199, 201, 204, 207–09, 212, 215, 219, 223, 232
song-contest 257
Song of Solomon 117
Spengler, Lazarus (1479–1534) 7, 119
Speratus, Paul (1484–1551) 20, 22, 37, 68, 106, 107, 163
Spitta, Philipp (1841–1894) 8, 46, 51, 100, 167, 174, 176, 229, 280
Stauber, Johann Lorenz (1660–1723) 3
Stockmann, Paul (1602–1636) 89
Störmthal 40
submission to God 12, 18, 61, 62, 73, 80, 186, 188
symbolism, xv, 12, 13, 17, 19, 32, 34, 44, 48, 53, 56, 58, 68, 80, 104, 105, 112, 116, 117, 129, 140, 145, 149, 157, 158, 189, 192, 193, 195, 199, 207, 216, 240, 254, 259, 269, 274, 279, 280, 288

Tafelmusik (table music) 238, 242, 274
tax-collector 17, 73, 271, 272
taxes 259
teachers/professors 246–48, 251, 252
Telemann, Georg Philipp (1681–1767) 46, 89, 271
Terry, Charles Sanford (1864–1936) 31, 76, 82, 92, 100, 103, 105, 107, 133, 140, 151, 153, 163, 171, 174, 185, 200, 203, 210 215, 226, 229, 233
thanksgiving 35, 127–29, 133, 137, 144, 167, 168, 174–76, 194, 214
Thomaskirche (St. Thomas's Church) 29, 48, 58, 151, 153, 228, 236, 244, 257, 274, 277, 279, 282, 284, 285, 287
Thomasschule (St. Thomas's School) 174, 246
Tietze, Christoph (1641–1703) 59
tone-painting 6, 8, 9, 16, 17, 19, 21, 22, 26, 30, 31, 33, 34, 44, 45, 48, 52, 53, 56, 64–66, 70, 71, 74, 76, 81, 85, 86, 89, 91, 92, 95, 100, 104, 110, 113, 115, 121, 122, 125, 135, 138, 140, 143, 145, 146, 148, 149, 153, 154, 156, 157, 164–66, 170–73, 176, 181, 182, 185, 189, 191, 193, 195, 197
Tonus Peregrinus (plain-chant) 199, 200
Torgau 87
transfiguration 212
Trinity 13, 41, 55, 62, 122, 133, 145, 162, 198, 225
trio (later forms) 5, 218, 232, 233, 250, 271, 287
Tunder, Franz (1614–1667) 5

vanity 31, 163, 217, 222, 256, 257
vernacular (Saxon slang) 272
Vetter, Daniel (d. 1721) 77
Vistula (River) 266, 267–269
Vulpius, Melchior (1560–1616) 129

Walther, Johann (1496–1570) 53
Walther, Johann Gottfried (1684–1748) 198
Walton, William 135
War of Polish Succession 141, 143, 167, 168, 174
wealth 17, 32, 33, 73, 162, 163
wedding 3, 16, 82, 117, 177, 242, 274
Wegelin, Josua (1604–1640) 153
Weimar 236, 238
Weingärtner, Sigismund (fl. 1607) 94
Weiss, Christian, Jr. (1703–1743) 145, 163
Weiss, Christian, Sr. (1671–1737) xiv, 31, 33, 38, 43, 45, 48, 50, 58, 59, 64–66, 68, 72, 74–76, 84, 92, 96, 103, 107, 141, 200, 226
Weissel, Georg (1590–1635) 286
Werner, Georg (1589–1643) 289
Whittaker, W. Gillies 21, 35, 43, 63, 111, 132, 179, 180, 200, 203, 226, 228, 229, 232, 270
Wiederau 82, 179, 269
Wildenfels, Anarg von (c. 1490–1539) 57
Wilhelm Ernst, Duke of Saxe-Weimar (1662–1728) 6, 13, 25, 238
Wittenberg 85

Zacharias 71, 179–81
Zeboim 96
Zelter, Carl Friedrich (1758–1832) 77
Ziegler, Christiane Mariane von (1695–1760) xiv, 107, 124, 141, 144, 146, 148, 153–56, 159, 176
Ziegler, Kaspar (1621–1690) 163
Zimmermann, Gottfried (?–1741) 236, 253, 257
Zimmermann's Coffee House 259, 263, 264
Zimmermann's Garden 257, 261
Zion 92, 98, 110, 120, 127, 170, 206, 278